BRITAIN'S ECONOMIC PERFORMANCE

Second edition

The new and substantially ... *...nce* provides a unique assessment of the ... ...ate of the supply side of the economy and will prove essential reading for all who take the economic problems of Britain and Europe seriously.

The 1990s have seen strong export growth, low inflation, and declining unemployment. But nagging doubts persist. Is the recovery sustainable? Or are we on the verge of yet another boom and bust cycle. Moreover, why has investment not recovered as quickly as in previous cycles? As we delve deeper, we find that many of the underlying problems remain. At the same time entirely new questions for economic policy have arisen. The new edition focuses on the enormous economic, social and technological questions that the 1990s are posing for Britain as we move toward a new millennium.

New features of this edition include:
- examination of Britain's role in the EU and the implications of the social chapter;
- the challenge from Asia and the Pacific and the new technologies;
- discussion of the changing policy agenda in the 1990s;
- analysis of the structure of British industry since the end of the Cold War;
- assessment of the resources available for an industrial strategy in the year 2000.

Britain's Economic Performance examines the evidence in six sections, each fundamental for our understanding of competitive performance: the political and macroeconomic framework; international trading performance; investment and innovation; the labour market and the social framework; European integration; and finally, structural change and microeconomic policy. Each section has its own overview providing an extensive review of the UK record, highlighting the issues that arise and the controversies that have ensued. Individual chapters are devoted to the in-depth analysis of critical issues. The questions posed by European integration as well as the macro-economy form entirely new chapters.

Utilising a team of highly experienced, policy-oriented applied economists, the new edition of *Britain's Economic Performance* will prove as indispensable a source of reference, analysis, and guidance as the first.

BRITAIN'S ECONOMIC PERFORMANCE

Second edition

Edited by Tony Buxton, Paul Chapman and Paul Temple

London and New York

First published 1998
by Routledge
11 New Fetter Lane, London EC4P 4EE

Simultaneously published in the USA and Canada
by Routledge
29 West 35th Street, New York, NY 10001

© 1998 Tony Buxton, Paul Chapman and Paul Temple

Typeset in Garamond by RefineCatch Limited, Bungay, Suffolk

Printed and bound in Great Britain by
MPG Books Ltd, Bodmin, Cornwall

British Library Cataloguing in Publication Data
A catalogue record for this book is available from the British Library

Library of Congress Cataloging in Publication Data
A catalogue record for this book has been requested

ISBN 0–415–14873–1 (hbk)
ISBN 0–415–14874–X (pbk)

CONTENTS

v

CONTENTS

CONTENTS

vii

FIGURES AND TABLES

FIGURES

TABLES

CONTRIBUTORS

Tony Buxton was an economics lecturer at Salford and Sheffield Universities before spending nine years at NEDO as an Economic Adviser. He is now a Principal Lecturer in Economics at London Guildhall University. His writings include published articles on industrial economics and macroeconomics and two editions of NEDO's *British Industrial Performance*.

Dr Paul Chapman is a lecturer in economics at the University of Dundee who also worked as an Economic Adviser at NEDO during 1991 and 1992. His publications have covered a wide variety of economic policy issues, including training, unemployment and regional labour markets. He is the author and co-author of two books on training policy.

Paul Temple is an economics lecturer at the University of Surrey, having recently been a Research Fellow at London Business School. He has lectured at universities in Britain and the United States and has also worked in television. Between 1989 and 1992 he was an Economic Adviser at NEDO, working on issues related to pay and productivity and international competitiveness. Recently published work includes studies on industrial policy and on the role of industrial standards and UK trade performance.

Sir Geoffrey Chandler, CBE, began his career as a journalist with the BBC and *Financial Times*, subsequently spending twenty-two years with the Royal Dutch/Shell Group in a variety of posts at home and abroad. He was Director General of NEDO between 1978 and 1983, Director of Industry Year 1986, and Industry Adviser to the Royal Society for the Encouragement of Arts, Manufactures and Commerce (RSA) until the end of 1992.

Martin J. Conyon is a Warwick Research Fellow at the University of Warwick. Previously he was a lecturer in economics at Queen's College, University of Oxford. His current research interests are in the area of corporate governance and economic performance. He has written a number of articles on executive pay and managerial labour markets.

Ciaran Driver has lectured in economics and statistics at a number of London Universities. He was at NEDO for three years until 1986, and is now

Reader in Economics at the Management School at Imperial College of Science and Technology. He has written books on employment and investment, including *Investment, Expectations and Uncertainty*, 1992 (with David Moreton) and has published numerous journal articles.

Professor George Hadjimatheou has been the Head of the Economics Department at London Guildhall University since 1990. Earlier employment included lecturing posts at Thames and Kingston Universities. He has written books on housing and mortgage markets, consumer theory, and macroeconomic modelling, and has published numerous articles in academic journals.

Mohammad Haq has over twelve years of commercial experience in the international energy industry. He is currently Research Fellow at London Guildhall University where his interests include the privatised energy sector in the United Kingdom and the emergence of derivatives-based trading in these markets, and the econometric modelling of occupational attainment and choice in the UK labour market.

Dr Ewart Keep is a Senior Research Fellow in the Industrial Relations Research Unit at Warwick Business School. He graduated from Royal Holloway College, University of London, in modern history and politics in 1979, and was subsequently employed in the CBI's Education and Training Division, before moving to Warwick University to undertake a PhD on industry-level collective bargaining. Since 1985 he has undertaken research within the IRRU on British training policy, and personnel policies for the education system's workforce.

Valerio Lintner has been a researcher at the European University Institute in Florence and a lecturer in European Economics at the University of North London. He is currently a Principal Lecturer at London Guildhall University and a visiting lecturer at the Université Paul Valéry Montpellier. His writings include books on the European Community, on the European economy and on economic policy-making in the EU, as well as numerous contributions to books and a number of journal articles.

Dr Tony Mananyi has taught economics at Napier, London Guildhall, Edinburgh and Essex Universities. He is now a Senior Lecturer in Economics at the University of North London. Previously a consultant to the Lothian Region Development Authority, Scotland, he has publications in academic journals in the area of market efficiency.

Ken Mayhew has been a Fellow of Pembroke College, Oxford since 1976. From 1989 to 1990 he was Economic Director at NEDO. After reading

Modern History at Worcester College, Oxford, and obtaining an MSc (Econ) from the LSE in 1970, he worked as an economic assistant at HM Treasury (1970–2), and as an Assistant Research Officer and Research Officer at the Oxford Institute of Economics and Statistics from 1972–81. From 1986 to 1988 he was Chairman of the Oxford University Social Studies Board. Until recently he was Chairman of the Committee for the Oxford Management School. He is an Associate Editor of the *Oxford Review of Economic Policy* and former editor of the *Oxford Bulletin of Economics and Statistics*. He has worked as a consultant for various private and public sector organisations at home and abroad. His research interests include labour markets, organisational theory and design, macroeconomics, and his publications include: *Pay Policies for the Future* (edited with D. Robinson), 1983; *Trade Unions and the Labour Market*, 1983; *Providing Health Care* (edited with P. Fenn and A. McGuire), 1990; *Improving Incentives for the Low Paid* (edited with A. Bowen), 1990; *Reducing Regional Inequalities* (edited with A. Bowen), 1991.

Dr Derek Morris has been a Fellow and Tutor in Economics, Oriel College Oxford since 1970 and is currently vice chairman of the Monopolies and Mergers Commission. From 1981 to 1984 he was Economic Director of NEDO. He has been a Director and Chairman of Oxford Economic Forecasting since 1984 and is an associate editor of the *Oxford Review of Economic Policy* and is on the editorial board of *Oxford Economic Papers*. Author of numerous books and articles, primarily in the field of Industrial Economics; these include *Industrial Economics and Organisation* (with D. Hay) in 1991; *Unquoted Companies* (with D. Hay) in 1984; *Industrial Enterprises and Economic Reform in China, 1980–89* (with D. Hay) in 1993; *The Economic System in the United Kingdom*, 3rd edition 1984.

Simon I. Peck is a research fellow at the Centre for Corporate Strategy and Change, Warwick Business School. Current research interests are in the area of corporate governance, firm restructuring and performance.

Dr John Philpott is an economist and has conducted research on labour market issues since completing his doctoral thesis at Oxford in the early 1980s. In 1987, having worked for a few years in higher education, he was appointed Director of the Employment Institute, an independent policy 'think tank'. In 1992, following the amalgamation of the Institute and Action Trust he was appointed Director of the Employment Policy Institute (EPI). He edits and contributes to EPI's monthly journal, *Economic Report*, and has written widely on labour market issues and is a frequent contributor to media discussions on employment policy. He has acted as consultant to a number of national and international organisations, including the OECD, the International Labour Organisation and the United Nations. From 1993 to 1996 he was Specialist Adviser to the UK House of Commons Select Committee on

Employment. He is author of *Working for Full Employment* (Routledge, 1996). His report, *A National Minimum Wage: Economic Effects and Practical Considerations* was published by the Institute of Personnel and Development in August 1996.

Dr Martha Prevezer is a Research Fellow at the Centre for Business Strategy, London Business School. She has worked as an economist with the Bank of England and as an Economic Adviser at NEDO from 1988 to 1992. Her research interests include the economics of both technology and capital markets. Her publications include *Capital Markets and Corporate Governance* (edited with Nicholas Dimsdale) for Oxford University Press (1994) and *The Dynamics of Industrial Clustering: International Comparisons in Computing and Biotechnology* (edited with P. Swann and D. Stout), Oxford University Press.

Dr Nicholas Sarantis is Hang Seng Professor of International Finance, and Director of the Centre for International Capital Markets, at London Guildhall University. He has worked as economic consultant on macroeconomic forecasting, and was Senior Lecturer/Reader in Economics at Greenwich and Kingston Universities for sixteen years. He has published numerous journal articles in the broad areas of empirical macroeconomics, investment, inflation, and exchange rates.

Dr Andrew Sentance is Director of the Centre for Economic Forecasting at the London Business School. Prior to joining LBS in January 1994, he was Director of Economic Affairs at the Confederation of British Industry (CBI). Until the end of 1993, he was a member of the Treasury Panel of Independent Forecasters (formerly known as the seven 'wise men') which provides advice to the Chancellor of the Exchequer. He is an established commentator on current economic issues and has published widely on a range of macroeconomic topics.

Margaret Sharp is Senior Fellow and Director of Research at the Science Policy Research Unit (SPRU). Her interest in industrial policy stems from the time she spent at NEDO at the end of the 1970s and early 1980s, and she has written extensively in the area, including *Europe and the New Technologies* (Pinter, 1985) and in Freeman, Sharp and Walker (eds), *Technology, and the Future of Europe* (Pinter, 1991).

Peter Swann is Professor of Economics and Management of Innovation at Manchester University, and director of research at Manchester Business School. Before this he was Associate Professor of Economics at London Business School, and Reader in Economics at Brunel University. He was editor of the journal *Economics of Innovation and New Technology* from 1989 to 1996.

PREFACE

Since going to press, the dramatic result of the 1997 May Day general election, however much it was anticipated, is rekindling debate about the economic challenges facing modern Britain. With hindsight, the ideology that bound the policies of the last administration, however liberating it may have been twenty years ago, has turned into a strait-jacket. But to what extent have the policy options really been extended? Some of the intellectual baggage has carried through to the new administration – the desire to be more fiscally and financially orthodox than its predecessor has for example placed the operation of monetary policy in the hands of the Central Bank; moreover the first Labour Budget was generally reckoned to be prudent, with the proportion of national income accounted for by public spending set to fall over the coming Parliament. Beyond fiscal and monetary orthodoxy there is, however, enough to encourage those who think that supply side reform, and the creation of an effective industrial policy, can assist in the medium term aim of reducing unemployment – not through the stimulation of the demand for low paid work but through the active promotion of quality in the resources of the economy and the consequent generation of international competitiveness.

Despite its attractions, there are clear risks in such a policy. Increasing the supply of well-educated, skilled, and motivated workers in the labour market is certainly a necessary step, but may not be enough. More needs to be known about how to stimulate the demand for such labour. This will depend heavily upon the effectiveness of the myriad of institutions and strategies which are necessary to harness the knowledge base of the economy towards the production of goods and services which meet the test of sophisticated international markets. While some of the necessary institutions exist, others may need to be created, and many would benefit from creative and imaginative reform. Likewise, corporate and other strategies need to embrace the changing opportunities and would be enhanced by the more effective coordination of investment.

The stress of both this volume and its predecessor has been on the role of the supply side in the generation of economic well being. As such, we hope it will prove useful in helping the new government to push forward its industrial agenda. It is of course far too early to say how precisely the new mood in the country might help to improve the economic fundamentals of the UK economy. But the debate about to begin should assist enormously.

The Editors

ACKNOWLEDGEMENTS

This book has its origins in the closure of the National Economic Development Office in 1992. One of the duties of the Office was to conduct independent analyses of aspects of the supply side of the British economy. The need for such work remains, and subsequent to the Office closing, a number of former members of the Office, as well as other interested recruits, have created a network of economists committed to the deeper understanding of Britain's economic performance which is so necessary if economic policy is to transcend the boundary between rhetoric and reality. The editors of this book would like to thank all those who have participated in discussions and have offered advice, especially the participants at a workshop at London Guildhall University in March 1996. They would also like to thank colleagues both at London Guildhall University and at London Business School, who have offered encouragement over the past eighteen months. Family and friends are thanked for their forbearance for the many enjoyable editorial meetings. Funding from the Gatsby Foundation for part of the project is also gratefully acknowledged.

The Editors

1

INTRODUCTION

Tony Buxton, Paul Chapman and Paul Temple

As we approach the millennium, the state of the economy is as close as ever to the heart of political and economic debate with economic prospects the subject of much speculation. The longer-term growth of the UK economy, of around 2.5 per cent, has generally been less than that of other major capitalist economies over the post-war period. In the long term one of the fundamental aims of economic policy should be to raise this underlying rate of growth; understanding how this can be achieved is the main objective of this volume. However, more short-term considerations such as an over-heating economy and balance of payments crises have in the past diverted attention from this fundamental objective. The UK economy has long been subject to cyclical changes but the post-war period has seen a succession of severe cycles. The amplitude of economic cycles has increased recently, so that the apparent horrors of the 1950s and 1960s now look like mere hiccups rather than the economic shocks which bring down governments.

So what are the United Kingdom's economic prospects? Looking first at the short run, by the second half of the 1990s, the recovery from the slump in the first two years of the decade was well under way. At the end of November 1996 in his speech introducing the last budget before the general election, the Chancellor, Kenneth Clarke, felt able to claim:

> The British economy is in its fifth successive year of steady, healthy economic growth, with falling unemployment and low inflation. These are the best circumstances we have faced in a generation. This is a Rolls-Royce recovery, built to last. This time – unlike so many previous recoveries – healthy growth has been accompanied by the best inflation performance for nearly 50 years. And restrained growth of earnings has been good news for jobs.

Rolls-Royce motor cars are indeed built to last, but very few people own one. The Rolls-Royce analogy is therefore an appropriate reference to the effects of economic policies since 1979 – very few people have benefited, and some are absolutely worse off – and this may well continue into the 1990s recovery. People with very high incomes have gained the most and

1

those with the lowest have suffered the worst. Even in areas where success has been claimed, there is doubt. Inflation has been put at the forefront of policy, yet in the late 1980s the annual rate rose to nearly 10 per cent. Furthermore, in the EU in 1996, only Greece, Portugal, Spain and Italy had higher rates of inflation than the United Kingdom.

In any case, the foundations of the recovery in the 1990s should be scrutinised. It is right to point to low inflation as a signal that capacity had not yet being stretched, and low earnings growth may give the same message. But in the relatively early stages of recovery this is quite common, because capacity is available to raise output without excess demand and Mr Lawson made similar claims in the 1980s. The number of jobs created also rises as a recovery gets under way, and this is not surprising. The true determinant of a successful recovery is that demand is not artificially or temporarily stimulated. It requires several features, including success in international markets, efficiency of domestic firms to remain competitive, and adequate capacity.

Competitiveness is a longer-term issue and is discussed shortly, but the essential feature of a short-run recovery is that it should be investment- and/or export-led, to avoid capacity and/or balance of payments difficulties. The 1990s recovery seems virtuous because exports have risen rapidly, more than twice as fast as GDP. The exit from the Exchange Rate Mechanism (ERM) and the consequential devaluation of sterling undoubtedly played a part here, but basing a recovery on a devaluation is ultimately a futile exercise – a kind of 'fool's gold'. It is worth noting that the late 1970s' recovery also saw a huge rise in exports, by nearly the same amount relative to GDP as in the 1990s. This was despite a rising pound, based on the potential respite from the United Kingdom's perennial balance of payments problem which was, in the view of the foreign exchange markets, to be delivered by North Sea oil. Spending on exports was the only category of expenditure to rise faster than GDP in the late 1970s' recovery, much like the present one, but that was not regarded as a sound recovery, either at the time or in retrospect.

The more important source of a sound recovery in the short run is arguably from the capacity derived from investment in fixed capital. In the recovery since 1992, fixed investment growth has been weak. In the late 1980s, fixed investment rose strongly. Much of it was simply to replace that lost in the huge trough in the 1979–81 period and perhaps also because the 1980s cycle lasted so long so that in the end companies invested strongly. It is possible though that the factor which should be given recognition in the 1990s' recovery is this high investment growth of the late 1980s, which has meant that capacity, particularly with respect to exports, has not restrained output. The resultant capital cannot be effective for long, however, partly because it is inevitably insufficient to satisfy increasing demand, and partly because it is not endowed with sufficient advanced technology. The absence of strong investment in fixed capital in the 1990s is therefore likely to provoke the bottlenecks of old, and either raise inflation or require remedial economic policy to restrain demand and generate another stop in the familiar stop/go cycle. By the end of 1996, the Bank of England was once again concerned that capacity would be insufficient to match the increase in domestic demand, and was calling for interest rate rises to combat it – a policy which would itself reduce capital expenditure and potential capacity.

In the short run, therefore, there is no room for complacency and this was recognised by the new Chancellor, Gordon Brown, in his first budget. In the longer term the competitiveness of the economy is what determines the speed of economic development. Is there room for complacency here?

THE FACTORS BEHIND COMPETITIVENESS

This book is based on the belief that the sources of differences in long-term economic growth rates can be understood by utilising and developing the concept of national competitiveness. At the level of the individual firm, success or failure is clearly based on competitiveness – the ability to compete and as a consequence to be successful and grow. The translation of the concept to the national level is more problematic, but it can be expressed in a number of ways, the most important of which is that competitive economies will find that the sectors of the economy which are exposed to competition from overseas, whether in goods or in services, will tend either to grow relatively quickly or to disappear entirely. This is a consequence of comparative advantage and a changing international division of labour, and has several favourable repercussions on the rest of the economy. Because the tradable sector relies heavily for its success upon technological advance its growth provides a larger channel for beneficial spillovers. In terms of macroeconomic policy there may be more favourable external financing and the Government should find that its fiscal problems are simpler while real interest rates may be lower, encouraging investment which may further boost competitiveness.

In Britain, the concept of competitiveness first came to the fore as the focus of attention shifted in the early 1960s from concern with maintaining full employment (which had largely been achieved) to one of growth performance; it became clear that growth in Britain was lagging behind that of its neighbours in Europe. Policy discussions were directed to the rapidity with which the balance of payments deteriorated whenever faster rates of demand growth were experienced. Although this was correctly diagnosed as a competitiveness problem, it was seen in very conventional terms, as largely a matter of costs and prices, soluble, with a given exchange rate, by a period of more rapid productivity growth (as for example envisaged in the National Plan of 1965), slower wage growth or, as events turned out, by the 'one-off' devaluation of sterling in 1967. Although many apparently believed that devaluation represented a quick macroeconomic fix to Britain's problems, it was also widely supposed that labour market institutions were responsible for creating the need for devaluation in the first place. It was no surprise therefore that many of the proposals for the reform of those institutions also date from the late 1960s. However, political considerations ensured that such proposals were never seriously acted upon until the inflationary implications of the second oil shock encouraged governments everywhere, but especially in Britain, to put the control of the price level at the very top of the economic agenda.

By the early 1970s some economists were convinced that a freely floating exchange rate might relieve the economy of the awkward balance of payments problem, but this depended upon an ability to control wages and prices. But by the middle of the decade, and with the rapid acceleration of inflation in a devastating wage-price-devaluation spiral, it was increasingly asserted that the principal problem of competitiveness faced by the economy was not one which could be assisted by sterling devaluation alone; rather it was primarily one of 'non-price competitiveness' – that British producers could not get delivery right, or their marketing, or the specification that consumers desired. Moreover, rising exchange rates in Germany and Japan did not seem unduly to harm their competitive positions in world markets. Meanwhile devaluation and depreciation of the pound could actually be making matters worse by encouraging producers to concentrate on price-sensitive sectors of the market, rather than on more sophisticated sectors where longer-term growth might be quicker, and making them reliant on further devaluations. In many respects the devaluation was a consequence of economic weakness rather than a cure for basic problems; there must be a concern in this respect about the basis for growth since 1992. Of course this does not mean that the currency cannot be overvalued, as it so plainly was in the 1960s and in the early 1990s, but growth following devaluation is no economic miracle.

The whole experience of two decades suggested, however, a deeper question, related not so much to the individual producers themselves, but to the *structural* aspects of the economy in which decisions are made. After all, apart from simplistic explanations founded upon generalised management failure, how could it be true that British management was *consistently* under-performing? Again we may turn to the role that idiosyncratic national institutions play in conditioning corporate strategies, i.e. to a notion of *structural competitiveness*, referring to the fact that national institutions (especially in training, education, labour markets, capital markets, and the physical infrastructure) have consistent effects on individual firm performance. The United Kingdom, for example, has very distinctive patterns in the organisation and financing of industry, in the provision of education and training, in the support by government of R&D, and in the way in which many institutions combine to affect the operation of the labour market. Structural competitiveness is fundamental in explaining why the national economy continues, despite the importance of the processes of globalisation and economic integration, as an essential unit of analysis. Differences between nations in their relative economic performance display remarkable persistence over time, and it is highly improbable that the search for the causes of this can ignore differences in national institutions.

Of course some of this was recognised by the incoming Conservative government in 1979, which subsequently maintained a very consistent view about the nature of the institutional reform required to resolve many of Britain's economic problems. Institutional reform in Britain was directed primarily at the labour market, whose idiosyncratic institutions, including both the trade unions and methods of pay bargaining, were held to be deeply inimical to industrial success. The guiding ideology was of course that markets should wherever possible be left to their own devices. If there was any 'model' for reform, it was to be based upon practices observed in the US, which, rightly or wrongly, is held to be the prime example of the *laissez-faire* approach to capitalism. After two decades of labour market reform, the 'flexibility' of the UK labour market is now frequently espoused as a source of national competitive advantage, especially within the EU, where reform has not been taken as far, and indeed in many instances is perceived to be moving in the other direction. Clearly this difference constitutes a major source of friction for Britain's membership in the EU. The results of the labour market reform programme can also now begin to be judged. Certainly unemployment rates have declined in the 1990s, and now compare favourably with some nations in Europe. But the costs have been considerable, particularly in relation to the growing inequalities between households and the increased polarisation between 'job-rich' and 'job-poor' households.

A common theme underpinning many of the contributions to this volume is that the emphasis on the reform of the labour market has become less relevant to improving competitiveness, but there are a host of factors to which policy must attend in addressing a moving target. Arguably what matters most for the advanced economies is their ability to generate investments based upon the generation and utilisation of knowledge as a resource, and hence to shift the pattern of specialisation into earlier stages of the product cycle. In such a world, government action needs to be founded not just on a philosophy of intervention in markets as a last resort, but upon a philosophy of public good provision – in areas such as education and training, cooperative R&D, and the coordination of investment, i.e. areas where public investment is *complementary* to private investment and most likely to generate additionality. The importance of these areas is at least partially recognised in the three 'competitiveness' White Papers, but the principal question – how government can best assist the private sector in *increasing* the resources devoted to the accumulation of technological capability – has not been systematically addressed. At the very least, this would require a systematic and frank audit of Britain's current institutional structure, but such an audit has yet to be carried out. We hope that the current volume goes some way to redress this situation.

The explanation of differences in economic growth rates underpinning our approach can be contrasted with some alternatives. The textbook, neo-classical approach emphasises two fundamental forces in the growth process – population growth and technological change – which are themselves unexplained. The investments required to adapt to these opportunities are signalled by prices and coordinated by markets. Differences in national per-formance reflect the flexibility of producers to the signals thrown up, as well as to the inherent potential of economies – their 'endowments' in terms of the supplies of various factors of production. While the approach recognises that market failures may occur, this does not by itself make a case for intervention, since the idea of 'government failure' is pervasive in some influential circles – the view that even if markets are not working as well as they might in theory, there is no necessary reason why intervention should improve matters – politicians, regulators and others charged with the public interest are more likely to act either incompetently or simply in their own self-interest.

In the British case, thinking about policy has also been influenced by the Austrian School, who adopt a more dynamic view of economic growth, emphasising the role of the entrepreneur in spotting and acting upon favourable profit opportunities. In the 1980s much was heard about the creation of an 'enterprise culture'. The encouragement of enterprise extended well beyond traditional areas of business, into new territory, especially the public sector e.g. in health provision through the creation of health service trusts and associated 'quasi-markets'.

A rather different school of economists (based mainly in the US) emphasises the institutional framework of the economy and its relationship to the competitive process. Institutions are no mere reflection of market forces, but are shaped in specific periods and may function rather better in some contexts than in others. Compared to the pace of developments in technology, institutional change can be very slow, and mismatch or institutional failure a real possibility. In the United Kingdom, for example, the centralisation of political authority and the adversarial nature of political debate may be exactly opposed to the smooth functioning of more liberal-ised markets. In Germany the more decentralised power structure, combined with a similar market-oriented culture, may have operated more effectively in promoting competitiveness.

The framework we have adopted in this study is consistent with the approach taken in the previous edition of *Britain's Economic Performance* and owes something to all of these approaches; it has also been informed by other, more specific developments in economic thinking, some of which are worth spelling out.

Some otherwise orthodox economists have taken a major leap forward by placing much greater emphasis upon the role of investment processes, not simply in tangible forms of plant, equipment, building and so on, but also in intangible forms – education, training, research and development, marketing, etc. The key point in their reasoning is that investment processes are also essentially learning processes on the part of individuals and organisations. Significantly, the owners of private firms cannot capture all the benefits from investment in the form of higher profits, and hence the social returns from investment will exceed private returns. Clearly, this provides considerable scope for policy intervention, but its effectiveness will depend upon the agents or institutions mobilised for that purpose.

At the same time, views of the nature of technology have been changing – moving away from the idea that technology can best be thought of in terms of 'codified' information (e.g. sets of blueprints) which can readily be transferred from one location to another, to a view of technology which is substantially more 'tacit' in nature, consisting of the skills of both individuals and teams and the specific competencies of firms. These factors in turn depend upon the *prior investment record* of the firm – in R&D, training and so on. In short, technology is much more costly to transfer than is commonly supposed, and depends upon the past history of firms and institutions. It follows that recessions may do much more damage to an economy's technology base than is apparent from the current loss of output. Certain types of company acquisition may have a similar effect. The importance of continuity within firms is well illustrated in the case of Japan, where management seems to realise more acutely that valuable *assets* are disappearing when a worker is made redundant. The problem is partly that the value of such assets is very difficult to assess from the outside, and the governance structures of economies such as the United Kingdom and the US may be inimical to these kinds of investment.

In short, the view of economic performance that we are putting forward can be thought of as a synthesis of a number of perspectives. The question of competitiveness cannot be reduced to either the effectiveness of markets or the behaviour of firms; institutions and infrastructure, both conceived in the broadest terms, really matter. Moreover, the appropriateness of institutions changes over time. The Government has a vital role to play in ensuring that these changes are consistent with the evolving pattern of international specialisation. Without that, there is no room for complacency in the longer term any more than in the short run.

PLAN OF THE BOOK: SUPPLY-SIDE THEMES

The contributors to this book may not themselves subscribe to all (if any) of the views above; nevertheless we have placed their efforts within a loose framework suggested by the idea of structural competitiveness. Unravelling the elements of structural competitiveness is the task of interpretation we have set ourselves. The book is grouped into six parts, corresponding to major supply-side themes. Each part has its own 'overview', intended to draw the reader's attention to the main issues and present a judicious mix of fact and relevant theory.

Part I sets out both the political and the macroeconomic scene. In the past, Britain's peculiar political framework has contributed to macro-economic policy errors and a comparative neglect of industry.

Part II looks specifically at the United Kingdom's trading performance. The overview charts the general parameters of Britain's overall performance in relation to other major economies, its growth record and its susceptibility to recession. It is argued that the balance of payments is fundamental to understanding the United Kingdom's relative growth performance. The remaining chapters analyse UK trade performance, employing the fundamental distinction between price and non-price competitiveness.

Part III examines investment and innovation, which are the foundations for competitiveness. The overview tracks the comparative record of the United Kingdom over the past decade or more for a number of indicators. Subsequent chapters discuss the roles of fixed investment and human capital, as well as the implications of corporate governance structures, including topical issues of short-termism and the impact of the takeover mechanism.

The labour market forms the basis for investigation in Part IV. The overview challenges the relevance of the simple model of how labour markets work. It examines many of the costs attached to labour market reform, including the impact on the distribution of both income and jobs across households. Remaining chapters question the value of flexibility in the jobs market and of new measures directed at vocational education and training.

Part V forms an entirely new section for the second edition; it evaluates Britain's place in Europe and the challenges that increasing integration pose for industry. The overview tracks the key political and economic developments surrounding the current phase of integration, while the other chapter analyses the prospects for the United Kingdom in a monetary union.

Part VI looks at issues relating to the rapidly changing economic world in which Britain exists. The overview examines the changing relationship between economic policy and the evolving international division of labour. Other chapters discuss deindustrialisation, technology policy, and the phenomenon and policy implications of industrial clustering in high technology industries.

Part I

THE POLITICAL AND MACROECONOMIC FRAMEWORK

2

THE POLITICAL FRAMEWORK
The political roller coaster
Sir Geoffrey Chandler

For some forty-five years from the end of the Second World War party politics imposed their own particular burden on a British industry already suffering from the self-inflicted wounds of low skills, poor training and inadequate investment. The political process was wholly inimical to industrial success. The Labour Party's exaggerated belief in the efficacy of the state vied with the Conservative Party's exaggerated belief in the efficacy of the market to bring damaging fluctuations of policy towards industry. In its crudest and most visible form the impact was manifested in the obsession with ownership rather than efficiency. It was visible not only in the fluctuations between rival administrations, but also within administrations, as the ideological rigidities with which each government entered office were tempered by industrial imperatives.

By the early 1990s these trends appeared to have run their course, or at least been modified by the recurrent failure of initiatives regardless of their political provenance. Repeated disappointment of expectations about the behaviour of the economy had forced a deeper scrutiny of the complex of causes underlying Britain's long relative economic decline and descent to the bottom of the major industrial league. While the search for scapegoats, whether in management, the City, the trade union movement or government, was never likely to disappear entirely as a national sport, there were signs of an emergence of some consensus about the role that government should play in industrial success, beyond the simple provision of a framework. If it was accepted that industrialists must ultimately solve the problems of industry, it was now also understood that politics and the political process played a role in industrial success.

This is not only because in a mixed economy (whatever the changes to the boundaries of ownership) government will remain a huge investor, supplier to and purchaser from industry, significantly influencing the private as well as the public sector; nor simply because as legislator and tax-gatherer, government has immense impact on industrial competitiveness. It is also because the adversarial nature of British politics, exaggerated by an inequitable electoral process, had damagingly infected the two chief institutions of industry and the whole of national debate. This not only prevented what should be an attainable consensus within industry itself, but, until the changes of the 1990s, for a decade or more stifled debate altogether. There is the further reason that government, as the elected leadership of the country, has an inalienable responsibility for providing an honest perspective of the situation and pointing the direction ahead.

Britain's growth rate in the post-war period, fast by our own standards, helped to disguise the decline relative to our competitors. The creation of the National Economic Development Council[1] in 1962 by a Conservative government reflected some recognition of the problem and of the need for joint solutions; but while its roots were embedded deeply enough in principle to enable it to survive through subsequent changes of government for the next thirty years, its influence in practice remained less than its potential.

From 1962, the trend of relative failure continued inexorably, regardless of the complexion of government. In terms of conventionally measured gross domestic product per head – a crude approximation for standard of living – Germany and France had surpassed us in the 1960s, Japan in the 1980s and Italy by 1990. No government gave uniform support to the competitiveness of industry in all its policies, even where it declared the intention of doing so. Each chose initially to pursue those aspects of policy which were ideologically attractive to it and which, even if relevant to the problem, could only make a partial impact if other policies had a contrary effect. We witnessed not only sharp reversals of policy as governments changed, but also reversals of policy within the lifetime of governments.

Most economic policies affect industry, but government attitudes to industry are chiefly manifested in those policies whose primary aim is to influence industrial structure and performance, and it is these which can be collectively described as 'industrial policy'. In May 1979, with the change from Labour to Conservative, there were few points at which the contrast between governments was more sharply focused than here. For some three-and-a-half years the Labour Government's *Approach to Industrial Strategy* had provided a framework for its industrial policy, using the NEDC mechanism – in particular the tripartite sectoral committees and the NED Office – as an integral part of that approach. This was a supply-side policy in which priority was explicitly given to industrial development 'over consumption or even our social objectives',[2] although in practice many government actions and attitudes remained inconsistent with this priority.

The 'industrial strategy' (the modesty of the White Paper's title was soon omitted in the over-politicising of the exercise) made considerable sense so long as its limitations were recognised. Tangible results undoubtedly appeared inadequate in relation to the effort put in, but the achievement of joint understanding at sectoral level of the nature of the problems – their complexity and the need for joint solutions – meant that there were few managers, trade unionists or civil servants involved who did not learn from the exercise, even if that knowledge went little further. And the growing understanding at national level that our fundamental problem was one of competitiveness, insoluble through demand management alone, was assisted by the analytical work of both the committees and the NED Office.

The NED Council itself became chiefly the coordinator of the committees, giving them weight and authority, while broader policy discussion was emasculated, a process accentuated by the close bilateral relationship between the TUC and the Labour Government. Certain subjects, for example pay, were by common consent – including that of the CBI – explicitly taboo.

The Conservative victory of May 1979 brought radical change. Over the next sixteen years there were to be eleven Secretaries of State for Industry,[3] a rapid succession which if it happened in industry itself would be accounted indifference or incompetence. They differed in temperament, philosophy, approach and understanding, although all shared the new Government's objective of 'rolling back the frontiers of the State and improving the functioning of the market economy'.[4] The first, Sir Keith Joseph, doubted whether there should be a Department of Industry at all. The second, Patrick Jenkins, undertook to be 'the voice of industry in Cabinet', a concept anathema to his predecessor, extolling what government was doing for industry, rather than minimising it as undesirable. Paul Channon, number six, in 1987 presented a view of government policy as being 'designed to establish a framework for enterprise within which industry and commerce can thrive and therefore maximize the production of wealth in this country'.[5] He believed that 'the surest – indeed the only – route to this is through a properly functioning free market'. No phrase has proved more debilitating to constructive thought than the 'free market'. The market as we know it in practice is constrained by health and safety, environmental and employment regulations reflecting the views of society at a particular point in history, posing no pragmatic or ideological obstacles to further limits to its freedom. But the phrase was used, and is still used today, to caricature – with Manichean distinction – any suggested alternative as an East European style of command economy.

Lord Young, Channon's successor and with just over two years in the post one of the longer-serving incumbents, brought all the aids – and costs – of modern image-making into play to implement his 'Enterprise Initiative'. This initiative, with its implicit recognition that the market needed prodding and did not work successfully on its own, had more in common with Labour's 'industrial strategy' than with prevailing doctrines. Nicholas Ridley, following Lord Young and closer to Joseph in approach, reportedly believed that the DTI should be left to wither on the vine. Others lacked either the time, capability or inclination to make a mark beyond dogged adherence to the policies of increasing competition, 'levelling playing fields', and supporting small businesses. It was not until the appointment of Michael Heseltine in April 1992 that a role for government in industrial success was given explicit recognition and made the basis of policy.

Underlying the new policies of the Thatcher Government appeared to be a widespread ignorance of the nature and extent of the problems of industry. Manufacturing was no Frog-Prince to be awakened by the kiss of monetary policy or fiercer competition, but a Rip Van Winkle, which, with notable exceptions of excellence to be found in individual companies in almost every sector, had slept for a century while its competitors moved ahead in the development of human resources and application of technology.

A new paradigm emerged: of a country whose wealth would henceforth be dependent on services, on profits remitted from overseas investment, and on North Sea oil. Manufacturing was seen as a balancing item, which, if temporarily eclipsed by the impact of oil and an oil-based value of the pound sterling, would automatically revive as oil declined. That the reverse was true – that manufactures would need to continue to be the most significant element in our international trade, that traded services, while growing fast and enjoying a positive balance of payments, were losing market share as had manufacturing earlier, that the nature and time-scale of manufacturing did not allow it to be switched on and off – was then an unfamiliar thought.

The British problem was that individual examples of excellence remained individual and did not spread to other parts of their sectors. This was not lack of knowledge: each NEDC sectoral committee could point clearly to the elements required for higher productivity for each part of industry they dealt with. The resistance to change of the industrial environment as a whole stemmed from other factors: from the failure of the conventional stimuli to better management – shareholders, non-executive directors, an involved workforce, the trade unions – and from the deep-seated handicap of an unsuitable education, inadequate training and anti-industrial attitudes. It was astonishing that in a political atmosphere where sporting metaphors abounded – the creation of level playing fields (that is, the equalising of competitive conditions) and getting our competitors to play cricket – little thought was given to the quality and training of the players themselves, which most of the electorate would know were fundamental whatever the state of the pitch. It naively postulated a latent industrial competence which, once the fetters were removed, would take its rightful place in the world.

In addition, as the trade unions were put on the defensive and their influence modified by legislation long overdue and welcomed both by the country and majority of trade unionists, a new and corrupting concept entered the scene. This was 'the right to manage'. 'I have given you back the right to manage', said the Prime Minister, Margaret Thatcher, at a CBI annual dinner. It was a 'right' frequently invoked by the Coal Board in the 1984–5 dispute, by ministers,[6] and even used, so pervasive did the concept become, by the former official conciliator, Sir Pat Lowry of the Advisory Conciliation and Arbitration Service.[7] It was a concept which ignored the experience and example of successful managers; it implied wholesale ignorance of the work of behavioural scientists and pioneering employers who over the years had demonstrated that effective management is by consent rather than authority, requiring all the human and intellectual skills a manager can summon; it ran counter to the recognition, to which at least lip-service was paid by successive presidents of the CBI, of the need for the better involvement of the workforce. It assisted a management style characterised as 'macho' which might be briefly successful in financial terms, but would lay no foundations for a long-term future.

The NEDC sat only on the periphery of the power centres of Westminster and Whitehall. But because it was the only regular forum for national economic debate, other than Parliament; because the sectoral committees and the Office were the only entities voicing an unpoliticised view of the needs and problems of industry; and because Sir Geoffrey Howe, the new Chancellor in 1979, with a considerable degree of courage and optimism, initiated a series of macroeconomic discussions in which all aspects of government policy were for the first time for many years put on the table, NEDC reflected with remarkable clarity the conflicts and contradictions of the time. Furthermore, for much of the 1980s, the Council was the only forum for government and trade union dialogue and indeed CBI and TUC dialogue.

Given this climate, if any discussion of industrial policy was to be continued at national level in the NEDC, it had to be done in a fashion which did not offend too obviously against prevailing beliefs. In a paper for the October 1981 NEDC,[8] widely accepted by the CBI, TUC and also government, the Office approached the issue by examining the industrial policies pursued by our continental competitors. It noted that the wide spectrum of policy measures operated on the Continent since the war had almost all been pursued by the United Kingdom at some time over the same period. But UK performance had been signally worse than that of our competitors. While recognising that the factors determining industrial success were complex and varied, precluding the selection of any single policy, institutional framework, or type of expenditure, certain characteristics appeared to be common and to have played a contributory role in success.

These characteristics were continuity and stability of policy; concentration of effort with mutually reinforcing packages of measures; a realistic view of long-term priorities, considering systematically how the structure of industry might look in the longer term; an element of choice or selectivity; massive investment in human resources; and, finally, consensus (whether explicit or implicit) and commitment, both at national and company level.

None of these characteristics was dependent on a particular political or economic philosophy; they were common to countries which adhered strongly to market principles, such as West Germany, as well as to those with more *dirigiste* philosophies, such as France. None appeared beyond our own capabilities.

A second paper in April 1982[9] examined the record of the United Kingdom over the preceding twenty years in terms of the characteristics identified in the first paper. The central phenomenon emerging from this was an underlying continuity and stability in the elements of UK industrial policy, obscured by significant discontinuities at a general level. While capital incentives, regional and competition policy, support for research and development, trade policy, public purchasing, and standard-setting were free from major fluctuations over a long period, this apparent continuity was overlain – and therefore destroyed in practice – by significant political change. This included the experiment with national planning in the mid-1960s; the move towards disengagement in 1970; its reversal in 1972; attempts to introduce a more central role for government in industrial performance in the mid-1970s; its abandonment and replacement by the 'industrial strategy'; and a renewed focus on disengagement from 1979. A further phenomenon was that these major changes were generally short-lived and were succeeded by convergence back to an identifiably more continuous progression of policy development.

THE STIFLING OF DEBATE

The inexorable conclusion was that ideology, however relevant to the distribution of income and wealth, was inimical to its creation. But the damage had been not only in the uncertainties added to those already inherent in industry, but also in the distortion or discrediting of ideas which would have been valuable in themselves had they been presented with a greater sense of the realities and needs of industry. There is logic in a disengagement which puts decisions nearer to the market-place and further from politicians and civil servants: but disengagement needs to be qualified in a world where the market is comprised of governments which play a significant role in industry: it must be matched to our competitors' actions.

The 1977 Bullock Report[10] damaged sensible national discussion about participation and involvement within companies – a human and industrial necessity – by a political rather than pragmatic point of departure. A narrowly doctrinaire conclusion was allowed to set back progress on an aspect of human relations in industry in which we continue to lag woefully behind our competitors, and possibly in some cases was used as an excuse to do so. Sir Terence Beckett, Director-General of the CBI from 1980, repeatedly said that Bullock had 'poisoned the well'. But he never proposed digging another. And while the need for employee involvement was frequently urged at CBI conferences, it was never effectively followed up.

Disengagement made sense for Mrs Thatcher, pushing back responsibilities to where they should lie and seeking to make the market operate more effectively as a stimulus to industrial performance. But most thinking industrialists would argue that government policies remained inadequate for the real challenges they faced in a world where many other governments played a more perceptive and constructive role in relation to industry's complex problems. Moreover, the coining of the ironic phrase 'picking winners' – in other words politicians and civil servants attempting to second-guess the market and failing – contributed nothing to the argument when used to caricature all government intervention.

The NEDC potentially provided a forum for debate of these issues; but even with a chairman such as Sir Geoffrey Howe, who from his appointment as Chancellor in 1979 saw a use for the Council, many significant issues were proscribed, sometimes by one, sometimes by all three parties. The problem of pay settlements unrelated to productivity and greater than country or company might be able to afford has emerged in every economic downturn and was particularly acute in 1979. Incomes policies were deemed to have failed, although it was more accurate to say that their aftermath was considered worse than the success they temporarily enjoyed in restraining increases. But as a low-wage, though high labour-cost, economy it has never proved enough to attempt simply to preach wages down. There were a number of ways in which the subject could have been approached: the potential trade-offs within companies between training and investment on the one hand and pay restraint on the other; the better involvement of company employees enabling them to understand their mutuality of interest; or some form of incomes determination – a phrase devised to meet the TUC's legitimate objection that 'pay' did not relate to all types of income.

We had the spectacle of trade unionists advocating settlements they must have known to be destructive to competitiveness and therefore ultimately jobs; of managements doing nothing to inform or involve their workforce. None the less, all proved undiscussable subjects, even if pay itself became an element in some macroeconomic discussions and the parties eventually agreed to the creation of a small tripartite working group on involvement (the Steering Group on Joint Arrangements at Company Level) under the chairmanship of the Director General. The Government meanwhile resorted to exhortation on pay restraint for the private and cash limits for the public sector.

The ill-conceived and discredited national economic planning of the 1960s had left planning too as a non-discussable subject ever since – the British tradition of throwing out the baby with the bathwater. Any Council discussion which appeared to touch in any way on a government role in planning or strategy provoked caricature and trivialisation from the Government team. But it was precisely because we did not know the answer to these problems, or because past attempts at solving them had failed, that rational discussion of the limits and possibilities was necessary.

THE POLITICISING OF INSTITUTIONS

The policy-swings from government to government were increased rather than diminished by industry's chief institutions, the CBI and TUC. Each lent weight to party political views, rather than slowing the pendulum by using its unrivalled experience of industry as a counterweight to dogma. Under Labour governments the trade union movement sought legislation to strengthen its own position, regardless of the impact on industrial success and regardless of management response. Under Conservative governments the CBI acted similarly. Politics predominated over industrial interest.

The CBI had forged close links with the Conservative Party during its years in opposition. At its first annual conference under the new regime, in November 1979, the closing address of the Director-General, Sir John Methven, contained the striking image that Britain was 'drinking at the Last Chance saloon'.[11] Methven was by temperament a diplomat and politician, who had done much to put the CBI on the map by the initiation of its annual conference. While in no way matching the TUC annual conference as a serious policy-making occasion, it provided a media-opportunity compelling the presence of jounalists and obtaining wide coverage. Its debates were stilted and any resolutions unpalatable to the leadership quietly ignored. But at least it acted as a sounding-board for some of the views of this vastly heterogeneous organisation.

The metaphor of 'the Last Chance saloon' could well have implied the belief that business and industry could only flourish under a Conservative government. But Methven also called on business leaders to go out on the shop floor and in the schools and in the pubs to present the true economic position. The nation had to find a way to talk, to argue and work together like reasonable and responsible people in search for common ground. 'The unions have tried it their way. Now let's try it our way.' Methven's premature death the following year left unknown the manner in which he might thereafter have led the CBI. But an extraordinary private discussion, published posthumously (the journalist concerned asserting that death should put on the record what in life had been off)[12] suggested an antipathy to the trade union leadership which would have done little for a reasonable search for common ground.

His successor, Sir Terence Beckett, previously chairman and managing director of Ford, was a very different character – a straightforward industrial manager plunged into an unfamiliar political world. His first annual conference in November 1980 was to prove a watershed both for him and for the CBI. Spurred by the protests of some of his members to call for an easing of the current recession, Beckett spoke out. 'You had better face the brutal fact that the Conservative Party is in some ways a rather narrow alliance. How many of them in Parliament or the Cabinet have actually run a business? This matters. They do not all understand you. They think they do, but they do not.' Those in industry, he said, had 'to take the gloves off for a bare-knuckle fight', because effective and prosperous industry was vital.[13]

Beckett was right on most counts, but fighting the battle at the wrong time. He directed his criticism not only at the Government's monetary policies, but also at industry's own inadequacies, including the failure to involve and motivate employees. But only the first was heard. Keith Wickenden of European Ferries and Jeffrey Sterling, chairman of Town and City Properties, immediately resigned; and from a meeting with the Prime Minister the following day, unpropitiously planned before his speech, Beckett emerged expressing enthusiasm for Mrs Thatcher and calling it 'a very encouraging meeting'.[14] From then on the CBI was effectively muzzled, not by government, but by itself. Its diverse membership, the contribution of some member companies to Conservative Party funds, the seduction and flattery of senior industrialists by private meetings with ministers, and, for some, the hope of honours, all helped to neuter the CBI as an independent industrial voice.

Criticism of the Government was only permitted in the context of the Government's own monetary policies. The fundamental relationship between government and industry was not a discussable subject, although at the 1986 annual conference members present voted overwhelmingly for a 'coherent industrial strategy' for which James McFarlane, Director-General of the Engineering Employers' Federation, had skilfully argued, calling not for a return to the past, but for an intelligent synergy between government and industry which matched that of our competitors. The vote, carried in the teeth of opposition from the leadership, was thereafter ignored. If the sobriquet 'the Tory Party at work' was unfair to the CBI as a permanent appellation, nevertheless there were occasions, not least during the election campaigns of 1987 and 1992, when public support for that party was voiced by leading CBI members, which fully merited the description.

The trade unions, 'their' party defeated, could expect to exercise little or no influence. The TUC congress after the election called for the reversal of government measures, import controls and the abolition of cuts, with no discussion of how such measures might be resourced – themes which would be repeated annually. Abuse of a 'reactionary' government characterised most contributions, and the President, Tom Jackson, emphasised the need to plan relationships with a future Labour government.

Alienated by legislation they regarded as anti-union, and also, with greater justification, by the social insult some ministers heaped upon them, union leaders none the less for most of the period successfully fought off calls to leave the NEDC and continued to play their part both in Council and on the sectoral committees in some of which they made a real contribution. But the unions' inadequate research and analytical capability – disproportionately small in relation to their role and membership – made them the weakest members of NEDC.

Moreover, with the Labour Party in opposition, the tendency to regard the TUC as a surrogate for it made its representatives in NEDC acutely conscious of their constituency outside. It is conventional wisdom that the trade unions constitute an albatross round the Labour Party's neck: it is too little recognised that the reverse is also true, and that the relationship hampers the contribution to industrial effectiveness that the unions might otherwise make in the interests of their members.

It might rationally be expected that the TUC and CBI could find some agreement at least on fundamentals. But the absence of any formal contact for many years, other than through the NEDC, meant that mutual ignorance was reinforced by mutual suspicion and hostility at both institutional and, in some cases, personal level.

THE SELECTIVITY OF DATA

If reasonable discussion was inhibited by unwillingness to tackle certain subjects, it was also hampered both by inadequacy and selectivity of data. Until the White Paper of 1994 there had been little indication that any government in the post-war period – or for that matter the City or industry – had fully understood the extent and nature of Britain's lack of industrial competitiveness or, which is crucially important for devising prescriptions, the length of our relative decline, now measurable over a hundred years or more. Little in their actions demonstrated a long-term commitment to tackle so deep-seated a problem. Low inflation, competitive interest and exchange rates are necessary, but insufficient, conditions of success – 'hygiene factors' which, if wrong, will prevent growth, but if right will not transform performance or touch the fundamental causes of relative decline.

Statistics comparing British performance with that of our main industrial rivals were neither readily available nor popular. Comparisons unfavourable to the United Kingdom were condemned as 'gloom and doom' or as 'knocking Britain', rather than as a challenge and spur to action. The charge of 'moaning minnies' and of 'whingeing', while hardly contributing to intellectual debate, managed to suppress protest on the part of otherwise robust industrialists. Forecasts of domestic performance were more plentiful – and more prominent in the media – than analysis and fact. Government statistics charted domestic performance which might show improvement against an inadequate past, but told nothing of our standing in the market in which we operated.

The independence of the NED Office, together with its economic and statistical capability, gave it its one weapon in a world where power lay elsewhere. Both at micro- and macro-level its comparative analyses could illuminate problems and even stimulate action.

At the macro-level the Office in July 1980 produced its first edition of *British Industrial Performance*,[15] a booklet intended to illustrate the underlying historical trends of British industry compared to our competitors over the preceding twenty years and the interdependence between broad economic policies and specific industrial performance. The data were purely historical, but the parties to Council, in particular the Government and TUC, argued over what should be included, the first anxious to illustrate any signs of upturn since they took office and to reveal the imperfections of the labour market, the second to minimise these imperfections and show the pain that industry was suffering. The booklet was indeed intended not as an academic economic record, but as a challenging backdrop to NEDC discussions illustrating the seriousness of the task we faced. More ambitiously, it was hoped that it could have a widely educational impact in a country ignorant of where it stood.

The draft of a second, more detailed, edition was put to the Council in March 1983, having been agreed with the Office by the staffs of the three parties. The historical comparisons, even though it was possible to illustrate some stabilising of the UK share of international trade, remained sombre. Electioneering was already in the air and the Council was at its most sensitive. The President of the CBI, Sir Campbell Fraser, chairman of the failing Dunlop company, damned the document as being so gloomy that people would want 'to get the first boat out of the country', and moved for its rejection. Beckett did not believe publication would be productive, because there was not a single item of cheer in it. The Government, surprised, acceded. So too reluctantly did the TUC, agreeing to a postponement of two months. This was later to become the basis of a bizarre election canard when the minutes of the meeting were leaked to the press and the paper described as 'a secret report highlighting the grim prospects for jobs and industry in Britain . . . deliberately held back'.[16] After the Conservative victory of 9 June this innocent historical document, whose statistics deliberately covered a period of time to show the continuity of relative decline under both Labour and Conservative governments, was duly published without demur and without a figure changed.

A third issue of *British Industrial Performance* was published in 1985; a fourth, and last, in 1987. For the next few years, until the Competitiveness White Paper of 1994, the United Kingdom's position in the world was obscured by the predominance of purely domestic data. Indeed, from the more than a thousand pages, numerous graphs and tables of Nigel Lawson's memoirs[17] it is impossible to tell how the United Kingdom fared competitively over the period of which he writes in terms of most major economic or industrial yardsticks.

THE DEEPER CAUSES

The mid-1980s presented the paradox of a flourishing City and cash-rich country accompanied by growing awareness of the basic flaws in our industrial capability. A series of seminal reports quantified the United Kingdom's deficiencies in vocational education and training, shop-floor skills and management qualifications and training.[18] A number of initiatives were started in response to their recommendations, but all were based on the Government's principle of voluntaryism, rather than seeking pragmatically the most effective way in which we might match our competitors. The Management Charter Initiative would embrace those companies which traditionally gave thought to the development of managers; it would not transform a climate where amateurism was still too common. The Training and Enterprise Councils (TECS) were saddled not only with the responsibility of encouraging training – the most fundamental need – but of tackling unemployment and promoting enterprise. Underfunded and with diverse objectives, they would not touch the anti-training ethos prevalent in industry. There was not even any attempt by government to use market forces to encourage the spread of good practice by requiring the publication of training plans in annual reports. Concentration on financial measurements built in short-termism both for companies and investors.

There was in addition a growing realisation that attitudes towards industry played a role in our performance – that we were an industrial country with an anti-industrial culture. The timing and nature of the Industrial Revolution and a narrowly academic education still rooted in a nineteenth-century ethos had contributed to shaping the views of a society which, although ultimately dependent on industry, regarded participation in it as intellectually and morally inferior to the professions.[19] Some might cavil at this analysis, but it was sufficiently compelling to obtain support across the political and institutional spectrum for the designation of 1986 as Industry Year by the Royal Society for the Encouragement of Arts Manufactures and Commerce (RSA). This campaign, targeted towards practical action through local working groups across the country and continued for a further three years under the banner of Industry Matters, had significant results in helping to transform awareness in primary and secondary schools and teacher-training institutions of the nature of industry and of its potential as a partner in delivering the curriculum. It was fortunate in coinciding with changes in education that brought a wider range of human capabilities into formal teaching and examination, many of these being particularly apposite to the needs of industry.

The sustained Industry Year campaign inevitably triggered institutional jealousy and political ambition. The CBI leadership (though not its members, whose efforts were to intensify) as early as September 1986 declined to support the continuation of the campaign beyond the end of the year.[20] The Department of Trade and Industry introduced its own scheme for industry–education links in December 1987, its civil servants emphasising that the credit would need to redound to the Secretary of State and his Enterprise Initiative, with a resultant fragmentation of what was becoming a nation-wide effort with its own momentum.

THE RECKONING

In July 1987 the Chancellor, Nigel Lawson, drastically reduced the NEDC mechanism, having first secured the connivance of the CBI President, David Nickson, whom he praised for his understanding of the climate needed for business success.[21] The CBI had not effectively barked, let alone bitten, for many years: it was safe to pat its titular leader on the head. By contrast the NEDC committees and the Office, with their sectoral analyses and international comparisons of performance, could still discomfit. Their final silencing, from which according to his memoirs Lawson had been dissuaded by Margaret Thatcher, was effected at the end of 1992 by the new Chancellor, Norman Lamont.

Lawson's criticism of the Council as a waste of ministerial time was no more than a self-fulfilling prophecy; his view of the organisation as part of 'the corporate state' simply reflected the shallowness of debate which had characterised the previous years. The Council had in practice long ceased to fulfil the function for which it had been created. Its chief value now was to provide a higher media profile for the work of the committees and of the Office. The sensitivity of politicians to unpalatable analysis and the reluctance of the parties to NEDC to engage in debate meant that the disappearance of the Council itself was a small loss, even if it removed the last non-parliamentary forum for discussion and mutual education about industry and the economy. The extinction of the sectoral committees and the Office, however, meant that there would now be no comparable body, accepted as independent and free of any political slant, arguing the corner for industry on the basis of collective experience and statistical analysis.

What we had seen had been no consistent supply-side policy. It had been shaped by what was politically acceptable, rather than what was industrially necessary. Government policies had shown themselves capable of controlling inflation, also of creating it and generating recession and boom, not of significantly influencing the foundations of competitiveness across the broad spectrum of industry. There had been genuine gains: the reform of the trade unions; the encouragement of self-employment and indeed of 'enterprise' until political overuse devalued the word. The diminution of government intervention in industrial disputes was also welcome, though the institution of 'beer and sandwiches' at No. 10 Downing Street was replaced by ministerial appearances on television when they felt their appointed managers were inadequately equipped for the task. The encouragement of a customer orientation, whether in the remaining public sector or the newly privatised monopolies, helped to make those entities more responsive to the consumer. But these reforms, important though they were, simply removed some of the archaic institutional and attitudinal clutter which hindered effective management. The fundamental changes required in the training of management and workforce continued to be left to the principle of voluntaryism which had long shown itself inadequate except for a minority of companies which in this, as in other requirements for market success, adapted to match their competition. Ministers simply continued to assert that government was impotent to play a role in these matters.

As the 1992 election approached it remained doubtful if much had been learnt from the preceding thirteen years. In the depths of the longest post-war recession, with unemployment again rising towards three million, a significant balance of payments deficit and a level of poverty wholly unacceptable in an advanced nation, there was little sign of new thinking. The Foreign Secretary, Douglas Hurd, asked in the pre-electoral period why government rejected intervention in industry, could only respond 'It's this business of "picking winners". It hasn't worked in the past'.[22] Even if the economy might be considered outside a Foreign Secretary's domain, nothing could better illustrate the shallowness of debate and staleness of prevailing shibboleths. In the economic policy debate of 24 September the Prime Minister, John Major, declared 'The essential conditions for Britain's economic success are low inflation, low taxes, free trade and freedom from excessive state interference. I am happy to reaffirm those principles today. The Government stand for a low inflation, low tax economy – and so, I believe, do the British people.'[23] There was nothing new here: only the familiar 'hygiene factors'. That nearly 60 per cent of the British electorate may have voted for something else was ignored.

THE NEW REALISM

By the early 1990s the underlying elements for industrial success – education, training and attitudes – were at least for the first time on the national agenda, even if they had been identified in principle more than a hundred years before.[24] Some progress was being made in all: the question remained whether it would be fast enough to keep up with the pace of change in competitor countries, let alone catch up with their level of achievement, or whether a narrow political philosophy, party conflict, and lack of national consensus about ends and means would condemn us to remain in our bottom place in the industrial league.

The scope and effectiveness of the Government role was also now being challenged, not least by the CBI. The politicisation of its members diminished by the removal of Margaret Thatcher from the scene, the manifest disarray of the successor administration, deep concern about the state and conduct of the economy – all contributed to a new realism in the organisation. Moreover, manufacturing, the Cinderella of the 1980s, was now seen as a priority. A CBI Manufacturing Advisory Group, reporting in Autumn 1991, recommended the creation of a National Manufacturing Council, which was duly set up early the following year 'to focus on the key strengths and weaknesses of UK manufacturing industry in relation to its main competitors, to ensure that it is developed and equipped within the shortest realistic timetable to compete with the best in the world'. The Council set targets for UK manufacturing – to increase productivity by more than 5 per cent a year through the 1990s; to double by the year 2000 investment per employee in plant and machinery, skills and innovation; to secure an extra 1 per cent of world trade, equivalent to £10bn a year, by the end of the decade. In a series of documents, foreshadowing the Government White Papers, the CBI set out the comparative figures of the United Kingdom's competitive position which had met such resistance from their representatives ten years earlier.[25] Perhaps most significantly, in direct contrast to its attitudes in the past, the CBI now called on government 'to change the culture and provide leadership with a positive industrial strategy to secure international competitiveness'.

With John Major's return to office in the 1992 election government policy towards industry also began a radical change. What was to prove the longest recession since the war, persistently high unemployment, a backdrop of growing inequality,[26] and a change of cast in both the main political parties, all contributed – at least on the surface – to a shift from the divisive dogmas of the 1980s. These dogmas could still be found within the Cabinet and the Conservative Party, primarily reflected in attitudes towards Europe and the handling of the economy. But if Michael Portillo and John Redwood remained the most prominent and articulate standard-bearers of the Thatcherite past, it was Michael Heseltine, as President of the Board of Trade and later to become Deputy Prime Minister, who set the stamp of his own approach on the Government's attitude to assisting industrial success. At the first Conservative Party conference after the election victory, Heseltine indicated his readiness to match French, German and Japanese government help to their companies by intervening in industry 'before breakfast, lunch, tea and dinner'. More specifically, after thirteen years in which the phrase had been taboo or rubbished, he stated his unequivocal belief in the need for an 'industrial strategy', emphasising that government was 'not powerless' to help to do things overdue by a hundred years in the interests of competitiveness.[27]

Any immediate impact this might have had was overwhelmed by the fiasco of the pit closure announcement, but it nonetheless laid the foundations for a new government industrial policy. This was to find expression in the two White Papers on Competitiveness of 1994 and 1995.[28]

These publications, intended to be produced annually, provided an analytical picture of the United Kingdom's competitive place in the world for the first time since NEDO's last issue of *Britain's Industrial Performance*. Although inevitably tempered by the language of public relations, they were remarkably frank by contrast with the Government's previously Panglossian approach. An introduction by the Prime Minister to the first of these stated 'To achieve this [commercial and industrial success] we seek a new partnership between government and industry.' A further quotation, from his address to the CBI Annual Dinner, prefaced the document: 'All our policies – not just our economic policy – need to be focused on the future strength of the British economy.'

If this had a resonance with the 'Industrial Strategy' of the late 1970s, it was reinforced by Heseltine's reinstatement of sectoral sponsorship at the DTI. A further echo of the work of the NEDC sectoral committees was the emphasis put on 'benchmarking' by both the CBI and the Department. A persistent phenomenon of British industry has been the existence of world-class companies in a number of sectors, accompanied by a large proportion of laggards. A 1994 study by IBM Consulting and the London Business School showed the United Kingdom matching Germany in its proportion of leading companies, but with a significantly higher percentage of companies lagging badly in key aspects.[29]

'Benchmarking' enables companies to measure their own performance against the best industry standards as a means towards improving their own competitiveness and was an attempt to remedy the failure of the market to encourage best practice to spread. In what was now planned the President of the Board of Trade was at pains to emphasise the greater magnitude over what had gone before. 'The opportunities in the DTI eclipse a thousandfold what I think NEDO was able to achieve ... Within the DTI the spirit of what was intended [in the NEDC] will be carried through on a scale not yet realised'.[30] The development of 'Business Links' across the country to provide a range of services, in particular to small business, added to the DTI's armoury of support. The regionalisation of government in England also promised the opportunity – if taken – of bringing a greater two-way flow of contact between local industry and government, even if falling well short of the impetus provided by the Scottish and Welsh Development Agencies. The watchwords became deregulation and competitiveness, responsibility for both of which was retained by Heseltine on his elevation to Deputy Prime Minister. For some, deregulation constituted the healthy removal of unnecessary and burdensome bureaucracy; for others, it could threaten the removal of employment rights, particularly in small businesses where unionism was weak or non-existent.[31] Indeed what had once been a declared national objective of a high-wage, high-productivity, high-profitability economy now appeared to seek low wages as a prime means of achieving competitiveness and attracting inward investment.

A NEW CONVERGENCE?

The forces that were changing Conservative attitudes were also changing the Labour Party. In addition, Labour was forced to come to terms with the traumatic impact of a fourth electoral defeat in a row. A new leader, Tony Blair, carried through the abolition of Clause IV of the Labour Party constitution which had long advocated, in the popular interpretation of a sophisticated form of words, wholesale nationalisation. Freed of this burden, the party refused to be tempted into promising the renationalisation of the privatised monopolies with the exception of the railways (even here, the means of restoring public control remained flexible). For the first time since the war it seemed that a change of government might promise a converging rather than divergent agenda. The national agenda had shifted towards the right and the most significant outcome of the Thatcher era might well now prove New Labour.

The Labour Party's stated policies on taxation, inflation and industry appeared little different from those of the Government. Blair sought a 'constructive partnership' with business and expressed himself as not being 'in favour of either [business or trade union special interests] having an undue influence over government policy'.[32] Blair's presence at the 1995 CBI Annual Conference and shadow ministers' approaches to business brought an outward shifting of business attitudes which the Government, discomfited by the weakening allegiance of what it regarded as its staunchest ally, did its best to counter, though by rubbishing rather than reason.[33]

Real differences between the parties remained the minimum wage and the Social Chapter, to both of which the Labour Party had committed itself. Within industry there were many managers who supported the first, if not at the levels currently being suggested by some trade unions. The second was seen by business in general as threatening additional costs and barriers to efficiency, not least through a statutory involvement of the workforce, though the subsidiaries of many British-based transnational groups were already living with its implications on the Continent.

But allegiances were shifting, even if not being transferred; and it was still too soon to hope that industry might fight its corner with strict political neutrality. Company donations to the Conservative Party, a dubious practice in a democracy based on one person one vote, were diminishing, even if only on grounds of expediency – concern with elements within the Conservative Party expressing hostility to Europe and thus to the effective working of the Single Market – rather than principle. In 1994 the media group Pearson gave £25,000 to both the Labour and Conservative Parties, having previously subscribed only to the second. The new CBI Director General, Adair Turner, expressed the view in an interview with *The Times* that the CBI should be neutral at the next election.[34] It was, however, a view unlikely to prevail among his membership as electoral pressures mounted, and as early as April 1996 the CBI was constrained to distance itself from a campaign promoted by its President-Designate, Sir Colin Marshall, extolling the Government's economic record.[35]

While Blair led Labour away from its doctrinal past and began to dismantle its close constitutional links with the trade unions, a new General Secretary of the TUC, John Monks, began to diminish on his side a political linkage which had for so long inhibited trade union freedom of thought and action on industrial policy. In addition, trade union sponsorship of Members of Parliament was modified to shift support from the individual members to the constituency.

If convergence now appeared in prospect, it was at the level of the leadership rather than in the ranks of the two major parties. The fragile unity of both front benches was sustained on the one hand by an increasingly precarious hold on power as the Government's parliamentary majority crumbled, and on the other by a determination to gain office after long exile from it. In the wings of both the major parties sat dissenting elements, unrepresentative but still potent, which only a more equitable electoral system could safely relegate to the minority sidelines where, arguably, they belonged.

THE CULTURAL PROBLEM

The CBI's National Manufacturing Council had called on government 'to change the culture'. But 'culture', embodied in attitudes towards industry, was also the responsibility of companies and their institutions. The campaign of Industry Year '86 and Industry Matters had made a lasting impression on education, but little on industry. In 1996 two new initiatives pursued similar objectives. The West Midlands Festival of Industry and Enterprise, or Industry '96, was 'organised to underline the vital role that West Midlands plays in the life of the country'. The Year of Engineering Success 1997, launched in September 1996, was intended 'to increase awareness of engineering, across all ages and backgrounds, through the most public participation exercise ever mounted in support of engineers and engineering which are vital to the nation's success and prosperity'. Whether the short lead-times allowed for these campaigns and the unspecific nature of their targets would allow them to be more than cosmetic exercises remained to be seen. But the perceived need for the repetition of such initiatives illustrated the persistence of the United Kingdom's cultural barrier to recognition of the importance of industrial success.

That the problem of the standing of engineers lay as much within the profession as outside it was underlined by the need for the Engineering Council to launch itself anew in 1996 for the purpose for which it had been set up fifteen years earlier – the unification of the engineering profession and its thirty-nine institutions. Whether its vitiating institutional fragmentation would now be overcome was unclear, but so long as the observer could contrast the undistinguished offices of the Council with the Victorian splendour of many of its component institutions conviction would be difficult.

The reputation of industry in general was damaged by the significant salary increases received by the senior executives of public utilities after their privatisation, which coincided with the 'downsizing' of their workforce and policies of wage restraint for the shop floor. The creation of the Greenbury Committee by the CBI to examine the question of top salaries did little to appease public and political anger, and even Howard Davies, now free of the institutional constraint of his Director Generalship of the CBI, could comment that top pay was handled badly by many companies and that 'some companies have moved outside their licence to operate in the past couple of years'.[36]

The 'licence to operate' in a more critical society was the concept which underlay a new RSA initiative, Tomorrow's Company. This brought attention to the need for successful businesses to be driven by values which would include all stakeholder relationships,[37] with a less exclusive focus on shareholders and financial measures of success. Admirable in intent, unexceptionable in its conclusions, the report[38] was unlikely, without a determination to find measures of success other than the financial bottom line, to make little greater impact than the Watkinson Report of 1973[39] which had dealt, though far less creatively, with the same problem.

THE HUMAN DIMENSION

If the United Kingdom was to compete in the market for skill-intensive and intellect-intensive services and products in which the prosperity of the older industrial countries must lie, education and training would be fundamental to success. The 1994 World Economic Forum Competitiveness Report[40] showed the United Kingdom ranking 32 out of 41 countries for in-company training, 34 for the willingness of workers to retrain and learn new skills, and 37 for the ability of its educational system to meet the needs of a competitive economy.

Advances, however, had been made by the mid-1990s. Participation in higher education had risen significantly from 13 per cent of those eligible in 1979 to some 30 per cent by 1994. The introduction of National Vocational Qualifications, wholly appropriate in principle to need, if difficult to administer, provided the opportunity for measured advancement and the attainment of skills in virtually every field. But education remained a party battleground, with levels of investment, methods of funding and control, and the principle of selection some of the chief points of contention. Meanwhile the A-level examination, despite the almost universal condemnation of the narrow specialisation it imposes at a premature age, remained impervious to radical change, although the proposed introduction of a new Applied A-level examination was intended to provide parity of esteem between vocational and academic subjects.

The growing evidence that early education, particularly nursery education, was crucial to later learning and ultimately to economic success led to both main parties putting emphasis here. But government pilot schemes and its attempt to widen policy issues between the parties, countered by a series of opposition initiatives, meant that politics, rather than a badly needed consensus on education, prevailed.

For training the TECs remained the principal vehicle where companies failed to provide their own in-house training. Born of a political desire to diminish the role of government, rather than as a considered means of diminishing the United Kingdom's training deficit, TECs had come under increasing criticism for the inadequacy of their resources, the unrepresentative nature of their governance, and their inability to deliver effectively any of the objectives they had been set. The anomaly of these hybrid bodies – government-funded monopolies in the form of private limited companies – was highlighted in 1995 by the failure of the South Thames TEC, with attendant damage to the training institutions with which it had contracted. Three years earlier the chairman of the National Training Task Force, Sir Brian Wolfson, had called on the Cabinet to abandon its philosophy of 'voluntaryism' and to introduce a levy on company payrolls to ensure that money was spent on training.[41] The weight of political capital invested by government in the TECs ensured that this plea went no further, but in 1995 the Labour Party indicated that in power it would seek some statutory framework for training, not in the form of a levy, as was initially mooted, but possibly an obligation for companies to become Investors in People. What had long been abundantly clear was that voluntaryism had failed.

THE FOG OF WAR

Although the next general election was unlikely to take place until May 1997 (the last politically practicable date), electioneering was dominating the political scene by late 1995. It could be claimed with some justification[42] that four policy approaches had made 'a particularly favourable contribution since 1979' leading to a significant growth in manufacturing productivity. These were privatisation, inward investment, the growth of small businesses, and labour market policies. But none, except the third, were exempt from severe actual or potential disadvantages. The crowning failure of the United Kingdom to run its publicly owned enterprises effectively, with freedom from politics, would continue to haunt us if the privatised utilities were to regard the obligation to their shareholders as their prime objective and the companies as properties to be freely bought and sold on the international market. The dominance of foreign ownership in certain sectors of industry and foreign-owned companies' significant share of the total export of manufactures (put at two-fifths by Eltis and Higham[43]) could mean a growing vulnerability to strategic decisions made elsewhere, even if in the short term the gains in technology, investment, and particularly management were wholly to be welcomed. Labour market policies, in particular trade union reform, had made a significant contribution to industrial stability; but now, as the Government sought 'clear blue water' between itself and the opposition, there was danger that the inequalities in society arising from new patterns of employment and unemployment could be increased, rather than diminished, by further legislation.

With the Government in disarray from internal dissension and external pressures, with an opposition wholly untried in government, there was opportunity for an industrial voice both to reinforce the aspects of economic management that found agreement between the parties – strictly controlled inflation, moderate taxation – and also to emphasise the needs of industry with political impartiality. But while allegiances were clearly shifting, while the CBI was once again talking constructively to the TUC, it remained clear that without greater business leadership than was evident, the touchstone of an actual election would revive old battle lines. At the relaunch of the Engineering Council Michael Heseltine had chided engineers (and accountants and industry trade associations) for their failure to provide a coherent voice to government and the public at large.

In 1996 government ministers, from the Prime Minister downwards, repeatedly proclaimed the United Kingdom to be 'the enterprise centre of Europe'. The Chancellor of the Exchequer, Kenneth Clarke, proclaimed his policy to be to 'stick to good enterprise economics, not boom and bust'.[44] The elements necessary to a competitive economy were improving, but the country's infrastructure, both physical and human, still lagged far behind our main competitors. (Transport had suffered even worse than industry in the rapid rotation of Secretaries of State: eleven since 1979; five since 1990.) Moreover the United Kingdom had become a society in which social cohesion had been severely damaged by the inequalities between those in and out of work, between full- and part-time workers, between the inner cities and the wealthier suburbs. If competitiveness were to be achieved and maintained, it would need to be done in a manner which diminished rather than enhanced these inequities.

The jockeying of the main parties for electoral advantage, however, debased the currency of public debate, nowhere more so than on the issue of taxation. Apart from the Liberal Democrats, whose lack of expectation of power could allow them frankly to promise higher taxation for the purpose of education, the parties substituted charge and counter-charge for serious argument about how their undertakings for health and education could be consistent with promises of lower or constant tax.

Debate on relations with the European Community was equally trivialised by fear of alienating an electorate assumed to be incapable of digesting serious discussion. The growing interdependence of national economies, the internationalisation of trade and production, and the European Single Market had all helped to change the world for Britain, as for its main trading partners, and to diminish the scope for independent action. As the weakest major economy in the Community, the United Kingdom could ill afford to go it alone in an increasingly competitive world or to jeopardise its attraction to inward investors as a springboard into the Single Market. Yet important arguments about the way in which British interests might best be furthered were reduced to simplistic soundbites about sovereignty and the single currency. The boundary between reasoned Euroscepticism and xenophobia was increasingly narrowed, sometimes by the reality, more often by the caricature, of decisions made in Brussels, and swept away, for the tabloid press at least, by the Government's ill-considered 'beef war' against its European partners. If there was growing convergence between parties on economic matters as the decade progressed, there was a sharpening of difference on constitutional issues and relationships with Europe, both of which could have more dramatic effects on our economic performance than economic policies themselves.

The political scene of the mid-1990s was undoubtedly different from the 1980s. But it would take an election to reveal the extent and nature of that difference and whether the political process might now assist industrial success or, at the least, do it no further harm.

NOTES

Some of the material for this chapter appeared in the *RSA Journal*, vol. CXXXI, no. 5319, February 1983 and *The Three Banks Review*, no. 141, March 1984.

1 The NEDC comprised three parts – the Council itself, the sectoral committees and the Office. Where the context is clear, they are referred to in this fashion; where there may be doubt they are prefaced by NED.
2 *An Approach to Industrial Strategy*, Cmnd 6315.
3 Secretaries of State for Trade and Industry since 1979: Sir Keith Joseph, Industry, May 1979–September 1981; John Nott, Trade and President Board of Trade, May 1979–January 1981; John Biffen, Trade and President of the Board of Trade, January 1981–April 1982; Patrick Jenkins, Industry, September 1981–June 1983; Lord Cockfield, Trade and President of the Board of Trade, April 1982–June 1983; Cecil Parkinson, Trade and Industry, June 1983–October 1985; Norman Tebbit, Trade and Industry, October 1983–September 1985; Leon Brittan, Trade and Industry, September 1985–25 January 1986; Paul Channon, Trade and Industry, 25 January 1986–13 June 1987; Lord Young, Trade and Industry, 13 June 1987–24 July 1989; Nicholas Ridley, Trade and Industry, 24 July 1989–14 July 1990; Peter Lilley, Trade and Industry, 14 July 1990–11 April 1992; Michael Heseltine, President of the Board of Trade, 11 April 1992–June 1995; Ian Lang, President of the Board of Trade, June 1995–. Source: Department of Trade and Industry.
4 Nigel Lawson (1992), *The View from No. 11. Memoirs of a Tory Radical*, London: Bantam Press, p.52.
5 October 1987, 'Why is there a DTI?' *RSA Journal*, vol. CXXXV, No. 5375.
6 For example, Lord Glenarthur, Parliamentary Under-Secretary of State in the Home Office, spoke of the 'absolute right to manage' in the context of the prison officers' dispute. BBC *Today* programme, 24 April 1986.
7 June 1988, 'The industrial relations outlook: confrontation or cooperation?', *RSA Journal*, vol. CXXXVI, no. 5383. The reference is omitted in the published text, but its use in the lecture is revealed in a published question and answer.
8 *Industrial Policies in Europe*, NEDC (81) 51.

9   *Industrial Policy in the UK,* NEDC (82) 25.
10 *Report of the Committee of Inquiry on Industrial Democracy,* Cmnd 6706.
11 *Daily Telegraph,* 12 November 1979.
12 *The Guardian,* 1 May 1980. Article by John Torode based on a discussion with Methven which had taken place three months earlier. The story was repudiated by the president of the CBI, Sir John Greenborough (*Guardian,* 8 May 1980), but, whatever the journalistic impropriety of revealing what had been said in confidence, the presumption must be that Torode did not fabricate his story.
13 *The Times,* 12 November 1980
14 *The Times,* 13 November 1980.
15 *British Industrial Performance,* NEDC, July 1980. Revised March 1981.
16 *Daily Mirror,* 23 May 1983.
17 Lawson, *op. cit.*
18 *Competence and Competition. Training and education in the Federal Republic of Germany, the United States and Japan,* NEDC, Manpower Services Commission, 1984; *The Making of Managers. A report on management education, training and development in the USA, West Germany, France, Japan and the UK,* Manpower Services Commission, NEDC, British Institute of Management 1987 (the Handy Report).
19 Key sources for this are: Corelli Barnett (1972), *The Collapse of British Power,* London: Eyre Methuen; *ibid.* (1986) *The Audit of War,* London: Macmillan; and Martin Wiener (1981), *English Culture and the Decline of the Industrial Spirit 1850– 1980,* Cambridge University Press.
20 The president of the CBI, David Nickson, pleading other priorities for the organisation, said that the continuation of the campaign would have the CBI's 'passive acceptance rather than whole-hearted or enthusiastic support'. Meeting with RSA representatives, 3 September 1986.
21 Lawson, *op. cit.,* p. 717.
22 BBC *World at One,* 12 February 1992.
23 Hansard, vol. 212, no. 52.
24 See, for example, *Report of the Endowed Schools* (Schools Enquiry), Royal Commission, 1867–8; and Lyon Playfair (1852), *Industrial Instruction on the Continent,* both cited by Barnett.
25 *Competing with the world's best,* CBI Manufacturing Advisory Group. Autumn 1991; *Making it in Britain,* CBI National Manufacturing Council annual reports I–IV, 1992–5
26 *Income and Wealth,* Joseph Rowntree Foundation, February 1995. This report, produced by an enquiry team which included both Howard Davies, Director General of the CBI, and John Monks, General Secretary of the TUC, showed that between 1979 and 1992 income of the poorest 10 per cent of the population fell by 20 per cent, compared with an increase of 36 per cent in average incomes, leading to greater inequality than at any time since the war.
27 BBC *Today* programme, 15 October 1992.
28 *Competitiveness: Helping business to win,* Cm. 2563; *Competitiveness: Forging ahead,* Cm. 2867.
29 Cited in *Competitiveness: Forging ahead,* p.115.
30 'The Future of Britain's Manufacturing Industry'; answer to question, *RSA Journal* vol. CXLI no. 5442, August/September 1993.
31 A leaked letter from Mr Ian Lang, President of the Board of Trade, to Mr Heseltine revealed – by warning against them – that there were plans to remove employment rights from workers in small firms: *The Times,* 8 March 1996. The letter had been leaked to the BBC the previous day.
32 Interview in *The Times,* 13 November 1995.

33 Applause for the speeches of Tony Blair and Michael Heseltine to the CBI's Conference were timed at 55 and 39 seconds respectively: *The Times*, 14 November 1995

34 *The Times*, 13 November 1995.

35 *The Independent*, 11 April 1996.

36 BBC Radio 4, 15 September 1995.

37 The concept of industrial stakeholders – employees, customers, community, as well as shareholders – long predated Tony Blair's application of the term to the country as a whole.

38 *Tomorrow's Company: the role of business in a changing world*, RSA, June 1995.

39 *The Responsibilities of the British Public Company*, CBI, September 1973.

40 *World Competitiveness Report 1994*, International Institution for Management Development and World Economic Forum Report. Cited in *Tomorrow's Company*.

41 *The Independent*, 14 December 1992.

42 Walter Eltis and David Higham (1995). 'Closing the United Kingdom Competitiveness Gap', *National Institute Economic Review*, November.

43 *Op. cit.*, p.80. The anomalous contrast between an unqualified embrace of inward investment and insular hostility towards 'Europe' is underlined by Will Hutton (1996), *The State We're In*, revd edn, London: Vintage, p.322.

44 BBC *Today* programme, 7 March 1996.

3

UK MACROECONOMIC POLICY AND ECONOMIC PERFORMANCE

Andrew Sentance

In many respects, the 1950s and 1960s can be seen as a disappointing period for UK economic performance. Between 1950 and the early 1970s, the UK economy grew at just over half the rate of our major European competitors. Measured in terms of GDP per head (at purchasing power parity exchange rates), living standards in Germany overtook those in the United Kingdom in 1961, and the average French citizen was richer than his/her British counterpart by 1969.[1] Meanwhile, Britain's share of world trade halved between the mid-1950s and the early 1970s – with the UK share of exports in a group of leading manufacturing nations falling from one-fifth to just one-tenth (CBI, 1991). Over this period there was a growing perception of Britain falling behind other competitor nations – failing to grasp the potential created by the 'white heat of technological revolution' and missing out on the trading opportunities within the fledgling European Common Market.

But in terms of the conventional benchmarks of successful macroeconomic policy, the 1950s and 1960s were a golden age of 'full employment' and low inflation which disappeared in the 1970s and has not been regained since. The United Kingdom was not alone in experiencing less favourable macroeconomic conditions after 1970 than before. Inflation rose world-wide in the late 1960s and the early 1970s and was given further momentum by the first oil price hike in 1973. As the authorities acted to curb inflation, unemployment rose in all the major industrialised economies and it increased further in the wake of the inflationary pressures generated by the second oil shock in 1978/9.

These shocks played an important part in undermining the relative stability that characterised the British economy in the 1950s and 1960s. However, they do not explain why UK macroeconomic performance after 1970 deteriorated not only in relation to the preceding decades but also in relation to other major economies which were affected by similar shocks. In the 1970s, our inflation rate was significantly higher than those of other major

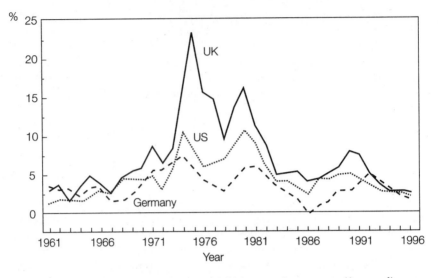

Figure 3.1 UK inflation record, 1961–96 (% increase in consumers' expenditure deflator)

industrialised economies – except Italy – and it remained relatively high through the 1980s (Figure 3.1). The average level of unemployment in the United Kingdom was the highest of the G7 economies in the 1980s, though recent performance has been more encouraging. Since 1970, the UK growth rate has been one of the most volatile in the industrialised world (Oulton, 1995) and the British economy has experienced more recession years than other major economies.[2] (Currie and Sentance, 1994.)

This chapter discusses the contribution of macroeconomic policy to these disappointing aspects of UK economic performance. It reviews the conduct of British macroeconomic policy over the last three decades and addresses three main questions. What have been the key failures in the operation of macroeconomic policy? To what extent have policy-makers learned from their mistakes and addressed these problems? And what lessons does past experience offer for the future conduct of macroeconomic policy?

THE OPERATION OF MACROECONOMIC POLICY

Macroeconomic policy primarily involves the regulation of the amount of expenditure (demand) in the economy, with the objective of influencing the direction of the economy in the short term – in particular the level of output and employment and the rate of inflation. Policies which stimulate demand will exert an upward influence on output and employment. Higher demand may also spill over into higher prices – either as a direct response from

36

companies to stronger demand conditions (for example because of capacity constraints) or because of upward pressure on wages through the labour market. In an open economy, the exchange rate – which affects output through its impact on competitiveness and inflation through the prices of imported goods and services – can be an important channel through which the levers of macroeconomic policy, in particular interest rates, affect economic performance.

There are two main channels available to the national authorities to influence demand conditions: monetary policy and fiscal policy. Through monetary policy, the authorities seek to influence private sector lending and borrowing decisions by changing the terms and conditions on which banks and other financial institutions have access to money from the central bank. The main lever for exercising control over the financial system is the interest rate at which the central bank supplies short-term money to the market. In the past, the authorities have used various forms of regulation to reinforce their control of the monetary system, including direct restrictions on consumer credit and controls on international financial flows. However, the increasing sophistication of financial markets greatly reduced the effectiveness of such restrictions on financial institutions as tools of monetary policy and the United Kingdom was in the vanguard of the international movement to deregulate its financial system in the 1980s.

Fiscal policy – the Government's decisions on its own spending and revenue-raising – is a less flexible though no less powerful channel for influencing the level of demand. Government spending and tax plans are normally set on an annual cycle and can therefore be adjusted less frequently than interest rates. However, despite this lack of flexibility, fiscal policy can exert a powerful influence on demand. The strong demand-led booms of the early 1970s and the late 1980s were fuelled by expansionary fiscal policy as well as monetary laxness.[3] A more recent example shows how fiscal policy can play a more positive role in demand management. The braking influence of the tightening of fiscal policy over 1994 and 1995 helped the UK economy to stay on a steady growth and low inflation course in the mid-1990s without a significant tightening of monetary policy.[4]

STABILISING THE ECONOMY

The instruments of fiscal and monetary policy provide policy-makers with powerful levers with which they can influence the direction of the economy in the short term. But though monetary and fiscal policy have the power to raise the rate of growth substantially in the short term by increasing the level of demand, the main contribution that macroeconomic policy can make to economic performance over the longer term is as a stabilising influence on the course of the economy.

There are two aspects to this stabilising role. First, macroeconomic policy underpins the financial stability of the economy by maintaining a low and stable rate of inflation and avoiding large and unsustainable government deficits. While inflation can be tolerated if it continues at a low and predictable rate, high inflation distorts the operation of markets, generates uncertainty and redistributes wealth in an arbitrary fashion – discouraging investment and disrupting the process of wealth creation.[5] As Keynes commented: 'There is no subtler, no surer means of overturning the existing basis of society than to debauch the currency. The process engages all the hidden forces of economic law on the side of destruction, and does it in a manner which not a man in a million is able to diagnose.' (Keynes, 1919) Persistently high government deficits are also a potential source of inflation and high public borrowing may also 'crowd out' productive investment, inhibiting the growth potential of the economy.

The second stabilisation role played by macroeconomic policy is in relation to the real economy. It is clearly beneficial to long-term economic performance to reduce fluctuations in output and employment – increasing the predictability of the business climate and avoiding the destruction of human and physical capital that occurs in prolonged downturns. However, there are practical constraints on the ability of economic policy-makers to 'fine-tune' the economy so that it proceeds on a steady growth path. Lags in the production of economic statistics, delays in policy implementation and the slow and uncertain response of the economy to policy changes can result in the Government exacerbating the next boom rather than preventing the current slump. In addition, if macroeconomic policy seeks to offset real shocks to which the economy needs to adjust – such as structural changes in the labour market or an oil price hike – this can lead to inflation.

Because of the difficulties associated with output stabilisation, policy-makers have come to emphasise medium-term financial stability – low inflation (stable prices) and sound public finances – as the main objectives of macroeconomic policy. However, this does not mean that stabilisation of the real economy is no longer a valid policy objective. Rather, it reflects the fact that financial instability and volatility in the real economy are correlated over the longer term. Countries which have high and volatile inflation rates have tended to experience greater fluctuations in output growth (IMF, 1996) because of the destabilising effect that inflation can have on private sector decisions and on policy interventions.[6] Large and persistent government deficits can have a similar destabilising effect. Therefore if the stabilisation of output and employment is to be effective, it needs to be conducted within a framework which ensures that the policies being pursued are consistent with financial stability over the medium term.

THE 'GOLDEN AGE' OF THE 1950s AND 1960s

In the 1950s and 1960s, financial stability in the United Kingdom and other major economies was largely maintained by the exchange rate link to a low inflation dollar under the Bretton Woods system. The commitment to maintain the value of sterling at a certain parity against the dollar ($2.80 until November 1967, when the pound was devalued to $2.40) held back inflation in the tradable sector of the economy (mainly manufacturing) and hence in the economy more generally. If UK producers of tradable goods raised prices more rapidly than the US and other countries, the balance of payments would deteriorate, exerting downward pressure on the currency. To maintain the value of the pound, demand conditions would need to be tightened through the use of monetary or fiscal policy.

While US inflation remained low and stable, this exchange rate commitment ensured that UK economic policy was consistent with low inflation. Movements in the balance of payments acted as an important barometer of the need to tighten demand conditions – hence the preoccupation with the balance of payments in the policy debates of the 1950s and 1960s. This balance of payments constraint on economic policy could be eased by devaluation – but only at the risk of higher inflation. Following the 1967 devaluation of sterling it was not surprising that UK inflation picked up (from 3.6 per cent in the three years before 1967 to 5.5 per cent in the three years afterwards).

The Bretton Woods regime was generally successful in maintaining financial stability within the British economy in the 1950s and 1960s. Inflation was low, at around the European average, with consumer prices rising on average at an annual rate of 3.5 per cent between 1952 and 1970 (excluding the inflation induced by the Korean War in 1951/2). And public finances were well managed. The public sector borrowing requirement averaged just 2.1 per cent of GDP in the 1950s and 1960s, with government debt falling in relation to GDP over this period (Pain and Young, 1996).

This period also saw an unusual degree of stability in the real economy. Between 1950 and 1970, the British economy operated at close to full employment, with the jobless total fluctuating between just 1 per cent and 3 per cent of the labour force. In these two decades, there was only one year in which national income contracted in the United Kingdom – 1958 – when it fell by just 0.1 per cent. Indeed, the growth of output was much more stable than in other (faster-growing) economies. (Whiting, 1976.)

In addition to the stabilising influence of the fixed exchange rate regime, this period of high employment, stable growth and low inflation in the UK economy was supported by two other factors. First, the international economic climate was relatively stable. The UK economy was not buffeted by any major shocks of the sort which became commonplace in the 1970s and 1980s. Second, the equilibrium unemployment rate or NAIRU

39

(non-accelerating inflation rate of unemployment) was low, making it possible to run the economy at close to full employment without generating serious inflationary pressures.[7] There were, of course, normal fluctuations in demand across the cycle, leading to periods of strong growth and rising inflation. But these cyclical movements in output and prices did not pose any major conflicts or dilemmas for economic policy-makers. At times of strong demand, both the desire to stabilise output and keep down inflation pointed to a tightening of policy, and vice versa at times of weak demand. The policies which were required to maintain the financial stability of the economy were therefore consistent with stabilising the growth of the economy at a high level of employment.

THE END OF THE 'GOLDEN AGE'

The late 1960s and early 1970s marked a watershed which saw the disappearance of the three conditions which had underpinned this 'golden age': the Bretton Woods system; favourable labour market conditions; and the absence of major shocks. The 1967 devaluation weakened the external monetary anchor which had helped to preserve low inflation in the 1950s and 1960s. The early 1970s saw the anchor disappear altogether as US inflation picked up in response to the increasing strain of financing the Vietnam War and an acceleration in wage increases which was experienced across the industrialised world. The link between the dollar and the price of gold was suspended in 1971 and the next year saw the Bretton Woods exchange rate system collapse altogether, ushering in an era of floating exchange rates. This shifted the burden of maintaining financial stability back onto national economic policy, though some countries grasped the implications of this change more rapidly than others.

The late 1960s and early 1970s also saw growing wage pressures, suggesting that the maintenance of full employment was ceasing to be consistent with low and stable inflation. The long period of full employment, rising union membership and relatively generous unemployment benefit systems had shifted the balance of power in the labour market, encouraging employees to press more aggressively for wage increases.[8] This phenomenon was not confined to the United Kingdom. Other European countries faced similar problems of wage pressures and industrial unrest. Over the period 1968–73, hourly earnings in manufacturing industry rose on average by 11.5 per cent per annum in the United Kingdom, but they also rose by 10.6 per cent in Germany, 11.8 per cent in France and by 15.3 per cent in Italy.

The final ingredient that undermined the harmonious economic climate of the 1950s and the 1960s was the oil-price shock of 1973/4, which followed on the heels of a wave of commodity price inflation. The oil price trebled between mid-1973 and early 1974, injecting further inflationary pressure into oil-consuming economies and making the task of macroeconomic management even more difficult. Though the rise in oil prices was inflationary in terms of its impact on prices and costs, its impact on the level of demand was deflationary (as higher import prices for oil-consuming countries squeezed real incomes). However, it was not possible to alleviate this deflationary impact without running the risk of pushing inflation up still further. In the face of the inflationary pressure generated by an increase in external costs, a squeeze on demand was required to prevent a wage-price spiral.

Challenges for economic policy

These shocks that hit the international economic system in the early 1970s overturned the benign conditions under which economic policy in the 1950s and 1960s had been able to operate. Policy-makers found themselves in a much more volatile international environment, with no external anchor to maintain financial stability. What is more, this was not a temporary phase. The first oil-price shock was followed by a second in 1978/9. These external shocks continued – to a lesser extent – through the 1980s which saw a period of high real interest rates and exchange rate volatility. The dollar doubled in value against European currencies between 1980 and 1985, before falling back sharply over the next three years. In the late 1970s and 1980s, the UK economy was also affected by the advent of North Sea oil and the impact of financial deregulation. 1990 saw another more short-lived oil-price shock from the Gulf War, followed by the economic fallout of the breakdown of Communism and the unification of Germany.

Nor did the labour market background become any more favourable to macroeconomic management through the 1970s and into the early 1980s. The wage pressures that were emerging in the late 1960s were an indication that the equilibrium unemployment rate, or NAIRU, had shifted upwards from the 2–3 per cent rate of unemployment that appears to have been compatible with steady low inflation for most of the 1950s and 1960s. An average of various estimates compiled by Cromb (1994) puts the NAIRU at 5.7 per cent of the labour force in the late 1970s and 7.0 per cent in the mid-1980s. In addition to the wage pressure created by rising union membership, this rise in unemployment also reflected structural change in employment which created a mismatch between available workers and job vacancies by skill and by region.[9] The loss of manufacturing jobs in the late 1970s and the early 1980s created a pool of unemployed manual workers in the traditional manufacturing regions, such as the North of England and the Midlands, while the new jobs created in the mid-1980s were in non-manual occupations and in the South, including a rapid expansion of employment in business and financial services.

These developments undermined the harmonious relationship between full employment, low inflation and sound public finances that had existed in the 1950s and 1960s. Developments in the labour market meant that stabilising the growth of output at a high employment level in the short term was no longer necessarily compatible with longer-term financial stability. In the face of major inflationary shocks, demand management had to be focused on the control of inflation rather than maintaining full employment. In addition, the rise in unemployment and the increased volatility of output placed additional strains on the management of public finances. A more rigorous framework was therefore needed to contain public deficits and debt.

Policy failures in the early 1970s

UK policy-makers were slow to pick up on the implications for macro-economic policy of the changed economic climate that was emerging – in particular, the need for domestic macroeconomic policy to shoulder the burden of maintaining financial stability which had previously been borne by the exchange rate link to the dollar. Rather, their initial response was to seek to use monetary and fiscal policy to maintain a high level of employment, while holding back the inflationary consequences using prices and incomes policies. The result was a major financial crisis in 1975, with inflation rising to over 25 per cent and government borrowing reaching almost 10 per cent of GDP. Rising unemployment was prevented for a while, but only at the expense of escalating inflation and a large public sector deficit.

The foundations for this crisis were laid by the Heath/Barber boom in 1972/3 when the early-1970s Conservative government embarked on an expansion of both monetary and fiscal policy to head off a rise in unemployment that was threatening to push the jobless total above one million. Restrictions on the banking system were relaxed from 1971 as part of an early experiment in financial deregulation under the banner 'Competition and Credit Control'. The bank base rate was cut to 5 per cent towards the end of 1971, even though inflation was still running at around 10 per cent per annum. And March 1972 saw the introduction of an expansionary budget by the then Chancellor of the Exchequer, Anthony Barber, with tax reductions totalling £1.2bn – around 2 per cent of GDP (Blackaby, 1978).

This relaxation in both monetary and fiscal policy set the scene for a very strong demand-led boom, arguably the most violent the UK economy has seen over the post-war period. (The Lawson boom of the 1980s was longer, but the growth rate was not so strong.) By the end of 1972, GDP was 4.5 per cent up on 1971, though this was still short of the target of 5 per cent set by the Chancellor in his 1972 budget. The economy gathered further momentum as it moved into 1973, and GDP growth in that year is now recorded at 7.5 per cent – a post-war record (see Figure 3.2). As a result of this strong growth, severe inflationary pressures were being placed on the UK economy even before the OPEC oil price hikes in the autumn and winter of 1973. By July 1973, one-third of manufacturers were reporting to

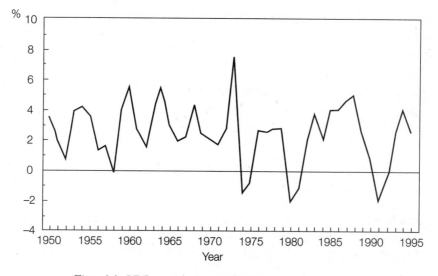

Figure 3.2 GDP growth since 1950 (% per annum change)

the CBI that a shortage of physical capacity was holding back their output, with 43 per cent indicating a constraint from shortages of skilled labour – rising to over 50 per cent in October.

To hold back the inflationary consequences of this strong growth, the Government relied heavily on incomes policy – though attempts were also made to slow the growth of demand during 1973 by raising interest rates. A three-stage reduction in the rate of pay increases was introduced towards the end of 1972. In the face of such strong upward pressures on inflation created by the growth of demand, it is not altogether surprising that the attempt to hold down inflation in this way was not successful. Stage 3 of the incomes policy was challenged by mineworkers in the winter of 1973/4. The Prime Minister, Edward Heath, chose to make this challenge a test of 'who rules the country' and when he lost the February 1974 election, the new Labour government abandoned (for a while at least) any attempt to control inflation with incomes policies.

This left the economy without any real defence against the inflationary pressures emerging in the wake of the Heath/Barber boom and the first oil-price shock. Moreover, instead of tightening economic policy to counter the effects of rising energy prices, the incoming Labour government initially sought to maintain demand to counter the deflationary impact of the shock on the real economy, by relaxing fiscal policy. Public borrowing was allowed to rise rapidly, with the PSBR reaching 9.0 per cent of GDP in 1974/5 and 9.2 per cent in 1975/6. Not surprisingly, inflation soared, reaching 20 per cent at the beginning of 1975 and peaking at 26.9 per cent in the summer of that year.

THE MID-1970s WATERSHED

These developments brought about a reassessment of the role of macro-economic policy in the management of the UK economy over the period 1975/6. It was becoming clear that attempts to stabilise the growth of output at a high employment level were proving ineffective. By stimulating demand to try and offset problems in the labour market and subsequently the first oil-price shock, the United Kingdom had ended up with the highest rate of inflation in the developed world. Yet the recession had not been prevented – merely delayed.

Medium-term financial stability – the control of inflation and public finances – had to assume a much greater role in the formation of macro-economic policy. The Labour government in power in the mid-1970s was already beginning to recognise the need for this shift of emphasis (Healey, 1989) but the sterling crisis of 1976, which saw the Government apply to the International Monetary Fund (IMF) for a special financing facility, acceler-ated the change.[10] As part of the conditions which were attached to the loan, public spending plans were cut in order to bring down the deficit and the Government adopted a system of money supply targets to assist in the reduction of inflation.

In autumn 1976, the shift in the emphasis of macroeconomic policy was confirmed by the Prime Minister, James Callaghan. He told the Labour Party conference: 'We used to think that you could spend your way out of reces-sion and increase employment by cutting taxes and boosting spending. I tell you in all candour that this option no longer exists, and that in so far as it ever did exist, it only worked by injecting a bigger dose of inflation into the system.' In other words, full employment was no longer compatible with low and stable inflation. In the face of the pressures building up in the labour market and major shocks to the international economy, macroeconomic policy had to give priority to reducing inflation and curbing public borrowing.

During 1977/8, the Labour Government achieved some success in restor-ing financial stability. Inflation fell to 8.3 per cent in 1978 as demand was restrained and incomes policies slowed wage growth. Meanwhile, public borrowing was curbed through cuts in capital spending and public sector pay restraint and the PSBR fell to 3.6 per cent of GDP in 1977/8. However, neither the reduction in inflation nor the squeeze on public borrowing was sustained. During 1978, demand conditions eased and fiscal policy relaxed in the run-up to the general election, with the deficit expanding to over 5 per cent of GDP in 1978/9. With demand management policies no longer bearing down on inflation, the burden of the Government's anti-inflationary policy fell on incomes policy. Though wage restraint had played a useful supporting role in the reduction of inflation in 1976 and 1977, it was incap-able of bearing the full load. As in 1972/3, the attempt to reduce wage growth against the background of an expanding economy failed. The squeeze on pay settlements broke down during 1978 – culminating in the 'winter of discontent' – with the result that inflation picked up again in 1979.

The Medium Term Financial Strategy

The election of a Conservative government under Margaret Thatcher in 1979 saw a consolidation of the macroeconomic policy shift that had begun in the mid-1970s. The commitment to medium-term financial stability became much more explicit and the Government's policies for achieving it were laid down in a Medium Term Financial Strategy (MTFS), which was launched in the 1980 budget. The MTFS was overtly monetarist and saw the role of controlling public borrowing as reducing the Government's contribution to monetary growth. As the 1980 Financial Statement and Budget report clearly stated:

> The Government's objectives for the medium-term are to bring down the rate of inflation and to create conditions for a sustainable growth of output and employment. To reduce inflation it will progressively reduce the growth of the money stock and will pursue the policies necessary to achieve this aim. Control of the money supply will over a period of years reduce the rate of inflation.
>
> (HM Treasury, 1980)

The monetary squeeze was indeed successful in bringing down inflation, though the process was not helped by a number of early policy mistakes which actually pushed up inflation and raised inflation expectations.[11] By June 1983, the rate of inflation had fallen to 3.7 per cent, and it remained at around 4–5 per cent through the mid-1980s (Figure 3.3). Public borrowing was also successfully restrained throughout the 1980s and the deficit was eliminated altogether by the end of the decade. Unlike the 1970s, the PSBR did not rise sharply in the early 1980s recession – largely due to the 1981 Budget, which saw rises in taxation and cuts in public expenditure implemented at the trough of a very deep recession. Public borrowing was contained at around 3 per cent of GDP during the mid-1980s, with restraint of public spending allowing taxes to be reduced. The emergence of a budget surplus towards the end of the 1980s reflected the beneficial impact of the consumer boom on public finances rather than any fundamental shift of policy.[12]

MACROECONOMIC PERFORMANCE SINCE 1980

The 1980s therefore saw a clear improvement in the financial stability of the UK economy. But there was a price to be paid. Unemployment rose sharply

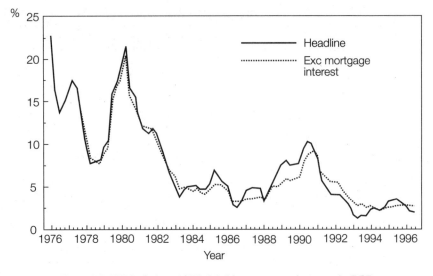

Figure 3.3 UK inflation, 1976–96 (% per annum increase in RPI)

in 1981 and 1982, with the jobless total rising above 3 million in 1983 and remaining above that level until mid-1987.[13] Though the equilibrium unemployment rate had risen over the 1970s and the 1980s, structural changes in the labour market cannot fully account for the extent of the mid-1980s unemployment problem. Between 1983 and 1987, UK unemployment averaged 10.7 per cent of the labour force, whereas most estimates of the equilibrium rate of unemployment for the mid-1980s are in the range 7–8 per cent (Cromb, 1994). Taking the 1980s as a whole, UK unemployment was higher than in any other G7 economy (Table 3.1).

The most plausible explanation for this prolonged period of high unemployment in the mid-1980s was the very sluggish adjustment of the labour market to major shocks, including shocks to demand generated by macroeconomic policy. The emergence of a hard core of long-term unemployed – accounting for half of total male unemployment – contributed to this process of sluggish labour market adjustment.[14] The severity of the demand squeeze in 1980 and 1981 undoubtedly contributed to this problem. A gentler disinflation in the early 1980s, accompanied by a more constructive programme of 'active labour market' policies in the first half of the 1980s, could have mitigated the unemployment consequences.[15]

This legacy of high unemployment was accompanied by other disappointing aspects of UK macroeconomic performance. First, though the UK inflation differential with other major economies narrowed after 1983, it did not disappear altogether, as Table 3.2 shows. The inflationary pressures generated by the consumer-led boom in the late 1980s meant that the United Kingdom missed the opportunity to reduce inflation created by the oil price

Table 3.1 Unemployment in major industrialised economies

	% of labour force, standardised OECD definition			
	1964–73	*1974–9*	*1980–9*	*1990–6*
United States	4.5	6.7	7.2	5.9
Japan	1.2	1.9	2.5	2.6
Germany*	0.8	3.2	5.9	6.8
France	2.2	4.5	9.0	10.9
Italy	5.5	6.6	9.5	10.9
UK	3.0	5.0	10.0	9.0
Canada	4.8	7.2	6.8	9.9

Source: OECD Historical Statistics, updated from *OECD Economic Outlook.*
* West Germany, prior to 1992.

Table 3.2 Inflation and volatility in major industrialised economies

	Inflation rate (%) *		Growth volatility (%) *	
	1970–82	*1983–95*	*1970–82*	*1983–95*
United States	7.9	3.6	2.5	1.7
Japan	8.1	1.5	2.7	1.9
Germany**	5.2	2.4	2.3	1.6
France	10.1	3.8	1.6	1.5
Italy	14.4	6.7	2.8	1.3
UK	13.1	4.8	2.5	2.0
Canada	8.6	3.7	2.6	2.2

Source: IMF Financial Statistics OECD.
* Inflation is measured by the % annual increase in consumer prices. Growth volatility is the standard deviation of the GDP growth rate.
** West Germany prior to 1992.

fall of the mid-1980s. It is only in the wake of the early 1990s recession that a climate of low and stable inflation has at last been re-established in the United Kingdom.

Second, relatively high inflation has been associated with a more volatile economy. Table 3.2 also shows that the 1980s and early 1990s were a much more volatile period for the United Kingdom than for other major economies.[16] Though the UK economy saw an increase in volatility after 1970, the 1970s and early 1980s were a volatile period for all major economies, in the wake of the two major oil price shocks of 1973/4 and 1978/9. Table 3.2 shows that the UK record is fairly average over this earlier period. It is the volatility of the UK economy generated by the boom-bust cycle of the late 1980s and early 1990s that is particularly unusual.

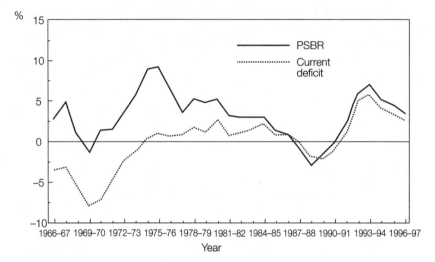

Figure 3.4 Public finances, 1966/7–1995/6 (% of GDP)

Third, the improvement in UK public finances over the 1980s was not sustained. Though the public sector borrowing requirement (PSBR) had been eliminated and public sector debt was being repaid, all this progress came unstuck in the early 1990s. The combined impact of tax cuts made in the late 1980s, a relaxation in the control of public spending and the recession combined to push the PSBR to a peak of over £45bn (7.1 per cent of GDP). Though the deficit has since been reduced substantially – with the assistance of substantial tax rises in 1994 and 1995 – the PSBR has averaged 5 per cent of GDP over the five years 1991/2–1995/6. The deterioration in the public sector current balance – which excludes the impact of cuts in investment and asset sales – has been even more marked (Figure 3.4).[17]

THE LAWSON BOOM

To a large extent, these problems all boil down to one big problem: the Lawson boom of the late 1980s. In the three years 1986–8, the economy grew at an average rate of 4.5 per cent a year and consumer spending rose at an annual rate of 6.5 per cent. Unemployment halved between mid-1986 and mid-1990, falling from 3.1 million to below 1.6 million. Interest rates were raised to 13 per cent during 1988 and to 15 per cent in 1989, which succeeded in slowing the economy down. But the inflationary consequences of the boom continued to be felt until 1990, by which time the economy was already moving into recession. GDP fell by over 2 per cent in 1991 and unemployment climbed to nearly 3 million by the end of 1992.

It was the strength of this boom and the depth of the following recession which were responsible for the excessive volatility of the UK economy in the late 1980s and early 1990s. The late-1980s boom was also the main cause of the United Kingdom's disappointing inflation performance. Inflation was pushed up by the strong growth in the late 1980s, reaching a peak of 10.9 per cent in the autumn of 1990 (9.5 per cent on an underlying basis, excluding the impact of mortgage interest rates). Prior to that inflationary episode, inflation had dropped to around 3 per cent in 1986 in the wake of the mid-1980s drop in oil prices. If that fall had been consolidated by the restraint of demand, UK inflation performance over the 1980s would have been broadly in line with other countries.

The Lawson boom and the following recession also contributed to the problems of managing public finances. The consumer-led growth of the late 1980s was particularly favourable to government revenues as both income and expenditure taxes rose strongly. The resulting improvement in public finances – with the Government budget moving into surplus – encouraged both a relaxation in public spending and cuts in taxation. The depth of the recession – and the approach of the 1992 general election – added to the pressure to reduce taxes and raise spending still further.

The boom of the late 1980s and the following recession are often attributed to the cumulative effect of a series of economic policy mistakes and misjudgements in the face of a major shock to demand created by financial deregulation. However, such a spectacular economic policy failure requires a more coherent explanation. In fact, the failure lay in the design of the Medium Term Financial Strategy itself. While the objectives of the MTFS – low inflation and the control of public finances – were correctly specified, the economic policy mistakes of the late 1980s arose from deficiencies in the framework which was put in place to achieve them.

The monetary framework

First, the monetary framework which was meant to underpin the control of inflation broke down in the first half of the 1980s and was not replaced with a satisfactory alternative mechanism for monitoring and regulating demand conditions. According to the original formulation of the MTFS, controlling the growth of broad money (sterling M3) was the centrepiece of the anti-inflationary strategy, with a declining path being set for the growth of the money supply for a number of years ahead. The basis of this approach is the existence of a stable relationship between the money supply and the level of demand (measured at current prices) in the economy. If such a stable relationship exists, control of the money supply can ensure that the growth of demand is consistent with low inflation.

The notion of controlling the amount of money as a means of regulating demand sounds deceptively simple. However, it will only work satisfactorily in practice if there are effective policy instruments to adjust the amount of money in circulation and if there is a stable relationship between the growth of the money supply and the level of demand. In the early 1980s, financial deregulation greatly complicated both of these relationships. The direct restrictions which had been used to restrict the activities of banks in the late 1970s were abolished, making control of the money supply wholly dependent on adjusting short-term interest rates. In addition, the growth of interest-bearing accounts and the abolition of controls on international capital movements boosted the growth of broad measures of money, such as M3 and M4, and weakened their relationship with the growth of demand in the economy (Figure 3.5).

These problems made the operation of the MTFS monetary framework difficult from the outset. In 1980 and 1981 the targets which had initially been set for monetary growth were massively exceeded. This had two effects, both of which intensified the depth of the early 1980s recession: first, monetary policy was tightened further to meet the money supply targets, resulting in interest rates being pushed up in the second half of 1981 in the wake of a deflationary budget and alongside sharply rising unemployment; and second, the failure to hit the targets undermined the credibility of the Government's commitment to achieve low inflation, slowing the deceleration of wages and prices (Minford, 1991). Though the targets for monetary growth were eventually achieved in 1983/4, the attempt to accurately target a measure of broad money in an era of financial deregulation was widely seen as a failure. The response of the authorities was to shift the emphasis away from controlling the growth of sterling M3 towards an approach based on looking at a range of indicators, including the exchange rate and M0 – a narrow measure of money, made up mainly of notes and coin.[18]

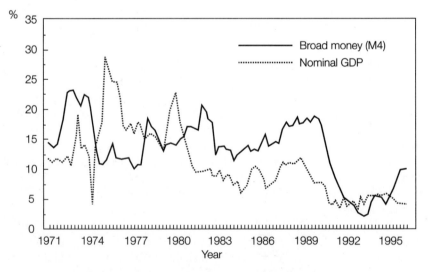

Figure 3.5 Broad money and nominal GDP (% per annum growth)

Because the authorities were trying to take into account a wide range of indicators, the control of inflation came to rely increasingly on a judgmental assessment of monetary conditions. It was this judgmental approach, coupled with attempts to stabilise the sterling exchange rate against the Deutschmark,[19] that opened the way for excessively lax monetary policy in 1987 and the first half of 1988. As Figure 3.6 shows, interest rates were cut from 11 per cent in early 1987 to a low point of 7.5 per cent in May 1988, at a time when domestic demand was accelerating. Some have argued that the crucial mistake was to abandon the original monetarist framework in the mid-1980s. (See, in particular, Congdon, 1992.) However, that line of argument fails to recognise the difficulties in interpreting and assessing the signals provided by the growth of broad money throughout the 1980s. Rather, the problem lay in not replacing the system based on monetary targets with a viable alternative framework for ensuring that demand conditions were consistent with continuing low inflation.

There are three directions in which monetary policy could have moved to fill the gap left by the demise of the monetary targets originally set out in the MTFS. The most obvious would have been a shift to targeting the growth of spending directly using a framework based on the growth of money GDP or nominal domestic demand.[20] Nominal domestic demand grew by 10.3 per cent during 1986 and accelerated to 11.9 per cent over the course of 1987 – rates of growth which were clearly incompatible with inflation in low single digits. Though there were problems with national accounts statistics in the late 1980s (Pickford, 1989), the estimates available in early 1988 clearly

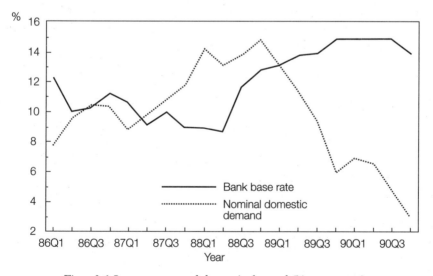

Figure 3.6 Interest rates and domestic demand (% per annum)

signalled the unsustainable growth of expenditure.[21] If these figures had received more serious attention, interest rates would have been raised earlier and more decisively in 1988. Moreover, if the control of expenditure had been more central to the framework for controlling inflation, there would have been a stronger official interest in identifying and correcting statistical errors.

The second alternative framework for UK monetary policy was membership of the ERM – using the DM as an 'external anchor' for UK monetary policy, playing the role that the dollar had fulfilled under the Bretton Woods agreement. The CBI came out in support of ERM membership in 1985 and Nigel Lawson made a case for joining then. It is sometimes argued that because the experiments with informally targeting the exchange rate in 1987 and early 1988 contributed to the policy errors of the Lawson boom, full membership of the ERM would have been more disastrous. However, if sterling had joined the ERM in late 1985 (before the depreciation which followed the oil-price fall of the mid-1980s) the rate of entry would have been around DM3.50 rather than the DM3 chosen later in the 1980s. A higher exchange rate – and the influence on expectations of a clear commitment to low inflation that ERM membership was seen to imply – could have resulted in a much more successful operation of monetary policy in the late 1980s.

The third direction that the United Kingdom could have followed in its monetary policy would have been to move more quickly to the system of inflation targets that was established in 1992. In the 1985 Mansion House speech in which he announced the abandonment of broad money targets, the Chancellor Nigel Lawson announced that inflation would be the 'judge and jury' of the success of his policy. If he had formalised this into an inflation target, monetary policy might have responded more quickly to inflationary pressures that were emerging in the labour market and in the housing market.

Destabilising fiscal policies

Monetary policy was not solely responsible for the strength of the late 1980s boom. A stimulus from fiscal policy also played a part. There were substantial net tax cuts in the budgets of 1986, 1987, 1988 and 1989, with the basic rate of income tax being reduced from 30 per cent to 25 per cent and the top rate of income tax from 60 per cent to 40 per cent. This tax-cutting strategy was encouraged by the improving short-term position of public finances, which reflected the boost to revenues created by the strength of consumer demand. The result was that the Government budget moved into surplus despite the fact that fiscal policy was being eased, with a debt repayment of £3.5bn (0.8 per cent of GDP) in 1987–8, rising to £14.7bn (3.0 per cent of GDP) in 1988–9, with smaller surpluses in the two succeeding years. These surpluses encouraged policy-makers to play down the inflationary risks from the tax cuts of the late 1980s, arguing that they were supported by a sound budgetary position. However, when the boom unwound, the apparent strength of public finances turned out to be a mirage.

Though there is an obvious temptation for government to reduce taxes when the budgetary position is improving, in terms of demand management, the tax cuts of the late 1980s were undoubtedly destabilising. In fact, when demand is growing strongly, it makes sense to use both fiscal and monetary policy to restrain the growth of demand and head off inflationary pressures. In other words, tax rises would have been more appropriate in the late 1980s than tax cuts.

Once again, the roots of the problem went back to the original design of the Medium Term Financial Strategy, in which the reduction of public borrowing, the growth of the money supply and the rate of inflation were seen as inextricably linked. A reduction in the contribution to monetary growth from public borrowing was identified as a key mechanism through which inflation would be curtailed. However, because the budgetary position is affected by the cycle, this approach actually encourages destabilising interventions. Periods of weak activity undermine tax receipts and push up unemployment benefits, raising borrowing while the reverse will be true in a boom. If policy-makers seek to offset these movements with policy changes, they will find themselves raising taxes and cutting expenditure in a recession and cutting taxes and raising expenditure in a boom – i.e. accentuating fluctuations in growth and possibly also exacerbating inflationary pressures.

The 1981 Budget had provided an earlier example of this destabilising use of fiscal policy, when Sir Geoffrey Howe raised taxes and cut public spending at the trough of the recession. In the early 1980s, there was a stronger argument that a tough budget was needed to reinforce the credibility of the Government's determination to restore financial stability. Supporters of the budget point to the fact that it coincided with the turning point in economic activity, with the recovery beginning in the second quarter of 1981 and continuing thereafter. However, the budget undoubtedly had the effect of holding back economic growth, which was initially very weak – with GDP rising by 1.9 per cent in the first year of recovery (1981Q1–1982Q1).[22] If such a tough budget was required, monetary policy should have been relaxed to a greater extent to offset it.

The role of the supply side

The Government's approach to the supply side of the economy in the late 1980s played a supporting role to these failures in monetary and fiscal policy. In principle, measures to improve the effectiveness and efficiency of the supply side of the economy should support the operation of monetary and fiscal policy by making output more responsive to demand and by raising the potential growth of output. However, notwithstanding these possible long-term benefits, the supply-side agenda being pursued by the Conservative Government in the 1980s encouraged the inflationary excesses of the Lawson boom in two ways.

First, a number of measures which were taken to improve the longer-term efficiency of the economy had the effect of raising demand in the short term. The most obvious candidate here is the process of financial market deregulation itself. The desire to cut marginal tax rates also boosted demand, and sales of council houses and privatisation receipts contributed to the improvement in public finances, which encouraged the relaxation in fiscal policy.[23] Second, there was a general perception that supply-side policies had raised the long-term growth rate so that the strong growth seen in the late 1980s would not pose an undue strain on the economy. However, policy-makers greatly over-estimated the extent to which the sustainable growth rate had risen. It is possible to detect some improvement in productivity growth in manufacturing industry and there are also signs of an improvement in labour market performance.[24] However, non-manufacturing productivity – which dominates the productivity trend across the economy as a whole – rose at the same rate in the 1980s as in the 1970s. (Sentance, 1995).

Just as the attempt to maintain full employment contributed to the rise of inflation in the 1970s, basing macroeconomic policy assessments on an optimistic assumption of the economy's long-term growth potential encouraged the excesses of the Lawson boom. Even in a situation where the long-term potential of the economy has increased, there may be 'speed-limit' constraints created by shortages of capacity and skills as the investment processes of the economy struggle to keep up with the growth of the economy.

THE EXCHANGE RATE MECHANISM

The decision to join the Exchange Rate Mechanism (ERM) of the European Monetary System in October 1990 was a reaction to the failure to control inflation over the late 1980s. If the decision had been taken five years earlier – before the Lawson boom got into full swing – the policy might have been more successful (see Chapter 16). However, sterling joined the ERM just at the point when UK and German economic conditions were diverging sharply. German unification boosted growth in the early 1990s, creating a tightening of monetary policy. However, the United Kingdom was moving into recession in the wake of the severe squeeze that had been applied to demand by the high level of interest rates during 1989 and 1990, with GDP dropping by over 2 per cent in 1991. That recession required a loosening of monetary policy.

These tensions did not become apparent at first. UK inflation fell sharply – dropping to around 4 per cent by the beginning of 1992 (5.7 per cent excluding mortgage interest) – and UK interest rates moved down to German levels. However, few signs of recovery were apparent over the course of 1992 (though the economic statistics now show that a weak recovery had begun over the course of the year, with the first quarter marking the trough in economic activity) and the financial markets began to question the credibility of the United Kingdom's policy of ERM membership at a central rate of DM2.95, which required British interest rates to be held above German rates. On 16 September 1992, a wave of speculative selling of sterling forced the withdrawal of sterling from the ERM.

ECONOMIC POLICY POST-1992

The forced departure of sterling from the ERM created something of a vacuum in UK economic policy-making. The credibility of UK macroeconomic policy had been badly undermined by the Lawson boom. It virtually disappeared following the humiliating events of the autumn of 1992. Policy-makers faced the task of building a credible and reliable framework which would not be subject to the problems which surrounded the original MTFS framework. In addition, they faced the challenge of repairing public finances. The impact of the tax reductions of the Lawson era had been compounded by further discretionary policy changes in the recession and an erosion of the local tax base by the failed introduction of the community charge (the poll tax).

The gap in the monetary framework left by sterling's departure from the ERM has been filled by an approach based on a target for the inflation rate (measured by the annual increase in the retail prices index excluding mortgage interest). The current system of inflation targets is the latest attempt to find a satisfactory framework for the control of inflation. Interest rate decisions are based on an assessment of future inflation conditions, with the aim to keeping the rate of increase in the price level below a target level (4 per cent in the short term and 2.5 per cent in the medium term). That assessment is based on information, analysis and judgements from the Bank of England as well as the Treasury. Each quarter the Bank of England publishes a comprehensive *Inflation Report* which contains analysis of a wide range of factors affecting the outlook for inflation, including developments in the real economy and the performance of the labour market.

This monetary framework has operated reasonably well over the four years in which it has been in operation, with underlying inflation averaging 2.8 per cent over the four years 1993 to 1996, while the economy has grown steadily and unemployment has fallen by a third. The fact that both the Chancellor of the Exchequer and the Governor of the Bank of England are involved in monetary policy decisions helps to safeguard against major errors of judgement. And the framework is comprehensible in that the target variable is based on a concept (a variant of the retail prices index) which economic agents understand. However, the new framework has yet to be severely tested by a major shock to the economic system and it remains to be seen how it would perform in a more turbulent economic climate.

The approach to the control of public borrowing also reflects the lessons learned in the 1980s. Instead of tightening fiscal policy at an early stage of the recovery, a delayed programme of tax increases was announced in two stages during 1993. These tax increases began to take effect during 1994 and against the background of a growing economy and tight control of public expenditure, they have produced a reduction in the PSBR from 7.1 per cent of GDP in 1993/4 to 4.5 per cent in 1995/6 and a projected 3.5 per cent in 1996/7. The rate of reduction of public borrowing has not been as great as earlier, more optimistic official projections; the 1996 budget saw the introduction of a package of measures to tackle tax avoidance and tax evasion, which ministers believe have contributed to the weakness of tax revenues.

CHALLENGES AHEAD

Both the performance of the UK economy and its policy-makers have exceeded the dismal expectations in the wake of sterling's departure from the ERM, when many respectable forecasters were projecting a future of persistently high unemployment and rising inflation. The situation is promising, but success is not guaranteed. There are three key challenges ahead which will determine whether the United Kingdom continues on the road to macroeconomic stability, or takes another diversion down more familiar but less fruitful paths.

The control of inflation

First, the framework for controlling inflation is likely to be tested by a pick-up in consumer demand and growth in 1997. Official projections, published in the autumn 1996 budget (H.M. Treasury, 1996) indicated a rise in the growth of consumer spending to over 4 per cent in 1997 with GDP growth forecast to pick up to 3.5 per cent. These figures are broadly in line with those being published by independent forecasters in late 1996. Growth of this order is not in itself a serious inflationary threat. However, at the time of writing, the Bank of England *Inflation Report* is warning of a gradual upward drift in inflation over the next two years, away from the medium-term target of 2.5 per cent or below. This points to the need for interest rates to rise, though there are a wide range of views about the timing and scale of the necessary adjustment. Some commentators are highlighting the mistakes that were made in the Lawson Boom, when the strength of consumer demand was persistently underestimated.[25]

This situation highlights two issues which have been actively debated since the introduction of the inflation target framework. First, given that policy levers affect inflation with a delay of up to two years, should there be an intermediate target for demand which guides policy-makers' decisions on interest rates? At present, the Bank of England's inflation forecast effectively plays the role of this intermediate target (Svensson, 1996). However, forecasts can be wrong and may lack credibility.

One possibility is to return to targeting the money supply, as envisaged under the original MTFS. There are currently 'monitoring ranges' for two monetary aggregates – M0 and M4 – though the ranges are wide (0–4 per cent for M0 and 3–9 per cent for M4) and the signals provided by these indicators do not appear do be given much weight in monetary policy decisions. Putting greater weight on these monetary measures to guide policy decisions would risk a return to the problems encountered in the early 1980s. A more promising approach would be to monitor and target the rate of growth of spending directly (rather than indirectly, through the money supply). One proposal on these lines is to set a target range of 4–6 per cent for nominal domestic demand, adjusting policy to keep the growth of spending within these limits[26] (Sentance and Nixon, 1995.) Keeping spending growth at around 5 per cent ensures it is consistent with the medium-term growth of the economy (around 2.5 per cent) and the Government's medium-term inflation target.

The second issue highlighted by the monetary policy decisions that must be taken in 1997 is the possible influence of political factors. A general election must be held by the summer of 1997 and a change of government is a distinct possibility. Though there is likely to be broad continuity of macro-economic policy in the event of the election of a Labour government, there are still some risks to inflation associated with a change of government (Sentance, 1996). One way of isolating monetary policy from political influences both before or after the election would be to make the Bank of England independent of government and assign it the task of setting interest rates to meet the inflation target.

An independent central bank could be seen as a further development of the moves which have taken place since 1992, which have given the Bank of England a greater role in monetary policy through the publication of the *Inflation Report*, the involvement of the Governor of the Bank in interest-setting decisions and the publication of the minutes of meetings between the Governor and the Chancellor. The arguments here are finely balanced. An independent central bank could reinforce the credibility attached to the inflation target but would involve the handover of monetary policy to a largely untested institution. The case for such a move would be stronger if there was evidence of monetary policy being manipulated for short-term political gain in the past. In fact, the major monetary policy errors of the 1980s were mistakes of competence and judgement and the main area where political influences have been felt on economic policy has been in the operation of fiscal policy. Because 'two heads are better than one', restricting the Bank to an advisory monetary policy role may provide a better safeguard against future errors of competence, even though there is a greater exposure to political risks.

Controlling public borrowing

The second major macroeconomic policy challenge for the late 1990s is the need to reduce public borrowing to sustainable levels. Whatever the political complexion of the Government in power, it will face the need to bring public borrowing down to a more sustainable level. Borrowing for the financial year 1997/8 is now projected to fall to 2.5 per cent of GDP, but is only on the border of the level of borrowing which is sustainable over the medium-term, based on the view that government should aim to stabilise and if possible reduce the level of public debt in relation to GDP. It provides little margin for error in face of an unexpected downturn or other unforeseen shocks, restricting the ability of policy-makers to use fiscal policy to stabilise the economy.

Official projections see borrowing continuing to fall over the medium term, with the 1996 budget indicating that balance will be achieved by the turn of the century. But these projections rely on extremely tight control of public expenditure. Over the next three years, public spending growth will be held to around 0.5 per cent a year in real terms, after increases below 1 per cent in the last two years. This flies in the face of experience even under a Conservative government. The public spending share of GDP has fluctuated a great deal with the cycle and there have been temporary periods of severe spending restraint. But as we get richer, we expect levels of public service to rise, with efficiency savings absorbed by other upward pressures on public spending. As a result, the main elements of current public spending rise with national income (i.e. at over 2 per cent a year) in the medium term – as Figure 3.7 shows. Even the Conservatives have not been prepared to make the radical changes to the public sector which might have broken this link.[27]

Cuts in public investment and reduced financial support for nationalised industries do allow the Government to claim that overall public spending has been falling as a share of the economy. The Private Finance Initiative is being used to reduce public investment still further, by using private capital, rather than public funds, to finance major projects. But the scope for further privatisation is diminishing and the Government is reaching the limit of its ability to squeeze public spending with creative mechanisms of this sort. Moreover, cuts or delays in necessary infrastructure investment can hold back the growth of the economy. If, as seems likely, the pressures to increase spending build up in response to the current squeeze, there may well be the need to raise taxes again in the next Parliament to keep down public borrowing.

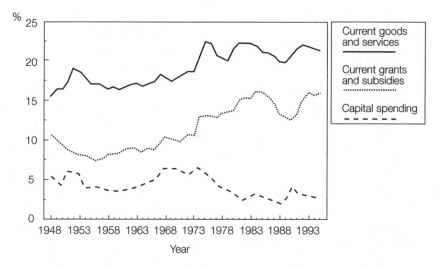

Figure 3.7 Main components of government spending (% of GDP)

EUROPEAN MONETARY UNION

The third challenge facing UK economic policy-makers is European Monetary Union (EMU). A group of countries, including Germany and France, are likely to go ahead with plans laid down in the Maastricht Treaty and form a currency union at the beginning of 1999. A decision will be taken in the first half of 1998 on the issue of which countries meet the convergence criteria and join the currency bloc, though the United Kingdom has to notify its intention to join before the end of 1997 because of the opt-out negotiated at Maastricht.[28]

The decision to join EMU will reflect political factors as well as economic criteria and both major parties have promised a referendum on the issue. However, on purely economic grounds, a decision by the United Kingdom to enter EMU at an early stage would represent a large step in the dark that could very easily harm the promising macroeconomic scenario that is in prospect. The practical step that the United Kingdom would take if it did sign up in 1999 would be to fix its exchange rate for all time against the other participating currencies, including Germany, and accept the interest rate set by the European Central Bank, which would reflect an assessment of monetary conditions in the currency union as a whole, rather than in the United Kingdom. Fiscal policy would also be constrained to some degree under a 'stability pact' currently being negotiated.

There would be three large risks associated with a UK decision to join EMU in 1999. The most significant is exchange rate misalignment. The volatility of the pound against the Deutschmark in recent years is in stark contrast to the experience of the French franc and the other currencies

59

which followed the discipline of the narrow bands of the ERM in the 1980s. These countries form a 'core' whose inflation and interest rates are already closely aligned with Germany and which have maintained a broadly stable exchange rate relationship for ten years (when the last FFr/DM realignment took place in the ERM). In a low inflation climate, getting the exchange rate 'wrong' by 5–10 per cent could be very disruptive for macroeconomic performance. A stronger track record of exchange rate stability would reduce this risk but is not yet evident.

The second EMU risk concerns the conduct of monetary policy within the new currency union. In the early stages of EMU, it will be hard to assess monetary conditions – just as it was in the wake of financial deregulation. Moreover, the currency union is likely to be dominated by a 'core' of countries surrounding France and Germany, whose cycle has been out of synchronisation with the United Kingdom in recent years. There is therefore a serious risk that in the early stages of EMU, the monetary policies that are applied within the currency union will not be suitable for the UK economy, again disrupting macroeconomic performance.

The third EMU risk surrounds fiscal policy. The 'stability pact' that is currently being negotiated would place limits on the scope for countries to use fiscal policy for stabilisation purposes. Arguably, the opposite is required, giving countries some fiscal flexibility to offset shocks to offset the loss of exchange rate flexibility. Here, there is a clear tension between medium-term financial stability – which the stability pact is aimed to ensure – and the stabilisation of output within the economy. While the disciplines of the stability pact make sense for a group of convergent economies, it could well compound the problems of early UK entry, again exerting a destabilising influence on the economy.

While these risks of early UK entry into EMU are clear, it may well be in Britain's long-term interests to join a European currency union eventually. Indeed, signalling that the United Kingdom had no interest in joining could reinforce the impression that Britain's interests are diverging from the EU and undermine political and economic cooperation in other areas. The UK macroeconomic policy framework will therefore probably need to embrace exchange rate stability against the Euro[29] as one of its objectives after 1999 – though experience in the Lawson boom and within the ERM shows that this should not override the need to maintain sound financial conditions in the domestic economy. Achieving this balancing trick may result in a rather prolonged transition to full UK participation in EMU.

CONCLUSION

A key lesson from the United Kingdom's experience of macroeconomic management over the last thirty years is that financial stability – low inflation and a sound public sector financial position – is a precondition for satisfactory management of the real economy. That financial stability was provided in the 1950s and 1960s under the Bretton Woods exchange rate regime. It was undermined by the turbulence of the mid-1970s and later in the Lawson boom. However, subject to further moves to reduce public borrowing and intelligent operation of the inflation target regime, financial stability has now been restored to the UK economy. Subject to growth not proceeding too fast in the short term, macroeconomic policy should then be able to allow the economy to return to the true equilibrium unemployment rate, which is probably below 6 per cent of the labour force (Sentance, 1995).

Another lesson of UK economic management is that sudden lurches towards an untested policy framework can have unpredictable and damaging effects. That is the lesson from the monetarist experiment of the early 1980s and indeed the hasty move to join the ERM in 1990. That is the worry surrounding EMU entry in 1999: for all the potential long-term benefits of being inside rather than outside a stable currency union, EMU entry could represent yet another destabilising lurch in policy from which the United Kingdom would take years to recover.

NOTES

1 UK GDP grew by 3.0 per cent a year between 1950 and 1973, compared with 5.9 per cent in West Germany, 5.1 per cent in France and 5.5 per cent in Italy over the same period (Temple, 1994). Data on GDP per head at purchasing power exchange rates is taken from OECD National Accounts (latest edition).

2 Since 1970, the United Kingdom has experienced six years in which GDP has declined, compared with five in the United States, three in Germany, two in Canada and Italy and one in France and Japan. It is worth noting that notwith-standing the length of the Japanese 'recession' in the early 1990s, GDP has risen in each calendar year, albeit by around 1 per cent or less in the four years 1992 to 1995.

3 The public sector borrowing requirement expanded from 1.6 per cent of GDP in 1971/2 to 5.8 per cent in 1973/4, with a tax-cutting budget in 1972 and significant increases in public spending in 1973. Tax cuts were made in the budgets of 1986, 1987, 1988 and 1989.

4 Interest rates were raised by just 1.5 percentage points between their low point in 1994 to reach a peak of 6.75 per cent in early 1995. This peak was below the lowest point interest rates had reached in the 1980s (7.5 per cent in May 1988).

5 The problems caused by inflation would be much less serious if it could be fully anticipated, in which case households and firms could 'see through' the effects of changes in the average level of prices. But in practice, high inflation has been associated with a volatile inflation rate – making it difficult if not impossible to anticipate changes in the price level. Moreover, at very high rates of inflation, even the costs of anticipated inflation – the need to constantly adjust prices and economise on the use of money (because it is declining in value rapidly) – can become significant.

6 High inflation can contribute to higher volatility in the real economy by increasing

uncertainty about business conditions and confusing the signals provided by changes in relative prices. However, perhaps its biggest destabilising effect on the real economy is the cost of squeezing inflation out of the system, which normally results in a recession of some sort. Two out of the last three UK recessions have resulted from policies that were applied to squeeze out inflation.

7   The equilibrium unemployment rate, or NAIRU, is a development of the 'natural rate' of unemployment concept introduced by Friedman in his 1967 address to the American Economic Association (Friedman, 1968). The concept is based on the notion that structural characteristics of the labour market predominantly determine the unemployment rate which is consistent with stable inflation. Attempts to keep unemployment below that level will ultimately lead to accelerating inflation, while a reduction in inflation requires unemployment to be held above the equilibrium unemployment rate for a while.

8   In the United Kingdom, the proportion of union members in the workforce rose from around 45 per cent in 1966/7 to over 50 per cent by 1970, reaching a peak of nearly 60 per cent of employment in 1979. For a family with one earner on average earnings, social security benefits as a percentage of wages rose from 30–35 per cent in the 1950s to 40–45 per cent by the late 1960s, fluctuating around that level in the 1970s and early 1980s. (Layard and Sentance, 1986.)

9   For detailed accounts of the factors responsible for the rise in the equilibrium unemployment rate between the 1960s and the 1980s, see Minford (1983) and Layard, Nickell and Jackman (1991, 1994).

10   The PSBR amounted to 9.0 per cent of GDP in 1974/5 and 9.4 per cent in 1975/6. However, Denis Healey, who was Chancellor of the Exchequer at the time, has since argued that the United Kingdom would not have needed the loan negotiated with the IMF if the Government and the financial markets had known the true state of UK public finances, which were healthier than Treasury forecasts suggested (Healey, 1989: 432–3). The PSBR fell to 6.4 per cent of GDP in 1976/7 and to 3.6 per cent in 1977/8 (helped by expenditure cuts agreed with the IMF), though the deficit widened again to 5.3 per cent of GDP in 1978/9.

11   VAT was raised from 8 per cent to 15 per cent in 1979, adding about 3 per cent to the retail prices index. The Government also made significant increases in public sector pay, following the Clegg Report in 1980, giving a confusing signal to private sector pay bargainers at a time when wage increases needed to adjust downwards to lower price inflation.

12   The OECD estimates that the UK 'structural' budget deficit – which attempts to correct for cyclical influences – fluctuated between 2 per cent and 3 per cent of GDP between 1984 and 1990. (OECD, *Economic Outlook*, June 1996, Annex Table 31.)

13   The unemployment figures refer to definitions in use at the time. If unemployment is measured on a basis consistent with current definitions, it only exceeded 3 million in 1985 and 1986.

14   This process is sometimes known as unemployment 'hysteresis', in which the path of the non-inflationary unemployment rate is heavily influenced by past shocks. See Budd, Levine and Smith (1988), for an analysis of this issue.

15   More active labour market policies, which aimed to provide training and job-search facilities for long-term unemployment, were implemented in the late 1980s and helped to support the reduction of unemployment over the period 1986–90.

16   Canada is the most volatile of the G7 economies since the early 1980s but this is accounted for by the fact that it is a major producer of energy and minerals and hence is more exposed than other economies to fluctuations in the prices of these commodities.

17 The fact that the UK public sector was running a current deficit for most of the 1980s and 1990s – and hence reducing the national savings rate – may have contributed to poor UK investment performance. UK fixed capital spending as a share of GDP averaged 17.5 per cent in the 1980s, compared with 19.0 per cent in the US and 20–21 per cent in other major European countries. Between 1990 and 1995, UK investment has averaged 16.2 per cent of GDP compared with 16.5 per cent in the US. Again, this is substantially below other major European countries: France – 18.5 per cent; Italy – 20 per cent; Germany and Spain – 22 per cent. In addition, though UK investment was not far below the US average over the 1990s, the profile over the recovery has been very different. US investment picked up strongly over the recovery to reach 17.5 per cent of GDP in 1995, compared to 15 per cent in the United Kingdom.

18 The 1985 Financial Statement and Budget Report stated that 'the significance of the broad aggregates as monetary indicators has somewhat diminished. Equal weight will be given to the performance of M0 and £M3, which will continue to be interpreted in the light of other indicators of monetary conditions. Significant changes in the exchange rate are also important. It will be necessary to judge the appropriate combination of monetary growth and the exchange rate needed to keep financial policy on track: there is no mechanistic formula' (HM Treasury, 1985).

19 The Government sought to keep the pound at around DM3 during 1987 and early 1988.

20 Arguably nominal domestic demand – the sum of private and public consumption and gross investment – is the superior measure, as strong growth of demand can divert production from exports and encourage imports, as it did in the late 1980s, with the result that money GDP growth understates demand pressures. (Money GDP is domestic demand plus exports less imports.)

21 The figures available in March 1988 showed domestic demand rising by 10.7 per cent in 1987 and 10.1 per cent in 1986 – not far short of the revised estimates currently available (11.9 per cent and 10.4 per cent).

22 Over this period, the impact of the budget can also be seen in the components of demand which were affected by the fiscal squeeze: consumer spending fell by 0.2 per cent and public sector investment was cut by 8.6 per cent.

23 Virtually the whole of the surplus on public finances in 1988/89 was accounted for by asset sales: £7bn from privatisation proceeds and about £6bn from sales of council houses and other buildings and land.

24 The average of a range of estimates of the equilibrium unemployment rate for the late 1980s quoted by Cromb (1994) suggest that it has fallen back to 6 per cent and may have fallen further in the early 1990s. See Sentance (1995) and Robinson (1996) for an assessment of the evidence on this issue.

25 The March 1988 budget forecast growth of consumer spending of 4 per cent in 1988, with GDP growth of 3 per cent. In the event, consumption grew by 7.5 per cent and GDP by 5 per cent!

26 Successfully targeting a spending measure of this sort depends on the reliability and timeliness of national accounts data. However, the cost of mistakes in macroeconomic policy are arguably sufficiently large to justify investments in this area.

27 For a detailed exposition of these arguments, see Hall, O'Sullivan and Sentance (1996), which sets out a detailed econometric analysis of UK public spending and revenues since the mid-1970s.

28 The criteria set down specific thresholds for assessing price stability, the sustainability of low inflation, exchange rate stability and the soundness of public finances. These include a threshold of 3 per cent for the budget deficit in 1997

and a benchmark for public debt of 60 per cent of GDP – though there is some scope for flexibility in applying these criteria.

29 The Euro is the agreed name for the new single currency.

REFERENCES

Budd, A., Levine, P. and Smith, P. (1988) 'Unemployment, vacancies and the long-term unemployed', *Economic Journal*, vol. 98.

Blackaby, F.T. (1978) *British Economic Policy, 1960–74*, Cambridge: Cambridge University Press.

Confederation of British Industry (CBI) (1991) *Competing with the World's Best*.

Congdon, T. (1992) *Reflections on Monetarism*, Aldershot: Edward Elgar.

Cromb, R. (1994) *The UK NAIRU*, Government Economic Service Discussion Paper No. 124, London: HMSO.

Currie, D.A. and Sentance, A.W. (1994) 'An end to boom and bust – Can the Chancellor deliver?', *Economic Outlook*, vol. 18, no.9, pp. 20–3.

Friedman, M. (1968) 'The role of monetary policy', *American Economic Review*, vol. 58, pp. 1–17.

Hall, S., O'Sullivan, J. and Sentance, A.W. (1996) 'UK fiscal policy over the medium term', in C. Allen and S. Hall (eds), *Macroeconomic modelling in a changing world*, Chichester: Wiley.

Healey, D. (1989) *The Time of my Life*, London: Penguin Books.

H.M. Treasury, (1980) *Financial Statement and Budget Report*, London: HMSO.

——— (1985) *Financial Statement and Budget Report*, London: HMSO.

——— (1996) *Financial Statement and Budget Report*, London: HMSO.

International Monetary Fund (IMF), (1996) 'The rise and fall of inflation – Lessons from the postwar experience', *World Economic Outlook*, October.

Keynes, J.M. (1919) *Economic Consequences of the Peace*, London: Macmillan, chap. 6.

Layard, R. and Sentance, A.W. (1986) *How to Beat Unemployment*, Oxford: Oxford University Press.

Layard, R., Nickell, S. and Jackman, R. (1991) *Unemployment*, Oxford: Oxford University Press.

——— (1994) *The Unemployment Crisis*, Oxford: Oxford University Press.

Minford, P. (1991) *The Supply Side Revolution in Britain*, Aldershot: Edward Elgar, chap. 4, pp. 56–73.

Minford, P. with D. Davies, M. Peel and A. Spraque, (1983) *Unemployment, Cause and Cure* Oxford: Basil Blackwell.

Oulton, N. (1995) 'Supply side reform and UK economic growth: What happened to the miracle?', *National Institute Economic Review*, no.154, pp. 53–67.

Pain, N. and Young, G. (1996) 'The UK public finances: Past experience and future prospects', *National Institute Economic Review*, no.158, pp. 27–35.

Pickford, S. *et al.* (1989) *Government Economic Statistics – a Scrutiny Report*, London: Cabinet Office.

Robinson, P. (1996) 'The myths and realities of structural change in the United Kingdom labour market', *Economic Outlook*, vol. 21, no. 1, pp. 12–17.

Sentance, A.W. (1995) 'Are we entering a new golden age of economic growth?', *Economic Outlook*, vol. 20, no. 1, pp. 12–21.

——— (1996) 'All change? Prospects for the United Kingdom economy under "New" Labour', *Economic Outlook*, vol. 20, no. 3, pp. 6–13.

Sentance, A.W. and Nixon, J. (1995) 'Keeping the lid on inflation', *Economic Outlook*, vol. 19, no. 3, pp. 6–13.

Svensson, L.E.O. (1996) *Inflation forecast targeting: implementing and monitoring inflation targets*, Bank of England Working Paper no. 56.

Temple, P. (1994) 'Understanding Britain's economic performance: The role of international trade', in *Britain's Economic Performance*, London: Routledge.

Whiting, A. (1976) 'An international comparison of the instability of economic growth', *Three Banks Review*, no.109.

Part II

INTERNATIONAL TRADING PERFORMANCE

4

OVERVIEW: GROWTH, COMPETITIVENESS AND TRADE PERFORMANCE[1]

Paul Temple

> It is the great multiplication of the production of all the different arts, in consequence upon the division of labour, which occasions, in a well governed society, that universal opulence which extends itself to the lowest ranks of the people.
>
> (Adam Smith, *The Wealth of Nations*, Book I chapter 1)

INTRODUCTION

Today the question of Britain's economic performance remains as fascinating as ever. Having undergone its third major recession in the post-war period, the rhetoric of the recovery has emphasised the combination of an expanding economy without the re-emergence of inflation – evidence in the eyes of some that the persistent relative economic decline which spanned more than a century is now firmly in the past. Others, however, argue that progress is largely a chimera created in part by the poor performance of other European economies. On this view, any gains achieved through the economic policies of the last twenty years amount to a belated period of catching up with other major economies and have been bought at the expense of rapidly rising, and possibly unsustainable, levels of inequality. Moreover, it has been argued that the policies have not created the institutions capable of assisting in the generation of sufficient numbers of adequately compensated jobs which would be necessary to bring about a more general increase in prosperity.

This overview provides essential background to the ongoing debate by outlining some of the principal features of Britain's economic performance. In order to provide some historical context for current controversies, Britain's progress is examined first over the longer term – from the last decades of the nineteenth century when doubts first began to surface. The modern period from the watershed year of 1973 is then examined in more detail.

In order to see how Britain stands today in relation to other comparable economies, to understand how it got there, and to assess the extent of any recent improvement in its performance, we first of all need some elementary concepts enabling us to compare and contrast the economic progress of nations. This is the purpose of the next section. The chapter then examines the path of Britain's relative economic decline from the last decades of the nineteenth century through to the period sometimes referred to as the 'Golden Age' which marked the thirty years following the Second World War and which ended in 1973. The next section then describes the contours of the period since 1973, which was characterised by a slowing of economic growth in all the major economies. This period is explored further by using the conventional economic technique of growth accounting, commenting also upon the more recent framework provided by endogenous growth theory. A different, and possibly richer, approach is then examined, based on the relationship between economic growth and increasing international specialisation. It is argued that a sea change has occurred in the determinants of international specialisation and that as a consequence, growth performance in the developed economies is now much more dependent on the ability of the developed economies to generate and utilise knowledge. The following section comments on the challenges this presents for economic policy, relating them to the concern in many countries with the concept of competitiveness. The chapter then concludes.

INTERNATIONAL COMPARISONS OF GNP

If we accept at the outset that the primary purpose of economic activity is the promotion of well-being, then economic progress for a nation can be described in terms of the ability of its economy to increase the well-being of its citizens. Any assessment of economic performance therefore begins with an attempt to measure 'well-being' or 'wealth'. We first of all consider some frequently employed concepts.

There is no simple way of gauging the progress made by a nation in terms of well-being. Nevertheless, economists do frequently make use of the concept of *gross national product* (GNP). For a nation this is defined as the total income from economic activity earned by its citizens. This measure has, however, been increasingly criticised as being too narrow from the perspective of wealth creation, and it is indeed important to bear in mind a number of points. First, that GNP measures only marketed goods and services, ignoring for example the contribution of unpaid domestic labour in raising children and supplying other household services. Second, that neither benefits from the environment or the costs of resource depletion are included in the GNP total. So when, for example, coal is mined, the activity of mining is included in GNP but nothing is deducted for the natural resources which are used up. Third, GNP essentially measures a flow of income, and cannot

70

necessarily be expected to deal adequately with the fact that much well-being is derived from the consumption of existing assets – whether of television sets or motor cars. However the argument is not clear-cut; since the production of durable assets is included in the total, these flows are measured to the extent that its future utility is represented in the purchase price of the asset.

These points of criticism were picked up recently in the Report of the Dahrendorf Commission, *Wealth Creation and Social Cohesion* (1995), which referred to the 'fetishism' commonly attached to GNP figures. Economists are, however, habituated to thinking in terms of aggregate measures of economic activity and as the Commission itself admitted, GNP does have a place as part of a more general 'wealth audit', which would not only attempt to ameliorate some of the problems with GNP, but would include a much wider variety of social, political, and environmental indicators to give a broader perspective as to what people actually value.

If we likewise accept that GNP figures have some relevance, we can get an idea of *average* living standards by dividing the GNP estimate by population, to obtain GNP *per head*. In the United Kingdom for 1994, and according to official data, GNP (measured at market prices) amounted to £678 billion and was distributed among an estimated population of 58.4 millions – a level of GNP per head of around £12,500. How does this figure square up with that of other nations? Such a comparison can only be performed by converting GNP per head in each country into a common currency. The most appropriate way of doing this is to use purchasing power parity (PPP) rates of exchange, whose use, like that of GNP is also a source of debate[2]. However, if we are still willing to suspend our disbelief we can make comparisons of the sort depicted in Figure 4.1. The figures are drawn from the 1996 *World Bank Development Report* and use PPP exchange rates developed in an ambitious attempt to compare price levels around the world. The resulting GNP comparisons are made relative to the US for 1994, so that the UK level of 69.4 implies that GNP per head was estimated to be over 30 per cent below that of the US, which had the highest recorded level. The United Kingdom was, however, more evenly matched with her major EU partners. Levels in both France and Germany were estimated to be about 10 per cent ahead of the United Kingdom, although it should be remembered that the German figure is heavily influenced by the incorporation of the eastern part of the country in 1991.

Comparisons outside the largest six economies (the G6) are also illuminating. Much has recently been made for example about the newly industrialised 'tiger' economies of the Pacific – South Korea, Hong Kong, Singapore, and Taiwan. Today, the GNP per head of Singapore and Hong Kong comfortably *exceeds* that of the United Kingdom. However, it needs to be remembered that these are essentially city states with relatively small populations (around six million in the case of Hong Kong and less than three million in the case of Singapore) and for this reason a simple comparison is of dubious value. More

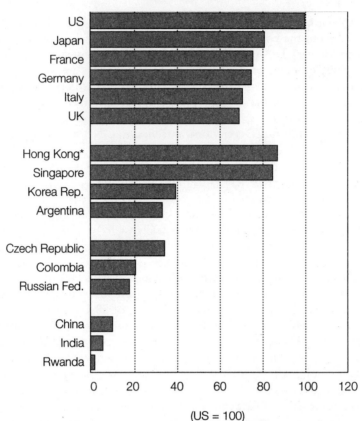

Figure 4.1 GNP per head in 1994 relative to US. Estimated using PPPs
Source: *World Bank Development Report 1996.*
Note: *Hong Kong figure is for 1993.

pertinent is the case of South Korea, which had an estimated population in 1994 of 45 millions. Here, GNP per head was still less than three-fifths of the UK figure. In fact South Korea has a very similar level of GNP per head to Argentina. In their turn, these levels are some way ahead of those found in Central and Eastern Europe. The figure for the Russian Federation is less than one-fifth of that for the US. Way below even these levels it can be seen that the poorest economy in 1994 was Rwanda, with an income per head little more than 1 per cent of that of the US.

It needs of course to be stressed that all these comparisons are based on *average* income. No account is taken of the *distribution* of incomes within these economies, and hence there can be no presupposition that these figures reflect (to any great extent) *typical* standards of living. In general, the more equal the distribution of income, the more these average figures genuinely

72

reflect typical patterns of consumption. In fact, the distribution of income has shifted markedly in many economies over recent years, and in the advanced economies, and especially in Britain, it has become significantly less equal (as Chapter 13 shows in more detail, below). We comment on this further below, and it forms an important element in the overview discussion of the labour market in the chapter below.

Comparisons such as these do not clearly bring out the factors behind Britain's disappointing long-run economic performance, nor the possibility that recent economic progress has ended the cause for that disappointment. For this we need to consider comparisons over time; accordingly, the next two sections review Britain's economic record both over the long period, and then for the more recent past.

RELATIVE ECONOMIC DECLINE 1870–1973

Dissatisfaction with Britain's economic record has a long history, with clear origins before the beginning of the twentieth century, when economic concerns were inextricably linked to perceived military decline, especially in relation to Germany.

In order to broach the question of Britain's economic record over the long run, it is convenient to distinguish the historical period of decline from what we might usefully call the 'modern' era. Perhaps the most obvious year for this chronological division is 1973. Most historians now use this as the year which marked the end of a remarkable period of post-war economic growth, now sometimes referred to, but not perhaps recognised at the time, as the 'Golden Age' – when historically high rates of expansion combined with very low levels of unemployment, modest levels of inflation, and a benevolent business cycle. The century beginning in 1870 might then be considered in two further periods – the first from 1870 to 1913, which was the period when Britain's supremacy as an industrial power, built up during the industrial revolution in the first half of the nineteenth century, was challenged, primarily by the US and Germany, and then overturned. The period between 1913 and 1950 was of course overshadowed by two wars and a powerful inter-war recession; one of the most significant features of the latter was a general decline in volumes of international trade.

Long-run estimates of the growth of output and income are generally available in terms of gross *domestic* (as opposed to national) product (GDP) – e.g. Maddison (1991). This may be defined as income arising from productive activity taking place within a specified region. The difference between GDP and GNP is attributable to the difference between income arising from productive activity carried out domestically but paid to overseas residents, and income earned from productive activity carried out overseas but received by domestic residents. So profits earned by Nissan Motor arising from its UK operations but repatriated to Japan constitute a part of the United

73

Kingdom's GDP but not its GNP. Likewise profits from the overseas operations of ICI which are remitted as dividends to UK citizens are a part of GNP but not GDP. However because the balance between these two kinds of flow is typically small for the major economies, the fact that GNP is a more appropriate indicator of national wealth need not detain us at this point.

The basic progress of GDP for five economies (the United Kingdom, France, Germany, the US, and Japan) over the three periods is depicted in Figure 4.2 in terms of *levels* of GDP per head, and in Table 4.1 in terms of *growth rates*.

Figure 4.2 shows comparative levels of real GDP in each of the benchmark years, based on both the prices and PPPs of 1984. In 1870 it can be seen that the United Kingdom had a substantial lead in terms of GDP per head over the other four economies, with levels very close to double those in Germany and 36 per cent ahead of the US. Such were the differences in growth rates between the US and Britain in the period up to the First World War, however, that the US emerged with clearly the highest level of GDP per head by 1913. As Table 4.1 shows, growth rates were also significantly faster than Britain in all the other economies during this period, but not sufficiently so to catch up or overtake.

The decades between 1913 and the end of the Second World War were

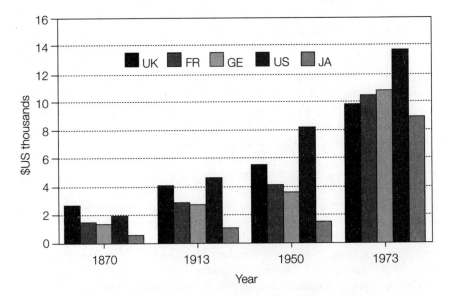

Figure 4.2 The progress of GDP per head in five economies
Source: Maddison (1987).
Note: GDP valued at 1984 prices and 1984 PPPs.

74

Table 4.1 Average annual percentage growth rates of GDP in five economies

GDP					
	UK	*France*	*Germany*	*Japan*	*US*
1870–1913	1.9	1.5	2.8	2.3	3.9
1913–50	1.3	1.1	1.3	2.2	2.8
1950–73	3.0	5.0	5.9	9.3	3.6
GDP per capita					
1870–1913	1.0	1.3	1.6	1.4	1.8
1913–50	0.8	1.1	0.7	0.9	1.6
1950–73	2.5	4.0	4.9	8.0	2.2
GDP per hour worked					
1870–1913	1.2	1.6	1.9	1.9	1.9
1913–50	1.6	1.9	1.0	1.8	2.4
1950–73	3.2	5.0	5.9	7.6	2.5

Source: Maddison (1991).

disastrous for the international economy. As Table 4.1 demonstrates, growth was everywhere slower; however, with the exception of the US, per capita GDP growth was actually very similar across the economies, so that by 1950, the United Kingdom still maintained a significant lead over the continental economies and even more so over Japan. More significant, however, was the substantial overall lead of the US in 1950 – nearly one half higher again than Britain in terms of GDP per head, and well over double that of Germany. Built up over at least eighty years, the faster trend rate of growth of both GDP and GDP per head in the US meant that the substantial lead was to become, as most historians would now agree, a potent source of profitable investment and 'catch up' in the Golden Age after 1950.

Although GDP (or better, GNP) per head is the relevant concept if we are interested in the progress of living standards, if we are interested in relative economic efficiency, GDP per person employed (or for preference, per hour worked) is superior because it provides a measure of labour productivity. Table 4.1 also includes Maddison's estimates of the growth of GDP per hour worked in the periods under scrutiny. What stands out is that progress in the trans-war period is now rather similar to the period 1870–1913, and that the slower growth of GDP and GDP per head basically reflected a slower growth of labour input rather than labour productivity; indeed, in Britain, France and the US, progress is actually faster in the trans-war period than in the earlier era. For Britain, leadership having been surrendered, the overall growth in labour productivity is more or less on a par with the other economies which are following the US.

By 1950 however, the US was actually able to increase its lead substantially in terms of labour productivity, increasing considerably thereby the scope for catch-up elsewhere. In the main, the opportunities were grasped by the major economies, as is attested by the historically rapid rates of expansion of nearly all the indicators, especially outside the US. For the US itself, labour productivity growth (at least in terms of hours worked) was remarkably similar across the two periods.

In the light of this, the degree of progress made by of Britain between 1950 and 1973 must be seen as exceptionally disappointing, even though it represented an unprecedentedly rapid rate of growth from the point of view of Britain's own history.

The idea that catch-up is a useful way of thinking about economic growth now has a long history and is widely accepted in both the theoretical and empirical literature. It needs to be remembered in this context that, as Abramovitz (1986) has pointed out, there is nothing automatic about such a process, and indeed one of the major points of departure for economic history since the Industrial Revolution has been the progressive *divergence* in productivity levels between what are now regarded as the advanced economies, and the rest of the world. The missing ingredient that allows a potential for catch-up to be realised, is what Abramovitz termed '*social capability*', a catch-all concept embracing not simply educational levels of the workforce but the obstacles to growth raised by vested interests and the institutional context within which those interests operate.

Discussion of the causes of relative economic decline over the century reviewed is beyond the scope of this chapter; the literature is both vast and growing. A useful introduction to the issues can be found in Coates (1994), many echoes of which will be found throughout this book. Here, however, as elsewhere in the book, we concern ourselves with the question of whether the period since 1973 has resulted in something of an economic revival, or whether fundamental economic weakness can be regarded as continuing throughout the post-war period.

THE PERIOD SINCE 1973

There are a number of important reasons for using the soubriquet 'modern' (rather than simply recent) to describe the whole of the period since 1973.

Perhaps the most important reason is the fundamental change in the basis of the process of international specialisation after 1973; discussed more fully below, it has involved a switch from a process of growth and specialisation based on catch-up and convergence with the technologically most advanced economy in 1950 – the US – to one in which growth is being increasingly dominated by the ability of economies to generate investment based on the generation and exploitation of knowledge.

There are, however, other reasons for describing 1973 as a watershed. The following are perhaps the most important.

1 For most OECD economies, 1973 was statistically a post-war peak in terms of economic growth. Most indicators of the growth of aggregate economic activity (GDP) as well as of labour productivity turn down after that point. In the United Kingdom for example, if the average annual growth from 1950 is recorded for successive years after, say, 1960, the series would peak in 1973.

2 By 1973 the scope for catch-up in productivity levels between the followers and the unequivocal leader in 1950 – the US – had diminished considerably. Further, many other obvious sources of rapid productivity growth and investment opportunity in the OECD had all but exhausted themselves. We need to include here factors such as the potential for employment to switch away from low productivity agriculture into higher productivity activity in manufacturing or certain service industries; until the 1970s these industries were consequently faced with a highly elastic labour supply. Maddison (1991) estimated that for sixteen advanced economies, the mean percentage of employment in agriculture fell dramatically from nearly 25 per cent in 1950 to 17.5 per cent in 1960 and just 9.3 per cent in 1973. The subsequent decline (to 6.0 per cent in 1987) has been much more modest. Note that Britain, which had a comparatively low level of employment in agriculture in 1950, was much less well placed from this point of view, but correspondingly was less affected by the loss of this source of productivity advance.

3 The early 1970s also marked a number of other events which were crucial in defining and shaping economic policy. Some were of a temporary nature, but others were more permanent. Among the latter, pride of place should go to the demise of the international monetary order which had been instigated by the Bretton Woods Conference in 1944. Primarily this meant that international exchange rates became free to fluctuate on a day-to-day basis[3] – albeit that for most of the period and for many of the countries, this took the form of a 'managed' float. Beyond this we should mention both the build-up of excess demand for the world's primary commodities in the early 1970s – exacerbated by the very strength of the boom in 1972 and 1973 – and the OPEC cartel oil-price rises of 1973–4. In fact, in the full period since 1973, these factors have proved only temporary. Recent years have seen weakness in primary commodity prices, especially those destined for use as industrial inputs. Nevertheless, the combination of rising oil and commodity prices, in tandem with the system of fluctuating exchange rates imparted a powerful impetus to inflation. It was a supply shock of sufficient force to have produced a significant shift in priorities, so that today the control of inflation remains on top of the macroeconomic policy agenda.

As regards economic aggregates, some of the main features of the period since 1973 can be gleaned from Table 4.2, which introduces Italy to the five nations considered in Table 4.1. The clearest feature of all is of course the marked slow-down in measured rates of growth of output, output per head, and labour productivity (GDP per person employed). The United Kingdom is no exception in this regard, but compared to the other economies, it is clear that the slowdown has been less severe. Nevertheless, the fact remains that aggregate GDP grew more slowly over the whole period than in any of the other economies. However, relatively rapid rates of population growth in the US and France meant that the growth of GDP per head in the United Kingdom was more or less on a par with those economies, although some way below Germany, Italy, and above all Japan.

The choice of 1993 as the end-point is dictated by data availability as at the time of writing, but this is not ideal since in that year economies were at very different stages of the business cycle. In this sense, we may not be measuring the growth in economic *capacity* in each economy very accurately, since 1993 may be a year in which capacity *utilisation* varied widely between the

Table 4.2 Average annual percentage rates of growth in six countries, 1960–93

GDP	UK	France	Germany	Italy	US	Japan
1960–73	3.1	3.4	4.3	5.3	3.9	9.6
1973–93	1.6	2.1	2.2	2.3	2.4	3.6
1973–most						
recent peak	1.9	2.3	2.3	2.5	2.5	3.8
GDP per capita						
1960–73	2.6	4.3	3.7	4.6	2.6	8.3
1973–93	1.4	1.5	2.1	2.3	1.4	2.9
1973–most						
recent peak	1.8	1.7	2.3	2.7	1.6	3.1
GDP per person employed						
1960–73	2.8	4.7	4.1	5.8	1.9	8.1
1973–93	1.7	1.9	1.8	2.2	0.7	2.5
1973–most						
recent peak	1.6	2.0	1.9	2.0	0.6	2.7
GDP per hour worked						
1960–73	3.4	3.3	5.1	6.6	2.4	9.1
1973–89	2.0	3.2	2.3	2.2	1.0	3.1

Source: OECD Historical Statistics 1960–93; Maddison (1991) for data on hours worked.

economies. A crude way of adjusting for this possibility is to measure output growth between cyclical peaks, i.e. when capacity is more or less fully utilised. While 1973 marked a peak for all the economies, the peak around 1990 varies somewhat.

Recorded growth between the 1973 peak and the most recent peak is also depicted in Table 4.2. The relative depth of the 1990s recession in the United Kingdom makes no difference to the rankings in terms of GDP growth, but does push the United Kingdom slightly ahead of France and the US on a *per capita* basis.

Table 4.2 also includes two very basic measures of the *efficiency* with which resources were employed – GDP per person employed and GDP per hour worked – both measures of labour productivity. Here the most remarkable feature is the extremely low rates of growth recorded for the US. This is true not only in comparison with the US's own record in the post war-period, but for all economies over the period 1870–1993. The slow-down in US labour productivity has of course spawned an intense debate over the past fifteen or so years, but the key point is that the marked slow-down of the leading economy provides us with some presumption that the period after 1973 is characterised by a very different climate for growth. Outside the US, the slow-down is of course more understandable in terms of the diminished possibility for catch-up.

Trend rates of growth convey only part of the performance characteristics of GDP statistics. Also of relevance, from a welfare perspective, is the degree to which GDP growth is volatile, and an economy is prone to alternating periods of boom and slump as opposed to steady rates of expansion. There are various, essentially arbitrary, ways of measuring periods of boom and slump. A relatively severe slump might be defined as a period when output growth fell more than two percentage points below trend – for the United Kingdom this would mean negligible or negative growth. Conversely a boom might be defined as a period in which growth exceeded the trend by more than two percentage points. Given such a definition, Table 4.3 shows the outcome.

More than half the years in the United Kingdom were periods of boom or recession by this definition, higher than in any of the other economies – considerably so in the cases of France, Italy, and Japan.

Table 4.3 Years of boom and recession (percentage of all years 1974–94 in which growth more than 2 percentage points different from trend)

	UK	France	Germany	Italy	US	Japan
Boom	29	5	24	10	24	19
Recession	24	14	14	14	19	5

Source: OECD.

Figure 4.3 illustrates a rather more general approach, based on the distribution of the deviation of annual rates growth from their mean over the period 1974–94. It compares the experience of the United Kingdom with the combined experience of the other G6 economies. A relatively steady growth path would imply a unimodal distribution with little dispersion. This is the experience for the rest of the G6, whose total observations are illustrated in the right-hand panel. The United Kingdom, by contrast, does not display a unimodal distribution, but has peaks some distance from the mean.

The extra volatility of the UK economy displayed in these simple comparisons does not give any indication as to its cause. One recent commentator at least (Oulton, 1995) has suggested that avoidable macroeconomic policies have been the main contributory factor to the poor record in this regard, and one which has damaged the trend rate of growth itself. This is certainly an interesting proposition, and the question of the role played by policy in the both the creation of the Lawson boom of the late 1980s and the subsequent recession, certainly needs addressing (see Chapter 3 above). It is, however, perfectly possible that the difficulties with macro policy stemmed not from simple error or from political pressure, but from the poor performance of the supply side.

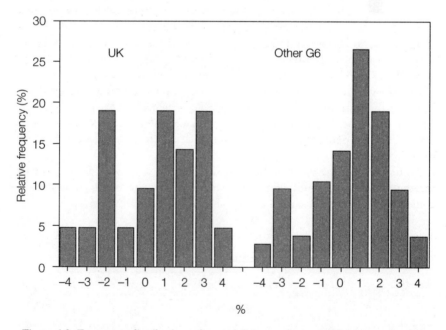

Figure 4.3 Frequency distribution of annual G6 growth rates: differences of actual growth rates from mean

To summarise the period since 1973, it seems clear that the figures contained in Table 4.2 do not suggest any remarkable turnaround in Britain's overall economic performance. However, they do suggest that the regime change that accompanied the period since 1973 has not harmed Britain as much as other economies. According to the various measures of the growth of GDP and the efficiency with which goods and services are produced, the United Kingdom now lagged only slightly behind, or just matched, the other major European economies, although as Figure 4.1 makes clear, there is still a gap in real levels of GDP per head with France and Italy which recent performance has not made up, and cannot be expected to make up quickly, if at all. Broad parity with Germany is largely a result of the incorporation of the eastern Länder. With hindsight, however, the really important historical questions may concern the lost opportunities in the period up to 1973, the precise causes of which remain highly contentious.

THE ECONOMIC REGIME SINCE 1973

What factors explain the very different situation that appears to have confronted the OECD economies in the period since 1973? As we might expect, for any such complex social process as economic growth, a variety of approaches are available. Perhaps the first port of call for the traditional economist is the 'growth accounting' framework, established by Solow and Dennison and exploited today by Maddison (1991). This approach attempts to explain growth on the basis of measurable inputs into the production process (primarily labour and capital), ascribing any residual element to 'technological progress', a phenomenon which is considered a catch-all for all other factors and largely outside the remit of economic analysis.

It is clear from Table 4.2 that inputs of labour have not contributed in any major way to the slowdown in G6 GDP growth. It shows that, by and large, the slowdown in GDP growth occurring between 1960–73 and 1973–93 was very similar to that in GDP per hour worked. It is of course possible that the period since 1973 has witnessed a weakening in the growth of the *quality* of the labour force, i.e. as its effectiveness is augmented by education and training or by other changes in the composition of the labour force. Maddison (1991) finds no evidence that any of these factors can provide anything other than a modest impact on the growth of labour quality. By and large, increasing levels of educational attainment in the advanced economies have been sustained – mainly in the form of increasing enrolment rates in tertiary education. Most workforces have experienced a more rapid increase in the proportion of females since 1973, but the impact of this is hard to quantify given the fact that anti-discrimination laws preclude the use of wages as an indicator of skill attainment.

The same things cannot be said with respect to capital inputs. Table 4.4 shows growth rates of both employment and gross capital stock both before

81

Table 4.4 Growth accounting: business sector only

	UK	France	Germany	Italy	Japan	US
GDP growth (annual ave. %)						
1960–73	3.4	5.9	4.4	5.6	12.2	3.4
1973–93	2.0	2.3	2.2	2.6	3.9	2.4
1973–most						
recent peak	2.2	2.5	2.4	2.8	3.9	2.5
Employment growth (annual ave. %)						
1960–73	−0.2	0.5	−0.1	−0.6	1.3	1.7
1973–93	0.1	−0.2	0.2	0.4	1.0	1.8
1973–most						
recent peak	0.3	−0.1	0.3	0.6	1.1	2.1
Capital stock growth (annual ave. %)						
1960–73	3.4	4.9	6.0	5.6	13.2	3.7
1973–93	2.3	3.1	3.0	2.6	6.3	3.3
1973–most						
recent peak	2.5	3.2	3.0	2.8	6.4	3.5
Total factor productivity growth (annual ave. %)						
1960–73	2.5	3.8	2.2	3.9	7.0	1.0
1973–93	1.2	1.3	1.0	1.4	1.2	0.0
1973–most						
recent peak	1.2	1.4	1.1	1.4	1.1	−0.1

Source: OECD/NIGEM.
Note: France: GDP and capital 1963–73 and employment 1965–73 only; Japan employment 1962–73 and GDP 1973–92; UK all data from 1961.

and after 1973 for the business sector only (i.e. excluding government and the household sector), so that capital excludes dwellings. Note that the use of gross figures excludes the possibility that the contribution of an asset declines with age prior to its ultimate retirement. It shows that the growth of the capital stock slowed markedly after 1973 in all the economies except the US. Since 1973, the experience in all the economies has been for the capital–output ratio to be rising, as the growth rate in GDP has fallen short of the growth of the capital stock.

In theory, growth accounting provides a means of assessing the precise contribution of each factor of production (considered independently) to output growth by making assumptions about both the nature of technology (constant returns to scale) and the existence of perfect competition in both product and factor markets. Under these circumstances, the contribution of each factor is measured by its share in total income. Typically, the share of capital (profits) in total income is of the order of one-third to two-fifths of total income, with the remainder constituting the share of labour. On this basis, for example, a simple calculation reveals that the sharp fall in capital stock growth in Germany, from 6.0 per cent per annum to only 3 per cent after 1973, 'explains' about one half of the fall in the GDP growth rate of 2.2 percentage points (i.e. approximately 0.37 times the decrease in the growth rate of the capital stock, or about 1.1 percentage points). Nevertheless this is the largest proportion for any of the six economies.

Note that, despite the higher weights attached to employment growth, changes in this factor were generally small enough to have made a more modest impact on the growth rate than the deceleration in capital stock growth. Nevertheless, it is clear that, within the growth accounting framework at least, this phenomenon explains only a small part of the deceleration in GDP growth after 1973. The 'residual' element to economic growth (i.e. after deducting from the growth in output the estimated contribution of labour and capital), is known as *total factor productivity* growth, and in all six cases this factor provides the major item in accounting for the decline in growth. For the productivity leader, the US, movements in total factor productivity growth are frequently ascribed to technical progress, so that some have inferred from the slowdown of total factor productivity growth in the US, that slower technical progress has characterised the period since 1973. However, direct evidence for such a phenomenon is lacking. The UK experience is similar, in that total factor productivity growth plays the lead role (if one difficult to interpret) in slowing GDP growth. It is worth noticing, however, that the United Kingdom has not experienced nearly as sharp a rise in the capital–output ratio as the other economies.

The simple framework underlying these growth accounting exercises has been challenged in the more recent literature generally referred to as 'endogenous' or just 'new' growth theory. A key feature in this body of theory is the existence of 'externalities' to capital investment, which implies that effects on output are not incorporated in the profit share, so that its use underestimates the *social* rate of return to investment.

There are a number of versions of endogenous growth theory. One version, attributable to Rebelo (1991), emphasises the role of so-called 'broad capital' – an amalgam of both physical and human capital. In the long run, the ratio of broad capital to output is a constant. If this were true, it would have considerable policy ramifications, since any rise in the rate of investment in broad capital could permanently raise the long-run or sustainable growth rate of the economy. Thus tax policies, or some other policy instrument capable of increasing the inducement to invest, could influence the long-run rate of growth. This particular model pays little explicit attention to the role of technological change; an alternative makes technological change endogenous (in sharp distinction to the Solow model) by making the rate of growth of labour productivity directly proportional to the share of labour allocated to innovative activity (Grossman and Helpman, 1991). As in the

Rebelo model, an increase in this share would permanently raise the growth rate.

While the assertion that there are categories of capital which are not subject to eventually diminishing returns appears rather implausible, the idea that there are significant differences between the social and private rates of return to investment (however defined) does have appeal. In principle, the impact of investment on output (i.e. the social rate of return) can be estimated statistically, and the deeper question of what kinds of capital generate externalities can be addressed, although the ability of economists to measure such fundamental concepts as human capital falls way short of the powerful statistical techniques available today. However, a whole literature has been devoted to examining differences in international growth rates along these lines. In a particularly exhaustive study of this kind, Levine and Renelt (1992) regressed cross-country differences in per capita growth rates for over one hundred countries (both developed and less developed) over the period 1960–89 against a variety of explanatory variables. They showed that the only 'robust' explanatory variables – in the sense that their significance was not affected by the inclusion or exclusion of other variables – indicated a positive association of growth with differences in (i) the physical investment share, (ii) the share of trade in GDP and (iii) the secondary school enrolment rate, while indicating a negative association with (iv) the initial level of real GDP (in 1960). The latter association is commonly believed to support a 'conditional convergence' hypothesis, whereby a poorer country (other things being equal) will grow faster than a rich country. However, aside from problems of sample selection in these studies, and statistical problems arising from the cross-sectional approach, there is also the possibility that an apparently poorer country is simply experiencing a temporary deviation below its long-run growth path, producing an apparent catch-up which is no more than a statistical artefact.

As noted by Crafts (1992), and Crafts and Bean (1996), the statistical procedures adopted by Levine and Renelt and others can be used to illumine the United Kingdom's own performance by comparing its actual with its predicted growth rate. Interpreting a variety of specifications in the literature, he finds that the principal story was that, given its initial position relative to the US, the size of its public sector, and its investment record in both physical and human capital, growth was unaccountably slow in the period 1950–73. This broadly is the conclusion we reached in the previous section. Rather than pursue the implications of new growth economics in more detail, the remaining sections of this overview seek to pursue the growth process from a different, if not necessarily competing, perspective – that of the relationship between growth and the process of international specialisation.

INTERNATIONAL SPECIALISATION, ECONOMIC GROWTH, AND TRADING PERFORMANCE

A different approach to understanding variations in economic growth and performance takes its cue from Adam Smith's vision of the growth process, and the emphasis which he placed on the 'division of labour', i.e. increasing specialisation made possible by a growing market. For small or medium-sized economies, the ability to specialise is heavily dependent upon an economy being able to trade goods and services internationally; for large economies, and in particular the US, the size of the economy and the strength of population growth may make international trade less important. Indeed, this difference almost certainly contributed to the productivity gap which opened up in the trans-war period, when growth in many other countries was constrained by the rise of protectionism.

A vital feature of Smith's view of economic growth was the idea that market growth engenders gains in productive efficiency – so that increasing returns prevail. Where these effects are strong enough, cumulative processes begin to dominate progress, and an early lead, due possibly to some minor historical event, may become a more permanent advantage as learning and other effects begin to take hold.

Great importance therefore attaches to the sector of the economy engaged in international trade, in explaining increasing economic prosperity. Figures 4.4(a) and 4.4(b) show just how close the association between productivity (GDP per person employed) growth and export performance has been since 1960 – a relationship which appears to cross the 1973 divide. That the US features as something of an outlier in both figures, may be because of the significantly smaller role that exporting plays compared to the domestic market. A number of observations are important. First, in comparing the two charts, it can be seen that the convergence in growth rates of GDP per capita observed between the two periods, is parallelled by the convergence in export growth rates; the rapid change in export shares occurring prior to 1973 has moderated somewhat. Second, it is important to notice the extent to which export growth exceeds growth of both GDP per person employed, or indeed of GDP itself. The export sector is therefore highly dynamic compared to other sectors of the economy.

In fact there are a number of mutually reinforcing explanations of this strong link between an economy's trading performance (as exemplified by its export growth rate) and the long-run or sustainable rate of expansion on the other. Perhaps the most obvious relates to the external constraint that is widely believed to limit the rate at which individual national economies can expand – an idea based on Harrod's foreign trade multiplier, but particularly associated with the late Lord Kaldor and more recently with Godley and Thirlwall[4]. The simplest version of this hypothesis maintains that there is a close positive relationship between the overall growth rate of an economy

85

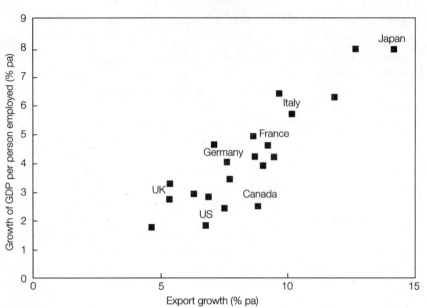

Figure 4.4(a) Growth of exports and labour productivity 1960–73
Source: OECD Historical Statistics, 1960–93.

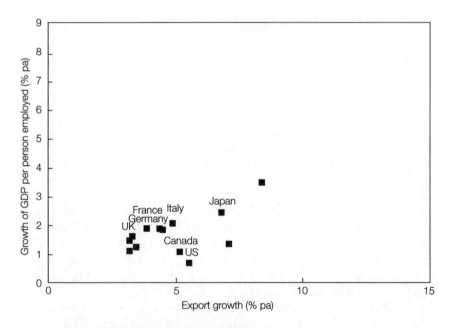

Figure 4.4(b) Growth of exports and labour productivity 1973–93
Source: OECD Historical Statistics, 1960–93.

and that of its import bill. If, in addition, the growth of exports is determined by the increase of world trade and what we might loosely term the competitiveness of its exports, then there will be a limit to the rate at which the domestic economy can expand without the growth of imports exceeding that of exports, with a consequential and eventually unsustainable deterioration in the balance of payments on current account. The reasons why such a deterioration is likely to be unsustainable need, however, to be assessed. Certainly to some extent, relative movements in price levels (brought about either through movements in the exchange rate or through relative rates of inflation) between the domestic economy and the rest of the world may be able to modify any tendency for imports to grow faster than exports. But this possibility tends to exaggerate the potential either for exchange rate movements to effect long-run changes in relative prices or in the degree of substitutability between domestic and foreign production. Indeed, many goods essential for the economy cannot easily be produced domestically. This is most obvious in the case of certain raw materials, but now applies to many technologically sophisticated manufactured products as well. In any event, if relative prices cannot move sufficiently, then faster rates of growth in one country relative to its trading partners will tend to show up as an increasing deficit in its balance of trade and payments.

There may also be circumstances in which a widening deficit on current account is sustainable because the counterpart to the deficit is an increase in long-run private sector borrowing. An example might be a net inward flow of long-term investment (e.g. direct investment in UK-based productive assets). However it should be noticed that, in the United Kingdom's case, although direct inward investment has in the past decade or more been substantial, outward investment has nearly always been even larger. But where the borrowing is short-term, speculative pressure on the exchange rate is likely to force the authorities to raise short-term interest rates, as witnessed during the years of the Lawson boom in the late 1980s. More generally, however, mounting deficits are associated with increasing risk on the part of the lender and may be accompanied by short-term capital outflows, exacerbating the pressure on governments to undertake deflationary measures to reverse the situation. Certainly for the United Kingdom, there can be little doubt that the balance of payments on the current account acted as a major feature in the 'stop-go' economic cycle of the 1950s and 1960s, or indeed of the late 1980s.

On this view it is clear that the competitiveness of the tradable sector as a whole is vital in explaining overall economic performance – not just that part producing exports, but also that part competing with imports. Attaching clear meaning to the idea of competitiveness therefore involves a consideration of the processes which drive the pattern of international specialisation. These may well have undergone deep and fundamental revision in the period since 1973. In the period before 1973, we saw that the stock of investment *incountrnul.*

opportunities available to the OECD economies outside the US was considerable. The skills of the workforce needed to complement such an investment programme does not seem to have been a major drawback, with, in most instances, the vast majority of populations receiving a full secondary education. The potential for the ready *transfer* of technology from, primarily the US, to elsewhere in the OECD was considerable. The problem was largely one of generating resources for investment. Moreover, the smaller countries had suffered in the trans-war period, relative to the US, because of the disruption and dislocation to the process of international specialisation. The rebound effect in the 1950s and 1960s, as markets became more integrated, made itself felt in the exceptionally high rates of export growth experienced and which are so vividly illustrated in Figure 4.4(a). The period since 1973 has seen major changes to this picture. Not least, increasing capital mobility, linked partly to the growing importance of the transnational corporation, has meant that the process of international specialisation between the advanced economies and the developing world is today largely driven by differences in the educational structure of the workforce. These differences are to be found in secondary school enrolment but even more so in terms of a higher level of tertiary education. Accordingly we would expect a pattern of specialisation in the OECD economies which follows a knowledge-based path, making increasing use of skilled labour.

Some writers, such as Brown and Julius (1993), have advanced a more specific hypothesis, arguing that the advanced economies will increasingly specialise in sophisticated services – in finance, insurance, consultancy, and so on. The evidence for this proposition is much weaker. As Table 4.5 makes clear, in all of the G6 economies, goods still make up the bulk of exported goods and services today. The US and, to a much lesser extent, France, do appear to have made some shift into service exports since 1973. UK exports are actually less service intensive than they were in 1973 (see below, Chapter 18), although this is partly a consequence of the advent of North Sea oil exports in the mid-1970s. However, even allowing for this, *manufactured*

Table 4.5 Services exports as a percentage of total exports of goods and services

	1973	1993
France	18.2	23.9
Germany	14.2	14.3
Italy	22.5	24.5
Japan	—	13.5
UK	30.4	23.2
US	20.1	30.1

Source: OECD/NIGEM.

exports formed a bigger proportion of UK exports in the early 1990s than they did in 1979 (Temple, 1994). Clearly then, outside the US, these figures do not support the hypothesis of a very strong trend toward specialisation in services.

What, however, is the hard evidence for the more general proposition that the United Kingdom and other advanced economies are following a pattern of international specialisation which is leading to a more intensive use of skills and knowledge in the production of exports? One way of measuring the knowledge intensity of production is through research and development (R&D) expenditures which, although they omit many activities which we would wish to include, have the merit at least of being internationally comparable and moreover are likely to be correlated with other activities (such as design and innovation), which are also knowledge–intensive in character. Frequently, these expenditures are expressed as a proportion of GDP – typically forming 2–3 per cent in the G6 economies. To counter the argument that this figure is not large enough to explain widely divergent outcomes in GDP growth, it needs to be pointed out that it has generally been rising across the OECD, and more importantly that R&D expenditure is a heavily concentrated activity, with perhaps about three-fifths of total R&D occurring within manufacturing (Prevezer and Temple, 1994) with a further slice concentrated in telecommunications and services related to computing – i.e. within the tradable sector or in areas important for the transmission of technological change. Further information regarding investment in R&D is supplied in Chapter 8 below.

As Figure 4.5 shows, the ratio of R&D expenditures to value added in manufacturing in the G6 economies has increased considerably in the period since 1973. Today this ratio stands above 8 per cent for the US, which is around two-thirds of its ratio of physical investment to output.

In explaining this rising research intensity it is useful to distinguish between two different possible sources. The first depends upon the fact that some branches of manufacturing are more research intensive than others, and that these ('high-tech') sectors grow faster than the rest of manufacturing. This can be thought of as a 'levels' effect, since it does not rely on any industry experiencing a rise in its research intensity. The second possibility is that all industries are tending to become more research-intensive, which we might call the 'rate' effect. Each possible process actually corresponds to commonly used ways of describing industrial change. The levels effect corresponds to the 'sunrise, sunset' phenomenon, where new research-intensive industries replace older, more mature industries. The rate effect on the other hand might be said to reflect a general shift into earlier stages of the product cycle.

Breaking down the aggregate rise into both these sources is a simple exercise in decomposition which is illustrated in Table 4.6 for the manufacturing sectors of the G6 economies and based upon twenty–two

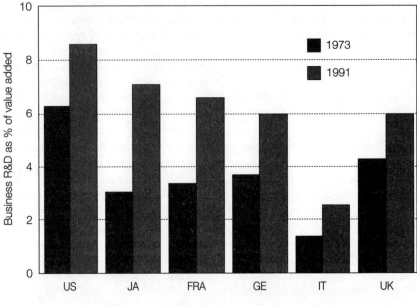

Figure 4.5 The growth of research intensity in manufacturing
Source: OECD.

Table 4.6 The growth in research intensity in G6 manufacturing and its decomposition (1973–91)

	Total (%)	Rate	Level	Interaction
France	93.8	57.8	31.5	4.5
Germany	63.6	41.6	25.4	−3.5
Italy	92.6	70.5	8.8	13.3
Japan	128.7	100.0	18.8	9.9
UK	39.5	15.7	27.7	−3.9
US	37.9	23.0	20.2	−5.3

Source: OECD Anberd/STAN 1994.
Note: Italy 1973–91 only; Germany 1976–91.

individual industries. Note that the discrete time period chosen for the analysis (1973–91) means that the decomposition is not exact, so that there is also a small interaction effect.

Having observed that for all six economies, both effects are positive, the remarkable feature of Table 4.6 is that the relative importance of each factor is not similar across countries. While the US and – even more so – the United Kingdom have comparatively small rate effects, they form the chief driving force elsewhere, especially in the cases of Japan and Italy.

At this point it seems natural to ask which of the two factors is more closely related to economic performance. Here we must be careful; while the best measure of performance at the economy-wide level may well be labour productivity growth, this is not so clear at the level of an individual sector such as manufacturing. Here the best barometer of success in a competitive capitalist environment is provided by the growth of output. This is justifiable not just because, in a capitalist society, successful entities will tend to grow faster than their less successful counterparts, but also because the linkages between manufacturing and the rest of the economy mean that its size is of fundamental importance. Not least, this is because of the way in which manufacturing acts as a conduit for technological change elsewhere in the economy – a factor emphasised in a number of studies (e.g. Geroski, 1994; Swann, 1993). However, using output growth as the preferred performance measure, simple correlation coefficients suggest a very strong correlation between the growth of output and the rate effect (0.91), and virtually none between growth and the level effect (−0.02). The same kind of picture emerges when the manufacturing sector of each of the six economies is divided into a research intensive sector (mainly chemicals and engineering) and the more traditional industries (food, clothing, textiles, furniture, etc.) and performance is compared as in Table 4.7. Although for example Japan has certainly moved heavily into the research-intensive sectors, this should not detract from the fact that it has also experienced steady expansion in its more traditional sectors. This is even more clear in the case of Italy, which has been successful in many traditional areas such as clothing and textiles. Although all six economies have been experiencing more rapid rates of expansion in the research-intensive sectors, the most successful (fastest growing) manufacturing sectors of the six – namely Japan and Italy – have also seen the fastest growth in their traditional industries as well. In both

Table 4.7 Growth of manufacturing output in G6: annual percentage growth, 1979–93

	Research-intensive sectors	*Other*
France	2.0	0.9
Germany	2.0	0.4
Italy	3.4	1.9
Japan	7.6	2.0
UK	1.2	0.1
US	2.1	0.5

Source: OECD/STAN.
Note: Italy 1973–87; Germany 1976–91.

these economies the traditional sectors have actually been growing faster than the research-intensive sectors in the United Kingdom.

The evidence therefore suggests that the important factor in generating growth in manufacturing has been the ability to increase the knowledge intensity of investments across manufacturing, and that success is not just about shifting resources into so-called high-tech sectors. In other words, the best way of thinking about competitive performance of the advanced economies may be in terms of a pattern of comparative advantage which is shifting into earlier stages of the product cycle – not just in terms of invention and innovation, but also in terms of the rapid diffusion of new technology and organisational best practice.

THE CHALLENGE FOR ECONOMIC POLICY: THE CONCEPT OF COMPETITIVENESS AND THE ROLE OF INSTITUTIONS

If the pattern of international specialisation, for both the OECD and, within the foreseeable future for the advanced economies of South East Asia, is indeed being based upon knowledge intensive activities, then this poses considerable challenges for economic policy. Two sets of considerations are especially important, one related to economic efficiency, and one related to economic equity.

1 That broad similarities in the educational structure of the workforce between the different advanced economies will not be sufficient to guarantee similarity in outcomes. It is widely recognised that the commercial exploitation of knowledge involves not only risk and uncertainty but also considerable market failure not only in the generation and transfer of knowledge but also in the exchange of knowledge-intensive goods and services (e.g. the hiring of skilled labour). National competitive performance will depend upon the extent to which institutions, both within and outside government, are able to eliminate or at least ameliorate those market failures. In this sense, far from diminishing national differences, the impact of international economic integration may serve to emphasise their importance.

2 That international specialisation along the lines suggested will tend to raise the demand for skilled labour and lower that for unskilled. This will accentuate any tendency toward increasing inequality in the distribution of income. This much has repeatedly been noted in the literature but its importance in relation to other factors (especially technological change more generally and the impact of labour market deregulation) is less clear. Most economists have believed that the impact of competition from the less advanced industrial economies (the 'South') has been small, given the rather low level of import penetration from these economies. However,

the conventional wisdom has been challenged by Wood (1994), who points to the possibility that *potential* competition from the South has been important in forcing producers to abandon unskilled labour intensive processes so that the impact on the demand for labour is much greater than the actual trade flows suggest. In Wood's view, up to 1990 about 12 per cent of employment in advanced economy manufacturing had been displaced because of increasing competition from the South. While not many economists would agree to the full extent of the impact claimed by Wood, many would agree that the rapid growth of unskilled labour-intensive imports has resulted in a considerable negative shock to the demand for unskilled labour. Whether this produces a commensurate rise in unemployment, depends to an extent upon the flexibility of the wages of unskilled labour in the non-tradable sector of the economy. The more flexible downwards they are, the greater the increase in inequality will be, but any rise in unemployment will be contained (for a discussion and model simulation, see Rowthorn, 1995).

Against this background, economic prosperity will depend upon the abilities of economies to generate investments which are consistent with the progressive international division of labour and which are able to meet the economic and social problems posed by the general decline in the demand for unskilled labour.

The perception that the process of international economic integration is increasing levels of unemployment always carries with it the likelihood of a political agenda which embraces protectionism, and the current climate is no exception. It is against this background that the current concern of Britain and other European economies with the idea of competitiveness needs to be addressed. There is certainly a danger, observed for example by Krugman (1994), that competitiveness may be no more than a mask for protectionism. It is therefore necessary to define more precisely how competitive performance is to be measured, and Krugman is surely right to emphasise that measures based upon such things as the trade balance (especially, in this context, the trade balance of Europe or the US with Japan), are entirely inappropriate in this regard, since one of the ways of improving the trade balance is through protectionist measures, which hinder the progressive development of international specialisation and the progress of technology. A similar thing can be said for export shares (Sentance, 1996) since this indicator tells us nothing about whether the denominator (world exports) is either rising or falling.

However, if the competitiveness of the tradable sector of the economy is defined in terms of its ability to *grow* in the face of more open global markets, then policies seeking to improve competitiveness may be viewed as a quite legitimate objective, not only for local and national governments but also for supranational organisations such as the European Commission. In

93

the context of knowledge-based specialisation, competitiveness policies are essentially promoters of technological change.

If the foregoing analysis is correct, then the challenge for the OECD economies will be in the creation of an economic climate favouring investment based upon innovation and product development. Here the role of institutions will be paramount, first and foremost because technology has both private and public good dimensions. No government is neutral in this regard, however pro-market its policy stance may be, because it is everywhere (at least in the advanced economies) responsible for much of education, for much scientific activity, and for the development of what is termed the 'technological infrastructure'. The latter is closely related to the public good element of technology, and embraces training provision and skill certification, industrial standards, the degree of protection for industrial property, and so on. Governments are therefore, in one way or another, largely responsible for assets which are complementary to, and which consequently raise the productivity of, private-sector investment in R&D, training, and physical capacity. In short, the development of the technological infrastructure will raise the incentive of firms to generate firm specific competencies. To the extent that policies in this regard are successful, the problem posed by rising levels of inequality may be diminished, since they will tend to increase the supply of skilled labour and reduce the supply of unskilled labour. Notwithstanding this effect, which may have a long-term character, there is a further challenge for the advanced economies to fashion redistributive instruments which increase employment for unskilled workers (these might include subsidies for their employment in the non-tradable sector of the economy).

In Britain the Government has produced a trio of White Papers embracing the concept of competitiveness as providing the basic framework for government economic policy (HMSO, 1994, 1995, 1996). The Government's understanding of the idea of national competitiveness is defined in terms of 'the ability of a country to increase its living standards', while at the same time ensuring that its goods and services meet the test of international markets. This is linked closely in its view with the progress of overall labour productivity. Little attention is paid, however, to the question of the distribution of the product or the levels of employment generated, although the latter is an important element of the recent European Commission's White Paper on competitiveness (CEC, 1994). Most importantly, there is little discussion in the UK documents of the theoretical underpinnings of the approach adopted, although some glimpses are to be found in an essay by Eltis and Higham (1995), who stress the importance of 'broad capital' (see above). No especial role is afforded to trading performance in this regard, nor is there any detailed institutional audit which would enable the reader to compare the competitiveness of its institutions with those abroad.

The centrality of institutions in understanding why growth paths differ is now generally recognised. This is evident from the increasing references to concepts such as 'Euosclerosis' – used to describe the inflexibility of European institutions, especially in the labour market – or the various national 'models' of capitalism – the Swedish model, the Japanese model, the US or 'Anglo-Saxon' model, and so on. One popular thesis, originally advanced by Olson (1965), maintains that differences in growth outcomes can be understood with reference to the nature of collective action and institutions. On this view narrowly defined collective bodies are able to shift the distribution of income in their favour through instruments (cartelisation, subsidies, etc.) which have distortionary effects on the allocation of resources and hence reduce growth. The narrowness of the membership, however, ensures that the slower growth is far less important than the extra rents exacted through the redistribution of income. The incentive changes, however, as the membership forms a significant fraction of the income-earning capacity of the country – the institution becomes *encompassing* – and the slower growth engendered becomes important. Something of this sort appeared to have informed creation of institutions which were fashioned in the wake of the Second World War; this was generally simpler in the case of occupied countries, than in those such as Britain, which were never occupied. Contrast, therefore, the industry-wide unions formed in Germany with the fragmented union representation found in Britain either side of the war. A number of writers (e.g. Crafts and Bean, 1996) have focused on the impact of bargaining between unions and management on the investment decision. They note that the returns to investment may fall short of the increment to output if workers are able, after the event, to extract some of that increment as wages. Essentially, this is an alternative explanation as to why private rates of return to investment may fall short of social rates of return. Crafts and Bean see in this a vehicle for poorer economic performance in the United Kingdom, because the multiple union bargaining prevalent in Britain was more likely to prevent a cooperative outcome in which the workers eschew possibilities for opportunism. Elsewhere in Europe, Eichengreen (1996) saw institutional mechanisms for preventing the exercise of opportunism as important in generating high levels of investment in the 'Golden Age'. However as the returns to investment declined with diminished scope for catch-up after 1973, the opportunity costs for such cooperative action rose with the institutions themselves thereby tending to exacerbate the initial problem created by fewer investment opportunities. In Britain it may be noticed, where institutions may be have been less helpful in regard to generating high investment levels, the impact of the interaction between the two influences on growth would have been much less severe.

The suggestion in all this was that labour market institutions were critical for economic performance in the 'Golden Age'. Moreover, they were also important for success given the inflationary shocks of the 1970s. What is less clear, however, is whether labour market institutions are going to be as

95

fundamental to the competitive performance of the tradable sectors of the OECD economies in the future. Here, pride of place must surely go to potential market failures which inhibit investment, not because of any trade union power, but because of the riskiness and difficulties of appropriating the benefits from devoting more resources to the purposive generation of knowledge, a topic developed at length in Part III of this book.

CONCLUSIONS

In reviewing Britain's economic performance from a longer perspective, it may well be that the most important story concerns the lost opportunities of the early post-war period. There can be little certainty about the causes of this failure, but the emphasis of orthodox studies has been to blame, and the emphasis of policy to reform, the institutions of the labour market, especially the trade unions. However, on the basis of the evidence of this overview it may well be that the emphasis of current policy in correcting perceived reasons for failure in the 1950s and 1960s has left Britain vulnerable to the challenges of today.

In more concrete terms, if a poorly performing labour market was important in explaining the reason for Britain's failure to exploit more fully the economic opportunities of the 'Golden Age', it does not follow that the operation of the labour market will be the key to success in the next millennium. Nevertheless recent government pronouncements all regard the 'flexibility' of the labour market as the cornerstone of Britain's competitiveness. While nobody would wish to argue that an inflexible labour market is the foundation of success, the whole emphasis nevertheless ignores the problem of generating investments consistent with the process of international specialisation – a process dominated in the advanced economies by the need to exploit their knowledge base. Here the record is much bleaker. The evidence from manufacturing shows that the ability of individual industries to increase the research intensity of their investments has been much weaker than elsewhere – comparative advantage has not moved as decisively into earlier stages of the product cycle. If this analysis is correct, although the steep process of relative economic decline observable in this period was to some extent arrested in the period since 1973, there can be little room for complacency.

When it comes to the question of policies which might stimulate knowledge based investments, partly because of the complexities of the processes involved, it does not seem likely that progress can be made on the basis of very simple theorising about the role of markets and the need to restrict the scope of government. The point is that governments, whether at a local, national, or supranational level, play a central role themselves in the development of knowledge as a resource, and in all probability only they can provide the coordination of the investment process necessary if the challenges of the present are to be met.

NOTES

1 Funding from the Gatsby Foundation gratefully acknowledged.
2 The PPP rate of exchange is an imaginary rate found by valuing the same bundle of goods and services in the different currencies, so if that bundle costs £100 in the United Kingdom but $150 in the US, the PPP exchange rate would be £1 = $1.50. PPP rates of exchange can and often do differ significantly from actual rates of exchange. They also have their own difficulties which stem from the fact that relative prices differ from one country to the next. In this case, the valuation of different bundles of goods and services may yield quite different PPP rates of exchange. This would not matter if the composition of consumption were more or less the same everywhere, but this is manifestly not the case. The problem is exacerbated when comparisons are made between economies with very different standards of living and the composition of the 'appropriate' bundle of goods and services differs widely. The relevance, for example, of a box of computer diskettes amongst the bundle selected, will almost certainly differ between Zaire and Frankfurt. The problem remains when comparisons are made over time; in 1950 the computer diskette had probably not even been conceived! Finally, recent research at the National Institute has shown that significant differences in the quality of goods and services being valued may mean that PPP estimates are misleading for yet another reason (Jarvis and Prais, 1995).
3 Note, however, that the Bretton Woods system was far from being a fixed exchange rate regime. Outside a narrow band, discrete changes were possible for reasons of fundamental disequilibrium on the balance of payments.
4 Recent applications of the idea can be found in Thirlwall (1980), or Coutts and Godley (1990, 1992). The basic idea behind the balance of payments constraint can be explained more formally as follows: if movements in the price levels prevailing in the different economies are, over time, counterbalanced by movements in the exchange rate, then the growth rate of an economy consistent with balance of payments equilibrium, G_b, can be expressed as $\varepsilon W/\pi$ where W is the rate of growth of income in the 'rest of the world', ε is the world income elasticity of demand for exports and π is the domestic income elasticity of demand for imports. Thirlwall (1979) shows that G_b predicts actual national rates of growth with some accuracy.

REFERENCES

Abramovitz, M. (1986) 'Catching up, forging ahead, and falling behind', *Journal of Economic History*, vol. 46, pp. 385–406.
Brown, R. and Julius De A. (1993) 'Is manufacturing still special in the world order?' in R. O'Brien, (ed.), *Finance and the International Economy*, Oxford: Oxford University Press.
CEC (1994) *An Industrial Competitiveness Policy for the European Union*, Brussels COM(94) 319.
Coates, D. (1994) *The Question of UK Decline*, London: Harvester Wheatsheaf.
Coutts, K. and Godley, W. (1990) 'Prosperity and foreign trade in the 1990s: Britain's strategic problem', *Oxford Review of Economic Policy*, vol. 6. No. 3, pp. 82–92.
—— (1992) 'Does Britain's balance of payments matter any more?', in J. Michie (ed.) *The Economic Legacy, 1979–1992*, London: Academic Press.
Crafts, N.F.R. (1992) 'Productivity growth reconsidered', *Economic Policy*, vol. 15, pp. 387–426.

Crafts, N.F.R. and Bean, C. (1996) 'British economic growth since 1945', in N.F.R. Crafts, and G. Toniolo, (eds) *Economic Growth in Europe since 1945*, Cambridge: Cambridge University Press.

Eichengreen, B. (1996) 'Institutions and economic growth', in N. Crafts and G. Toniolo (eds) *Economic Growth in Europe since 1945*, Cambridge: Cambridge University Press.

Eltis, W. and Higham, D. (1995) 'Closing the competitiveness gap', *National Institute Economic and Social Review*, November, pp. 71–84.

Geroski, P. (1994) 'UK productivity growth', in *Market Structure, Corporate Performance, and Innovative Activity*, Oxford; Oxford University Press.

Grossman, G.M. and Helpman, E. (1991) *Innovation and Growth in the Global Economy*, Cambridge, Mass.: MIT Press.

HMSO (1994) *Helping Business To Win*, Cm 2563, London: HMSO.

—— (1995) *Forging Ahead*, Cm 2867, London: HMSO.

—— (1996) *Creating the Enterprise Centre of Europe*, Cm 3300, London: HMSO.

Jarvis, N. and Prais, S. (1995) 'The quality of manufactured products in Britain and Germany', *National Institute of Economic and Social Research*, Discussion Paper no. 88.

Krugman, P. (1994) *Peddling Prosperity*, New York: Norton.

Levine, R. and Renelt, D. (1992) 'A sensitivity analysis of cross-country growth regressions', *American Economic Review*, vol. 82 no.4 pp. 942–63.

Maddison, A. (1991) *Dynamic Forces in Capitalist Development*, Oxford: Oxford University Press.

Olson, M. (1965) *The Logic of Collective Action: Public Goods and the Behaviour of Groups*, Cambridge: Cambridge University Press.

Oulton, N. (1995) 'Supply side reform and UK economic growth: What happened to the miracle?', *National Institute Economic Review* November pp. 53–69.

Prevezer, M. and Temple, P. (1994) 'Britain's economic performance: The strategic dimension', *Business Strategy Review*, vol. 5, no 3, pp. 35–48.

Rebelo, S. (1991) 'Long-run policy analysis and long run growth', *Journal of Political Economy* vol. 99 no. 3 pp. 500–21.

Rowthorn, R. (1995) A Simulation Model of North-South Trade, ESRC Centre for Business Research Working Paper Series WP9 May.

Sentance, A. (1996) 'Europe's economic malaise: A problem of competitiveness?', *Business Strategy Review*, vol. 7, no. 2, Summer, pp. 37–44.

Swann, P. (1993) *Can High Technology Services Prosper When High Technology Manufacturing Cannot?*, CBS Working Paper Series, London Business School.

Temple, P. (1994) The evolution of UK trade performance since 1979: Pointers for industrial policy *Centre for Industrial Policy and Performance* Discussion paper no. 8, University of Leeds.

Thirlwall, A. P. (1979) 'The balance of payments constraint as an explanation of international growth rate differences', *Banca Nazionale del Lavoro Quarterly Review*, March.

—— (1980) *Balance of Payments Theory and the United Kingdom Experience*, London: Macmillan.

Wood, A.J.B (1994) *North-South Trade, Employment, and Inequality*, Oxford: Oxford University Press.

5

QUALITY SPECIALISATION IN UK TRADE[1]

Paul Temple

INTRODUCTION

Despite its obvious importance and relevance for economic performance in general, the basis of the overall pattern of specialisation in UK trade is seldom discussed. This chapter adds to what is known by examining the pattern of specialisation in UK manufacturing trade according to 'vertical' differences in quality – i.e. differences in the quality of goods which result from a superior set of characteristics.[2] Such differences may reflect a more innovative product or one which makes the greater use of skilled labour.

Unfortunately, observing the characteristics of even a limited set of goods[3] can be very labour-intensive, so that recourse must be made to other methods if observed differences in quality are to form the basis for an investigation of underlying specialisation patterns of whole economies. In this chapter, an alternative approach, based on 'willingness to pay' as measured by observed unit values in international trade, is adopted.

The chapter first of all discusses the 'traditional' theory of international specialisation, i.e. one based on national resource endowments. It is argued that, appropriately formulated, the traditional approach is consistent with intra-industry trade which takes place according to vertical differences in quality. Other perspectives on patterns of specialisation in trade should perhaps be viewed as complementary, rather than as substitutes, for the traditional view. Differences in unit values observed at a very detailed level of trade classification are then used to consider the relative importance of vertically, as opposed to horizontally distinguishable trade flows. The question of the basic pattern in UK trade is then explored, before turning the approach to the question of foreign competition from trade with Asia. Finally, the relationship between specialisation according to quality and trade performance is considered.

THE TRADITIONAL THEORY OF INTERNATIONAL SPECIALISATION

The traditional theory of international trade and specialisation is based on the idea of comparative advantage, with countries trading according to the pattern of comparative costs which, in their turn, are determined by so-called 'resource endowments'. In other words, a region or country which is especially rich in a particular resource will specialise in goods or services which make relatively heavy use of the resource in question. In contrast to the pattern of resource endowment, the approach regards other possible reasons for trade – such as access to technology, or differences in tastes or preferences between groups of consumers, or increasing returns phenomena leading to 'lock-in' by historical circumstance – as being of secondary importance. The hypothesis also carries with it some important implications, especially that the opening up of trade will raise the demand for the resource which is in abundance – increasing its price relative to other resources or factors of production.

There is obviously some general validity in the basic proposition of the traditional approach – countries which are well endowed with natural resources ('land'), such as Canada or Australia, tend to export resource-intensive products such as minerals or certain kinds of foodstuffs. Other countries, with abundant supplies of poorly educated labour, will tend to export products – maybe certain kinds of textile product – which require much labour with little qualification but make little use of highly qualified labour.

Despite the obvious relevance of examples where trade clearly follows patterns of resource endowments, and the continuing importance of the theory for teaching purposes, the approach is far less well established in the empirical analysis of trade flows. Several alternative approaches can be identified. One strand, the literature on trade between the developed economies, in noting the extent to which bilateral trade within industries is of a two-way nature, has emphasised the ability of producers to differentiate their products as an important source of trade (for a survey, see Greenaway and Milner, 1986). Another strand has emphasised the importance of technology, arguing *inter alia* that technology is not easily transferred from one country to another and that lags in the process can be a fundamental and persistent source of trade flow as national firms and industries build up specific technological competencies which cannot be costlessly or timelessly imitated (e.g. Posner, 1961; Dosi *et al.*, 1990). While the relevance of either of these strands cannot be doubted, it is possible to argue that they are, at least in part, complementary to the received doctrine. To see this it is necessary to regard the traditional approach as referring to a higher level of abstraction – not appropriate for dealing with the minutiae of the commodity composition of trade, in which detailed historical circumstance (including, for example, the history of firm-specific investments) may be vital, but useful nonetheless for dealing with very broad patterns of trade and their evolution over lengthy periods of time.

One reason why the traditional theory of international trade has not attracted more attention in the empirical analysis of trade or, where it has been used, has produced somewhat contradictory results, has been its failure to consider adequately the question of factor mobility, for it is of course the immobility of factors which is the basis of comparative advantage, since mobile factors cannot command different prices in the long run. Of course 'land' is the classic immobile factor, but it is widely recognised that this is not the key feature in a large part of the trade involving developed economies. Therefore, with some degree of deference to reality, the typical textbook treatment assumes that 'labour' and a factor of production called 'capital' are immobile. By implication the developed economies possess a comparative advantage in goods (or services) utilising capital relatively intensively. But it is soon apparent that capital has many different forms which make it a slippery concept. Some types of capital are clearly highly mobile. Machinery, for example, is highly tradable in international markets, and even if buildings are not, the services of builders and architects most certainly are. On the other hand, there are aspects of capital which are immobile – roads, railways and other physical infrastructure – and these aspects are important, in the most general way, in distinguishing the developed economies from the rest of the world.

The view that the relative abundance of capital is at the heart of the pattern of comparative advantage of the developed economies is at considerable variance with the simple fact that there does not appear to be any major divergence in profit rates in different parts of the world, a fact that may be explained in part by the fact that one form of capital – financial capital – is highly mobile internationally. Of course, if (homogeneous, undifferentiated) labour and capital were the only factors of production, then the equality of rates of profit, together with equal access to technology would mean that the wages of labour would be equalised everywhere. This demonstrably has not happened, although it is currently possible to observe forces tending to bring them into equality.

The persistence of differences in wages means that we must look beyond capital, for some other immobile factor of production. It is natural to think of skilled labour fulfilling that role (e.g. Wood, 1994), although it needs to be made clear that in modern production, the effective utilisation of labour force skills requires the complementary input of what, for want of a better choice of term, might be called the 'technological infrastructure'. This concept might be used to embrace any number of aspects of technology which are to a greater or lesser extent, immobile. We may wish to include here many factors which operate at a national (or indeed a more local) level – things such as education and training and the institutional mechanisms which link

101

them to firms (such as the relevance of the curricula, or the idiosyncrasies of the qualification system); the system of industrial standards; the existence of institutions promoting cooperative R&D; the presence of effective legal means to protect intellectual property, and so on. In short the technological infrastructure amounts to a collection of public goods which enable skilled labour to operate effectively. None of this is of course to deny that production may be intensive in the use of skilled labour without the need for any degree of sophistication in the technological infrastructure, and this is indeed the case in some craft-based industries. We may assume, however, that such goods are rather exceptional.

Armed with this concept of skilled labour, augmented by a motley collection of more or less public goods called the technological infrastructure, it is not at all clear that the presence of a comparative advantage may be expected in any particular range of industries. Although we might expect some advantage in those that are routinely described as being 'high-tech' – in electronics and electrical engineering, fine chemicals, aerospace and so on – closer inspection reveals that much of the output of these industries is highly standardised and quite possibly 'low-tech'. On the other hand, in more traditional industries – textiles, furniture, footwear and clothing for example – it is perfectly possible to conceive of output being very intensive in the use of marketers, designers and other skilled occupations. Italian success in many of these industries is well recognised, and believed to be based on the deployment of skilled labour in areas such as design. The implication may be that the pattern of advantage may reside as much in earlier stages in the product cycle than in any established set of industries, however finely defined.

It follows from the earlier discussion that in order to examine trade data for evidence regarding the resource intensity of trade, an industry-based approach is clearly inadequate and this may partly explain why attempts to understand the nature of trade flows on the basis of generalisations about the resource intensity of production in different industries, have frequently produced strange results – as originally exemplified in Leontief's attempt to infer the resource intensity of US imports on the basis solely of US input–output tables and which gave rise to the famous 'paradox' according to which the US was importing the more capital-intensive products (Leontief 1953).

THE PATTERN OF SPECIALISATION IN UK TRADE

The question of the pattern of specialisation in UK trade is of course an important one. In the past, some studies have indicated that the United Kingdom may in some sense display a 'perverse' pattern (which may make the economy vulnerable to a relatively rapid process of import penetration from low wage cost economies). For example, in a study of UK net exports covering the years 1910, 1924, 1930, and 1935, Crafts and Thomas (1986) found that net exports were positively related to inputs of unskilled labour and negatively to inputs of human capital. For a more recent period, Katrak (1982) found that although the relative skill intensity of exports exceeded that for imports in the period 1968–78, the ratio was declining rapidly. Both these studies, however, made the assumption, in common with Leontief, that inferences about the nature of imports could be made on the basis of domestic production technology. A different approach, not subject to the same charge, makes use of unit values in international trade (i.e. prices actually paid per kilogram or per tonne or per unit) which are used to deduce vertical differences in quality, on the basis of consumer willingness to pay.[4] As reported by Swann below (Chapter 6), some studies of UK trade in the 1970s, based on unit values, did show a tendency, when compared with France or Germany at any rate, for the United Kingdom to export cheap and import dear. However, using more recent data for the period 1978–87, Oulton (1990 and 1993), while noting important cross-sectoral differences, could not detect any such systematic tendency for the United Kingdom.

But what is the relationship between vertical differences in quality and the relative intensity of inputs of skilled labour? In the modern world, perhaps the most important source of differences in consumer willingness to pay can be summed up as 'product development' – i.e. the recognition that the preponderance of technical progress is of an incremental kind, in which some products fulfil existing needs rather better than other more basic products. It is likely that such products will not only make greater demands on specialised skilled labour inputs, but may also experience rather higher income elasticities of demand than the products that they replace. By contrast, a developed economy specialising in more standardised goods suggests a pattern of trade more vulnerable to competition from low-wage cost economies. This is of course the pattern of specialisation suggested in a number of highly specific studies emanating from the National Institute for Economic and Social Research, according to which the problem of a labour force with inadequate training has caused producers to adopt technologies of production which are relatively intensive in the use of unskilled labour (e.g. Jarvis and Prais, 1989; Steedman, 1987 and 1988; Steedman and Wagner, 1987 and 1988).

These considerations suggest that evidence using unit values can be used to provide an important characterisation of the pattern of UK specialisation in international trade. This leads to the following questions:

1 How important are vertical differences in UK trade and how far can these vertical differences explain the pattern of intra-industry trade?
2 On the basis of its exports, does the United Kingdom specialise in high-quality or low-quality goods?
3 On the basis of quality, what is the nature of the competition from emerging economies?

4 What is the relationship between quality specialisation and trade performance?

The remainder of this chapter is an attempt to illumine UK trade data at a very detailed level of classification, namely the eight-digit codes that make up the Harmonised Nomenclature of the trade classification. Across manufacturing this classification amounts to some 8,000 commodity groups. All data are for 1992.

HORIZONTAL VERSUS VERTICAL DIFFERENTIATION IN UK TRADE

For some, the phenomenon of intra-industry trade has long been held to be at variance with the orthodox doctrine of resource-based comparative advantage. However, it is clear from the above discussion that this view applies strictly only to *horizontally* differentiated goods, i.e. goods which differ in their characteristics but which cannot command a price premium because the characteristics of any one are not clearly superior to another (a blue against a red car, for example). International exchange of horizontally distinguishable goods is based on differences in consumer tastes. With one recent exception (Greenaway *et al.*, 1995), empirical work, while emphasising the importance of intra-industry trade, has not generally considered the distinction between horizontal and vertical differences in quality.

Empirical investigation of intra-industry trade has generally made use of the Grubel-Lloyd index (GL). For any group of commodities constituting an 'industry' it may be defined, either in terms of bilateral trade or multilateral trade as:

$$GL = 1 - \{\,|\,(X_i - M_i)\,|\,/(X_i + M_i)\}$$

where X_i, M_i are the aggregate exports and imports of industry i.

If the flow of trade is predominantly one-way, the sum of the absolute values of the difference between exports and imports will be close to the total value of trade in that industry, and the index will be close to zero. On the other hand, if the trade is relatively balanced in each commodity, the index will be closer to unity.

In this exercise exports and imports are allocated to one of 197 four-digit industries of the 1980 Standard Industrial Classification (SIC).[5] The distribution of the indices calculated on a multilateral basis is shown in Figure 5.1(a). It confirms the commonly reported finding (contingent to an extent on how broadly an industry is defined) regarding the extent of intra-industry trade, with a modal class interval of 0.8–1 and an average of 0.70.

But how big are the contributions of horizontal and vertical intra-industry trade to the total index? In each industry, it is possible, although this of course is essentially arbitrary, to distinguish trades according to whether the *relative* unit value of a trade (calculated as the logarithm of the export unit value less the import unit value of the corresponding trade) falls within a specified range; in this case the range used is ±0.2. This is slightly wider than the range used in a recent study by Abd-el-Rahman (1991) and in between the two ranges employed by Greenaway *et al.* (1995). A trade inside this window of approximately 40 per cent is classified as horizontally differenti- ated, otherwise it counts as vertically differentiated. The contribution to the total GL index of horizontally differentiated trade is then made up of the GL index for this group multiplied by the weight of such trade in the total trade $(X + M)$ for the industry. The distribution of resultant percentage contributions are shown in Figure 5.1(b). It can be seen that in this case the modal class interval is 0–20 per cent with an average of 24 per cent. In very few industries does horizontally differentiated intra-industry trade contribute over half to the total.

Evidently, vertically distinguished trade is a more significant component of intra-industry trade: while not directly supporting to the relevance of the orthodox theory in explaining trade flows, the results are at least consistent with it.

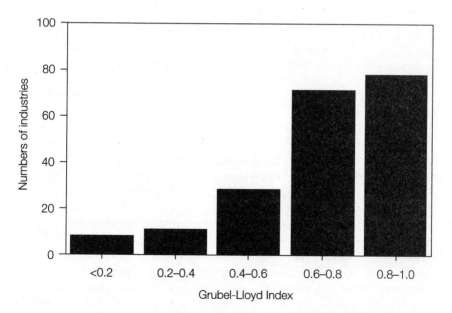

Figure 5.1(a) Total intra-industry trade by 4-digit industry

105

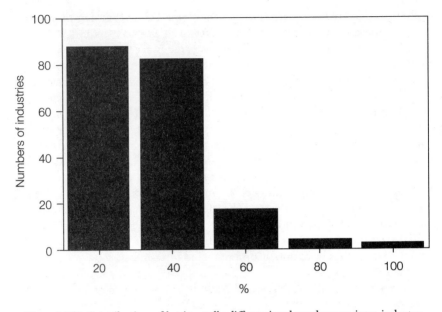

Figure 5.1(b) Contribution of horizontally differentiated products to intra-industry trade

ARE UK EXPORTS SPECIALISED ACCORDING TO QUALITY?

To what extent are UK exports specialised in terms of quality? If the discussion above concerning the traditional theory of international specialisation is correct, we should predict that the United Kingdom, as an advanced economy, should be relatively specialised in goods of rather high quality.

To help answer this fundamental question unit value 'norms' were estimated for each commodity group on the basis of the geometric mean of the observed unit values across twelve major OECD economies.[6] In order to ensure that there is some competition, these were only calculated when the number of observations exceeded three.[7] For descriptive purposes the value of the trade flows were then categorised according to one of three categories – high-quality, medium-quality, or low-quality. The demarcation was based upon whether the logarithm of the recorded unit value exceeded the logarithm of the norm unit value by 0.2 or more (high-quality) or fell short of the norm by 0.2 or more (low-quality).

Table 5.1 shows the composition of UK imports by quality for the major OECD economies and for the EU. Low-quality imports are the most important group, but there are clear differences between the economies. High-quality imports are relatively important in the United Kingdom's imports from both the US and Japan, and even more so from Switzerland,

Table 5.1 Quality specialisation in UK imports from selected OECD economies, 1992

| | % of value of imports in quality range | | |
	Low	Medium	High
Total	46.0	33.0	21.0
EU	45.0	38.7	16.4
US	26.0	35.5	38.5
Japan	43.8	21.1	35.1
Germany	40.7	43.7	15.6
France	37.5	47.0	15.4
Italy	54.2	30.8	14.9
Belgium/Lux.	53.7	32.2	14.1
Netherlands	46.2	37.1	16.7
Denmark	46.9	33.0	20.0
Spain	50.9	40.4	8.7
Norway	56.5	30.4	13.1
Sweden	40.1	40.5	19.4
Switzerland	14.8	21.5	63.7
Canada	52.4	28.7	18.9

indicating perhaps that there are important trading bloc characteristics in the quality composition of trade. Low-quality imports from the EU are almost as important in the composition of total EU imports as they are from the world in general.

In ascertaining the United Kingdom's pattern of specialisation, the key question is how measures of trade performance *vary* over the quality range. Table 5.2 considers one such measure – an estimated export–import ratio.[8] It can be seen that, with the exception of Switzerland, where the reverse is the case, the normalised export–import ratio is greatest in the high-quality range. However, it is by no means always the case that trade performance is better in the medium-quality range than in the low-quality range. Nevertheless it is reasonable to conclude that UK exports are relatively specialised in the high-quality range.

THE QUALITY COMPOSITION OF TRADE WITH THE ASIAN ECONOMIES

One of the most important developments in international trade in recent decades has been the growing importance of exports of manufactured products from the developing economies. In the 1950s this phenomenon was relatively insignificant, perhaps 5 per cent of total manufactured exports (Yates 1959); by 1994, this share (excluding the transition economies of

Table 5.2 Estimated export–import ratios by quality, 1992

	Low	Medium	High	Total
Total	0.8	0.8	1.3	0.9
EU	0.9	0.8	1.2	0.9
US	0.9	0.7	1.0	0.9
Japan	0.1	0.3	0.5	0.3
Germany	0.7	0.7	1.0	0.8
France	1.0	0.7	1.4	0.9
Italy	0.7	0.8	1.7	0.9
Belgium/Lux.	0.9	1.1	1.3	1.0
Netherlands	0.8	0.8	1.4	0.9
Denmark	1.1	0.8	1.3	1.1
Spain	1.3	1.0	5.2	1.6
Norway	0.8	1.2	3.1	1.2
Sweden	0.7	0.6	1.1	0.7
Switzerland	0.9	0.7	0.3	0.5
Canada	0.7	0.8	2.4	1.1

central and eastern Europe) had grown to over 20 per cent, constituting growth in volume of a factor of over 40, with the vast preponderance of the exports destined for industrial economies (Cairncross, 1996). In fact, the overwhelming proportion of this increase has been largely confined to a handful of Asian economies, spearheaded by the four so-called 'tigers' – South Korea, Taiwan, Singapore, and Hong Kong – which between them supplied something like one half of total manufactured exports from the developing economies in 1990 (Cairncross, 1996). Other Asian economies are also becoming important, however. For the purposes of this chapter we include five as constituting 'other industrialising Asia' (OIA): China, Philippines, Indonesia, Malaysia, and Thailand. The OECD economies generally have significantly higher wage rates than the tigers, which in their turn have higher wage rates than other industrialising Asia (McGiven, 1996).

One consequence of a very rapid growth in exports from the Asian economies has been a large increase in import penetration in the advanced economies. Combined with large-scale unemployment, this process may ultimately be the harbinger of advanced economy protectionist measures in an attempt to boost jobs. One of the reasons for the protectionist sentiment is not simply the rate of growth of imports, but the simultaneous emergence of a trade deficit, illustrated in Figure 5.2. It shows that in 1992 the United Kingdom had a deficit in manufactured goods trade with each of the industrialising economies. However it still needs to be remembered that the sums involved are not huge. Total manufactured imports from all the countries shown in 1992 stood at just over £10 billions, which was around 10 per cent of the United Kingdom's total manufactured import bill.

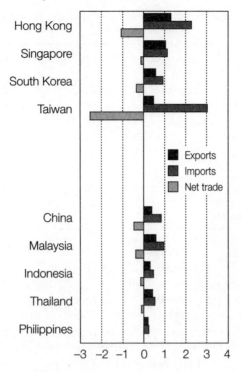

Figure 5.2 Manufactured goods trade with industrialising Asia 1992 (£b)
Source: *Business Monitor* MA20, 1993.

But what precisely is the nature of the competition, and more especially, to what extent is the specialisation based on low-quality manufactures and to what extent has the competition advanced into medium-quality or even into higher-quality manufactures?

It is evident from Table 5.3 that, whether from the four Asian Tigers or from other parts of industrialising Asia, the imports are overwhelmingly of low quality. However it should not be supposed that the pattern is quite universal. The figures for Singapore suggest some variation with a high proportion of high-quality goods. Although this may be the result of simple error – much of the result is attributable to a single commodity (computer disk storage units) – it may also reflect the possibility that where foreign direct investment is important, the expected trade patterns may be overturned. Some evidence for this is presented in Temple (1995), where it is shown that although the basis of specialisation is in low-quality production and in the more traditional sectors (textiles, clothing, footwear, leather, furniture), the proportion of high-quality imports of office machinery and data processing equipment is already above that of the EU.

Table 5.3 Quality composition of UK imports from
industrialising Asia, 1992

	% of value of imports in quality range		
	Low	*Medium*	*High*
Hong Kong	86.6	10.6	2.8
Singapore	45.7	11.7	42.6
South Korea	83.1	13.3	3.6
Taiwan	86.5	8.9	4.6
Malaysia	86.9	10.5	2.5
Thailand	79.2	8.9	12.0
China	91.7	5.8	2.5
Philippines	81.3	12.4	6.2
Indonesia	94.1	4.9	1.1

The pattern of comparative advantage is therefore largely as expected.
Note that the opportunity to export higher-quality manufactures is limited by
the generally lower real incomes in the Asian economies. However, with real
earnings advancing more rapidly in these economies than in the OECD area,
it may be expected that the opportunities for OECD exports of higher-
quality products to the Asian economies will increase. At the same time, the
advancing economies of Asia will find their pattern of advantage supplanted
by other economies with lower wage costs. They will be forced to produce
higher quality, more innovative products. The important point is that the
whole process is not a zero sum game, and that as economic catch up in
living standards occurs, we can expect trade flows to become more even,
with consumers and firms in the OECD economies benefiting from the
general stimulation to technological change occurring elsewhere. As with
any technological change, this does not of course necessarily mean that all
economies or regions will be winners.

The picture of trade presented so far is simply a snapshot view. The
dynamism of the Asian economies makes it essential that some idea is gained
of how these patterns are evolving. Figure 5.3 is based on a more comprehensive study of imports contained in Temple (1995). It shows cumulative distributions (ogives) for the value of imports against quality for both
groups of economies for two years – 1988 and 1992. While the overall
pattern is a stable one, the shift observable is instructive. The evolution of
the pattern in the tiger economies is taking them closer to that observed for
the OECD economies, with a reduced share in the lower-quality range.
The pattern is reversed in the OIA economies, where 1992 saw a higher
proportion of lower-quality products among imports.

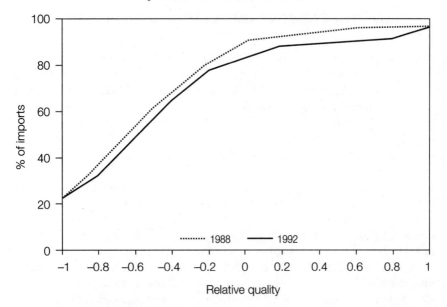

Figure 5.3(a) Quality composition of UK imports, Asian tiger economies

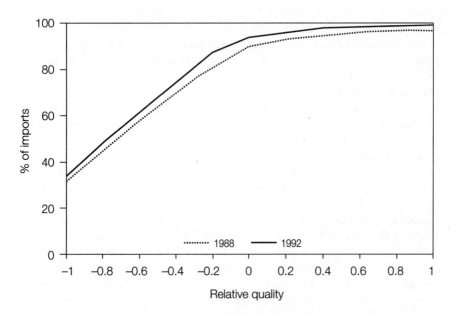

Figure 5.3(b) Quality composition of UK imports, Other Industrialising Asia

QUALITY SPECIALISATION AND TRADE PERFORMANCE

While measures of the nature of quality specialisation are of interest in their own right, they need to be combined with performance measures if they are to provide useful evidence regarding the competitive structures and the nature of competitive processes in international trade. If, for example, we observe increasing specialisation in high-quality products in an industry, this could be for one of two opposed reasons. The first might be that the industry is particularly innovative in areas where demand growth is strong, so that specialisation in high quality products is combined with strong trade performance in that industry. This might be described as a particularly 'dynamic' specialisation path. The other possibility is that observed specialisation is the result of a lack of competitiveness in lower-quality products, so that exports of these products simply disappear from the observed structure. The latter process was shown by Horn *et al.* (1985) to have been important in the development of the UK machine tool industry; they found that the relative unit value of UK exports of machine tools increased dramatically between 1976 and 1983 (from 37 per cent below the EU average to 14 per cent above it), despite the rapid loss of market share.

The phenomenon of increasing competition in manufacturing from the Asian and other developing economies suggests that the latter process is likely to be more important in general. At the level of individual industries, this would imply a negative relationship between the extent of specialisation in high quality exports and trade performance. A basically negative relationship for UK imports was found in an earlier study (Temple, 1995). The European economies and Japan displayed patterns in which relative specialisation in high-quality products was found to be related to a comparative disadvantage. The US, however, presented something of an exception, in that in some traditional industries there was some specialisation in low-quality imports. A possible explanation of this is the considerable difference in productivity levels that apparently continues to exist between the US on the one hand and Japan and Europe on the other.

Table 5.4 illustrates a similar phenomenon to that found for imports in the pattern of UK trade for 1992, with a relationship estimated by ordinary least squares across 196 four-digit manufacturing industries. The measure of trade performance used as the independent variable was the logarithm of the export–import ratio, while the indicator of the extent of quality specialisation was the logarithm of the export–import ratio in high-quality trade normalised by the aggregate export–import ratio. It can be seen that a negative relationship was found for manufacturing as a whole, even when some allowance for possible heterogeneity was made by using divisional dummies. Estimated at a more disaggregated level, the relationship is strongest in 'other manufacturing' (SIC Division 4) where competition from the Asian

Table 5.4 Trade performance and quality specialisation

		Dependent variable = log (relative quality specialisation) independent variable = log (export–import ratio)	
	Constant	Estimated coefficient	t-ratio
All manufacturing	0.34	−0.22	−3.2
– with divisional dummies	0.64	−0.18	−2.5
Metals and chemicals	0.23	0.22	1.3
Engineering	0.21	−0.25	−2.3
Other manufacturing	0.55	−0.35	−3.5

economies is more intense. The relationship was insignificant in chemicals and metals, although closer inspection shows that this result is attributable to one or two outliers.

These results confirm the importance of considering the extent of quality specialisation only in relation to trade performance. Given the patterns observed, the extent of quality specialisation is inversely related to trade performance, which is consistent with a more rapid growth of imports at the lower-quality end, where domestic production is more easily supplanted. The fact that a large portion of EU imports are still in the low- and middle-quality ranges where, on a bilateral basis (see Table 5.2), trade performance is inferior to that in the high-quality range, suggests that EU imports (if unprotected) are possibly rather vulnerable to displacement.

CONCLUSIONS

The discussion and empirical analysis in this chapter suggest that vertical differences in quality are an important way of analysing trade flows and one which is consistent with the orthodox approach to trade because the extent of these vertical differences within industries is sufficient to reject the idea that they are produced by common techniques of production. In addition, the extent of horizontal quality differentiation in trade flows has possibly been over-stressed in the literature.

The United Kingdom was found to be relatively specialised in high-quality exports – a pattern to be expected in a mature industrial economy. However, it seems to be relatively specialised even compared with other comparable economies. This finding is compatible with a generally weak trading performance, so that what seems to have happened is that UK exports have disappeared in areas where the competition (and probably the price

113

elasticities of demand) are the greatest – essentially a niche or 'boxing-in' effect. On the other hand, the pattern of exports is now less vulnerable to competition from the rapid industrialising economies of Asia, which is consistent with the fact that the UK share of OECD exports, after decades of decline, has now stabilised.

The improved picture for exports which all this implies is at some variance with studies – such as those conducted by the National Institute – which tend to depict UK producers as relying on less-skilled labour than counterparts in France or Germany. However, it is very important to distinguish between production for export and production for the domestic market. Today, exporting from the United Kingdom is a highly concentrated activity, mainly in the hands of large multinational firms; according to Eltis and Higham (1995), something like 40 per cent of UK exports are accounted for by foreign-owned multinationals. Moreover, perhaps four-fifths or more are accounted for by large transnational corporations (UNTCMD 1988). The potential for a clear gap in performance between these world class firms and the rest of UK manufacturing is clear and there is some evidence that, in contrast to Germany, UK manufacturing is characterised by a long tail of poor performance (IBM Consulting/LBS, 1994), a possibility re-emphasised in the 1996 Competitiveness White Paper (HMSO, 1996). A long 'tail' of poorly performing domestically oriented firms may still be making manufacturing extremely vulnerable to import penetration. A study by Temple and Urga (1997) shows that, in contrast to studies of exports, no improvement in competitive performance can be detected by looking at the behaviour of imports. One possible explanation for the continuing existence of a long tail is the progress of the real exchange rate – where upward shocks (especially in the period 1979–81 and again in the late 1980s) followed by long periods of a low real exchange rate encouraged producers to enter more price sensitive sectors of markets.

NOTES

1 Funding from the Gatsby Foundation gratefully acknowledged.
2 Vertical differences in 'quality' occur where general agreement would exist among consumers about a ranking of products according to either their intrinsic attributes (e.g. better functionality) or because of superior pre- or post-sales service. In this sense, a television incorporating teletext is clearly of superior quality to a similar television not incorporating the feature. With 'horizontal' differences in quality, by contrast, no agreement on a ranking would be reached: the television sets might differ only in colour or some other facet of styling.
3 This is the methodology behind the so-called 'hedonic' method.
4 Of course, differences in unit values could be interpreted as relating to differences in prices. Although there are a number of ways in which the inherent identification problem could be solved, no attempt is made to do so here. It is assumed in the analysis that competition generally forces prices of goods of similar quality into

equality and that remaining differences amount to purely random error (for further discussion, see Temple, 1995).

5 The allocation of each eight-digit commodity code to a four-digit industry was accomplished using correlators kindly supplied by the Department of Trade and Industry.

6 The twelve countries used were France, Belgium, the Netherlands, Germany, Italy, Norway, Sweden, Denmark, Switzerland, Canada, the USA, and Japan.

7 Of course, not all manufactured trade is thereby included – a norm must be established and not all UK exports can be compared with such a norm. Nevertheless, the total of manufactured exports that could be so allocated was £69 billion, – compared to an estimated total of £78 billion. A higher proportion of manufactured imports was, however, allocated, which tends to inflate the apparent size of the trade deficit. However, it is not believed that this caused serious distortion to the results.

8 The proportion of total trade which could be allocated to one of the quality ranges, although large, was less than unity, and slightly greater for imports than exports. Accordingly, the estimated export–import ratio was based on the within-sample estimates of the proportions of imports and exports in each of the ranges and total trade with each country taken from *Business Monitor*, MA20, 1993, Tables 3 and 4.

REFERENCES

Abd-el-Rahman, K. (1991) 'Firms' competitive and national comparative advantages as joint determinants of trade composition', *Weltwirtschaftliches Archiv*, vol. 127, pp. 83–97.

Cairncross, Sir A. (1996) 'Exports of manufactures from Developing Economies' *Royal Economic Society Newsletter*, October, pp. 3–4.

Crafts, N.F.R. and Thomas, M. (1986) 'Comparative advantage in UK manufacturing trade', *Economic Journal*, vol. pp. 96, 629–45.

Dosi, G., Pavitt K. and Soete, L. (1990) *The Economics of Technical Change and International Trade*, London: Harvester Wheatsheaf.

Eltis, W.E. and Higham, D. (1995) 'Closing the competitiveness gap' *National Institute Economic and Social Review*, November.

Greenaway, D. and Milner, C. (1986) *The Economics of Intra Industry Trade*, Oxford: Basil Blackwell.

Greenaway, D., Hine, R. and Milner, C. (1995) 'Vertical and horizontal intra-industry trade: a cross industry analysis for the UK', *Economic Journal*, vol. 105, pp. 1505–18.

HMSO (1996) *Creating the Enterprise Centre of Europe*, Cm. 3300, London: HMSO.

Horn, E.J., Klodt, H. and Saunders, C. (1985) 'Advanced machine tools: production, diffusion, and trade' in Sharp, M. (ed.) *Europe and the New Technologies*, London: Francis Pinter.

IBM Consulting/LBS (1994) *Made in Europe: A Four Nations Best Practice Study*, London: London Business School.

Jarvis, V. and Prais, S.J. (1989) 'Two Nations of Shopkeepers: training for retailing in France and Britain', *National Institute Economic Review*, May, pp. 58–74

Katrak, H. (1982) 'Labour skills, R&D, and capital requirements in the international trade and investment of the United Kingdom', *National Institute Economic Review*, vol. 101, pp. 38–47.

Leontief, W. (1953) 'Domestic production and foreign trade: the American capital position reexamined', *Proceedings of the American Philosophical Society*, vol. 97.

McGiven, A. (1996) 'Trade with Newly Industrialising Economies', *Bank Of England Quarterly Bulletin*, February, pp. 69–78.

Oulton, N. (1990) 'Quality and Performance in UK Trade 1978–87', *NIESR Discussion Paper* no. 197, London: NIESR.

—— (1993) 'Workforce Skills and Export Competitiveness: An Anglo-German Comparison', Paper prepared for CEPR Conference on *The Skills Gap and Economic Activity*, London, April 19–22.

Posner, M. (1961) 'International trade and technical change' *Oxford Economic Papers*, vol. 13, pp. 323–41.

Steedman H (1987) 'Vocational training in France and Britain: Office work', *National Institute Economic Review*, May, pp. 58–70.

—— (1988) 'Vocational training in France and Britain: Mechanical engineering and craftsmen', *National Institute Economic Review*, November, pp. 57–70.

Steedman, H. and Wagner, K. (1987) *National Institute Economic and Social Review*, May, pp. 40–57.

—— (1988) 'A second look at productivity, machinery, and skills in Britain and Germany', *National Institute Economic Review*, November, pp. 84–95.

—— (1988) 'Productivity, machinery, and skills: Clothing manufacturing in Britain and Germany', *National Institute Economic Review*, July, pp. 40–57.

Temple, P. (1995) 'Quality specialisation and quality competition: A study of UK imports', paper presented to 22nd Annual EARIE Conference, Juan Les Pins, France.

Temple, P. and Urga, G. (1997) 'The competitiveness of UK manufacturing: Evidence from imports', *Oxford Economic Papers* (forthcoming).

UN Transnational Corporations and Management Division (1988) *Transnational Corporation in World Development: Trends and Prospects*, New York: UN.

Wood (1994) 'Prosperity and foreign trade in the 1990s: Britain's strategic problem', *Oxford Review of Economic Policy*, vol. 6, no. 3, pp. 82–92.

Yates, P.L. (1959) *Fifty Years of Foreign Trade*, London: Allen & Unwin.

6

QUALITY AND COMPETITIVENESS

Peter Swann

INTRODUCTION

In much of the debate about British industrial competitiveness, price competitiveness and cost considerations are taken to be paramount. From this perspective, the appropriateness of business strategy and industrial policy hinges on whether they help to increase productivity and thus reduce unit costs.

This chapter will argue that as a practical matter, quality considerations – broadly interpreted to include product performance, design, delivery, after-sales service, marketing and other non-price factors – are on average as important or even more important than price in determining British industrial competitiveness. This is not to deny that price is always an important factor. Nor does it deny that there are some consumers who will always buy the cheapest product in a market, regardless of quality. Moreover it is clear that there are some markets for *commodities* – that is, products capable of little distinction – where price is always paramount. But as Deschamps and Nayak (1995: p. 29) have put it so succinctly, 'this is not a commodity world'. This chapter will assert that in most of the markets in which Britain is currently competing, and especially in the markets in which we would wish to compete, the broad range of quality factors, taken together, are more important than price.

This perspective suggests a rather different set of criteria on which to judge business strategies and industrial policies. The issue is not just what they do to the cost base, but more what they can do to enhance quality – broadly defined.

The arguments used to support these assertions are part theoretical and part empirical. The theoretical argument, essentially, is that in most markets there are many more quality dimensions on which to differentiate a product or service from the competition than price dimensions. Accordingly it is more likely that the decisive factor influencing consumer choice will be a quality factor than a price factor. The steps of this argument are a little unfamiliar, and are therefore developed in more detail later in the chapter.

117

While there is a small but interesting mix of empirical literature on these issues, gleaned from different markets, and using a variety of methodological approaches, it has to be said that there is no comprehensive evidence on this question across all markets. Those approaches that attempt to paint an overall picture of UK quality competitiveness have to use indirect approaches that can only measure quality imperfectly. Nevertheless, what evidence there is does support our central thesis. This chapter summarises the evidence from this diverse literature.

We start, however, with two important preliminaries. The first is to define quality, and to clarify our use of terms in this chapter. The second is to contrast the direct and indirect approaches to the measurement of quality.

DEFINING AND MEASURING QUALITY

Perhaps the first issue to be resolved is one of definition. Within the social sciences and business studies there are two rather different uses of the term 'quality'. In economics and marketing, the quality of a product is defined broadly to include performance, design, style, distinction, branding, desirable features, level of service, and indeed reliability. A high-quality product may have any or all of the above. By contrast, in operations management a much narrower definition is used, which refers to the process as much as the product. Here, when talking of quality control or total quality, the term quality is taken to mean (primarily) freedom from defects. For a given product specification, what proportion of those produced on a particular production line are defect-free? These two distinct uses of the term can sometimes cause confusion, but they reflect the somewhat different concerns of these two fields of business studies. In this study we adopt the first, broader definition.

There is another important reason why the distinct usage is confusing. It relates to the way in which costs and prices are thought to relate to quality. For the economist or marketer, prices and costs are expected to increase as quality (broadly defined) increases. This relationship is indeed of key importance in segmenting markets into 'up-market' and 'down-market'.

In operations management, conversely, the notion that price and cost must, eventually at least, increase with quality (freedom from defects) is considered to be misleading. It is perhaps accepted that for a given state of a production process, quality (freedom from defects) can only be improved by the use of further labour inputs, hence resulting in increased costs. But as the process is further refined and optimised, costs should fall as the incidence of defects falls – and quality increases.

Each language has its own logic, but in this report we adopt the broad definition of quality because buyers as a group are concerned with a wide range of quality issues. Reliability of products is one issue, but not the only one.

118

Measuring quality: direct and indirect approaches

There are still some difficult issues to be faced in actually measuring quality (Steenkamp, 1989). For some products it is clearly possible to assemble the sorts of measures identified in product surveys published in the specialist trade press and consumer magazines, for example *Which?* These studies can make some measurements of the more readily quantifiable aspects of quality, such as product features, performance, and reliability. This approach works well when the product is sold in a finite number of models. A good example of this is in consumer white goods (fridges, cookers and washing machines). It is much harder in the case of products that are usually sold in a customised fashion, such as large-scale machine tools.

While the economics literature has generally been content with the 'object-ive' measures of product quality that can be assembled in this manner, the marketing literature has tended to be critical of it. From the marketing perspective, quality is in the eye of the beholder, and is not easily amenable to 'objective' measurement of this sort. From the marketing perspective, the correct way to assess the competitive position of products is by reference to consumer perceptions of them; analysis based on 'objective' characteristics is very much a second best (Wind, 1982). Moreover, some of the more subtle aspects of quality (design, flexibility, finish, styling, and so on) are barely amenable to objective measurement. And finally, as Bacharach (1991) notes, the product characteristic itself is often simply an answer to a question: 'Does the product do this?' Since these questions emanate from individuals, in response to their own concerns and needs, it is difficult to say that the set of characteristics used to define a product is entirely objective. While con-sumer perceptions may correlate with 'objective' measures, such correlation is unlikely to be perfect.

Despite these difficulties, studies based on 'objective' characteristics are important, because that remains one of the few *direct* ways of measuring quality. The main difficulty is that this research approach is very labour intensive, and only a few scattered studies across a small group of sectors are found.

A related approach has been the technique of computing unit values, which is much less labour intensive, and can be performed on an economy-wide basis. This is very useful, as we see later, but it only really works so long as high price is definitely indicative of high quality, and not poor value for money.

Most economic studies, in contrast, have tended to 'measure' quality indirectly, because this is seen as the best way to gain an overall impression of the role of non-price factors in all sectors of the economy. Some of these approaches use measures such as research and development, innovations, patents, or data on the level of skills in the workforce, or the quality of material inputs. Others use measures that could indicate the general level of quality that could be expected in a sector, such as the number and use of standards.

QUALITY OR PRICE? THEORETICAL ARGUMENTS

There are theoretical grounds to expect quality to be of greater importance than price in many competitive settings. If there are a large number of dimensions to quality (as evidence suggests; see Hjorth-Andersen, 1986), then we shall argue that aspects of quality (broadly defined) will be of greater significance than price, both in purchasing decisions, and as a source of competitive advantage.

The logic behind this argument needs a little explanation.[1] Take the simplest case of a market with two products, differentiated on one dimension of quality, and one price: a low-price low-quality product, and a high-price high-quality product. It seems fair to argue that for those who buy the low quality low-price product, the most important factor is price: the lower price is more important than the associated reduction in quality. Conversely, for those who buy the high-price high-quality product, the most important factor is quality: the enhanced quality is more important than the price premium.

This argument is easily extended to the case of a market with four products, differentiated in terms of two quality dimensions and price. In an obvious notation, suppose that the product prices and qualities are as follows:

Product	Price	Quality characteristic 1	Quality characteristic 2
1	low	low	low
2	medium	high	low
3	medium	low	high
4	high	high	high

For all of those who buy product 1, the most important factor is price: whatever their second-choice product would be, the reason they prefer 1 must be because it is cheaper – despite its inferior quality. Conversely, for all of those who buy product 4, the most important factor must be quality: whatever their second-choice product would be, the reason they prefer 4 must be because it is of higher quality – despite its premium price.

For those who buy product 2, there are three possibilities. If their second choice would have been 1, then the main factor behind their decision to buy product 2 is quality: they prefer 2 because it scores better on characteristic 1, despite its higher price. If their second choice would have been product 3, then again, the main factor behind their decision to buy product 2 is again quality: product 2 scores better on characteristic 1 despite its inferiority in

120

characteristic 2, and price doesn't come into it. It is only if their second choice would have been product 4 that the main factor behind the decision to buy product 2 can be price. In two cases out of three, the choice is made on grounds of quality, and only in one is the choice made on grounds of price. A similar sort of argument applies, *mutatis mutandis*, to those who choose product 3.

Consider the simplest uniform case where equal numbers buy products 1,2,3 and 4, and where the proportions of those buying 2 and 3 in each of the three categories are equal. In this case it is apparent that for slightly over half (7/12) of the consumers, quality is a more important factor than price in their decision, while for slightly under a half (5/12) it is the other way round. Thus in this case where products are differentiated in two quality dimensions, as opposed to one, the relative importance of quality as a factor in consumer choices is increased.

The significance of the argument is that as the number of quality dimensions continues to increase (and the number of price dimensions stays at one) then the relative importance of quality factors in consumer choices continues to increase. The maths of this are a little intricate, but when the number of quality dimensions reaches five to ten or more, then quality factors (as a group) are predicted to be very much more important than price.

Now, of course, the scenario described in the previous paragraph makes some strong and special assumptions. Uniformity is an unlikely situation. If for example, the bulk of demand chooses the cheapest product, then price may continue to be the most important factor, simply because there aren't many of the different quality-conscious consumer types identified in the preceding argument. On the other hand, casual reflection suggests that such a distribution of demand is relatively uncommon. In many markets, it is not the bottom of the range product that captures the bulk of consumer demand.

There are good theoretical reasons why the number of quality dimensions in product markets can reach quite a high level – five to ten or more (Swann, 1990). There is also empirical evidence of this (Hjorth-Andersen, 1986; Swann and Taghavi, 1992). Moreover, the argument is that innovating companies will only add new quality dimensions in this way if there is a demand for such characteristics. If there is not, it is unlikely to be a profitable activity. Of course, one of the predictions of the product life-cycle is that while the number of quality dimensions may continue to rise over the life cycle, the prevalence of imitation means that the number of dimensions on which products are actually differentiated may start to fall during the maturity stage. This lack of differentiation is exactly what we expect to observe in a commodity market.

To use this framework to quantify the relative importance of quality and price as factors in consumer choices would be beyond its scope. Nevertheless the arguments advanced above provide an interesting background to the empirical evidence, to which we now turn.

121

SURVEYS OF BUYERS AND SOURCES OF COMPETITIVE ADVANTAGE

The two central questions for this chapter are these. How does quality influence trade performance? And how do British products compare to imported products in terms of quality? The main evidence pertinent to these questions can be grouped into six categories. Each strand of the literature has something to say about both questions. Each approach, moreover, has its strengths and weaknesses. In general, there is a trade-off between the quality of evidence obtained and the ability to offer a comprehensive coverage of the economy. This section, and those that follow, summarise some of the leading approaches.

Some striking evidence about the relative importance of price and non-price factors in industrial competitiveness has come from surveys of buyers. Perhaps the first survey of this type was done by NEDO (1965). This study surveyed UK machine tool users who had bought foreign rather than British tools. The study found that the vast majority of buyers indicated that they had bought imported products because the product was superior, because there was no equivalent specification in the United Kingdom, because foreign manufacturers were willing to meet their special needs, or because of better delivery or after-sales service. Only 5 per cent indicated that price was the main factor in their decision.

There have been a few comparable studies since, notably by Rothwell (1979, 1981) and Moody (1984). These surveys found that amongst those buying imported products, non-price factors were much more important than price, while amongst those buying British products, price was one of the most important factors. While the Rothwell (1981) study of agricultural machinery is quite old, it is still widely cited because of the interesting comparisons it offers. As Figure 6.1 shows, the main reasons for purchasing

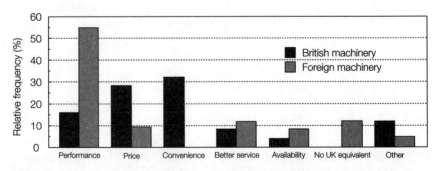

Figure 6.1 Reasons given by British farmers for purchasing foreign built and British built agricultural machinery, 1972–7
Source: Data from Rothwell (1981, Table 6).
Note: Relative frequency is percentage of all reasons given by all respondents.

imported products were performance, unique specification and service, while the main reasons for buying British machinery were price and the convenience of having a local manufacturer.

A related body of evidence comes from surveys that ask firms where their competitive advantage lies – on the price or non-price side. Indeed, in view of von Hippel's (1988) thesis that customers are often one of the most valuable sources of innovative ideas, these two approaches have a lot in common. The first of this type was by Kravis and Lipsey (1971), relating to the USA, and similar studies have been carried out for the United Kingdom by Hooley *et al.* (1988), Ughanwa and Baker (1989) and Roy (1990). (Further references are contained in Design Council, 1990 and Walsh *et al.*, 1992.) In terms of international comparisons, the picture here is less pessimistic: just as with foreign companies, many British companies consider that their distinctive competitive advantage lies in delivering some aspect of quality or service, broadly defined. This is generally a much more important source of competitive advantage than price.

The study by Hooley *et al.* (1988) is important because of the very large sample (1,380) of companies covered, and one which was representative of British industry in terms of the industrial sectors and range of company sizes covered. As Figure 6.2 shows, most companies indicated that their competitive advantage derived from various non-price factors, notably company or brand reputation, product performance, product quality or design, distribution and after-sales service. Price was only a significant source of competitive advantage in about 7 per cent of companies. (Note that in Figure 6.2, the percentages do not sum to 100 per cent because some companies cite more than one factor.)

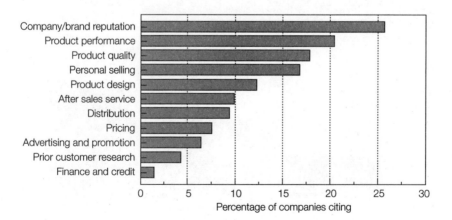

Figure 6.2 Percentage of companies citing different factors as a source of competitive advantage
Source: Based on Hooley *et al.* (1988, Table 10).

Unfortunately there are, to our knowledge, too few studies of this sort to draw firm conclusions about underlying trends. Moreover, as noted before, these studies refer to a diverse group of industries. There is also a potential technical problem. In responding whether the purchase of an imported product was made for price or non-price reasons, the consumer is making an implicit comparison with at least one other product, but it is not immediately apparent which one(s). A simple example will make this clear. When explaining why a German car was bought, the consumer may signal that he bought the imported car on grounds of quality. But if asked, 'Why didn't you buy a Rolls-Royce?' the response might be, 'I bought the imported car on grounds of price.' Such puzzles can be resolved, but they do introduce an element of ambiguity into data of this sort.

Despite these problems, one conclusion seems quite clear. In most competitive settings, quality (broadly defined) is more important than price as a source of competitive advantage, and as a reason for consumers' purchasing decisions. This observation receives further support from other studies below. This, moreover, is in line with the theoretical arguments advanced above.

UNIT VALUES

One across-the-board measure of non-price competitiveness in a wide range of sectors is the unit value. This approach, pioneered by Stout (1977), looks directly at the question, 'Does the United Kingdom import dear and export cheap?', by comparing the average price of exports in a sector (the export unit value) with the average price of imports (the import unit value).

Stout (1977) found that export unit values were frequently lower than import unit values in the United Kingdom – see Figure 6.3. For twenty-six

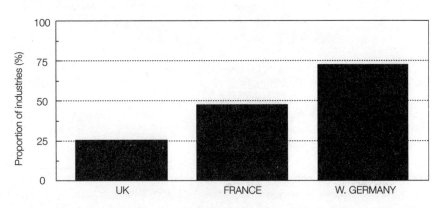

Figure 6.3 Proportion of industries where export unit value exceeds import unit value, by country, 1974
Source: Calculations based on Stout (1977).

out of thirty-five NEDC Sector Working Groups (about three-quarters), UK export unit values were lower than UK import unit values. Contrast this figure with about a half in France and about three-quarters in Germany. This suggests that there was a clear quality shortfall in United Kingdom exports compared to UK imports. In addition, the ratio of export unit value to import unit value (the *relative unit value*) was typically lower in the United Kingdom than in France and (especially) Germany. For the thirty-five industries considered, the UK relative unit value was lowest in twenty-two cases, second lowest in ten cases and largest in only three cases.

The unit value technique is very useful in exploring non-price competitiveness, but there is one potentially important ambiguity to bear in mind. If the unit value of UK exports is lower than the unit value of UK imports, then the price of the average UK export is certainly lower than the price of the average UK import. But what does this mean? Does it imply that imports to the United Kingdom are relatively 'up-market' products (of high quality and price)? Or does it imply that imports to the United Kingdom are bad value for money (high price but not necessarily high quality)? The technique, in itself, offers no solution to this puzzle, though some recent developments may shed light on this – see below.

There is moreover another potential problem with the technique. When a single unit value is calculated at an aggregate level (that is, across a wide range of industrial sectors) it is difficult to interpret; differences between export and import unit values may simply reflect the very different composition of exports and imports, and may not say anything about quality *or* value for money.

Recognising these problems with the relative unit value as a measure, Brech and Stout (1981) suggested a method by which changes in unit values could be decomposed into a change in a *product mix* index and a change in a *price* index. The product mix index reflects the changing composition of exports as between products of high and low unit value. They found that improvements in price competitiveness resulting from devaluation in the 1970s tended to lead to a down-market movement in the product mix – that is, towards products of lower unit value. This finding has been an important part of the argument against devaluation as a means of enhancing long-term competitiveness.

Oulton (1990), in a more recent study, has performed a very thorough analysis of unit value data over the period 1978–87. He found that although there were wide variations across different sectors, there was no systematic tendency for the unit values of UK imports to exceed those of UK exports. As Figure 6.4 shows, when UK exports to *all industrial economies* are considered, the position is better than in the Stout (1977) study, and moreover the position improves over the period 1978–87. Nevertheless, the figure illustrates perfectly the rather complex pattern of relative unit values. The quite optimistic pattern in respect of trade with all industrial economies is

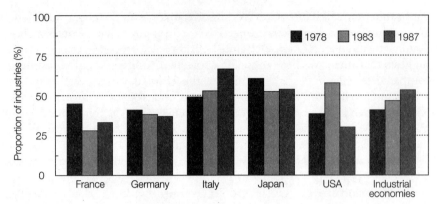

Figure 6.4 Proportion of UK industries where export unit value exceeds import unit
value, by trading partner, 1978–87
Source: Based on Oulton (1990, Table 12).

not matched in all cases. In trade with France, Germany and USA, UK
export unit values lie below import unit values in a majority of industries. In
short, there are some sectors and trading partners for which the unit values
of British exports are above those of UK imports, but these are offset by
other sectors and trading partners where the reverse is true. Oulton's (1993)
later article came to a similar conclusion in respect of UK and German
exports to the USA.

Recent work by Temple (1995a, 1995b) has sounded a cautionary
note, however. He observed that the pattern of unit values observed for
the United Kingdom depends on the country or group of countries
with which it is being compared. At the nine-digit level available in
overseas trade statistics, Temple shows that the distribution of UK relative
unit values across different commodity groups has a wide variance. The
general message is that in trade with almost any other major country,
there are some sectors where UK exports are of high value relative to
imports, and other sectors where UK exports are of relatively low
value. Temple also cautions us against uncritical acceptance of relative unit
value results, observing that the United Kingdom shares a problem with
some other EU countries which rely heavily on low quality trade among
themselves. He concludes that the traditional approach of measuring relative
quality by unit values may underestimate the extent of low quality specialisation in key areas of UK trade.

Unit values offer one of the most accessible ways to make systematic
comparisons of non-price competitiveness across all sectors, but the
decomposition of unit values into price and quality effects remains an area
where further research is needed. In earlier unpublished work, the present
author studied whether more can be gleaned from unit values by using them

in conjunction with trade data. One example is instructive. Using 1989 data for a number of three-digit manufacturing industries, the present author found that the distribution of UK relative unit values (exports to imports) is similar to that observed for comparable German industries. But on average, the German trade balance in each sector is considerably more favourable. This suggests that while the unit values may be similar, the German figures are more likely to represent high quality, which in turn are favourable to German trade.

Despite the various difficulties visited above, the balance of evidence seems to support the following conclusion. In comparing Stout's (1977) results with those of Oulton (1990), the systematic shortfall in UK non-price competitiveness of the 1970s did not sustain to the end of the 1980s. Some sectors of British industry still undoubtedly export cheap and import dear, but the average picture at the end of the 1980s was one of rough parity.

INDIRECT ECONOMETRIC APPROACHES TO MEASURING NON-PRICE COMPETITIVENESS

Some studies have sought to make inferences about quality competitiveness from the results of standard econometric trade models. One such approach compares (a) the elasticity (or responsiveness) of UK imports with respect to UK income to (b) the elasticity (or responsiveness) of UK exports with respect to world income (or world trade).

Such approaches make use of the following basic argument. Economic theory suggests that demand for high quality products will be relatively income elastic but price inelastic. This means that demand is responsive to changes in income but not responsive to changes in price. This, crudely, is because as people get richer, in general (though not invariably), they like to trade up to higher-quality products, while at the same time the price of a desirable product becomes less of a deterrent to purchase. Conversely, the income elasticity of demand for low-quality products will be low. While the income elasticity of demand is not an unambiguous measure of quality, such an approach provides some useful supplementary evidence.

In reviewing the evidence, Thirlwall and Gibson (1992) conclude that the UK income elasticity of imports was traditionally quite high, while the elasticity of UK exports with respect to world trade was traditionally quite low (well below one). The high elasticity of demand for UK imports with respect to UK income indicates that these imports are of high quality. Conversely, the low elasticity of demand for UK exports with respect to world income or world trade suggests that British exports are of relatively low quality.

But in a widely quoted study, Landesmann and Snell (1989) found that the elasticity of UK exports with respect to world exports rose over the 1980s. Figure 6.5 shows that following a definite decline in the elasticity of UK exports in the early 1980s, there was a distinct increase by 1986. As argued above, one interpretation of this is that the relative quality of UK exports had risen. This interpretation is consistent with the differences between the Stout and Oulton studies noted above.

NON-PRICE FACTORS AND TRADE PERFORMANCE

A number of studies have sought to estimate the effects of non-price factors on the United Kingdom's trade performance, using a variety of indirect measures of quality, including R&D expenditures, patents, standards or innovation counts. None of these are perfect indicators of quality, but they are useful measures that can be applied across a wide range of industries. Moreover, there are some correlations amongst these various measures. Archibugi and Pianta (1992, Figure 3.1) show a very close correlation in the cumulative R&D expenditures (1982–8) and cumulative patents granted in the US (also 1982–8) across fourteen countries. But neither R&D nor patents are particularly closely correlated with innovation counts (Pavitt *et al.*, 1987). Swann *et al.* (1996) look at the correlation between UK statistics on R&D, patents, counts of innovations produced, innovations used, and a count of standards by sector. This found that R&D tended to correlate quite closely with the standards count, while patents correlated more closely with innovations produced by sector.

Some of the most important studies are those by Buxton *et al.* (1991), Fagerberg (1988), Greenhalgh (1990), Greenhalgh *et al.* (1994), Hughes

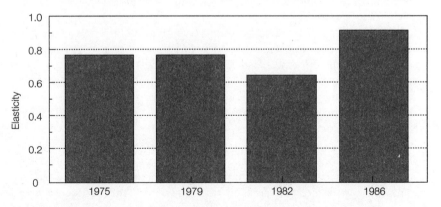

Figure 6.5 Elasticity of demand for British exports with respect to world exports, 1975–86
Source: Based on Landesmann and Snell (1989, Figure 8).

(1986a, 1986b), Pavitt and Soete (1980), Schott and Pick (1984), Wakelin (1994), Walker (1979). Fagerberg (1988) concludes that the main factors influencing differences in international competitiveness and growth across countries are technological competitiveness and the ability to compete on delivery, and not cost-competitiveness, as so commonly assumed.

One of the largest studies of this sort is by Greenhalgh *et al.* (1994), and the findings with respect to innovation are summarised in Figure 6.6. This indicates that trade performance in each industrial sector is significantly enhanced by innovative activity in that sector. In most cases, innovations enhance the trade ratio by up to 15 per cent – a very substantial effect.

Swann *et al.* (1996) carried out a similar study using data on standards counts as the measure of non-price competitiveness. As Figure 6.7 indicates, this found that UK strength in standards was certainly associated with stronger export performance, and indeed an improvement in the balance of trade. There was also evidence that standards can act to open up trade, and enable increased imports to the United Kingdom.

Other studies have used alternative indirect measures of quality. Landesmann and Snell (1990) used quality measures based on unit values in an econometric analysis of trade performance. Owen and Wren-Lewis (1993) used cumulative investment expenditure as an indicator of product quality, and found that it has a very significant effect on UK export performance – though this could relate to factors other than product quality.

One other econometric approach has been to treat quality (or non-price competitiveness) as a 'latent' or unmeasurable variable, and to measure non-price competitiveness as part of the modelling exercise. Using such techniques, Anderton (1992) finds a persistent downward trend in UK exporting,

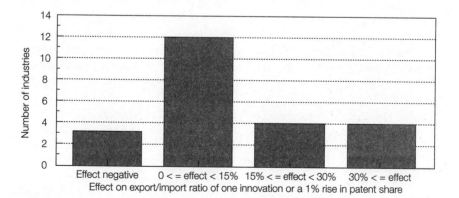

Figure 6.6 Effect of innovations on trade balance in 23 UK industrial sectors
Source: Based on Greenhalgh *et al.* (1994, Table 3).

129

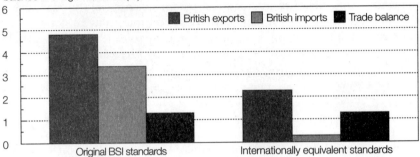

Average effect of 10 BSI standards on exports, imports and trade balance in 3-digit industries (%)

Figure 6.7 Effects of British standards on trade performance 3-digit industries, 1985–91
Source: Swann *et al.* (1966, Figure 1).
Note: Percentage effect on trade balance is not exactly equal to difference between percentage effects on exports and imports, as explained in the text.

which is interpreted as the consequence of a downward trend in UK non-price competitiveness. There is some evidence, however, that this trend was levelling off during the 1980s. That lends some support to the findings of Landesmann and Snell (1989), noted above. But it is important to remember that this approach uses no independent measure of quality or non-price competitiveness, but simply attributes the unexplained residual to such factors.

Figure 6.8 summarises a slightly different approach to this question. Temple and Swann (1995) examined in what respects the industrial sectors that contain Design Council award-winning companies differ from the rest. As the figure indicates, sectors with award-winners tend to perform better than the rest on most criteria: higher exports, higher standards registrations (Kitemark and BS5750 Part 1 diffusion), higher employment, value added, export performance, a higher trade ratio, import penetration and tradability (exports plus imports divided by sales). These observations have two implications: first, that sectors with Design Council award-winners (and in which design is recognised to be strong) tend to perform better in trade terms; second, that the Design Council awards seem to do a good job in 'picking winners'.

This section lends further support to the conclusion relating to quality as a source of competitive advantage, noted above. Quality is as important, and probably more so than price in determining trade performance in most competitive situations.

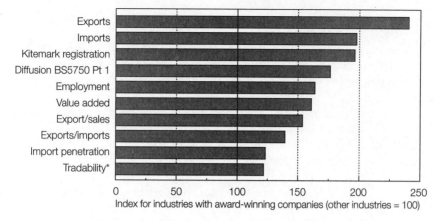

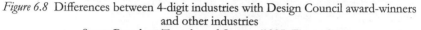

Index for industries with award-winning companies (other industries = 100)

Figure 6.8 Differences between 4-digit industries with Design Council award-winners
and other industries
Source: Based on Temple and Swann (1995, Figure 3).
Note: * Tradability = (exports + imports)/sales.

DIRECT MEASUREMENT OF QUALITY

Given the inevitable ambiguities in the aggregative studies described above, the detailed measurement of quality competitiveness in particular sectors is an important part of the picture, even if it relates only to a few sectors. These studies used detailed data on product characteristics, obtained from surveys in the specialist trade and consumer press, including *Which?* The economic analysis and measurement of quality has a long history (Griliches, 1971, 1990; Lancaster 1971, 1990; Triplett, 1990), but few attempts have been made to compare the competitiveness of products made in different countries. More effort has been directed at examining whether inadequate treatment of quality advance tends to overstate inflation and understate productivity growth (Griliches, 1990; Oulton, 1995).

Swann (1987) examined the relative quality competitiveness of British and imported products in the UK market for fridges and fridge-freezers. He found that British products generally scored well in terms of value for money, but they also tended to reach a lower score than imported products in terms of various measures of product quality. In later work, Swann (1994) also found that in this market, British products were more likely to compete in niches with other British-made products than with imported products. This national clustering seems to imply that far from competing across the whole quality spectrum, British producers (and those of other nations) were focusing their product ranges on particular parts of the quality spectrum.

131

Cubbin and Murfin (1987) examined the evidence on the quality competitiveness of British products compared to imported products in the UK car market. They found that the value for money of British cars had improved relative to that of imported cars over a ten-year period, and moreover that UK cars appeared more price and quality competitive than most.

Swann and Taghavi (1992) examined quality competitiveness in eighteen British consumer markets. The study applied recent developments in consumer choice theory to divide products into three categories: uncompetitive; competitive by virtue of value for money; competitive by virtue of quality. Figure 6.9 shows the balance of quality competitiveness between British and imported products. In a number of markets, a larger proportion of competitive British products (than imported products) achieve their competitiveness by virtue of quality. But in some other markets, notably fridges, washing machines and handsaws, the reverse is true.

A series of studies performed at the National Institute of Economic and Social Research also provide important evidence on this. Summarising a number of studies, Jarvis and Prais (1995) conclude that in a selection of consumer goods (clothing, garden tools, and biscuits) British products are generally of inferior quality to German products. Figure 6.10 summarises the results for one of the products considered, biscuits. This shows how the United Kingdom has a relatively small proportion of high-quality manufacture, while Germany has a relatively high proportion of high-quality manufacture.

The NIESR study suggests that these quality differentials are related to the higher skills of the workforce in Germany than in Britain. More skilled

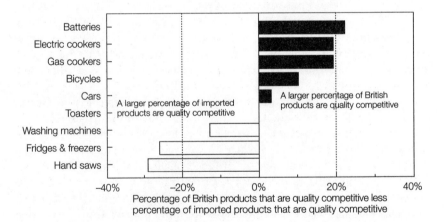

Figure 6.9 Balance of quality competitiveness between British and imported products, 1983–7

Source: Based on Swann and Taghavi (1992, Table 27.1).

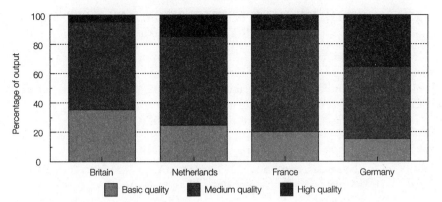

Figure 6.10 Composition of biscuit output, by quality grade in Britain, the
Netherlands, France and Germany
Source: Based on Mason *et al.* (1994, Table 6).

operatives find it easier to change production methods, which allows for
the production of shorter runs of specialised and high-quality products.
German manufacturers make use of designers with more extensive experience. And it is also suggested that German consumers are more quality-
conscious, and this provides a stimulus to high-quality production in
Germany.

These findings are consistent with the earlier work from the National
Institute stressing that the quality deficit in British products is due to the
skill deficit of the UK workforce (Oulton, 1989; Britton, 1993; Mason and
Wagner, 1994). But there are two unresolved puzzles. If British consumers
are not particular about quality, and this is why British manufacturers do
not find it profitable to invest in improving quality, then why do some
British consumers say (in buyer surveys, as noted earlier) that they are
driven to buy imported products because of their desire for quality? Second, what is the direction of causation here? Are British manufacturers
consigned to produce mediocre quality because they cannot employ skilled
workers? Or is it because British manufacturers have chosen to compete in
the middle market, that they do not have any need for highly skilled
employees?

The *neutral* results (in Swann and Taghavi, 1992) are in line with those of
Oulton (1990) using unit values: there was no systematic tendency for British
products to be of lower or higher quality than imported products. It is worth
stressing, however, that this comparison is made between British products
and *the average import*. If attention is focused instead on imports from high-
quality countries (e.g. Germany), then the picture is less rosy for the United
Kingdom – as the National Institute have shown.

133

MEASUREMENT OF OTHER ASPECTS OF NON-PRICE COMPETITIVENESS

Knowledge about other aspects of non-price competitiveness is even more limited, though there are a few important landmarks. The classic study of delivery times and trade performance (Steuer *et al.*, 1966) showed that production delays can readily translate into lost export orders, and this was cited as part of the explanation for the deterioration in performance by the UK car industry in the 1970s (Central Policy Review Staff, 1975). Unfortunately again, there are few direct measures of delivery times, though some of the econometric studies listed above in the section on non-price factors and trade performance (notably Greenhalgh, 1990; Greenhalgh *et al.*, 1994) have used data on the incidence of strikes as an indirect measure of disruption to supply, and found that this leads to reductions in export sales.

Data on reliability are perhaps a little easier, at least for individual sectors. *The Economist* (1992) reported that only 2.8 per cent of Japanese cars break down each year, compared with 4.8 per cent of German cars, 5.6 per cent of British cars, 7.2 per cent of French cars and 10.2 per cent of Italian cars.

Pre-sale and post-sale services may be as important as product quality, if not more so, in securing improved trade performance (Samli *et al.*, 1992). But it is difficult to identify data on comparative performance in these factors. In the same way, the excellent study by Buckley *et al.* (1992) gives a very detailed picture of the strategies firms use to service international markets, but little comparative evidence on UK performance in this respect. Swann (1987a) found that it was the network of supporting products and services around a particular family of microelectronic components – and not just the intrinsic quality of the core component – that would be decisive in establishing that design as an industry standard. But again we have little systematic evidence of how the United Kingdom measures up on this front.

The World Competitiveness Reports (WEF/IMD, various years) offers one of the few glimpses of these 'softer' aspects of non-price competitiveness by surveying leading business people in major industrial countries. On factors such as delivery times, product development lead times, quality of the product and quality of service, the United Kingdom ranks around half-way down the table. The problem with this source is that some of the softer measures are based on a very small sample of data.

Sentance (1996) and OECD (1992) provide a useful summary of what data of this type are available on a comparable basis across countries. Patent data is the easiest, with R&D next, while fully comparable innovation count data are still some way off. Information on national expenditures on other intangible investments are very scarce.

There are other interesting fragments that we do not describe here, but the point remains, that they are fragments. To advance the debate, there is a strong need for regular and systematic measures of British non-price competitiveness, comparable to the indices of export and import prices, productivity by sector, and other aspects of price competitiveness. As one of the main conclusions of this report is that non-price factors are more important than price in a majority of competitive settings, it must be a major priority to bring data on non-price factors up to the standard expected of data on price competitiveness.

What can we conclude from this empirical literature summarised above? First, that in a majority of competitive settings, quality is a more important source of competitive advantage than price. This proposition is supported by surveys of buyers, companies, econometric evidence and indeed theoretical analysis. Second, that the United Kingdom's competitive position with respect to quality has probably improved over the last twenty-five years. This is supported by evidence from unit value studies, direct measurements of quality, and some econometric studies. But thirdly, that there is still some considerable scope for further improvements in quality – particularly in comparison to the 'high-quality' economies, such as Germany. This proposition is supported by evidence from unit value studies and direct measurements of quality.

It is no longer appropriate to conclude that, in general, the United Kingdom imports dear and exports cheap. It is easy to think of counter-examples: Stout and Swann (1994) show that at the top end of the car market, UK exports in 1992 (by value) were 2.7 times greater than UK imports. But the studies by NIESR and others have shown that there are still too many markets in which British quality falls below that of major trading partners.

POLICY IMPLICATIONS

As we said at the start, a perspective which emphasises the role of quality as well as price in competitiveness will direct our attention to the effects of business strategy and industrial policy on quality. A concern about price competitiveness focuses attention on downsizing, flexible labour markets, wage inflation, productivity growth, location of production in low-cost economies, and on the macroeconomic side, the control of inflation. But a concern about quality competitiveness focuses attention on skills, training, labour retention, technology transfer, standards, research and development, and other non-price strategies and policies. The other chapters of this book look at many of these issues in depth. The first group are of course very important. But so are the second group – equally, if not more so.

Two broad policy issues are worthy of attention here. First, is it necessarily bad that UK non-price competitiveness falls below that of Germany and other countries? Is it more appropriate perhaps for the United Kingdom to aim for price competitiveness rather than quality competitiveness? Or to put it differently, how far up the non-price competitiveness league table should the United Kingdom aim to rise, given that a position of number one, across the board may be implausible? The answer to such questions really depends on the density of demand in different market segments. In some cases demand may be heaviest at the bottom end of the market, and in the mid-market, while demand at the top end of the spectrum is thin. This suggests that even if margins on high-quality sales are large, the volume of such sales is low. But the risk of relying on sales at the bottom end of a market is that a general increase in economic welfare will tend to shift consumers to demand higher levels of quality and service, and to move away from the bottom end of the market.

Second, even if a lack of quality competitiveness compared to high-quality countries is a bad thing, is it a market failure which policy intervention would put right? Is this problem an issue of public policy, or is it simply a matter for the management of companies in question? Gresham's Law – or the story of 'lemons' (the US slang for a faulty second-hand car) – is one reason why markets may fail to supply sufficient quality, and why there may be a role for standards and certification to correct the market failure (Akerlof, 1970; Leland, 1976). But a more powerful rationale for policy comes from the virtuous circle of diffusing best practice. Quality in the United Kingdom may be poor relative to Germany (say) because best practice quality management has not diffused widely in the United Kingdom – at least not compared to Germany. This suggests that there continues to be an important role for institutions such as the Design Council and the British Standards Institution in disseminating best practice (Department of Trade, 1982; National Audit Office, 1990; David and Greenstein, 1990; OTA, 1992).

SUMMARY AND CONCLUSIONS

This chapter has surveyed some of the economic and related literature on quality and competitiveness. The *quality* of a product has been defined broadly, to include performance, design, features, style, branding, level of service, and indeed reliability. A high-quality product may have any or all of the above. This is in contrast to the narrow definition used in some circles, where 'quality' simply measures freedom from defects.

The evidence about the role of quality in competitiveness and the relative position of the United Kingdom is limited. There are no regularly published statistics on quality, comparable to the retail price index, for example. Direct measurement of quality, moreover, is labour intensive and the literature on this consists of a collection of scattered studies relating to different sectors. A larger part of the literature uses indirect approaches to measuring quality, such as unit values, innovation counts, standards, R&D and patents. These have the advantage of allowing a more comprehensive picture to be drawn, but they are nevertheless imperfect measures of quality.

Despite these reservations, the following conclusions can be drawn. First, in a majority of competitive settings, quality (defined broadly) is a more important source of competitive advantage than price, and sometimes much more important. This is not to deny the importance of price, but simply to emphasise that business must not get stuck in a one-dimensional view of competition. This view is supported by evidence from econometric studies and surveys, and indeed by theoretical considerations.

Second, while different studies do not all point in the same direction, the balance of evidence is that the average UK competitive position *vis-à-vis* quality has improved somewhat over a twenty-five-year period. The evidence for the mid-1960s and early 1970s indicates that in a majority of industries, Britain was exporting cheap and importing dear, and that quality was a major reason for purchasing imported products. But by the mid-late 1980s, the picture had improved to one of rough parity. In about half of all industries, Britain exports dear and imports cheap, while in the other half the reverse is found. This conclusion receives some backing from econometric studies, and from studies making direct measurements of quality.

Third, despite this, for many sectors, and in trade with a number of countries (notably Germany), Britain still suffers a shortfall in quality, so there is scope for further improvement in quality. It seems clear that further improvements in product quality (defined broadly) can be a continuing source of competitive advantage. A number of national institutions, including the Design Council and British Standards Institution, can play an important role in achieving this.

NOTE

1   The mathematical details of this argument are set out in an unpublished note available from the author.

REFERENCES

Akerlof, G. (1970) 'The market for "lemons"', *Quarterly Journal of Economics*, vol. 84, pp. 488–500.

Anderton, R. (1992) 'UK exports of manufactures: Testing for the effects of non-price competitiveness using stochastic trends and profitability measures', *Manchester School of Economic and Social Studies*, vol. 60, no. 1, pp. 23–40.

Archibugi, D. and Pianta, M. (1992) *The Technological Specialisation of Advanced Countries: A Report to the EC on International Science and Technology Activities*, Dordrecht: Kluwer.

Bacharach, M. (1991) 'Commodities, language and desire', *Journal of Philosophy*, vol. 87, no. 7, pp. 346–68.

Brech, M.J. and Stout, D.K. (1981) 'The rate of exchange and non-price competitiveness: A provisional study within UK manufactured exports', *Oxford Economic Papers*, vol. 33, pp. 268–81.

Britton, A. (1993) 'Economic prosperity and the quality of production', *National Institute Economic Review*, vol. 145, August, pp. 6–10.

Buckley, P.J., Pass C.L. and Prescott, K. (1992) *Servicing International Markets: Competitive Strategies of Firms*, Oxford: Blackwell Publishers.

Buxton, A.J., Mayes, D. and Murfin, A. (1991) 'UK trade performance and R&D', *Economics of Innovation and New Technology*, vol. 1, no. 3, pp. 243–56.

Central Policy Review Staff (1975) *Future of the British Car Industry*, London: HMSO.

Cubbin, J.S. and Murfin, A.J. (1987) 'Regression analysis versus linear programming in the analysis of price-quality relationships: An application to the determination of market shares', *Oxford Bulletin of Economics and Statistics*, vol. 49, no. 4, pp. 385–99.

David, P.A. and Greenstein, S. (1990) 'The economics of compatibility standards: An introduction to recent research', *Economics of Innovation and New Technology*, vol. 1, no. 1/2, pp. 3–41.

Department of Trade (1982) *Standards Quality and International Competitiveness* Cmnd 8621, London: HMSO.

Deschamps, J-P. and Nayak P.R. (1995) *Product Juggernauts: How Companies Mobilize to Generate a Stream of Market Winners*, Boston, Mass: Harvard Business School Press.

Design Council (1990) *Design and the Economy*, London: Design Council.

Economist, The (1992) 'New factories for old', *The Economist*, vol. 325, October 3, pp. 18–19.

Fagerberg, J. (1988) 'International competitiveness', *Economic Journal*, vol. 98, pp. 355–74.

Greenhalgh, C. (1990) 'Innovation and trade performance in the United Kingdom', *Economic Journal*, vol. 100 (Conference Supplement), pp. 105–18.

Greenhalgh, C., Taylor, P. and Wilson, R. (1994) 'Innovation and export volumes and prices – a disaggregated study', *Oxford Economic Papers*, vol. 46, pp. 102–134.

Griliches, Z. (1971) (ed.) *Price Indexes and Quality Change*, Cambridge, Mass.: Harvard University Press.

—— (1990) 'Hedonic price indexes and the measurement of capital and productivity: Some historical reflections', in E.R. Berndt and J.E. Triplett (eds), *Fifty Years of Economic Measurement*, Chicago, Ill.: University of Chicago Press.

Hjorth-Andersen, C. (1986) 'Monopolistic competition or spatial competition or something else: Empirical evidence', Cykelafdelingen Memo. 94, Kφbenhavns Universitets Φkonomiske, August.

Hooley, G.J., Lynch, J.E., Brooksbank, R.W. and Shepherd, J. (1988) 'Strategic market environments', *Journal of Marketing Management*, vol. 4, no. 2, pp. 131–47.

Hughes, K. (1986a) *Exports and Technology*, Cambridge: Cambridge University Press.

—— (1986b) 'Exports and innovation: A simultaneous model', *European Economic Review*, vol. 30, no. 2, pp. 383–99.

Jarvis, V. and Prais, S.J. (1995) 'The quality of manufactured products in Britain and Germany', *National Institute of Economic and Social Research Discussion Paper*, no. 88.

Kravis, I. and Lipsey, R.G. (1971) *Price Competitiveness in World Trade*, New York: Columbia University Press.

Lancaster, K.J. (1971) *Consumer Demand: A New Approach*, New York: Columbia University Press.

—— (1990) 'The economics of product variety: A Survey', *Marketing Science*, vol. 9, no. 3, pp. 189–206.

Landesmann, M. and Snell, A. (1989) 'The consequences of Mrs Thatcher for UK manufacturing exports', *Economic Journal*, vol. 99, pp. 1–27.

—— (1990) 'Structural shifts in the manufacturing export performance of OECD economies', *DAE Working Paper*, no. 9011, Department of Applied Economics, University of Cambridge.

Leland, H. (1976) 'Quacks, lemons and licensing: A theory of minimum quality standards', *Journal of Political Economy*, vol. 87, pp. 1328–47.

Mason, G. and Wagner, K. (1994) 'Innovation and the skill mix: Chemicals and engineering in Britain', *National Institute Economic Review*, vol. 148, pp. 61–72.

Mason, G., van Ark, B. and Wagner, K. (1994) 'Productivity, product quality and workforce skills: Food processing in four European countries', *National Institute Economic Review*, vol. 147, pp. 62–83.

Moody, S. (1984) 'The role of industrial design in the development of new science-based products', in R. Langdon (ed.) *Design and Industry*, London: Design Council.

National Audit Office (1990) *Department of Trade and Industry: Promotion of Quality and Standards*, London: HMSO.

NEDO (1965) *A Survey of Investment in Machine Tools*, London: NEDO.

OECD (1992) *Technology and the Economy: The Key Relationships*, Paris: Organisation for Economic Cooperation and Development.

OTA (1992) *Global Standards: Building Blocks for the Future*, Congress of the United States Office of Technology Assessment, Washington D.C.: US Govt. Printing Office.

Oulton N. (1989) 'Trade unions, product quality and the structure of international trade', in J. Black and A.I. MacBean (eds.) *Causes of Changes in the Structure of International Trade, 1960–85*, London: MacMillan.

—— (1990) 'Quality and performance in UK trade, 1978–87' *NIESR Discussion Paper* no. 197, London: National Institute for Economic and Social Research.

—— (1993) 'Workforce skills and export competitiveness: An Anglo-German Comparison', CEPR Conference on *The Skills Gap and Economic Activity*, London, April.

—— (1995) 'Do UK price indexes overstate inflation?', *National Institute Economic Review*, vol. 152, pp. 60–75.

Owen, C. and Wren-Lewis, S. (1993) 'Variety, quality and UK manufacturing exports', *International Centre for Macro-Modelling Discussion Paper*, no. 14, University of Strathclyde, May.

Pavitt, K. and Soete, L. (1980) 'Innovation activities and export shares', in K. Pavitt (ed.) *Technical Innovation and British Economic Performance*, London: Macmillan.

Pavitt, K., Robson, M. and Townsend, J. (1987) 'The size distribution of innovating firms in the UK: 1945–1983', *Journal of Industrial Economics*, vol. 35, no. 3, pp. 297–316.

Rothwell. R. (1979) 'The relationship between technical change and economic performance in mechanical engineering: Some evidence', in M.J. Baker (ed.) *Industrial Innovation: Technology, Policy, Diffusion*, London: Macmillan.

—— (1981) 'Non-price factors in the export competitiveness of agricultural engineering goods', *Research Policy*, vol. 10, pp. 260–88.

Roy, R. (1990) 'Product design and company performance', in M. Oakley (ed.) *Design Management: A Handbook of Issues and Methods*, Oxford: Basil Blackwell.

Samli, A.C., Jacobs, L.W. and Wills, J. (1992) 'What presale and postsale services do you need to be competitive', *Industrial Marketing Management*, vol. 21, no. 1, pp. 33–41.

Schott, K. and Pick, K. (1984) 'The effect of price and non-price factors on UK export performance and import penetration', Discussion Paper, University College London.

Sentance, A. (1996) *Innovation and Design in a Changing World Economy*, Research Report to the Design Council, London.

Steenkamp, J.B.E.M. (1989) *Product Quality: An Investigation into the Concept and How it is Perceived by Consumers*, Assen/Maastricht: Van Gorcum.

Steuer, M., Ball, J. and Eaton, J. (1966) 'The effect of waiting times on foreign orders for machine tools', *Economica*, vol. 33, pp. 387–403, November.

Stout, D.K. (1977) *International Price Competitiveness, Non-Price Factors and Export Performance*, London: NEDO.

Stout, D.K. and Swann, P. (1994) 'The non-price competitiveness of British firms', in K. Hughes (ed.) *The Future of UK Competitiveness and the Role of Industrial Policy*, London: Policy Studies Institute.

Swann, P. (1987a) 'Industry standard microprocessors and the strategy of second source production', in H.L. Gabel (ed.) *Product Standardization and Competitive Strategy*, Amsterdam: North Holland.

—— (1987b) 'International differences in product design and their economic significance', *Applied Economics*, vol. 19, no. 2, pp. 201–13.

—— (1990) 'Product competition and the dimensions of product space', *International Journal of Industrial Organisation*, vol. 8, no. 2, pp. 281–95.

—— (1994) 'Quality, competitors and competitiveness', *Business Strategy Review*, vol. 5, no. 3, pp. 21–34.

Swann, P. and Taghavi, M. (1992) *Measuring Price and Quality Competitiveness: A Study of 18 British Product Markets*, Aldershot: Avebury.

Swann, P., Temple, P. and Shurmer, M. (1996) 'Standards and trade performance: The United Kingdom experience', *Economic Journal*, vol. 106, pp. 1297–1313.

Temple, P. (1995a) 'Quality specialisation and quality competition: A study of UK imports', unpublished Paper, Centre for Business Strategy, London Business School, September.

—— (1995b) 'Patterns of quality specialisation in UK trade', Working Paper 151, Centre for Business Strategy, London Business School, November.

Temple, P. and Swann, P. (1995) 'Competitions and competitiveness: The case of British design awards', *Business Strategy Review*, vol. 6, no. 2, pp. 41–52.

Thirlwall, A.P. and Gibson, H.D. (1992) *Balance of Payments Theory and the United Kingdom Experience*, 4th edn, Basingstoke: Macmillan.

Triplett, J.E. (1990) 'Hedonic methods in statistical agency environments: An intellectual biopsy', in E.R. Berndt and J.E. Triplett (eds), *Fifty Years of Economic Measurement: The Jubilee of the Conference on Research in Income and Wealth*, Chicago, Ill.: University of Chicago Press.

Ughanwa, D.O. and Baker, M.J. (1989) *The Role of Design in International Competitiveness*, London: Routledge.

von Hippel, E. (1988) *The Sources of Innovation*, Cambridge: Cambridge University Press.

Wakelin, K. (1994) 'The impact of technology on bilateral OECD trade', in *Proceedings of the EUNETICS Conference*, Strasbourg, October, vol. 2, pp. 1301–28.

Walker, W.B. (1979) *Industrial Innovation and International Trading Performance*, Greenwich, Conn.: JAI Press.

Walsh, V., Roy, R., Bruce, M. and Potter, S. (1992) *Winning by Design: Technology, Product Design and International Competitiveness*, Oxford: Blackwell Publishers.

Wind, Y. (1982) *Product Policy: Concepts, Methods and Strategy*, Reading, Mass.: Addison-Wesley.

World Economic Forum/International Institute for Management Development (various years) *World Competitiveness Report*, Geneva/Lausanne: WEF/IMD.

7

ECONOMIC POLICY AND THE INTERNATIONAL COMPETITIVENESS OF UK MANUFACTURING

Tony Buxton and Tony Mananyi

INTRODUCTION

Exports of goods and services accounted for 28 per cent of GDP in the United Kingdom in 1995. This is a substantial proportion and illustrates the great importance of trade to the UK economy. The equivalent figure in 1950 was 23 per cent, and while the percentage varies across the economic cycle there is no evidence that the United Kingdom is becoming any less dependent on international trade; indeed it may be more so. The United Kingdom's relative dependence on international trade means that assessing the determinants of performance is vital.

The United Kingdom's traditional trading strength lay in its manufacturing sector, yet in the post-war years the United Kingdom's share of world manufactured exports fell quite rapidly. In the mid-1980s, however, the decline was halted and to some extent was reversed, as discussed in Chapter 4. Similarly, the balance of trade of UK manufactures got steadily worse until in 1983 it went into deficit for the first time. In the 1990s, however, there is again some evidence that the decline has been halted.[1] This evidence begs the question: has there been a fundamental improvement in the trading performance of UK manufacturing, and if there has, what is the reason? In particular, has it been the changes in economic policy by the Conservative administration in the 1980s and 1990s which have had the desired effect?

This chapter therefore attempts to provide evidence on whether UK manufacturing has fundamentally improved its trading performance. It does this within the context of key relevant changes in UK economic policy which have taken place since 1979. The likely effects of these are incorporated into a manufacturing export model. This is then estimated over the period 1970–93 to assess the effects of policy changes. The results are both interesting and important.

ECONOMIC BACKGROUND

In this section, two principal elements of recent thinking and policy are discussed as an introduction to the econometric model. In each case, variable and structural changes to the model are distinguished. In other words, while economic policy may be able to affect one of the determinants of export performance – a change in the size of one of the variables, say price via a new exchange rate regime, policy may also influence the importance of that determinant – a structural change so that the influence of any variable is strengthened even though the variable itself is unchanged. The two effects may be complementary or not, and this is argued to be central in assessing the efficacy of policy.

Supply-side policy

The UK economy has undergone considerable change since 1980. Policy objectives have moved away from the long-standing ones and have focused on inflation, a stable macro-stance and 'supply-side' strategy to improve the workings of the micro-economy. The *raison d'être* of 'supply-side' policies is that resources are allocated optimally by markets provided that the markets are free and competitive. Measures are designed to remove impediments to markets working better – reducing market imperfections. Economic agents are then able to respond more quickly and efficiently to changing market conditions. In carrying out policy therefore the aim is to improve overall efficiency of the economy by changes in the basic climate.

Respectability for this view is of course steeped in the historical development of economic thought, not least of which involves Adam Smith's 'invisible hand', but often draws upon authors such as Hayek. Writing between the wars in response to the emerging disbelief in market clearing, he claimed the 'spontaneous order' of the free market to be superior, in terms of social welfare, to any form of 'planned social order'. Essentially, though, the recent theoretical advances have been in bolstering the traditional invisible hand/ *laissez-faire* faith. Here, not only must competitive market conditions prevail, but the authorities can significantly improve the overall efficiency of the economy by changes in the basic climate. The instrument which holds the whole thing together is Say's Law. This ensures that all markets clear. Any resources which are not bought or sold are unused through choice. This 'law' has often been regarded as a worthless identity where even if all markets do clear the equilibrium may not be unique or at a high level of resource utilisation, but has been defended as a matter not of logical impossibility for excess supply to exist, but that as a matter of fact it never persists long enough to matter. This empirical version of Say's Law forms the fundamental basis of neo-Austrian analysis, the more positive side of supply-side theory. And on top of that was developed the notion that governments could not do anything else to improve the economy in the long run and would more normally provoke the opposite if they tried.

This all meant that market forces should prevail because that ensures the optimal allocation of resources, and should be allowed to do so. The Government in this scenario is therefore mandated to keep out of economic activity, in practice ranging from cutting out the derided 'picking winners' on the expenditure side to the important improving incentives by lowering rates on the taxation side. In general, the philosophy could be used as a justification for any economic policy or, more sceptically, for not having any at all. In practical terms in the United Kingdom, the policy approach has two broad strands. The first is to deregulate markets. This amounts to reducing market power, where it exists, of both labour and capital, to raise the responsiveness of each to changes in market forces. The most widely canvassed example is the series of trade union reforms, but also significant were reductions in producer power, for instance in financial markets. The second is to provide incentives to individuals to work more efficiently and cause firms to raise output and investment and stimulate entrepreneurship. The most infamous of these measures is the series of income tax cuts which arguably helped the Conservative Party to win its post-1979 general elections.

The effectiveness of supply-side policy can be evaluated in many ways, but as far as manufacturing industry is concerned, the performance of labour productivity has been central to the debate. Productivity grew rapidly in the late 1980s, and the word 'miracle'[2] was often used to describe the claimed turnaround that took place compared with the 1970s and which was professed to have arisen out of the new economic policies.[3] The issue was therefore whether the UK economic policy changes of the 1980s had a fundamental effect, or whether it was just another cyclical recovery. On the positive side the potential for catch-up on the other countries was thought significant. But other countries had not been standing still. They too had to respond to the increased harshness of international competition as impediments to free trade were lowered and removed and the world economy became more competitive. The process of 'catching-up', however, may be easier than setting the pace, so that the UK economic policy changes in the 1980s may have had a stronger effect than elsewhere. Also the 'supply-side revolution' which most countries strove to achieve may have been more beneficial to the UK economy because reform was much more radical.

The freeing-up of markets and the return of the 'right to manage', the 'enterprise culture' and the 'fear factor'[4] in the United Kingdom may have made firms more responsive and competitive in world markets. The 1980s also saw an acceleration in the use of stock control systems such as 'just in time' and 'right first time', and of team-working and similar methods. The effects of these can be dramatic and may not only raise the level of productivity but also increase the economy's growth rate by establishing flexibility so that firms can respond quicker to changing demand patterns. A related factor is the redesign of products[5] to eliminate some operations and components, a route adopted by the Japanese which the United Kingdom has been following. In summary, the combination of a deep recession between 1979 and 1981, supply-side measures, particularly relating to trade union reform, a stable macroeconomic stance, and a relatively long recovery may therefore have created the conditions for a sustainable improvement in manufacturing productivity growth.

On the negative side, however, the apparent improvement may have been merely cyclical and structural. The length and strength of the recovery might have simply reflected the depth of the 1979–81 slump which was undoubtedly severe and saw the end of many companies. This may have boosted efficiency simply by the 'batting average' effect, where low productivity companies were put out of business. Additionally those that went to the wall may have been potentially the most dynamic, but in investing in the longer term stretched themselves too far when the recession deepened and lengthened, which may have implications for the future.[6] Furthermore in the latter part of the 1980s the economy was run at a very rapid rate so that output growth was very fast and productivity may have benefited simply in a 'Verdoorn' manner not dissimilar to the past, and which would not constitute fundamental improvement.[7]

The way in which productivity can improve trade performance is basically in making costs lower than they would otherwise be, which in turn can improve price competitiveness. The standard method of analysis[8] is to evaluate unit labour costs – ULC – the cost of labour required in relation to the output it produces:

$$ULC = WC/TO \qquad (7.1)$$

where WC are wage costs and TO is total output. This can be measured by comparing average wage costs with the amount of output produced per person by dividing the top and bottom of equation 7.1 by employment, giving:

$$ULC = AW/PR \qquad (7.2)$$

where AW is wage cost per person, or average wages, and PR is output per person, or labour productivity. This formulation helps to identify how supply-side policy might work on price competitiveness. First is the direct effect of productivity, which lowers ULC as it rises. Labour productivity in UK manufacturing did indeed grow much faster in the 1980s cycle, 1979–90, than the second 1970s' one, 1974–9 – 4.60 per cent per annum, compared with 1.08.[9] This meant that productivity relative to the United Kingdom's main competitors increased during the 1980s whereas it had declined in the 1970s. This is illustrated in Figure 7.1 where the United Kingdom is compared with a weighted average[10] of the other G6 economies.

The 1990–2 slump in activity meant that the miracle was curtailed. Since the trough in 1992.1, however, manufacturing productivity in the United

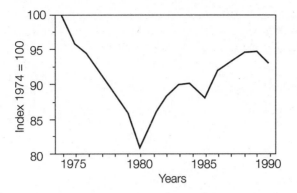

Figure 7.1 UK manufacturing relative to other G6: labour productivity
Source: IMF.

Kingdom has grown at a fairly rapid rate, not too dissimilar to that seen in the three-year period up to the peak in 1990.[11] The strong performance of productivity may therefore be continuing, although its source, strongly depending upon labour-shedding,[12] may not induce long-term confidence.

But also fundamental is the ratio of *AW* to *PR*. This relates to the much-discussed UK malaise of paying ourselves too much in relation to the extent to which our productivity performance improves. Under this scenario, raising productivity is of little value in an international setting if it all goes into wage increases, because the downward effect on costs and therefore prices is negated. The turn-around in the comparative ratio of *AW* to *LP* was quite dramatic in the 1980s. In the 1974–9 cycle, in relation to the main competitor economies, UK wages grew around 10 per cent faster than productivity, whereas productivity growth exceeded wages by less than 2 per cent over the (longer) 1980s cycle. The annual changes are shown for the two cycles in Figure 7.2.

The net result is that productivity growth improved dramatically in the 1980s, and may be continuing to do so, but also that the extent to which wage growth exceeded productivity diminished.

Both of these are strong plus points for supply-side policy. But the indirect effects of these on competitiveness are critical. Even though these two aspects of *ULC* improved, unless they helped at least to maintain price competitiveness, then the effect on trade performance may be negated. The distinction between these direct and indirect effects is important. Under the new policy regime, any rise in *ULC* could have less effect on reducing competitiveness than in the past because, say, the expectation is that productivity will not be eroded to the same extent by wage increases. But it is important that the effect of *ULC* on competitiveness is not worsened because that would reduce export effectiveness. In other words the elasticity of *ULC* in relation to competitiveness must be at least maintained or the

145

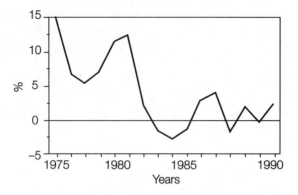

Figure 7.2 UK manufacturing relative to other G6: growth of wages less productivity
Source: CSO, IMF.

improvement in the variables themselves could be offset. This is the key empirical question which is addressed later.

Technology policy

A second key development in economic thinking in the 1980s was attempts to erase the United Kingdom's reputation for poor quality of product. This was typified by late delivery dates and inadequate after-sales service. But many other aspects of non-price competitiveness[13] can be identified which can be usefully encompassed by consideration of quality. While price may be of central importance, competition in design and process, in selling, and in matching design to markets are arguably also crucial. Strong impressionistic evidence suggests that UK non-price competitiveness and product quality, delivery date, design, reliability and after sales-service improved over the 1980s,[14] and may well have contributed significantly to overall competitiveness in the short run and, if maintained, in the longer term as well.

The theoretical measurement of quality is of course quite straightforward. For any given product, with perfect markets, quality is reflected in price. Under imperfect competition (Krugman, 1980), the variety of goods which a country can produce is a factor determining the position of its demand curve. These can be approximated in a number of ways and are discussed later.

Product quality can be improved in a number of ways but 'technical change' is an often-used umbrella. Governments have for many years played an active role in the process of technical change. The justification for government help is in terms of perceived market failure, arising from 'externalities': increasing returns, public goods or indivisibilities (Stoneman, 1987). Government policy affects all aspects of innovation, however, from the macro-stance to the provision of appropriability laws. Direct innovation

146

policy can either attempt to increase the stock of knowledge or to improve its effectiveness and dissemination. The former is often in the shape of R&D assistance, and the latter can involve helping firms to bring new technology to the market-place by improving technology transfer and diffusion.[15] The interrelationship between private and public R&D finance is important partly because the Government carries out much of its own R&D but also provides much finance for the private sector, particularly manufacturing. The decisions of firms and government are not made independently, however, and interactions – crowding in and crowding out – are inevitable. The policy of the 1980s and 1990s has been to reduce the role of the public sector in actively promoting, as well as carrying out, R&D where allocations seem inadequate – any market failure is seen as insufficient automatic justification for public spending support: the market knows best. The way that this has affected the overall picture and the extent to which private spending has substituted the public is the subject of this section.

For many years, research and development expenditure was virtually equated with[16] technical change and innovation. Now it is regarded by many as only a small part in the process of innovation as a whole. Notwithstanding, R&D arguably requires attention not least by virtue of the performance of the two most successful post-war large economies – if R&D is unimportant, why do the Japanese and Germans do so much of it (as discussed in Chapters 8 and 19)? There is also a growing literature which shows the important role of R&D in trade performance (Anderton, 1992; Buxton et al., 1991; Greenhalgh, 1990; Greenhalgh et al., 1994; Sedgley and Smith, 1994; Woods, 1995). An early criticism of the attention paid to R&D was that it meant different things to different people in different firms and industries, to say nothing of countries. To some extent this problem has been reduced by the international use of the so-called 'Frascati Manual' (OECD, 1981) so that survey figures are standardised. Published R&D statistics still suffer from many limitations, of course, due to their nature and measurement. Nevertheless, the data are regularly collected and recognised amongst the OECD countries as a relatively consistent indicator of trends in technological input. With these caveats in mind, Figure 7.3 shows how R&D in UK manufacturing has changed over the last two decades in relation to that of the other main industrial economies.

Explanations for the relative decline in the United Kingdom's R&D performance have been many and varied and continue a lingering debate relating to company and industry distribution; basic research versus applied and development; and many aspects of the 'new learning'.[17] But the most straightforward explanation relates to the Government's contribution to the total, reflecting a policy of reducing its own R&D assistance to private industry and hoping for crowding-in of private expenditure. Much has been made in the past of the fact that, despite much government assistance to R&D, such spending may be 'inappropriate' in various ways – too much on

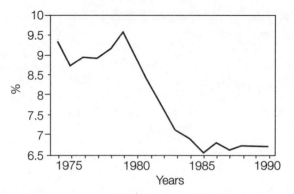

Figure 7.3 UK manufacturing relative to other G6: business performed R&D
(*Source*: OECD)

defence, purloining top scientists, picking winners, etc., and combinations of these arguments, despite solid ones to the contrary.[18] In the 1980s while these issues were still debated, the undoubted influence of government on the total was that it had reduced its contribution. This broad approach of letting companies spend their own money was designed on the one hand to reduce the Government's contribution allowing the private sector to 'crowd in' in the hope that such expenditure would be more 'efficient', viz. generate more technical change per unit of expenditure. On the other the Government saw its role as promoting diffusion and technology transfer and to promote the effectiveness of R&D spending.[19]

As a result of this policy, between 1981 and 1994, government funding of intramural R&D in UK manufacturing industry fell by over 60 per cent in real terms.[20] Other funding, including from overseas, rose by 44 per cent, so that research actually carried out by that sector increased by just under 10 per cent – at less than 0.75 per cent per annum, not a very good performance. To the extent that government policy aimed to withdraw financial help to private industry so that the 'market' could decide on the optimal allocation of expenditure therefore, the policy seemed to be to some extent successful. Given Figure 7.3, however, the apparent 'crowding in' which took place was insufficient to get real expenditure in total rising at the same rate as the United Kingdom's main competitors, although the downward trend may have been arrested.

As with price competitiveness, there are potentially two separate effects of changes in quality – the direct one in the variable itself, and the indirect one of the effect on overall competitiveness of any given value of the variable. As a result, even though R&D spending itself might fall, perhaps in relation to the past or international competitors, this might not matter if its effectiveness rises to compensate. This is the second key empirical question which is addressed in the empirical analysis.

148

MODELLING COMPETITIVENESS

International competitiveness traditionally revolved around price because the 'product' was regarded as relatively standard. Once differences in quality are considered, competitiveness can take on two meanings – price and what has become known as 'non-price'. Taking overall competitiveness as $COMP$:

$$COMP = COMP_0(PC, NPC) \qquad (7.3)$$

where PC is price competitiveness and NPC is non-price competitiveness. These are considered in turn.

Price competitiveness

International price competitiveness means that prices must be relative to those of competitors, which in this case are those of competing countries:

$$PC = PC_0(REP) \qquad (7.4)$$

where REP is relative export price, or:

$$REP = REP(P^x/P^a) \qquad (7.5)$$

where P^x is UK export prices and P^a is prices abroad. Prices are generally related to costs and in the standard model of course, marginal costs. While all costs are important, labour is often regarded as the key element in pricing, particularly as it is regarded as more variable and therefore more marginal than others. As discussed earlier, this is put in terms of ULC so if wages are low in relation to output, prices are lower. The exchange rate also affects prices, as do costs other than labour, giving:

$$P^x = P^x_0(ULC, EER, F) \qquad (7.6)$$

where EER is the effective exchange rate,[21] and F is other costs or influences on price. Then from equation 7.2:

$$P^x = P^x_1(AW/PR, EER, F) \qquad (7.7)$$

Taking equations 7.4–7.7 and separating AW and PR to test for structural changes:

$$PC = PC_1(AW, PR, EER, P^a, F) \qquad (7.8)$$

This treatment has similarities to Greenhalgh (*op. cit.*) and Greenhalgh *et al.* (*op. cit.*) where unit costs are labour plus materials, and productivity is not distinguished separately. The terms in F used by them involve innovations, capacity utilisation and strikes, reflecting reliability of supply.

The UK economy's trade performance has been much discussed in relation to bottlenecks where even if demand from abroad is strong, supply is constrained either because total capacity is limited or because of switching to the more profitable home market when demand allows it. Therefore while the actual measurement of capacity is not easy, it is clear that it should be included in the model, giving:

$$F = F(CU) \tag{7.9}$$

where CU is a measure of capacity utilisation, giving:

$$PC = PC_2(AW, PR, EER, P^a, CU) \tag{7.10}$$

Again the 1980s were thought to have addressed this capacity problem so that it was diminished and trade performance would be less constrained by it. Recent evidence (Driver, 1996) suggests that the capacity stance has worsened because firms have (finally) learnt from repeatedly having their fingers burnt as expected demand which justified the investment has been whisked away by policy turnarounds. This aspect of planning as well as strategy is vital in trade performance. Again though, as well as the extent of capacity itself, it is its effect on supply and therefore trade performance which is crucial. Even if, say, capacity utilisation had fallen, it would not matter if its effect on trade had diminished. This is an empirical question which is addressed later.

Non-price competitiveness

Non-price competitiveness is more difficult to assess, but is usefully encompassed by consideration of quality. There are a number of methods which have been adopted to indicate relative quality. The most theoretically respectable is the construction of Hedonic price indices, starting with Court (1939) and developed by, for instance, Griliches (1979). It is well known though that calculation of such an index for a single product, for a single country can be a very big piece of work; to repeat the exercise for different products and countries is even more so.[22] The alternative is to use proxies which either reflect quality itself, such as standards (Swann *et al.*, 1996 and chapter 6), or to approximate the likely determinants of quality change such as R&D (Owen and Wren-Lewis, 1992). As with prices, quality must be a relative concept. Therefore the equivalent of equation 7.8 for non-price competitiveness (*NPC*) can simply be described as:

$$NPC = NPC_0(RQ) \tag{7.11}$$

where RQ is a measure or measures of relative product quality.

The argument adopted here is that relative quality depends to some extent on relative research expenditure, so that:

$$RQ = RQ(RRD) \tag{7.12}$$

where RRD is relative R&D spending, so that:

$$NPC = NPC_1(RRD). \qquad (7.13)$$

Or:

$$NPC = NPC_2(UKRD, CRD) \qquad (7.14)$$

where $UKRD$ and CRD are UK and competitors' R&D spending respectively.

Using equations 7.10 and 7.14 in 7.3:

$$COMP = COMP_1(AW, PR, EER, P^a, CU, UKRD, CRD) \qquad (7.15)$$

The next stage is to model equation 7.15 in an export equation.

MODELS OF EXPORT PERFORMANCE

Basics

Recent empirical work has taken standard export equations in which supply is essentially assumed perfectly elastic, and tested for supply-side/other effects either by checking stability and/or using proxy variables for other 'non-price' effects. This approach is an approximation to a fully specified general equilibrium model (Krugman, 1989). New trade theory models which start from micro foundations include Barker (1977), Krugman (1979, 1980, and 1989), Lancaster (1966) and Ethier (1982), where essentially export demand may shift as a result of changes in the relative 'quality' range of goods or the variety which a country produces. In principle, prices should reflect this, but lags and learning effects may make this improbable.

Practitioners then build on this using proxies either for the determinants of changes in quality, such as R&D, or indicators of quality itself, such as standards. In addition, supply-side effects are often modelled to reflect improvements in say costs, such as productivity, and constraints on delivery, such as capacity utilisation. The present model takes on aspects of these.

The analysis of trading performance is therefore carried out here by including 'competitiveness' in a demand model. A standard export demand equation has relative price, income and 'tastes' – everything else. Here price is the main competitiveness variable because the 'product' is relatively standard. Taking this 'standard' export equation but allowing competitiveness to take on two meanings – price and 'non-price' gives:

$$X = X_0(COMP, WEX, T) \qquad (7.16)$$

where WEX is 'world' export volumes of manufactures as a measure of world demand, and T is tastes. Specifying these variables and X can be done in a number of ways, but the aim in this chapter is particularly to include the effect of productivity as the driving force behind any improvement in export performance plus the influence of non-price competitiveness. In this way the effect of the supply-side revolution and technology policy can be assessed. So from equations 7.3, 7.4, 7.13 and 7.16, the basic model is:

$$X = X_1(REP, RRD, WEX, T). \qquad (7.17)$$

And the full model, from equations 7.15 and 7.16 is:

$$X = X_2(AW, PR, EER, P^a, CU, UKRD, CRD, WEX, T) \qquad (7.18)$$

Estimation of some form of equation 7.17 therefore is of a basic demand equation which includes non-price competitiveness, while equation 7.18 tests all aspects of the theory described above. In practice, the appropriate model appears to be somewhere between the two.

Dynamics

There are a number of approaches that may be adopted to capture the dynamics of export performance. Landesmann and Snell (1989) examine whether there had been a significant improvement in the export perform-ance of UK manufacturing, using the log version of equation 7.16 without the non-price competitiveness term, RQ, for the period 1970–86. They focus on the income elasticity coefficient as the catch-all for export competitive-ness. They conclude, with a number of caveats, that there had been a struc-tural shift in this parameter since 1979. The analysis is disputed by Holly and Wade (1991) who find the opposite but also find other evidence that it is the supply-side of UK exports which accounts for the improvement in com-petitiveness. Much of this controversy of course centres on the definition and measurement of 'competitiveness'.

The approach adopted here is similar to these, but more extensive. The starting point is the specific model in equation 7.16 omitting non-price com-petitiveness and estimated in the way that Landesmann and Snell did, but over a longer time period. In other words, only lagged REP and WEX plus dummy variables are included. Landesmann and Snell also only considered the dynamics of WEX as reflecting possible improvements in export per-formance. The aim is to estimate a satisfactory version of this; to look at the dynamics of the variables; and then estimate the full model particularly in relation to the two policy shifts discussed earlier.

Empirical results

The data are seasonally adjusted quarterly from 1970 to 1993 and two dummy variables are included, as described in the appendix, but the estim-ation period is truncated at the start by lags, and at the end by the method of interpolation of the R&D series. The results for the equivalent of Landesmann and Snell are given in Table 7.1. All variables are in logs.

These results are very similar to Landesmann and Snell. The autocorrela-

ECONOMIC POLICY AND COMPETITIVENESS

Table 7.1 Regression results for manufactured export volumes:
1970.1–1992.4

Variable	Coefficient	t-values
Constant	3.65	10.80
REP_{-7}	−0.62	−7.40
WEX	0.83	33.08
D_1	−0.10	−2.33
D_2	−0.10	−2.28

$R^2 = 0.94$ $F(4,81) = 305.93\ [0.00]$ $e = 0.0589$ $DW = 0.42$

RSS = 0.2817 for five variables and eighty-six observations

tion is problematic as they also found. Nevertheless, we proceed on the basis that the estimators are consistent and the magnitudes of the coefficients are reasonable and not to be used for forecasting. To capture the dynamics, they used recurring sample periods of seventeen quarters to generate the coefficient changes to the model. The (similar) estimation procedure here is recursive regression starting with the first 17 observations, again for the longer time period. The results are shown in Figures 7.4 and 7.5. The result which Landesmann and Snell report is the rise in the coefficient on *WEX* in the 1980s. This is the same in the present model, with the rise continuing over the later sample period. Figure 7.4 shows, however, that the rise in the late 1980s and 1990s is to a large extent simply making good the fall in the early 1980s.

Landesmann and Snell do not report the profile of the coefficient on REP_{-7}, but Figure 7.5 shows our results. According to this, price elasticity, in relative terms rose sharply in the early 1980s and continued to do so throughout the sample period but not as fast as earlier.

Having more or less replicated Landesmann and Snell's results and then extended them, then to the extent that supply-side effects are contained in the coefficient on *WEX*, the extended data series does not suggest much net improvement. But this model omits the influence of non-price competitiveness which is argued above to be an important influence on overall competitiveness and therefore on export performance. The full model in equation 7.18 includes this, but also goes further in breaking down the *REP* variable, and estimation of this is therefore the next stage.

The estimated results for the full model, equation 7.18, were not economically or statistically sensible for any lag structure. The model which provided reasonable results was:

$$X = X_3(REP,\ SUKRD,\ WEX) \qquad (7.19)$$

153

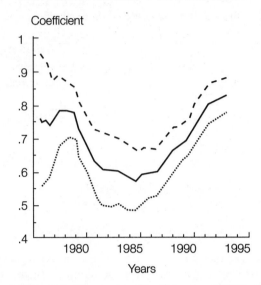

Figure 7.4 Recursive Regression (Coefficient on LWEX ± 2*SE)

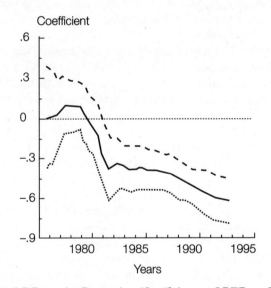

Figure 7.5 Recursive Regression (Coefficient on LREP$_{-7}$ ± 2*SE)

where *SUKRD* is the stock of UK R&D capital, rather than the flow of expenditure.[23] This is therefore an intermediate model between equations 7.17 and 7.18 and means that the interpretation of the results in terms of policy changes is less straightforward than was hoped for. In particular, the effects of supply-side policy on any improvement in UK relative productivity and the relation between productivity and wages could not be estimated directly. Instead, it must be inferred from the behaviour of the coefficient on REP. Similarly the effects of changes in technology policy must be inferred from the coefficient on UKRD rather than on relative R&D.

The results for equation 7.19 for the whole data set are reported in Table 7.2.

The coefficient on REP_{-7} is about the same as in Table 7.1, but the WEX coefficient is much lower, while the dummy variable ones are about the same.

The dynamics are again examined using recursive regression. The course of the coefficients estimated here is graphed in Figures 7.6, 7.7 and 7.8. Landesmann and Snell concentrated entirely on the income elasticity, and it was discussed earlier that they found a rise in this coefficient using recursive regression and this was interpreted as support for the 1980s' policies relevant to international competitiveness, particularly non-price. This generated a certain amount of controversy but it was argued earlier that non-price competitiveness is better proxied by a separate variable, in this case R&D. Nevertheless, to the extent that the world demand coefficient also reflects competitiveness improvements, Figure 7.6 tells an interesting story.

The rise in the estimate in the early 1980s is similar to that of Landesmann and Snell, who argued that this suggested that there had been success for the supply-side policies of Mrs Thatcher's administration. Arguably, however, their result is due to model misspecification, since the results given here suggest that the rise is simply a blip in a slight downward trend. The extent to which this is a success story is therefore debatable. Figure 7.6 suggests that when non-price factors are included, given the decline in the coefficient after the blip, then the opposite is true – that the elasticity has declined under supply-side policies.

The improvement both in UK relative productivity and its relation to

Table 7.2 Revised regression results for manufactured export volumes: 1970.1–1992.4

Variable	Coefficient	t-values
Constant	−4.22	−2.02
REP_{-7}	−0.58	−7.55
WEX	0.57	7.23
D_1	−0.10	−2.62
D_2	−0.11	−2.78
$LSUKRD_{-10}$	0.80	3.77

$R^2 = 0.95$ $F(5,77) = 265.25 \ [0.00]$ $e = 0.0541$ $DW = 0.39$

RSS = 0.2250 for six variables and eighty-three observations

155

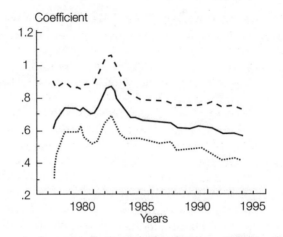

Figure 7.6 Recursive Regression (Coefficient on LWEX ± 2*SE)

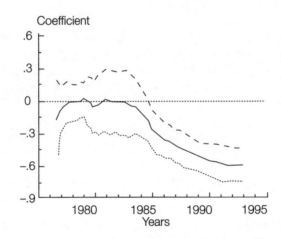

Figure 7.7 Recursive Regression (Coefficient on LREP$_{-7}$ ± 2*SE)

wages was discussed earlier and was argued to have had an important effect on UK relative export price increases compared with the trend in the 1970s. Figure 7.7 suggests that the relative export price elasticity has risen (become more negative) over the 1980s and 1990s.

This means that any fall in relative prices will generate a larger rise in export volumes. This in turn implies from equation 7.7 that any improvement in relative productivity and/or change in the relation between wages and productivity has a bigger effect on exports than it did before the policy changes – there is evidence for improvements from supply-side policy. This is an important result since it suggests that, to the extent that supply-side policy has improved international competitiveness, the improvement appears double-edged, lowering the differential between relative wages and productivity on the one hand and at the same time lowering its effect on export volumes. In other words, any improvements in the variable itself are intensified by changes in their effect. The result is in fact triple-edged, having coefficient/variable interactions. If relative productivity and/or the relation between wages and productivity improves, export volumes will be affected in the opposite way, downwards, more than it did before supply-side policy. This means that the policy works only as long as the values of the variables do not rise, because if they do, export volumes will fall faster than they would have done in the absence of the policy change. In fact, *REP* did rise over the period following the implementation of supply-side policy so that the combination of both rising coefficient and variable had the effect of reducing exports. This is obviously not the desirable result as far as the policy is concerned, but means that, for it to work, the variable itself has to fall – the coefficient change is not enough and is in fact counter-productive.

Figure 7.8 provides comparable evidence for the coefficient on *SUKRD*.

The discussion earlier suggested that technology policy in the United Kingdom meant that government contributions to industry R&D had declined and that the effect was a steady fall in spending relative to the other G6 economies, particularly in the early 1980s. The hoped-for crowding-in of private expenditure seems not to have taken place, although some flattening out of the ratio is evident in Figure 7.3. Figure 7.8 suggests, however, that despite the decline in spending, there was a steady rise in its effectiveness over about the same period. This suggests some success for the United Kingdom's technology policy change.

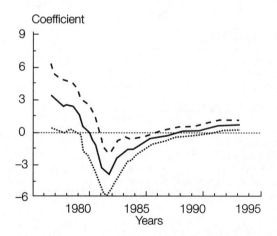

Figure 7.8 Recursive Regression (Coefficient on LSUKRD$_{-10}$ ± 2*SE)

However, the coefficient on R&D at the end of the sample period was only about one-third its size around 1980. The chosen sample period does not allow us to say whether the decline until about 1982 was a continuation from earlier. If it was, then it could be argued that the technology policy of the 1980s and 1990s has reversed the downward trend. In the absence of such evidence however it must be concluded that the policy has merely succeeded in partially reversing the downward movement in the effectiveness of R&D, which the technology strategy itself generated between 1979 and 1982.

CONCLUSIONS

This chapter has merged two crucial aspects of recent economic policy changes affecting the supply-side and technology characteristics of the economy. Part of the aim of the policy changes was argued to be to affect the economic variables which influence exports. But a concomitant change can be in economic behaviour for any given state of the variables. This was tested by formulating a model of manufacturing exports including price and non-price competitiveness and estimating it and its dynamics.

The final equation omitted some of the variables in the full model. The dynamics were estimated using the recursive regression approach. The results suggest that changes in economic behaviour have indeed taken place under the new policies since 1979. However, the net effect of the changes in variables and in their influence suggests that supply-side policy has not improved competitiveness and technology policy has at best returned the effectiveness of R&D to what it was, while at the same time lowering the amount of UK research spending, which is likely to have the effect of storing up trouble for the future.

NOTES

1 The numbers are as follows:

	1990	1991	1992	1993	1994	1995
Deficit, £m. (BOP basis)	11,647	3,627	7,089	8,168	7,522	7,823

Source: ONS.

2 Ball(1989) for instance.
3 'There can be no doubt that the transformation of Britain's economic performance during the eighties, a transformation acknowledged throughout the world, is above all due to the supply side reforms we have introduced to allow markets of all kinds to work better.' Chancellor (Nigel Lawson), Institute of Economic Affairs special lecture, 21 July 1988.
4 Metcalfe (1989), Hughes (1992), and Jackman *et al.* (1990) respectively.
5 HMSO (1995).
6 Oulton (1987).

7 NEDC (1988). Other contributors to the debate include Bosworth (1989), Feinstein and Mathews (1990), Glyn (1992), Kay and Haskell (1990), Muellbauer (1986), Muellbauer and Murphy (1989), and Spencer (1987).

8 Hughes (1993), for instance.

9 Quarterly peak to peak, 1974.2–79.2 and 1979.2–90.2 although the hiccup in output in 1985 can imply two cycles in manufacturing in the 1980s.

10 The weights are exports.

11 The annual growth rate was 3.39 per cent between 1992.1 and 1995.4, and 4.34 per cent between 1987.2 and the peak in 1990.2. Given that productivity in the period leading up to a peak is generally the fastest within an economic cycle, the rates are roughly comparable.

12 Buxton (1996).

13 See Chapter 6.

14 Buxton (1994) and NEDC (1989), for instance.

15 HMSO (*op. cit.*).

16 'Often confused with' are the words of the *Competitiveness* White Paper (*loc. cit.*) p. 136.

17 See Chapter 8 of this volume.

18 Stoneman (1992) and Dasgupta and Stoneman (1987) discuss the issues.

19 HMSO, *loc. cit.*

20 Some of the fall was because the UK Atomic Energy Authority was denationalised in 1986. Stoneman (*op. cit.*) has some estimates of the effect.

21 *ULC* are measured in home currency: see Chapter 17.

22 The seminal study of Gordon (1990), which combines the hedonic approach with the conventional specification method for a wide range of US durable consumer and producer goods, was first drafted in 1974.

23 See Chapter 8.

24 The OECD generates annual figures, in some cases by interpolating. This data were made quarterly using the method of Lisman and Sandee (1964).

REFERENCES

Anderton, R. (1992) 'UK exports of manufactures: Testing for the effects of non-price competitiveness using stochastic trends and profitability measures', *Manchester School*, vol. 60, pp. 23–40.

Ball, Sir J. (1989) 'The United Kingdom economy: Miracle or mirage', *National Westminster Bank Quarterly Review*, February, pp. 43–59.

Barker, T. (1977) 'International trade and economic growth: An alternative to the neo-classical approach', *Cambridge Journal of Economics*, vol. 1, no. 2, pp. 153–72.

Bosworth, D. L. (1989) *The British productivity miracle*, Coventry: Institute of Employment Research, University of Warwick.

Buxton, T. (1994) 'The competitiveness of UK manufactured exports', in T. Buxton, P. Chapman and P. Temple (eds) *Britain's Economic Performance*, London: Routledge, pp. 57–75.

—— (1996) 'Maintaining international competitiveness: Is the UK reverting to labour shedding and is it working?', *The Business Economist*, vol. 27, no. 1, pp. 38–49.

Buxton, T., Mayes, D. and Murfin, A. (1991) 'UK trade performance and R&D', *Economics of Innovation and New Technology*, vol. 1, no. 3, pp. 243–56.

Court, A. T. (1939) 'Hedonic price indices with automotive examples', in *The Dynamics of Automobile Demand*, New York: General Motors Corporation, pp. 99–117.

Coutts, K. and Godley, W. (1992) 'Does Britain's balance of payments matter any more?', in J. Michie (ed.) *The Economic Legacy 1979–92*, London: Academic Press, pp. 60–7.

Dasgupta, P. and Stoneman, P. (eds) (1987) *Economic Policy and Technological Performance*, Cambridge: Cambridge University Press.

Dicks, G. (1991) 'What remains of Thatcherism?', *Economic Outlook*, vol. 15, no. 5, pp. 6–14.

Driver, C. (1996) 'Tightening the reins: The capacity stance of UK manufacturing firms 1976–1995', in J. Mitchie and J. G. Smith (eds) *Creating Industrial Capacity*, Oxford: Oxford University Press, pp. 75–92.

Ethier, W. (1982) 'National and international returns to scale in the modern theory of international trade', *American Economic Review*, vol. 72, no. 3, pp. 389–405.

Feinstein, C. and Mathews, R. (1990) 'The growth of output and productivity in the UK', *National Institute Economic Review*, vol. 133, pp. 78–90.

Glyn, A. (1992) 'The "productivity miracle", profits and investment', in J. Michie (ed.) *The Economic Legacy 1979–92*, London: Academic Press, pp. 77–87.

Gordon, R. J. (1990) *The Measurement of Durable Goods Prices*, NBER, Chicago: University of Chicago Press.

Greenhalgh, C. (1990) 'Innovation and trade performance in the United Kingdom', *Economic Journal*, vol. 100, pp. 105–18.

Greenhalgh, C., Taylor, P. and Wilson, R. (1994) 'Innovation and export volumes and prices – a disaggregated study', *Oxford Economic Papers*, vol. 46, pp. 102–34.

Griliches, Z. (1979) 'Issues in assessing the contribution of research and development to productivity growth', *Bell Journal of Economics*, vol. 10, pp. 72–116.

HMSO (1995) *Competitiveness: Forging Ahead*, Cm 2867, London: HMSO.

HMT (1989) 'Helping markets work better', *Economic Progress Report*, No. 203, August, London: HMSO, pp. 4–8.

Holly, S. (1995) 'Exchange rate uncertainty and export performance: Supply and demand effects', *Scottish Journal of Political Economy*, vol. 42, pp. 381–91.

Holly, S. and Wade, K. (1991) 'UK exports of manufactures: The role of supply side factors', *Scottish Journal of Political Economy*, vol. 38, no. 1, pp. 1–18.

Hughes, A. (1992) 'Big business, small business and the "enterprise culture"', in J. Michie (ed.) *The Economic Legacy 1979–92*, London: Academic Press, pp. 296–311.

Hughes, K. (1993) 'Introduction: UK competitiveness and industrial policy', in K. Hughes (ed.) *The Future of UK Competitiveness and the Role of Industrial Policy*, London: PSI, pp.1–6.

Jackman, R., Layard, R. and Nickell, S. (1990) *Unemployment*, Oxford: Oxford University Press.

Kay, J. A. and Haskell, J. E. (1990) 'Industrial performance under Mrs Thatcher', in T. Congdon *et al.*, *The State of the Economy*, London: IEA, pp. 8–20.

Keegan, W. (1994) 'In my view', *The Observer Business*, 20 November, p. 2.

Krugman, P. (1979) 'Increasing returns, monopolistic competition and international trade', *Journal of International Economics*, vol. 9, pp. 469–79.

—— (1980) 'Scale economies, product differentiation and the pattern of trade', *American Economic Review*, vol. 70, no. 5, pp. 950–9.

—— (1989) 'Differences in income elasticities and trends in real exchange-rates', *European Economic Review*, vol. 33, no. 5, pp. 1031–54.

Lancaster, K. (1966) 'A new approach to consumer theory', *Journal of Political Economy*, vol. 74, pp. 132–57.

Landesmann, M. and Snell, A. (1989) 'The consequences of Mrs Thatcher for UK manufacturing exports', *Economic Journal*, vol. 99, March, pp. 1–27.

Lisman, J. H. C. and Sandee, J. (1964) 'Derivation of quarterly figures from annual data', *Applied Statistics*, vol. 13, pp. 87–90.

Metcalfe, D. (1989) 'Water notes dry up, the impact of the Donovan reform proposals and Thatcherism at work on labour productivity in British manufacturing industry', *British Journal of Industrial Relations*, vol. 27, pp. 1–31.

Muellbauer, J. (1986) 'Productivity and competitiveness in British manufacturing', *Oxford Review of Economic Policy*, vol. 2, pp. i-xxv.

Muellbauer, J. and Murphy, A. (1989) *How Fundamental Are the UK's Balance of Payments Problems?*, Oxford: Nuffield College.

NEDC (1987) *British Industrial Performance*, London: NEDO.

—— (1988) 'Pay and productivity', Memorandum by the Director General, London: NEDC(87)8.

—— (1989) 'Trade performance', Memorandum by the Director General, London: NEDC(89)9.

OECD (1981) *The Measurement of Scientific and Technical Activities (The Frascati Manual)*, Paris.

—— (1986) *Flexibility in the Labour Market*, Paris.

—— (1991) *Employment Outlook*, Paris, July.

—— (1994) *Employment Outlook*, Paris, December.

Oulton, N. (1987) 'Plant closures and the productivity "Miracle"', *National Institute Economic Review*, No.132, August, pp. 71–91.

Owen, C. and Wren-Lewis, S. (1992) 'Variety, quality and UK manufactured exports', London: HM Treasury Academic Panel Paper AP(92)5.

Sedgley, N. and Smith, J. (1994) 'An analysis of UK imports using multivariate cointegration', *Oxford Bulletin of Economics and Statistics*, vol. 56, no. 2, pp. 135–50.

Spencer, P. (1987) *Britain's Productivity Renaissance*, First Boston, Credit Suisse.

Stoneman, P. (1987) *The Economic Analysis of Technology Policy*, Oxford: Clarendon Press.

—— (1992) 'Why innovate?', in A. Bowen and M. Ricketts (eds) *Stimulating Innovation in Industry*, London: Kogan Page.

Swann, P., Temple, P. and Shurmer, M. (1996) 'Standards and trade performance: The UK experience', *Economic Journal*, vol. 106, pp. 1297–1313.

Thirlwall, A. (1992) 'The balance of payments and economic performance', *National Westminster Bank Quarterly Review*, May, pp. 2–11.

Thirlwall, A. and Gibson, H. D. (1992) *Balance of Payments Theory and the United Kingdom Experience*, 4th edn, London: Macmillan.

Woods, R. (1995) *Investment, R&D and Manufactured Trade*, London: HMT Academic Panel.

APPENDIX

Definitions and sources of the data are as follows:

- Export volumes, X, UK export prices, P^x and prices abroad, P^a, (and REP): *Monthly Review of External Trade Statistics*, ONS;
- Average wages, AW and productivity, P: *Economic Trends*, ONS;
- Capacity utilisation, CU, CBI;
- Research and development, RD: OECD, DSTI(STAN/ANBERD), 1994,[24] deflated with the GDP deflator and converted into 1985 dollars; the rest of the G6 are US, Japan, France Germany and Italy;
- World exports, WEX: ONS;
- 1972 dummy, D_1: +1 in 1972.Q3; −1 in 1972.Q4, 0 otherwise;
- 1979 dummy, D_2: +1 in 1979.Q1; −1 in 1979.Q2, 0 otherwise.

Part III

INVESTMENT AND INNOVATION

8

OVERVIEW: THE FOUNDATIONS OF COMPETITIVENESS
Investment and innovation

Tony Buxton

> Just as the introduction of looms is a special case of machinery in general, so the introduction of machinery is a special case of all changes in the productive process in the widest sense, the aim of which is to produce a unit of product with less expense and thus to create a discrepancy between their existing price and their new costs. Many innovations in business organisation and all innovations in commercial combinations are included in this.
>
> (J.A. Schumpeter, *The Theory of Economic Development*, English edn, p. 112)

The fundamental source of competitiveness which can enable rapid growth in the long run is investment and innovation. The most widely addressed type of investment is in 'fixed' capital – plant and machinery, buildings and vehicles. But labour is also obviously of considerable importance in the productive process. Improving labour's efficiency requires investment in education and training. It is well known that 'innovation' can enhance product quality and also improve the efficiency with which labour and fixed capital combine. Many factors influence innovation, but investment in 'intangibles' is one of the main sources, and promotional expenditure, education and training, and research and development (R&D) are the three most often discussed. Promotion abroad of UK goods and services is an increasingly important aspect of international competitiveness, but has yet to receive the empirical back-up which it undoubtedly warrants. The same is not true of R&D, which is seen as vital in the process of innovation by increasing the stock of 'research' capital, or of spending on education and training which can raise the stock of 'human' capital. This chapter explores aspects of investment and innovation over the last twenty-five years.

The traditional inputs into the productive process are of course capital

165

and labour. Yet much evidence over a long period of time suggests that these play a far smaller part in economic growth than 'other' inputs, the contributions of these often being aggregated into a single entity labelled the 'residual' or 'technical change'.[1] Innovation has arguably been an integral contributor to this. In view of its historical importance and its likely accelerating role in the future, innovation is given central attention here, although fixed capital and labour are not forgotten. Indeed they cannot be since both labour and fixed capital are key vehicles in the introduction of innovation. This chapter therefore begins with a comparative analysis of an important input into technological change – R&D – and of technological output – royalties. It then turns to expenditure on fixed capital and finally to inward investment, the extent to which investment by overseas companies in human capital contributes to the economy.

INNOVATION

Innovation is often analysed within the context of Schumpeter's (1942) trilogy of the process of technological change: invention, innovation and diffusion. Invention is the creation of new ideas or of technological knowledge; innovation is the process of converting new ideas into marketable products or processes; diffusion is the adoption of the innovation by others. The overall literature on technological change has been surveyed *ad nauseam*; Baldwin and Scott (1987) and Cohen and Levin (1989) are competent compilations. The focus of much research into innovation has been of the technological kind, product and process, and therefore on the main measurable input, R&D expenditure; its effectiveness, often measured by patents; and its effects, through the diffusion of technology, on economic growth and other measures of performance. But a whole host of other innovation questions have been asked.[2] The tempo has risen recently, however, with widespread recognition that the process of innovation is far wider, and that successful implementation requires the satisfaction of a long series of conditions from an original idea to the international market-place. This appreciation is not new, of course, as evidenced for instance by Rothwell's (1980) survey,[3] but has now taken a strong hold in the literature. The theoretical difficulties related to property rights have been studied in depth, yet their practical aspects have mushroomed as internationalisation has grown. The technological human experience necessary to cope with advancing innovation is increasingly a problem as education institutions grapple with the requirements of industry and training becomes more specialised. Marketing is now seen as an integral part of the process where the most advanced technological developments may fail if not linked to the needs of the user. Similarly, design is now recognised as an ongoing part of the development process, not a once-and-for-all contribution. Stock control methods have meant that innovations may be introduced faster and more effectively. And as part of this, the importance of liaison with suppliers, of both current and capital inputs, is increasingly seen as necessary to ensure success in innovation.

The importance of competition as a stimulant to innovation has long been debated. Schumpeter (*op. cit.*) and his celebrated 'creative destruction' began the debate by positing whether large firms in relatively monopolistic industries were required in order to 'create' new technology; 'destruction' then came about as new products and processes were copied and competition eventually eroded market power. His work developed into the notion of 'bigness and fewness' where innovation requires big expenditure because technology is expensive and this requires a monopolistic or oligopolistic industry structure. Galbraith's (1952) subsequent famous fiction,[4] and Arrow's (1962) theoretical analysis of the incentive to innovate set in train voluminous studies of the effect of firm size, industry structure and industry characteristics on numerous aspects of technical change (Cohen and Levin, *op. cit.*).

But the benefits of cooperation are more and more seen as having considerable potential. Collaborative research has obvious attractions, but also many difficulties, particularly relating to appropriability (Katz and Ordover, 1990). Similarly 'technology transfer' – how new technology can be used in practice[5] – has long been prominent in evaluating the effectiveness of UK R&D – good ideas are plentiful, but exploited by foreign companies rather than home producers (Ray, 1989, for instance). Financial aspects of successful innovation have also attracted attention more recently, with the debate on 'short-termism' relevant here. And encompassing many aspects of all of these is the importance of management and business strategy. This includes non-technical aspects of technological innovation – where to put the new machinery – as well as non-technical innovation itself – how to rearrange the existing equipment, reminiscent of the 'embodied' and 'disembodied' technical change classifications.

Governments have for many years played an active role in the process of technical change because of perceived market failure, arising from 'externalities'; increasing returns, public goods or indivisibilities (Stoneman, 1987). Government policy affects all aspects of innovation, from the macro-stance to the provision of appropriability laws. Direct innovation policy can attempt either to increase the stock of knowledge or to improve its effectiveness and dissemination. The former is often in the shape of R&D assistance, and the latter can involve helping firms to bring new technology to the market-place by improving technology transfer and diffusion. The interrelationship between private and public R&D finance is important partly because the Government carries out much of its own R&D but provides much finance for the private sector. The decisions of firms and government are not made independently, however, and interactions – crowding in and crowding out – are inevitable. The call of the 1980s, which continued into the 1990s, was to

167

reduce the role of the public sector in actively promoting, as well as carrying out, R&D where allocations seem inadequate, and the effects of this can be seen in what follows.

All these are part of the 'new learning' in the economics of innovation.[6] Yet despite the progress of the new, it is important to keep sight of the old. To make improvements in the future we must forgo current consumption, and to generate innovation we must invest in it by allocating current resources. Such spending will by no means always change technology and will certainly not be comprehensively picked up in published R&D statistics[7] but is self-evidently a necessary condition. The effects of R&D as well will not wholly come through in the traditional measures of technological output – such as the so-called 'technological balance of payments' – the difference between royalties received and paid abroad.

R&D expenditure

The age-old problem in the study of innovation is that the direct spending on technology, mainly R&D, and its impact on patents and royalties, are far easier to measure than the many indirect ones such as the complementary investment in the marketing necessary to carry it through.[8] However, the study of published records of inputs of technology and outputs from it can point to trends and areas of inadequacy in aspects of the process of innovation, especially the extent to which the United Kingdom has progressed relative to competitor economies. The empirical analysis therefore begins with R&D expenditure.

For many years, research and development expenditure was virtually equated with technical change and innovation.[9] Now it is regarded by many as only a small part in the process of innovation as a whole. None the less, this variable arguably requires attention, not least by virtue of its maturity. An early criticism of the attention paid to R&D was that it meant different things to people in different firms and industries, to say nothing of countries. To some extent this problem has been reduced by the international use of the so-called 'Frascati Manual' (OECD, 1981), so that survey figures are standardised. Published R&D statistics still suffer from many limitations, of course, due to their nature and measurement. Nevertheless the data are regularly collected and recognised amongst the OECD countries as a relatively consistent indicator of trends in technological input.

There are three main ways of categorising the institutions which carry out research: business enterprise, government, and 'other' – mainly quasi-public, though non-profit-making bodies such as universities. These three also provide the funds – 'other' here including quasi-charitable bodies such as trusts, and funds from abroad, often from foreign-owned companies. In addition, when making comparisons, various levels of aggregation – inter-industry and inter-country – and time-scales are possible. Furthermore, until recently, particularly in the United Kingdom, data were available only on a bi- or triennial basis which sometimes necessitated interpolation or comparisons between cyclically different time periods.[10] What follows therefore has its limitations, but the aim is to compare the performance of the United Kingdom over the recent past with earlier years and with its main competitors.[11]

In 1994 £12.6bn was spent on R&D in the United Kingdom. This is compared with £99.6bn allocated to fixed capital, nearly eight times more. In view of the comments earlier about their relative contributions to economic growth, this may seem surprising but is partly explained by the extent to which these investment flows boosted the corresponding stocks and is discussed later. Also the complementarity of the two is relevant. The more usual R&D comparison is with GDP, showing the percentage of total resources which are allocated to investment in research – gross expenditure on research and development (GERD). In 1994 the United Kingdom's GERD/GDP ratio was 2.19 per cent. This is compared with the same statistic over the last two decades in Figure 8.1.

The graph suggests an improving performance in the 1970s and a declining one in the 1980s and 1990s.[12] However, the relatively high percentage in 1981 reflects to some extent a steep fall in GDP since that year was the bottom of the early 1980s recession.[13] Furthermore, after 1986 the proportion of R&D spending fell at a time when the economy was running at a rapid rate and resources were relatively easy to come by. And there is cause for other misgivings about the experiences of the 1980s and 1990s. The first of these springs from a comparison with the other G6 countries, shown in Figure 8.2.

In the 1972–89 comparison,[14] the UK ratio was about average. In the 1990s, however, Figure 8.3 shows the United Kingdom's ratio has been

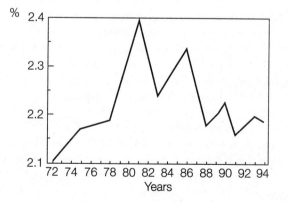

Figure 8.1 UK R&D relative to GDP: gross R&D expenditure as % of GDP
Source: ONS/author's estimates.

169

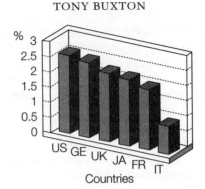

Figure 8.2 G6 R&D relative to GDP: average 1972–89
Source: OECD.

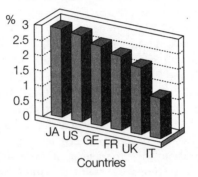

Figure 8.3 G6 R&D relative to GDP: average 1990–4
Source: OECD.

behind the other G5 nations, with Italy improving rapidly. By this measure, the United Kingdom has fallen well behind in the 1990s.

So far the analysis has been in nominal terms, which is the way the data are collected. In Figure 8.4 an attempt is made to compare real R&D expenditure. A specific R&D deflator is required for this, but in practice, in the absence of an 'official' one, researchers use the GDP deflator. This has obvious difficulties[15] but is used here nonetheless because, over a long period, the picture is strongly indicative.

Figure 8.4 again shows that in the 1970s the United Kingdom was about average, but by the mid-1990s it was left far behind by the others. In Japan, real expenditure on R&D increased more than fourfold between 1972 and 1994, and in West Germany and Italy by about two-and-a-half times. The United Kingdom raised real spending by only 20 per cent during this period and expenditure actually fell in the recessions in the 1980s and 1990s – a truly dismal performance.[16]

170

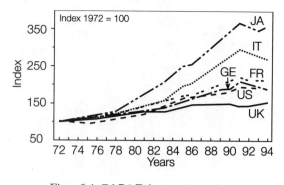

Figure 8.4 G6 R&D in constant prices
Source: OECD.

Although R&D investment – the flow of expenditure – is important, it is the 'stock of knowledge' which is critical in the contribution to economic growth, and the definition of R&D in the Frascati Manual discussed earlier takes this on board. An important development in the literature has been relating this concept to R&D expenditure.[17] It has been done by considering R&D as contributing to a stock consisting of the (depreciated) accumulated spending of the past. The stock of 'R&D capital' which results is then analogous to the stock of fixed capital and contributes to output in a similar way, viz.: providing a flow of services.

There are a number of difficulties in estimating R&D stock, however. The rate at which the stock depreciates is unknown, and the private and social rates may not be equal because of different perceived rates of obsolescence and the extent of 'spillovers' – firms benefiting from the expenditure of others – which may be endogenous to the innovation process. Also there may be a lag before R&D expenditure affects the stock.[18] And all of these difficulties are probably different across industries and perhaps countries. On top of these difficulties is the basic practical problem of estimating a consistent long-run series of constant-priced R&D figures.

The method used here to estimate international trends in R&D capital follows that of (amongst others) Griliches (1980). This involves computing the stock of R&D capital (RDC) in an initial year, and then depreciating at a fixed rate.[19] R&D capital for any subsequent year is then calculated by depreciating the previous year's stock and adding the new expenditure.[20] The assumed rate of depreciation is 10 per cent.[21] In Figure 8.5, the annual growth of R&D capital in each of the G6 is estimated from expenditure figures in constant-priced own currencies over the 1970s and 1980s compared with the 1990s.

Japan's stock of R&D capital grew the fastest in both periods. In addition, while all countries experienced a relative decline in the 1990s, the United Kingdom's fall has been proportionately the worst.

171

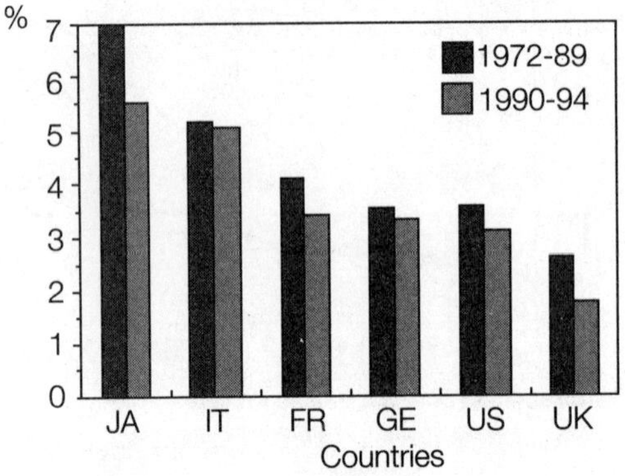

Figure 8.5 G6 growth of R&D stock: annual growth rate, 1972–89 and 1990–4
Source: OECD/author's estimates.

The growth of GDP and the stock of R&D capital is probably a two-way process, where rapid expansion of the economy can release resources for R&D spending on the one hand, or high R&D expenditure can generate fast GDP growth. The combination of the two can generate a virtuous circle which Japan has probably gone some way to achieving. But if, as argued earlier, innovation is the main driving force behind competitiveness, and investment in R&D is a key way to promote innovation, which the Japanese experience suggests it is, then the important direction of causation is from R&D to GDP growth, albeit with a lag, so that countries which increase their stock of knowledge the quickest eventually achieve the fastest growth of their economies. This to some extent is borne out in GDP growth figures, but also is portentous for the future – the United Kingdom's poor performance in the 1990s, continuing the trend in the 1980s,[22] means that the stock of knowledge which the United Kingdom has to call upon to improve competitiveness in the late 1990s and beyond may prove wanting.

Explanations for the relative decline in the United Kingdom's R&D performance have been many and varied, and continue a lingering debate relating to company and industry distribution, basic research versus applied and development, and many aspects of the 'new learning' discussed earlier. But the most straightforward explanation relates to the Government's contribution to the total. Much has been made in the past of the fact that, despite much government assistance to R&D, such spending may be 'inappropriate' in various ways – too much on defence, purloining top scientists, picking winners, etc., and combinations of these arguments, despite solid ones to the contrary.[23] In the 1980s and 1990s while these issues were still debated, the undoubted influence of government on the total was that it had reduced its contribution.

This had one or two aspects. Between 1972 and 1994, government financing of intramural R&D in UK business fell from 33 per cent to 12 per cent.[24] Figure 8.6 shows that almost all of this decline took place in the 1980s and 1990s.

Figure 8.7 takes this fall further by showing the level of real spending over the 1980s and 1990s. It shows that to some extent, private spending took over from public so that the total actually rose by nearly one-third. The increase may have been greater but for the recession in the early 1990s.

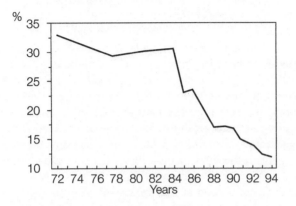

Figure 8.6 Source of funds for UK business R&D: per cent government finance, 1972–94
Source: CSO.

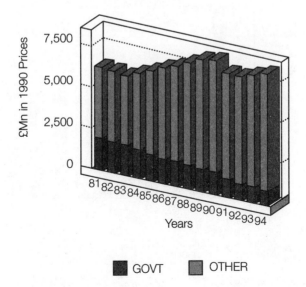

Figure 8.7 Real UK business R&D 1981–94: government financed and other sources
Source: NSO.

173

To the extent that government policy aimed to withdraw financial help to private industry so that the 'market' could decide on the optimal allocation of expenditure, the policy seemed to be to some extent successful. Given Figure 8.4 earlier, however, the apparent 'crowding in' which took place was insufficient to get real expenditure in total rising at the same rate as our main competitors. But this aggregate picture hides the fact that 'crowding in', in the sense that where government removes financial assistance the private sector takes over, did not in fact take place in the 1980s.[25] Figure 8.8 suggests that this continued in the 1990s by showing real spending in 1989 and 1994 in six broad sectors of the economy.

In the 'crowding-in with more effective spending' scenario, the reduction in government assistance is at least made up by a rise in private. This more or less happened in 'other'. In electrical machinery, the big fall is compensated by about half. In aerospace, the other main sector with a reduced government contribution, private spending fell. On the other hand, the two sectors which received increased government support also saw an expansion of private spending – the opposite of the crowding-in argument. Needless to say, the reallocations in spending which took place may have been made by the Government in the light of indications that the usual criteria for public assistance, mentioned earlier, required it, having regard to our competitors. But another way of looking at this which suggests that they may not have done so is that the percentage of total business R&D which was financed by government fell from 17 per cent to 12 per cent over the period 1989–94.

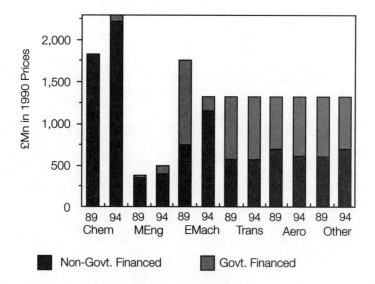

Figure 8.8 Finance of R&D in UK manufacturing: government and non-government, 1989 and 1994
Source: ONS.

Figure 8.9 takes this further, with another international comparison. The percentage of GERD which was financed by governments in the G6 in 1989 had West Germany and Japan below the others, particularly the latter. Much of the explanation for this lies in their lack of defence industry. In the 1990s, however, these two countries increased their relative government contributions. The UK government reduced its contribution even faster over this period, so that by 1994 the United Kingdom was the lowest except for Japan, despite the huge UK commitment to defence.

Finally, the changing role of government R&D, as well as the extremely skewed company distribution of spending in the United Kingdom, with expenditure concentrated into a very small number of firms, can be seen in the analysis of R&D by firm size. Table 8.1 shows this for the same three years in the 1970s, 1980s and 1990s.

Taking the first row for illustration, Table 8.1 shows that the five largest R&D spending companies in the United Kingdom in 1978 spent 41 per cent of total intramural R&D expenditure; that they received 76 per cent of the Government finance for private industry R&D; and that the amount which these firms themselves contributed to their own R&D was only 68 per cent that of the Government. The figures for each individual year are revealing and show that the vast majority of industry R&D is carried out by the largest 100 companies in terms of R&D, but this fell significantly between 1978 and

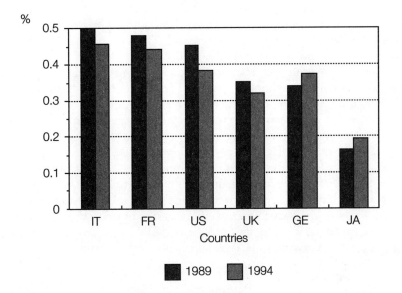

Figure 8.9 G6 government finance of R&D: percentage of total, 1989 and 1994
Source: OECD.
Note: FR and JA 1993.

Table 8.1 The 100 UK enterprises with the largest R&D expenditure as a percentage of the total: 1978, 1989 and 1994

Enterprises with the largest R&D	Intramural R&D			Government R&D			Private/Government finance		
	1978	1989	1994	1978	1989	1994	1978	1989	1994
Largest 5	41	32	20	76	64	37	68	208	328
Largest 10	53	46	36	82	76	46	98	270	556
Largest 20	67	62	49	91	84	54	123	346	597
Largest 50	83	77	63	96	94	75	161	396	543
Largest 100	91	86	71	99	96	79	181	446	624

Source: ONS.

1989. A case against this change would involve diseconomies of scale, but on the other hand, helping small(er) companies was an important aspect of the industrial policy, such as it was, of the 1980s and early/mid 1990s administration.

Table 8.1 also demonstrates that these companies received virtually all the R&D finance which the Government provided for private industry, but again the proportion has fallen. Finally the table shows how the private contribution, relative to government, changes as company size (measured by R&D) falls, and how this changed in the 1980s and 1990s. In 1978, the biggest five companies received the most government support but provided a much smaller amount themselves. By 1989, this had been reversed so that their contribution was twice the Government's. This change was true all the way down the line and continued in the 1990s.[26]

The UK government's reduction in contributing to R&D is not in doubt. So what is current technology policy? The answer is that 'government policies in innovation are designed to encourage innovation in its widest sense and help UK firms to exploit it most effectively' (Competitiveness, 1995). Under this policy the Government tries to raise awareness of innovation, spread best practice, facilitate cooperation between firms, establishes incentives for academics, research facilities and firms, secures access to world technology, ensures government activities contribute to competitiveness, encourages skills, and reduces regulations which inhibit innovation.[27] These seem laudable aims which essentially attempt to improve the effectiveness of private spending. Whether they can act as a viable alternative to public spending on research remain to be seen and is assessed in Chapter 19.

Patents and royalties

Patents and royalties are frequently used as indicators of technological output,[28] but both have shortcomings. There are a number of factors that affect patenting propensities so that there are important differences across countries in patent applied for/granted ratios. Some of these are because of differences in the degrees of protection offered. Patenting fees also differ, as the time taken for a decision to be made by patenting offices varies between countries. Furthermore there are variations in technical aspects due to differences in scientific understanding.

Royalties are paid on a patent if another person or company wishes to use it. Arguably it is therefore a good indicator of the worth of a patent, although problems abound relating to the propensity to patent across countries and industries.[29] By this measure, though, the UK record compares well with the other G6. Figures for the 'technological balance of payments' – the net receipts for the use of patents, licences, trademarks, designs, inventions, know-how and closely associated technical services – are shown in Figure 8.10 for the 1980s and early 1990s.

Until the early 1980s the United Kingdom was a net exporter of technology by this measure. This compared starkly with Japan and Germany,[30] which over the 1980s experienced deficits. This may indicate of course that these countries are better able to exploit available technology and/or that UK companies are reluctant to seek technological potential elsewhere. By 1994, Japan's net payments had become positive, reflecting its growth of R&D capital discussed earlier. Figure 8.10 as a whole backs up the frequently cited belief that the United Kingdom is good at ideas and inventions but poor at exploiting them. Having said that, starting in 1983 the balance took on a downward trend and by 1986 was negative, although less so than the others except the US. This may mean that the United Kingdom has begun to

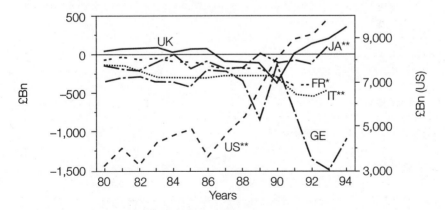

Figure 8.10 Technological balance of payments: 1980–94 (£Bn using PPPs)
Source: OECD.
Note: * FR 1992; ** IT, JA, US 1993.

emulate Japan and West Germany, but the decline may not be entirely unconnected with the relative demise of UK R&D discussed earlier. By the early 1990s, however, the balance became positive, so the picture is mixed.

FIXED INVESTMENT

Fixed capital is central to much economic analysis, not least that relating to economic cycles. For that reason, amongst others, it was much debated in the 1980s. The recovery from the recession of the early part of the decade was often related to changes in investment in stocks, while the extent of scrapping in that period and the consequent loss of capacity as well as the enhanced value of new capital, endowed with the latest technology, was much analysed, particularly in relation to the sustainability of the rapid expansion in the late 1980s (NEDO, 1988).

Investment in fixed capital has many aspects and a multitude of comparisons are possible in providing a balanced overview of the United Kingdom's experience. Nonetheless the story can begin by charting fixed investment in the United Kingdom over the twenty-five years since 1970. Investing in the future requires the forgoing of current consumption, and the extent to which society chooses to do this is often approximated by the amount of resources which are allocated to investment out of the total – the proportion spent out of GDP. This is graphed in Figure 8.11.

As expected, the path is broadly similar to the economic cycles in these years, with big peaks in 1974 and 1990 and to a lesser extent in 1979, and a very deep trough in the early 1980s and 1990s – the latter being historically very low.

Investment in 'building' takes place in dwellings and commercial property.

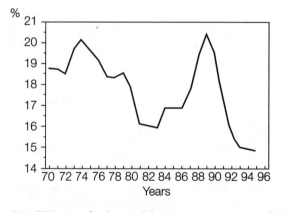

Figure 8.11 UK gross fixed capital formation: percentage of GDP
Source: ONS.

The domestic property boom of the 1980s is well known and was accompanied, *pari passu*, by a big hike in commercial property prices, partly because of the expansion of financial and other city-based services. The effect of this can be seen in Figure 8.12 where the amount of expenditure on buildings, plant and machinery and vehicles each in relation to GDP is graphed.

The very rapid increase in building in total portrayed in Figure 8.12 was due to growth in both dwellings and non-dwellings until 1988, but after that was predominant in the non-dwelling sector, which continued to rise rapidly after the dwellings sector had turned down. Its legacy was a huge surplus of floor-space, particularly in London, in the early 1990s. Plant and machinery, often thought to be the driving force behind economic growth, fell very sharply in the 1990s, to an historical low. Similarly, if the sustainability of economic recovery from recession requires high investment, particular in plant and machinery, then the prospects for the later 1990s are not good.

Figure 8.13 makes an international comparison by graphing the volume of fixed investment in the G6 economies over the same period in relation to the levels which prevailed in 1970.

Japan is again way out in front, having increased its spending by over 150 per cent. This involved relative stagnation in the early 1980s but very rapid growth after 1983, followed by a big fall in the early 1990s. Overall, the United Kingdom's experience was about average.

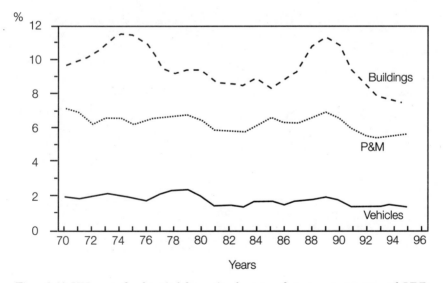

Figure 8.12 UK gross fixed capital formation by type of asset: as percentage of GDP
Source: ONS.

In the analysis of economic growth, many attempts have been made to assess the relative contributions of labour, capital and 'technology'.[31] Their importance depends on the services from the three, not just the net flow into them over any time period. And the influence of each on GDP growth is the increase in each weighted by its importance. The growth of the stock of fixed capital is therefore in the end the key measure of the performance of fixed investment in its contribution to economic growth. Figure 8.14 shows

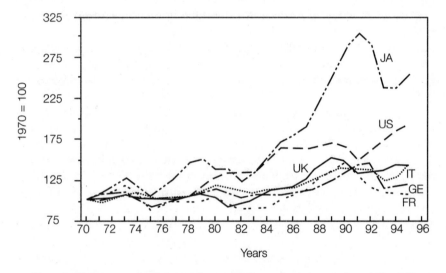

Figure 8.13 G6 gross fixed capital formation, constant prices: index 1970 = 100
Source: OECD.

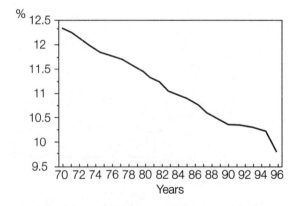

Figure 8.14 UK relative fixed capital stock: UK/other G5 using exchange rates
Source: OECD.

fixed capital in the United Kingdom in relation to the other G5[32] economies. The apparent flattening out of the downward trend in the late 1980s was soon reversed in the early 1990s, and the net result is not promising.

INWARD INVESTMENT

The United Kingdom has a long history of investing overseas, and the consequential profits have significantly helped the balance of payments. In the 1990s, a big part of UK industrial policy has been to attract inward investment[33] and is a principal aspect of the claim of the United Kingdom becoming the 'enterprise centre of Europe'.[34] The argument is that as well as providing employment, inward investment improves competitiveness by encouraging suppliers to improve quality, and product development, thereby improving profitability, level of exports, labour quality and creating an enhanced technology base.[35]

Figure 8.15 compares the G6 economies' world-wide outward and inward investment stocks in 1992. The United Kingdom's inward investment stock is second only to that of the US, but its outward stock is higher than its inward. Japan has the second highest outward stock but negligible inward – no one invests in Japan.

Much of the rationale for the United Kingdom's policy is to attract non-EU companies, particularly from the US and Japan. Non-EU companies which export to the EU from their own country must pay import duties, but foreign-owned ones located in the EU do not, provided that they source a significant amount of their inputs from within the EU.[36]

Figure 8.16 shows the stocks of US and Japanese inward investment into the large EU economies. The United Kingdom has about 40 per cent of the outward stocks of both the US and Japan in the EU. The policy of attracting these countries to invest here certainly seems to be working therefore,

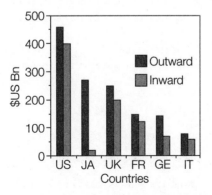

Figure 8.15 G6 foreign direct investment: stocks in 1992
Source: OECD.

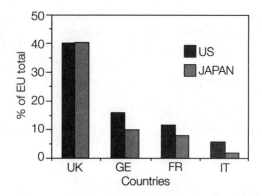

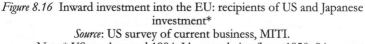

Figure 8.16 Inward investment into the EU: recipients of US and Japanese
investment*
Source: US survey of current business, MITI.
Note: * US stock at end 1994; JA, cumulative flows 1950–94.

although these stocks have obviously been built up over many years.
Whether the policy is a good alternative to others is debatable, and is
discussed in Chapter 18.

HUMAN CAPITAL

The last aspect of investment is in human beings. Arguably this is the most
important and fundamental, since everything stems in the end from people. 'Human' capital is that which is embodied in the labour force in the form
of the skills and the productive potential of the people. Spending on education and training contributes towards increasing or maintaining the stock of
human capital in an analogous sort of way to expenditure on R&D and fixed
capital. The resources devoted to education and training come from the
private and the public sectors so that the stock of human capital depends on
both.

In view of the high priority given to human capital in the 1990s, the United
Kingdom's relative performance is given a full treatment in Chapter 12.

SUMMARY

Summary of this chapter is relatively easy. The usual proxies for the inputs
into innovation suggest that the United Kingdom's traditionally weak position became weaker during the 1990s and that government scientific policy
must bear at least part of the blame. On the output side of innovation, the
picture seems rosier to the extent that the technological balance of payments
improved significantly. But this may simply be a symptom of the United

Kingdom's increasing inability to exploit its own ideas – the central theme of the Conservative Government's technology policy.

In terms of fixed capital, the situation is better, with the United Kingdom third only to Japan and the US in the period 1970–95 in the growth of fixed investment. This masks the huge fall in investment in the early 1990s and the continuing downward trend in the United Kingdom's stock of fixed capital in relation to its main competitors.

The contributions of innovation and fixed capital would not therefore be expected to improve the United Kingdom's relative competitiveness in the medium to long term.

NOTES

1 Abramovitz (1956), Fabricant (1954), Solow (1955) originally, and Maddison (1987), for instance, more recently, where the 'residual' accounts for up to 90 per cent of GDP growth.
2 Kamien and Schwartz (1982, pp. 12–13) provide a useful enduring checklist.
3 Pavitt's (1980) comments on Rothwell at the time included:

> Rothwell also identifies some other specifically British weaknesses in innovative activities: the inadequacy of market intelligence in many of the world's most important markets; and the poor links that often exist between product design and production engineering, with the result that new British product designs are sometimes unnecessarily difficult and costly to make. Rothwell stresses that the management of innovation is demanding and difficult, requiring a high level of professional and technical competence. It is here that the most important changes in British management will have to take place.
>
> (*Op. cit.*, p. 11)

One wonders whether they have.

4 There is no more pleasant fiction than that technical change is the product of the matchless ingenuity of the small man forced by competition to employ his wits to better his neighbour. Unhappily, it is a fiction. Technical development has long since become the preserve of the scientist and the engineer. Most of the cheap and simple inventions have, to put it bluntly, been made.

> (*Op. cit.*, p. 91)

5 To be distinguished from diffusion which refers to the wider use of existing technology that has already been transformed into an innovation. (Stewart and Nihei, 1987).
6 Freeman and Soete (1990) contains a number of relevant readings.
7 Hollander (1965) for instance some time ago established that firms devote a considerable amount of their resources to technological innovation which is outside their formal R&D operations.
8 Kuznets (1962) for instance provides an early discussion.
9 'Often confused with' are the words of the 1996 *Competitiveness* White Paper.
10 In the United Kingdom, benchmark surveys are now carried out every four years together with annual sample surveys in the intervening years covering the 100 enterprise groups spending most on R&D but ensuring all product groups are covered fully.

183

11 When there are gaps in the data, the series, in this and subsequent graphs, are interpolated. To make the comparisons consistent, the data for other countries are interpolated for the same years as the United Kingdom.

12 The greater volatility after 1983 is because before then the series is interpolated between the biennual and triennial surveys of R&D spending.

13 Stoneman (1992) has a discussion.

14 1972 was chosen because the next survey was in 1975, so that 1989 is approximately cyclically comparable.

15 The biggest is that, since a substantial proportion of R&D spending is on personnel, wage and salary changes are more important than the prices of other inputs which, because they are subject to the effects of technological change, tend to rise less quickly.

16 The position may actually be worse if the correct deflator was used.

17 Minaisian (1961) is an early example, and Griliches (1979) notably more recent.

18 The difficulties are not fundamentally dissimilar to those relating to fixed capital.

19 The actual calculation is: $RDC(t) = RD(t)/(r - d)$

> where $RDC(t)$ is R&D capital at time t
> $RD(t + 1)$ is R&D expenditure at time $t + 1$
> r is the growth of R&D expenditure during $(t + 1)\tilde{}(t + n)$
> d is the rate of depreciation of R&D.

20 $RDC(t + 1) = (1 - d)RDC(t) + RD(t)$.

21 As an 'intangible', R&D capital is unlike fixed capital where the rate can often be estimated from the length of life of the asset. It is broadly agreed, however, that the depreciation rate of R&D is low – knowledge remains useful for long periods. Griliches (*op. cit.*) actually assumes a zero rate, but the compromise here is 10 per cent. Clearly the lower the rate, the greater the influence of the past is on present stock values and therefore the greater is the error should the assumption be wrong. Individual observations may therefore have large inaccuracies but the trends are unlikely to be systematically biased.

22 Buxton (1994).

23 Stoneman (*op. cit.*) and Dasgupta and Stoneman (1987) discuss the issues.

24 Some of the fall was because the UK Atomic Energy Authority was denationalised in 1986. Stoneman (1992) has some estimates of the effect.

25 Buxton, *op. cit.*

26 Clearly the actual companies in the size groups are likely to have changed. In view of Figure 8.8, chemical companies are likely to have progressed up the ladder.

27 *Competitiveness (op. cit.)* has more discussion.

28 But there are others, particularly diffusion indices, Pavitt and Patel (1988), for instance.

29 Some companies patent everything 'just in case', others rarely do.

30 Remembering that German unification in 1990 had a big effect.

31 See page 165.

32 Figures for Italy are unavailable.

33 Cowling and Sugden(1996) and Eltis and Higham (1994).

34 The *Competitiveness* White Paper, *op. cit.*

35 *Competitiveness, op. cit.*

36 To avoid the creation of 'screwdriver economies' where foreign companies use home-made components and simply assemble them in Europe. The so-called '60 per cent rule' – now not often quoted and always a rule of thumb in reality – required at least that amount of local content in order to avoid duty.

REFERENCES

Abramovitz, M. (1956) 'Resource and output trends in the United States since 1870', *American Economic Review*, vol. 46, pp. 5–23.

Arrow, K. (1962) 'Economic welfare and the allocation of resources for inventions', in R.R. Nelson (ed.) *The Rate and Direction of Inventive Activity*, Princeton, N.J.: Princeton University Press, pp. 20–9.

Baldwin W.L. and Scott, J.T. (1987) *Market Structure and Technological Change*, London and New York: Harwood Academic Publishers.

Buxton, T. (1994) 'Overview: the foundations of competitiveness: investment and innovation', in Buxton *et al.* (eds) *Britain's Economic Performance*, London: Routledge.

Cohen, W.M. and Levin, R.C. (1989) 'Empirical studies of innovation and market structure', in R. Schmalensee and R. Willig (eds) *Handbook of Industrial Organisation*, vol. 11, Amsterdam: North Holland.

Cowling, K. and Sugden, R. (1996) 'Capacity, transnationals and industrial Strategy', in J. Michie and J.G. Smith (eds) *Creating Industrial Capacity*, Oxford: Oxford University Press, pp.289–308.

Dasgupta, P. and Stoneman, P. (eds) (1987) *Economic Policy and Technological Performance*, Cambridge: Cambridge University Press.

Eltis, W. and Higham, D. (1995) 'Closing the competitiveness gap', *National Institute Economic and Social Review*, November, pp. 71–84.

Fabricant, S. (1954) *Economic Progress and Economic Change*, Princeton N.J.: Princeton University Press.

Freeman, C. and Soete, L. (eds) (1990) *New Explorations in the Economics of Technical Change*, London: Pinter Publishers.

Galbraith, J.K. (1952) *American Capitalism*, Boston, Mass.: Houghton Higgins.

Griliches, Z. (1979) 'Issues in assessing the contribution of research and development to productivity growth', *Bell Journal of Economics*, vol. 10, pp. 72–116.

—— (1980) 'R&D and the productivity slowdown', *American Economic Review*, vol. 70, no. 2, pp. 343–8.

HMSO (1995) *Competitiveness: Forging Ahead*, CM 2867, London: HMSO.

Hollander, S. (1965) *The Sources of Increased Efficiency: A Study of Dupont Rayon Plants*, Cambridge, Mass.: MIT Press.

Kamien, M. and Schwartz, N. (1982) *Market Structure and Innovation*, Cambridge: Cambridge University Press.

Kuznets, S. (1962) 'Invention and activity: problems of definition and measurement', in R.R. Nelson (ed.) *The Rate and Direction of Economic Activity*, National Bureau for Economic Research, Princeton, N.J.: Princeton University Press.

Maddison, A. (1987) 'Growth and slowdown in advanced capitalist economies', *Journal of Economic Literature*, vol. 25, no. 2, pp.649–98.

Minaisian, D. (1961) 'Technical change and production functions', mimeo, Presented at the Annual Meeting of the Econometric Society.

National Economic Development Office (1988) 'Pay and productivity in the UK', Memorandum by the Director General, London, NEDC(88)21, June.

OECD (1981) *The Measurement of Scientific and Technical Activities*, (The Frascati Manual), Paris: OECD.

Pavitt, K. (ed.) (1980) *Technical Innovation and British Economic Performance*, London: Macmillan.

Pavitt, K. and Patel, P. (1988) 'The international distribution and determinants of technological activities', *Oxford Review of Economic Policy*, vol. 4, no. 4, Winter.

Ray, R.F. (1989) 'Full circle: The diffusion of technology', *Research Policy*, vol. 18, pp. 1–18.

Rothwell, R. (1980) 'Policies in industry', in K. Pavitt (ed.) *Technical Innovation and British Economic Performance*, London: Macmillan.

Schumpeter, J.A (1942) *Capitalism, Socialism and Democracy*, New York: Harper & Row.

Solow, R.M. (1955) 'Technical change and the aggregate production function', *Review of Economics and Statistics*, vol. 39, pp. 312–20.

Stewart, C. and Nihei, Y. (1987) *Technology Transfers and Human Factors*, Lexington, Mass.: D.C. Heath and Co.

Stoneman, P. (1987) *The Economic Analysis of Technology Policy*, Oxford: Clarendon Press.

—— (1992) 'Why innovate?', in A. Bowen and M. Ricketts (eds) *Stimulating Innovation in Industry*, London: Kogan Page.

9

THE CASE OF FIXED INVESTMENT

Ciaran Driver

INTRODUCTION

When uncertainty is ever present, prudence is the only strategy – don't borrow, don't innovate. don't diversify and when in recession, 'bunker down' and don't spend.

(Sir John Egan, former Chairman Jaguar Cars, *The Evening Standard* 23 October 1991)

Two major recessions have weakened the British economy by promoting uncertainty and discouraging long-term investment. Of course, costs have been squeezed and labour productivity increased; but it is important to see the larger picture. The fruits of higher productivity have mostly been consumed, not invested, because that was part of the grand accord between industry/government and those in work. In exchange for greatly increased work intensity and less job security, wages per head of those in work rose.[1] It is doubtful whether productivity could have risen so fast without this accord. But since the 'bunkered' economy is in no shape to mop up the surplus army of displaced workers, the enduring legacy of the 1980s economic policies is mass unemployment. If the problem with the Lawson boom of the late 1980s was that demand increased too rapidly, we may expect that it will be beyond the end of the century before employment drops to its 'equilibrium' level. Put differently, for about twenty years actual employment will have been a million higher than its equilibrium level. When it is realised that this is an optimistic scenario based on the belief that it is labour market reforms – rather than technology, training or investment – that galvanises an economy, the scale of the policy challenge becomes evident. Indeed, previous government projections, and those of many independent commentators, are more sanguine, predicting unemployment still at around two million by the end of the century.

What is an appropriate policy response? The economy needs long-run supply-side policies: poor performance cannot be cured by macroeconomic shocks, which seem to be most powerful in inducing real recessions and

Table 9.1 Gross fixed capital formation (current prices) as a ratio of GDP (market prices)

	UK	EC(12)	FR	WG	IT	J	USA
1961–70	18.3	19.1	23.8	24.9	24.6	32.2	18.3
1971–80	19.1	22.6	23.9	22.3	24.0	31.6	19.3
1981–90	17.5	19.9	20.4	20.1	20.9	29.2	18.6
1993	15.5	19.6	19.6	21.4	19.3	31.2	15.3

Source: European Commission.

nominal booms (Allsopp, Jenkinson and Morris, 1992). So much is merely commonplace. But there are sunk costs in the old regime, which is still defended by influential sniper fire and entrenched political support. Change will be slow and grudging, and arguments will have to be won point by point.

This chapter takes up the issue of fixed capital formation. Gross fixed capital formation – capital investment in buildings, plant and machinery and vehicles is lower in the United Kingdom as a ratio of output than most major competitors.[2] Comparative data on this are recorded in Table 9.1.

THE IMPORTANCE OF CAPITAL INVESTMENT

Capital investment is important not only because productivity gains are largely dependent on it, but because it is discretionary in its timing. If the recovery path of capital investment followed current expenditure as an alert cat follows a mouse, there might be little to lose sleep over. But problems arise when the cat itself behaves sleepily. The complacency of some commentators on investment stems from a failure to take this point seriously. The *Financial Times* journalist Samuel Brittan, for example, argues that it is wrong to focus on investment simply because it is a volatile component of demand: 'when there is a deficiency of total spending . . . consumer spending is just as good at plugging the hole' ('Economic Viewpoint', *Financial Times*, 25 March 1993).

In a purely accounting sense, Brittan is right. Consumer expenditure not only accounts for a much larger fraction of GDP than business investment, but strong cyclical recoveries seem to be characterised by an early surge in consumer expenditure before investment responds. When we look deeper, however, at the structure of economic causation and the sustainability of the recovery, it is clear that the investment response is crucial. The validity of Brittan's view rests heavily on his second belief, that 'if output can be increased without inflationary effects, the capacity will be created by business' ('Economic Viewpoint', *Financial Times*, 8 April 1993).

Here we are dancing over thin ice. To avoid digression let us bypass the question of whether a significant output increase can simply be facilitated by a conquest of wage inflation.[3] We focus rather on investment confidence and the time-scale of non-inflationary growth needed to inspire it. Initial investment stimulus is preferable to a consumer-led stimulus because the former generates sustainable income-related consumption in its wake – the multiplier, enhanced by productivity gains, is more reliable than the accelerator. That of course should be familiar to all students of the Lawson boom of the 1980s and the Barber boom of the 1970s, when the initial investment response in productive sectors was insufficient to prevent capital shortage stoking up inflation. The experience of the inter-war period is also salutary in this respect. Investment failed to respond to output due to a lack of confidence (Matthews, Feinstein and Odling-Smee, 1982, p. 384).

The pattern of investment in the United Kingdom in recent years is complicated by the extensive structural change that has characterised the economy. There has been a marked switch from manufacturing which has necessitated increased capital in growing service industries, especially finance (Milne, 1991). This transformation involved a rise in business investment in the mid-to-late 1980s, especially during the Lawson boom. Throughout the period, however, there was a trend fall in manufacturing investment and the investment–output ratio also fell in this sector. As there was also a switch from long-lived assets such as buildings and plant in favour of short-lived equipment, the fall in the growth of the capital stock was even more marked. Comparative cross-country evidence for manufacturing and for the total economy are given in Kitson and Michie (1996) and Bond and Jenkinson (1996). Both of these studies suggest that the United Kingdom has tended to invest comparatively less in fixed assets than have other advanced economies. Certainly a serious deterioration in manufacturing investment relative to Europe from the 1970s is evident in Table 9.2.

The 1990s' recovery in the United Kingdom has been marked by sluggish investment for the business sector as a whole, as shown in Figure 9.1. In the

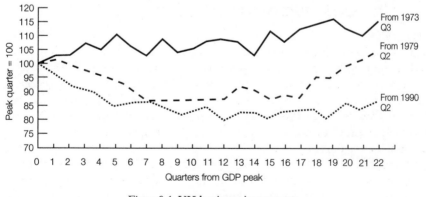

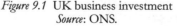

Figure 9.1 UK business investment
Source: ONS.

189

Table 9.2 Volume index of investment in
manufacturing industry (1981 = 100)

	UK	EUR*
1977	136	106
1978	145	108
1979	141	108
1980	124	110
1981	100	100
1982	95	96
1983	95	93
1984	109	99
1985	113	111
1986	119	117
1987	125	122
1988	141	132
1989	142	143
1990	141	152
1991	120	147
1992	127	139
1993	123	131

Source: European Economy, February 1993, based on
EC investment survey.
Note: *Excluding the five new German Länder.

following section we look at two possible reasons for the hesitant performance of capital investment in recent years: the inability of firms to fully
appropriate private profit from the technological advance embodied in new
capital; and the role of risk and uncertainty.

FIXED INVESTMENT: EXTERNALITIES SPILLOVER AND APPROPRIABILITY OF RETURN

The question of whether the social rate of return to fixed investment
exceeds the private rate of return is one of the most interesting questions in
economics today. If it does, countries which happen to have a rapid
growth in the capital stock may have higher output growth as well. Of course
the issue is one of context. The United Kingdom had a high rate of
capital growth in the 1960s which did not lead to sustained rapid growth,
possibly because of the sectoral composition of investment, or the lack of
complementary skills.

Despite this caveat, recent evidence suggests that capital growth confers
benefits beyond those captured by the private return to capital represented
in a firm's production function. There are several plausible reasons for this.
There may be spillovers of technology from one firm to another; specialisa-

tion of production may occur, lowering costs; and follower firms may benefit from the standard-setting and market testing that the leader performs.

Perhaps surprisingly it has been US economists who have made the running in pointing to the importance of fixed investment and technology for high growth. The original contribution of US economist Dale Jorgenson in the 1960s gave us the modern neoclassical theory of investment. As is well known, the basic version of this theory states that the rates of savings and investment are irrelevant to growth. But now Jorgenson and his co-worker Ralph Landau have reassessed this view, reopening the question of whether technology can be regarded as exogenous – a disembodied input separate from the supply of new capital goods (Jorgenson and Landau, 1989).

While Jorgenson's own position is equivocal – he argues that the productivity element in the growth accounting equation has gained in importance, and is silent on the capital–productivity nexus, Landau stresses the endogeneities which make any accounting for growth hazardous: 'Technical change itself is largely determined by capital investment (human and physical) as well as by R&D' (*ibid.*, p. 503).[4] Landau (1992) further argues (against the Samuel Brittan view set out earlier) that investment is quite likely to be less than optimal because heightened risk and uncertainty have shortened pay-back periods. Indeed this has occurred just as technology has lengthened gestation periods for capital supply. Thus 'supply is no longer assured even if demand is stimulated' (*ibid.,* p. 56).

In the opinion of these authors, technology has accentuated the opportunities of capital investment to increase productivity simultaneously with heightening the risk that individual companies may not themselves be able to appropriate the gains from investment. This view is supported by economists working on technological trends (Mowery and Rosenberg, 1989, p. 236).

If these spillovers can be demonstrated to be widespread and important, they cut across the inconclusive empirical debate on new growth theory over the causal influence of investment on growth (de Long and Summers, 1992; Clarke, 1993; Outton and Young, 1996). The existence of spillovers provides an *a priori* argument that investment should be encouraged beyond the usual private marginal return condition.

RISK, INVESTMENT AND TYPES OF INVESTMENT

The existence of business risk presents a complementary argument that the economy might be well served by an investment rate higher than the private optimum. Marginal investments, while not acceptable in terms of private risk, may nevertheless be justifiable on welfare grounds, since society as a whole can avoid borrower and lender risk of default (Meltzer, 1989). Capital investment should be pushed beyond the point of zero private risk-adjusted return.

Empirical evidence provides some support for the view that demand risk depresses investment (Artus and Muet, 1990; Driver and Moreton, 1992; Price, 1995). This suggests the need to stabilise expectations and to arrange incentives which will counter the negative effect of risk on private investment. Investment incentives tend to have large deadweight losses, so it is important to identify the categories of investment which are most affected by risk. We will focus here on the two main categories used in European business surveys: expansionary investment, including new products, and efficiency investment, which generally involves technology to reduce labour or material inputs.[5]

Capital investment responds to demand and cost pressures. In theory, market signals will provide information on the best response, with companies allocating their capital budgets in a way which makes the marginal return from a unit of efficiency investment just equal to that on a unit of enlarged capacity. This theoretical reasoning abstracts, however from both risk and spillover, as argued below.

Efficiency investment is less risky for firms and probably has quicker payback. It relies more on engineering cost estimation than on gauging demand, i.e. more on local knowledge. Potentially offsetting this are spillover effects which have ambiguous influences depending on whether technological or market influences dominate. Technological spillover of benefits will cause firms to be more cautious in development work. On the market side, if there are significant costs in pioneering and testing new markets the expansionary type of investment may be constrained. The business literature is rich in its description of influences that affect the appropriability of private profit and which therefore suggest that private business decisions on the type of investment may be biased (Porter, 1988). On my reading of this literature and the associated literature on appropriability of various types of R&D expenditure, investment seems likely to be biased towards the cost-cutting type.

These considerations suggest that in an environment of market risk, firms may be tempted to invest a higher proportion of resources in efficiency investment as compared with expansionary investment than would be the case in a less risky environment. From the firm's point of view this may be a rational response, but it drives a wedge between the interests of the individual firm and the economy or society as a whole.[6] Some readers will find the distinction between the two types of investment irrelevant: cost-cutting investment ought in theory to spur expansion via vigorous price-cutting. Nevertheless, a casual look at the data is enough to dispel the notion of a simple link between efficiency investment and growth. UK manufacturing productivity boomed in the 1980s but manufacturing output stagnated. In part this was due to the level of rent extracted by the remaining workforce. But the same phenomenon affected the USA in this period, masked only by growth in the computer industry (Clarida and Hickok, 1993). And the worker rent story simply does not apply in the US context. It appears that higher efficiency investment in the US led to an increased proportion of price-sensitive goods in exports but a reduction in the proportion of quality-sensitive capital goods which are characterised by learning by doing and economies of scale. Cutting the critical mass of an industry and excessive capital deepening has also been criticised as destroying value even from the standpoint of private firms (Clayton and Carroll, 1995).

EXPANSIONARY INVESTMENT OVER THE CYCLE

The issue of which type of investment is appropriate is partly one of timing. Expansionary investment tends to rise in a boom in relation to other types of investment (efficiency or replacement). But the change in gear is often not effected until companies are sufficiently sure of impending recovery to risk investments that have to be validated by market growth. Indeed Figure 9.2 shows that the proportion of expansionary capital authorisations is strongly associated with contemporaneous capital shortage.

This caution may be rational from an individual firm's point of view, but it destabilises the economy and ends in deflation. Some evidence on firm behaviour in this regard is presented in Table 9.3, where the proportion of

Table 9.3 Explanation of expansionary investment. Sample period maximum consistent with data availability: 1980.1–1987.4

t-statistics in parentheses		
Dependent variable EXP		
CONSTANT	0.292	(4.55)
EXP(−1)	0.505	(7.88)
CAPSHORT	0.424	(8.64)
CAPSHORT*UNCER	−0.181	(−2.49)
R^2 = 0.96		
D.W. = 2.34		
LM(1) = 0.9 (1.27)		
LM(4) = 1.8 (4.24)		
J-B = 0.83 (2)		

Key: EXP: proportion of responses giving reason for authorization as expansionary investment (CBI data); CAPSHORT: percentage replies with output constrained by plant capacity (CBI data); UNCERT: dispersion across twelve forecasting teams of one-year ahead GDP forecasts (Investor Chronicle data, as transformed in Driver and Moreton 1992) *Diagnostics:* D.W.: Durban–Watson statistic; LM(1), (4): LM test for first- and fourth-order autocorrelation, *F*-form; J-B: Jarque-Bera statistic for normality of residuals distributed as $\chi^2(2)$

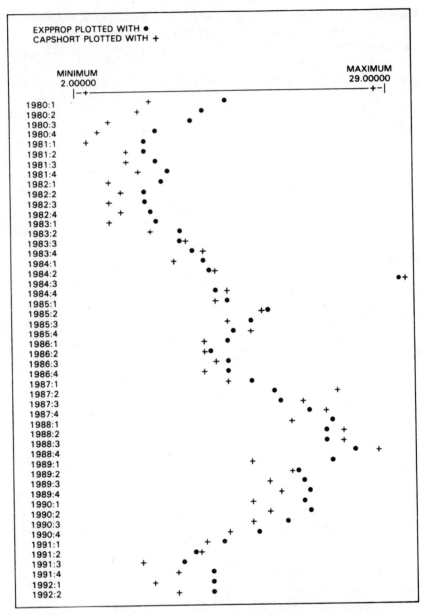

Figure 9.2 Time plot of expansionary investment intention proportion (EXPROP) and
proportion experiencing capacity shortage (CAPSHORT)
Source: CBI Industrial Trends Survey.

expansionary investment is related to capital shortage, and capital shortage interacted with demand uncertainty. A significant negative interaction effect is present, suggesting that firms will not react decisively to expansionary signals in the presence of uncertainty.

From these figures, a doubling of the uncertainty index when the capacity shortage is at its mean level would virtually eliminate the expansionary effect. The implications of all this are serious for employment prospects. The spectre of capital shortage unemployment is haunting Europe and the United Kingdom. By this is meant unemployment that, whatever its original cause (obsolescence, wages, demand shocks), cannot be resolved in reasonable time simply by altering relative factor prices. A significant increase in expansionary investment is a necessary condition for resolving unemployment: nevertheless stimulus provided to the private sector to engage in that expansion does not appear to date to have been markedly successful.

POLICY MEASURES

Investment is a proper subject for intervention, whether by regulation, tax or direction. This is because business risk biases investment below what it would be in the absence of risk. (Aiginger, 1987; Driver and Moreton, 1992.) Despite textbook claims, there is no clear way of diversifying risk since full information is not available to investors and in any case managers, who make the decisions, are vulnerable to bankruptcy. This makes companies shirk commitments that society as a whole would be happy to bear. Furthermore the benefits of large capital projects frequently have spin-off benefits which do not enter into private calculations of the profit that is appropriable by the investors.

More investment is needed; but only more investment of the right sort. In this paper we have reached some conclusions on this. Equipment investment raises the growth rate more than might be thought, because of spin-offs. On the other hand, equipment investment of the cost-cutting kind may take undue precedence over expansionary investment at times of uncertain demand. Academic consensus is that tax and subsidy measures generally only affect the timing of investment, rather than its quantity. This suggests a focus on the timing of different types of investment to satisfy the objective of stable and sustainable growth.

I have suggested that the timing of the relative proportions of expansionary investment and efficiency investment is suboptimal. In particular, too little expansionary investment takes place in anticipation of the upturn. These are important points for the design of policy on investment. It appears, for example, that it would be wrong simply to attempt to stabilise investment, though stabilisation may be necessary for the small-firms sector that acts in an uncoordinated risk-accepting way. For the important large-

195

firm sector, the aim should be to accelerate expansionary investment in advance of output recovery. In the United Kingdom, a countercyclical investment programme – the Accelerated Project Scheme – was introduced in 1975 with some success, though it did not focus on expansionary investment.

A more systematic approach might involve a variant on the Swedish Investment Fund System. Although primarily intended in Sweden as a stabilisation system, it can also be used to favour certain categories of investment and to alter their timing (Pontusson, 1992; Taylor, 1982: Comment). The essence of the approach, illustrated in Figure 9.3, is that companies voluntarily place profits in a tax-free fund, to be released selectively at later periods.

Given the aim of accelerating expansionary investment, the release of funds could be conditional on a high proportion of this type of investment in advance of the upturn. The scheme does not have to be self-financing and can incorporate permanent subsidies to particular types of investments that are thought to generate large spin-offs.

The introduction of an IFS in Britain was last considered in the mid-1970s when the Machine Tools Economic Development Committee of NEDO supported the proposal. Ironically the resulting NEDO report (NEDO, 1978), while recognising the intrinsic merit of the scheme, rejected it because of the then operation of free depreciation. Introducing the report, Lord Roll suggested that the scheme might be relevant in Britain 'if the tax regime were to change'. Given that these changes – initiated by Nigel Lawson in the mid-1980s – have now been implemented, it presents us with an opportunity to implement an effective capital investment policy. There will be pressure to introduce automatic accelerated depreciation provision to encourage investment generally.[7] However, this should be avoided. Investment is a proper

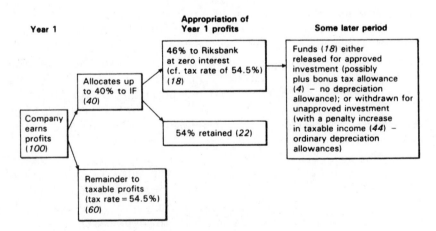

Figure 9.3 The Swedish investment reserve fund system
Source: NEDO (1978).

196

subject for planning and coordination. The recent history of British economic performance suggests misallocation of private investment reflecting extremes of herd behaviour, on the one hand, and risk-aversion on the other.

Elsewhere I have proposed an alternative scheme for encouraging investment in advance of an upturn (Driver, 1996). This aims to take advantage of the existence of risk-loving firms in the economy, i.e. the scheme rewards existing risk-takers rather than persuading risk-averse firms to increase their exposure to risk. Firms would be retrospectively awarded incentives if investment put in place was greater than some target (either historical or comparative), but at the same time was insufficient to produce overcapacity in the industry, i.e. if rival firms were to invest too little. Despite the difficulties in defining the target and the reference industries, the scheme has the advantage that incentives are only paid when the marginal value of investment is positive. The scheme could also increase the risk for rival companies of *not investing* if permanent market share advantages accrued to the investing firms.

CONCLUSIONS

Capital investment affects the chances of sustainable growth. Put differently, the conditions for growth depend not only on labour market considerations, but on the confidence that is both signalled and generated by capital investment.

The investment decision is one in which there is more than usual scope for private and social interests to diverge: consequently it is the arena where state involvement is likely to bear greatest fruit. The resistance to giving priority to investment probably hinges on a distrust of corporatism and the replacement of individual by collective decision-making. However the pendulum has swung so far in that direction in the United Kingdom that the clock is no longer ticking.

The policy lesson is that for risky long-run investments, markets may not capture the social rate of return any more than is the case with new technology. If these externalities or spillovers are strong there is a compelling case for public support and direction to be given to fixed investment. The downside is that this public support will be also be misguided and wasteful. A balanced approach to these concerns is surely possible.

NOTES

1 Hourly labour costs in manufacturing are still a quarter lower in the United Kingdom than the EC average, partly reflecting low non-wage costs.
2 For cross-country comparisons, the net figure is preferable. As the United Kingdom has tended to have a higher ratio of shorter-lived assets, that will inflate the gross figure compared with other countries. The net figures are even less favourable to the United Kingdom (*European Economy*, 1989).

3 Brittan abstracts from the starting point of mass unemployment with greatly increased capital intensity of production. What scale of output increase is automatically facilitated by a conquest of (wage) inflation? Is it likely to be sufficient to make a dent in unemployment? We have been around this track before (Bean, 1989). When unemployment is due to capital shortage, it cannot be resolved by labour market flexibility because labour can only be substituted for capital on new projects. Expansion of the capital stock is needed at a very rapid rate if unemployment is to be contained, but that expansion is constrained by demand uncertainty.

4 This point has, of course, been made repeatedly over many decades by writers from heterodox schools such as Cambridge (UK) and by other political economists.

5 These categories should not be confused with the asset class of capital investment – equipment or structures – introduced earlier. Cost-saving investment may well require moving to a greenfield site and expansionary investment may imply an even higher capital intensity.

6 This last point has greatest force at a time of mass unemployment when there is no indication that the pressure of unemployment is performing any transformative role. The appropriate calculation is then not the savings made by the firm or the public sector on efficiency investment, but the difference between these savings and the extra tax burden of incremental unemployment. Does it make social sense to have automatic ticket barriers at tube stations, or self-service at petrol stations? Studies done by NEDO economists during the 1980s suggest that this difference is frequently negative, supporting the case for marginal employment subsidies. Although often unremarked, such subsidies also have the effect of enhancing the return from expansionary as opposed to efficiency investment, since there is only limited substitutability between labour and capital. Furthermore, in a world where much unemployment results from a mismatch of qualities inherent in the unemployed and those demanded by employers, those ejected from low-productivity jobs have a high probability of exit from the labour market, with no transformative gain to the economy.

7 The Investment Fund System in Sweden was abolished by the Social Democrats as part of tax reform in 1989–90 as the emphasis shifted towards a general encouragement of investment through a reduction in profit taxation.

REFERENCES

Aiginger, K. (1987) *Production and Decision Theory under Uncertainty*, Oxford: Basil Blackwell.

Allsopp, C., Jenkinson, T. and Morris D. (1992) 'The Assessment: Macroeconomic policy in the 1980s', *Oxford Review of Economic Policy*, vol. 7 no. 3.

Artus, P. and Muet, P.A. (1990) *Investment and Factor Demand*, Amsterdam: North Holland.

Bean, C. (1989) 'Capital shortage', *Economic Policy*, April, pp. 11–54

Bond, S. and Jenkinson, T. (1996) 'The assessment: Investment performance and policy', *Oxford Review of Economic Policy*, vol. 12, no. 2, pp. 1–29.

Clanide, R.H. and Hickok, F. (1993) 'US manufacturing and the reindustrialization debate', *World Economy*, March, pp. 173–92.

Clark, P. (1993) 'Tax incentives and equipment investment', *Brookings Papers on Economic Activity* vol. I, pp. 317–48.

Clayton, C. and Carroll, C. (1995) 'Building business: Evidence from Europe and North America', *Panorama*, EU.

de Long, J.B. and Summers, L.H. (1992) 'Equipment investment and economic growth: How strong is the nexus?', *Brookings Papers on Economic Activity* vol. 2, pp. 157–211.

Driver, C. (1996) 'Tightening the reins: The capacity stance of UK manufacturing firms 1976–95', in J. Michie and J. Grieve Smith (eds) *Creating Industrial Capacity: towards full employment*, Oxford: OUP.

Driver, C. and Moreton, D. (1992) *Investment, Expectations and Uncertainty*, Oxford: Basil Blackwell.

Jorgenson, D. and Landau, R. (1989) *Technology and Capital Formation*, Cambridge, Mass.: MIT Press.

Kitson, M. and Michie, J. (1996) 'Britain's industrial performance since 1960: Underinvestment and relative decline', *The Economic Journal* vol. 106, no. 434, pp. 196–212.

Landau, R. (1992) 'Capital investment: Key to competitiveness and growth', *Brookings Economic Review*, Summer, pp. 52–6.

Matthews, R. Feinstein, C.H. and Odling-Smee, J.C. (1982) *British Economic Growth 1856–1973*, Oxford: Clarendon.

Meltzer, A. (1989) *Keynes' Monetary Theory*, Cambridge: CUP.

Milne, A. (1991) 'Non-Manufacturing Investment and UK aggregate demand', *Economic Outlook*, June, London Business School.

Mowery, D.C. and Rosenberg, N. (1989) *Technology and the Pursuit of Economic Growth*, Cambridge: Cambridge University Press.

National Economic Development Office (NEDO) (1978) *Investment Reserve Schemes*, London: NEDO Books.

Oulton, N. and Young, G. (1996) 'How high is the social rate of return to investment?', *Oxford Review of Economic Policy*, vol. 12, no. 2.

Pontusson, J. (1992) *The Limits of Social Democracy: Investment policies in Sweden*, Ithaca, N.Y.: Cornell University Press.

Porter, M.E. (1988) 'The technological dimension of competitive strategy', in R.A. Burgelman and M.A. Maidique (eds) *Strategic Management of Technological Innovation*, Homewood, Ill.: Irwin.

Price, S. (1995) 'Aggregate uncertainty, capacity utilisation and manufacturing investment', *Applied Economics*, vol. 27, pp. 147–54.

Taylor, J.B. (1982) 'The Swedish investment funds system as a stabilisation policy rule', *Brookings Papers on Economic Activity*, vol. 1, pp. 57–105.

10

THE STOCK MARKET AND PROBLEMS OF CORPORATE CONTROL IN THE UNITED KINGDOM[1]

Derek Morris

INTRODUCTION

A major and long-standing source of controversy in the analysis of the United Kingdom's economic performance has been the role of the City, and more specifically the London Stock Exchange, in influencing industrial performance. On the one hand the City represents one of the two major financial centres in the world, provides highly knowledgeable and flexible markets for all manner of financial instruments, includes some of the largest investing institutions in the world and, in conventional terms, has one of the most efficient stock exchanges anywhere providing an easily accessible market for corporate control. This in turn is seen by many as a key discipline on industrial companies' managers and a crucial mechanism for allocating or reallocating resources to their most efficient uses. On this view the City is not only a major contributor to GNP and overseas earnings but a significant and more pervasive contributor to economic welfare.

An alternative view is that the City has had a baleful influence on industrial performance over many decades. On this view the City originally grew as an adjunct to trading rather than production, has been dominated by individuals and institutions with little or no understanding of industry, its workings or its financial needs, is to only a limited extent a source of funds, is often poor at evaluating companies or their opportunities and is obsessed with immediate profit at the expense of successful longer-term development. It is frequently pointed out that a number of countries, most noticeably Germany and Japan, have been notably more successful without any comparably developed institutional arrangements to match the market for corporate control in the United Kingdom.

Many in the financial, business, academic and political areas have addressed this controversy, theoretically, empirically and, in many cases, purely speculatively but with little sign of resolution. This no doubt in part reflects the fact that the issue is unavoidably political, being concerned with the disposition and use of power and the consequences for the level and distribution of economic welfare. In part it also reflects quite severe problems of data, methodology and interpretation in analysing the issue, to which we refer later. Whatever the cause, the result is to generate serious policy dilemmas concerning how companies should best be governed, whether or how stock market behaviour should be regulated, what role shareholders can or should play in controlling companies and in particular whether takeovers should be made more or less difficult.

Our purpose here is primarily to review various relevant strands of literature and analyses which only partly intersect, to see what can be distilled concerning this issue, looking at both theoretical considerations and evidence. We will, however, in the course of this, make reference to ongoing analysis concerning the vexed question of 'short-termism', i.e. the allegation that in some way stock markets of the type existing in London inhibit managers from acting in the best long-term interests of their companies.

Our approach is first to summarise briefly some relevant recent literature on forms of corporate governance and control. This starting point, examined below, looks at different types and structures of company ownership and the basic considerations which are likely to be important in determining the interaction of the industrial and financial sectors of an economy. This chapter then looks in more detail at the motives, consequences and effectiveness of the takeover mechanism in a developed stock market such as exists in the US and the United Kingdom. We attempt to draw out from a large number of different studies and indeed different approaches to this issue some reasonably well supported working conclusions concerning the role of takeovers and their consequences. The chapter moves on to the more specific but much less well understood area of short-termism. It looks at two models of rational short-termist pressures which have appeared in the literature and then provides some new perspectives on this issue. The section also reviews the evidence on short-termism, such as it is, and brings out some of the methodological problems in identifying short-term pressures or its consequences in any rigorous or systematic manner.

The chapter then looks at both the traditional and more recent analysis of the economic behaviour of professional managers, their objectives, activities, the constraints on them and resulting performance. This throws new light on the welfare implications of different types of corporate ownership and control. A key element in the paper is then an attempt to integrate these insights with the earlier analysis of short-termism. Some empirical work that may be interpreted as relevant to the overall picture that emerges of the impact of the stock market on industrial performance is then examined which points the way forward in exploring further these ideas. Conclusions are then presented.

201

CORPORATE GOVERNANCE: SOME BASIC CONSIDERATIONS

Not only elementary economics textbooks but many more advanced analyses of industrial behaviour view firms as individual and indivisible decision-taking units where the decision-taker owns the firm, controls its resources and decisions and receives the profits or accepts the losses made. In practice much of the industrial assets base in the United Kingdom is owned and controlled by large, and sometimes enormously large, companies characterised by many thousands of employees, tens or even hundreds of product lines, multidivisional structures, complex organisational structures, dispersed decision-taking, internal planning mechanisms for allocating resources rather than market coordination and a high degree of separation between the owners who have a legal title to the assets of the company and the managers who direct its activities.[2] This raises a number of questions, not least why in Coase's (1937) famous question there are such 'islands of conscious power' in a sea of market transactions, why some resource allocations should occur through market transactions while others (in some cases identical ones) occur through planning and direction internal to a firm, and how efficiency is affected by these considerations. Our present concern is a narrower and subsidiary one, namely the different possible ways in which the various functions of a firm are carried out, how they are integrated, and through what institutional arrangements.

We start by presenting brief working definitions of ownership and control.[3] *Ownership* lies in (i) the legal power to appoint managers and determine their remuneration, and (ii) the bearing of, or reassignment through contracts of residual (uninsurable) risk, the latter conceived of as the surplus (positive or negative) accruing after meeting all contractual obligations. *Management* lies in the direct control and immediate direction of resources, human and otherwise within a company, in the context of spot market transactions and contracts with agents external to the firm and utilising various types of contract, usually incomplete in the sense that they do not define all possible eventualities, responsibilities, etc., within the firm. Thus even though many people are both owners and managers simultaneously, the conceptual distinction is clear.

In practice the distinction is rendered less clear by the existence of directors on the senior board of a company. These are appointed by the owners and may be thought of as their representatives charged with the responsibility of ensuring that the owners' interests are maximised. Much has been written recently about the need for more non-executive directors who will pursue this responsibility more effectively and more single-mindedly than has often been the case in the past. This is primarily because many if not most directors are executive and hold the most senior managerial responsibilities for directing and controlling resources. In the case of the single owner-manager-director this creates no problem, but where owners and managers are different and their interests diverge, considerable tensions can arise concerning the proper role and duties of the board. The most obvious such tensions arise where directors are inefficient managers or determine their own remuneration. Still further complications can arise where, as is often argued, directors should, either on ethical grounds or efficiency grounds, try to take into account or even represent the interests of other so-called 'stake-holders' in a company besides the owners, e.g., employees, suppliers, customers, etc.

Despite these complications we can use these simple definitions to identify two main characteristics of companies that serve to delineate differing broad classes of corporate 'governance', where this catch-all term is used to span the whole ownership-control nexus: These are, first, the extent of overlap of ownership and managerial control and, second, the degree of concentration of ownership. While in principle we might define a third, namely the extent to which individual owners have their own direct representation on company boards, in general this is closely related to ownership concentration. Where the latter is high, typically large shareholders will have one or more nominees on a board; where ownership is highly dispersed this is unlikely to occur.

These two fundamental characteristics potentially generate four broad types of corporate governance:

1 Concentrated ownership with high management–ownership overlap. This is the governance structure of the typical unquoted company in the United Kingdom and the US. Most if not all of the shares of such companies are held, directly or indirectly, by a small number of shareholders who are also directors holding key management positions.[4]

2 Concentrated ownership with relatively little overlap between ownership and managerial control. This is the typical form of governance in Japan and most European countries. While there may be a large number of shareholders and an active stock market, for many companies the majority of shares are held by a relatively small number of institutional shareholders, including banks, other financial and industrial companies, suppliers and customers. Many of these will have directors on the boards of the companies in which they hold equity and this general structure is frequently characterised by a series of interlocking shareholdings and directorships.

3 Unconcentrated ownership with relatively little overlap between ownership and management. This is the typical structure for quoted companies in the United Kingdom and US. Individuals and institutions tend to hold relatively small proportions of the shares of any one company, and frequently operate their dispersed investments on a portfolio basis, i.e. spreading investment across a range of shares with different risk–return

characteristics.[5] Managers may well hold shares in their company but these holdings will typically represent only a small proportion of the total shares issued.

4 The final category will be of less interest in our discussion, namely un-concentrated ownership with high management–ownership overlap. This typically applies in partnerships where many or all of those involved in an undertaking each hold a portion of the overall equity. The under-taking is fully owned by the managers but no individual or group has a disproportionately large share.

Before going on to examine some of the differences between these struc-tures, three comments are necessary. First, in some cases a statistically small shareholding may for most of the time be quite sufficient to provide substan-tial ownership rights. A shareholding of 2 or 3 per cent, particularly if held by managers, may in normal circumstances repeatedly provide majorities at annual shareholders' meetings, partly because many dispersed shareholders regularly decline to get involved and also because many who do frequently assign voting rights to a proxy established by the largest shareholders. This may of course break down in difficult or more controversial circumstances.

Second, although the management–ownership overlap, or lack of it, is important, from the point of view of objectives and incentives it is also important to identify the proportion of a manager's remuneration depend-ent on his or her ownership of shares or, directly or indirectly, on share performance, for example via share options, profit or share price-related bonuses, etc. There may be much greater convergence of owners' and man-agers' interests where 80 per cent of the latter's remuneration comes from share-related sources, even though the manager holds only a very small fraction of the shares than cases where the managerial share holding is higher but is not the main source of managerial remuneration.

Third, the four-way classification of corporate governance above, and the typical real-world counterparts mentioned, may appear too dichotomous in that, in principle, there could be a whole spectrum of degrees of ownership concentration and management–ownership overlap, generating a highly heterogeneous pattern of governance. In practice this is largely not the case. While exceptions exist, most undertakings fall rather clearly into one or other of the categories described. This is not an historical accident. There are quite powerful economic forces which make intermediate combinations of ownership concentration and management–ownership overlap relatively non-viable. These are most easily understood in terms of the basic pro-position that owners must either have a fairly high degree of control *or* a high degree of marketability of their ownership rights. This is because, in the absence of both, an owner has no protection or strategy for dealing with poor performance and poor returns. *Ex hypothesi*, the owners cannot step in to change performance as they have no control, nor can they easily sell the ownership right to escape the consequences of any further deterioration. While it cannot be said that there will never be any attraction to such investments, which have characteristics similar to many types of pure gamble, the combination of lock-in and lack of control make this an unlikely basis for corporate governance.

Concentrated ownership structures of the type described above typically confer powerful control functions, either because, as in unquoted companies, the owners are the managers or, as in countries such as Germany and Japan, directors representing major shareholders sit on company boards. Control is also exercised in partnerships. Unconcentrated ownership of the type reflected in the UK and US stock markets does not readily provide influence or control, but such rights are tradable in a highly liquid market. Other theoretical combinations do not provide the necessary functions. For example, the issuing of small parcels of shares to a large number of investors in unquoted companies is very rare. Managers may hold some shares for incentive reasons, inheritance sometimes results in a number of individuals uninvolved in the company obtaining an incomes stream, and government incentives for this type of investment exist, but this does not alter the basic premise. Some companies do have a substantial minority shareholder, typically another company, but this does not greatly reduce the concentration of shareholding and is almost always associated with a presence on the board. Even here many unquoted companies see the existence of such a shareholding as a first step, desirable or otherwise, towards quotation, primarily because the shareholder in question may wish to have the opportunity to sell, or may at some point sell to others who wish to have such opportunities. While in theory a majority shareholder group can block this, the presence of minority shareholders on boards, and the scope for competitors, suppliers or customers to become involved may make this difficult.

An alternative hybrid, namely moderate ownership concentration with moderate management–ownership overlap, does exist but is again relatively rare. Typically this involves a company which was unquoted being floated but with the original entrepreneur or family retaining a sizeable grip on the management's structure and composition. In effect most shareholders have marketability, and the small number who might face constraints on this because of the size of their holdings retain a significant measure of management control.

It is worth adding that we have in the above largely ignored another distinction, often made, between individual and institutional shareholdings. This is not unimportant, particularly if it can be demonstrated that institutional investors can get better information, operate more efficient portfolios, exercise superior investment skill or respond to different incentives, though none of these suggestions is uncontroversial. But the main control-type distinction is between concentrated shareholding generating ownership control and unconcentrated holdings permitting managerial control. Highly dispersed shareholdings are both compatible with and just as much associated with institutional shareholdings as with individual ones.

Corporate governance structures involving concentrated ownership representation and/or control in quoted companies of the type for example generally observed in Germany, we refer to (following recent terminology) as 'inside control'. Dispersed ownership of quoted companies in contrast we refer to as 'outside control'. It should be stressed that day-to-day control in the latter case is by managers and the more traditional term for such a structure is 'managerial control'. This, however, sidesteps the crucial question of how much discretion managers have when dissatisfied shareholders can sell shares, perhaps precipitating a takeover and a change of management. Hence outside control is quite different in form and effect from inside control but none the less provides some type of ultimate control for owners.

The concentrated shareholding we typically find in unquoted companies we term 'entrepreneurial control' and, though we have little to say on it, the typical partnership format we term 'joint control'.

Though we will have cause to refer to entrepreneurial control later, most recent analysis and comment has concerned the differences between, and respective virtues and deficiencies of, insider and outsider control systems. That concentration of ownership is a crucial aspect is seen from the fact that of the 200 largest companies in Germany, nearly 90 per cent have at least one shareholder with a stake of at least 25 per cent of issued equity. In the United Kingdom in two-thirds of the largest 200 companies no single shareholder holds more than 10 per cent of the equity.[6] In addition, however, another feature of insider control in Germany and Japan is reciprocal shareholdings. It is not uncommon for 20 per cent of the shares of a company to be held by other firms in which the company itself holds shares. In the United Kingdom such arrangements are virtually non-existent.[7]

These differences in ownership structure and the differences in board composition to which they give rise generate at least three main differences in behaviour or efficiency characteristics. First, they generate quite different agency relations. When one or more principals (shareholders) recruit one or more agents (managers) to act for them, there is a fundamental agency problem in trying to establish a remuneration schedule which will induce the agents to act as the shareholder would want, in a world where the agent's actions or efforts are not fully observable and company performance is the outcome jointly of the agents' input and the state of the world in which they find themselves. In order to ensure the same profit maximisation strategy that the principals would themselves pursue, the agents must, as the principals themselves would, keep all of any additional profit arising from additional effort. The principals can only be rewarded, therefore, via a lump-sum payment from the agents (as for example in a franchise arrangement) if the contract is to generate efficient incentives. This, however, loads all risk on the agents, because the principal gets a guaranteed sum in all states of the world. This is not efficient from the risk-sharing point of view, particularly if, as is likely, managers are risk-averse because all their income is linked to their job, whereas shareholders are risk-neutral because they can diversify across a number of companies.[8]

The two key factors in this are information, i.e. how well can the principals observe, monitor and measure the input of agents; and risk, i.e. how well is it distributed across the parties. In principle, inside control will reduce and perhaps even eliminate the information asymmetry. Under outside control this asymmetry entails a need for some signalling mechanisms by which managers can indicate their views of company prospects and in a manner such that shareholders can systematically attach credibility to those views. In practice much of this function appears to be borne by earnings announcements and dividends. The effectiveness of this, and possible distortions to which it gives rise are considered below. Against the informational advantages of inside control the greater concentration of shareholdings reduces the extent to which risk is diversified away, though it does, at the same time, tend to align the risk exposure of shareholders and managers. Where inherent risk is high, for example for small, single product and/or speculative investment companies, the latter effect may well make outside control preferable.[9] But many such companies will not in any event be quoted on any stock market. Where companies are large enough and diversified enough to reduce the need for portfolio-based diversification of risk, and this appears to be the typical case for quoted companies, then the superior informational characteristics of inside control will tend to make it the preferable form of corporate governance.

The second main difference follows directly from the superior monitoring which inside control permits. Because deteriorating performance and its causes can more easily be detected, corrective action can be instigated earlier, can occur more gradually and with shareholders being better informed in the process. Outside control may result in longer delay before deteriorating performance is observed, indeed strenuous efforts may be made to conceal it; a short-, or even medium-term response by shareholders may be difficult or impossible, apart from selling shares; and corrective action if it occurs may well only be via the threat of takeover.[10] Modest or piecemeal restructuring which would benefit shareholders may not be achievable and significant restructuring may not be feasible without ownership change. This is in sharp contrast to inside control where there typically is little if any correlation between industrial restructuring and/or management control on the one hand, and ownership on the other. In Germany, for example, hostile takeover is extremely rare[11] but it is far from obvious that this has been disadvantageous to the performance or development of German industry. Clearly it does not imply that there is no effective disciplinary mechanism for ensuring managerial effectiveness.

The third main difference lies in the consequences of the board structure associated with each type of control. Inside control typically involves the presence on boards of directors appointed by the owners. This means:

1 that effective ownership lies largely in the corporate sector itself, whereas most shares in the United Kingdom are owned by financial institutions, in particular pension funds, life assurance companies and investment trusts.

2 Because such directors are representatives of other companies they act for organisations which are quite likely to have an ownership stake for many years, and perhaps generations. This may well generate a longer-term perspective than in the typical UK or US case where such representation is relatively rare.

3 The existence of two-tier boards, with the supervisory board having representatives of employees, trade unions and, in many cases, suppliers and purchasers, means that governance reflects a wider group of 'stakeholders' than just owners, thereby reducing the extent of conflict between shareholders and other parties and the inefficiencies in operation to which such conflicts can lead. A broader spectrum of advice is available and this all reinforces the longer-term stability of inside control.[12]

In contrast, in the United Kingdom, emphasis is placed on the protection of shareholders' rights and maintenance of a fair market in those rights. This can directly curtail the dissemination of information to shareholders, because of the need to ensure that none are discriminated against through receiving it later than others (insider dealing), and to employees and others because of the potential for conflict with the owners who alone are represented on the board.

In many respects these differences appear to favour inside control systems. However, to expand on an earlier conclusion, it seems better to conclude that inside and outside control have different strengths and weaknesses. Outside control may well be best where diversification of risk is important, or where there are divergent views on the risk–return characteristics of company investment projects. The superiority of inside control appears to lie in the fact that it is more appropriate to the conditions that actually face most developed industrial sectors, namely diversified companies relying on complex long-term relationships with customers and suppliers, needing to develop and retain skilled labour and attempting to identify and exploit new products and new models on the strength of those relationships and human skills.

Before proceeding, reference should be made to entrepreneurial control in unquoted companies. In most of the above respects these should function in a manner similar to inside control ones. Agency problems are minimised though potentially at some cost in terms of less risk reduction; and monitoring and adjustment of behaviour in the light of performance is likely to be easier and less discontinuous than in outside control. Control lies within the corporate sector and may be exercised in the light of longer-term perspectives and greater stability, though this may well be family-based rather than enterprise-based. Against this there is little if any institutional representation of shareholders other than the owner-managers, and minority shareholders, who may often have received shares through inheritance, constitute a pressure on management to maintain a dividend stream that would otherwise be unnecessary.

If for most large diversified companies inside control is likely to be superior, it must be asked why outside control as found in the United Kingdom and US does not gradually disappear, to be replaced by a more efficient form of governance. As we shall see, however, there may well be quite strong economic forces that prevent outside control mechanisms evolving into inside control (though EC deregulation may well push inside control in the opposite direction).

We conclude therefore that there are agency, monitoring and representation problems in the governance structure of the typical UK quoted company which would in principle militate against corporate efficiency. Support for the system of governance of these companies must therefore be based on the view that an active stock market provides an effective discipline on managers to organise and develop their companies efficiently. The primary way in which this will occur is via the threat of takeover as a result of poor performance, and it is to this that we now turn.

TAKEOVERS AND STOCK MARKET EFFICIENCY

Theoretical considerations

The pure theory of takeover or merger is both straightforward and familiar. If managers of companies are fully efficient in their use of resources, act only in the best interests of their shareholders and if the stock market is fully efficient in the use of all information,[13] then mergers will occur if and only if they generate increased market power and/or efficiency gains. The latter may encompass rationalisation of production, economies of scale or scope[14] in production distribution or research and development, better economies in obtaining finance, reduction of risk, better information about the market-place or reduction in transactions costs.[15] While none of these gains necessarily require a merger, as opposed to internal growth, in most cases merger is quicker, less risky, avoids temporary increases in excess capacity and/or competitive pressure and can also offer a low-cost way of overcoming barriers to entry.

While some mergers no doubt occur for such reasons, even at a purely theoretical level, we need to take account of at least two other interrelated elements: the assumptions on which the above picture is based may not hold;

and there can be other reasons for mergers to occur. With regard to the first, if managers are not fully efficient then, given that the share price reflects this, there is scope for another company capable of improving performance to take over the firm and realise a higher valuation. These *allocational* takeovers, or the threat of them, are seen by many as the prime means by which an efficient stock market in corporate control enforces efficient behaviour on the part of managers. A firm's efficiency, profitability and valuation can drop below their maximum only to the extent that the takeover mechanism has transaction costs associated with it. In most cases, and certainly for all sizeable takeovers, this leeway is likely to be very small.

In a seminal article, Grossman and Hart (1980) suggest that the efficient working of this mechanism may be inhibited by a free-rider problem. If a bid is conditional upon 50 per cent acceptance, then each of a large number of dispersed shareholders has an incentive to reject a bid for an underperforming firm. If the bid fails, no shares are bought and those rejecting the bid lose nothing. If it succeeds, those who accepted obtain the bid price but those who rejected the bid gain the necessarily still higher value of the shares once the new management have eliminated the inefficiencies. Desirable allocational takeovers may therefore fail, weakening, perhaps substantially, the disciplinary role of the stock market. Grossman and Hart go on to show that this problem can be avoided if, after the takeover, the raider, as the majority shareholder, can use this position to transfer wealth to another company in which it is the sole shareholder, diluting the share price of the acquired company and eliminating the gains from free-riding.[16] But such practices are normally prohibited because, while they might have advantages in relation to the takeover mechanism, they could also be used much more generally to extract wealth from minority shareholders, and it is not in practice possible to distinguish for regulatory purposes between such cases.

Other means of overcoming the problem exist in theory; for example, legislation permitting compulsory acquisition of minority stakes post-merger can prevent free-rider gains.[17] But in the United Kingdom this operates only where the main shareholder holds more than 90 per cent, so that in a takeover which gives the acquirer between 50 and 90 per cent of the target company's shares, the free-rider problem remains.[18] Building up a 'toehold' stake at pre-raid prices in principle can generate sufficient profit to cover the cost of paying maximum value in the takeover itself, thereby overcoming the free-rider problem, but building up toe-hold stakes prior to a bid is heavily regulated, as are sudden early morning mass-share acquisitions ('dawn raids'), individuals acting together ('concert parties') and other ways of trying to acquire sizeable holdings at pre-raid prices. Unconditional bids, and the actions of arbitrageurs (who buy up shares at prices that reflect the fair gamble on a takeover succeeding but then acquire sufficient shares to be able actually to influence the result), also affect the free-rider problem but in practice do not overcome it.[19] There can be no presumption therefore that a market for corporate control, however liquid, flexible or informed about fundamental values, will necessarily constitute a mechanism for eliminating managerial inefficiency.[20]

A further motive for takeover emerges if we no longer assume that share prices always reflect 'fundamentals', i.e. that they do not systematically deviate from the present value of the future cash flows appropriable by the shareholders. Testing this directly is difficult because the discount rate used by shareholders in such a calculation is unobservable, may vary through time and will be dependent on the perceived risk of individual shares. The familiar capital asset pricing model (CAPM) predicts that this risk will depend on the covariance of a share's return with the market portfolio, but this may or may not hold in practice and, even if it does, this may also vary through time, with the expected value again being unobservable.

Indirect tests, based on the efficient market hypothesis[21] (EMH) tended to show that investors utilise all past and current share-price information and that share prices reflect all publicly available information but not generally *all* information, i.e. including privately held ('inside') information.[22] This rather reassuring picture has, however, been increasingly questioned in recent years. At a theoretical level Grossman and Stiglitz (1980) have argued that informationally efficient markets are impossible in competitive equilibria. If they did exist then full information on fundamental value could be freely obtained simply by observing share prices, in which case no one would have any incentive to incur the cost of acquiring the necessary information about and from companies themselves. Equilibrium requires that share prices only partly reflect fundamental values, such that there is a return to investigating fundamentals and obtaining superior information which is not fully reflected in the share price. This suggests that in equilibrium there will be some investors (e.g. fund managers in investing institutions) who will engage in acquisition of information and make a superior return sufficient to cover the cost of so doing. One study in the US by Ippolito suggests this result, though most earlier studies in this field found little if any evidence that institutional investors do make higher returns.[23] In any event, share prices are not fully revealing and there can be an incentive to find and buy undervalued companies. These have been termed 'merger bargains' or 'acquisitional takeovers'.

It might be thought that such takeovers would lead to the correction of the mispricing which gave rise to them but this is by no means certain. If a better informed trader makes a bid, then this signals that the fundamental value is higher than the bid price. Except where one needs to liquidate an investment it is not rational to sell to a better informed investor. While in practice this does not inhibit acquisitional takeovers occurring, it may well interfere with the efficient functioning of the stock market.

At a more empirical level, numerous studies have suggested that share prices fluctuate far more than can be explained by shifts in fundamental values, that share prices over-react to good or bad news; and that fads or speculative bubbles occur from time to time which cause share prices substantially to depart from fundamental values, followed by generally rather sharp correction.[24] While few such studies can be said definitively to demonstrate that stock markets are not efficient in pricing shares,[25] the general weight of them leaves little grounds of support for the efficiency hypothesis.

Nor are such results necessarily in conflict with earlier support for at least some forms of the efficient markets hypothesis. Summers (1986) presents a simple model in which share prices are subject to negative serial correlation. This permits excess volatility, over-reaction and bubbles to occur. He then shows that quite substantial valuation errors in this model are consistent with the efficient markets hypothesis not statisically being rejected. As a result, the fact that neither formal tests of the EMH nor presumably, therefore, investors themselves can identify systematic errors which would permit excess returns to be made, does not mean that market valuations do not vary substantially from fundamental values. Finally we may add that, in the absence of fully effective insider trading, however efficient the stock market might be in its use of available information it will not reflect fundamental values where, as is quite likely in many cases, the latter is fully known, if at all, only to 'insider' managers.

In addition to allocational and acquisitional motives for merger as a result of inefficiency and mispricing respectively, a further motive which it appears may play a highly significant role in takeovers is the managerial pursuit of higher salaries, status, power and security through increased size.[26] Many of the problems and costs of growth can be avoided through growth by acquisition, not least those associated with competing market demand away from competitors where growth is via internal expansion in existing markets. The significance of such managerial mergers is three-fold. First, the acquisition of an efficient, well-managed company may be preferable to that of an inefficient one because, although the former does not provide opportunities for post-merger gains, it makes the expansion process much easier and less costly. Second, a company's strategy for growth, in terms of acquisition of resources, personnel, technology etc., market positioning, product development and the like, may in many cases most effectively be pursued via takeover. Third, and somewhat ironically, the factors inhibiting the efficient functioning of allocative and acquisitional takeovers may themselves be weakened in a world where managerial takeovers can occur. The latter may systematically entail bid prices above fundamental value, because the bidder acquires greater size to compensate for the capital loss. With regard to allocative takeovers, this can inhibit free-riding because in the event that the takeover was a value-reducing managerial takeover, the free-rider loses by not having sold out. With regard to acquisitional takeovers, a bid from a better informed investor no longer necessarily implies higher fundamental value and hence it may be perfectly rational to sell. Shares can on this approach still end up incorrectly valued in relation to fundamentals but at too high a level reflecting the premiums which growth-oriented raiders will pay, as opposed to too low a level, reflecting investors' reluctance to sell to more informed bidders. In practice, of course, elements of both types of deviation from present value may exist.[27]

To summarise this section so far, if stock markets are fully efficient in their use of information, and managers, purely pursuing shareholders' interests, are also fully efficient, then mergers may occur in pursuit of market dominance or real efficiency gains available only from the merged entity. In the absence of those conditions, mergers may occur as the result of, and as a discipline on, managerial inefficiency, as a result of misvaluation of share prices, or as a result of managerial pursuit of growth. In terms of social efficiency, we infer first that pursuit of dominance is undesirable, of real efficiency gains desirable; second that stock market mechanisms to correct managerial inefficiency and inaccurate share prices may be inadequate and perhaps substantially so; and third that while growth maximising has traditionally been seen as undesirable because of the non-profit-maximising use of resources it entails, we will have cause to question this conclusion later.

In recent years the list of motives for merger has been extensively added to. Historically conglomerate mergers were seen as a means of reducing risk,[28] but this is an 'uneasy case'[29] given that all such gains to shareholders from merging are equally and more cheaply available by holding an appropriately constructed portfolio of shares in individual companies. It may be that small investors cannot diversify sufficiently to achieve this; or that shareholders have less reliable information on what constitutes the efficient combination of companies in terms of risk and return. In addition, a conglomerate firm will typically experience a lower risk of default which cannot be replicated purely by portfolio diversification, and this may also reduce the cost of debt finance. But the strongest motivation is once again likely to be managerial. If managers are risk-averse, with most of their human wealth tied up in the firm they manage, then they have an interest in the survival and stability of that firm which does not apply to an investor holding shares in the firm as part of a diversified portfolio. It may not be possible to recruit managers at all for some high-risk–high-return companies which investors would like to have as part of their portfolio unless the managers have substantial profit-sharing or profit-related remuneration. In terms of traditional concepts of allocative efficiency, mergers designed to reduce managerial risk may well be undesirable. The same, of course, holds if the objective is increased size to reduce the risk of being taken over.[30]

Another motive for merger which has received increasing attention lies in the potential tax advantages. Acquisition of a firm with losses that can be set against taxable profits of the acquirer may generate gains completely independent of any considerations previously referred to.[31] In the US until recently this applied to past losses whereas in the United Kingdom it only applies in effect to losses of the acquired 'division' after the merger, though this could still be a significant motive.

In addition as company taxation will result in lower share prices than otherwise, purchase of another company may be a cheaper way of acquiring assets than purchase of new capital equipment etc., even if the former has some associated adjustment costs. Equally, where capital gains tax is lower than income tax on dividends, acquisition through cash offers is a way of channelling funds from the corporate sector to the personal sector at lower net cost in terms of taxation than payment of dividends.[32] Finally, if a merger lowers risk and, as a result, raises the optimal debt–equity ratio, then this also will lead to a tax saving.

Not unrelated to this is the free cash-flow theory of merger associated with the work of Jensen (1986). Cash flow in excess of that necessary to finance all profitable investment opportunities may not all be paid out to shareholders, either because of tax considerations or because managers prefer to pursue their own objectives with these funds. This may to some extent also reflect the need to reduce cash holdings lest they cause the company to become the target of a raid by another company anxious to obtain liquid resources quickly and/or cheaply.

A final reason for mergers which has become a focus of attention recently is the role of takeovers in allowing the owners of a company in effect to cancel or rewrite existing commitments.[33] Managers and other employees may find themselves redundant even though prior to the takeover they had a reasonable expectation of, and in some cases a legal contract determining future employment. Assets may be sold, divisions closed, existing contracts with suppliers or customers terminated, investment, training and research and development activity curtailed or halted even though, in the absence of a takeover, these might not have occurred, or have taken place more gradually and in a manner that allowed the other parties involved to adjust to such changes. The incentive for owners to eliminate or reformulate existing implicit commitments arises because initial arrangements between owners, managers and other parties will be made in the light of the then prevailing circumstances and economic conditions. As the latter change, so an information asymmetry builds up between the managers who have better knowledge about these changes and the shareholders who do not.[34] A principal–agent problem emerges and, unless the shareholder can distinguish between poor managerial performance and externally determined deterioration in performance, there is an incentive for a raider who *can* so distinguish to take over the company and generate a new set of efficient contracts appropriate to the changed circumstances. Even if the raider cannot assess the cause of the suboptimality it may still rewrite any *ex-post* inefficient contracts after a takeover more easily and more readily than incumbent owners.[35]

There is therefore no shortage of explanations for takeovers, and little reason to presume that they will necessarily or even normally tend to promote greater productive efficiency, superior resource allocation or higher economic welfare for consumers. The incidence of takeovers and their impact depend on the informational properties and asymmetries in the stock market, the accuracy of stock market valuations, the motives, incentives and control of managers, the tax system and organisational arrangements and contracts, as well as the more obvious factors of the scope for synergistic gains and the impact on product market competition.

Empirical evidence on takeovers

Evidence on the efficiency of the takeover mechanism is of four types: comparisons of pre- and post-merger performance; comparison of the characteristics of acquiring and acquired companies; examination of share price and company valuation effects; and analysis of the effects of anti-takeover provisions in company articles. We consider evidence from both the US and the United Kingdom because these represent the two major markets where outside control and hostile takeovers are prevalent.

In the first category, the most thorough recent investigation is that by Ravenscraft and Scherer (1987). Their analysis of 6,000 acquisitions involving 471 corporations in the US between 1950 and 1976 revealed that post-merger performance was generally poor. In the case of roughly one-third of the takeovers, the acquisition was subsequently sold off, generally having had negative operating income in the last year before resale. The profitability of the other two-thirds also declined on average, especially in conglomerate mergers.[36] The only systematic exception was slightly improved profitability where the merging firms were of roughly equal size. These results are consistent with a large number of earlier examinations of pre- and post-bid performance. In particular Meeks (1977), in a study of 233 acquisitions in the United Kingdom between 1964 and 1972, found that apart from the year in which the merger occurred, profitability showed a mild but definite decline.[37]

These results, however, are not necessarily inconsistent with mergers generating gains, if for example the mergers resulted from an expectation of a deteriorating economic environment, the effects of which were partially offset by the merger.

A recent study by Healy, Palepu and Ruback (1992) of fifty large mergers in the US between 1979 and 1984 found that, although the ratio of pre-tax cash flow to market value of assets fell on average in the five years after merger, it fell less than industry averages, so that on this measure of performance, which is largely unaffected by accounting conventions, depreciation provisions, tax considerations, etc., the merged firms did relatively better after merging. They also found that this relative improvement is strongest where the merged firms are mainly in the same line of business; that the relative improvement is associated with higher asset productivity rather than

215

higher profit margins; that longer-term expenditure on investment and research and development does not suffer; and that the relative improvement can explain much of the rise in equity value at the time of merger. This, however, obscures the fact that over the five years after the merger, not only is the performance of merging firms lower than before the merger but both cash flow and assets of these firms increase much less than in the corresponding industries. The ratio improves relatively because the merged firms' assets growth is exceptionally low relative to industry average, whereas cash flow is only half that of the industries concerned. It appears likely therefore that these mergers were predominantly in industries where cash flow in relation to assets was likely to decline, and led to a process of retrenchment, i.e. severe restraint on, or contraction of investment in order to improve average operating performance in the face of industry decline.

Turning to comparisons of acquiring and acquired firms, both with each other and with firms not involved in mergers, there is at best only weak evidence that raiders are more profitable and their victims less profitable. Singh (1971) found that the latter did have lower profit and growth rates than other firms in the same industry but that the difference was never statistically significant. Size appeared to be the main discriminant with large firms exhibiting a much lower probability of takeover than small or medium-sized firms. Within a given size class profitability was significant over a two-year period but only for the highest and lowest deciles. However, over a six-year period firms with below-average profitability were twice as likely to be taken over as those above the average. A later study by Singh (1975) provided general further support for the significance of size and only limited evidence of a profitability effect.

Such results lend relatively little support to the view that the main role of the stock market is to provide a forum in which the control of less efficient companies can be reallocated to more efficient management. Other studies are still more damaging to this view. Levine and Aaronovitch (1981–2) could find no characteristics other than size and stock market assessment to distinguish raiders and victims; and in an analysis of 287 US companies acquired in the period 1962–72, Mueller (1980) found that these victim-firms had slightly *higher* returns on capital than either the average for their industry or a control group matched by size and industry. Harris, Stewart and Carleton (1982) found a similar result for 106 acquired US companies in the period 1974–7, though the difference was not statistically significant. More recently, Ravenscraft and Scherer's evidence, based on a sample which includes a substantial number of unlisted acquisitions, also found that acquired firms tended to have higher profitability than other firms and here the difference was quite large and significant.[38] In addition there was no evidence that units subsequently sold off were less profitable prior to merger than those which were held on to. In a somewhat different type of study, Morck, Schleifne and Vishny (1989), using stock market-based measures of return, found that poor performance by a firm was much more likely to lead to takeover if the whole industry was performing poorly, but more likely to result in internal reform if the firm was underperforming the industry. This is consistent with the above in that companies actually acquired would not necessarily be performing less well than other similar companies, and suggests that internal reform triggered by existing shareholders is the main mechanism by which inefficient management is disciplined, rather than the takeover mechanisms.[39] Against this, Martin and McConnell (1991) found that the pre-bid performance of firms in which the top manager was replaced after the takeover was significantly worse than its industry average. However, this was not true for takeovers where the top manager was not replaced, suggesting that some takeover may be disciplinary on managerial inefficiency but others not. They also found that takeover targets tended to be in industries which were performing better than average, further indicating the significance of motives other than exploitation of incumbent management inefficiency.

As an interim conclusion, the main thrust of these types of study is that the more traditionally assumed motives for takeover provide at best only a limited explanation for the evidence. In particular, takeovers seem rarely to be in pursuit of either significant monopoly power or conventional synergistic effects, and in many cases appear unrelated to the penalising of inefficient management. Results also tend to exclude significant financing or tax advantages. Rather, three other conclusions emerge. First, following Ravenscraft and Sherer, pursuit of growth, together with 'hubris', i.e. excessively optimistic estimates of what can be achieved as a result of takeover, is one main explanation. The hubris effect is not necessarily implausible. Suppose there are no real gains from takeover but raiders make random valuation errors. If the latter are negative no bid is made but if they are positive a bid is made and the raider overpays (Roll, 1986). In this situation only a conviction on the part of the raider that he can do better will explain why bids continue to be made. This can to some extent be tested in the light of the share-price movements which takeovers generate (see below). Second, following Healy et al., takeovers may play an important role in defending firms against severe downturns in performance. Post-merger performance still deteriorates but some mergers may permit rationalisation which to some degree mitigates the consequences of cyclical or industry decline.

Third, it is also consistent with the results described that takeovers are, to a substantial degree, a means by which companies can pursue not just expansion but strategic development aims, for example, through building up product ranges, geographical coverage, security of supply, wider distribution, etc. None of these need necessarily increase market power, nor provide any conventional economies of scale observable in subsequently enhanced profit performance. Takeovers may merely represent quick, cost-effective and potentially more stable ways of achieving such company development than internal investment programmes. If so there would be no reason to expect acquirers systematically to be more profitable than acquirers, nor to expect that the latter would systematically tend to be less profitable before a bid or exhibit improvement in profitability after a bid. Indeed in many cases an efficient well-run company may be a more attractive target through which to achieve such aims.[40] Thus, while we would not wish by any means to discount all the other motives for merger, a predominant aim may be the restructuring or strategic development of firms operating in an outsider control world where the assets and goodwill of other companies are easily accessible via the stock market. If so, then it is the strategy of acquirers, rather than the inefficiency of acquirees, towards which attention mainly needs to be directed.

We now examine the third type of evidence, namely the movement of share prices during and after takeovers, of which there are now a large number of studies. An early study in the United Kingdom by Firth (1919) found that, on the day a bid was announced, average gains in the target companies' share prices were 22 per cent (though 80 per cent of the firms had exhibited abnormal gains in the month preceding the bid). But the average movement in the bidding firm's share price was a marginally greater *fall*, suggesting a transfer of wealth from the acquiring firm's shareholders to those of the acquiree, rather than any net gain. The great majority of more recent studies, however, both in the US and the United Kingdom, while confirming that the target firm's shareholders gain significantly, indicate that the raider's share price changes relatively little and if anything on balance tends to rise slightly, suggesting net gains of merger even if nearly all of the gain accrues to the shareholders of the target firm. A survey of studies by Jensen and Ruback (1983) found that target company shareholders on average gained 30 per cent in tender offers, 20 per cent in mergers and 8 per cent in proxy battles, while raiders gained 4 per cent in tender offers and nothing in mergers. A major study by Bradley, Desai and Kim (1988) of 236 takeovers between 1963 and 1984 found that 95 per cent of target companies and 47 per cent of raiders exhibited positive share-price effects, and that the cumulative abnormal return for target shareholders was 31.77 per cent, for raiders 0.97 per cent, and in total 7.43 per cent.[41] Factors such as competitive bidding by raiders and the entry of 'white knights' (i.e. an alternative bidder whom the target firm's management perceive as being a sympathetic vehicle for displacing a hostile bid) both tend to eliminate the small acquirers' shareholder gains. There are also some indications that positive bidder returns may have fallen through the 1960s and 1970s, turning negative though not statistically significantly in the 1980s.[42] A study of 1,800 takeovers in the United Kingdom between 1955 and 1985 by Franks and Harris (1989) generally echoes these results with the bidder gaining either fractionally or by amounts not significantly different from zero.[43] However, it should be noted that a study by Dennis and McConnell (1986) found that convertible preferred stock of acquiring firms showed positive gains which, even though common stock exhibited little if any gains, were enough to generate an increase in the overall share value of acquiring firms.

It seems reasonable to conclude that takeovers typically raise the combined share value of the raider and target companies substantially, and that it is the shareholders of the target company who obtain most if not all of that increase. This raises two important questions. First, what are the sources of the bid premium? Bhagat Scheiffer and Vishny (1990) found that on average around 10 per cent to 20 per cent of the rise in the target company's share price could be explained by cost savings arising from lay-offs of employees or managers (though in some individual cases this was a complete explanation) suggesting a combination of improved efficiency and rewriting of implicit contracts. Tax advantages, though quite frequent, tended to explain only about 5 per cent to 15 per cent, but were particularly important in management buy-outs (MBOs) (often helped by high leverage) acquisitions by partnerships and, unsurprisingly, by companies carrying tax losses. Across the sample of sixty-two hostile takeovers as a whole, 30 per cent of the bid premium was covered by later sell-offs. While this might in part reflect initial underpricing and in some cases was a way of paying off the debt incurred in the original takeover, it appears that much of this was due to the initial takeover, frequently but not always in the form of an MBO, representing an essentially temporary step in the process of reallocating assets ftom one public company to another in the same industry. Many such sell-offs were part of a process of concentration or reconcentration on core lines of business. As a result a much higher proportion of takeover activity may ultimately be associated with companies' strategic development and/or acquisition of market power than would be inferred from the initial takeover viewed in isolation. In a number of cases, sell-offs were primarily designed to unscramble unsuccessful conglomerate mergers that had been encouraged by abundant liquidity, availability of debt instruments to finance takeovers and lenient anti-trust provisions. More minor sources of the bid premium were overpayment by the raider's management and cutting back on excessive investment out of cash flow by the target company.

Increases in market power and strategic development can to some extent be distinguished by looking at the effect of a merger on the share price of rival companies. Stillman's (1983) study of rival firms in eleven horizontal mergers found virtually no evidence of wealth increases such as would be expected if the merger, via increased concentration, were to lead to higher market prices. In two other studies Eckbo (1983, 1985) found some signs of abnormal returns to rival companies' shareholders, but rejected the view that this was due to increased market power arising from the merger. This was based on correlations with the changes in market structure, and on the share response to challenges to the merger under anti-trust legislation. He concluded that the response reflected identification of cost savings in the merger process that were potentially applicable throughout the industry.

A substantial study by Slutsky and Caves (1991–1), using a somewhat different approach, found that real synergies explained very little of the bid premium, and that financial synergies arising from the opportunity to infuse more capital to a financially constrained or heavily leveraged firm was more important. The existence of a rival bidder tended to lead to higher premiums despite lower opportunities for real gains. Nearly half of the explained variance in bid premiums is associated with the structure of shareholdings (concentration and/or managerial fraction) in the target or raider company, indicating that the market for corporate control does exercise some effect on managers whose activities depart too far from their shareholders' objectives, but also that managers in raider companies tend to overpay in pursuit of growth, especially where rival bidders are present. Cash bids also tended to increase the premium in comparison with share tender offers.

The significance of overbidding in the presence of rival bidders is supported by Franks, Harris and Mayer (1987) as is a hubris-type belief by bidding managers in previous undervaluation of the target company's shares. Also, Franks and Harris (1989) find that not only contested bids but revised bids and the existence of pre-merger equity stakes held by the raider all increase the premium.[44]

The difference between cash and tender offers is significant not only for the bid premium. Travlos (1987) found that raiders' stock returns were average for cash bids but negative for stock offers, perhaps because the use of stock rather than cash is a signal that the bidding firm is overvalued. This is consistent with Brown and Ryngaert's (1991) finding that more efficient raiders tend to use cash to avoid any undervaluation of shares following a tender offer. This in turn fits with Franks *et al.*'s (1987) evidence that post-bid performance tends to deteriorate after tender offers but not after cash ones.

Therefore, overall bid premiums in takeovers appear to have a number of causes, corresponding to a range of previously identified motives, but with the emphasis on the gains from reorganisation of an industry's assets, financial synergies, the consequences of managerial growth objectives coupled with overoptimism concerning the benefits of the takeover, and the reduction in agency problems associated with management control.

The second question concerns whether the evidence for increased shareholder wealth in takeovers can be reconciled with the earlier evidence that post-merger performance often tends to deteriorate, and with the evidence on the relative profiles of raiders and target companies. The evidence on post-merger rates of return tend to direct attention away from synergistic, market power or managerial inefficiency explanations, and also those based on tax advantages or contract revision; even though any of these could be consistent with the share-price evidence. A more consistent explanation would seem to be inefficiency in stock market valuations, leading to acquisitional mergers based not on improvements in performance but on buying assets when they are undervalued. The bid would reveal the true value and hence raise share valuation, the effect would be almost totally on the share price of the acquired firm and there would be no post-merger real gains to be realised.

Franks and Harris (1989) argue that, at least in relation to *failed* bids, acquisitional takeovers can be distinguished from allocational ones because the former, having revealed underpricing of a company's shares, will result in no subsequent reduction in share price after the bid has failed, whereas the latter, being based on synergistic, efficiency or market-power gains that occur only if the bid goes through will, if unsuccessful, be followed by a reversion of the share price to its earlier level. In an analysis of sixty failed bids between 1981 and 1984 they found on average no reduction in target company share prices in the ten months subsequent to the bid suggesting a preponderance of acquisitional mergers. However, as Williams (1992) has argued, this may be too strong an inference because a failed allocational bid may galvanise the existing management to improve its efficiency, thus justifying the higher share price into the longer term. In addition, evidence from the US indicates that the target company's share price does eventually tend to drift back down unless another bidder appears, suggesting that there might be efficiency, synergy or market-power gains to be had from merger, though not any particular merger (Bradley *et al.*, 1988). Moreover, Pound (1988) found that the consensus forecast by stock market analysis of standalone earnings of companies involved in mergers did not change significantly at the time of a bid, and in the case of failed bids was largely correct, suggesting that the bid premiums might reflect real gains available from the merger rather than previous misvaluation. Thus mispricing by the stock market, though no doubt part of the explanation for bid premia but no post-merger improvement, cannot be accepted uncritically.

Apart from misvaluation, this survey of the evidence also directs attention towards three other explanations. First, it is entirely consistent with mergers being a key element in the pursuit of growth by managers and in the strategic development of companies. Takeovers motivated by either of these would typically not lead to any post-merger improvement in profitability, but would lead to a rise in the share price of a target company even if its pre-bid price was an accurate reflection of the present value of future earnings. There would still be a preference, other things being equal, for acquisition of an underpriced company, and this might still play some role in the pattern of takeovers, but the main driving force would be expansion, if necessary paying above the present value; and/or strategic development of the raider's products and market position. The continuation of a higher share price after a failed bid would reflect that a target company was still 'in play', in particular if arbitrageurs had taken sizeable positions in the company; but in the absence of a new growth-maximizing bidder, the price would lapse back towards its original earnings-related value.

The second additional explanation that fits these results is Roll's hubris hypothesis, namely that raiders' management systematically tend to over-estimate their ability to manage an acquisition effectively. The bid would reflect this optimism, generating share-price increases concentrated almost wholly on the target company. Post-merger performance would none the less tend not to improve, and failed bids would be followed by share-price declines if it became clear that no one else shared the same confidence concerning the scope for post-merger improvements. We have already seen that the hubris explanation is quite plausible and the evidence so far provides significant support.

Finally, the evidence is consistent with takeovers being defensive moves to avoid some or all of the consequences of increased competition or industrial decline in the future. Share values would rise because of the relative improvement in a firm's prospects, but post-merger performance would still decline because of the deteriorating economic environment Target companies would tend to be those most able to help the merged company survive and hence there would be no great tendency for target companies to be relatively weak performers.

We conclude therefore that the stock market provides only a limited role in the efficient reallocation of resources, from less to more efficient management teams. Instead, it mainly provides (i) opportunities for acquisitional mergers as a result of share-price misvaluations, (ii) a vehicle by which management teams can pursue growth objectives and development strategies relatively easily, (iii) a means for achieving retrenchment or greater consolidation in the face of expected downturns in business but, also, (iv) scope for over-optimistic evaluations by managers of the potential which they can derive from assets currently under the control of other managers. While no doubt there are occasions when an outside management can come in and do better, the evidence suggests that more often the outside management merely has less adequate information and, as a result, too optimistic a view of what is possible.

We now turn briefly to the fourth source of evidence, namely that on the effects of anti-takeover provisions in company articles. These include requirements for super majorities (e.g. 67 per cent or even up to 90 per cent) of shareholders to approve changes in management control; fair-price amendments limiting and/or defining the bid price that can be accepted by the firm; staggered board appointments so that at any one time relatively few of the board can be removed; and various types of so-called 'poison pills', e.g. in the event of a bid, the power for managers to issue preferred stock to shareholders with rights attached, the purchase of which by the raider would make the takeover very – perhaps prohibitively – expensive. Such provisions, not surprisingly, reduce the probability of takeover and hence help to entrench the existing management.[45] At the same time they give managers greater bargaining power, in the event of a bid, to achieve a higher price. The former effect would tend to lower share prices, the latter increase it.

Although the overall effect appears in practice to be small, most evidence to date tends to suggest that the former effect dominates.[46] It is surprising therefore that such provisions are adopted, given that they require majority approval by shareholders. The usual explanation is that management are able to persuade shareholders of the potential for obtaining a higher price from a bid, even though the overall effect on share prices subsequently is negative; and/or that highly diversified shareholders typically just go along with management proposals.[47]

Similar effects may be involved in the negotiation of 'golden parachutes', i.e. very favourable pay-offs to managers if they lose their jobs.[48] These may not in practice be in the shareholders' interests but can be presented as a mechanism for ensuring that managers will not fight a takeover which is in the shareholders' interests simply to defend their own security.

While this evidence is far from conclusive it is in general consistent with the conclusion above that managerial motivation and managerial perceptions are of primary significance in the incidence and effects of takeovers.[49] If takeovers were mainly concerned to obtain efficiency, synergistic or market-power gains, then shareholders would have little incentive to approve anti-takeover provisions. If, on the other hand, there is a danger that under-valuations will occur then strengthening management's bargaining position is attractive but share prices should then rise. However, if managers know that efficiency on their part is no guarantee against takeovers motivated by growth, strategic development, retrenchment and/or excessive optimism, they will have strong incentives to persuade shareholders to adopt anti-takeover provisions. The resulting fall in the likelihood of takeover will none the less generate a negative effect on share prices.

Overall, therefore, while there is no reason to reject any of the motives for merger that have been discussed, the evidence taken as a whole indicates that the most significant factors are managerial growth and development strategies, restructuring and consolidation, and errors of valuation, primarily over-optimistic ones by acquiring companies' managers, but also to a lesser extent by stock market investors generally. The effects of all this on economic welfare and the associated policy implications we turn to later.

THE STOCK MARKET AND SHORT-TERMISM

The debate over short-termism

The previous section looked at the motives for, and consequences of, takeover activity in a stock market. We now go on to consider what impact, if any, the existence of outsider control in a dispersed equity market has on managerial behaviour. While part of this relates to evidence on the relationship between share prices and investment, considered later, we start by looking at the most prominent issue in this area, namely the short-termism debate.

Many industrialists are quite concerned that the existence of largely atomistic shareholders, be these individuals or institutions, ready to sell at the first sign that share prices might fall, forces managers to adopt unnecessarily short-term time horizons in their investment decisions and profit planning, to the long-term detriment of company performance and indeed the national economy. This situation is often contrasted with the insider-control mechanisms in Germany and Japan which allow managers to pursue, and shareholders' representative's to acquiesce in longer-term stratagies, particularly with regard to research, innovation and product development, which eventually generate much superior performance. Reference is often made to the generally very short time horizons, often three months or less, over which financial institutions' fund managers are assessed, a phenomenon not present in the insider control structure.

Many if not most of those in the financial world strongly disagree. They argue that sensible investment involves identifying companies with high present values, which may reflect short or long-term profit potential and indeed more generally both. The short time horizons for assessing fund managers are seen as irrelevant because if new information becomes available concerning long-term profit potential this will tend to be reflected in today's share price and fund managers will want to identify and invest in such opportunities now, with the capital gain reflected in the current three-monthly review. More generally it seems rather implausible to many of them that investors, whose only rationale is to identify good profit opportunities, should systematically miss or ignore good opportunities. If this were the case, could not *some* investors identify the profit opportunities, invest, hold until fruition and outperform the market?

For some while, economists had relatively little to say about this issue, and such evidence as there was seemed generally adverse to the myopia thesis (see below). More recently some models of myopic behaviour have emerged to explain why rational agents might adopt excessively short-term time horizons, and the issue has been subject to more rigorous empirical investigation. The next section looks at three theoretical approaches, and this is followed by an assessment of the empirical evidence.

Models of myopic behaviour

The signal jamming model

The most common line of argument in support of short-termism is based on the existence of asymmetric information in an outsider-control structure. It is assumed that managers have reasonably sound knowledge of their firms' profit prospects and investment requirements, and associated trends in dividends, retentions and other key expenditure variables. There are none the less likely to be sizeable stochastic elements in all of these in the light of the economic environment, competitive pressures, innovative developments etc. Where ownership is highly dispersed across many shareholders, the latter will have much less detailed, useful information and, typically, much less incentive for any one of them to improve this situation. In such circumstances the growth of dividends and/or earnings can be used and taken as a signal of the sustainable position of the firm; and it is well known both that managers do try to smooth the dividend stream over time, and that investors regularly use dividends and earnings as a key guide to share valuation (Stein 1988, 1989). This means that share prices will be very responsive to dividends or earnings, and this is perfectly rational given the signalling role that their announcement performs.[50]

With insider control, actual or suspected share misvaluations are not particularly significant, because there is little scope if any for a hostile raider to buy up shares, but this is not the case with outsider control. Overvaluation brings no penalties, but undervaluation increases the threat to takeover creating a one-way incentive to raise current dividends or earnings even if this is at the expense of longer-term profit. For example, the dividend can be raised by cutting investment but, more pervasively, earnings can be increased by cutting above-the-line product or process R&D or other longer-term development expenditures, e.g. training, marketing, export market development, etc., or capital investment, again because of its associated running costs; by setting higher prices in the presence of switching costs (which will boost short-term profits at the expense of longer-term ones) or conversely by excessive discounting of durable products to generate a short-term profit boost, again at the expense of the longer-term. Development of links with suppliers and purchasers, recruitment and maintenance and repair expenditure are all other areas where short-term improvements in earnings can readily be made by cutting back, at the cost of longer-term efficiency.

The stumbling block in this line of argument has always been the question, if the stock market does force managers systematically to act in these short-termist ways, why don't investors perceive this and allow for it in their valuation procedures? Stein's hypothesis is that they *do* recognise the problem, but managers are subject to a prisoners' dilemma (Stein, 1988, 1989). If managers could coordinate their activities so that none behaved in a short-term manner then there would be no distortion, a situation investors would prefer. But any one manager failing to act in this way would be perceived as less effective than all others, because investors know that the dividend or earnings signal is normally distorted and would presume that this was still occurring. There is an equilibrium degree of distortion, which investors can systematically allow for, but from which no one management can depart without poorer performance being inferred. An interesting property of this model, therefore, is that investors can and do infer the 'correct' position, by allowing for the equilibrium distortion, but managers none the less systematically find that some longer-term expenditures have to be forgone if a drop in the share price is to be avoided.

Stein argues that, in principle, the problem could be solved by investors getting detailed information about firms and their managers, so that they do not have to rely on dividend or current earnings signals, and such activity is of course important. But if shareholders are highly dispersed, as typically they are in an outsider-control structure, then it will often not be worth any one investor incurring the costs of this, but coordination of such activity by investors may well be impractical. Even if some shareholders followed this strategy they would still be exposed to the risk of capital losses in the event of managers ceasing to act short-term (because of the response by the other shareholders) unless they could buy most or all of the shares. This implies that there will be less pressure on managers to act short-term in companies with more concentrated shareholdings, the advantages of which might offset any increase in risk resulting from a more concentrated holding. It would also be entirely consistent with insider control, *ceteris paribus*, being a more efficient ownership structure.

Two other inferences may be drawn from this signal-jamming model. First, the pressure to act short-term will tend to be more serious in relation to less tangible expenditures such as product and process research and development, marketing, building up customer and supplier networks, etc. Long-term investment in some types of plant and machinery may be subject to the same problem, but it will usually be much clearer as to why the investment is being made, what the likely pay-off will be and the risks involved, etc., thereby facilitating the transmission of information to investors without having to rely on signalling mechanisms.

Second, the holding of shares by managers, which is generally thought of as a way of improving the profitability of managers may, in this model, make things worse because the managers have an additional disincentive to carry out longer-term plans which reduce the current share price. Only if managers hold a controlling proportion of the shares, as is typically the case in unquoted companies, will this cease to hold.

The mispricing arbitrage model

An alternative but not incompatible explanation for short-termism is provided by Schleifer and Vishny (1990). Consider a capital market in which the interest rate equals the rate of return on assets, in which some mispricing of assets may occur, and in which arbitrageurs, who can borrow at the prevailing interest rate, attempt to profit from such mispricing. In the simplest case the arbitrageur is indifferent how long it takes for the mispricing to emerge, because the present value of an investment in an underpriced share is independent of the period necessary for price correction to occur.[51] In practice the arbitrageur faces two risks; that he may need to liquidate early at a time when the mispricing is worse; and that if price correction takes a long time, the fundamental value of the company may deteriorate. Both these risks are greater the longer the interval before the share price corrects itself.

There are two main consequences of these risks. First, the cost of funds to the arbitrageur will rise above the rate of return and, second, because the capital market does not have full information on the skill of individual arbitrageurs, it will to some extent credit-ration the latter.[52] As a result, first, the present value of mispricing arbitrage falls the longer the period to price correction, and second, with limited funds there is an opportunity cost of any individual arbitrage operation.[53] These raise the costs of longer-term arbitrage. Because in equilibrium the return to short and long-term arbitrage must be equal, there must be a higher gross return on long-term arbitrage, which in turn implies more mispricing of assets whose mispricing is revealed later. Managers, however, try to avoid mispricing because the disutility of underpricing, with its concomitant threat of takeover, is much greater than any utility from overpricing. Managers will therefore systematically tend to avoid longer-term investments where fundamental value is only likely to be revealed after a long time.

Three mechanisms can exacerbate this pressure towards short-term investment. First, arbitrageurs can reduce their cost of funds by demonstrating success, but this may increase the incentive to make short-term gains from short-term mispricing. Second, if arbitrageurs tend to avoid longer-term mispricing because of the higher costs involved, then the market pressures towards price correction will be weaker in the case of long-term assets, exacerbating the effects described. Third, if managers do invest in longer-term assets, then there may be scope for a takeover, followed by adjustment to shorter-term investments which reduce the arbitrage costs, making the company more valuable and providing a capital gain for the raider. In this model, therefore, long-term behaviour by managers may lead directly to an increased takeover threat.

Sunk costs and externality effects

In recent years growing emphasis has been placed on the role of sunk costs in determining competitive behaviour and outcomes, and in particular on the incentives to firms to increase sunk costs as a form of strategic entry deterrence. This has also revealed the potential for sunk costs incurred for other reasons, 'innocently' to deter entry.[54] The significance of sunk costs for ownership and control issues, however, has not been addressed.

In a different context there has been revived interest in the potential for investment and other types of expenditure to have externality effects, for example by lowering prices of inputs to other firms, hence increasing their profitability, investment and growth, thereby generating faster economic growth.[55] Here again, however, the implications for ownership and control remain unexplored. This section summarises recent attempts by the author to explore the interactions between sunk costs, various types of externality, the stock market and short-termism.[56] For simplicity we imagine that a firm, in investing and producing for a market, incurs initial fixed costs which are sunk and subsequently incurs variable costs which are linearly dependent on output. Traditional models have focused on the extent to which firms can obtain strategic advantage in later periods by adopting levels of investment or techniques of production which involve higher sunk costs initially and lower variable costs subsequently. This advantage occurs because, in the event that another firm considers entering the market, the first entrant will consider only its non-sunk costs in determining its price–output strategy, whereas the later entrant, having as yet incurred no cost, will have to consider all its costs. This results in a more favourable outcome for the first entrant.

In practice there are numerous other ways in which increased investment today may lead not just to higher profits in the future but to a strategic change in the future terms of competition with other firms. First, higher investment will tend to be associated with a lower average age of the capital stock, more recent technological advance, higher productivity levels and greater competitiveness.[57] This, together with consequent higher profits and higher market share, will typically generate more opportunities for future competitive activity, including product development, greater market knowledge, greater security of demand and lower financing costs, all of which can put the firm in a strategically stronger position in the future. More generally, following Scott's (1986, ch.6) analysis of the growth process, any investment will typically create new opportunities for investment. The set of profitable opportunities will not therefore in general decline as a result of the taking-up of one of those opportunities, but will be maintained as a result of the investment carried out. High investing firms, which traditionally would be thought to have moved down their investment demand schedule to a point characterised by low returns at the margin and few further opportunities, may therefore find themselves facing new cost and demand conditions, new product opportunities etc. which were not available previously. In some cases opportunities may become available to other firms and there is a straight externality effect of the original investment. In other cases only the investing firm will be in a position to exploit the new opportunities.

This naturally leads on to a second link, via learning-by-doing. In many firms the key to corporate success is not just the right investment decisions, nor even just recruitment of the appropriately skilled personnel, though both will be necessary. Of much greater importance will be the often highly specific knowledge of the product and the market, of relationships with customers and suppliers, the technology and production processes involved and how all these can best be integrated. Where such effects are important (and it is arguable that this is the typical case) investment may create future investment opportunities which cannot be foreseen initially but which accrue only to the investing firm by virtue of the experience it gains, in one or more aspect of the firm's activities from implementing the investment. Whether the latter involves new technology, new products or new markets, development of new skills, or just embodies new employment, production or distribution arrangements, the result may be the creation of new opportunities, previously unforeseen, which are highly specific to the firm concerned, and which can give it a strategic advantage in future competition with other firms.

The consequence of these various effects is that, in principle, any investment expenditure may generate four different types of profit:

1 the excess of revenue over costs in the shorter term as a result of undertaking the investment;
2 subsequent longer-term profits as a result of maintaining the investment;
3 additional profits in the longer term as a result of lower cost (or higher revenues) attributable to the initial investment via the new opportunities, learning effects, etc., described above;
4 further profits deriving from the strategic competitive advantage which follows from the cost (or other) advantages generated.

We now focus on four crucial characteristics of a sunk-cost investment which has the knock-on effects described and hence the profit profile outlined above. First, managers will find it progressively harder to identify, still less quantify the profit consequences as one goes down the list. The shorter-term conventional profits will typically be assessed in terms of discounted cash flow (DCF) or other cruder types of investment analysis technique. Managers are likely to be aware of the second but they will generally be harder to quantify. The third and fourth may well be considerations that influence their thinking and judgement but, by their nature, these are likely to be highly judgemental, very imprecisely assessed, unquantifiable and often, as a result, much more marginal to any decision.

Second, any such problems may be an order of magnitude larger for the typical shareholder in an outside control issue. Assessment of any but the first source of profits may be extremely poorly informed, highly speculative and very prone to swings in fashion, sentiment and the like. Even investment analysis of the sort undertaken by financial institutions may find it very difficult to assess adequately, if at all, the longer-term consequences.

Third, the structure of the profit profile means that there will typically be a level of investment beyond which the present value of profits under headings 1 and 2 will fall, but the present value of the profits under 3 and 4 will still rise. Thus an assessment which largely or wholly focuses on the first, or first and second sources of profit will generate lower investment than one which incorporated all elements of the profit stream.

Finally, the higher the level of sunk-cost investment, the longer the period until the later elements of the profit profile appear, and the greater the risk that a negative shock to the firm's economic position will render it vulnerable to losses, a falling share price and perhaps takeover. This will be evident to both managers and shareholders at the time that the investment is made.

The combination of sunk-cost investment and what may be termed *inter-temporal externalities* (which may accrue to other firms but which will in part accrue to the investing firm), together with the resulting profit-and-risk profiles and the problems of shareholder assessment, can generate a situation in which the net present value of the total profit stream of new investment is positive but the share-price response is negative and the risk exposure to negative shocks increased, in both cases reducing the security of managers and inhibiting the investment. Neither effect will be very pronounced in an insider-control world where managerial security is not greatly threatened, if at all, by a falling share price, but could be acute in an outside-control one where the shorter-term costs and risks of new investment are a more dominant influence on share prices than longer-term externalities.

In practical terms the consequence is likely to be either the omission of the externality effects in DCF calculations, or the use of higher rate-of-return hurdles than otherwise, which in turn reduce the present value of the later profits more rapidly. Managers may want to override the more quantitative shorter-term calculations to reflect their assessment of the externality effects but will often be reluctant to do so because of the potential damage to their own security. The result is a systematic tendency for mangers to focus on shorter-term returns where share-price fluctuations matter. As before we would expect these effects to be less severe where managers have majority control, or ownership control is concentrated in a small number of relatively well-informed investors.

The crucial and to some extent unifying features of these three models of short-termism are the informational asymmetry that exists between managers and shareholders in an outside control structure and the generally poor incentives for highly dispersed shareholders to correct this. Given these problems we might expect to see growing institutionalisation of shareholdings in financial intermediaries which can specialise in the acquisition of information, and growing concentration of shareholdings in an individual company. However, there may well be powerful forces constraining such institutions to a 'local' optimum, i.e. profit-maximising behaviour within the context of current institutions and forms of operation, even though different forms of operation might be superior. Typically under outsider control, investing institutions are highly skilled at assessing a large number of companies relatively quickly, in part using the financial signals used earlier, and in constructing and managing optimal portfolios of shares in a range of companies. They will not generally be well equipped to focus on a small number of companies and become involved in their direction such that they can pursue an inside-control strategy. In these circumstances any attempt to shift towards the latter approach may well reduce profits, but the alternative of a wholesale change in both strategy and personnel will be impractical. Thus even if the costs of short-termism outweigh the gains from diversification of risk under outside control, the latter may well rationally persist, perhaps indefinitely.

Empirical evidence on short-termism

Early investigations for the most part found little evidence for short-termism. For example, McConnell and Muscarella (1985) found that share prices tend to respond positively to the announcement of planned investment increases and negatively to announced reductions. In similar vein, Chan, Martin and Kensigner (1990) found that share prices tended to rise in response to increases in research and development expenditure in high technology industries even though earnings might decline, and that this effect was larger than a negative effect in low-technology industries.[58] Other studies by Hirschey, (1982) and by Pakes (1985) gave similar results.[59] Such evidence is not conclusive, however. If investors do exhibit myopic behaviour then this would tend to inhibit longer-term strategies and associated expenditures from occurring. In some cases firms might find ways of overcoming the problem, *ex hypothesi*, generating higher investment or R&D *and* a positive share-price response. This would not necessarily imply that there were not many other cases, and perhaps a majority where myopic behaviour prevented managers from taking a longer-term perspective. Also if managers for any reason are systematically myopic then again there would be a positive share-price response in those cases, perhaps infrequent, where managers eschew such behaviour.

A study by the Office of the Chief Economist of the Securities and Exchange Commission in the US found that, contrary to what might be expected from myopic behaviour, high R&D companies were no more likely to be taken over than low R&D ones.[60] But here again interpretation is important. It is quite possible that companies which are more likely to be taken over have to cut R&D as the myopia thesis would suggest. This might lower the threat of takeover to the norm but result *ex post* in the probability of takeover being the same for low and high R&D companies.[61] The only really telling evidence is a study by Muellbroek *et al.* which finds that firms which introduced anti-takeover provisions subsequently exhibited significant reductions in their R&D intensity (ratio of R&D expenditure to sales) relative to their industry averages. That firms might introduce such provisions and simultaneously cut R&D is not necessarily inconsistent with the myopia thesis, because an increased threat of takeover would cause both to happen; but significant decrease in R&D *after* incorporating the provisions does suggest that the stock market values R&D and that managers who are more secure from takeover face less pressure to engage in such risky activity.

Even here some caution is necessary. Over one-quarter of the sample were subsequently the target of a takeover bid. This high proportion suggests that the sample of firms introducing such provisions was heavily skewed towards those which, for one reason or another, were likely takeover targets. The provisions and the subsequent R&D cuts may both have been a response to this, with the former capable of being introduced much more quickly. Muellbroek *et al.* seek to eliminate this explanation by stating that similar results apply to the subset of firms for which no bid was subsequently made, but the fear of takeover may quite possibly have existed throughout the sample rather than in just those receiving a bid.

A rather different strand of literature questions whether a company's share price is of any great significance at all in influencing investment expenditure. Surveys indicate that over half of investors had not altered their discount rate in three years, despite equity yields varying between 4.95 per cent and 11.55 per cent. The 1987 stock market crash appeared to have almost no effect on investment intentions being generally regarded as merely the end of a speculative bubble. Mullins and Wadhwani (1989) found that stock market variables matter more in the US and the United Kingdom in determining investment than in Germany or Japan (where they have virtually no discernible effect) once the usual determinants of investment such as output relative prices, etc., have been taken into account. However, the effect in both the US and the United Kingdom is primarily via the debt–equity ratio which probably reflects the information content of this variable in outside control structures. In neither country does Tobin's q (the ratio of stock market value to replacement cost of assets) add any additional explanatory power. The yield on equity, as measured by the dividend yield plus the growth of the dividend, is significant in the United Kingdom though the effect is small, and not significant in the US.

These result are consistent with another study by Morck, Schleifer and Vishny (1990). This distinguishes between the stock market as:

1 passive informant, i.e. managers assume that it reflects the same fundamentals as those which determine investment; and
2 active informant, i.e. managers use share prices as a source of information. If the latter reflected only fundamentals then they would not influence investment independently but if they are swayed by 'sentiment' as opposed to fundamentals, then they can constitute an additional determinant of investment:
3 a source of funds, so that variations in equity prices influence investment via the cost of equity funds,
4 a short-term pressure, such that share-price movements can influence investment separately from fundamentals and financing costs.

Models 2 and 4 may be distinguishable in that sentiment will be more influential at the aggregate level, while stock market pressure will be more influential at the level of the individual company.

Morck *et al.* examine the extent to which stock returns, financial variables and a combination of them add anything to fundamentals (such as sales, cash flow, etc.) in explaining investment. They find that sentiment and finance do have identifiable effects and that the former is primarily a market pressure phenomenon rather than an 'active informant' one; but the effects are quite small. However, interpretation is again very important. If sentiment affects investment, which in turn influences sales growth, cash flow, etc., then stock returns may add little to fundamentals in explaining investment even though, *ex hypothesi*, they are influential. Some exogenous shocks can systematically lower stock market prices but raise investment opportunities – for example, lower capital prices, higher oil prices, etc. The problem also remains that some investments may not occur because of the share-price reaction it would lead to. Thus short-term pressures may exist but for that very reason neither the investment nor the stock price response occurs which might constitute statistical evidence for short-termism. More generally, it is neces- sary to establish a full simultaneous investment model which includes stock market activity and the links between it and investment in both directions if short-term pressures are empirically to be identified using this methodology.

Many of these difficulties, however, and, indeed, the whole debate on short-termism, have been transformed by a seminal empirical study in 1993 by Miles (1993).[62] This starts from the premise that, in the absence of any short-termism, the price of a share will represent the present value of the expected future stream of dividends up to the time when the share is sold, plus the present value of the expected share price when it is sold. Further- more, actual returns will only differ from expected returns randomly. Empirically therefore we would expect:

$$P_t = \sum_{i=1}^{n} \left[\frac{D_{t+i}}{(1+r)^i} \right] + \frac{P_{t+n}}{(1+r)^n}$$

where P_t is the share price in period t, D_t is the dividend in period t, and r is the discount rate in period t, assumed equal to the risk-free rate plus a risk premium, which can be derived for any company from the capital asset pricing model.

Miles then suggests four different ways in which this could be modified to allow for the possibility of short-termism.

1 Too high a discount factor may be used. This would mean that the basic equation would have to be rewritten as:

$$P_t = \sum_{i=1}^{n} \left[\frac{D_{t+i}}{(1+r)^{bi}} \right] + \frac{P_{t+n}}{(1+r)^{bn}}$$

where b is above unity.
2 Alternatively, short-termism could be interpreted as a systematic under- estimating of longer-term cash flows. This could be incorporated by

233

rewriting the basic equation as:

$$P_t = \sum_{i=1}^{n} \left[\frac{D_{t+i} \cdot x^i}{(1+r)^i} \right] + \frac{P_{t+n} \cdot x^i}{(1+r)^i}$$

where x is less than unity.

3 A third approach would be to allow for the use of a higher discount rate after some arbitrary period, for example five years. This would give:

$$P_t = \sum_{i=1}^{5} \left[\frac{D_{t+i}}{(1+r)^i} \right] + \frac{P_{t+5}}{(1+r+a)^5}$$

where a was above zero.

4 Finally, it is possible to combine the approaches by applying a b-type or x-type factor, but only after a certain number of years. This would give:

$$P_t = \sum_{i=1}^{5} \left[\frac{D_{t+i}}{(1+r)^i} \right] + \frac{P_{t+5}}{(1+r)^{\alpha 5}}$$

and

$$P_t = \sum_{i=1}^{5} \left[\frac{D_{t+i}}{(1+r)^i} \right] + \frac{P_{t+5} \cdot \lambda}{(1+r)^5}$$

where α was above unity and λ was below unity.

The following table indicates the empirical results obtained by Miles for the period 1980-8.

Coefficient	Expected value if myopia	Estimated value	t-statistic
b	>1	1.68	5.6
x	<1	0.93	30.6
a	>0	0.16	3.8
α	>1	2.03	6.3
λ	<1	0.53	6.1

In every case, irrespective of how precisely short-termism is modelled, the evidence is statistically significant and suggests a substantial degree of short-termism. Illustratively, the value of b implies that cash flows expected in five years' time will be discounted as if they were due in nine years' time. The estimate of x suggests that cash flows expected in five years' time are underestimated by 40 per cent relative to a rational expectation of them. The other estimates, by assuming that all myopic behaviour occurs only after five years, generates even more excessive discounting in the later years. While it is always possible to interpret the results as reflecting varying and, in fact, rising risk premia throughout the period, Miles views this as a rather unlikely explanation.

While these results cannot be said conclusively to confirm the existence of myopic behaviour by investors, they constitute quite strong evidence, and certainly place the onus on those who would dispute the existence of such behaviour to show how this can be reconciled with the evidence. In relation to the models of myopia described above, Miles' results tend mainly to favour the mispricing arbitrage and intertemporal externalities approaches. The equilibrium condition in the arbitrage model that longer-term projects should be subject to greater underpricing would reveal itself in over-discounting, or undervaluing of longer-term cash flows, as found by Miles. Inadequate recognition of the overspill effects of investment in the longer term, as hypothesised in the intertemporal externalities approach, would again lead to under-estimation of longer-term cash flows.

The signal-jamming approach, in contrast, suggests that investors cor-rectly assess companies' earnings potential, albeit managers are nonetheless forced by security considerations systematically to favour short-term pro-jects. However, if for other reasons investors do place excessive emphasis on shorter-term earnings, then this would of course exacerbate the pressure on managers to favour shorter-term projects arising from the signal-jamming process.

In summary, drawing out reasons why rational investors and managers might systematically act in a myopic fashion has been difficult and contro-versial. It has been exacerbated by the methodological difficulties involved in finding reliable methods for identifying such behaviour, if it does exist. The development of a theoretical underpinning in recent years, together with recent evidence have probably switched the best judgement in favour of such behaviour, and this is important because myopic behaviour could lead to fairly large-scale and persistent under-investment in a country like the United Kingdom with a dispersed stock market, in which information asymmetries and the threat of takeover are likely to be predominant features; but the issue will no doubt remain a very lively one for some time to come. The policy debate will also continue over whether takeovers should be made easier in order to improve the disciplinary effect on managerial efficiency, or more difficult in order to avoid the alleged dangers of short-termism.

MANAGERIAL OBJECTIVES, GROWTH AND THE MYOPIA DEBATE

The previous sections focused attention on the information asymmetry characteristics of outside – as opposed to inside – control mechanisms. We now look at the other major distinction, namely the different locations of power that emerge from these control structures. We start from what is now the main framework for analysing the economic characteristics of different company control mechanisms, namely the Marris model.[63] This views managers as equating the growth of supply of funds with the growth of demand, the latter ultimately achieved through diversification. The growth of funds is a positive function of the profit rate, while the growth of demand, after some point, is a negative function of it. The latter relationship derives from the lower margins necessary to increase growth through lower prices, higher marketing, more research and development, etc., and from the tendency, again after some point, for faster growth to raise the capital–output ratio as a result of progressively less successful diversification in pursuit of ever-faster growth. The equilibrium growth rate can be increased by managers who are assumed to pursue growth for the greater salaries, status and power it affords, but this eventually entails lower profitability, higher gearing and/or new equity issues, all of which jeopardise the share price and hence raise the threat of takeover. The basic model is then one of growth maximisation subject to a takeover constraint. The extent of this discipline depends on how easy or difficult it is for shareholders to enforce their own objectives, and these enforcement costs will in turn reflect such things as the concentration of shareholders, the availability of ready benchmarks of achievable profitability and the like.

From this perspective, two inferences have traditionally been drawn. First, managerially controlled firms will tend to have higher growth rates but lower profit rates than owner-controlled firms because the latter, unlike the former, will have a direct concern for the profits they receive. Second, anything which reduces enforcement costs and, therefore, in the event of substantial non-profit-maximising behaviour by managers, makes takeover more likely, will improve resource allocation and economic welfare.

Further analysis has, however, indicated that both of these inferences may well be incorrect. With regard to the economic welfare effects, the seminal work is due to Odagiri (1981). He first argues that, in the industrial sector of an economy containing both growth maximisers and profit maximisers, the former will come to dominate, primarily because they will systematically be prepared to pay more for assets than the latter, reflecting the additional utility they get over and above the present value from increased levels of assets. Increasingly therefore we can think of the whole industrial sector in terms of a representative Marris-style enterprise, with the growth and profitability of the sector reflecting the strength of the growth motivation of managers and the extent of enforcement costs. If, as Odagiri argues is the case in Japan, growth motivation is powerful because managers rarely achieve greater salary, status or power through changing companies, and if enforcement costs are high because the stock market offers relatively little disciplinary effect via the threat of hostile takeover, then growth will be rapid. If, as in the US, there is a very flexible managerial labour market and a very flexible and effective market for corporate control, then industrial growth will be much lower. Similar comments apply to Germany and the United Kingdom, respectively.

Empirical support for this view relies not only on the faster rate of internal diversification and growth exhibited by Japan in comparison with the US and United Kingdom. Evidence also indicates that Japan has typically had quite a low profit rate, which at first sight is surprising in such a successful economy, but is fully explicable within the Marris-Odagiri framework; new product development has typically been faster and product life-cycles shorter than in the US, even though this may reduce profits prematurely on existing products, because it drives growth; export markets have played a major role in providing growth opportunities, rather than a marginal role in providing profit opportunities; investment and R&D have been much higher and dividends lower in Japan and Germany than in the US and United Kingdom; and the refined DCF criteria, test discount rates and disaggregate profit centres so often emphasised in UK and US investment techniques and management literature are relatively rare in Japan, replaced by criteria relating to market share, future growth, product diversification and innovation.[64]

The paradox in all this of course is that it is weak or ineffective markets – the managerial labour market and the market for corporate control – which generate faster growth and higher economic welfare in Japan. The dynamic welfare gains from growth as a result of ineffective markets exceed any static welfare gains traditionally associated with profit maximisation and efficient markets.

Turning to the other inference from the Marris model, namely that owner-controlled firms will be more concerned with profits than growth, this also appears flawed. In a detailed study of large unquoted companies, which were very largely owned, directly or indirectly, by the senior managers, Hay and Morris (1984) found that most were if anything more growth-oriented than comparable quoted companies owned by dispersed shareholders and controlled by salaried managers, for two reasons. First, in most cases the managers wished to pass the company on to the next generation. The major threat to this was inheritance and capital transfer taxes, liability for which could force a sale of the company to raise the necessary funds.[65] As earnings and/or dividends were the main determinants of the valuation of the company for capital taxation purposes, there was a strong incentive not to go above a profit rate necessary to finance expansion. Second, these companies, unlike quoted companies in the United Kingdom, experienced no threat of takeover if they should decide to go for longer-term, larger-scale and/or riskier projects which might enhance growth and long-term profitability, but which would, for reasons examined in the previous section, generate a potentially dangerous fall in share price if there had been a market for them and substantial non-managerial shareholdings.[66]

Empirically it was found that in the 1970s, unquoted companies both grew faster *and* were more profitable.[67]

The work of both Odagiri and Hay and Morris serves to strengthen the significance of the Marris framework, if not all the specific inferences. Nearly all companies are likely to have substantial growth motivation; quoted managerial companies are the most subject to disciplinary pressure to maximise profits; and economic welfare is likely is to be highest where this pressure is weakest.

This view of the ownership–control nexus throws new light on the question of short-termism. At one level it could generate a quite different interpretation of the traditional conflict between managers who believe that investors are myopic, and financial institutions and others who would dispute this. If managers behave as depicted in the Marris model, then rather than it being investors who fail to see the desirability of long-term investment which the managers sensibly work to pursue, it is the managers who in pursuit of their own goals try to over-invest, with the profit-maximising owners having, as best they can, to curb this through selling shares as a response.

While elements of this are almost certainly present, this none the less ignores both the analysis of short-termism in the previous section and the implication of the Marris model drawn out by Odagiri. Consideration of these leads on to a second, more comprehensive interpretation. We start by assuming an optimal investment[68] programme, I^*, which is defined as a set of investment decision over time, including both short- and long-term investment projects which, in the traditional manner, would maximise the present value of the earnings of the company. The investment programme actually pursued can differ from this for two main reasons. The short-term pressures described earlier will tend to reduce investment below I^*, to I, because they will systematically tend to discriminate against the longer-term components of I^*. This will, however, raise share prices. Managers will nevertheless want to invest more than I. This may be because of potential externalities which are not reflected in the present value but the inclusion of which we equate with the welfare optimum as derived in the Marris-Odagiri approach. However, the more powerful reason may well be the pursuit of managerial objectives which are helped by higher investment expenditure and greater growth. These forces may, if unfettered, raise investment partly towards or even beyond I^*. Thus, in an outside-control world where takeover is easy, investment may well fall short of I^*. At the other extreme, a highly developed inside-control structure is likely to see investment approach or even exceed I^*. The crucial element stemming from this analysis is that in the case of outside control, if takeover opportunities are limited, the relatively unfettered pursuit of growth by managers for their own purposes may well be welfare enhancing because it tends to offset the reduction in investment below I^* caused by outside control, and therefore tends to generate an investment programme nearer to I^*. It need not be the case that managers have any greater insight into the externality effects of, or incentives to obtain, these benefits, though in practice both may be true. Rather it is that weak control of managerial pursuit of growth leads to the type of investment programme which generates these effects, whereas tight restrictions on such activities would prevent them being realised.

Within this framework, managers operating under an outside-control structure will tend to view investors as creating short-termist pressures which depress investment below the level they wish to pursue, and below I^*. Investors, however, will see managers as trying to invest beyond the level which maximises their share price. Inside control then has three separate advantages. First, it tends to eliminate short-term pressures stemming from signal-jamming and arbitrage, raising actual investment, I, above I'. Second, the weakness or absence of the takeover mechanism permits more scope for managerial objectives to raise I above I' towards I^*. Third, in as far as inside control permits greater recognition of, and ability to appropriate externality effects, it directly encourages I to approach I^*. Thus the pursuit of managerial objectives, though distorting activity from conventional profit-maximising levels, offsets the distortions due to short-termism and tends to encourage investment with externality effects of the type elaborated upon above.

As in the myopia debate so here, evidence until recently has been very thin. Reference has already been made to the work by Hay and Morris which showed unquoted companies in the United Kingdom investing more, growing faster and generating more profits than equivalent quoted ones, and this is important evidence that outside control may not be the optimal mechanism for generating maximum economic performance.[69] There are, however, two caveats to this.

First, more recent work by Hay and Morris, updating their earlier study, found that, while similar results held through the recession of the early 1980s and up to around 1983–4, the difference in performance diminished and, in the major upswing of the later 1980s, reversed.[70] This may not necessarily undermine the view that outside control generates short-term pressures which reduce performance because there are indications in the data that unquoted companies exhibit more stable performance, experiencing less of a decline in recessions but less improvement in an expansionary phase. But attempts to identify this explicitly measuring the *persistence* of performance give ambiguous results.[71] There are signs of slightly greater persistence in unquoted companies over three years but the difference is small, and from one year to the next it is quoted companies that exhibit greater persistence.

The second caveat is that we cannot assume that any difference in performance between quoted and unquoted companies stems only from the control problems inherent in outside control, still less that it is short-termist problems. Though both assumptions are plausible, there are other differences, most notably that in most unquoted companies the majority if not all of the shares are owned by the managers or their associates. This alignment

239

of motives of managers and owners may have an advantage quite separate from any resulting from the absence of a ready market in ownership rights.

An alternative approach is to look at shareholder concentration in quoted companies. In the United Kingdom, Leech and Leahy (1991) obtained data on share holdings for a sample of 470 quoted companies, 325 of which were in *The Times 1000* list of largest UK companies and covering 32 per cent of companies on the London Stock Exchange. They then split this sample into 'owner-controlled' companies, where shareholder concentration was sufficient to give them effective control, and 'managerially controlled' companies, where shareholder concentration was insufficient. In practice, as they point out, it is very difficult to say what degree of concentration of shareholding is necessary to locate effective control with the shareholders rather than the managers, and they carried out all their analysis with six different measures, three relating to the size of the largest shareholder and three, using earlier work by Cubbin and Leach (1983), relating to the probability that the largest shareholder could, given certain assumptions, obtain majority support in any future contested vote. Allowing the data to determine which measure statistically gives the best results they found that on average 'owner-controlled' companies generated 1.89 per cent higher margins, 4.54 per cent higher return on shareholders' capital, 5.06 per cent per annum faster growth of sales and 10.59 per cent per annum faster growth of net assets. They were also associated with higher company valuation and lower salary of the highest-paid director but these were not quite statistically significant. While the higher profitability is not surprising, the substantially higher growth performance suggests that the reduced threat of short-term takeover pressures as a result of concentrated share ownership permitted these companies to pursue longer-term strategies which eventually generate higher profits as well.

Here again there are two caveats. First, Leech and Leahy also include specific measures of shareholder concentration and the preferred measure is associated with lower valuation, lower profit margins and lower assets growth. However, because concentration and control are included in the same equations this is an association, given the control type. On the preferred control definition, with regard to the negative effect on growth, 86 per cent of the sample are classified as managerially controlled. Thus, given that concentration is insufficient to shift control from the managers, and given therefore that the problems of outside control are likely to be at their most acute, a higher concentration of shareholding to some degree inhibits managerial pursuit of growth because it is easier for a few shareholders to sell shares and thereby generate a takeover threat. The lower margins and valuations of managerially-controlled companies, when shareholder concentration is higher, may reflect parallel short-term pressures that inhibit longer-term profitable opportunities, but could also indicate the Japanese situation where greater freedom to pursue longer-term strategies, though welfare enhancing, is at the expense of persistently lower margins.[72]

The second caveat is that, while on their preferred definition of owner control based on a probabilistic voting model, the great majority of quoted companies are managerially controlled, none the less in 91 per cent of Leech and Leahy's sample, the largest shareholder held over 5 per cent of the shares; in 54 per cent, the largest three shareholders together had a controlling interest; and in all but one, the largest ten had majority control. If these small groups acted together, a matter on which there is no evidence or data, then much tighter ownership control would be possible. Given the advantages of owner control, this cannot be ruled out. Against this, it is not clear that Leech and Leahy would find the results that they do if this coalition potential were being exploited on an appreciable scale.[73]

Comparable studies in the US do not exist, but a study by Holderness and Sheehan (1988) compared the performance of quoted companies with a majority shareholder (a condition that applied to only 5.3 per cent of Leech and Leahy's sample) with that of matched pairs of quoted companies exhibiting dispersed shareholdings. This found much higher levels of capital investment amongst corporations with company majority holdings, much higher advertising expenditures amongst individual majority holders and much higher research and development expenditure in both groups than their dispersed shareholdings counterparts. However, these differences were in part due to an outlier, with median differences tending to be much smaller (though all still in the same direction) and in some cases not statistically significant. In a different type of study, Wruck (1989) found that on average a public sale of shares, which typically increases the dispersion of shareholdings, resulted in a negative average abnormal return, whereas private sales, which typically increase the concentration of shareholdings, resulted in a 4.5 per cent positive average abnormal return. There is a significant range of concentration over which the effect of the latter is negative, but this may reflect management purchases and growing management entrenchment which would permit longer-term and/or more growth-oriented strategies but reduce share valuation.

This leads on to the other area which has been examined, namely the effect of managerial shareholdings. A study by Masson and Madhavan (1991) found that the value of a firm rose on average with managerial shareholding. Morck, Schleifer and Vishny (1988) found that increases in management shareholdings up to 5 per cent of the total and above 25 per cent raised stock market valuation (as measured by Tobin's q) but lowered it in the 5–25 per cent range. They interpret the positive effect up to 5 per cent as reflecting increasing alignment of shareholder and management interests, and the negative effects from 5–25 per cent as reflecting increasing managerial entrenchment, dominating any incentive alignments. Other evidence in both the US and United Kingdom is not consistent with this non-linear relationship[74] but, even if overall there is a positive relation between managerial shareholdings and valuation, this unfortunately does not help much in examining myopia. High valuation despite, or indeed because of, the lower threat of takeover would be entirely consistent with the short-termist thesis, but it would not be rejected even if valuation fell, if the stock market was indicating by this its lack of recognition of the longer-term investment opportunities now able to be exploited. It is the impact of managerial shareholding on investment, both tangible and intangible, and on growth which needs to be focused upon, with stock market valuation being a derivative consideration. Indeed, paradoxically, if liquid stock markets are myopic, then higher managerial shareholdings in such markets may exacerbate the problem because managers not only face a constraint on longer-term strategies, but also an incentive not to pursue them.

Overall, therefore, there is some support for the view that more concentrated share ownership generates better performance in quoted companies if it is sufficient to generate ownership control, such that shorter-term pressures arising from the dispersed sale of shares are weakened. But the specific relationships between shareholder concentration and managerial shareholdings on the one hand, and myopia, investment, growth and stock market valuation on the other, remain unclear. We are still only in the building phase of a more comprehensive picture of such governance relations, but at least some of the characteristics of dispersed versus concentrated shareholdings are beginning to emerge.

CONCLUSIONS

Ownership of corporations in the form of equity shares owned by investors and traded on open markets, such as exists in the United Kingdom is one (but only one) of a number of forms of ownership. We have looked at reasons for believing that the information flows and incentive effects associated with such institutional arrangements may create significant problems for companies which, at least in the circumstances in which many UK quoted companies find themselves, are potentially detrimental to corporate performance. Detailed review of the evidence on takeovers suggests, first, that a market in corporate control may play an important role in permitting or facilitating corporate restructuring, retrenchment and the pursuit of corporate strategies. But evidence from other countries suggests that this is not the only institutional arrangement able to provide such opportunities. Hostile takeovers in the United Kingdom appear to provide what in several other industrial economies is provided by internal restructuring, implemented administratively. Second, the stock market does not provide a particularly strong, effective or efficient mechanism for disciplining poor managerial performance or for creating incentives to correct the latter, even though there can be no doubt that it does have some such effects. In addition the stock market frequently exhibits valuation errors both by investors and acquiring companies, particularly over-optimistic valuations by the latter. These can create opportunities for, or generate takeover activity which has zero or negative effects on company performance.

With regard to the question of whether trading of equity on a liquid stock market generates short-term pressures on companies which prevent them pursuing longer-term welfare-enhancing strategies, it has previously been argued that this is theoretically implausible and rejected by the evidence. However, we have seen, first, that there are a number of reasons why these pressures might systematically occur in developed stock markets. These revolve around the problems of transmitting signals to investors in outside control systems; arbitrage processes coupled with the asymmetric effects of under- and over-valuation; the role of sunk costs, risk and intertemporal externalities; and the dynamic gains from managerial growth strategies which may offset some or all of any short-term pressures generated by the stock market. All of this is consistent with the generally superior performance of companies, both in the United Kingdom and abroad, which are not subject to the economic effects of public quotation on a stock exchange. Concentrated shareholdings which generate inside control reduce the information asymmetry problem, reduce therefore the need for signalling mechanisms which can create short-termist pressures, minimise the significance of the mispricing of shares, make negative shocks more survivable and reduce the threat of long-term implicit contracts being invalidated. Above all, they provide a context in which longer-term growth-oriented strategies can be pursued without the threat of takeover which would otherwise inhibit them.

Second, early evidence against short-termism was in fact insufficient to reject it. If myopia does exist, then the longer-term investments which would depress share prices and generate a confirmatory negative relationship between them are precisely the ones that firms will systematically avoid. Against this, direct estimates of the discount rates used by investors suggest that short-term pressures do exist, though the precise reasons need clarification. To arrive at a definite conclusion will require further analysis, in the light of the theories we have examined, of the interrelation between ownership structure, investor and management behaviour and company performance measured not only by profitability but by investment, innovation and growth.

In the meantime, policy can be based only on our present state of knowledge. This suggests, at a minimum, greater scepticism towards the view that a highly developed stock market and ready scope for hostile takeover are bound to improve industrial efficiency overall. Rather it indicates leaning more towards greater constraints on such activity, either relying more on the pursuit of growth by managers to provide longer-term efficiency gains, and/or encouraging greater ownership concentration, the development of structures which bring about more direct ownership involvement in companies, and greater emphasis on internal monitoring systems, all substantially less constrained by external stock market pressures than is the case at present. In the context of current growing European integration, this suggests governments should be wary of a process of harmonisation in relation to equity markets if it involves deregulation designed to encourage more extensive, more open and more liquid equity markets such as exist already in the United Kingdom. There is little evidence that this is necessary, still less that it is sufficient to promote corporate efficiency or long-term economic growth.

NOTES

1 This paper is one of several resulting from research into the dynamic efficiency characteristics of companies and their determinants, financed by the Economic and Social Research Council grant no. L102251013.
2 For an elaboration and quantification of these characteristics see Hay and Morris (1991, pp. 273–81).
3 While the location of ownership and of managerial control of companies in the United Kingdom may appear obvious, there is considerable uncertainty and some semantic confusion about the concept of corporate control. Also, while legal title to ownership may generally be clear (though even this is problematic in some non-trivial cases such as insolvency) the discretionary powers which ownership provides depend heavily on the legal and institutional arrangement surrounding patterns of ownership. For a detailed analysis of the concepts of ownership and control, see Hay et al. (1993, ch. 12). In the context of ownership reform, in China and other economies in transition, the concept of ownership and control are far from clear-cut, but the analysis of them is equally applicable to Western capitalist economies.
4 For a detailed analysis of the ownership and management structure of unquoted companies in the United Kingdom, see Hay and Morris (1984).
5 The crude capital asset pricing model (CAPM) suggests that *all* investors rationally should hold the *same* portfolio of shares, albeit in differing ratios to their so-called riskless holding of interest-bearing bonds, depending on their risk preferences. However, different companies might provide the same risk and covariance with the rest of the market as each other so that portfolios which are identical from the point of view of the model might contain different companies' shares. For a description of the CAPM, problems with it and empirical testing of it, see Hay and Morris (1991, pp. 499–505).
6 See Franks and Mayer (1992).
7 See Kester (1992).
8 For a formal statement of the principal–agent problem, and possible resolutions of it, see Hay and Morris (1991, pp. 311–17).
9 For example, the strength of small biotechnology companies in the US and United Kingdom may be partly attributable to this. More speculatively, outside control may have some advantages in economies more exposed to fluctuations and/or external shocks.
10 To use the useful but often overlooked approach of Hirschman, inside control permits a 'voice' option if performance is poor, i.e. complaint, investigation and adjustment without severing formal or informal contracts, whereas outside control tends to generate an 'exit' response, sale of shares and severance of the economic relationship involved. As Hardie points out, the information flows and decision possibilities in inside control are much richer because they do not have to

be standardised, whereas outside control regimes require established accountancy procedures and reporting conventions, within which it may be much more difficult to convey idiosyncratic information. See Hardie (1990)

11 Franks and Mayer (1992) report that there have been only four hostile takeovers in Germany since the Second World War.

12 See Jenkinson and Mayer (1992).

13 The notion of stock market efficiency is considered in more detail below. Here full efficiency implies that all formation available at any time, including evidence of systematic errors in the past, is used to determine share prices. The latter therefore do not systematically err from the present value of future earnings, there are no share 'bargains' to be had and no methods by which any investor, on the basis of 'inside' or 'outside' information, can systematically beat the market index.

14 Economies of scope occur when two products are related such that the marginal cost of producing one is dependent on the level of output of the other.

15 See Hay and Morris, (1991, ch. 14) for a fuller discussion of most of these issues. For discussion of the information advantages of horizontal mergers in a stochastic market, see Gal-Or (1988). While merging firms generally gain from greater precision of information and the reduction in the number of rivals whose behaviour must be predicted, they only gain from consequent changes in responsiveness to information if competition is of Bertrand form, i.e. in prices. In Cournot (quantity) competition, there is no such incentive to merge.

16 It can be shown that if $d > C/n$, where d is the dilution per share, C is the costs of takeover and n is the number of shares in total, then provided that shareholders in the largest company expect dilution, there will be no free-rider problem.

17 See Yarrow (1985).

18 Many bids are made conditional on 90 per cent acceptance, but reserve the right to reduce this figure. The raider generally cannot, and would not wish to pre-commit to this, given that 50.1 per cent gives control.

19 See Hay and Morris (1991, p. 516).

20 In this context 'inefficiency' covers both underperformance and pursuit of alternative objectives.

21 For the seminal work in this area see Fama (1970).

22 For a recent survey of this evidence see Fama (1991).

23 See Ippolito (1991), Sharpe (1996) and Jensen (1968).

24 For a survey of work on the excess volatility approach see Shiller (1987). On the over-reaction hypothesis, fads and bubbles, see de Bondt and Thaler (1985, 1987), Blanchard and Watson (1982), Biba and Grossman (1987), Flood and Hodrick (1986) and West (1988).

25 Dividends may be smoothed by managers to reflect only sustainable earnings changes, resulting in dividends being more damped than the price of the shares which entitle an investor to these dividends. See Marsh and Merton (1986). Also, in response Shiller (1986). Bubbles could be the result of rational shifts in expected returns. See Fama and French (1989). For more explicit rejection of the efficient markets hypothesis see Lehmann (1990).

26 For the main analysis of these motives and their effect on the economic behaviour and performance of firms, see Marris (1963).

27 Note that even if allocational and acquisitional takeovers become fully efficient in this way, this by no means guarantees resource allocation efficiency in the economy as a whole. Assets may still be transferred from more efficient to less efficient but growth-maximising managers. See below, however, for potential offsetting mechanisms.

28 Unless there is perfect positive correlation between the earnings streams of two

firms, their merging will always reduce the ratio of the standard deviation of earnings to their mean.

29　See Levy and Sarnat (1970).

30　That larger size does in general reduce the probability of being taken over is one of the few empirical results in this field which finds almost universal support. See the discussion of empirical studies below.

31　See, for example, Hayn (1989), who shows that loss carry-forwards and expiring tax credits are significant attributes of target firms in the US. In addition, mergers are more likely to be completed (or in some cases will only be completed) where the tax liability on gains from the sale of equity are deferred, usually as a result of the bid being a share rather than a cash offer. These results are consistent with, and may offer some partial explanation for, the widely observed fact that much if not all of the investor wealth gains in a merger accrue to the shareholders of the acquired firm. (This is discussed later in the chapter.) It is similarly consistent with increased merger activity in boom periods when successful firms typically have higher tax liabilities.

32　See 'Takeover activity in the 1980s', *Bank of England Quarterly Bulletin*, vol. 29 (1989), pp. 78–85. If such considerations were important, they are unlikely to be so now, given recent changes in relative rates of personal taxation of income and capital gains.

33　See, for example, Franks and Mayer (1990).

34　See Scharfstein (1988).

35　This has important effects on what commitments are possible *ex-ante*. In addition the forms of legal contracts will reflect the threat of takeover and influence the probability of takeover.

36　A detailed examination of the share price movements of thirteen leading conglomerates indicates that, contrary to general perception, they did not make higher returns for their shareholders than other companies. There is no inconsistency therefore between their performance and returns to shareholders. See Ravenscroft and Scherer (1987, pp. 207–10).

37　For a survey of other supporting results see Hay and Morris (1991, pp. 524–5).

38　Ravenscraft and Scherer (1987). The inclusion of unlisted companies does, however, introduce additional problems of valuing assets.

39　They also found that internal reform was more likely if the firm was managerially controlled, but takeover more likely if the firm was effectively run by the founder or some other individual entrepreneur. The effectiveness of internal reform processes is considered further below.

40　In an interesting 'comment' on the article by Franks and Mayer (1990). Malinvaud argues that many takeovers appear not to be motivated by considerations of poor target company performance.

41　See also Malatesta (1983) for further support.

42　See Jarrell, Brickley and Netter (1988).

43　In addition, Franks, Harris and Titman (1991) have shown that the negative abnormal post-merger performance found in some studies may be due to the use of incorrect benchmarks for assessing risk in the estimation of abnormal returns.

44　Bid premiums also appear to have jumped in 1973–4 as a result of the oil shock, more volatile economic considerations, etc., which increased the heterogeneity of investors' expectations. See Nathan and O'Keefe (1989).

45　See, for example, Jarrell and Poulson (1987).

46　See, for example, McWilliams (1996), Jarrell and Poulson (1987, 1988), Linn and McConnell (1983), Malanesta and Walkling (1988), Rytgaert (1988).

47　See Jarrell and Poulson (1987).

48 See Harris (1990).
49 Further support for this comes from evidence on defensive corporate restructuring by managers in response to takeover bids, which can be large and costly in terms of shareholder wealth. See Dann and DeAngelo (1988). Note, however, that neither managerial resistance to a bid, nor some other frequently observed characteristics of takeover such as sequential and mistaken bidding, the emergence of white knights, etc., *necessarily* indicate that managers are not trying to maximise shareholder value. See Giammarino and Heinkel (1986).
50 In fact, Nickell and Wadhwani (1987) provide empirical evidence that investors systematically place too much weight on current dividends in their valuations.
51 Formally, let the share price be P_0, the fundamental value be F_0, the interest rate i, and the time to correction n. Assuming that the fundamental value grows at rate i, the fundamental value at time n is $F_0(1+i)^n$. The payment to the supplier of funds is $P_0(1+i)^n$. The present value of the gain as represented by the difference between these two is given by

$$PV = \frac{(F_0 - P_0)(1 + i)^n}{(1 + i)^n} = F_0 - P_0$$

which is independent of n.
52 See, for example, Stiglitz and Weiss (1983).

53 $$PV = \frac{F_0(1 + i)^n - P_0(1 + i')^n}{(1 + i')^n}$$

where i' is the higher cost of funds to the arbotrageur; dPV/dn is then negative.
54 See Hay and Morris (1991, pp. 95–100) for a survey of these issues.
55 For the seminal works, see Scott (1986), Romer (1986, 1990a, 1990b). For a recent survey of the issues, see Boltho and Holtham (1992).
56 For the formal model on which this is based, see Morris (1996).
57 For an elaboration of the mechanism see Morris and Stout (1985).
58 This result raises the possibility that institutional investors are rather specialised with those analysing high-technology industry understanding and geared to respond to R&D announcements, but those looking at low-technology industries focusing more on earnings *per se*. There may also have been 'clientele' effects, i.e. investors with high marginal income tax rates preferring to invest for capital gains in long-term opportunities. This could make R&D investment more attractive for these investors than low marginal tax-rate payers more concerned with immediate income.
59 More tentative support comes from Ben-Zion (1984) and from Cockburn and Griliches (1988).
60 Referred to in Stein (1988).
61 See Stein (1988).
62 The exposition in the text is a highly simplified version of Miles' argument. For a critique and reply, see Satchell and Damant (1995).
63 See Marris (1963). For a summary and assessment of Marris's work see Hay and Morris (1991, ch. 10).
64 See Odagiri (1992), especially ch. 8.
65 While it might be thought sufficient to sell only a minority of the shares, thus still ensuring management control, this was rarely if ever possible, because a minority stake in an unquoted company would provide neither control nor marketability. A holder of such a stake would therefore have no way of avoiding or offsetting poor managerial performance. In practice therefore the only realistic options, in the

event that personal funds were insufficient to pay the tax liability, were flotation, sale or break up of the company.

66 There are some unquoted companies, nearly all first-generation ones, where the main motive of the founder-managers is to maximise the value of the company and then float or sell it to make the maximum capital sum on retirement. These were more prevalent in the 1980s but were not generally amongst the larger unquoted companies in the UK.

67 See Hay and Morris (1984). Subsequent work for the 1980s indicates that this pattern persisted in the first half of the 1980s but not in the second half. This may reflect that unquoted companies were less responsive in the short term to *either* the recession of the early 1980s *or* the rapid expansion of the economy in the later 1980s. See Hay *et al* (1991).

68 'Investment' should here be interpreted in the broadest possible sense to include R&D expenditure, product and market development, training, etc.

69 See Hay and Morris (1984). For a review of other studies in this vein, see Hay and Morris (1991).

70 Hay *et al.* (1991).

71 Morris (1993).

72 Only one other UK study has looked at shareholder concentration, but this is mainly concerned with managerial shareholding and the problems of departure from 'one share-one vote'. See Curcio (1992). Current research by the author, utilising shareholder concentration data over a six-year span for all quoted companies in the United Kingdom, is aimed at identifying the impact of concentration independent of any control type to which it might give rise.

73 We also note Schleifer and Vishny's (1986) work which, having found comparable evidence in the US of shareholder concentration, points out theoretical reasons why the incentive to start compiling larger shareholdings might be small if shareholdings are initially highly dispersed.

74 See, for example, Jarrell and Poulson (1988), Curcio (1992), Jensen and Warner (1988).

REFERENCES

Ben-Zion, U. (1984) 'The R&D and investment decision and the relationship to the firm's market value: some preliminary results', in Z. Griliches (ed.), *R&D, Patents, and Productivity*, Chicago: University of Chicago Press.

Bhagat, S., Schleifer, A. and Vishny, R. (1990) 'Hostile takeovers in the 1980s: the return to corporate specialization', *Brookings Paper on Economic Activity* (Microeconomics), pp. 1–84.

Blanchard, O. and Watson, M. (1982) 'Bubbles, rational expectations and financial markets', in P. Wachtel (ed.), *Crises in the Economic and Financial Structure*, Lexington.

Boltho, A. and Holtham, J. (1992) 'New approaches to economic growth', *Oxford Review of Economic Policy*, vol. 8, pp. 1–14.

de Bondt, W. and Thaler, R. (1985) 'Does the stock market overreact?', *Journal of Finance*, vol. 40, pp. 793–805.

de Bondt, W. and Thaler, R. (1987) 'Further evidence on investor overreaction and stock market seasonality', *Journal of Finance*, vol. 42, pp. 557–8.

Bradley, M., Desai, A. and Kim, E. (1988) 'Synergistic gains from corporate acquisitions and their division between the stockholders of target and acquiring firms', *Journal of Financial Economics*, vol. 21, pp. 3–40.

Brown, D. and Ryngaert, M. (1991) 'The mode of acquisition in takeovers: taxes and asymmetric information', *Journal of Finance*, vol. 46, pp. 657–70.

Chan, S., Martin, J. and Kensigner, J. (1990) 'Corporate research and development expenditures and share value', *Journal of Financial Economics*, vol. 26, pp. 255–76.

Coase, R. (1937) 'The nature of the firm', *Economics*, n.s. vol. 4, pp. 386–405.

Cockburn, I. and Griliches, Z. (1988) 'Industry effects and appropriability measures in the stock market's valuations of R&D and patents', *American Economic Review*, P&P vol. 78, pp. 419–23.

Cubbin, J. and Leach, D. (1983) 'The effect of shareholding dispersion on the degree of control in British companies: theory and measurement', *Economic journal*, vol. 93, pp. 351–69.

Curcio, R. (1992) 'Managerial ownership of shares and corporate performance: an empirical analysis of UK companies 1972–86', Working Paper No. 290, Centre for Economic Performance, London School of Economics.

Dann, L. and DeAngelo, H. (1988) 'Corporate financial policy and corporate controls', *Journal of Financial Economics*, vol. 20, pp. 87–127.

Dennis, D. and McConnell, J. (1986) 'Corporate mergers and security returns', *Journal of Financial Economics*, vol. 16, pp. 143–87.

Diba, B. and Grossman, H. (1987) 'On the inception of rational bubbles', *Quarterly Journal of Economics*, vol. 102, pp. 697–700.

Eckbo, B. (1983) 'Horizontal mergers, collusion, and stockholder wealth', *Journal of Financial Economics*, pp. 241–73.

Eckbo, B. (1985) 'Mergers and the market concentration doctrine: evidence from the capital market', *Journal of Business*, vol. 58, pp. 325–49.

Fama, E. (1970) 'Efficient capital markets: a review of theory and empirical work', *Journal of Finance*, vol. 25, pp. 380–423.

Fama, E. (1991) 'Efficient capital markets II', *Journal of Finance*, vol. 46, pp. 1575–617.

Fama, E. and French, K. (1989) 'Business conditions and expected returns on stocks and bonds', *Journal of Financial Economics*, vol. 25, pp. 23–49.

Firth, M. (1979) 'The profitability of takeovers and mergers', *Economic Journal*, vol. 89, pp. 316–28.

Flood, R. and Hodrick, R, (1986) 'Asset price volatility, bubbles and process switching', *Journal of Finance*, vol. 41, pp. 831–42.

Franks, J. and Harris, R. (1989) 'Shareholder wealth effects of corporate takeovers: the UK experience 1955–85', *Journal of Financial Economics*, vol. 23, pp. 225–49.

Franks, J. and Harris, R. (1989) 'Shareholder wealth effects of UK takeovers', in J. Fairburn and J. Kay (eds), *Merger and Merger Policy*, Oxford: Oxford University Press.

Franks, J., Harris, R. and Mayer, C. (1987) 'Means of payment in takeovers: results for the UK and US', CEPR Discussion Paper 200.

Franks, J., Harris, R. and Titman S. (1991) 'The post-merger share price performance of acquiring firms'. *Journal of Financial Economics*, vol. 29, pp. 81–96.

Franks, J. and Mayer, C. (1990) 'Capital markets and corporate control: a study of France, Germany and the UK', *Economic Policy*, vol. 10, pp. 191–231.

Franks, J. and Mayer, C. (1992) 'Corporate control: a synthesis of the international evidence', mimeo.

Gal-Or, E. (1988) 'The informational advantages or disadvantages of horizontal mergers', *International Economic Review*, vol. 29, pp. 639–61.

Giammarino, R. and Heinkel, R. (1966) 'A model of dynamic takeover behaviour', *Journal of Finance*, vol. 41, pp. 465–80.

Grossman, S. and Hart, O. (1980) 'Takeover bids, the free-rider problem and the theory of the corporation', *Bell Journal of Economics*, vol. 11, pp. 42–64.

Grossman, S. and Stiglitz, J. (1980) 'The impossibility of informationally efficient markets', *American Economic Review*, vol. 70, pp. 393–408.

Hardie, J. (1990) 'Comment', on J. Franks and C. Mayer, 'Takeovers', *Economic Policy*, pp. 191–223.

Harris, R. (1990) 'Antitakeover measures, golden parachutes and target firm shareholder welfare', *Rand Journal of Economics*, vol. 21, pp. 614–25.

Harris, R., Stewart, J. and Carleton, W. (1982) 'Financial characteristics of acquired firms', in M. Keenan and L. White (eds), *Mergers and Acquisitions: Current Problems in Perspectives*, Lexington.

Hay, D. and Morris, D. (1984) *Unquoted Companies*, Basingstoke: Macmillan.

Hay, D. and Morris, D. (1991) *Industrial Economics and Organisation*, Oxford: Oxford University Press.

Hay, D., Morris, D., Evans, S. and Macey-Dare, R. (1991) *The Performance of Quoted and Unquoted Companies in the 1980s*, Oxford: Institute of Economics and Statistics.

Hay, D., Morris, D., Liu, G. and Yao, S. (1993) *State-owned enterprises and economic reform in China*, Oxford: Oxford University Press.

Hayn, C. (1989) 'Tax attributes as determinants of shareholder gains in corporate acquisitions', *Journal of Financial Economics*, vol. 23, pp. 121–53.

Healy, P., Palepu, K. and Ruback, R. (1992) 'Does corporate performance improve after mergers', *Journal of Financial Economics*, vol. 31, pp. 135–75.

Hirschey, M. (1982) 'Intangible capital aspects of advertising and R&D expenditures', *Journal of Industrial Economics*, vol. 30, pp. 375–90.

Holderness, C. and Sheehan, D. (1988) 'The role of majority shareholders in publicly held corporations', *Journal of Financial Economics*, vol. 20, pp. 317–46.

Ippolito, R. (1991) 'Efficiency with costly information: a study of mutual fund performance 1965–84', *Quarterly Journal of Economics*, vol. 104, pp. 1–23.

Jarrell, G., Brickley, J. and Netter, J. (1988) 'The market for corporate control: the empirical evidence since 1980', *Journal of Economic Perspectives*, vol. 2, pp. 49–68.

Jarrell, G. and Poulson, A. (1987) 'Shark repellants and stock prices', *Journal of Financial Economics*, vol. 19, pp. 127–68.

Jarrell, G. and Poulson, A. (1988) 'Dual-class recapitalisations as antitakeover mechanisms; the recent evidence', *Journal of Financial Economics*, vol. 20, pp. 129–52.

Jenkinson, T. and Mayer, C. (1992) 'Corporate governance and corporate control', *Oxford Review of Economic Policy*, vol. 8, no. 3, pp. 1–10.

Jensen, M. (1968) 'The performance of mutual funds in the period 1945–1964', *Journal of Finance*, vol. 23, pp. 389–416.

Jensen, M. (1986) 'Agency costs of free cash flow, corporate finance and takeovers', *American Economics Review*, P&P vol. 76, pp. 323–9.

Jensen, M. and Ruback, R. (1983) 'The market for corporate control: the scientific evidence', *Journal of Financial Economics*, vol. 11, pp. 5–50.

Jensen, M. and Warner, J. (1988) 'The distribution of power among corporate managers, shareholders, and directors', *Journal of Financial Economics*, vol. 20, pp. 3–24.

Kester, W. (1992) 'Industrial groups as a system of contractual governance', *Oxford Review of Economic Policy*, vol. 8, no. 3, pp. 24–44.

Leech, D. and Leahy, J. (1991) 'Ownership structure, control type classifications and the performance of large British companies', *Economics Journal*, vol. 101, pp. 1418–37.

Lehmann, B. (1990) 'Fade, martingales and market efficiency', *Quarterly Journal of Economics*, vol. 105, pp. 1–28.

Levine, P. and Aaronovitch, S. (1981–2) 'The financial characteristics of firms and theory of merger activity', *Journal of Industrial Economics*, vol. 30, pp. 149–72.

Levy, H. and Sarnat, M. (1970) 'Diversification, portfolio analysis and the uneasy case for conglomerate mergers', *Journal of Finance*, vol. 25, pp. 795–802.

Linn, S. and McConnell, J. (1983 'An empirical investigation of the impact of "antitakeover amendments" on common stock prices', *Journal of Financial Economics*, vol. 11, pp. 361–99.

McConnell, J. and Muscarella, C. (1985) 'Corporate capital expenditure decisions and the market value of the firm', *Journal of Financial Economics*, vol. 14, pp. 399–422.

McWilliams, V. (1990) 'Managerial share ownership and the stock market effects of antitakeover amendment proposals', *Journal of Finance*, vol. 45, pp. 1627–40.

Malatesta, P. (1983) 'The wealth effect of merger activity and the objective functions of merging firms', *Journal of Financial Economics*, vol. 11, pp. 155–81.

Malatesta, P. and Walkling, R. (1988) 'Poison pill securities', *Journal of Financial Economics*, vol. 20, pp. 341–76.

Marsh, T. and Merton, R. (1986) 'Dividend rationality and variance bounds tests for rationality of stockmarket prices', *American Economic Review*, vol. 76, pp. 483–98.

Martin, K. and McConnell, J. (1991) 'Corporate performance, corporate takeover and management turnovers', *Journal of Finance*, vol. 46, pp. 671–87.

Marris, R. (1963) *The Economic Theory of Managerial Capitalism*, London: Macmillan.

Masson, R. and Madhavan, A. (1991) 'Insider trading and the value of the firm', *Journal of Industrial Economics*, vol. 39, pp. 333–54.

Meeks, G. (1977) *Disappointing Marriage: A Study of the Gains from Merger*, Cambridge: Cambridge University Press.

Miles, D. (1993) 'Testing for Short-Termism in the UK Stock Market', *Economic Journal*, vol. 103, pp. 1379–96.

Morck, R. Shleifner, A. and Vishny, R. (1988) 'Management ownership and market valuation', *Journal of Financial Economics*, vol. 20, pp. 293–315.

Morck, R., Shleifner, A. and Vishny, R. (1989) 'Alternative mechanisms for corporate control', *American Economic Review*, vol. 19, pp. 842–52.

Morck, R., Shleifner, A. and Vishny, R. (1990) 'The stock market and investment: is the market a sideshow?', *Brookings Papers on Economic Activity*, pp. 157–215.

Morris, D. (1996) 'Sunk costs, shocks and myopia', Working Paper, Institute of Economics, Oxford.

Morris, D. and Stout, D. (1985) 'Industrial policy', in D. Morris (ed.), *The Economic System in the UK* (third edn), Oxford: Oxford University Press, pp. 851–93.

Muellbroek, L., Mitchell, M., Mulherin, J. *et al.* (1990) 'Shark repellents and managerial myopia: an empirical test', *Journal of Political Economics*, vol. 98, pp. 1108–17.

Mueller, D. (1980) 'The United States, 1962–72', in D. Mueller (ed.), *The Determinants and Effects of Mergers*, Oedgeschlager: Gunn & Hain.

Mulins, M. and Wadhwani, S. (1989) 'The effect of the stock market on investment', *European Economics review*, vol. 33, pp. 129–61.

Nathan, K. and O'Keefe, T. (1989) 'The rise in takeover premiums: an exploratory study', *Journal of Financial Economics*, vol. 23, pp. 101–20.

Nickell, S. J. and Wadhwani, S. (1987) 'Myopia, the "dividend puzzle" and share prices', Discussion paper 272, Centre for Labour Economics, London School of Economics, February.

Odagiri, H. (1981) *The Theory of Growth in a Corporate Economy*, Cambridge: Cambridge University Press.

Odagiri, H. (1992) *Growth through Competition, Competition through Growth*, Oxford: Oxford University Press.

Pakes, A. (1985) 'On patents, R&D, and the stock market rate of return', *Journal of Political Economy*, vol. 93, pp. 390–409.

Pound, J. (1988) 'The information effects of takeovers', *Journal of Financial Economics*, vol. 22, pp. 207–28.

Ryngaert, M. (1988) 'The effect of poison pill securities on shareholder wealth', *Journal of Financial Economics*, vol. 20, pp. 377–417.

Ravenscraft, D. and Scherer, F. (1987) *Mergers, Sell-offs and Economic Efficiency*, Brookings Institution.

251

Roll, R. (1986) 'The hubris hypothesis of corporate takeover', *Journal of Business*, vol. 59, pp. 197–216.

Romer, P. (1986) 'Increasing returns and long-run economic growth', *Journal of Political Economy*, vol. 94, pp. 1002–37.

Romer, P. (1990) 'Capital labour and productivity', *Brookings Papers on Economic Activity: Microeconomics*, pp. 337–67.

Romer, P. (1990) 'Endogenous technical change', *Journal of Political Economy*, vol. 98, pp. S71–S102.

Sarnat, M. (1970) 'Diversification, portfolio analysis and the uneasy case for conglomerate mergers', *Journal of Finance*, vol. 23, pp. 795–802.

Satchell, S. E. and Damant, D. C. (1995) 'Testing for Short Termism in the UK Stock Market: A Comment' and D. Miles, 'Testing for Short Termism in the UK Stock Market: A Reply', *Economic Journal*, vol. 105, pp. 1218–55.

Scharfstein, D. (1988) 'The disciplinary role of takeovers', *Review of Economic Studies*, 55, pp. 185–99.

Schleifer, A. and Vishny, R. (1986) 'Large shareholders and corporate control', *Journal of Political Economy*, vol. 94, pp. 461–88.

Schleifer, A. and Vishny, R. (1990) 'Equilibrium short horizons of investors and firms', *American Economic Review*, P&P vol. 89, pp. 148–53.

Scott, M. (1989) *A New View of Economic Growth*, Oxford: Oxford University Press.

Sharpe, W. (1966) 'Mutual fund performance', *Journal of Business*, vol. 39, pp119–38.

Shiller, R. (1986) 'The Marsh–Merton model of manager smoothing of dividends', *American Economic Review*, vol. 76, pp. 499–503.

Shiller, R. (1987) 'The volatility of stock market prices', *Science*, vol. 235 (2 January), pp. 33–7.

Singh, A. (1971) *Takeovers*, Cambridge: Cambridge University Press.

Singh, A. (1975) 'Takeovers, economic natural selection and the theory of the firm', *Economic Journal*, vol. 85.

Slutsky, A. and Caves, R. (1990–1) 'Synergy, agency, and the determinants of premia paid in mergers', *Journal of Industrial Economics*, vol. 39, pp. 277–96.

Stein J. (1988) 'Takeover threats and managerial myopia', *Journal of Political Economics*, vol. 96, pp. 61–80.

Stein, J. (1989) 'Efficient capital markets, inefficient firms: a model of myopic corporate behaviour', *Quarterly Journal of Economics*, vol. 104, pp. 655–70.

Stiglitz, J. and Weiss, A. (1983) 'Incentive effects of terminations: applications to the credit and labour markets', *American Economic Review*, vol. 73, pp. 912–27.

Stillman, R. (1983) 'Examining antitrust policy towards horizontal mergers', *Journal of Financial Economics*, vol. 11, pp. 225–40.

Summers, L. (1986) 'Does the stock market rationally reflect fundamental values', *Journal of Finance*, vol. 41, pp. 591–601.

Titman, S. (1991) 'The post-merger share price performance of acquiring firms', *Journal of Financial Economics*, vol. 29, pp. 81–96.

Travlos, N. (1987) 'Corporate takeover bids, methods of payment and bidding firms' stock returns', *Journal of Finance*, vol. 42, pp. 943–64.

West, K. (1988) 'Bubbles, fads and stock price volatility tests: a partial evaluation', *Journal of Finance*, vol. 43, pp. 639–56.

Williams, M. (1992) 'Do empirical studies help identify the welfare effects of merger', Working Paper (Institute of Economics, Oxford).

Wruck, K. (1989) 'Equity ownership concentration and firm value: evidence from private equity financing', *Journal of Financial Economics*, vol. 23, pp. 3–28.

Yarrow, G. (1985) 'Shareholder protection, compulsory acquisition and the efficiency of the takeover process', *Journal of Industrial Economics*, vol. 34, pp. 3–16.

11

RECENT DEVELOPMENTS IN UK CORPORATE GOVERNANCE

Martin J. Conyon and Simon I. Peck

INTRODUCTION

The growing interest in the mechanisms by which companies are owned and governed bears testimony to the fact that there is an increasing belief that the institutions of ownership and control can directly affect economic performance (see Nickell, 1995). Corporate governance broadly refers to the accountability and decision-making structures and processes in organisations. The efficacy of these structures in the United Kingdom has recently been called into question. Witness the collapse of leading companies (e.g. Polly Peck); alleged company financial irregularities (e.g. Robert Maxwell and Barings); perceived excessive compensation and severance for top executives (e.g. the privatised utilities); and in some instances fraud and deceit (e.g. BCCI). It is easy, though, to pick instances of calamity which turn out to be not the case generally, or unfounded for the majority of companies Our aim in this chapter is to consider the broad academic evidence relating to recent developments in UK corporate governance.[1]

Our main objective is to evaluate the adoption and impact of various governance institutions on economic performance in relation to the United Kingdom. The analysis will focus mainly on the internal governance reforms. For example we shall look at management pay mechanisms, incentive systems, management dismissal, boards of directors, organisational design and the role of equity stakes. Derek Morris (Chapter 10) analyses fully the evidence relating to stock markets and the take-over mechanism as instruments for aligning managerial and shareholder interests

This chapter proceeds as follows. First, we specify the conditions under which corporate governance issues are relevant. Second, we detail some key governance mechanisms for controlling management. Third, we evaluate changes in boardroom governance in the wake of the critically acclaimed Cadbury Committee (1992) recommendations. Finally, we offer some concluding remarks.

MODELS OF CORPORATE GOVERNANCE

Corporate governance, broadly conceived, refers to the mechanisms by which companies are controlled, directed and made accountable. Many practical forms of governance exist and these are often tailored to the demands of a particular company, institution, time period, and culture or country. For instance, there is the often-quoted difference between the Anglo-Saxon model of governance that stresses a unitary board structure, and the German tradition of a dual board system (see Charkham, 1995; Nickell, 1995; Jenkinson and Mayer, 1992; Kay and Silberston, 1995). In this section we are less interested in describing the present British governance scene, which we leave until later, but instead focus on why governance should matter at all. This is important: without a theoretical conception of corporate governance it is difficult to imagine how policy can be formulated.

Hart (1995) provides a coherent analysis of the conditions under which corporate governance issues are important. Two conditions must be met. First, an agency problem (conflict of interest) must exist between members of the organisation (e.g. owners, managers, consumers or suppliers). Second, transactions costs must be prohibitive, such that the agency problem cannot be resolved by a well-defined contract (this implies that contracts are incomplete).

The issue of corporate governance arises when one departs from an orthodox model of the owner-managed firm, principally involving the separation of ownership and control. Under this separation, ownership confers the right to hire and fire management (and determine their remuneration), and the bearing of uninsurable risk, with the rights to the 'residual' (the surplus accruing after all contractual obligations have been met). Management implies the direct control of all the firm's resources (capital, human, etc.) and the ability to direct the use of these resources.

This is the classic agency problem (Jensen and Meckling, 1976; Tirole, 1988; Hart, 1995). Unlike the orthodox model, where managerial effort and other types of cost can be rewarded or reimbursed directly, the principal–agent model is characterised by imperfect and asymmetric information. In particular, an informational advantage resides with the agent such that their behaviour, or level of effort, creates potential for opportunistic behaviour. The scope for such opportunism motivates the need to set explicit incentives for the agent in such a way as to minimise the associated agency costs (e.g. by making pay contingent on observed accounting measures such as profit or shareholder returns).

The basic model of moral hazard describes an incentive problem in which a risk and effort averse agent whose actions/effort (a) influence the welfare of the principal (y), enjoys an informational advantage concerning his observable effort; $y = y(a, \varepsilon)$ where ε is a random shock variable with mean zero and known variance. The term y may be thought of as shareholder wealth or profit. The pay-off to a higher level of effort stochastically dominates that to a lower level. This pay-off, whose probability distribution is affected by the unobservable effort, is verifiable, however, and provides an enforceable argument in the optimal (but second-best) contract set by the principal (see Hart, 1995). Subject to the constraints imposed by ensuring the participation and the individual rationality of the agent, the argument focuses on defining the optimal contract or sharing rule $s(y)$. The enforceable contract in the basic moral hazard case is nonetheless second-best, owing to the conflict between efficient incentives and efficient insurance (risk-sharing). The alignment of incentives through the dependence of rewards upon outcome inefficiently distributes risk from the principal to the risk-averse agent. The optimal solution to the moral hazard problem is only available where monitoring is perfect and costless, but clearly imperfect monitoring may provide gains on the second-best sharing rule (Zajac, 1990; Hart, 1995). As Holmstrom (1979) shows, *any* signal of the individual action is of value if it possesses an association with the observed pay-off.

These principal–agent considerations alone may be necessary, but are not in themselves sufficient to provide a role for governance structure (see Hart, 1995, p. 679). The reason is that although agency issues (moral hazard) suggest contracts that relate agent rewards to observable profits rather than effort, these contracts are nevertheless incomplete. They are complete, though, in the sense that the contract specifies the parties' obligations in possible future states of the world contingent on these obligations being observable and verifiable. In a general model the contract would, as a matter of detail, specify the conditions under which management should be rewarded, the conditions that management is replaced, the conditions for the adoption of new technologies, the conditions under which workers are hired and fired, etc. The point is that agency contingencies are governed by a contract and this is the lesson drawn from standard principal–agent solutions.

This makes a role for corporate governance difficult to find. The form of the governance structure (e.g. the appropriate mix between executive and non-executive directors on the main board) only matters when some action needs to be taken in the future that has not been specified in the originating contract. As Hart (1995) remarks, 'in a comprehensive contracting world, everything has been specified in advance, i.e. there are no "residual" decisions'. Governance structure in such a world is deemed irrelevant.

Governance structure matters in a world of transactions costs and incomplete contracts. Given an agency problem, governance structures can be seen as a mechanism for making decisions that have not been specified in the initial contract. Transactions costs in writing contracts may be considerable and numerous. Hart (1995) identifies three:

1 The cost of specifying all eventualities and their resolution during the lifetime of the contract;

2 The costs of negotiating with all the contract parties about the plans;

3 The costs of formally writing down the contract such that they can be enforced by a third party in the event of a dispute arising.

Where prohibitive transactions costs are present, the parties are not able to write a comprehensive contract. So, incomplete contracts, in conjunction with the agency costs of incomplete and asymmetric information, provide a role for governance mechanisms. Corporate governance, in this framework, is seen as a mechanism for enacting decisions about events that have not been specified in an initial contract.[2]

CORPORATE GOVERNANCE MECHANISMS

Management compensation

How are rewards used by companies to align management and shareholder interests? Specifically, we are interested in, first, whether managerial pay is adequately tied to company performance, and second, whether the adoption of high-powered incentive schemes results in better corporate performance.

A contract approach to the relations between owners and managers will only work in a first-best world if it is possible to monitor and evaluate the effort of individual managers and this effort is actually capable of influencing the overall performance of the firm. The ability and incentive to 'shirk' in a team environment is well known (Alchian and Demsetz, 1972). The solution to the problem is to employ a monitor to evaluate effort, but the issue of who monitors the most senior executives is critical. One solution is to make senior executives' compensation dependent upon corporate performance. A central academic theme in this area is therefore whether directors' pay is adequately tied to measures of corporate performance.

Figure 11.1 details the average highest-paid directors' compensation (salary, bonus, benefits and pensions) between 1989 and 1996. Values are expressed in 1995 prices. The sample of companies is drawn from the population of Datastream FT All Share listed companies. Of interest are the levels and growth in remuneration. Mean compensation of £230,000 in 1989 rose to £436,000 in 1996[3] – about a 190 per cent rise. Most of this increase occured in the period post-1992, when top pay has increased at 14.8 per cent per annum.[4] Table 11.1 illustrates the 1995 cross-section distribution of top pay. Notice that median pay is £260,000, compared to the mean which is £351,000. This suggests that looking at the growth in mean earnings (as above) will probably give a different picture than looking at the growth in median earnings.

Many UK authors have tried to estimate how sensitive executive compensation actually is to measures of company performance. The usual way in

256

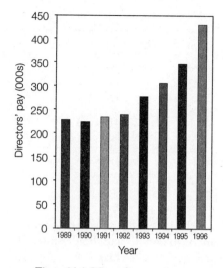

Figure 11.1 Mean directors' pay

which such empirical models proceed is to estimate a simple reduced-form equation, rather than the parameters of a structural model informed by a specific principal–agent model (see Conyon, Gregg and Machin, 1995). So, a standard regression equation would model the compensation of an individual director *i* at time *t* as:

$$\Delta \log(\textit{Compensation})_{it} = \alpha + \beta \ \textit{Performance}_t + \varepsilon_{it}$$

where the term β is the reaction coefficient reflecting the sensitivity of director compensation to corporate performance. The magnitude of the coefficient is often interpreted as reflecting the operation of principal–agent type mechanisms, with higher values of β suggesting closer alignment of owner and management interests. An important feature of this modelling procedure is that by estimating in differences the β estimate is free from company fixed effects bias (see Murphy, 1985). There has now been a certain amount of UK research estimating such models, but there is a much more extensive US literature (see Bruce and Buck, 1995). So, what estimates of β have been reported in the literature?

The US literature has often found that the link between directors' compensation and company performance is weak. In an often-cited analysis of US executives, Jensen and Murphy (1990) estimated that the pay–performance relation (including pay, options, stockholdings, and dismissal) is $3.25 for every $1000 dollar change in shareholder wealth. Such a small pay-for-performance sensitivity might be a matter of concern for shareholders and policy-makers since the small private returns to chief executive officers

Table 11.1 Highest directors' pay (1995)

Percentile	Highest directors' pay (£000s)		
5	117		
25	183		
50	260	Mean	351.6
75	412	Std Dev.	333.8
95	866	Obs	731

Source: Datastream International, item 244. Pay includes salary, bonus, benefits and pension contributions as constructed by Datastream.

(CEOs) for significant changes in shareholder worth imply little direct incentive for top management to pursue shareholder interests.[5]

The existing UK evidence, too, suggests that directors' cash compensation is only weakly related to company performance, i.e. that estimates of β are small or insignificant (see Conyon, Gregg and Machin, 1995). Before looking at the evidence in detail, it is important to stress some general caveats when using UK data.

First, the measure of compensation typically used in UK studies is a time series on the salary and bonus of the highest-paid director. This contrasts with the relevant unit of analysis, which is the individual executives. So, when the individual who is the highest-paid director changes, this can cause problems for the estimated relationship between pay and performance. For instance, a large annual increase in the salary and bonus of the highest-paid director may reflect a recruitment payment for a new CEO, and not be a pay rise for a given individual director. The Greenbury Report (1995) contains recommendations which address this issue.[6]

Second, there is the controversial area of how to measure the director compensation variable. Until comparatively recently, most UK studies have used only the direct emoluments of the highest-paid director which are available from the company accounts. This measures only current compensation and excludes long-term compensation such as the estimated value of share options, equity holdings and other forms of deferred compensation. Bruce and Buck (1995) argue that by excluding these extra components of directors' overall compensation, the estimated relationship between compensation and performance may be biased (see also Conyon, Gregg and Machin, 1995). However, the primary reason why the wider compensation measures are typically not used in the UK context is due to lack of available and consistent data. Finally, there is the question of how to measure company performance. Some empirical models use market-based measures of corporate performance, such as shareholder returns or shareholder wealth, whereas others use accounting-based measures such as earnings per share or return on capital employed. It is not immediately apparent which is the correct performance measure to use, though since principal–agent mechanisms stress returns to shareholders, a market-based measure reflecting share price appreciation and dividend yield (i.e. total shareholder return) is often used.

Table 11.2 reports some recent UK evidence on the relationship between directors' pay and company performance. Some important themes emerge. First, estimates of the pay for performance relationship in the United Kingdom are small. This suggests that incentives are not very strong. Second, the statistical link between directors' pay and corporate performance in UK companies appears to have been decoupled in the period since 1989 (Gregg, Machin and Szymanksi, 1993) so that by the early 1990s one could not detect *any* relationship between the basic pay of UK executives and the stock market performance of their companies. Even allowing for the changing nature of compensation packages (i.e. towards more longer-term performance pay, in the form of stock options and other deferred mechanisms), Gregg *et al.* (1993) found little change in the estimate of β. However, the recent work by Main, Bruce and Buck (1996), based on a small sample of large UK companies, finds that the relationship between pay and performance is much stronger when total remuneration is used as the dependent variable (i.e. that which includes the Black-Scholes value of share options). More evidence on compensation determination (e.g. by looking at wider pay measures, competing pay models like tournament theory and assessing how pay is set in practice) is certainly needed.

In addition to rewarding managers based on their company performance, the owners of a company should make pay depend on performance relative to that of other companies operating in the same industry or sector (see Nickell, 1995; Tirole, 1988 or Holmstrom, 1982). The idea is simple: in the scheme outlined above owners want to reward effort, ε, but can only observe the outcome profits variable, y. That is, reward the former but ignore the latter. Some shocks, though, are common to an industry or a sector as a whole (e.g. industry profits may fall independent of the actions of the manager). To control for such shocks the owner of the company merely looks at the profit outcome of the company relative to other firms in the same industry. We would expect then to see managerial pay not only directly related to company performance but also to the performance relative to other companies (see Gibbons and Murphy, 1992).

The evidence on the whole issue is mixed, and still an under-investigated area in the United Kingdom. Antle and Smith (1986) and Barro and Barro (1990) found no strong association between executive compensation and relative performance using US data. Gibbons and Murphy (1992) assessed the impact of relative performance on compensation using data on 1,688 CEOs from 1,049 US corporations between 1974 and 1986. They found that compensation was significantly (negatively) related to industry and market

Table 11.2 Recent evidence on the compensation–performance relationship

Study	Data	Compensation measure	Performance measure	Estimated β (standard error)	Remarks
Jensen and Murphy (1990)	US data on 2,213 CEOs, 1974–86.	1. Change in salary and bonus. 2. Change in total pay (salary plus bonus, value of restricted stock, savings and other benefits) plus value of stockholdings.	Change in shareholder wealth.	1. 0.00022 (0.000002) 2. 0.000309 (0.000054)	Performance effects regarded as small.
Main (1992)	512 UK companies 1969–89.	Change in salary and bonus of highest-paid director.	Stock market return.	0.038 (0.012)	
Gregg, Machin and Szymanski (1993)	288 UK companies, 1983–91.	Change in salary and bonus of highest-paid director.	Change in shareholder returns.	1983–88 0.027 (0.013) 1989–91 −0.024 (0.022)	Effect of performance on compensation displays time heterogeneity. Disappears after 1988.
Main and Johnston (1993)	220 UK companies, 1990.	Salary and bonus of highest-paid director.	Risk-adjusted market return.	0.100 (0.135)	Cross-section evidence.
Conyon and Leech (1994)	294 UK companies, 1983–86.	Change in salary and bonus of highest-paid director.	Change in shareholder wealth.	0.052 (0.020)	Effects of governance discussed.
Conyon and Gregg (1994)	169 UK companies, 1985–90.	Change in salary and bonus of highest-paid director.	Shareholder return.	1985–87 0.076 (0.032) 1988–90 0.020 (0.036)	Role of unions, mergers and financial structure on director compensation evaluated.

Conyon (1995)	28 UK privatised companies, 1990–94.	Change in salary and bonus of highest-paid director.	Return on shareholders' equity, return on long-term capital.	0.0039 (0.0042)	Level models, rather than first differences; fixed effects.
Cosh and Hughes (1995)	44 companies in UK electrical engineering sector, 1989–94.	Level and change in CEO pay.	1. Return on capital employed; 2. Shareholder return.	1. −0.02 (0.05) 2. 0.11 (0.047)	Effects of shareholdings evaluated; relative performance effects considered.
Smith and Szymanski (1995)	51 quoted UK companies, 1981–91.	Level of directors' remuneration including performance-related pay, benefits and basic salary for all directors).	1. Sales; 2. Earnings per share.	1. 0.43 (0.06) 2. 0.03 (0.10) cross-section 1. 0.41 (0.20) 2. 0.03 (0.24) time series	Argue for the need to include effect of average executive pay as an 'outside option'.
Conyon (1996)	213 large UK companies, 1988–93.	Change in salary and bonus of highest-paid director.	Shareholder return.	0.061 (0.020)	Effects of boardroom controls evaluated: outcomes ambiguous.
Main, Bruce and Buck (1996)	60 large UK companies, 1983–89.	Board and top directors' remuneration: 1. Salary and bonus; 2. Total remuneration (including stock options).	Share performance.	For CEO: 1. 0.146 (0.113) 2. 0.729 (0.282)	Models include sector performance term and lagged dependent variable.
Conyon and Peck (1996)	96 FT-SE 100 companies, 1991–94.	Change in salary and bonus of highest-paid director.	Shareholder return dated at 1. Period t and 2. period $t-1$	1. 0.088 (0.052) 2. 0.054 (0.045)	Data derived directly from annual reports. Board structure effects on pay evaluated. Outcome ambiguous. No effect in panel models.

rates rates of return. In addition, they noted that firms operating in the wider market, rather than firms in the more narrowly defined industry group, are the more important comparison group. The UK evidence on relative performance is more mixed, and no papers to date address the issue directly. Conyon and Leech (1994) and Conyon (1996) find little support for the effect of share performance in other companies influencing executive compensation. Cosh and Hughes (1996) find that a measure of overall performance, defined as shareholder return net of the median total shareholder return for the sample in the relevant period, has a positive effect on compensation.

On the whole the evidence points to a positive, but potentially weak, association between managerial compensation and corporate performance, both in the United Kingdom and the US. Does this coupling of top pay to performance actually imply greater sustainable corporate profitability? Here, the evidence is disappointingly thin. Leonard (1990) examined the effect of executive compensation policies on the performance of 439 large US companies between 1981 and 1985. He found that companies with long-term incentive plans enjoyed significantly greater increases in return on equity than companies which did not have such schemes. Similarly, Abowd (1990) examined data on over 16,000 managers at 250 large US corporations to test whether the sensitivity of managerial compensation during this period was related to company performance in subsequent periods. Using both accounting and market-based measures of performance, he found a positive relationship between the power of compensation–performance relationship and subsequent company performance. At present there is no systematic UK evidence assessing the long-term corporate efficacy of linking pay to performance.

Management turnover

Related to the issue of management compensation is that of turnover. If management compensation is only weakly related to measures of performance, does this actually matter if poorly performing CEOs have a higher likelihood of losing their job? The key issue under scrutiny here, then, is whether the threat of management dismissal for poor company performance also provides incentives for CEOs to pursue shareholder interests? Econometric and event study analysis from the US tends to support this hypothesis. Weisbach (1988) and Jensen and Murphy (1990) both reported an inverse relationship between CEO turnover and net of market firm performance. Kaplan (1994) compared the relationship between executive turnover and firm performance in the US and Japan – countries which have markedly different corporate governance arrangements. He found that in both countries management turnover is negatively related to measures of company performance. The turnover consequences of poor performance, then, appear to be surprisingly similar in these two economies.

The existing published work on British management turnover is more limited. Cosh and Hughes (1997), in their study of the electrical engineering industry, found that CEO turnover was negatively related to net of market performance. They followed a standard strategy used by Weisbach of regressing board turnover on performance. Similar results are also found by Franks, Mayer and Renneboog (1995). They take two random samples of quoted companies: one from the lowest quintile of abnormal share price returns in the period 1984–5, and one from the middle quintile. Their results indicate a significantly higher proportion of board turnover in poorly performing companies compared with the zero abnormal return sample. Conyon (1996) also finds, in a sample of quoted companies between 1986 and 1994, that CEO turnover is inversely correlated with predated financial performance.

Overall, the amassed evidence as to whether management incentives generated by linking pay to performance, or indeed the threat of dismissal, actually work (by enhancing corporate performance) is not particularly compelling. Despite ongoing UK research, the picture is of a weak relationship between pay and profits, and some evidence of a management dismissal effect coming from poor corporate performance. However, as Nickell (1995) observes, there are some problems even with this existing evidence. Most of the work is static, in the sense that we know that other factors, which have not been considered fully, also generate incentives for managers. For instance, the role of career concerns (Gibbons and Murphy, 1992); promotion prospects (Gibbs, 1995; Nickell, 1995); tournaments (Lazear, 1995; Lazear and Rosen, 1981; Rosen, 1986; Becker and Huselid, 1992); product market competition (Nickell, 1996); macroeconomic shocks and financial pressure (Nickell, Nicolitsas and Patterson, 1995; Nickell and Nicolitsas, 1995). In sum, we still do not have a complete picture of how managerial pay structures and incentives actually affect company performance or align managerial and shareholder interests.

The board of directors

The board of directors, being directly elected by the shareholders to act on their behalf is, in principle, one of the major checks on management. The questions are, first, will they play a sufficient role in monitoring top management and ratifying their decisions, and, in some instances, seek to replace a company's CEO or management team (see Jensen, 1993)?; and second, will they affect dimensions of corporate governance in such a way as to enhance corporate performance?

Boards in the United Kingdom are unitary in structure (and so differ from the two-tier board governance arrangements in Germany). The unitary board is characterised by a mixture of executive (inside) and non-executive (outside) directors. The function of the executive directors is decision management while that of the non-executives, in contrast, is to exercise potential decision control (Fama and Jensen, 1983). It is reasonable to assume that executive directors will not self-monitor, or monitor effectively the performance of the CEO. The career of the executive director, after all, is closely tied to the incumbent CEO and so they do not possess sufficient incentives to remove them or to, say, restrict their compensation growth (Hart, 1995; Crystal, 1992; Jensen, 1993).

There are some reasons, though, to believe that non-executives might have sufficient incentives to monitor management. First, they need to signal their managerial competence to the external managerial labour market (Weisbach, 1988; Fama and Jensen, 1983). Non-executive directors who do not monitor the management team effectively will suffer a reputation loss in the labour market and a decreased probability of outside employment. Second, non-executive directors often already have expertise, either current or derived through career history, in decision control (Fama and Jensen, 1983). So, non-executive directors possess the relevant human capital to monitor the management team. Non-executive directors on UK boards tend to be older than the executives.

There are, however, ample reasons to believe that non-executives have insufficient incentives to monitor management. First, the legal structure in the United Kingdom is such that the executive–non-executive split is somewhat artificial since all directors are collectively responsible in law. So, how the *de facto* management responsibility of non-executives is reconciled with their monitoring duties is hard to establish. Litigation concerning managerial incompetence is also far less rife in the United Kingdom than the US so this hardly acts as a credible restraint on managerial excess.

Second, there seems to be a clear asymmetry of information between executive and non-executive directors. Executive directors are full-time company employees whereas the non-executives are not. Typically, non-executive directors spend only a fraction of their time at the company and, indeed, can be executive directors at other companies. This seems to build into the internal governance system an information bias in favour of the executive directors. Related to this are issues of how non-executives acquire information. Financial or strategic information comes from the executive team so how is its quality to be assessed? Do the non-executives have access to a secretariat? And so forth.

Third, even if one discounts the above information problems, are there adequate incentives to act in the face of poor company performance? The company equity holdings by non-executives are typically low, and so is the willingness to correct managerial mistakes. In addition, the compensation received by outside directors, along with their chances of reselection as a non-executive director, are influenced by the CEO. So, as Nickell (1995) aptly remarks: 'Why should they make a fuss, rather than keep quiet and collect their fees?'(p. 55).

The empirical evidence suggests that board structure is important for CEO turnover. Weisbach (1988) found that CEOs were more likely to be dismissed for poor company performance in companies with outsider-dominated boards than insider-dominated ones. The existing work from the United Kingdom is mixed. In the Cosh and Hughes (1995) study of the electrical engineering industry the proportion of non-executive directors on the main board has no effect on the probability of CEO dismissal. A similar outcome is found in the Conyon (1996) study which covers many industries: the effect of non-executives on CEO turnover is difficult to establish. However, Franks, Mayer and Reeneboog (1995) find that board turnover in the period 1985–89 is facilitated by a greater proportion of non-executive directors.

There is also little evidence to suggest that non-executives have restrained the growth in managerial compensation. In a sample of 220 large UK companies in 1990, Main and Johnston (1993) found that after controlling for company size and financial returns, top executive pay was higher the greater the proportion of non-executive directors. What is perhaps more surprising is that in companies with remuneration committees, the forum where top pay is set and which are usually dominated by non-executive directors, top executive pay was higher still. Conyon and Peck (1996) in their analysis of the FTSE 100 companies between 1991 and 1994 find that the proportion of outside directors had no effect on executive pay. However, top pay in companies which report the existence of a remuneration committee, after controlling for company size, was higher.[7]

Overall, we cannot see any compelling reasons or evidence to suggest that outside directors are particularly effective in correcting management failure within companies. This stems from an asymmetry of information between inside and outside directors and the lack of adequate incentives to act on such information if acquired. Indeed, recent US evidence suggests that it is not the mix between inside and outside directors *per se* that is important for performance, but that smaller boards are more effective, due to the difficulties of communication and decision-making within large boards; Yermack (1996) finds for 452 large US corporations an inverse association between board size and firm value. Companies with smaller boards in this study also display a stronger CEO pay, turnover and performance link.

Large institutional shareholders

It is a stylised fact that UK public limited companies have a large number of small owners. This creates quite specific agency relations; although the owners (shareholders) possess residual control rights in the form of votes, they are too numerous, small and uncoordinated to exercise this control on a day-to-day basis. This is delegated to their agents (a board of directors), who in turn delegate it to management. Widely dispersed shareholders have little incentive to monitor management, given that monitoring is not a costless activity, and any improved company performance that results from any individual expending resources in monitoring will, however, be enjoyed by all other shareholders. This is the classic free-rider problem (Stiglitz, 1985). If all shareholders effectively look to free ride, the result is no, or at least sub-optimal, monitoring of management.

Significant changes have taken place in the structure of ownership of UK companies since Berle and Means (1932) emphasised the importance of the separation of ownership from control; changes in the last thirty years are described in Table 11.3. The picture which emerges is one of a constant decline in the proportion of shares held directly by individuals (even allowing for the privatisation programme of the 1980s which had, arguably, as one of its aims, the creation a large body of small shareholders) and a corresponding increase in the institutional and overseas involvement. After a period of rapid growth, the proportion of shares held in unit trusts appear to have levelled off, and the low proportion of equity held by the banking sector is apparent.

The rise of the institutional shareholder has certainly affected the corporate governance landscape. Corporate managers have increasingly seen and been critical of the use of the 'exit' option of selling shares by institutions, rather than the use of the 'voice' mechanism (Hirschman, 1970) and engaging in dialogue with companies in which they hold stock – or as Charkham (1989) argued, pension fund managers have tended to act as 'punters', rather than as stewards of their clients' interests. This seems, on the face of it, a particularly compelling case, since as Table 11.3 illustrates, it is highly likely that any institution selling equity is probably finding it being bought by a very similar one.

The counter-argument is that company managers have been acting without regard to the owners of the company, or as Ball (1991) claimed, 'shareholders have been considerably neglected by companies'. In this light the recent debates over the alleged 'excesses' or ability to pursue their own

Table 11.3 Beneficial ownership of UK equity

Beneficiary owner	1963	1975	1981	1989	1993
Pension funds	6.4	16.8	30.6	30.6	31.5
Insurance companies	10.0	15.9	20.5	18.6	20.0
Unit trusts	1.3	4.1	3.6	5.9	6.6
Banks	1.3	0.7	0.3	0.7	0.6
Other financial	11.3	10.5	6.8	1.1	0.6
Individuals	54.0	37.5	28.2	20.6	17.7
Public sector	1.5	3.6	3.0	2.3	1.6
Companies	5.1	3.0	5.1	3.8	1.5
Overseas	7.0	5.6	3.6	12.8	16.3

Source: CSO.

agenda enjoyed by corporate management have focused attention on the institutional detail of corporate governance.

If the incentives for small dispersed shareholders to monitor management are weak, then the presence of a large shareholder may result in improved monitoring and corporate governance which is, in effect, the role undertaken by the banking sector in Japan and Germany.[8] The evidence suggests that this may also be becoming an important feature of UK corporate governance. However, unless the large shareholders own all the equity in the firm, the agency problems are, for sure, reduced, but not eliminated. In owning all the firm's equity, the separation of ownership from control is no longer an issue, but presumably, one of the gains from publicly listing a company, namely the ability to spread risk by portfolio diversification, is lost (Hart, 1995).

The issue of increased institutional activism does, however, raise some practical and legal problems. There is evidence to suggest that institutional investors meet on a regular basis with companies in which they hold stock (National Association of Pension Funds, 1990). However, if the subject matter of any of these meetings could be deemed commercially sensitive, then these meetings would fall foul of the UK's insider trading laws, i.e. the firm is not allowed to release potentially price sensitive information in a piecemeal fashion.

Second, there is no *a priori* basis for asserting that pension funds managers etc. have any feeling for the mechanics of running a company, or would be any good at it. Nor is there is any guarantee that a large shareholder would use their votes more 'intelligently', but may use their own voting power to improve their position at the expense of other shareholders. Also if institutional shareholders are to have a larger role to play in corporate governance, to whom should they be accountable, given that most institutions are themselves plcs?

There is some recent UK evidence to suggest that share-stakes matter for company reorganisation. Franks, Mayer and Renneboog (1995) examined the interrelationship between large share stakes, institutional investors, and board reorganisation. They examined the effects of particular categories of large shareholdings on management turnover. Ownership is split into three types: institutional investors (banks, insurance companies and pension funds), outside owners (industrial and commercial companies, individual and family investors) and inside owners (directors). They find significantly higher management turnover in boards of poorly performing companies in cases where there is concentrated ownership by outsiders. There is, though, no significant relationship between board turnover and the concentration of shares by institutional investors.

Moreover, Cosh and Hughes (1995) also find that the presence or absence of institutions as major shareholders makes no difference on the likelihood of CEO dismissal in the electrical engineering industry. They also find that the presence of institutions, on average, has no effect on the pay received by the CEO. This result is consistent with Conyon and Leech (1994) who could isolate a robust relationship between ownership structure and directors' compensation in a sample of companies between 1983 and 1986.

Company takeovers

All the governance mechanisms based on monitoring share the feature that those who expend resources in monitoring only receive a fraction of any gains. A (hostile) takeover is, in principle a much more powerful mechanism for disciplining management, since the rewards from identifying and taking over an under-performing company accrue entirely to the raider. As Grossman and Hart (1980) noted, if under an incumbent management a company is currently worth v, but if properly managed would be worth $v + g$, then a raider could buy all the company's equity for v, install new management and make a capital gain of g on the shares owned.

In reality the gains from hostile take-overs are likely to be rather lower, since small shareholders have an incentive not to tender to the raider, as they may be able to obtain a pro-rata fraction of the capital gain g simply by holding on to the equity themselves. As Grossman and Hart (1980) showed, if corporate law does not permit a successful raider to expropriate minority shareholders who do not tender, then it can be shown that the only successful bids are those that offer at the post-acquisition value of $v + g$. But once the costs of the takeover are taken into account, the result will be a net loss.

Much of the empirical evidence on the performance effects of take-overs reflects the rather lacklustre performance of the post-takeover firm. Ravenscraft and Scherer (1987) and Bradley, Desai and Kim (1988) found that most of the gains from a successful takeover accrue to shareholders of the target company rather than to the shareholders of the acquiring company. This could be due to he fact that some raiders are empire-builders. Empirical work on the takeover mechanism also suffers from a sample selection-problem, in that one can only actually measure the effects of take-overs that are visible or happen. Arguably in effect, what one fails to capture is the effect of the discipline of the takeover mechanism, even though a takeover may not occur. In sum, however, the weight of evidence suggests that it is not the managements of poorly performing companies that are penalised by the market for corporate control; rather well-performing companies are purchased, often at great expense. Further discussion can be found in Chapter 10.

RECENT POLICY RESPONSES

The Cadbury Committee

The best-known example of the reform and assessment of UK corporate governance procedures is contained in the Cadbury Committee report. Its recommendations on accountability and restructuring have become a tacitly accepted standard by which to judge the internal governance arrangements of companies.

In particular, the Cadbury Report recommended that 'boards should appoint remuneration committees, consisting wholly or mainly of non-executive directors, and chaired by a non-executive director, to recommend to the board the remuneration of executive directors in all its forms, drawing on other advice as necessary. Executive directors should play no part in decisions on their own remuneration' (Cadbury, 1992, para. 4.42). The importance of a remuneration committee is clear; in its absence there exists an opportunity for senior executives to award themselves pay rises which are not congruent with shareholder interests. Williamson (1985) comments that in the absence of an independent remuneration committee, it is akin to an executive director writing his employment contract with one hand and signing it with the other.

Second, while the report does not explicitly set numbers on the representation by non-executive directors, it does state that the 'calibre and number of non-executive directors should be such that their views carry significant weight in the board's decisions' (Cadbury, 1992, para. 4.8). Moreover, non-executives 'should be selected through a formal process', and this is taken as recommending adoption of nomination committees for the purpose of selecting non-executives.

The Cadbury Report also acknowledges that the head of a company occupies a particularly symbolic position. In particular it seeks to reduce what Boyd (1994) refers to as CEO duality, i.e. when a firm's CEO also serves as the chairman of its board of directors. The alternative is for the roles of the CEO and chairman to be separated. In this case 'an independent board chair will facilitate objective assessment of the CEO and top management team performance' (Boyd, 1994, p. 338). Until recently it was commonplace in leading UK firms for the chairmen of the board to also be the CEO, but the Cadbury committee recommended that there should be a clear division of responsibilities at the head of the company. To many commentators this was interpreted as meaning that the roles of chairman and CEO should not be combined. The function of the chairman is to organise board meetings and to take a lead in hiring, firing, and compensating the CEO. If the roles are combined then the CEO faces a potential conflict of interest in carrying out these roles. As Jensen (1993, p. 866) notes: 'for the board to be effective, it is important to separate the chairman and CEO positions'.

It is perhaps important to stress some aspects concerning the status of the Cadbury Report. First, the report does not confer a statutory obligation on the part of companies to comply with its recommendations. This may be important since, as Hart (1995, p. 686) comments, 'There is in fact a strong argument that a market economy can achieve efficient corporate governance without government intervention'. The argument, which has its roots in the Chicago tradition, is that the founders of companies have an incentive to choose corporate governance structures that maximise the total surplus they receive and will not, therefore, choose governance structures that are sub-optimal (see Hart, 1995, pp. 686–9, for more detail and qualifications). Second, the Cadbury code may be viewed as trying to persuade companies about what is regarded as best practice in boardroom structures, and corporate governance more generally. As Hart (1995, p. 688) concludes: 'the case for statutory rules is weak and so the Cadbury approach of trying to educate and persuade companies to make changes in corporate governance is probably the best one.'

Company responses

To what extent are the key Cadbury recommendations being adhered to, and what has been the effect on the compensation–performance relationship? On the issue of board composition, the evidence on non-executive directors suggests that they make up around 40 per cent of the main board (Conyon, 1994). This is significantly lower than in the US, where the figure is nearer two-thirds, but based on a sample of the largest UK companies, Conyon and Peck (1996) found that by the end of 1994, non-executives formed nearly half of the typical main board. This has been combined with a decline in the number of companies combining the posts of CEO and chairman. Conyon (1994) found that 77 per cent of quoted companies in his sample separated the roles of chief executive and chairman in 1993, compared to 58 per cent in 1988.

On the issue of remuneration committees, the evidence suggests the majority of companies have such a committee for the purposes of top pay-setting. Conyon (1996) found all of the FTSE 100 companies had adopted a remuneration committee; Cadbury (1995), reviewing compliance with the earlier Cadbury recommendations, found an overwhelming majority of the top 500 report the existence of a remuneration committee. The role of the Cadbury Report should not be understated. Conyon (1994), using a sample of 298 companies, found that since publication of the Cadbury Report in 1992 a significant minority (119 companies) had chosen to establish remuneration committees post 1992.

In terms of the structure of the remuneration committee, while Cadbury recognised that executives should play no part in setting their own pay, there is still an executive presence. Conyon (1995) found that the average number of non-executives on the remuneration committees of the FT350 companies in 1995 was 3.82, compared to the average size of such a committee, which was 4.23. Conyon and Peck (1996) showed that the proportion of non-executive directors on the remuneration committee had risen steadily from 68 per cent in 1991 to 91 per cent in 1994. Much is made of the fact that the chief executive absents himself from proceedings when his own pay is being set.

The situation concerning the adoption of nomination committees is quite different, though. The findings of the Cadbury (1995) investigations on compliance with the code of best practice illustrated a significant increase in companies of all sizes disclosing a nomination committee. The percentage of companies in the Top 500 disclosing the existence of a nomination committee rose from 5 per cent in 1991/92 to 50 per cent in 1993/94. Even among the largest UK companies, Conyon and Peck (1996) found the proportion reporting its existence to be around 11 per cent in 1991 and 72 per cent in 1994. The current situation in the United Kingdom contrasts with evidence from the United States. Lorsh and MacIver (1989, p. 20) reported that 84 per cent of the directors whom they surveyed revealed that the boards on which they served had nominations committees. More recently Monks and Minow (1995, p. 193) reported the results of a Korn Ferry study that showed that in 95 per cent of large US companies, potential boardroom candidates were recommended to the board by a nominating committee.

The UK situation is clearly different. There are far fewer companies with formal nomination committees. Conyon and Mallin (1995) are critical of this low adoption rate of nomination committees by UK listed companies. They argue that one way in which boardroom independence may be potentially enhanced is by having procedures for selecting and appointing directors that are transparent. In their absence, there exists the danger of interlocks whereby board members of one company sit on the boards of other companies; evidence from PIRC (1993) indicates that in the ten highest-paying FT100 companies, over half the members of each company remuneration committee serve, or recently served, as executive directors on other companies. The clear implication is that such interlocks are not in the interests of good governance. As Lorsh and MacIver (1989) commented, in relation to the changing US situation: 'The CEO's role in selecting directors, while still a factor in stacking the power deck in his favour, is less predominant as more nominating committees allow directors to participate in the process'. The current paucity of nominating committees represents a failure in contemporary governance arrangements.

CONCLUSIONS

This chapter has considered recent developments in UK corporate governance. Our review of some of the recent literature has suggested that many of the mechanisms provided under the Anglo-Saxon model have a number of shortcomings. The managerial pay-for-performance link does not appear to be particularly effective in aligning management and shareholder interests at present. Neither does the threat effect of CEO job dismissal in the event of poor corporate performance. The role and profile of the non-executive director has increased in recent years, yet again the evidence on their effectiveness appears inconclusive, as does the role of large institutional shareholders.

Given this evidence we would finally like to document some possible reforms in three broad areas: information disclosure and the role of management incentives, internal corporate governance reforms, and the use of regulatory and legal mechanisms.

Compliance with the Cadbury and Greenbury Committee reports has clearly improved the quality and quantity of information supplied to shareholders. Proper reporting of long-term performance pay (most notably stock options) and consistent valuation of pension funding is particularly important if a more precise measure of total compensation is to be given. There is a case for reforming the mechanisms for designing and implementing long-term bonuses and incentive schemes. As Conyon, Gregg and Machin (1995) note, the use of share appreciation schemes means that the stock base is not diluted. Second, the timing of exercise options should be codified as part of the contract, so as to remove the ability to make speculative gains from the timing of stock sales. Thirdly, the issue of the appropriate benchmark for the award of comparative performance bonuses should be made apparent to shareholders (e.g. companies in the same industry or sector).

It can be argued that the focus of recent policy measures in the United Kingdom has been an innovation in institutional structures in and around the boardroom. To this end, the policy has been successful. Companies are indeed complying with best practice as outlined in reports such as Cadbury, as noted above. While the adoption of remuneration committees is now standard, their independence can still be called into question because of the executive presence on them. The independence issue can be further addressed through the increased adoption of nomination committees, where as we have noted, compliance remains less than universal.

More generally, in focusing on structures, the debates on corporate governance have neglected policy that actually seeks to directly influence boardroom behaviour and incentives. They rest very heavily on the premise that by both introducing innovation in institutional structure and increasing the flow of information to shareholders appropriate pay-setting mechanisms will develop. Whether the insider power enjoyed by executives is able to withstand increased scrutiny is the issue; the evidence presented above appears to suggest that simply augmenting current corporate governance arrangements with board sub-committees will, in itself, have little impact on the behaviour and incentives of top management.

Finally, we turn to potential regulatory reforms. Certain commentators are in no doubt that these institutional innovations have little practical reality; Kay and Silberston (1995), for instance, call the independence of board committees a 'sham' and argue that they have 'proved to be a mechanism not for restraining excess but for justifying it'. This undoubtedly reflects the problems of predicting *ex-ante* responses to any form of policy intervention. For instance, it would seem hard to be critical of measures to promote increased information for shareholders. The Greenbury Report recommends that the compensation packages of all directors be detailed into their constituent parts (base salary, performance-related pay, stock options, etc.). While this increase in information is to be welcomed, the effect of increased information on future pay is unknown. For instance, there could be an upward ratchet effect on the pay for directors in companies that are currently perceived to be under-paying their executives.

All this begs the question of whether some form of regulation is deemed desirable to restrain the growth and levels of top pay in the United Kingdom. For Kay and Silberston (1995) this is a distinct option. In their proposals for a new Companies Act they suggest that 'the appointment of a CEO ... should be a for a fixed term of four years; salary and any bonuses should be determined at the beginning of that period'. The CEO is appointed by a selection committee drawn from non-executive directors and members from 'other businesses and professional advisors, and would be obliged to consult employees, investors, suppliers'. The difference from the current system is that the hostile takeover loses its role as ownership of the majority of equity confers no right to appoint executive management. However, for Kay and Silberston, the four-year review (with the possibility of one renewal) would make a real change to the behaviour of top executives, making them more like politicians(!), aware of the heterogeneity of interests that make up the firm. They do not, however, make any attempt to evaluate the costs of their proposals, and recognise that the 'quest for perfection in systems of corporate governance is a hopeless one'. Hart (1995), for one, is not convinced of the arguments for new statutory rules; corporate governance mechanisms are perfectly capable of evolving and adapting to changes if there are efficiency gains from doing so. In this sense 'codes', backed up by education and persuasion, are as far as governments should seek to go; they should not attempt to interfere with the free operation of existing governance mechanisms.

To align shareholder and managerial interests, and hence solve the latent agency problems associated with the separation of ownership from control, management must think and behave as if they were owners (Jensen, 1993). It could be argued that a policy that sought to generate incentives by 'force-feeding' management with equity may, however, have the effect of 'insulating' management if, indeed, they owned sufficient. Practically, this is unlikely in the majority of UK plcs with large proportions of free equity. Moreover, this measure would have the effect of putting executives' wealth at stake; in the absence of a weak disciplining effect from job loss, this may provide the necessary constraints on behaviour. The introduction of 'dual-class' shares may also be particularly appropriate here; the dual class refers to the fact that while both classes of shares entitle the owner to residual income, only one possesses voting rights.[9]

The arguments outlined above seem particularly timely in the light of recent calls to move towards some form of 'stakeholder' approach to the governance of the firm. We have shown that there is a paucity of evidence on the best way to organise corporate governance arrangements in a quite narrowly defined way. Once one seeks to extend the focus to embrace other groups (for example, trade unions, suppliers, etc.) then the problems of providing incentives for different groups, with a highly complex set of potential responses and incomplete set of performance measures, rapidly mount.

NOTES

1 Anyone coming to the corporate governance area for the first time can do worse than read *Barbarians at the Gate*, by Bryan Burrough and John Helyar. This mock-epic tells the story of the RJR-Nabisco takeover battle in the US during the 1980s and of its main actor, Ross Johnson, chief executive officer of the company. One instance of alleged management excess involved the use of the company's enviable fleet of Lear and Gulfstream corporate jets. Ross Johnson's German Shepherd dog, Rocco, had bitten a security guard. Burrough and Helyar report that the dog 'was smuggled onto a corporate jet and secretly flown out of Palm Springs to Winston-Salem, one jump ahead of the law'. Apparently, the dog was accompanied by a company vice president and was registered on the passenger list as 'G. Shepherd'! (Burrough and Helyar, 1990, pp. 129–30).

2 An alternative governance model has recently been advanced by Kay and Silberston (1995). They reject the principal–agent mechanism as a useful description of behaviour in the modern corporation. Instead, they emphasise the role of the board as 'trustees' and the corporation as a social institution.

3 The number of observations per year are 557 (1989); 580 (1990); 601 (1991); 604 (1992); 648 (1993); 716 (1994); 731 (1995) and 189 (1996).

4 Care should be taken with interpretations after about 1993 as the Datastream definition of highest director salary includes pension contributions.

5 It should be noted, however, that some recent work has suggested that the estimated relationship between pay and performance may not be inconsistent with principal–agent theory.

6 Paragraph B4 of the report argues that full details of all elements in the remuneration package of each director should be given by name. In future we would expect to see more complete disclosure of individual directors so that a relevant time series on individual director pay can be constructed.

7 In the panel data models (which control for the biases introduced by ignoring company-specific factors) there was no effect of remuneration committee existence, or remuneration committee structure, on executive pay in either the fixed or random effects models.

8 Mayer (1996) notes importantly, however, that there appear to be significant differences in the way in which banks operate in these two so-called 'bank orientated' financial systems. Surveying this evidence he concluded that there is more evidence of active involvement of Japanese than German banks in the rescuing of distressed firms.

9 For a review of the European experience of dual-class shares see Rydqvist (1992).

REFERENCES

Abowd, J. (1990) 'Does performance-based managerial compensation affect corporate performance?' *Industrial and Labor Relations Review*, vol. 43, pp. 52–73.

Alchian, A. and Demsetz, H. (1972) 'Production, information costs and economic organisation', *American Economic Review*, vol. 62, pp. 777–95.

Antle, R. and Smith, A. (1986) 'An empirical examination of the relative performance evaluation of corporate executives', *Journal of Accounting Research*, vol. 24, pp. 1–32.

Ball, J. (1991) 'Short termism – myth or reality?', *National Westminster Bank Quarterly Review*, August.

Barro, J. R. and Barro, R. J. (1990) 'Pay, performance and turnover of bank CEOs', *Journal of Labor Economics*, vol. 8, pp. 448–81.

Becker, B.E. and Huselid, M.A. (1992) 'The incentive effects of tournament compensation systems', *Administrative Science Quarterly*, vol, 37, pp. 336–50.

Berle, A. A. and Means, G. C. (1932) *The Modern Corporation and Private Property*, London: Macmillan.

Boyd, B.K. (1994) 'Board control and CEO compensation', *Strategic Management Journal*, vol. 15, pp. 335–44.

Bradley, M., Desai, A. and Kim, E. H. (1988) 'Synergistic gains from corporate acquisitions and their division between the stockholders of target and acquiring firms', *Journal of Financial Economics*, vol. 21, pp. 3–40.

Bruce, A. and Buck, T. (1995) 'Executive reward and corporate governance', in M. Wright, K. Keasey and S. Thompson (eds) *Corporate Governance* (forthcoming), Oxford: Oxford University Press.

Cadbury, Sir A. (1992). *Committee on The Financial Aspects of Corporate Governance*, London.

—— *Committee on the financial aspects of corporate governance: Compliance with the code of best practice*, London: Gee Publishing.

Charkham, J. (1989)' Corporate governance and the market for control of companies', Bank of England Panel paper 25.

—— (1995) *Keeping Good Company; A study of corporate governance in five countries*, Oxford University Press.

Conyon, M.J.(1994) 'Corporate governance changes in UK companies between 1988 and 1993', *Corporate Governance: An International Review*.

—— (1996) 'Directors' pay and turnover in large UK companies', mimeo, Univeristy of Warwick.

Conyon, M.J., and Leech, D. (1994) 'Top pay, company performance and corporate governance', *Oxford Bulletin of Economics and Statistics*, vol. 56, no. 3, pp. 229–47.

Conyon, M.J. and Mallin, C.A. (1995) 'A review of compliance with Cadbury', *Journal of General Management* (forthcoming).

Conyon, M. J. and Peck, S. I. (1996) 'Board Control, Remuneration Committees and Directors' Compensation', mimeo, Warwick Business School.

Conyon, M.J., Gregg, P., and Machin S. (1995) 'Taking care of business: Executive compensation in the UK', *Economic Journal*, vol. 105, pp. 704–15.

Cosh, A., and Hughes, A. (1995) 'Executive remuneration, executive dismissals and institutional shareholdings', University of Cambridge Working Paper, 19 (forthcoming *International Journal of Industrial Organization*).

Crystal, G. (1992) *In search of success: The overcompensation of American executives*, New York: W.W. Norton and Co.

Fama, E. and Jensen, M.C. (1983) 'Separation of ownership and control' *Journal of Law and Economics*, vol. 26, pp. 375–93.

Franks, J. Mayer, C. and Renneboog, L. (1995) 'The role of large stakes in poorly performing companies', mimeo, London Business School.

275

Gibbons R. and Murphy K.J. (1992), 'Optimal incentive contracting in the presence of career concerns: Theory and evidence', *Journal of Political Economy*, vol. 100, pp. 468–505.

Gibbs, M. (1995) 'Incentive compensation in a corporate hierarchy' *Journal of Accounting and Economics*, vol. 19, pp. 247–77.

Greenbury, Sir R. (1995) *Report on Directors Pay*, London: GEE Publications.

Gregg, P., Machin, S., and Szymanski, S. (1993) 'The disappearing relationship between directors' pay and corporate performance', *British Journal of Industrial Relations*, vol. 31, pp. 1–10.

Grossman, S.J. and Hart, O.D. (1980) 'Takeover bids, the free-rider problem and the theory of the corporation', *Bell Journal of Economics*, vol. 11, pp. 42–64.

—— (1983) 'An analysis of the principal–agent problem', *Econometrica*, vol. 51, pp. 7–45.

Hart, O. (1995) 'Corporate governance: some theory and implications', *Economic Journal*, vol. 105, pp. 678–89.

Hirshman, A.O. (1970) *Exit, Voice and Loyalty: Responses to Decline in Firms, Organizations and States*, Cambridge, Mass.: Harvard University press.

Holmstrom, B. (1979) 'Moral hazard and observability', *Bell Journal of Economics*, vol. 10, pp. 74–91.

—— (1982) 'Moral hazard in teams', *Bell Journal of Economics*, vol. 13, pp. 324–46.

Jenkinson, T., and Mayer, C. (1992) 'Corporate governance and corporate control', *Oxford Review of Economic Policy*, Autumn.

Jensen, M.C. (1993) The modern industrial revolution, exit, and the failure of internal control mechanisms, *Journal of Finance*, vol XLVIII, pp. 831–80.

Jensen, M. and Meckling, W.H. (1976) 'The theory of the firm: Managerial behaviour, agency costs and ownership structure', *Journal of Financial Economics*.

Jensen, M. and Murphy, K. (1990) 'Performance pay and top management incentives', *Journal of Political Economy*, vol. 98, pp. 225–64.

Kay, J. and Silberston, A. (1995) 'Corporate governance', *National Institute Economic Review*, August.

Lazear, E. (1995) *Personnel Economics*, Cambridge, Mass.: MIT Press.

Lazear, E. and Rosen, S. (1981) 'Rank order tournaments as optimum labour contracts', *Journal of Political Economy*, vol. 89, pp. 841–64.

Leonard, J. S. (1990) 'Executive pay and firm performance', *Industrial and Labor Relations Review*, vol. 43, pp. 13S–29S.

Lorsh, J. and MacIver E. (1989) *Pawns or Potentates: The reality of America's corporate boards*, Boston, Mass.: Harvard Business School.

Main, B.G.M. and Johnston, J. (1993) 'Remuneration committees and corporate governance', *Accounting and Business Research*, vol. 23, pp. 351–62.

Main, B.G.M. Bruce, A. and Buck, T. (1966) 'Total board remuneration and company performance', *Economic Journal*, vol. 106, pp. 1627–44.

Mayer, C. (1996) *Corporate Governance, Competition and Performance*, Paris: OECD.

Monks, R. and Minow, N. (1995) *Corporate Governance*, Oxford: Basil Blackwell.

Morris, D. (1998) 'The stock market and problems of corporate control in the UK', in Buxton, Chapman and Temple (eds) *Britain's Economic Performance* (2nd edn), London: Routledge.

Murphy, K.J. (1985) 'Corporate performance and managerial remuneration: An empirical analysis', *Journal of Accounting and Economics*, vol. 7, pp. 11–42.

National Association of Pension Funds (1990) *Creative Tension?*, London.

Nickell, S.J. (1995) *The Performance of Companies*, Oxford: Blackwell.

—— (1966) 'Competition and corporate performance', *Journal of Political Economy*, vol. 104, pp. 724–46.

Nickell, S.J. and Nicolitsas, D. (1995) 'How does financial pressure affect firms?', Applied Economics Discussion Paper Series No. 170, Institute of Economics and Statistics, Oxford.

Nickell, S.J., Nicolitsas, D. and Patterson, M. (1995) 'Does doing badly encourage management innovation?', Applied Economics Discussion Paper Series No. 175, Institute of Economics and Statistics, Oxford.

PIRC (1993) *Directors' Remuneration and Contracts*, London: Pension Investment Research Consultants.

Ravenscraft, D.J. and Scherer, F.M. (1987) 'Mergers, sell-offs and economic efficiency', Brookings Institution.

Rosen, S. (1986) 'Prizes and incentives in elimination tournaments', *American Economic Review*, vol. 76, pp. 701–15.

Rydqvist, K. (1992) 'Dual-class shares: a review, *Oxford Review of Economic Policy*, vol. 8 no. 2, pp. 45–55.

Smith, R. and Szymanski, S. (1995) 'Executive pay and performance: The empirical importance of the participation constraint', *International Journal of the Economics of Business*, vol. 2, no. 3, pp. 485–95.

Stiglitz, J E. (1985) 'Credit markets and the control of capital', *Journal of Money Credit and Banking*, vol. 17, pp. 133–52.

Tirole, J. (1988) *The theory of Industrial Organization*, Cambridge, Mass.: MIT Press.

Weisbach, M.S. (1988) 'Outside directors and CEO turnover', *Journal of Financial Economics*, vol. 20, pp. 431–60.

Williamson, O.E. (1985) *The Economic Institutions of Capitalism: Firms, markets, relational contacting,* New York : Free Press.

Yermack, D. (1996) 'Higher market valuation of companies with a small board of directors', *Journal of Financial Economics*, vol. 40, pp. 185–211.

Zajac, E.J. (1990) 'CEO selection, succession, compensation and firm performance: A theoretical integration and empirical analysis,' *Strategic Management Journal*, vol. 11, pp. 217–30.

12

HUMAN CAPITAL ISSUES

Paul Chapman

The importance of investment in human skills for economic performance has been recognised in economic analysis especially since the work on human capital theory notably by work at Chicago University.[1] This chapter examines some of the key economic issues involved in measuring and explaining the process of human capital acquisition. The chapter then examines the main human capital issues in the United Kingdom and the implications for economic performance. The policy focus will be on establishing some areas where the United Kingdom appears to be lagging behind and where there is good reason to believe this will ultimately diminish the chances of competing and growing as fast as other comparable countries.

Economists refer to the process of investing in education and vocational skills as human capital formation. This significant description is based on the view that investing in human skills is essentially comparable with investing in fixed capital. Many economists have attempted to explain the process of human capital accumulation in the same terms as physical investment. While this approach has been widely accepted, it has also been recognised that there are some significant differences. Most significantly, labour cannot be traded and scrapped like capital equipment. In any case our understanding of the process of investment and innovation is also limited.

Human capital theory is the main form of economic analysis of how individuals, workers and firms undertake education and training. Many of the human capital ideas have been around for a long time in economics but much specific technical development of human capital theory and most of the empirical work has been undertaken in the last thirty years. The most significant work was undertaken by a few American economists, especially Becker and Mincer. Blaug (1976) expressed some doubts which should not be ignored, but overall the ideas have proved sufficiently robust to support a considerable amount of empirical research. Much of this empirical research has been concerned with estimating the returns to education and training.

A very significant idea in the human capital literature has been the distinction between specific and general training. Becker (1962), introducing this distinction, argued that general training which was easily transferred between firms, was unlikely to be supported by firms because workers would be able to secure the benefits of such training (which broadly might be defined as including education). The notion of general training supports the view that firms will fear the poaching of skilled labour. The greater the general content of training, the more this fear is well founded. Specific training, on the other hand, as its name suggests, was not so easily transported between firms. It might be argued that firms would wish to bear some of the cost and consequentially receive some of the benefits of specific training. This basic distinction has proved rather more difficult to translate into real world situations, but nevertheless it is helpful in identifying one of the key problems (heterogeneity of human capital) which policy-makers face in deciding what support might be necessary to secure the levels of human capital required in the economy.

It is not essential to accept all of the conceptual apparatus of Becker's human capital theory to usefully apply it to economic policy. A working assumption in what follows is that there are real returns to human capital investment. This assumption is supported by the vast body of empirical studies across many countries documenting the returns to human capital investment. There is an alternative view that education and training are screening or signalling devices used by workers and employers to improve the job match between firm and worker.[2] The latter view, at least in an extreme form, may seem impossibly far fetched and it has not gained much support in the literature, nor has there been much empirical evidence in its favour. However, the idea of screening or signalling should not be so readily dismissed and it is arguable that some of the returns we are observing for human capital investment are very likely to be due to better matching, rather than the benefits of education and training in itself. Also some of the difficulties in correlating training and education with productivity and earnings differentials might be explained within a 'credentialist' theory.

MEASURING THE CONTRIBUTION OF EDUCATION AND TRAINING

It is possible to identify two main empirical approaches to support the view that investment in human capital is of considerable economic benefit. First, a number of studies have tried to identify the specific effects of education and training on wages and employment, largely following the method developed by Mincer (1962) and (1974).[3] Much of this work has been on the importance of education. The method has involved relatively simple data requirements and therefore it has been possible to generate a large body of research findings. Studies following this approach have provided a measure of the rate of return to human capital investment. Second, a number of studies have focused more on the link between productivity and training. We look briefly at some of the evidence from both these approaches.

The 'rate of return' approach

This method seeks to identify the return to human capital investment just as if we were looking at an investment in physical capital. The most widely adopted method of measuring rates of return is to construct some form of 'Mincerian earnings function', as in equation 12.1.

$$\ln Y = a_0 + a_1 S + f(x) + u \tag{12.1}$$

In equation 12.1 the log of earnings (Y) is explained by years of schooling (S) and some function (usually quadratic) of years of experience $(x$, often prox-ied by age); u is the standard random error component. From this type of equation the human capital proponents derive the rate of return from the coefficient a_1. The beauty of this approach is that estimation of the rate of return can be based on simple cross-section data and there is no requirement to collect information on cohorts of workers plotting their wage and employment history over time. Although such data sets exist (more so now than in the early 1960s), the estimation of earnings functions benefited from the widespread availability of simple cross-section data sets.

There are significant difficulties in interpreting returns to education. An important distinction is between the social and private rates of return; social returns take into account the state subsidies for education. It follows that social returns are typically below private returns. There has been a great deal of rationing of places especially in higher education and other distortions in the demand and supply especially in the United Kingdom. This suggests that we might place more importance on the very high private rates of return to higher education which have been typically measured.

While earlier studies found high rates of return on education, more recent studies of the importance of education have cast some doubt about the extent to which the widening gap in income distribution (across all countries) can be attributed to education differences. Schmit (1993) found that about 30 per cent of the widening gap between high-and low-paid over the period 1978–80 and 1986–88 could be explained by either more educa-tion or more experience. Gosling, Machin and Meghir (1994) also found that returns to education were only partly able to explain changes in income distribution. There also appeared to be significant variations across coun-tries in the extent to which growth can be accounted for by the role of education. The OECD(1994) reports on other studies which suggest the role of education might range from as little as 1 per cent up to nearly 30 per cent.

The more recent studies were undertaken when the supply of better educated workers was increasing, and despite this the gap between these and other workers appeared to grow. This was especially the case for young poorly educated workers. Hills (1995) reports on the growing problem of low-paid younger workers and the new phenomenon of flat earnings profiles, where more experience is not associated with higher earnings. This is especially serious for young workers who are starting with low earnings.

A further important finding from several studies is that the return to education appears to have increased during the 1980s (although the return may still be below what it was in the 1970s). This suggests that under-investment in education may have taken place, unless the return had been driven down too low in the early 1980s. Bell (1995) summarises some of the relevant findings concluding that there have been increasing returns to education (and experience) in the United Kingdom and the US during the eighties. Ashenfelter (1996) reports that the return on an additional year of schooling grew from around 6.2 per cent in 1979 to almost 10 per cent in 1993. This suggests that there may have been a substantial rise in under-investment in education (and possibly under-investment in training) in recent years.

Training and productivity

There are a number of problems in assessing the contribution of human capital formation to productivity. One difficulty is with the measurement of productivity itself. An important aspect of measurement which specifically concerns human capital is the measurement of 'labour quality' by relative wages. The contributions of capital and labour quality to total labour productivity can in principle be estimated and any residual attributed to measurement error or unknown factors. This method can be used to compare productivity per worker-hour across countries and to determine the extent to which such differences are related to labour quality which is a reflection of human capital investment.[4]

We can readily see how this approach might be implemented. Effective labour (l_e) is defined in equation 12.2.

$$l_e = [l_s (W_s / W_u) + l_u] / [l_u + l_s] \qquad (12.2)$$

where l_s is skilled labour and l_u is unskilled labour and (W_s / W_u) is the skilled–unskilled wage ratio. $l_e = 1$ if labour is homogeneous.

In addition to comparing labour productivity for the economy as a whole, or for a key sector of the economy, as in manufacturing, it is possible to consider the much more disaggregated industrial sector evidence. The main application of this method is to better identify the contribution of vocational training to both productivity growth and productivity differentials between countries. Focusing on industry data has arguably two main advantages. First, it may help to provide more accurate estimates of the overall contribution of human capital and other factors of production. Second, it identifies the industry specific contributing factors to growth in the different sectors of the economy.

There are many factors to take into account for comparisons of this kind.

One approach to reducing measurement error has been to focus on similar situations. The National Institute has carried out a series of productivity comparisons of 'matched plants' in the United Kingdom with plants in selected European countries, including Germany, France and the Netherlands. Daly, Hitchens and Wagner (1985) set out the methodology and report on findings for the UK and German metalworking industries.[5] This approach has been recognised as a major contribution to the study of vocational training. This National Institute research also provides a link with earlier important work on the contribution of education and training to economic growth.

Detailed industry studies are of major interest in their own right, but there are many problems with the matched plant research as a measure of the contribution of human capital to economic growth. The main stated purpose of the research was to examine the extent to which observed productivity differentials, measured on a comparable basis (using matched plants) can be attributed to differences in human capital and the related vocational training. All these studies attempt to explain productivity differentials, allowing for as many observable factors as possible with the residual attributed to human capital differences. It is the link between the residual productivity differences and unobservable differences in human capital which remain questionable in this research.[6]

It also appears that the industry-specific studies have been developed into economy-wide policy conclusions. One of the findings in the study of the metalworking industry was the superior maintenance of German machines. However, it is debatable whether this can be attributed to better supervision or whether the effectiveness of such maintenance may be related to the technical competence of operatives. Significantly, Prais and Wagner (1988) recognised that it is not always easy to detect to what extent greater skills at different levels are important. One of the main problems in translating the concept of marginal productivity from theory to the real world is the importance of team-working and the difficulties of determining the origins of higher productivity. This remains important despite the changes in the economy and the decline of heavy industry. To allocate marginal contributions of different groups of the workforce or to distinguish entrepreneurial contributions is to some extent arbitrary.

In general, estimates of the return to training have provided less satisfactory evidence in favour of the benefits of human capital accumulation than have studies of the return to education. In particular, studies of the returns to youth training have provided little evidence of positive returns and in many cases significant negative returns, although there are some exceptions such as Main and Shelley (1990). Previous work in the United States, notably Ashenfelter and Card (1985), found modest positive effects of training. Some of the difficulties in estimating the effects of training reflect the nature of training programmes. These programmes have evolved in part out of employment creation programmes and often training duration and quality were too low to be captured in econometric studies.

Overall there seems to be a strong case to argue that human capital investment is a key determinant of economic growth, even if it is sometimes difficult to measure all of the effects. There appears to be stronger evidence on the contribution of education rather than training towards higher productivity. A more contentious issue is not whether high levels of human capital investment are vital for economic growth but whether the required investment can be delivered by a market-based policy. It is therefore essential to examine the main arguments which have been developed about the effectiveness of free markets to provide the best framework and the necessary individual incentives and opportunities.

EXTERNALITIES, MARKET FAILURE AND POACHING

A free market view would be that we should not worry about shortfalls in human capital investment. The market should be allowed to take care of any perceived shortfalls. Alternatively, if the free market does not work, why can't we make it work effectively? Four major sources of market failure have been identified:

1 Arguably the most crucial issue concerns 'non-training firms', which poach skilled workers from 'training firms'. Firms face an environment in which training by all firms is efficient (Pareto optimal) but the outcome is no training (Nash equilibrium); this is one version of the well-known prisoner's dilemma game. Even the fear that non-training firms will recruit trained workers may be sufficient to deter the training firms.[7] The poaching problem has been the most common reason given for the lack of training.

There are some obvious remedies. Firms might seek to protect themselves by limiting training, or making it more specific. Policy action on levies and taxes can counter poaching. The United Kingdom at one time had the Industrial Training Board levy and more recently other countries, notably Australia, have had a payroll tax for this purpose. These measures have been criticised as 'distorting' the market, and impractical because training is inherently difficult to measure. One concern is how well these measures can take account of more indirect training activities, especially more informal 'learning-by-doing'.

More realistically, markets might develop their own mechanisms to accommodate the fear of poaching so that firms will be able to have some limited protection against the 'free-riders' who only recruit skilled workers – this is discussed below in the context of views of the labour market.

A more flexible labour market in which workers can more easily be hired and fired may in fact discourage training; it may encourage greater turnover (although the evidence for this in the United Kingdom remains weak) and this may lead to greater concern over poaching of skilled labour. Paradoxically then, the need for more intervention to encourage firms to invest in human capital investment would appear to be stronger in a world where the labour market is otherwise more 'competitive'. A new dilemma for economic policy is whether more flexible labour markets can be achieved without loss of long-term competitiveness through insufficient human capital accumulation. Alternatively it may be necessary to limit labour market flexibility to encourage more human capital investment.

2 The human capital model assumes that individuals will have free and easy access to finance if necessary. However, individuals may be deterred from human capital investment because of imperfections in the capital market.[8] In particular the property rights to human capital are unlike physical capital; human capital cannot be sold by the lender in the case of a loan default. Policies to promote access to capital to fund both training and education have been a significant development in recent years, with loans available for education and training. Arguably this particular market imperfection has been recognised and at least partially addressed, but it does not address whether allowing individuals control over the choice of training is necessarily best. Also the tendency has been to focus on those not in employment, with the presumption that resources are best allocated to those outside work.

3 Employment contracts may restrict employers and workers from achieving an 'efficient outcome'. Unless continual recontracting is allowed to reflect unanticipated changes in the value of human capital, some inefficiency is inevitable.[9] The problem of achieving the 'efficient' (market-based) outcome in real time is not of course specific to the issue of training; the whole issue of involuntary unemployment lends itself to an analysis along these lines. In the case of implicit contracts, recontracting will also be inefficient in a different sense, because of risk aversion by workers. The whole structure of the labour market has been radically altered by policies designed to improve 'labour market flexibility' and other changes which have led to more flexibility. The effect of these changes on contracts and the implications for training have been left almost entirely to firms, workers and the significant numbers out of work. What is clear is that the predisposition to leave more to the market may prove to be totally inappropriate for human capital decisions. It is also possible that job insecurity may have a more pronounced effect on productivity.

4 Finally, efficient markets depend on full information. But workers can only observe current market conditions in assessing training choices, while employers will generally find it difficult to assess the skills of potential recruits and find it difficult to assess the merits of alternative training for their employees. It is not surprising that employers' associations exist,

although they would arguably be more effective in a system with significant public support for such information. Employees do not know exactly
what skills are in demand or what training might best equip them in the
labour market. The issue is not that such problems exist, but what policies
might improve information flows.

Educational achievements are more easily defined and measured but the
absence of recognised vocational qualifications has been a more serious
information gap. Many countries, including the United Kingdom have
attempted to provide better records of competencies. The United Kingdom
has developed National Vocational Qualifications (NVQs) to measure
vocational attainment. The need for such a system became especially clear
with the decline in formal apprenticeship training in the 1970s and 1980s.
However, one of the many concerns has been whether these qualifications
especially at lower NVQ levels, are sufficiently rigorous. An extension of the
principle of formal qualifications has been the development of entirely individual 'records of achievement' which can be carried into and between jobs.
The use of this more informal and individual approach was briefly tried with
the development of the Youth Training Scheme (YTS) in the early 1980s,
but this was not found to be successful and provided another reason for
developing a more formal qualification system.

There is a fundamental problem in raising the level of information about
training. With more information, workers will be able to move more easily
between firms, exacerbating the poaching problems described above. This
fundamental implication of better certificated workers has not been
addressed and if more labour market flexibility also implies more job
changes, the position in the future may be substantially worse.

VIEWS OF THE LABOUR MARKET

Is the market failure hypothesis an adequate theoretical basis in itself for
understanding the training process? Are individuals deterred or prohibited by
imperfections in the capital market? Is it reasonable to suppose that firms
possess the information about the costs and benefits of training that is
required for the market to function efficiently? Is market failure relevant to
situations where the type of training differs substantially between firms?
Whatever the view taken on these fundamental questions, the concept of
market failure has been widely used to justify market intervention.

Labour markets operate quite differently within and between economies.
An important categorisation of labour markets is between internal labour
markets (ILMs) and occupational labour markets (OLMs). ILMs function in
much the same way as labour markets with only firm-specific skills, following
Becker's distinction between general and specific skills. ILMs are associated
with limited ports of entry into the firm, particular workplaces, internal

promotions, skills acquisition rather than certification, and greater job security. In these markets the firm will be more likely to pay for, and benefit from, training. OLMs are more like the competitive labour markets assumed in standard economic models where workers at all levels are much more mobile. Given the importance of labour mobility, it is clear that the structure of the labour market cannot be set aside in any discussion of training policy.[10]

Training may be categorised by three types of labour market situations: ILMs in which training takes place within the firm, OLMs in which firms recruit from other firms, and OLMs in which firms recruit new but trained labour market entrants. The impact of various training policies in these three types of labour markets will be quite different. For example a levy on non-training would be effective for within-firm training. Economy-wide training schemes would be mainly effective in promoting training for new labour market entrants. Finally, policies promoting more certification and labour mobility would be mainly effective outside the firm. Promoting certification can be counterproductive in ILMs. This supports the view that training policies are likely to be ineffective if they fail to take adequate account of industrial structure and variations in training needs. Economy-wide policies must by definition be wasteful, without some flexibility across industries.

This discussion does not provide a comprehensive account of all the economic issues which arise in an examination of human capital issues. It is also necessary to point out that the economic theory of human capital accumulation is incomplete and much may be required in terms of empirical validation of some of the central hypotheses. Many ideas, including the distinction between general and specific training, signalling, and labour market contracts are of more theoretical rather than practical interest. There are a number of key areas where more empirical information is necessary. However, a picture is emerging of the dangers of either allowing a completely unfettered market approach to training, or poorly conceived interventionist measures. It is arguably problematic to select any common policy themes from such wide-ranging ideas but it is clear that policy should recognise the diversity of labour markets and intervention, where it is necessary, needs to be very carefully designed if it is to be effective.

VIRTUOUS AND VICIOUS CYCLES

An extension of the prisoner's dilemma model of training is the dynamic equilibrium account of training proposed by Finegold and Soskice (1988). In this model there is a high-skill–high-wage or low-skill–low-wage equilibrium outcome. The economy can become locked into a vicious circle of low wages and low skills which is self-perpetuating unless some form of intervention is undertaken. This proposition has proven to be hugely popular with many economic commentators who find it an appealing counter to the market-orientated view that lower wages are an essential ingredient to economic success leading to higher employment.

This hypothesis can be seen as a dynamic version of the market failure hypothesis. Market failure leads to a lose-lose outcome because profit-maximising firms are constrained by policies which may have social aims including short-term employment creation but which produce some unintended side-effects. Taking stock of the dynamic equilibrium in which underinvestment in training occurs, it is clear why even the non-training firms lose. The economy under-invests, fails to grow as fast as it might otherwise do and the supply of trained workers is suboptimal. Policies aimed at strengthening firms in the wage bargaining process will add to this vicious circle of low wages and low skills. Firms will have every incentive to develop a low-skill production process to match the low wage structure; workers will have little incentive to upgrade skills.

This dynamic framework is supported by some of the empirical findings. Many studies have suggested a virtuous cycle in which those who are better educated and trained are more likely to participate in further training. If workers are entering the labour market with lower educational achievements, little training and few qualifications, then firms may not be inclined to offer further training. Firms will offer to train the already trained but not the untrained, although there are large variations across countries in training outcomes. In Germany and the USA those with university qualifications are four to five times as likely to receive further training, compared with unqualified workers, whereas in Japan the distribution is much more even.[11] Broadly the evidence suggests that to under-invest in education and training of young workers lays the foundations of future disincentives to train; a vicious cycle of 'undertraining' develops which is especially costly for young people.

The marginalisation of sections of society is reflected in the move towards more inequality in income distribution.[12] More generally there has been a great deal of discussion about increased social divisions and the idea of social exclusion, or the emergence of a new underclass.[13] Part of the problem is very clearly to do with education and training opportunities. If the labour market has changed as dramatically as some have argued, then movement out of any socially excluded group may be very difficult for the poorly educated, and the consequences for individuals and society could be very great. The vicious cycle for individuals may create a basis for a permanent underclass with limited scope for movement despite the greater income mobility and better lifetime incomes for those in the socially included group.

The creation of groups who are excluded from the benefits of growing real incomes and who may even face incomes which do not follow the normal upward lifetime patterns is of concern for social reasons. It will also ultimately be important for economic reasons if in an ageing population some young people fail to contribute much to society during their working lives. There appear to be vicious and virtuous circles for individuals and the economy whereby the better educated and trained tend to receive even more training than others.

POLICIES AND EVIDENCE

The discussion above indicates that there are substantial returns to education and training, that there are several reasons why lack of investment might occur in a free market and that there may be considerable social costs in under-investing in training and education. It follows that policy should strive to ensure that the UK investment in human capital is adequate. One indicator of an adequate rate of investment is that of performance relative to other countries based on input and attainment measures. Therefore the next step is to examine where the United Kingdom lags behind other countries and where there may be a consequential gap to be made up. We look at four areas where it has been argued that the United Kingdom may be lagging behind and where there is a policy interest:

1 education expenditure;
2 school enrolment rates;
3 education and training participation;
4 craft skills and training qualifications.

Education expenditure

Data on education expenditure should be treated with some caution and are probably of less value than comparisons of qualifications. Differences in how expenditure information is recorded and differences in institutional arrangements across countries are considerable. However, what information does exist is not especially encouraging, and at least casts doubt about whether sufficient resources are being devoted to human capital investment.

For example, in 1991 the percentage of GNP devoted to education in the United Kingdom was higher in the United Kingdom than in Japan, Spain, Germany, Australia or Italy, but generally lower than in Belgium, Canada, Denmark, France, Netherlands, Sweden and the USA. The figures on expenditure as a proportion of GDP are a little volatile between years and it is perhaps best to compare them over a number of years. This picture is less flattering for the United Kingdom, which is ahead of only Japan, Spain and Germany. The figures for 1987, 1991 and the average over 1987–91 are shown in Table 12.1 which is limited to public expenditure.[14]

School enrolment rates

While the United Kingdom has put a significant effort into providing training for young people, one of the main concerns for the sixteen plus youth

Table 12.1 Public expenditure on education as a percentage of GDP

	1987	1991	Average, 1987–91
UK	4.8	5.3	4.9
Australia	5.0	4.7	5.0
Belgium	5.2	5.4	5.2
Canada	7.2	6.7	7.1
Denmark	7.9	6.1	7.3
France	5.5	5.4	5.4
Germany	4.4	4.0	4.2
Italy	4.8	5.0	4.9
Japan	4.3	3.7	4.1
Netherlands	7.3	5.6	6.5
Spain	3.2	4.5	4.1
Sweden	7.1	6.5	6.9
USA	4.6	5.5	5.3

Source: Department for Education, *Education Statistics for the United Kingdom* (1990–94).
Notes: (a) 1987–91 averages are based on available years between 1987 and 1991.
(b) The data exclude private expenditure.

labour market must lie with the significant drop-out rate from formal education (measured also by the low enrolment rates at different ages). Training school leavers may be better than leaving them idle, but it is a dubious alternative to full-time education. The enrolment rates show the United Kingdom is nearly at the bottom of the international league. The enrolment rate falls markedly in the United Kingdom after the age of fifteen and lags significantly below most countries for those aged sixteen and above. The figures for those aged eighteen are shown in Table 12.2.

The growth in enrolment rates also offers only a little encouragement. The enrolment of seventeen-year-olds in 1984 was about 46.3 per cent but had risen to 58.7 per cent in 1990, although the recession in the United Kingdom may have accounted for some of this improvement, as leaving school or further education early was discouraged by the state of the labour market. Furthermore, other countries had been moving as fast as or faster than the United Kingdom. Some countries had shown remarkable progress; Australia improved its enrolment rate from less than 50 per cent in 1986 to more than 90 per cent by 1990. Spain, the nearest country to the United Kingdom in this league table, maintained a higher enrolment rate than the United Kingdom of 62.8 per cent in 1990 compared with 48.8 per cent in 1984.[15]

There has more recently been a greater policy interest in the initial stages of education (vouchers for nursery education, for example). Surprisingly the United Kingdom appears to have a more impressive record in this respect than some of the recent policy discussion might suggest. The enrolment rates for four-year-olds are given in Table 12.3.

Table 12.2 Enrolment percentages at age eighteen

Germany	80	Sweden	55.7
Switzerland	75.9	USA	55.0
France	75.0	Spain	52.0
Norway	74.8	Ireland	50.1
Finland	73.4	Portugal	42.0
Netherlands	72.7	New Zealand	32.7
Denmark	67.6	UK	25.7
Canada	59.2	Turkey	24.6

Source: OECD (1994, p. 130).

Table 12.3 Enrolment rates for four-year-olds

France	100.0	Japan	57.8
Belgium	99.4	USA	56.7
Netherlands	98.3	Ireland	55.3
Spain	93.5	Norway	53.5
New Zealand	92.6	Portugal	44.0
Germany	70.6	Switzerland	26.4
Austria	65.7	Canada	24.1
UK	60.7	Turkey	0.3

Source: OECD (1994, p. 134).
Note: France figure adjusted.

From these data it would appear that most concern should be directed to the very high drop-out rates from secondary-schooling rather than giving the highest priority to the under-fives. It is also clear that there is a case for concentrating more attention on those nearer to entering the labour market, rather then pre-school education.

Education and training participation

The United Kingdom has a high drop-out rate from secondary education, but a high proportion of these school leavers move into vocational training. If we take training and education together, the relative position of the United Kingdom is arguably more encouraging (Table 12.4).

Although the United Kingdom appears to have a significant number of people in training, a lot of this training is only part-time. The United Kingdom still lags behind many countries (Table 12.4) even when part-time training is included. This data do not provide any basis for assessing the quality of training in different countries and this has also been a matter of concern. Some of this concern is reflected in the debate on craft skills. Also it is important to reflect on the empirical studies cited earlier in this paper. These

Table 12.4 Participation in education and training of sixteen- to eighteen-year-olds

	1987	*1991*	*Average, 1987–91* *
Germany	92	89	91
Belgium	87	85	87
Netherlands	86	80	85
France	77	87	82
Denmark	79	79	79
Japan	79	79	79
USA	81	76	79
Canada	75	78	77
Sweden	78	76	76
UK	68	76	71
Australia	67	76	70
Italy	65	65	65
Spain	50	63	58

Source: Department for Education, *Education Statistics for the United Kingdom,* (1990–4).

studies found it difficult to establish a link between training and productivity suggesting that differences in training may be less significant than differences in education.

Craft skills and qualifications

There has been a significant increase in enrolment in further and higher education in the 1980s and 1990s. But one of the main findings of international comparisons of training provision is that the United Kingdom has tended to provide relatively well for academic qualifications but poorly for vocational qualifications. The evidence for this is not new, but it remains one of the long-term UK training problems. This illustrates that even if all of the arguments about the merits of a high-wage high-skill economy are accepted, it still remains an issue as to where scarce resources should be invested.

The United Kingdom has a comparatively good record on training qualifications for bachelor degrees, masters degrees and doctorates compared with many other leading countries including the US, Japan, Germany and France.[16] Even so, there is a significant gap even in higher-level skills (higher degrees and above). The National Institute research on training qualifications shows that at the craftsmen level the United Kingdom lags significantly behind other countries.[17] Other studies have supported this conclusion.[18]

There are difficulties in international comparisons of this kind, and many of the comparisons which are made are often of a superficial kind. For example, it has been argued that compared with Germany, our relative youth wage rate has been an obstacle to employing younger workers as apprentices.

A high relative wage tends to encourage employers to see young workers as employees rather than trainees. On the other hand the German VET system has been the focus of much attention and has been frequently cited as a benchmark for other countries, including the United Kingdom. It has also been argued that Germany provides much better for the 'middle' group of labour market entrants. In both countries more than 25 per cent of this group have obtained some form of academic qualification, such as a good set of GCSEs, but in Germany this group will also have considerable vocational and technical achievements.

In international comparisons generally, the United Kingdom compares unfavourably with other countries in terms of lower and intermediate skills. There is considerable evidence of the United Kingdom lagging behind other countries (including Germany), especially in terms of intermediate qualifications. In 1987 the proportion of the workforce with no qualifications was about 60 per cent in the United Kingdom, whereas it was below 30 per cent in Germany and the proportion of the workforce with lower intermediate qualifications was about 25 per cent in the United Kingdom compared with more than 55 per cent in Germany.[19] Such gaps cannot be eliminated in a short time, and if it is suggested that they have been quickly reduced we should be even more concerned about the relevance and quality of such training provision; investment in human capital must be seen as a long-term policy.

Another puzzling aspect of many international comparisons is the variation in qualifications which employers accept in different countries.[20] For example, two very different structures operate in the Germany and the United States. In Germany it is a necessity for workers to be qualified before they are likely to get a job and the route to further qualifications is through company training. In the United States, schooling is a much more important prerequisite to finding a job and also more important as a means of obtaining basic qualifications. The tendency to pick out 'good examples' of policy in other countries, including Germany, France, US and Japan, without regard for whether any specific policies are transferable, is open to many objections. It specifically ignores the social frameworks which exist in different countries. The scope for different approaches to training provision should not be underestimated; what works well in one country could be disastrous for another. Perhaps one of the more important insights from the comparison of the United Kingdom and Germany is social rather than economic; the value of craft and vocational skills is recognised in Germany but not in the United Kingdom.

A recent study of skills and education attainment by DFEE (1996) supports many of the conclusions in this paper. The evidence suggests that the United Kingdom continues to compare favourably in terms of higher-level qualifications, but less so at lower education levels and for intermediate skill levels. Comparing the United Kingdom with France, for example, using the

DFEE findings, the United Kingdom is behind on measures of the population reaching level 2 qualifications (level 2 is the equivalent of five GCSEs at grades A to C), behind at level 3 in general education, but ahead on vocational qualifications at level 3 (level 3 is equivalent to two A levels) and broadly comparable on higher degrees with France. Notably both France and the United Kingdom are significantly behind Germany in the achievement of level 3 vocational qualifications.

CONCLUSIONS

There is a body of evidence which suggests that investment in human capital remains a constraint on the competitiveness of the economy. The importance of this constraint has been considered from many perspectives, but the evidence suggests that Britain lags behind other countries in a number of areas.

This chapter identifies the main theoretical reasons why there may be difficulties for individuals in free markets to optimise levels of human capital – poaching, difficulties individuals may encounter in borrowing for the purpose of education or training, contract problems with firms who have no guarantee that workers will stay long enough to provide a return on training, and finally workers and firms need full information to determine optimal training and employment decisions.

There are also wider problems associated with the operation of labour markets. One of the problems for the proponents of a more market-based approach to training is whether adequate incentives for human capital accumulation are consistent with ever greater labour market flexibility. More labour market flexibility may encourage greater turnover and more poaching of skilled labour. There also appear to be strong virtuous and vicious circles which characterise the process of human capital accumulation. Well-educated workers are more likely to have better training opportunities and there is a virtuous circle of high-skilled firms with high wages creating a human capital incentive for workers to acquire the necessary education and training.

As the conditions required for optimum decision-making are so unlikely to be achieved, it is not surprising that various forms of policy intervention have proved necessary. A variety of policy measures have been put forward to remedy the widely recognised market failures. These measures include subsidies and tax relief to individuals and firms, institutional reforms to promote education and training, economy-wide training schemes financed by government, measures promoting certification, vouchers, government targets and guarantees, financial incentives to educational institutions, and education performance standards. These measures may have been well-intentioned, and each one may be explained individually on a clear logical basis. This paper has sought to spell out the wider strategic issues and until these are tackled, it seems unlikely that any future assessment of the United Kingdom's stance on investing in skills will be very different.

NOTES

1   See Becker (1962) and (1975) and Mincer (1958), (1962) and (1974).
2   See in particular Spence (1973).
3   See Main and Shelly (1990) for example.
4   See O'Mahoney (1992) for an application of this method comparing manufacturing productivity differences in the United Kingdom and Germany. Of the 22 per cent difference in productivity, about 10 per cent was due to labour quality and 9 per cent to capital differences. Only 4 per cent was due to other 'residual' factors.
5   The National Institute has undertaken many comparable industry studies using the 'matched plant' approach. These have been undertaken mainly in the manufacturing sector, including metal-working, furniture, clothing and biscuit production, but also hotels in the service sector. Detailed findings can be found in Prais (1990) and some further commentary on the methods used in Chapman (1993).
6   See Daly, Hitchens and Wagner (1985, pp. 60–1).
7   This has been recognised for a long time. See Oatey (1970) for example.
8   See Thurow (1970), for example.
9   See Hashimoto (1981) and Hashimoto and Yu (1980).
10 Marsden and Ryan (1991) argue that the United Kingdom is more closely described by an OLM structure.
11 See OECD (1994).
12 See Hills (1995) for example.
13 See Murray (1994) for example.
14 A case can be argued for including other types of expenditure (such as private expenditure on education) in this analysis. However, it is simplistic and possibly misleading to argue that such expenditures can be added to generate a total figure for investment in human capital. For example, there may be different (lower) returns to private expenditure and there may be negative externalities for the public sector of selection by income. On the other hand, by focusing on public expenditure, we focus on a part of human capital investment of more direct interest for policy where there is less doubt about what expenditure represents.
15 See OECD (1994).
16 See Prais (1989).
17 See Prais (1990).
18 See NEDO (1984) for example.
19 See O'Mahoney (1992).
20 See OECD (1994).

REFERENCES

Ashenfelter, O. (1996) 'Schooling, intelligence and income in America', mimeo, paper for the EEEG conference at the University of Leeds.
Ashenfelter, O. and Card, D. (1985) 'Using the longitudinal structure of earnings to estimate the effect of training programs', *Review of Economic Studies*, vol. 47, pp. 648–60.

Becker, G. S. (1962) 'Investment in human capital: A theoretical analysis', *Journal of Political Economy*, Vol. 70, Supplement, pp. 9–49.

—— (1975) *Human Capital*, 2nd edn, New York: Columbia University Press.

Bell, D. N. F. (1995) 'Earnings inequality in Great Britain: Some additional evidence', *Scottish Journal of Political Economy*, vol. 42, no. 3, pp. 290–309.

Blaug, M. (1976) 'The empirical status of human capital theory: A slightly jaundiced survey', *Journal of Economic Literature*, vol. 14, pp. 827–55.

Chapman, P. G. (1993) *The Economics of Training*, Hemel Hempstead: Harvester Wheatsheaf.

Daly, A., Hitchens, D. M. W. N. and Wagner, K. (1985) 'Productivity, machinery and skills in a sample of British and German manufacturing plants: Results of a pilot study', *National Institute Economic Review*, no. 111, pp. 48–61.

DFEE (1996) *The Skills Audit: A Report from an Interdepartmental Group*, Occasional Paper, DFEE and the Cabinet Office.

Finegold, D. and Soskice, D. (1988) 'The failure of training in Britain: Analysis and prescription', *Oxford Review of Economic Policy*, vol. 4, no. 3, Autumn, pp. 21–53.

Gosling, A., Machin, S. and Meghir, C. (1994) 'What has happened to wages', *IFS Commentary*, No. 43, London: IFS.

Hashimoto, M. (1981) 'Firm-specific capital as a shared investment', *American Economic Review*, vol. 71, pp. 475–82.

Hashimoto, M. and Yu, B. (1980) 'Specific capital, employment contracts, and wage rigidity', *Bell Journal of Economics*, vol. 11, Autumn, no. 2, pp. 536–49.

Hills, J. (1995) *Income and Wealth*, Joseph Rowntree Foundation, Enquiry into Income and Wealth.

Main, B. G. M. and Shelly, M. A. (1990) 'The effectiveness of YTS as a manpower policy', *Economica*, vol. 57, pp. 495–514.

Marsden, D. W. and Ryan, P. (1991) 'Institutional aspects of youth employment and training policy', *British Journal of Industrial Relations*, vol. 29, no. 2, pp. 497–505.

Mincer, J. (1958) 'Investment in human capital and personal income distribution', *Journal of Political Economy*, vol. 66, part 4, pp. 281–302.

—— (1962) 'On-the-job training: Costs, returns and some implications', *Journal of Political Economy*, vol. 70, no. 5, pp. 50–79.

—— (1974) *Schooling, Experience and Earnings*, New York: NBER, Columbia University Press

Murray, C. (1994) *The Underclass: The Crisis Deepens*, IEA.

NEDO (1984) *Competence and Competition: Training and education in the Federal Republic of Germany, the United States and Japan*, London: National Economic Development Office and The Manpower Services Commission, NEDO.

Oatey, M. (1970) 'The economics of training with respect to the firm', *British Journal of Industrial Relations*, vol. 8, no. 1, pp. 1–21.

OECD (1994) *The OECD Jobs Study: Evidence and explanations*, Part II, The adjustment potential of the labour market, Paris: OECD.

O'Mahoney, M. (1992) 'Productivity levels in British and German manufacturing industry', *National Institute Economic Review*, no. 139, pp. 46–63.

Prais, S. J. (1989) 'Qualified manpower in engineering: Britain and other industrially advanced countries', *National Institute Economic Review*, no. 127, pp. 76–83.

—— (ed.) (1990) *Productivity, Education and Training*, London: NIESR.

Prais, S. J. and Wagner, K. (1988) 'Productivity and management: The training of foremen in Britain and Germany', *National Institute Economic Review*, no. 123, pp. 34–47.

Schmit, J. (1993) 'The changing structure of male earnings in Britain, 1974–1988', *Centre for Economic Performance Discussion Paper*, no. 122, London: London School of Economics.

Spence, M. A. (1973) 'Job market signalling', *Quarterly Journal of Economics*, vol. 87, pp. 355–75.

Thurow, L. (1970) *Investment in Human Capital*, Belmont, Calif.: Wadsworth.

Part IV

THE LABOUR MARKET AND THE SOCIAL FRAMEWORK

13

OVERVIEW: THE PERFORMANCE OF THE UK LABOUR MARKET

Paul Chapman and Paul Temple[1]

There are activities in our culture in which it is socially acceptable and expected that individual pecuniary self-interest will be the overriding decision criterion; choosing a portfolio of securities for example. There are others in which it is not; choosing a mate, for example. The labour market is more complicated than either of course, and contains elements of both.

(Solow, 1980).

INTRODUCTION: THE LEGACY OF TWO DECADES

Twenty years ago Britain's labour market was widely supposed to be the major stumbling block to improved economic performance. The belief embraced both the nature of the country's idiosyncratic labour market institutions, and the extent to which the tax and benefit system interfered with economic incentives towards work and enterprise. The evidence cited included an inferior record on the inflationary effects of the two great supply-side shocks of the 1970s, lower productivity growth, a higher incidence of strikes, and lower levels of labour force skills and training provision.

The general unpopularity of rapid inflation and the widely perceived need to weaken union bargaining power encouraged the incoming government of 1979 to engage in what was perhaps the most radical labour market reform programme pursued among the advanced economies during the 1980s. Broadly, this programme pursued the following objectives.

- To reduce union power, chiefly via the Employment Acts of 1982, 1984, and 1988. These Acts reduced union immunities, while increasing the rights of the individual worker and the employer. In particular the ability of the employer to hire and dispose of labour was enhanced.
- To increase the incentive to work, by lowering the benefits to those out of work and making eligibility for benefits more difficult.

- To make labour market outcomes mimic more precisely those that would prevail in a free market, i.e. to reduce the redistributive impact of government. Measures adopted included the lowering of tax rates and abolition of wages councils. A wider dispersion of earnings was expected, *inter alia*, to increase incentives to undertake education and training.
- To encourage individual enterprise and self-employment though a variety of schemes such as the enterprise allowance.
- To reduce the Government's direct involvement in the labour market through privatisation and a reduction in central government responsibility for the pay and conditions of public sector workers.

While the reforms were inevitably part of a wider political agenda, they also had an efficiency objective. But such is the importance of the labour market for standards of living, that we cannot ignore the impact of the reforms on equity. It is precisely the tension between efficiency and equity that forms the backbone of this overview chapter.

However, while policy does appear to have had substantial influence, there have been other long-term changes, both nationally and internationally, which also have had major impacts on the labour market. Two particularly important features should be noted. First, there has been a marked decline in the demand for manual labour. Undoubtedly, the related factors of international competition and investment and technological change have contributed, although the extent to which each has contributed remains a contentious issue. Second, wider changes in society have affected the supply side of the labour market. Especially important has been the increased diversification of household types: more single-person households and lone parents, pensioner households, and couples without children – each type with differential access to the opportunities and rewards of the labour market.

These wider social and economic factors have interacted with the policy reforms to create an economy marked by considerably greater inequality. Any benefits coming from increased efficiency in the functioning of the labour market must be considered against the costs and risks of increasing inequality and social deprivation, a fact rather belatedly recognised by the OECD:

> High and persistent unemployment is only one manifestation of the poor labour market performance in many OECD countries. OECD societies also confront worrying inequalities which are straining the social fabric ... The risk now facing a number of OECD countries is that labour market exclusion can easily turn into poverty and dependence. Social protection systems can alleviate poverty, but they cannot promote participation in society unless they are closely tied to measures to tackle labour market problems.

(1996, vii)

300

It is essential therefore that the analysis of the labour market goes beyond the description of what has happened to employment and wages and the rate of unemployment, but also considers the impact of change on the household. However, further discussion cannot properly proceed in a theoretical vacuum. Accordingly, the following section briefly examines some models of the labour market. We then consider the changing relationship between paid employment and the household, before looking at the issue of unemployment from a number of perspectives. The chapter then briefly reviews some of the evidence at the microeconomic level, before concluding and suggesting some considerations for policy.

ALTERNATIVE MODELS OF THE LABOUR MARKET

A reform programme of labour market institutions of the kind outlined in the introduction could not have proceeded without theoretical guidance. In fact it is possible to argue that policy was based on a remarkably simple view of the operation of the labour market. In its most crude form, this was that labour market performance would be enhanced if it could be made to work more like the competitive spot market of neoclassical economic theory. On this view the labour market works best if the 'price' of labour is free to adjust to a level at which the quantity of employment desired by employers matches the amount of employment offered by workers. If actual prices are higher than this 'equilibrium' price, employers will respond by reducing the hours of work they offer. On this analysis, many observed labour market institutions are inefficient because they prevent the market clearing.

At the level of an individual labour market – say in the analysis of the demand for a particular kind of skilled labour within a particular travel to work area, the model has something to commend it. However, it is crucial to understand that this view has been extended routinely to the analysis of aggregate employment, i.e. to a macroeconomic view of the labour market. This version of the model is, for a variety of reasons, more controversial than its micro counterpart.

In relation to either version of the model, there are two sources of friction to the competitive market process which are generally regarded as important by advocates. The first is the impact of unionisation. Unions may affect labour supply by (for example) the threat of collective action to withdraw labour if certain terms and conditions, which may include the wage rate, are not met. In terms of the model, if the union wage exceeds the market clearing wage, then unemployment may result. Note that the emphasis on trade union activity as a source of market power is not generally matched by any emphasis on the possibility of power on the demand side of the labour market; such power is generally assumed to be a curiosity confined to single-employer towns (e.g. a mining town). The second source of interference in the market frequently considered important for its impact on the labour supply decision is the impact of the tax and benefit system upon either the incentive to enter employment in the first place, or to increase hours of work. The decision to enter the labour market is held to depend critically upon the existence of alternative sources of income – these take the form of social security benefits which constitute the so-called 'reservation wage' for the individual worker. The proportion of income earned when unemployed to that earned when employed, is known as the 'replacement ratio', which will depend in part upon the generosity of the benefits system, the impact of which would be to increase the elasticity of supply at lower levels of the wage.

A number of problems are manifest in both versions of the model. The precise nature of what is being bought and sold in the labour market is one particular area that requires more detailed consideration than it is generally given. In the standard textbook version, the numbers of hours purchased correspond to a definite amount of effort and, given the other factors of production required, a definite amount of output. By contrast the intensity of work is crucial to the 'efficiency wage' approach to labour market behaviour outlined below. Other problems relate to the importance of information in supply and demand decisions – in for example the 'matching' of the tasks needing to be performed in the workplace and the competencies of the individual needing to perform them, a process becoming increasingly important as the skill intensity of production rises.

Leaving such considerations aside, there are significant differences between the macro and the micro versions of the model. First and foremost, the concept of the wage rate needs very precise definition in a macro model. In a micro model, it is possible to argue that the prices of other goods and services, aside from the price of labour, are constant. In a macro model however, the interaction between wages and prices becomes crucial, so that while actual bargains in the labour market are always being struck in money terms, the real wage outcome is uncertain for both employers and employees, and dependent upon the ensuing rate of price inflation. Expectations of price inflation become central.

Beyond the considerable problem of the interaction between wages and prices in a macro setting, other macroeconomic factors may come into play which limit the aggregate level of employment and make the neoclassical cause of unemployment – an excessive real wage – an inappropriate, or entirely misleading, basis for policy. Both Keynesian and classical economic theory depart considerably from the neoclassical approach.

In Keynesian theory, for example, unemployment arises because of a lack of effective demand for output as a whole. Money wage reductions (which may bring about an equilibrium in the microeconomic market) may fail in the aggregate, because consequential price reductions prevent the real wage from falling. The appropriate policy response in this instance is to increase the effective demand for goods and services and not to force any particular group of workers to accept money wage reductions.

In a Keynesian world, full employment is prevented by insufficient effective demand. The assumption is made that physical capacity exists to employ all the available workforce. This assumption is also a part of the neoclassical model, where the underlying technology is always sufficiently flexible to be able to employ the existing workforce. If real wages are allowed to fall in the presence of unemployment, then more labour-intensive processes of production will be used and the demand for more labour-intensive goods and services will be stimulated; together these processes will be sufficient to restore full employment. However, for the classical economists (such as Smith or Ricardo), technology is never this flexible and capital is essentially complementary to labour; in such a world it may well be that lower real wages will not stimulate the demand for labour sufficiently and that unemployment may persist because of capital shortage. Although some modern economists have stressed the importance of capital shortage (e.g. Malinvaud, 1980, 1985; Rowthorn, 1995; Driver, 1994) and the need for capital accumulation to increase the number of jobs, this has not been the thrust of either the majority of writers or of the OECD in its *Jobs Study* (OECD, 1994), which stresses the role of labour market reform and deregulation in the creation of jobs – largely reflecting the neoclassical approach.

The last decade has seen the development of other models which challenge the neoclassical view of the labour market but from a more clearly microeconomic perspective. Perhaps the most obvious involves abandoning the assumption of perfect competition and recognises that firms bargain with employees over wages, and that firms themselves may possess product market power and be able to pass on at least some of any increase in wage costs in the form of higher prices. Many labour economists make use of these assumptions and it forms the basis of the so-called NAIRU framework outlined below. Beyond the relaxation of competitive assumptions, a further alternative – the efficiency wage approach – builds on the fact that when an employer pays for so many hours of work, he or she cannot monitor the actual effort that will be put in. In fact, it seems reasonable to suppose that effort will respond positively to increases in wages, and negatively to the probability of being hired elsewhere if caught shirking, which is of course related to the level of unemployment.

The intensity of effort is an important variable not just between different workers but also for the same worker(s) from one point of time to the next. In the competitive market-clearing model, this variable is rooted in the technology of production. While somehow fixing the intensity of effort through such technological devices as the production line may sometimes be an objective for employers, such attempts are neither all-pervasive nor necessarily successful. The efficiency wage approach therefore recognises a potential for shirking on the part of the workforce. Moreover, and especially in team-working situations, the monitoring of individual effort is costly or impossible. In one version of the model (Shapiro and Stiglitz, 1985), work itself has disutility, so there is an incentive to shirk. If unemployment did not exist, a worker caught shirking would immediately be rehired by another firm. On the other hand, if firms pay a higher wage to induce more effort from workers, real wages will tend to rise above market-clearing levels, producing unemployment. Unemployment now functions as a disciplinary device in its own right, raising the cost to the individual worker of being caught shirking.

The idea of a 'natural propensity to shirk' is not, however, a necessary (nor possibly an attractive) aspect of the approach. An alternative is the 'fair exchange' in the work-place in which workers are generally happy to offer effort in excess of an 'acceptable norm' in exchange for wages which are above the reservation wage. This is Akerlof's 'exchange of gifts' in which social norms play an important role in determining work-place behaviour (Akerlof, 1982).

Of course, model building would be a largely futile activity if it did not generate differing predictions about likely outcomes in changing economic circumstances. Many facts about the structure of wages, both between firms and between industries, tend to support the efficiency wage approach. The competitive model has fundamental difficulties in explaining why wages for similar workers and jobs apparently differ significantly and persistently both between firms in the same industry and across industries (see, for example, Layard et al., 1991).

One area of comparison is provided by the impact of minimum wage legislation, a facet of labour market policy which has divided the political parties in the United Kingdom and elsewhere. The objective for introducing minimum wage legislation has been to provide a low-cost means of enhancing the incomes of the low-paid and hence reducing an important source of poverty. However if the impact of a minimum wage is to raise wages above their current levels (so that the legislation actually bites), then neoclassical competitive wage theory predicts a substantial further cost as employers reduce their employment levels. Moreover, if an unprotected sector remains, the displaced workers may find even lower wages as the supply of labour in this sector is increased. There are also further employment effects if wage inflation takes hold, as workers seek to maintain relative pay differentials. By contrast, in the efficiency wage approach the employer has some monopsony power: employers who pay higher wages find it both easier to recruit and retain workers, so that the labour supply faced by the firm increases with the wage offered. In such circumstances the firm's profit-maximising wages are below the marginal cost of labour. An increase in that firm's wages resulting from legislation (at least one that is not too large) will actually increase the profit-maximising level of employment, by lowering the cost of hiring an additional worker.

Recent empirical evidence offers some support for the belief that the impact of minimum wage legislation may have negligible costs in terms of unemployment. Most important are the studies relating to the US where minimum wage legislation, both at state and federal levels, has created a variety of 'natural experiments'. Evidence from these has generally been mixed, and indeed several recent studies have highlighted cases in which an increase in the minimum wage has resulted in increased employment in certain low-pay jobs (e.g. Card, 1992a, 1992b; Card and Krueger, 1993). For the United Kingdom, Machin and Manning (1994) have studied the impact on employment of wages councils which, at their apogee in the 1960s, covered some 3.5 million workers but whose influence and coverage were reduced during the 1980s, with eventual complete abolition in 1993. These set legally enforceable minimum rates of pay and other conditions (such as holiday entitlement). As a proportion of average earnings, the minimum rate of pay set by the Wages Councils fell in the course of the 1980s and Machin and Manning found that this measure of 'toughness' helped to explain the change in employment of industries covered, but in the opposite direction to that predicted by neoclassical competitive theory, i.e. they found a positive relation between toughness and employment.

EMPLOYMENT AND THE HOUSEHOLD

The labour market and sources of household income

Some idea of the extent of the changes in the impact of the labour market on the household can be gained from an examination of how the source of aggregate household income has changed over the period from 1979 to 1994; this is done in Figure 13.1, where it can be seen that the importance of the labour market to the aggregate household sector has declined quite sharply – from 74 per cent of total income in 1979 to 65 per cent in 1994, with the importance of wages and salaries falling slightly more in proportionate terms – from 65 per cent to just 55 per cent of total income. The slightly larger fall in wages and salaries reflects the growing importance of self-employment income, but the major changes have been the increased importance of pensions (but not the basic state pension) and transfers in the form of a variety of state benefits – chiefly income support, family benefit, and unemployment benefit. By contrast with these movements, the share of interest, dividends and other forms of property income has remained relatively steady.

These changes in the sources of household income reflect fundamental changes in household composition – especially the growing importance of households without even a single worker. Evidence on the nature of these changes can be obtained from the sample of households in the long-standing Family Expenditure Survey (FES). The most striking change over the period 1979–94/5 in the sample reported is the rise in the proportion of households where the head of household is 'economically inactive' – a

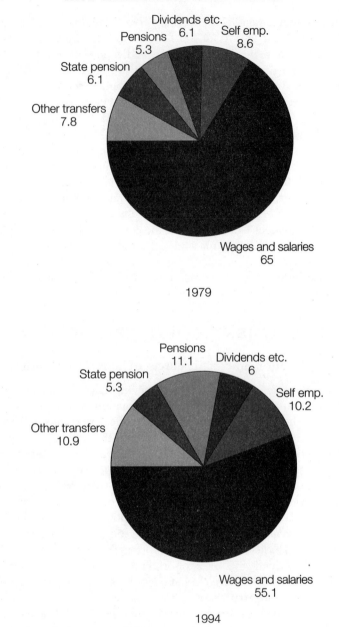

1979

1994

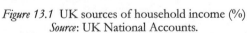

Figure 13.1 UK sources of household income (%)
Source: UK National Accounts.

categorisation which includes retired people but not the unemployed – from 30 per cent to 39 per cent of households. Of this change, only a small part is explained by the increased preponderance of households whose members are retired: households with one or two retired members rose from 22 per cent to 24 per cent of all households. Nor is the change explained by the unemployed, since these are counted as economically active. However, households in which the head was actively seeking (or about to obtain) a job in the week interviewed, i.e. unemployed, also rose from 2.9 per cent in 1979 to 5.3 per cent in 1994/95 – an important but less dramatic change than the surge in the economically inactive. Moreover, according to the FES, households without any member who is economically active form by far the greater proportion of the poorest households by income – over three-quarters of households in the two bottom income deciles were without a member who was in paid employment.

By way of contrast with the increase in 'no-earner' households, there has been an equally important rise in the proportion of working households where there is more than one worker. Therefore there has been a large shift in the distribution of jobs across households consistent with the idea of a polarisation between 'job-rich' and 'job-poor' households.

It is of course the precise status of the economically inactive that lies at the heart of the debate about the 'true' extent of unemployment in the United Kingdom. There are many reasons why a person of working age might appear in the data as economically inactive, such as tertiary education (where numbers have been increasing significantly), disability, and sickness, but there are also many who are discouraged (because of perceived difficulties in finding employment) and others who have family responsibilities but who would otherwise like a job.

Further evidence on the economically inactive may be obtained from the Labour Force Survey (LFS) which includes not only those individuals who are unemployed and actively seeking work (the definition of unemployment adopted by the International Labour Office) but also those who merely report that they would like a job. As the inaugural issue of the Employment Audit pointed out, adding the two together results in an individual jobless count of over 4 million people – twice as large as the standard LFS measure (Employment Policy Institute, 1996).

Another important change for households has been the rise in the importance of self-employment, although this change is of course very much in line with the intended reform of the labour market. Employment data suggest that the number of self-employed rose from 1.9 million in 1979 to 3.3 million in 1995 (from 7.2 per cent to 11.9 per cent of the workforce) – a rise of 75 per cent over the period.[2] However, it needs to be noted that the trend toward self-employment may have run its course, with the total number of self-employed having fallen in the 1990s – although this reflects full-time rather than part-time self-employment, with the latter category continuing to rise.

307

The proportion of self-employment in the United Kingdom is one of the largest in the OECD (*Employment Outlook*, 1992). To what extent does this indicate the development of the 'enterprise culture'? First it is important to notice that the rise in self-employment *income* has not matched the rise in self-employment. The rise in real household earnings from self-employment (estimated from the National Accounts data as above), rose by 71 per cent – by less than the increase in self-employment. This does not suggest that the creation of more self-employment owes much to the opening up of new and lucrative entrepreneurial possibilities. Indeed estimates, based on the LFS by Blanchflower and Freeman (1994), suggest that the rise in self-employment between 1979 and 1990 owed nothing to any rise in the rate of flow from employee to self-employed status which, they argue, would be a distinguishing characteristic of the enterprise culture. Using the General Household Survey they do, however, find that, after controlling for regional and human capital variables, the negative gap between a self-employed worker and his or her employee counterpart may have diminished in the course of the 1980s. This is of course quite consistent with a decline in the real value of average earnings of the self-employed, since the main source of increasing self-employment has been from the ranks of the unemployed, who are more likely to possess lower levels of human capital, to reside in a disadvantaged region, and to have a manual occupation. On balance, they suggest that the rise in self-employment should be regarded as a positive feature, although not on a scale sufficient to compensate for the loss of full-time male employment.

One final aspect of changes in the labour market needs to be mentioned in relation to the household – the fundamental shift in the nature of the kind of work supporting households. According to the FES, 41.1 per cent of heads of households were in a manual occupation in 1979 (whether employed or unemployed); by 1994/5, this percentage had declined to just 27.6 per cent. Among employees, this reduction was very similar for skilled (craft workers) or unskilled manual workers, so it is generally incorrect to speak of a decline in the demand for unskilled manual workers as opposed to skilled manual workers. Note, however, that the trend decline in the proportion of employment which is manual is very long-lived, displaying a rather steady trend over forty years, and, if anything, has slowed down in the 1990s (Robinson, 1996a).

A note of caution needs to be added to the descriptive statistics in this section. They are all views taken over a very short period of time. Households do of course change over time. Much less is known about the nature of these transitions and how a deeper knowledge of them might affect our view of the changes that have taken place. However, the rise in the degree of economic inactivity recorded above does give cause for concern regarding the waste of human resources and lost production opportunities. It may tell us less about the social distress caused by inactivity, which may depend upon the period over which unemployment lasts. A rapid churning of the unemployed or inactive may mitigate the distress somewhat. Thanks to the Labour Force Survey and other survey data concerning labour market transitions, we are able to say more today than previously, especially in relation to unemployment. We consider evidence relating to unemployment below.

The distribution of earnings and income

We have seen that the distribution of jobs across households has shifted markedly over the past fifteen years, with an enormous increase in the number of households, where nobody is employed. However, for most households income from employment remains the most important source of income, so that the distribution of earnings is also of fundamental importance in determining the trend in the distribution of income across households. In addition, the tax and benefit system plays an important role in determining how the distribution of private pre-tax income translates into disposable income.

The distribution of earnings in the United Kingdom has become markedly more unequal over the period under review. Two features are particularly important. First there has been an increase in the gap between manual workers and other groups (depicted in Figure 13.2). Second there has been an increase in inequality within nearly all occupational groupings, illustrated in Figure 13.3. Figure 13.2 shows that real manual earnings for the median employee increased only modestly over the period 1979 to 1994 – by approximately 1.1 per cent per annum for men and rather more (1.4 per cent)

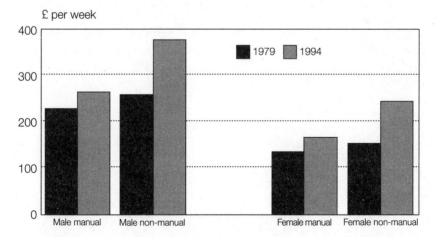

Figure 13.2 Growth of real median weekly earnings 1979–94, 1994 prices
Source: NES and own estimates.
Note: Full-time workers whose pay is not affected by absence.

for women. The comparable figures for non-manual categories are 2.5 per cent and 3.2 per cent. Note that the increase for non-manual women was sufficiently rapid in this instance for median earnings to overtake the median for manual men.

Figures 13.3(a–d) show how two summary measures of the occupational distribution of income – the decile ratio and the interquartile range divided by the median – shifted for both manual and non-manual groups between 1979 and 1990. Since most observations lie above the 45 degree line in all four panels, both measures indicate increasing within-occupation dispersion. There are some exceptions, but they are to be found in the public sector – primary, secondary and other teachers, firefighters, policemen. Other groups have found a very rapid increase in dispersion by either measure – journalists (a group for whom union influence declined markedly) and financial specialists having seen especially dramatic changes.

It seems as if there is no single compelling explanation for rising inequality in the distribution of earnings (e.g. Machin, 1996). Many would agree that both the pressure of technological change and competition in unskilled labour-intensive products from abroad have greatly reduced the demand for unskilled manual labour. Wood (1994) pointed out that the mere threat of international competition may also be helping to influence the nature of technological change. However, even a sharp decline in the demand for

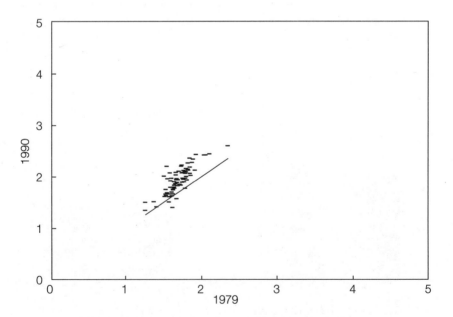

Figure 13.3(a) Decile ratios of incomes in manual occupations, based on weekly earnings (exc. overtime effects)

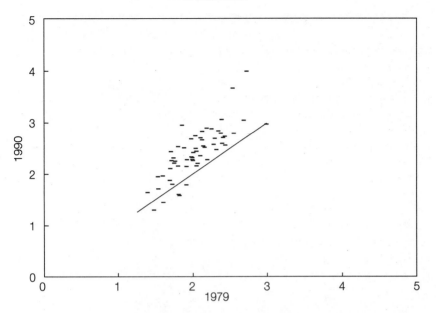

Figure 13.3(b) Decile ratios of incomes in non-manual occupations, based on weekly earnings (exc. overtime effects)

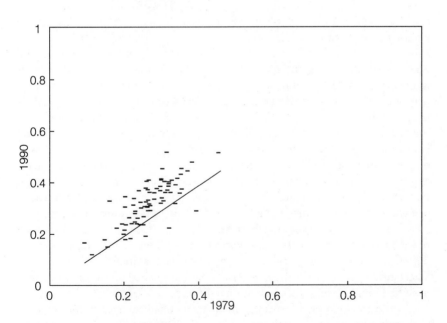

Figure 13.3(c) Interquartile range of incomes in manual occupations (expressed as proportion of median)

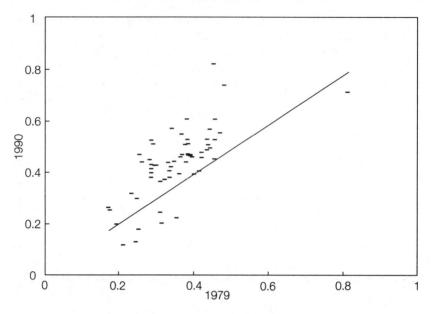

Figure 13.3(d) Interquartile range of incomes in non-manual occupations (expressed as proportion of median)

unskilled labour cannot explain the apparent increase in inequality within occupational groupings. Here institutional change spurred on by policy has almost certainly contributed. Both the influence of unions (e.g. Gregg and Machin, 1994, Gosling and Machin, 1995) and the prevalence of pay policies in the 1960s and 1970s almost certainly served to compress the structure of pay, while the abolition of wages councils was found by Machin and Manning (1994) to explain up to 20 per cent of the rise in income dispersion in the low-pay sectors of the economy – especially in catering, retailing, and hairdressing. Reform of methods of pay bargaining, and the fact that pay is now much more likely to be influenced by company performance, have almost certainly all contributed to the increase, albeit to an unknown extent. For what it is worth, Figure 13.3 does highlight the fact that the anomalous occupations – those which somehow bucked the trend of increasing inequality – were in the public sector, where union presence remains significant. One occupation at least – in this case journalism – where unions have been of diminishing importance, has shown one of the largest increases in inequality. These findings tend to confirm the role that diminished union presence may have had in increasing the occupational dispersion of earnings.

Beyond the increase in earnings inequality, policy changes in the form of changes in the tax and benefit system have also increased the inequality in the distribution of income across households. Indeed, a main aim of policy was precisely that – to reduce the redistributive impact of government. Atkinson (1996) shows that the rise in the Gini coefficient over the period 1979–94 for private pre-tax income was more or less reversed by the impact of the tax and benefit system, so that the post-tax Gini coefficient rose only modestly. Between 1984 and 1989 however, he shows that it is the Gini coefficient for post-tax income which climbs substantially, indicating that the redistributive impact of government decreased markedly over this period.

What, then, do the changes in the distribution of jobs, earnings, and changes in the tax and benefit system, add up to in terms of the distribution of disposable income across households? A pattern of rising inequality over the past fifteen years is now well documented. The Joseph Rowntree Foundation for example recently concluded that by 1990 the degree of income inequality had reached its highest level since the Second World War.

A study by Goodman and Webb (1994) uses methodology based upon the Department of Social Security (DSS) Households Below Average Income (HBAI) series, using data from the FES. The analysis uses a particular equivalisation of total disposable household income, which does not assess income on a per capita basis but according to an equivalence scale based upon the expenditure patterns of different household types. According to the scale, for example, a lone individual needs 61 per cent of the income of a two-adult household to maintain the same living standard, while a couple with one child aged three needs 18 per cent more income. Individuals are then grouped according to the equivalised income of the household to which he or she belongs. Figure 13.4 shows the UK Gini coefficient over the period

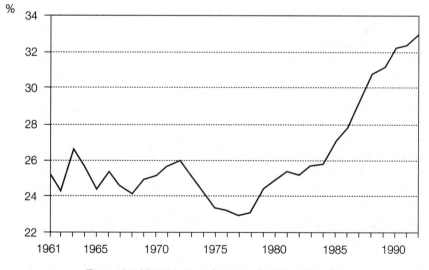

Figure 13.4 The Gini coefficient in the UK, 1961–92
Source: Goodman and Webb (1994) and own estimate.

1961–92. Relatively stable in the 1960s, it fell significantly in the mid-1970s before climbing substantially after 1977.

The Gini coefficient provides a useful overall measure of the degree of income inequality but is less informative about what is happening to any particular decile. For this it is useful to consider the evolution of the shape of the distribution. Goodman and Webb note that the frequency distribution today, compared to 1961, exhibits:

1 a much longer 'tail' at the top end, with very many more individuals living in households with incomes two or three times the mean;
2 a modal income which is now only half the national mean, compared to 80–90 per cent in 1961;
3 an increase in negative incomes after housing costs have been taken into account, reflecting both the increased importance of mortgage interest payments and the increased incidence of the self-employed recording losses.

In addition, Goodman and Webb report some evidence that the distribution is becoming 'bi-modal' (i.e. with twin peaks) which owes much to the increasing importance of economically inactive households and the relative decline in the one-earner household.

An international comparison of the distribution of household income has been conducted by Atkinson (1996) using a cruder equivalence scale (aggregate income divided by the square root of household size). A variety of measures tend to suggest that the US has the most unequal distribution of income, although this is driven mainly by the very low levels of income of the bottom decile (expressed as a proportion of median income), rather than the highest levels of income. In turn this seems to be a result of very low levels of pay – Freeman (1994) has shown that, using PPP rates of exchange, the lowest-paid in US employment actually earn much less than their European counterparts. On the other hand mainland Northern Europe – Scandinavia, Benelux and Germany – form a group with a discernibly more equal distribution of incomes than other European economies such as the United Kingdom, France and Italy. Where the United Kingdom does stand out is in the trend over time. Atkinson's analysis of indices of Gini coefficients over the period 1961–91 shows that only the United Kingdom has seen a major shift in the Gini coefficient – similar to the 30 percentage points shown in Figure 13.4. In France, Italy, and Finland it has been falling – with little evidence of rises even in the recent past. Germany, and surprisingly the US, show little change. The reason for the generation of debate on growing inequality in the US seems simply to be that the well-established trend toward greater equality observed in the 1960s reversed itself during the 1970s and 1980s.

Other international comparisons such as that of the OECD (1996) confirm that the United Kingdom is exceptional in the degree to which

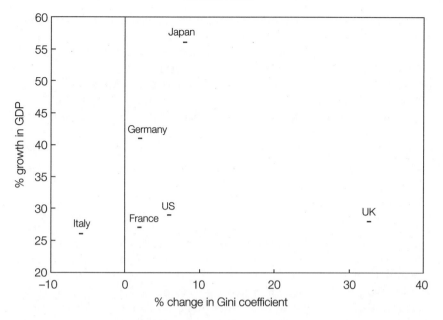

Figure 13.5 Growth in GDP and change in Gini coefficient, G6 economies 1980–91

inequality in the distribution of income has risen, if not in the comparative level of inequality. Taking the OECD as a whole, only New Zealand seems to have undergone a similar experience.

Rising inequality is of course consistent with the British Government's aim of reducing the impact of government and allowing market forces to shape incentives more powerfully. From this point of view the remarkable shift in the distribution of income may at least have some efficiency gains associated with it. Figure 13.5 does not, however, suggest that there is any obvious relationship between the increase in Gini coefficients for the distribution of income and the increases in GDP experienced, although it may of course be argued that a period of growing inequality was a necessary cost in the prevention of further relative declines in average living standards (see above, Chapter 4).

Dynamic considerations: the stability of income and employment

It is now widely recognised that estimates of income distributions based on 'snapshot' data may give a misleading impression of movements in inequality over time because the data do not refer to the same individuals or households. The observed rise in inequality in earnings or income may have less significance if the movement is largely explained by increase in instability of

315

earnings and income across households, i.e. if more households are experiencing short periods of low income.

In the United Kingdom there is very little evidence regarding the periods over which individuals experience low (or high) incomes. Using the New Earnings Survey (NES), Dickens (1995) found that among men, around three-quarters of the rise in inequality of hourly earnings was attributable to a 'permanent' increase. Also using NES data from 1976–91, Gregory and Elias (1994a,1994b) report that there are important differences between groups: thus only 8 per cent of young males had remained in the lowest quintile after eight years, while males in the prime age experiencing low pay had a much higher probability of remaining there. Women in both groups had a higher probability of remaining in the lowest quintile than the corresponding men. Another data set allowing individuals to be tracked is the British Household Panel Survey (BHPS). The nature of the survey means that comparisons are possible over only a two-year period. Work by Webb (1995) showed that for many, low-pay was a temporary phenomenon and that upward mobility was significantly greater for the low-paid than downward mobility for the high-paid, and although Sloane and Theodossiou (1996) report similar findings, they also show that women predominate among the low-paid, while experiencing a lower probability of leaving low-paid work. They also suggest that many of the low-paid are in multiple-earner households where household income is not low; moreover, and somewhat reassuringly, they find that training and education do significantly increase the probability of leaving low-paid work.

One study consistent with the view that low income is now more of a temporary phenomenon is the work by Goodman and Webb (1995) on patterns of expenditure (as opposed to income). Although the study is based upon a snapshot view, they find that the poor spend more than they earn and that the distribution of expenditure has shifted much less dramatically than the distribution of income. From elementary economic theory, the latter finding suggests that a greater proportion of individuals in households on low incomes may be experiencing purely temporary reductions in their income.

An aspect of the dynamics of income that has become more prominent recently is the issue of job security, quite possibly as a result of the much greater job losses among white collar groups which distinguished the most recent recession from that of the early 1980s, when the sharpest reductions were in manual jobs in manufacturing. Increasing uncertainty with regard to prospects in current jobs has of course inspired Hutton (1995) to speak of a '30–30–40 society', in which only 40 per cent of individuals enjoy any degree of predictability or security in relation to their future earnings.

A number of recent studies have sought to investigate the substance behind the hypothesis of increased job insecurity. Gregg and Wadsworth (1995) found that median job tenure fell by around 14 per cent between 1975 and 1993, but that the fall was rather larger for men than for women. However, some of this fall reflects increased churning of the same employees, an increase in self-employment, and more female workers who have lower job duration. Another feature of the findings is that full-time tenured jobs have not become less stable for those in them – job durations have not altered by much. Burgess and Rees (1996) find that, contrary to the popular conception, job tenure does not fall in a recession because quits fall as the rehiring probability falls. Moreover this research also establishes that, despite feelings to the contrary, the observed changes are most pronounced in the low-paid unskilled sectors. Gregg and Wadsworth (1995) and Burgess and Rees (1996) found that if we standardise for age, the job tenure of those at the lower end of the earnings distribution has fallen by most. Burgess and Rees also show that for men aged between thirty and fifty, average job tenure showed little change from 1975 to 1992 for the top 75 per cent of earners. By contrast, for the lowest 25 per cent of male earners, average job tenure fell from about nine years to about seven years over the same period.

Despite these empirical findings, it seems likely that there have been dramatic changes in confidence and attitudes to risk – not only because of the recent experience of recession itself but also because of the pervasive rhetoric of the new 'flexible' job market and the current management fashion for 'downsizing'. Workers in tenured jobs may fear that job-loss will permanently remove them from the primary labour market into the less stable secondary market, and with a consequential very large welfare loss. This is perfectly rational since it is clear that there are fewer tenured jobs today and that the flow of new jobs is increasingly geared towards temporary work, implying that the expected cost of losing a job has risen, even without a rise in the probability of losing a job.

The arguments surrounding the issue of job insecurity are therefore finely balanced. On the one hand, those arguing that there has been a fundamental increase in job insecurity base their case on small changes in job duration, the long-term trend in the nature of newly created jobs, the results of changes in the risk and cost of leaving the primary employment sector, and polls based on attitudes. On the other hand, the actual changes in labour market structure seem to be driven in part by increases in female employment, self-employment and part-time working. These changes may be desirable for many reasons, and to focus solely on the 'security' characteristics of jobs in such employment is unbalanced. There is some evidence (for older or low-skill workers) that job duration may have fallen but this is not widespread and not applicable to skilled prime-age males – but this may in turn reflect a reduction in the willingness of workers to quit jobs that they might, in a different climate, find unsatisfactory.

Clearly much that is new and important is being revealed by the consideration of income dynamics since the extent of the increasing volatility of income and employment has great significance for policy. Much more work

317

needs to be done, and in particular it needs to be established that the increased movement in and out of low incomes is sufficiently dispersed across the whole population to balance the clear evidence on the increase in income inequality.

MACROECONOMIC ISSUES: INFLATION AND UNEMPLOYMENT

The labour market reform programme of the 1980s had many objectives, but at the heart of the policy agenda was that labour market policy should support the anti-inflation monetary strategy. In this section we look at the ways in which the institutions of the labour market have been transformed, before discussing the evidence as to whether the labour market is now able to deliver better inflation unemployment outcomes.

Institutional change

The influence of the trade unions has declined considerably since the late 1970s. Membership of trade unions in the United Kingdom reached a post-war peak in 1979 at over 13 millions – a 'density' (the proportion of employees in employment belonging to a union) of over 50 per cent of employees in employment. By 1992 union membership had fallen to just over 9 millions, a density of 41 per cent. Membership is now concentrated in far fewer unions with much greater central control, but with considerably reduced financial strength. As an explanation of the decline in density, a simple composition argument (based especially on the shrivelling of manufacturing employment, where unions were always more important) may have accounted for about one half by the late 1980s (Booth, 1989). Beyond that, attention needs to be focused on the decreasing utility of membership. Evidence from the Workplace Industrial Relations Survey (WIRS) indicates that there has been a sharp reduction in the degree of recognition for unions at the work-place – from roughly two-thirds in 1984 to just over one half in 1990. Derecognition of unions over the same period outnumbered new recognitions two to one (Metcalf, 1990). In addition, legislative and other changes have more or less ended the phenomenon of the closed shop, while making the strike an unpromising approach in pursuing a trade dispute. More recent data on recognition has been made possible by the introduction of new questions into the LFS. This suggests that there are important differences in the extent of recognition: it is bigger in the public sector than the private sector, in large rather than small workplaces, and in private manufacturing than in private services. Overall levels of recognition in 1993 appeared to be similar at around one half of all workplaces to that reported in WIRS, although differences in the source of data make exact comparisons difficult (*Employment Gazette*, December 1994).

Management practices have also been changing rapidly, frequently initiating important changes in the nature of pay determination. Multi-employer negotiations (the so-called national industry agreement) have almost entirely ended. However, Walsh and Brown (1991) suggest that the decentralisation of pay to the individual company level does not mean that pay is now determined at the level of the individual workplace, but that it is increasingly being coordinated at divisional or company-wide level.

Debate over the appropriate institutional mechanisms for pay determination in terms of macroeconomic outcomes has been substantial. Calmfors and Driffill (1988) originally argued that there is a 'hump-shaped' relationship between the level at which pay is determined and economic performance. Economies with a heavily centralised system, such as Sweden and Austria, or substantially decentralised systems (where pay is determined at the company level), do better than economies with intermediate levels (at the industry level). The advantage of the centralised system is that parties to the wage bargain are more likely to take into account the impact of the bargain on inflation and unemployment. The advantage of the company-level bargain over the industry bargain hinges on a difference in the price elasticity of demand for the product of an individual firm as against that of the industry as a whole. The greater elasticity at the company level imposes a greater discipline on management not to grant pay increases. The argument has been strongly criticised by others. Soskice (1990), for example, argues that what matters is the degree of coordination in wage-setting, rather than where pay is actually set in practice.

The UK unemployment experience

Some idea of the continuing scale of the unemployment problem and the challenge that faces the United Kingdom can be gleaned from Figure 13.6(a), which shows 'standardised' rates of unemployment (unemployment as a percentage of the labour force). The standardisation across countries employs the definition of unemployment advocated by the International Labour Office (ILO). This defines an unemployed worker as an individual without a job who is actively seeking work. The upper panel highlights the commonly accepted fact that, in the course of the 1980s, a specific problem of European Union unemployment emerged. Whereas at the end of the 1970s, the US and the EU had very similar rates of unemployment, the US rate has continued to cycle around this level while the EU rate climbed during the 1980s to levels which were not reversed in the recovery. Moreover the recovery since recession of the early 1990s in Europe has not yet brought about a return to the rate of unemployment seen at the end of the 1980s. By contrast with both the EU and the US, Japan has witnessed very low rates of unemployment throughout, with perhaps a small tendency to rise. However even with the prolonged

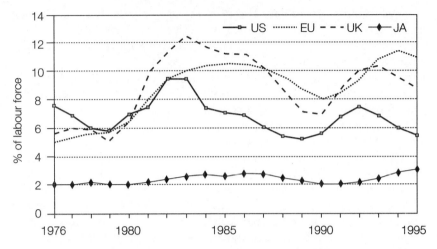

Figure 13.6(a) Standardised unemployment rates: US, EU, UK, JA (unemployed as percentage of labour force)
Source: OECD (ILO/OECD definitions).

stagnation in economic activity in Japan during the early 1990s, unemployment rates there have remained low.

In relation to this picture it is important to note that the UK experience matches that of the EU rather than that of the US or Japan. While the unemployment series has shown greater volatility than the EU as a whole, it has displayed a similar tendency for the rate to ratchet upwards with downturns in economic activity. The idea that has gained ground, that Britain's labour market, with allegedly greater flexibility, shares the same characteristics as the US market, does not as yet fit the facts. After four years of recovery, the unemployment rate in Britain in 1996 was still above levels recorded in 1990 and even further above levels in 1979, as well as being considerably above current US levels. Nevertheless, unemployment did start to decline reasonably rapidly in the 1990s' recovery compared to that of the 1980s, when unemployment had continued to rise for several years after the start of the recovery.

Figure 13.6(b) directly compares the United Kingdom with France and Germany. France displays the clearest 'ratchet' effect, with minimal reductions in unemployment associated with economic recovery. After a much worse experience in the 1980s, UK unemployment by 1995 matched that found in Germany, although the latter's experience reflects the considerable shock to the unemployment rate attendant upon the incorporation of the eastern Länder. There is some evidence, then, that the unemployment record in the United Kingdom has improved somewhat compared to other EU economies, but the idea that the labour market is now delivering a US pattern

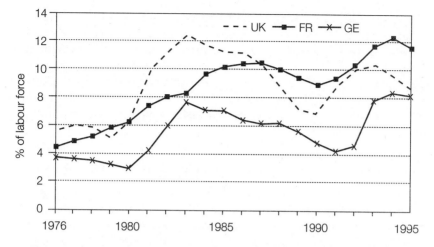

Figure 13.6(b) Standardised unemployment rates: UK, FR, GE (unemployed as percentage of labour force)
Source: OECD (ILO/OECD definitions).

of unemployment remains fanciful. However, Philpott below (Chapter 14) discusses much more fully the evidence for the more recent period of recovery.

It is important to be clear how the steady rise in European unemployment came about. The stock of unemployment evolves over time as a result of flows into and out of unemployment. Comparing 1988 with 1979, Bean (1994) shows that while the rate of entry into unemployment from employment changed little, the rate of outflow from unemployment virtually halved in the EU as a whole. In other words the rise in unemployment is associated with a marked fall in the probability of leaving unemployment for a job. Bean also noted the sharp rise in Europe in the proportion of the long-term unemployed (more than one year). Together, these facts suggest longer periods of unemployment, rather than more frequent spells of unemployment. Evidence for the United Kingdom is consistent with the European pattern, which is at odds with the view that a more competitive labour market will necessarily have beneficial effects on unemployment. Using LFS data, the *Employment Audit* (Employment Policy Institute, 1996) examines flow rates between employment, unemployment and economic inactivity between 1977 and 1994. Apart from a cyclical effect, the outflow rate from employment to unemployment has changed little, while that from employment to inactivity has risen a little. The major changes are a reduction in the outflow rate from unemployment into employment, and a very major increase in the flow from unemployment into inactivity. These tendencies were especially acute for men.

One final fact concerning unemployment in Britain and Europe needs to be addressed in any explanation, and that is the relationship between vacancies and unemployment. In general, a negative relationship between the rate of vacancies and unemployment is to be expected, as both are correlated with movements in economic activity. However, in the United Kingdom as well as elsewhere in Europe, the relationship appears to have shifted outward, with rather more unemployment associated with a given level of vacancies than before.

Explanations of rising unemployment using the NAIRU framework

In the post-war period the discussion of what determines the rate of unemployment has been inseparable from that of inflation, particularly since Phillips's (1958) proposition that there was a stable statistical relationship between increases in money wage rates and the level of unemployment implied that there was a policy trade-off between them, a view which was very influential in policy-making circles during the 1960s. However, accelerating inflation by the end of the decade (indicating the breakdown of the relationship) forced a retreat from this view, by almost all theoretical persuasions – whether monetarist or Keynesian. Since that time something of a consensus has emerged based upon the concept of a sustainable (or equilibrium) level of unemployment at which inflation is stable and has a tendency neither to accelerate nor decelerate. This is the so-called 'non-accelerating inflation rate of unemployment' or NAIRU (e.g. Layard, Nickell and Jackman, 1991), the theoretical construct discussed further by Philpott below.

In this framework, the fundamental aspect of the inflationary process is the interaction between labour costs and prices – the specific way in which rises in pay feed through into price rises, on the one hand, and the reaction of pay to rises in prices, on the other. In imperfectly competitive conditions, these can be considered in terms of a 'target' or aspirational real wage on the part of employees or their representatives. Bargaining, of course, takes place over the money wage required to meet this target real wage and hence is dependent upon the expected rate of price inflation. Since what matters to workers is what wages will buy in terms of consumer goods, they must bargain on the basis of an expected rate of consumer price inflation. It is generally accepted that the degree of labour market slack (measured by unemployment) will condition the target real wage.

Producers, operating in an imperfectly competitive product market, must set prices on the basis of a mark-up on the money wage that they anticipate. Their ability to do this, however, is constrained by the level of demand for output, which may be supposed to depend on unemployment. Note that the real wage that matters for producers and their employment decisions is the real product wage, the wage (including any taxes on employment or employer pension contributions) measured in terms of output prices, rather than consumer prices. The difference in movement between the real product wage and the real consumption wage is sometimes referred to as the 'wedge'. A divergent movement between consumer prices (as measured for example by the RPI in the United Kingdom) and producer prices (as measured by the deflator of GDP at factor cost) might be caused by real movements in the exchange rate or by changes in the rate of indirect taxes. If the target real wage of the workforce is defined net of income taxes, then changes in income tax rates can also change the wedge.

The NAIRU is the unique level of unemployment at which producers correctly anticipate changes in the level of wages and workers correctly anticipate changes in the level of prices, i.e. it is the level of unemployment consistent with stable inflation. Starting from a given level of NAIRU, there are some factors which influence only the short-run levels of unemployment and inflation and others which influence NAIRU itself. Among the former, adherents to the framework generally include levels of nominal demand. These have no permanent effects on unemployment but may, because of nominal wage or price rigidity, involve differential costs to the process of disinflation which began in earnest with the second oil shock of 1979. Although a number of studies have been able to establish that differences in nominal inertia do exist between countries (and in particular that it is higher in North America), they are not sufficient to explain the differential unemployment experiences of the later 1980s and 1990s.

Other factors may, depending upon the particular variant of the model, have either short- or long-run influences on unemployment. These factors may include productivity growth, which is known to have slowed in virtually all the OECD countries after 1973 (see Chapter 4). Target real wages may take time to adjust to lower productivity growth, if at all. In an earlier paper, the present authors indeed argued that the slower productivity growth was an important part in the emergence of inflation in the United Kingdom in the late 1980s (Chapman and Temple, 1994). The consensus is, however, that this factor contributed only a little to the rise in unemployment, and that wage bargainers do take into account changes in productivity growth. There is also debate as to whether the wedge between real take-home pay and the real product wage acts as a short- or long-run influence on unemployment. Theoretical considerations favour the short-run interpretation, as does the empirical work of Newell and Symons (1986). Moreover, a simple consideration of the determinants of changes in the wedge – the terms of trade or taxation – does not point to the importance of the wedge in explaining the observed differences in unemployment. Although the terms of trade moved against the European economies to a much larger extent than they did against the US in the 1970s, the weakness in oil and commodity prices since the middle of the last decade has more or less reversed the initial rise. Moreover, while the burden of taxation certainly rose faster in the EU than in the US, it does not appear to have risen faster than in Japan or in non-EU European economies, in both of which unemployment increases have not been as marked (Bean, 1994).

By contrast to these factors, the benefit system, trade union power and militancy, and structural mismatch, are generally regarded as long-run influences on unemployment and the NAIRU. We now take each of these factors in turn.

In general we would expect a more generous system of benefits to result in a higher level of the NAIRU. Moreover, a move to a more generous system is at least consistent with the observed outward movement in the UV relationship (see above). Although it is the case that the benefit system tends to be more generous in Europe and in the United Kingdom than in the US, the generosity of most systems has begun to decline generally through the tighter imposition of rules and other devices. In Britain a progressively stricter regime has been imposed, including more severe tests of availability for work. Most empirical work finds very small effects for the impact of the benefit system (see Bean, 1994). For the United Kingdom Layard, Nickell and Jackman (1991) find that of the rise of 6.2 percentage points in the NAIRU between 1960–8 and 1981–7, less than one percentage point is explained by the movement in the replacement ratio (the ratio of benefits to probable earnings).

Mismatch arises when those who are unemployed are not fitted to the vacancies being created; this may have technological origins with geographical, industrial, or occupational implications. An increase in mismatch will tend to raise the NAIRU by lowering the probability, other things remaining equal, that an unemployed worker will find a matching vacancy. As with unemployment benefits, an increase in mismatch would be consistent with the outward movement in the UV curve for the United Kingdom and Europe. A study by Jackman and Roper (1987) for several countries found no tendency for mismatch to increase in the late 1970s or early 1980s, so the evidence for mismatch being an important cause of rising unemployment is weak – a fact now generally recognised. More recently Robinson (1996) goes further than this, arguing that after the considerable shocks of the 1980s the structure of unemployment has changed over the period 1984–95, with unemployment now rather less-concentrated on less qualified manual workers, which in part reflects the rising levels of qualification among the workforce. He suggests that there has been no significant *further* deterioration of the unemployment rates of less-qualified workers.

Explanation of movements in the NAIRU based on union power focus on the ability of unions to achieve a given increase in the real consumption wage. One problem of employing such an explanation of changes in the NAIRU is that union power is clearly difficult to measure, although some studies have employed union density or a measure of industrial conflict. The important point here is that density, after rising in the 1970s, actually fell back in many European economies, as it did in the United Kingdom. This is difficult to reconcile with the observed unemployment pattern.

Clearly therefore the NAIRU framework offers plausible explanations of why unemployment started to rise after 1973 but not as to why it remained high. A number of empirical studies have shown that current levels of unemployment in the major EU economies have depended, to a much greater extent in the EU than in the US (or Sweden) upon previous levels of unemployment (e.g. Alogoskoufis and Manning, 1988, and Henry and Snower, 1997). In itself this casts great doubt upon the adequacy of the NAIRU framework, at least as outlined above. Consequently attention is now paid by labour market economists in theorising about mechanisms which explain persistence in rates of unemployment – so that the level of unemployment today depends not only upon the NAIRU but to a greater or lesser extent upon past unemployment. Mechanisms explaining persistence include the implications of bargaining by 'insiders' who are largely unaffected by workers outside the firm (Lindbeck and Snower, 1989), as well as the problems created by the real or imaginary skill depreciation of those who are out of work for a period and who consequently find it increasingly difficult to compete effectively for jobs.

A further explanation of the persistence in unemployment levels may be sought in the classical belief that the major constraint on output and employment arises from the capital stock. In this view, negative demand shocks to the economy may go uncorrected either by subsequent capital expansion or capital labour substitution. Figure 13.7 compares unemployment against capacity utilisation (the latter only for manufacturing) and confirms that a given level of capacity utilisation has been associated with rising unemployment in the EU but not in the US. Evidence from Chapter 4 also shows that, after 1973, the growth of aggregate investment fell substantially in the major European economies but not in the US. The significance of the idea of capital shortage has been developed, *inter alia*, by Rowthorn (1995) and Driver (1994), who argue that measures to stimulate investment may be necessary to reduce unemployment. In the view of Driver (1996), the Government plays an important part in the story by interpreting capacity constraints as a signal of incipient inflationary pressures that must be met with a tightening policy stance. In a similar vein, Allen and Nixon (1995) make a distinction between a short-run and a long-run NAIRU, where the former is defined by the fixity of the capital stock. They point to the negative impact on capital accumulation and the capital stock of raising interest rates whenever the short-run NAIRU is encountered and inflation starts to increase. Countervailing stimuli to investment may be appropriate. The chief question is therefore whether these capacity constraints represent more than just a 'speed limit' on the process of reducing unemployment, once its fundamental causes have been traced, or whether deliberate measures need to be taken to increase investment.

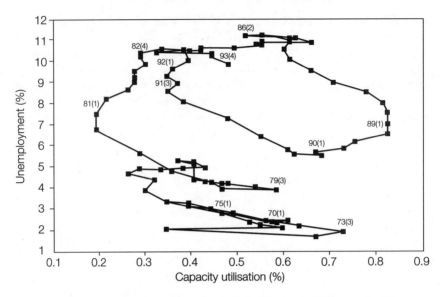

Figure 13.7(a) Unemployment and capacity utilisation in UK manufacturing

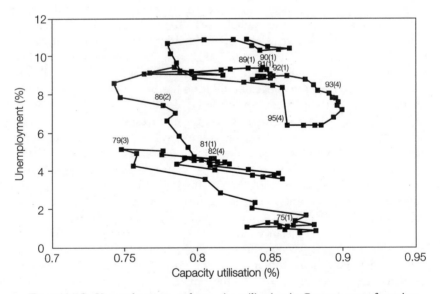

Figure 13.7(b) Unemployment and capacity utilisation in German manufacturing

Although the NAIRU approach has been widely adopted as the most appropriate framework for understanding the inflation–unemployment trade-off, it is clear it leaves many of the key questions unanswered. By the

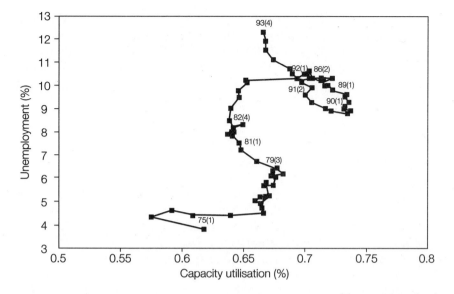

Figure 13.7(c) Unemployment and capacity utilisation in French manufacturing

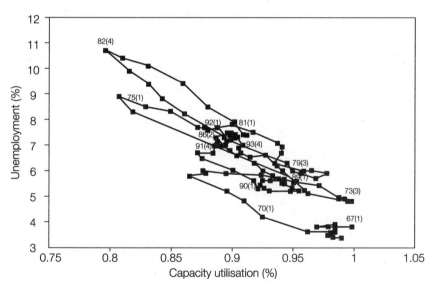

Figure 13.7(d) Unemployment and capacity utilisation in US manufacturing

mid-1990s the level of inflation was extremely low and it was unclear whether NAIRU had been substantially reduced or whether the economy was operating with considerable excess capacity of labour, a point developed

327

by Philpott below (Chapter 14). In addition, the conclusions of those adherents to the basic framework who stress the role of policies directed primarily at the labour market, may be ignoring the crucial need for measures elsewhere – particularly in the field of capital investment. Increased investment would of course serve a double need, increasing both capacity and the effective demand needed to attain high levels of utilisation.

Regional unemployment trends

Historically, great attention has been paid to the geographical location of unemployment. In Britain the regional pattern of unemployment has been an economic policy concern since the 1930s. Until the most recent economic recession, there has been, with only limited exceptions, a remarkable stability in the pattern of regional unemployment rates, stretching back to the 1920s. The pattern involved low unemployment rates in the South and Midlands, with unemployment significantly higher than the national average in the North and more especially in Northern Ireland. This degree of stability has been quite significant by international standards: an OECD study in 1988 showed that over the period 1975–87, although Japan and Italy had displayed similar degrees of stability, other economies had shown either only a small degree of stability (e.g. Germany) or, in the case of the US, none at all (OECD, 1988).

The stable pattern observed in the United Kingdom for much of the twentieth century has, however, begun to change over the course of the last fifteen years. The recession of the early 1980s saw rates of unemployment in the traditionally prosperous region of the West Midlands rise toward levels observed in the Northern region. At the same time, regional disparities in unemployment rates grew considerably, with disparities rising until the mid-1980s, prompting public debate about a 'North–South divide'. Disparities began to shrink in the boom years of the late 1980s, and have continued to shrink during the recession and subsequent recovery, although the most recent evidence suggests divergence may be returning.

The experience of the South East in the 1990s has been attributed to the greater downward shock to consumer spending occurring here (Evans and McCormick, 1994) because of the greater incidence of consumer indebtedness (mainly in relation to housing) and the consequent impact of sharp and unexpected increases in interest rates and the subsequently larger declines in house prices. By way of example, the Bank of England estimated that in 1994 almost 50 per cent of negative housing equity was held in the South East (Murfin and Wright, 1994). Looking at the overall regional pattern, it may be hypothesised that the peculiarities of the most recent economic cycle – and in particular the emergence of levels of indebtedness in the late 1980s, in the main negatively related to initial regional unemployment rates – have contributed to the reduction in regional disparities in the 1990s. The wealth effects of house price changes are, however, theoretically more uncertain, since a rise in house prices implies a rise in the cost of housing services, so that a positive wealth effect operates only for those planning to exchange some housing services for other goods and services (e.g. those 'trading down'); first-time buyers or those planning to move upmarket may have to curtail consumption of non-housing goods and services. Muellbauer and Murphy (1990), however, have observed that this argument ignores the role of housing as a source of collateral in a world where credit is rationed and borrowing on secured collateral is the cheapest, and maybe the only, means to increase borrowing.

In explaining the persistence (or not) of unemployment rates across regions, account must be taken of the various possible modes of adjustment. If wages and prices are flexible downward in the face of a rise in unemployment, then a region experiencing a negative shock to demand would find its goods and services becoming more competitive externally, and the rise in unemployment will be only temporary. Alternatively, the migration of workers to regions where there were greater job opportunities will also tend to reduce disparities through time. Without the operation of either of these mechanisms, and in the absence of other mechanisms – such as countervailing policy measures or other reasons for inward investment – unemployment will tend to persist. There is some empirical evidence of a distinction between the market for manual labour and that for non-manual labour (Hughes and McCormick, 1987, 1994). For manual workers Hughes and McCormick found evidence of wage convergence across the regions in the period 1970–93 and that (based on LFS data) only the West Midlands, albeit at a slow rate, experienced net outward migration of manual heads of household in the five regions with highest unemployment in the 1980s. Adjustment in the manual labour market thus took the form of increased unemployment among manuals and importantly, reduced labour force participation. For non-manuals, by contrast, they found both an increase in the dispersion of earnings in favour of the regions of relative employment growth and significant amounts of net inward migration. In consequence, there is very little difference in non-manual unemployment rates across the regions. It is sometimes suggested that the nature of housing tenancy has contributed to this asymmetry between the two groups, with social house tenure providing a constraint on labour mobility especially for the unskilled. While there has been some limited evidence supporting this contention it is unclear to what extent reform would increase mobility and whether reform within the existing constraint of security of tenure might be as effective.

Beyond the question of the persistence of regional unemployment differences, there is a deeper one relating to the cause of the disparities in the first place, and to explanations of divergence in regional rates of economic growth and job generation. The emphasis has been put on the mix of industries, with some regions suffering as the industrial structure of domestic and international demand shifts. Clearly this factor has been important in explaining, *inter alia*, the rise in unemployment in the West Midlands in the early 1980s. Empirical analysis based on a shift-share approach suggests that the South East tends to have a consistently favourable industrial mix (e.g. Gudgin, 1995) with most other regions having an unfavourable mix, but with the majority of the disparities in growth unexplained by the mix of industries. What appears to matter more in explaining disparities is the growth in external demand for a region's goods and services (Kaldor, 1981). As Gudgin (1995) shows, there is a strong relationship between a region's export base (primarily manufacturing) and the growth of overall employment. Differential growth patterns in this sector appears to relate to the so-called urban–rural shift – those regions heavily dependent upon large conurbations losing out to regions which are more rural. It is important that this effect is different to one based solely on costs, since there is no convincing evidence that conurbations have consistently higher costs than their hinterlands, although Tyler, Moore and Rhodes (1988) did show that distance from London was an important element in costs. More important than cost levels may be the potential for new investment in rural areas as opposed to conurbations (Fothergill and Gudgin, 1982). Even allowing for their industrial mix and the urban–rural shift, it is clear that northern and peripheral regions underperform. Basing himself on Porter (1990), Gudgin (1995) argues for the crucial importance of non-price competitiveness in explaining observed regional patterns in growth rates, and he shows that the South East outscores all other regions in terms of, *inter alia*, its ability to produce innovations and its supply of entrepreneurship. Proximity to London might also be added to the list, since London offers the greatest concentration of, and access to the range of business services – professional, technical, and financial, required for innovative investment.

While policy seeking to reduce variations in unemployment rates has been a continuous feature of the post-war period, both the underlying rationale and the associated instruments of policy have changed enormously, together with significant declines in the amount of regional assistance. Early policy focused on the belief that policy should aim at taking the work to the worker. This reflected the view that once the problem of the social and economic infrastructure had been solved, the bulk of manufacturing employment was actually 'footloose' and that given full employment nationally, little would be lost by preventing growth in certain regions. Reducing regional unemployment variations in this way would, it was argued, improve macroeconomic trade-offs – namely the Phillips' Curve and the balance of payments constraint. This approach became unsustainable with mounting unemployment, and negative restraints on development were abandoned.

In conclusion, in seeking explanations for the reduction in regional disparities in unemployment seen since the mid-1980s, labour market reform would not be very high on the list. The roles played by the peculiarities of the recession and by inward foreign investment may have been just as powerful.

MICROECONOMIC PERFORMANCE

We have spent some time discussing the possible impact of labour market reform on macroeconomic outcomes, in relation to pay and unemployment. But reform also has implications at other levels — the plant or company or industry — which are essentially microeconomic in character but which nevertheless may have a considerable bearing upon overall economic performance. These include, but are not restricted to, the possible losses of output through strikes, productivity gains, increased investment in both physical and human capital, and the incentive problems created by poverty and unemployment traps.

Strikes and industrial relations

An improvement in industrial relations partly resulting from the much diminished power of trade unions has been one of the great claims for recent policies. Quite how such an improvement can be measured is a tricky question, since negotiation in a climate of fear of dismissal and unemployment is clearly different to a situation where alternative employment is more plentiful. Attention is frequently drawn to the reduced number of working days lost through strikes. Certainly there were important differences between countries in the OECD in the 1970s and Britain, with Italy, was one of the more strike-prone, as Table 13.1 shows. Progress has been made since the 1970s, with the number of days lost normalised by the number of employees in the 1990s only one-eighth of their level in the 1970s. But other countries have also been making gains, as the record for Italy attests. In Germany, as in Japan and the Netherlands, strike incidence has always been very low.

Given the rise in unemployment and the declines in union density, the falls recorded in the United Kingdom and Italy and elsewhere in the OECD are perhaps unsurprising, although there may be a case for supposing that a number of legal changes, such as the introduction of compulsory balloting as well as the increased incidence of single-union bargaining, may have helped. In any event, at an aggregate level, and notwithstanding the considerable local impact that a strike may have, the numbers of days lost has always been insubstantial. Even at the 1970s level, days lost amounted to only a minute proportion (around 0.2 per cent) of total days worked.

Table 13.1 Days lost per 1,000 employees

	1970–9	1980–4	1985–9	1989–93
UK	570	480	180	70
US	na	160	90	200
France	210	90	60	90
Germany	40	50	—	30
Italy	1,310	950	300	360

Source: Employment Gazette, Dec. 1990, 1994.
Note: = less than five days per 1,000 employees.

A number of studies have looked at the effect of unionisation, union recognition and other institutional factors such as multiple unionism on various indicators of financial performance or productivity.

Whether individual firm or industry performance is adversely affected by unionisation is quite difficult to establish empirically. That there is a union wage differential is clear from the literature, but whether this is dependent upon product market power, and hence merely represents a redistribution of rents between profits and wages, is less clear. A review of the various studies conducted by Metcalf (1994) suggests tentatively that what is being observed is 'largely a matter of equity between labour and capital that has few implications concerning long-run economic senescence'. A slightly different link between unionisation and economic performance runs via its impact on investment. As Metcalf points out, the argument can certainly be made to run in different directions. On the one hand union pressure on wages may make firms anxious to invest more to substitute capital for labour. On the other hand investment may be reduced because of the fear that workers may be able to capture some of the anticipated gains – forcing a wedge between social and private rates of return that would not exist if the labour market were competitive. This particular possibility, initially developed theoretically by Grout (1984), has been explored further by Bean and Crafts (1996), who point out that the craft-dominated, multiple union system may have been especially detrimental to investment; in an industry-level empirical study, they indeed find that the presence of multiple unions may have depressed total factor productivity growth in the United Kingdom over the period 1954–86. However, Metcalf (1994) in the study already alluded to concludes that much of the evidence on the impact of unions on investment at least in the 1980s and 1990s points the other way with, if anything, a tendency for unionised workplaces to invest rather more in capital equipment and human capital.

Unions and bargaining systems may also have an impact upon productivity if the level of effort is itself variable – as in many of the discussions of 'overmanning' prevalent in the 1970s. A number of studies suggest that changes in working practices – whether made possible by the decline in union power or enforced by increasing product market competition – did lead to improvements in productivity. Studies using company accounts (e.g. Nickell, Whadhwani and Wall, 1992, and Gregg, Machin and Metcalf, 1991) have found that the improvement in productivity growth in the 1980s is associated with the degree of unionisation, but this has not been found by studies using industry data (Layard and Nickell, 1989; Bean and Symons, 1989, and Haskel, 1991). What the industry studies have found is that the improvement in the 1980s was associated either with the 1980–1 recession or with increased product market competition.

It is important to notice that if the improvement in productivity largely stemmed from a removal of restrictive practices, this implies a 'one-off' effect, rather than a sustainable improvement in trend productivity growth which will be maintained in the 1990s. Precisely the same problem of course relates to any increased investment that may have stemmed from changes in the balance of power in the workplace. However, even if one does not subscribe to modern endogenous growth theory where an increase in investment permanently alters the growth rate, the benefits to growth from a higher rate of investment are much more likely to be long-lived than a simple shake-out of inefficient practices.

Human capital formation

It has become a conventional wisdom to argue the case for higher investment in human capital. Many of the failures in UK provision, such as high rates of exit from education, low levels of vocational training and low educational attainment of a large percentage of the population, have been noted for some time. The real debate has for many years been about the extent to which greater investment in human capital can be met by purely market means. Many of the issues are dealt with elsewhere in this book (especially Chapters 12 and 15). However, it is useful to consider here some of the more important areas of change, and that in part at least, may have been as a result of policy.

The clearest change has been in the proportion of young people entering further or higher education. In 1986/7 47 per cent of sixteen and seventeen year-olds continued in full-time education; this proportion had risen to 71 per cent by 1994–5 (Robinson 1996a). The larger part of the rise was in forms of vocational education; here the introduction of National Vocational Qualifications (NVQs) and General National Vocational Qualifications (GNVQs) came at a time when the trend in the proportion of those undertaking vocational education had already begun to rise. The proportion of young people entering higher education at the age of eighteen has also increased, with gradually accumulating effects on the labour force itself. Between 1984 and 1995, according to the LFS, the proportion of the

333

working age population with a qualification in higher education rose from 12.2 per cent to 19.7 per cent (Robinson, 1996). For those in work, LFS evidence suggests the proportion of those receiving some form of training has been rising over the past decade, although it is very hard to establish the quality of the training received, or the way in which the pattern links to government policy in this area, which is based around the establishment of the TECs in 1990. National targets for education and training were set in 1991 for the year 2000 in relation to Foundation and Lifetime Learning (in terms of the percentage of the workforce with NVQs or their equivalent), and higher education. Only for the last of these are the targets likely to be reached.

One of the ways in which an improvement in training and education provision can be felt is in the reports of firms regarding skills shortages. For manufacturing this has been reported in the CBI Industrial Trends Survey for three decades. So far, the 1990s recovery in manufacturing has not been especially rapid, but as yet no skill shortages of the sort experienced in the late 1980s are in evidence.

Unemployment and poverty traps

In the United Kingdom, the problems of the 'unemployment trap' and 'poverty trap' and their implications for labour supply incentives have long been areas of policy interest. At the centre of the problem is a clear trade-off between targeting the benefits for those least well off, and hence containing the direct cost, and creating possibly undesirable disincentive problems.

The unemployment trap refers to the possibility that an individual or household might be better off not accepting a job offer. This may be a particularly important consideration for the United Kingdom, where low-paid jobs are more prevalent than in other EU economies. The problem created by policy and other factors over more than a decade is that the key variable in determining the incentive to work – the replacement ratio (see above) – is dependent not only on the generosity of benefits for the unemployed, which has clearly declined, but also on the earnings consequent upon taking a job (a so-called 'entry' job), which have also declined in relation to average earnings. Thus, while incentives and the problem of the unemployment trap may well have declined for some groups, especially single-person households, a significant problem remains especially for women whose partner may be unemployed, or for single parents. Family Credit was introduced in 1988 to replace the Family Income Supplement as the major means of providing in-work benefit and removing the unemployment trap. However the 'tax rate' on this benefit is quite high – benefits being withdrawn at a rate of 70 per cent as earnings rise; this can interact with the tax system and other in-work benefits to create an effective marginal rate of tax of 90 per cent or more. As Whitehouse (1996) notes, action on the unemployment trap may in this instance be creating an additional 'poverty trap' (extremely high marginal rates of taxation on the income from extra hours of work).

CONCLUSIONS: SOME POLICY CONSIDERATIONS

The labour market of today is clearly a very different beast to what it was twenty years ago. The new found 'flexibility' of the labour market is nowadays sometimes touted as a major source of national advantage. Certainly, the institutional changes have been considerable but in very few instances can clear-cut answers be given to questions about the efficiency of labour market performance. At the macro level, two of the major objectives for labour market reform, namely the poor performance of the UK economy with respect to inflation, and the recovery of levels of profitability – appear to have been achieved.

The rate of price inflation is now at a level not seen since the 1960s, and the major test for the labour market – the reaction to the significant sterling devaluation of 1992 – appears to have been passed. On the other hand, the background of falling inflation internationally, with continuing weakness in commodity prices, makes this outcome slightly less impressive. By late 1996, the United Kingdom still had a rate of consumer price inflation which was above that of the EU average (Office for National Statistics, 1996). Moreover it has been achieved with significantly higher long-term real rates of interest which today are probably higher than at any period since the 1930s. The profit share in the United Kingdom has also recovered to levels last witnessed in the 1960s, but this has been achieved by increasing capital utilisation at given rates of unemployment, increasing the importance of capital shortage as a feature for the policy agenda.

At the micro level, few would doubt that the changing framework and partial dismemberment of the systems of collective bargaining inherited from the past have resulted in much greater management prerogative and a much more quiescent workforce. But hard evidence that this is bringing tangible benefits beyond lower rates of strike activity is harder to sustain. The development of reforms to enhance the human capital of all the workforce have been given a much lower priority.

However, whatever the benefits that have come the way of the United Kingdom from labour market reform, there is a legacy that is effectively changing the political context. The interrelated problems of inequality and unemployment have now established themselves very high up the political agenda, and have set new challenges for labour market policy. Whatever the rhetoric, there is no doubt that the unemployment problem is greater today than it was in 1979 – and the dramatic rise in the number of no-worker households has put increasing strain on the fiscal resources of the state. The rapid increase in the incidence of low pay may eventually be providing businesses with inappropriate signals, encouraging competition in the global market-place on the basis of low cost, rather than on the exploitation of the skills and knowledge of the workforce and the technological infrastructure. Over the next decade both the natural growth of the labour force and the growth in labour force participation imply that many more jobs will be needed to reduce unemployment. Moreover, others will be drawn into the labour force if more jobs become available.

There is probably a consensus that part of the solution must be to increase the supply of skilled labour, although there is more debate about how to achieve this in terms of public finance. Providing more full-time education, an area where Britain continues to lag, particularly among the young, would help to achieve this, while reducing the number of jobs that need to be created. It would moreover help to reduce earnings inequalities, and provide a different set of incentives for business. There consensus probably ends.

It seems that a decisive turning point for the focus of labour market policy has been reached. The rewards of further deregulation seem more limited and may indeed be counterproductive. Minimum wage legislation may offer some assistance to some of the poorer households, but not to the long-term unemployed. While the compliance with the Maastricht convergence criteria is keeping fiscal problems and inflation to the fore, the problems raised by an economy which is much more unequal than in the recent past are beginning to gain ground. The problems of unemployment and workerless households, which are exacerbating the fiscal problem, have not disappeared. What will be required is for policy to place much greater emphasis on the conditions for greater investment, for a combination of higher levels of both capacity and demand are emerging as clearer priorities than further labour market reform.

NOTES

1 Funding from the Gatsby Foundation is gratefully acknowledged.
2 Figures from *Annual Abstract of Statistics* (1996 and 1990).

REFERENCES

Akerlof, G.A. (1982) 'Labour contracts as a partial exchange of gifts', *Quarterly Journal of Economics*, vol. 97 no. 4, pp. 543–69.
Allen, C. and Nixon, J. (1995) 'Two concepts of the NAIRU', *Centre for Economic Forecasting*, DP 28–95, London: London Business School.
Alogoskoufis, G. and Manning, A. (1988) 'On the persistence of unemployment', *Economic Policy*, vol. 7, pp. 427–69.
Atkinson, A.B. (1996) 'Income distribution in Europe and the United States' *Oxford Review of Economic Policy*, vol. 12 no. 1, pp. 15–28.

Bean, C. (1994) 'European unemployment: A survey', *Journal of Economic Literature*, vol. XXXII, pp. 573–619.

Bean, C. and Crafts, N. (1996) 'British economic growth since 1945', in N. Crafts, and G. Toniolo (eds) *Economic Growth in Europe Since 1945*, Cambridge: Cambridge University Press.

Bean, C. and Symons, J. (1989) "Ten years of Mrs T", *NBER Macroeconomics Annual*, pp. 13–72.

Blanchflower, D.G. and Freeman, R.B. (1994), 'Did the Thatcher reforms change British labour market performance?', in R. Barrell, (ed.) *The United Kingdom Labour Market*, Cambridge: Cambridge University Press.

Booth, A. (1989) 'What do unions do now?', University of Brunel (mimeo).

Bowen, A. and Mayhew, K. (1991) 'Regional issues in economics: setting the scene', in A. Bowen and K. Mayhew (eds) *Reducing Regional Inequalities* London: Kogan Page.

Bruno, M. and Sachs, J.D. (1985) *Economics of Worldwide Stagflation*, Oxford: Basil Blackwell.

Burgess, S. and Rees, H. (1996) 'Job tenure in Britain, 1975–92' *Economic Journal*, vol. 106, pp. 334–44.

Calmfors, L. and Driffill, J. (1988) 'Centralisation of wage bargaining and macro-economic performance', *Economic Policy*, vol. 6, pp. 13–61.

Card, D. (1992a) 'Do minimum wages reduce employment? A case study of California 1987–89' *Industrial and Labour Relations Review*, vol. 46, pp. 38–54.

—— (1992b) 'Using regional variation in wages to measure the effects of the federal minimum wage', *Industrial and Labour Relations Review*, vol. 46, pp. 22–37.

Card, D. and Krueger A.B. (1993) 'Minimum wages and unemployment: A case study of the fast food industry in New Jersey and Pennsylvania', Working paper, Princeton University.

Chapman, P. and Temple P.A. (1994) 'The question of pay', in T. Buxton, P. Chapman and P.A. Temple (eds) *Britain's Economic Performance*, London: Routledge.

Dickens, R. (1995) 'The evolution of individual male earnings, 1975–1990', mimeo.

Driver, C. (1994) 'The case of fixed investment' in T. Buxton, P. Chapman and P. Temple (eds) *Britain's Economic Performance*, London: Routledge.

—— (1996) 'Tightening the reins: the capacity stance of UK manufacturing firms 1976–1995', in J. Grieve Smith and J. Michie (eds) *Creating Industrial Capacity: Towards Full Employment*, Oxford: Oxford University Press.

Employment Policy Institute (1996) *Employment Audit*, no. 1, Summer.

Evans, P. and McCormick, B. (1994) 'The New Pattern of Regional Unemployment: Causes and policy significance', *Economic Journal*, vol. 104, pp. 633–47.

Fothergill, S. and Gudgin, G. (1982) *Unequal Growth, Urban and Regional Employment Change in the UK*, London: Heinemann.

Freeman, R.B. (1994) 'How labour fares in advanced economies', in R.B. Freeman (ed.) *Working Under different Rules*, New York: Russell Sage Foundation.

Goodman, A. and Webb, S. (1994) *For Richer, for Poorer*, Institute for Fiscal Studies Commentary no. 42.

—— (1995) *The Distribution of Household Expenditure 1979–92*, Institute for Fiscal Studies Commentary no. 49.

Gosling, A. and Machin, S. (1995) 'Trade unions and the dispersion of earnings in British establishments 1980–1990', *Oxford Bulletin of Economics and Statistics*, vol. 57, pp. 167–84.

Gregg, P. and Machin, S. (1994) 'Is the UK rise in inequality different?', in R. Barrell (ed.) *The UK Labour Market*, Cambridge: Cambridge University Press.

Gregg, P. and Wadsworth, J. (1995) 'A short history of labour turnover, job tenure and job security, 1975–1993', *Oxford Review of Economic Policy*, vol. 11, no. 1, pp. 73–89.

Gregg, P., Machin, S., and Metcalf, D. (1991) 'Signals and cycles: Productivity growth and changes in union status in British companies', University College London, Discussion Paper 91–15.

Gregory, M. and Elias, P. (1994a) 'The earnings transitions of the low paid in Britain 1976–1991 – a longitudinal study', *International Journal of Manpower*, vol. 15, pp. 170–88.

—— (1994b) 'Earnings transitions: Some panel evidence for Britain', papers of the sixth Annual EALE Conference, Warsaw, 22–5 September.

Grout, P. (1984) 'Investment and wages in the absence of binding contracts: A Nash Bargaining approach', *Econometrica*, vol. 52, pp. 449–60.

Gudgin, G. (1995) 'Regional problems and policy in the UK', *Oxford Review of Economic Policy*, vol. 11, no. 2, pp. 18–63.

Haskel, J. (1991) 'Imperfect competition, work practices, and productivity growth', *Oxford Bulletin of Economics and Statistics*, vol. 53, pp. 265–79.

Henry, S.G.B. and Snower, D. (eds) (1997) *Economic Policies and Unemployment Dynamics in Europe*, Washington, D.C.: IMF.

Hughes, G.A. and McCormick, B. (1987) 'Housing markets, unemployment, and labour market flexibility', *European Economic Review*, vol. 31, pp. 615–45.

—— (1994) 'Is migration in the 1990s narrowing the North–South Divide?', *Economica*, vol. 61, no. 244, pp. 509–28.

Hutton, W. (1995) *The State We're In*, London: Jonathan Cape.

Kaldor, N. (1981) 'The role of increasing returns, technical progress and cumulative causation in the theory of international trade and economic growth', *Economique Applique*, vol. 4. Reprinted in F. Targetti and A.P. Thirlwall, *The Essential Kaldor*, London: Duckworth, pp. 327–50.

Layard, R. and Nickell, S. (1989) 'The Thatcher miracle?' *American Economic Review Papers and Proceedings*, vol. 75, pp. 215–20.

Layard, R., Nickell, S. and Jackman, R. (1991) *Unemployment: Macroeconomic performance and the labour market*, Oxford: Oxford University Press.

Lindbeck, A. and Snower, D.J. (1989) *The Insider-Outsider Theory of Employment and Unemployment*, Cambridge, Mass.: MIT Press.

Machin, S. (1996) 'Wage inequality in the United Kingdom', *Oxford Review of Economic Policy*, vol. 12, no. 1, pp. 47–64.

Machin, S. and Manning, A. (1994) 'The effects of minimum wages on wage dispersion and employment: Evidence from the UK's Wages Councils' *Industrial and Labour Relations Review*, vol. 47, pp. 319–29.

Malinvaud, E. (1980) *Profitability and Unemployment*, Cambridge: Cambridge University Press

—— (1985) *The Theory of Unemployment Reconsidered*, Oxford: Basil Blackwell.

Metcalf, D. (1990) 'Industrial relations and the productivity "miracle" in British manufacturing industry in the 1980s', *Australian Bulletin of Labour*, vol. 16, pp. 265–76.

—— (1994) 'Transformation of British industrial relations?' in R. Barrell (ed.) *The UK Labour Market*, Cambridge: Cambridge University Press.

Muellbauer, J. and Murphy, A. (1990) 'Is the UK balance of payments sustainable?', *Economic Policy*, no. 11, pp. 348–95.

Murfin, A. and Wright, K. (1994) 'Regional differences and their importance for the UK economy', *Bank of England Quarterly Bulletin*, vol. 34, pp. 324–32.

Newell, A. and Symons, J.S.V. (1986) 'The Phillips curve is a real wage equation', *Centre for Labour Economics*, Discussion Paper, no. 246.

Nickell, S., Whadhwani, S. and Wall, M. (1992) 'Productivity growth in UK companies' *European Economic Review*, vol. 36, pp. 1055–85.

OECD (1988) *Employment Outlook*, Paris: OECD.

OECD (1992) *Employment Outlook*, Paris: OECD.

OECD (1994) *Jobs Study*, Paris: OECD.

OECD (1996) *Employment Outlook*, Paris: OECD.

Office for National Statistics (1996) *Retail Price Index*, 10 October.

Phillips, A.W. (1958) 'The relationship between unemployment and the rate of change of money wage rates in the United Kingdom, 1861–1957', *Economica*, vol. 25, pp. 283–99.

Porter, M. (1990) *The Competitive Advantage of Nations*, London: Basingstoke.

Robinson, P. (1996a) 'The myths and realities of structural change in the UK labour market', Centre for Economic Performance, mimeo

—— (1996b) 'Rhetoric and reality: The take up of new vocational qualifications', Centre for Economic Performance/Gatsby Foundation.

Rowthorn, R. (1995) 'Capital formation and unemployment', *Oxford Review of Economic Policy*, vol. 11, no. 1, pp. 26–39.

Shapiro, C. and Stiglitz, J. (1985) 'Equilibrium unemployment as a worker discipline device', *American Economic Review*, vol. 74, pp. 443–4.

Sloane, P.J. and Theodossiou, I. (1996) 'Earnings mobility, family income, and low pay', *Economic Journal*, vol. 106, pp. 657–66.

Solow, R. (1980) 'On theories of unemployment', *American Economic Review*, vol. 70, no. 1.

Soskice, D. (1990) 'Wage determination: The changing role of institutions in advanced industrialized economies', *Oxford Review of Economic Policy*, vol. 6, no. 4, pp. 36–61.

Tyler, P., Moore, B. and Rhodes, J. (1988) 'Geographical variations in costs and productivity', Department of Trade and Industry, London: HMSO.

Walsh, J. and Brown, W. (1991) 'Pay determination in Britain in the 1980s: The anatomy of decentralisation', *Oxford Review of Economic Policy*, vol. 7 no. 1.

Webb, S. (1995) *Poverty Dynamics: Issues and examples*, Aldershot: Avebury.

Whitehouse, E. (1996) 'Designing and implementing in-work benefits', *Economic Journal*, vol. 106, pp. 130–41.

Wood, A.J.B. (1994) *North-South Trade, Employment, and Inequality*, Oxford: Oxford University Press

14

THE PERFORMANCE OF THE UK LABOUR MARKET

Is 'Anglo-Saxon' economics the answer to structural unemployment?

John Philpott

Over the last seventeen years, the UK Government has taken significant action to promote a competitive labour market in the UK. . . . A free labour market is a flexible labour market. It is a market that maximises employment opportunities and labour productivity (and thereby living standards) by allowing market forces to achieve an efficient matching of supply and demand. Restricting the ability of individuals and their employers to respond to market forces creates rigidities which will lead to inefficiency and a reduction in welfare.

(Rt Hon. William Waldegrave MP, June 1996).[1]

The market-oriented approach to UK labour market reform has paid off in a steady drop in structural unemployment since the mid-1980s and in a relatively good job creation and unemployment record compared with many continental European countries.

(OECD, 1996a, p. 2)

INTRODUCTION

The above quotation from the Mr Waldegrave neatly summarises the philosophy underpinning the so-called 'Anglo-Saxon' approach to labour market policy pursued by successive Conservative governments in the 1980s and 1990s. Employment regulations (i.e. job protection laws, wages councils which set minimum rates of pay in a limited number of sectors, and legal immunities for trade unions) together with overly progressive tax systems and generous welfare protection, were highlighted as the fundamental causes of structural unemployment. A policy of deregulation was thus pursued to remove these so-called 'rigidities', in the belief that this would make the British labour market more flexible and adaptable and able to sustain a lower rate of joblessness.[2] Moreover, while the policy objective of reducing structural unemployment is in essence distinct from that of improving the competitiveness of the British economy, it is also often suggested that labour market reforms have contributed to increased productivity and played a role in attracting inward investment.[3]

At first sight, the endorsement of the OECD, also quoted above, indicates that Anglo-Saxon economics (or 'deregulated flexibility') has paid dividends. Unemployment began to fall much earlier than expected as the UK economy recovered from recession in the early 1990s and, for the first time in a generation of peaks and troughs in economic activity, the peak in unemployment following the 1990s recession was below the peak in the previous cycle experienced in the mid-1980s. Similarly, despite falling unemployment, wage pressure remained very subdued from 1993 to 1996, which has been taken as a sign of improvement in the underlying inflation/unemployment trade-off.

Yet many economists and commentators remain sceptical of the suggestion that the performance of Britain's labour market has greatly improved. And even those who are sanguine about prospects for job creation and aggregate unemployment – including the OECD – express concern that Britain remains a relatively low-wage, low-productivity economy exhibiting increased income inequality alongside a still high level of long-term joblessness.

The first edition of *Britain's Economic Performance* set out the theoretical rationale for the free market approach alongside an assessment of the performance of the labour market during periods of economic boom and bust in the 1980s and early 1990s. In the light of the experience of the 1990s' recovery, this chapter looks for evidence of increased flexibility in the British labour market and, from a policy perspective, considers the limits of the Anglo-Saxon approach when it comes to tackling structural unemployment.

'FLEXIBILITY': A FLEXIBLE CONCEPT

The (seasonally adjusted) count of people unemployed and claiming unemployment-related benefit peaked at just below three million (10.5 per cent of the workforce) in December 1992, having been on an upward trend during the previous 33 months (Figure 14.1). By June 1996 the total had fallen from this peak to just over 2 million, a rate of 7.7 per cent. The rate of fall was slow at first, then speeded up toward the end of 1994 before slowing again in 1995 and early 1996.

The peak in unemployment occurred much earlier in the economic cycle than had generally been expected. Changes in unemployment usually lag behind changes in output, and recovery in output following a period of recession usually precedes a fall in unemployment. The initial response of employers to increased demand for goods and services is normally to get

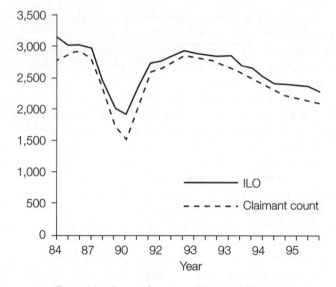

Figure 14.1 Unemployment 1984–95 (UK, 000s)

more output out of their existing workers. Only later, when employers are sure that demand is being sustained, will they hire new workers. Following the recession of 1979–81, for example, almost two years elapsed after the recovery in output before total employment began to rise, and the dole queue in fact continued to lengthen until 1986.

When the 1990s' recession bottomed out in mid-1992, therefore, most economic forecasters predicted that unemployment would continue to rise until at least well into 1994. So there was understandable surprise when unemployment began to fall in 1993 at a time when the recovery in output was barely noticeable. Indeed, government statisticians were so taken aback by the first monthly fall in unemployment that they ran rigorous double-checks on the figures before releasing them. At the time there were suggestions that, as an administrative count of jobless benefit claimants, the monthly unemployment figures were being influenced by changes in the rules governing benefit. But as Figure 14.1 indicates, the turning point in unemployment is evident also from the International Labour Office (ILO, or active job search) measure of unemployment obtained from the Government's quarterly household Labour Force Survey.

In attempting to explain the surprise fall in unemployment, some eco-nomists pointed to what they saw as an earlier than expected pick-up in the demand for labour after the recession, which was taken as evidence that the British labour market had become more 'flexible'. Before considering this possibility it is necessary to issue a health warning; the term 'labour market flexibility' needs to be handled with care. It is sometimes used as if a syno-

342

nym for deregulated labour markets, but flexibility in fact refers simply to the ease with which employment and/or wages can adjust or adapt to changing conditions of demand and supply in labour and product markets. Flexibility or adaptability can be hampered by labour market institutions and regulations; but by the same token flexibility can be hampered by lack of regulation if and where formal rules and procedures are necessary to prevent various forms of market failure.

One can distinguish between a number of broad types of flexibility: external flexibility, internal (or functional) flexibility, and wage flexibility (Beatson, 1995). *External* flexibility refers to the ease with which employers can adjust the number of employees they require in line with fluctuations in demand. *Internal* flexibility refers instead to the ability of employers to alter the hours worked by employees and/or the ease with which employees can be deployed to different tasks. Finally, *wage* flexibility refers to the responsiveness of wages to changes in supply and demand – in either relative terms or real terms. All these forms of flexibility can be considered either at the micro (workplace) or macro (economy-wide) levels. When discussing labour market flexibility it is therefore important to make clear which of these different types of flexibility is being referred to.

EXTERNAL FLEXIBILITY AND JOBS

Most explanations of the early fall in unemployment following the 1990s' recession rely on some notion of there having been an improvement in external flexibility during the 1980s. It is often argued that, unlike the pre-Thatcher/Major era, when Britain's labour market was more regulated and more strongly unionised, employers are nowadays better able to hire and fire staff in line with changes in demand.

Employment legislation, for example, has been diluted since the 1980s so as to extend from six months to two years the qualifying period of employment before an employee may challenge an employer on grounds of unfair dismissal, or become eligible for financial compensation in the event of redundancy. Similarly, the power of trade unions has been weakened by a step-by-step process of reform which, amongst other things, has somewhat reduced the ability of unions to stand in the way of proposed redundancies.[4]

Union density (i.e. the proportion of employees who are union members), which stood at around 50 per cent in the late 1970s, had fallen to around 35 per cent in the mid-1990s as measured by the Labour Force Survey, which excludes retired and unemployed union members. Legislation is not the only factor to have contributed to this decline – structural change and higher unemployment have also played a part – but it is clear that the influence of unions has waned. Britain's craft-based union system, it is often argued, had previously made it costly and difficult for managers to manage. In the 1980s, by contrast, following the fall in union influence, it may therefore have became easier for employers to change production methods and introduce new ways of working.

Taking weaker trade unions and employment protection together, employers may now find it easier to shed staff during downturns in demand, while also being more prepared to take workers on during the early stages of an upturn, in the knowledge that workers can be laid off easily and cheaply if the upturn proves short-lived. Allied to these changes affecting the demand for labour, cuts in the relative value of welfare benefits, tighter benefit rules, and the application of ever-tougher job search requirements on claimants since the mid-1980s should in principle mean that unemployed people cannot be choosy about jobs, and are more likely to take whatever vacancies are on offer.

To what extent can a shift in policy regime of this kind explain the early fall in unemployment following the 1990s recession? A number of studies have approached this question by first examining the responsiveness of employment to changes in economic conditions. Morgan (1996), for example, compares employment trends in the first three years following the trough in output in the 1980s with what occurred in the 1990s. In the 1980s, total employment fell two years into the recovery before rising in the third, whereas in the 1990s employment began to rise in the second year of recovery. The difference in experience amounts to around 1 per cent of total employment. By the same token, with growth in output broadly similar during the first three years of both recoveries, whole-economy labour productivity therefore recovered more slowly in the 1990s (although, as Table 14.1 shows, the tendency for employers to shed labour earlier than in previous downturns meant that productivity held up remarkably well during the 1990s recession).

Table 14.1 UK output and (labour) productivity, 1988–95
(1990 = 100, seasonally adjusted)

	Manufacturing		*Whole economy*	
	output	*output per person employed*	*output*	*output per person employed*
1988	95.9	93.6	97.3	100.7
1989	100.2	97.6	99.4	100.0
1990	100.0	100.0	100.0	100.0
1991	94.6	102.5	97.9	100.8
1992	94.0	108.3	97.4	102.9
1993	95.3	113.7	99.6	106.4
1994	99.3	119.1	103.6	110.0
1995	101.5	120.7	106.1	111.9

Source: Office for National Statistics, *Labour Market Trends.*

Two additional points are worth making about this finding, the first relating to the employment data used, the second to the issue of hours worked by people in employment.

As in the case of unemployment, there are two official measures of employment. One is provided by the same quarterly Labour Force Survey that produces the ILO measure of unemployment, the other comes from a data series known as the Workforce in Employment (WIE). The LFS – the basis for Morgan's study – is a large and detailed survey of households, and asks household members about the jobs they have and their job search behaviour. The WIE, by contrast, is based upon a survey of employers to which is added information on the numbers of self-employed people, people serving in the armed forces and those on work-related training programmes funded by the Government. One expects these two measures to tell broadly similar stories of events in the labour market. But as Table 14.2 shows, this has not been the case during the 1990s recovery.[5]

The WIE suggests a sharper fall in employment during the initial stages of the recovery than the LFS, and a more gradual improvement thereafter. The WIE data, which have been available for many years and which provide the basis for the 'traditional' view of the responsiveness of employment to changes in output, suggests that the experience of the 1990s was only little better than that of earlier cycles (this is also the conclusion of Blanchflower and Freeman (1994) who conclude that while there are signs that employment became more flexible in the 1980s, the improvement was 'hardly overwhelming'). Indeed, if one looks at the three-year period from mid-1992 to mid-1995, whereas total employment as measured by the LFS showed a net rise of 400,000, the WIE registered no net rise at all. The gap between the two measures had, by 1995, widened to 500,000.

Table 14.2 Total employment: Labour Force Survey and Workforce in Employment series compared (UK millions, seasonally adjusted 1992–5)

| | 1992 | | | | 1993 | | | | 1994 | | | | 1995 | |
	Spr Mar	Sum June	Aut Sepr	Win Dec	Spr Mar	Sum June	Aut Sepr	Win Dec	Spr Mar	Sum June	Aut Sepr	Win Dec	Spr Mar	Sum June
WIE	25.3	25.1	24.8	24.7	24.7	24.7	24.8	24.8	24.8	24.8	25.0	25.0	25.0	25.1
LFS	25.2	25.1	25.0	25.0	24.9	25.0	25.0	25.1	25.1	25.2	25.3	25.4	25.4	25.5

Source: Office for National Statistics, *Labour Market Trends*. See also Perry (1996).
Note: The LFS total comprises employees, the self-employed, people on government employment and training programmes and unpaid family workers. The WIE comprises employees in employment, the self-employed, people on work-related government training programmes and members of HM armed forces. The employees in employment series counts jobs while the LFS counts people. The two surveys cover slightly different periods each quarter; they are shown together here purely for convenience of presentation.

Irrespective of which measure of the number of people employed or jobs is used, it is also important to remember that the volume of employment – or the demand for labour – depends upon the number of hours being worked in the economy. Unfortunately, as Morgan (1996) notes, changes in the 1980s in the way in which hours data are collected in the LFS prevent a comparison of the responsiveness of total hours worked to changes in output in the British economy in the 1990s with earlier periods. However, Beatson (1995) makes some useful observations in this respect.

Beatson, like Morgan, concludes that employment in Britain has become somewhat more responsive to changes in output over recent years. But in addition he highlights the fact that UK employers are far more likely to adjust employment levels than hours worked when faced with a change in demand. For example, estimates drawn from some other major economies suggest that while the responsiveness of manufacturing employment to changes in output is broadly similar in the United Kingdom and Germany, total hours adjust only very slowly in the United Kingdom (Table 14.3). In other words, UK employers are far more reliant on external than internal flexibility as defined earlier (although one should note that according to these figures, UK manufacturing has still some way to go before matching the degree of flexibility apparent in the USA). Moreover, Beatson finds that hours worked in manufacturing have become less variable in the 1990s, indicating a further shift in the direction of external flexibility.

How one views this apparent increased reliance on 'hire and fire' may depend to some extent upon the degree to which one values employment stability – a factor that may have some bearing on employees' perceptions of job security. But interestingly, Beatson is unable to draw a firm conclusion on whether policy changes can account for this increase in external flexibility. Politicians and commentators may point to such things as weaker employment protection laws as a source of increased job flexibility, but Beatson is unable to find evidence to suggest that such rules hindered flexibility in the 1970s. What he does find is that external flexibility has been aided by the

Table 14.3 Speed of adjustment of employment and total hours (manufacturing 1973–90)

	Employment	Hours
Belgium	0.82	0.44
France	0.94	n/a
Germany	0.84	0.43
UK	0.84	0.71
USA	0.38	0.13

Source: Beatson (1966).

growth of both part-time working (there are now 6 million part-timers in Britain, mostly women) and self-employment (over 3 million people are now self-employed). There are also 1.5 million workers employed on temporary contracts. These forms of working offer employers the possibility of matching labour supply more closely to demand and – especially in the case of buying in the services of self-employed people – enables them to reduce the overhead costs associated with employing people full-time.

What remains unclear is how far this trend toward flexible forms of working results from free market employment policies as opposed to 'natural' structural change in the labour market. Thatcherite emphasis on free enterprise might help explain the sharp 1.2 million increase in self-employment since 1979 although, as Robinson (1994) notes, part-time employment has been growing steadily for fifty years and in fact grew more slowly in the 1980s than in the 1970s. It is nonetheless possible that policy has worked indirectly in this respect given that, prior to 1995, many part-time workers had fewer rights than full-timers under employment protection legislation with regard to unfair dismissal and redundancy payments.[6]

Although the legislative bias against part-time workers predated the Conservative Governments of the 1980s and 1990s, the fact that policy-makers stood out for so long against pressure to agree to equal rights for part-timers could be said have been working with the grain of structural change. In this respect, however, the TUC (1996) highlights that between the mid-1980s and mid-1990s the share of part-time employment in total employment increased faster in the Netherlands, Ireland, Belgium, France and Germany than in the United Kingdom, despite stronger employment protection for part-time workers in these countries. But regardless of this, a more fundamental structural development which may underpin the growth in part-time and flexible working is simply a shift away from employment in production industries to employment in services which have traditionally been somewhat more reliant on flexible forms of working. This, it is often contended, has changed the observed economy-wide relationship between changes in output and changes in employment because service employers can adjust their labour inputs in line with demand with far greater ease than is the case in production industries.

Whatever the precise source of increased external flexibility, it lies at the heart of one particular explanation of the early fall in unemployment in 1993, the so-called 'oversacking' theory. According to this explanation, employers – having shed labour early in the recession because of greater external flexibility – misread their employment requirements throughout most of 1992. Whereas output stabilised in the spring of that year, falling confidence in the summer and autumn meant that employers became too pessimistic about the prospects for demand for their products and laid off too many workers. This 'oversacking' became intense in the early autumn of 1992 amid the gloom that initially followed upon sterling's departure from the Exchange Rate Mechanism; it is argued that, as the gloom lifted at the turn of 1992/3, employers came to realise that they were operating with too few staff and began either rehiring or at least reducing the scale of previously announced redundancies.

THE RISE IN INACTIVITY

We have so far concentrated on the demand side of the labour market when trying to explain the earlier-than-expected fall in unemployment in the 1990s. But factors operating on the supply side also played an important role. Unlike the early 1980s, renewed growth in output following the 1990s' recession coincided with much slower growth in the labour force. One factor has been a drop in the numbers of 16–24 year-olds in the population. But in addition, fewer in this age group have been participating in the labour market (the percentage of economically active 16–19 year-olds fell from just over 70 per cent in the late 1980s to 60 per cent in the mid-1990s, that for 20–24 year-olds from 82 per cent to 77 per cent). To some extent this can be attributed to the recession and higher unemployment, but it would appear that there has also been a marked structural shift in the labour market behaviour of young people, many more now preferring to enter further or higher education (one in three young people now enter higher education in Britain, compared with one in seven in the mid-1980s).

What is surprising, more generally, is that despite rising employment and falling unemployment, and a policy environment that ostensibly increases work incentives for the jobless, the size of the total workforce remained fairly static during the first three years of recovery in the labour market. As Table 14.4 shows, the reason for this was a fall in the number of men of working age who were economically active, and a sharp rise (of 9 per cent) in the numbers who were economically inactive. Indeed the rise in the number of economically inactive men between winter 1992/3 and winter 1995/6 was equal to just over half the fall in male unemployment.

Table 14.4 Recovery in the British labour market (winter, 1992–5)

	Total employment			ILO unemployment			Economically inactive		
	male	*female*	*total*	*male*	*female*	*total*	*male*	*female*	*total*
92 winter (000)	13,407	10,654	24,061	1,993	946	2,939	2,522	4,760	7,282
95 winter (000)	13,794	10,991	24,785	1,520	755	2,274	2,753	4,722	7,475
change (000)	387	337	724	−473	−191	−665	231	−38	193
change (%)	2.89	3.16	3.01	−23.73	−20.19	−22.63	9.16	−0.80	2.63

Source: Office for National Statistics, Labour Force Survey.

In the absence of this 'shrinkage' of the male workforce, total unemployment would not have fallen as much as it has during the recovery and the worrying problem of very high male unemployment would look considerably worse. Almost one in ten men of working age were unemployed at the end of 1995. The male unemployment rate at that time was far higher than that for women (6.4 per cent) – the two rates having been roughly equal prior to the recession – while 50 per cent of unemployed males were long-term unemployed, having been without a paid job for over a year. But the rise in the number of economically inactive men suggests that the unemployment figures understate the full extent of joblessness.

The OECD (1996a) highlights in particular a sharp rise in non-employment (i.e. the sum of the unemployed and the economically inactive) among adult males aged 24–64 years with only basic education. Between 1971 and 1978 the non-employment rate for this group averaged 11 per cent; between 1987 and 1995 the average rate was over 30 per cent. According to the OECD, many of these non-employed have taken early retirement or extended sick leave, with many long-term welfare dependants receiving non-unemployment-related benefits. The existence of this group of 'hidden jobless' may signal failings in the free market approach to tackling unemployment (an issue to which we return below). Moreover, the possibility that the rise in inactivity more generally represents a structural change in labour market behaviour could have broader consequences for the economy by reducing overall output potential.

REAL WAGE FLEXIBILITY AND 'CORE' UNEMPLOYMENT

Whether or not one accepts that employment and unemployment in Britain have become more responsive to changes in output, increased external flexibility need not in itself mean a reduction in structural unemployment. Greater external flexibility could merely serve to make less stable whatever levels of employment (and unemployment) are being generated in the economy. Indeed, some economists argue that employment protection legislation has no impact on structural unemployment because while such legislation preserves jobs, it also deters employers from hiring because of the costs of shedding labour (see Layard, Nickell and Jackman, 1991, 1996). A truer test of improved labour market performance in the 1990s should thus be whether the economy is able to sustain a lower rate of unemployment without causing the labour market to overheat.

No market economy can operate without some unemployment. If there were no people unemployed, employers would be continually engaged in a desperate scramble for labour, while workers would exploit the situation to gain higher wages. Together, employers and workers would bid up pay and (by extension) prices in an ever-rising inflationary spiral. So some amount of unemployment is needed to contain inflation. This is the 'core' amount, known in various guises as 'structural' unemployment, 'equilibrium' unemployment, the 'natural rate' of unemployment or the non-accelerating inflation rate of unemployment (NAIRU).

Core unemployment reflects the underlying structural conditions of supply and demand in the labour market. At its root lies a struggle between employers and workers over how to share out – in terms of profits and wages respectively – real per capita output. When unemployment is low, workers find it easier to press for wage rises (which, if not matched by improved productivity, will raise wage costs). But assuming employers want to maintain their profitability they will pass on higher wage costs by raising prices. This in turn will reduce the real value of wages, causing workers to press for still higher wages. The outcome will be an inflationary wage/price spiral, unless unemployment rises to 'discipline' the wage bargaining process. Core unemployment is simply the amount of unemployment needed to accommodate objectives on both sides of the bargaining table so as to ensure that inflation remains stable. When unemployment is lower than this, inflation will rise, choking-off real demand which will in turn cause unemployment to rise back to the core rate, and vice versa.

One can elaborate on this simple account of core unemployment by incorporating the impact on wage bargaining of taxes, exchange rates, import prices, changes in labour market productivity and the degree of product market competition. Other determinants will include the nature of industrial relations systems (in particular union power and the structure of wage bargaining institutions), minimum wage laws, the operation of the benefit system and the degree of 'mismatch' between available job vacancies and the skills or location of unemployed people. A high degree of skills mismatch, for example, will mean not only that job vacancies remain unfilled but also that skilled workers will be in a stronger position to bid for higher pay.

Whatever the precise determinants of core unemployment, however, the key point to remember is that while the core can be reduced by appropriate structural/supply-side policies, it acts as a constraint upon the ability of policy-makers to cut the dole queue simply by lowering interest rates or cutting taxes and increasing public spending in order to boost demand.

It is important to remember that core unemployment is a theoretical concept – it cannot be observed directly, but has to be estimated.[7] But, as Table 14.5 shows, the range of estimates of core unemployment vary considerably. The variation reflects differences of estimating techniques and differences of opinion amongst economists about the precise determinants of core unemployment.

Estimates of core unemployment are a little lower today than a decade ago, although the general consensus amongst economists is that core unemployment remains somewhere between 1.75 and 2 million. The most

Table 14.5 Estimates of core unemployment (UK claimants)

	1969–73 %	1974–80 %	1981–7 %	1988–90 %	1995–6 %
NAIRU (range of estimates)	1.6–5.6	4.7–7.3	5.2–9.9	3.5–8.1	3.5–8.9
NAIRU (average estimates)	2.9	5.7	7.0	6.1	6.7
Actual unemployment	2.5	3.8	10.1	6.8	8.2
Number of estimates	11	13	15	5	9

Source: Coulton and Cromb (1994), updated for 1995–6 by Robinson (1996).

recent estimates range from just 3 per cent of the workforce – around one million unemployed – to as high as 9 per cent (the latter above the actual rate of unemployment in the mid-1990s). The low estimate assumes that the supply-side reforms of the 1980s have wrought a sea-change in the operation of the British labour market and, with actual unemployment in the mid-1990s of around 8 per cent, suggests considerable leeway for a more expansionary macroeconomic stance to government policy (Minford and Riley, 1994).

Minford (1996) points in particular to the role of trade union reform in this respect. We have earlier described the decline in union density and the reduced influence of unions over management discretion, but also significant has been a diminution in the pay-setting role of unions. The proportion of employees covered by collective bargaining arrangements has fallen from over three-quarters in the late 1970s to below a half (the lowest rate of coverage since the Second World War), with the most marked change having occurred in the private sector. Related to this has been a shift away from national, multi-employer and industry-based systems of pay determination toward more company-based bargaining.

Should one side with the core unemployment optimists or the pessimists? The jury is still out at the time of writing – with actual unemployment in mid-1996 still well above but gradually moving toward the average core unemployment estimate in Table 14.5 – but there are signs of a shift toward the optimists in recent years, with growth in both nominal and real wages remaining very subdued despite the fall in unemployment.

Prior to the recovery there were few signs of any fundamental improvement in the inflation/unemployment trade-off. As Robinson (1996a, 1996b)

351

notes, the so-called 'sacrifice ratio' (which measures the percentage point rise in unemployment required to bring about a given percentage point drop in wage inflation) was, at 0.5 per cent, identical in the 1980s and 1990s recessions. Moreover, there was little sign that real wages were becoming more responsive to unemployment. Although the average annual rate of growth of nominal earnings dropped sharply in the early 1990s – reaching an economy-wide low of just 3 per cent per annum in 1993 – inflation was already low. Real wages, by contrast, continued to grow during the recession, a fact conceded by Beatson who concludes that:

> While nominal earnings growth and inflation have varied considerably over the past 25 years, real earnings growth has been more stable – apart from 1976 and 1977, real earnings have increased every year usually between 1 and 4 per cent. Unemployment does not seem to have been much of a restraining influence on real earnings.
>
> (1995, 128)

Between mid-1993 and mid-1996, however, the rate of growth of nominal earnings remained between 3 and 4 per cent and, with retail price inflation of between 2.5 and 3.5 per cent for most of that period, real pay barely grew at all. Private-sector employers – operating in an environment where consumer expenditure was muted and product market competition more acute – seemed more concerned about keeping the lid on pay, while the Government maintained a freeze on public sector pay. Even by mid-1996, with the level of unemployment having fallen by well over three-quarters of a million below the post-recession peak, there were few signs of any marked pick-up in earnings growth. Indeed, such was the lack of wage pressure that even the Director-General of the CBI suggested that a resurgence of growth in earnings should be seen as a welcome development – rather than a risk to sustainable growth in output – so long as pay pressures did not accelerate out of hand.[8] Assuming a long-run rate of productivity growth of 2.5 per cent per annum, employees should on average be able to expect real wage gains of a similar magnitude. Given this, average nominal wage increases of up to 5 per cent per annum could sit comfortably alongside an official target for underlying inflation of 2.5 per cent – somewhat above the rates of pay increase being experienced in the mid-1990s.

Unfortunately, the apparent continued slack in the labour market, as evidenced by modest wage growth does not in itself necessarily make life easier for policy-makers since – despite an array of estimates – they can never be certain of the exact core constraint they face at any particular point in time. Moreover, even if it were thought that improvement in the underlying performance of the labour market was conducive to a more expansionary macroeconomic policy, policy-makers might still prefer to steer the economy on a stable growth path, rather than accelerate toward core unemployment and risk exceeding the so-called 'speed limits'. The latter term refers to the possibility of experiencing short-run capacity constraints (including skill shortages), even with unemployment above its core rate, if there is too rapid an expansion of demand.[9]

One can thus sympathise with the Governor of the Bank of England when he says that estimates of core unemployment are not to be taken as a reliable guide for macroeconomic policy. As Mr George put it in a speech on structural unemployment in 1994,

> As a practical matter, macroeconomic policy has to adopt a cautious approach, watching closely for early warning signs of incipient inflationary pressure which, in terms of the theory, would signal that we were approaching the 'natural' rate of unemployment – or approaching it too rapidly – and, as they begin to appear, to slow the expansion to its sustainable rate.[10]

What is interesting in this respect is that the Bank of England has been consistently more cautious about the rate of core unemployment than those economists and commentators who proclaim the merits of Anglo-Saxon economics. Only time will tell if the Bank has been too cautious in its appraisal of the degree of improvement in the British labour market – and how long it will take for unemployment to fall to its sustainable rate (assuming no unforeseen shocks to the system). But this issue notwithstanding, unless one accepts the view of the super-optimists, the core unemployment constraint is at best likely to be felt at somewhere in the 6–7 per cent range (1.5 to 1.75 million). So a key question remains: is Britain's deregulated new model labour market capable of providing opportunities for the chronic core jobless in the 1990s in the absence of new forms of policy intervention?

THE LIMITS OF RELATIVE WAGE FLEXIBILITY

Part of the underlying rationale for the policy of deregulated flexibility was that by placing more emphasis on profits than pay, the economy's potential for investment, higher productivity and job creation would be raised. In terms of raising the profit share, the policy can be said to have been stunningly successful. The share of wages and salaries in national income (which reached a peak of over 70 per cent in 1975) had by 1995 fallen to a forty-year low of 62 per cent. Despite this, however, rates of investment have been generally subdued while the pay-off in terms of extra jobs in Britain in the 1980s and 1990s has not been that spectacular, in European terms let alone in comparison with the United States (Table 14.6). Britain's record *vis-à-vis* the EU stands better comparison in terms of both the unemployment rate and the employment/population ratio (Tables 14.7 and 14.8), although it should be noted that British unemployment only fell below the EU average in 1993 while the employment/population was high by European standards prior to the Thatcher/Major era. (Moreover, as we discuss in more detail

Table 14.6 Employment growth (percentage change on previous year)

	1961–73 %	1974–85 %	1986–90 %	1991–3 %	1994–6 %
UK	0.3	−0.2	1.8	−2.1	0.6
EU	0.3	0.0	1.3	−1.0	0.3
US	1.9	1.8	2.1	0.2	1.6
Japan	1.3	0.7	1.5	1.2	0.4

Source: European Commission.

later, one should be careful to assess Britain's record with individual EU economies, not just in comparison with EU averages).

It is of course difficult to disentangle the impact of structural reform on job creation and investment from the impact of macroeconomic developments. It is arguable, for example, that an underlying improvement in the supply-side potential for job creation in Britain has been masked by macroeconomic instability and policy errors, such as resulted in the prolonged job-destroying recession of the early 1990s. But regardless of this, there are features of the changing *pattern* of job creation and pay in the past decade that highlight weaknesses in the deregulated approach to labour market policy.

In terms of pay, problems have arisen precisely because one outcome of government policy has been increased relative wage flexibility. Wage and income inequality has grown over the past two decades, which in turn results in part from the fact that lower-paid workers have seen their pay fall (in relative and in some cases absolute terms), while better-paid workers have experienced wage gains. According to the Joseph Rowntree Foundation's (JRF) *Inquiry into Income and Wealth*, hourly wages for the lowest-paid men in the United Kingdom hardly changed in real terms between 1978 and 1992 (and by the latter year were lower than in 1975). Men on average pay, by contrast, saw their hourly earnings rise by a third, while the highest-paid men enjoyed a 50 per cent increase.

Government policy has not been the underlying force behind growing inequality, which has been driven by a variety of factors. Most commentators have pointed to advances in trade and technology which have resulted in a shift in demand away from less skilled and toward more skilled workers as the major factors, although it would appear that even more important has been a widening of the pay gap within the different skill groupings, which has proved more difficult to explain (Robinson, 1996b). But whatever the forces behind the tendency for the labour market to generate more inequality, the point of relevance to the current discussion is that these forces have been underscored rather than resisted by policy in the United Kingdom. The JRF *Inquiry (op. cit.)* found that throughout the industrial world in the 1980s

354

Table 14.7 Comparisons of unemployment rates,
1991–5

	EU %	G7 %	UK %
1991	8.7	6.3	8.8
1992	9.4	6.9	9.9
1993	10.9	7.2	10.4
1994	11.3	7.0	9.5
1995	11.0	6.8	8.7

Source: Office for National Statistics, *Labour Market Trends.*
Note: OECD standardised unemployment rates
(annual averages).

Table 14.8 Civilian activity rates and employment/population ratios, 1972–92

	1972 Activity rate %	E/P %	1982 Activity rate %	E/P %	1992 Activity rate %	E/P %
UK	71.1	68.9	72.2	64.5	73.6	66.8
France	65.7	63.8	65.7	61.0	65.3	58.5
Germany	67.8	67.2	66.8	63.2	68.0	64.0
US	66.0	63.5	71.5	64.5	75.9	70.3
Japan	71.4	70.4	72.3	70.6	75.9	74.2
OECD	66.5	64.2	68.3	62.9	72.2	66.7

Source: Beatson (1995).

only New Zealand – which pursued a similar mix of free market policies – experienced a greater increase in income inequality than the United Kingdom. By 1990 British income inequality – reflecting much higher joblessness as well as more unequal earnings – was wider than at any time since the Second World War.

Relative wage flexibility has been enhanced by policies aimed directly at the labour market – such as the dilution and then abolition of minimum wage controls designed to encourage, in particular, the creation of low-productivity jobs – and also benefit reform which has sought to move more unemployed people off welfare into work in the hope that more such jobs are filled. But despite this, there remains a hard core of long-term jobless people on welfare – some, as we saw earlier, officially unemployed, others on other forms of benefit – who seem relatively immune to the policy. The explanation seems to be that downward pressure on pay rates in low productivity jobs has tended to reinforce work disincentives, while pressure on unemployed people to take jobs has tended to be thwarted by the broader characteristics of the jobs on offer.

For example, 'entry-level' jobs (i.e. of the kind open to people when they attempt to move from welfare to work) are increasingly very low-paid in Britain. Half of all such entry jobs in the mid-1990s paid less than half average (median) earnings and a third below a quarter of the average, reinforcing the welfare trap for many individuals (Gregg and Wadsworth, 1996a). Similarly, about half the net new jobs created in Britain in the 1990s have been part-time and three-quarters of new full-time jobs have offered only temporary contracts. Overall, the proportion of temporary jobs in total employment has risen by a quarter (from 5 to 7 per cent). Most of the part-time jobs have gone to women – either because such work is low-paid or is seen by employers and/or unemployed men as 'women's work' – while intricate rules for signing on and off benefit make it difficult for unemployed people to become reliant on temporary jobs. It takes time to process new claims for unemployment-related benefit, so unemployed people may be reluctant to take a low-paid job because they fear that if the job were to quickly disappear it would be difficult to sign back on for benefit (see McLaughlin, 1992, 1994).

Unskilled men in particular have tended to be squeezed out of the jobs equation – still effectively priced out of low-paid entry jobs and lacking the skills to obtain better-paid 'good jobs'. The perversity of the benefits system has also meant that many of these jobless men have been joined on welfare by their female partners. Means-tested benefits are assessed on the basis of family income – the partners of unemployed men may therefore find that they will reduce the overall family income if they take a job offering less than sufficient to 'float' the family off benefit completely. Since most jobs being taken by women at present are part-time and/or relatively poorly paid, this effectively shuts the women partners of unemployed men out of the labour market altogether.

A worrying side-effect of this is a polarisation in society between 'job-rich' families where both partners work and 'job-poor' families where neither partner works – the wife of an unemployed man is two to three times less likely to be in employment than the wife of a man in work. This polarisation has been demonstrated most by research undertaken by Gregg and Wadsworth (1996b). They stress that jobless families on welfare are not feckless – indeed, members of such families search harder for jobs than other people.

FROM WELFARE TO WORK

For this underlying core of unskilled unemployed, the essential policy choice lies between making them more employable, thus pricing them into better-paid jobs, or overcoming the limits to wage flexibility by pricing them into the types of jobs they can perform without new skills by means of subsidies or adjustments to taxes and benefits. It could of course be argued that state-funded welfare provision should be curbed or slashed, so that the core unemployed would be forced to seek jobs at whatever rates of pay are on offer. But as well as requiring a dramatic further dilution of the welfare state, such a move would not guarantee higher employment. As the US experience demonstrates, there are limits to wage flexibility as a solution to unemployment even in a minimal welfare environment, because anti-social activities such as crime effectively provide an alternative reservation wage (Freeman, 1995). This may in part explain the OECD's recent observation for developed economies as a whole that there is no strong correlation between relative wage flexibility – as measured by the the the incidence of low-paid work – and employment and unemployment rates for low-skilled workers (OECD, 1996b).

Within the British policy context, the Conservative Government has in the 1990s implemented or experimented with different ways of improving work incentives. A lower-rate tax band of 20p in the pound was introduced in 1992, while the less-skilled and lower-paid have been the focus of several changes to employee or employer National Insurance contributions (NICs). In terms of benefits, although the provision of out-of-work welfare benefits for the jobless has continued to be cut back and more closely linked to active job search – the switch from Unemployment Benefit to Job Seeker's Allowance in October 1996 being a classic example – ever greater stress has been placed on the use of in-work earnings supplements to encourage unemployed people into low-paid jobs. Around half a million working people were receiving Family Credit in the mid-1990s – at an annual cost of almost £1.5 billion – and (at the time of writing) a new in-work benefit, Earnings Top-Up, aimed at unemployed people without dependant children is due to be piloted. In addition to these subsidies paid to individuals, the Government is also experimenting with Workstart – a subsidy paid for up to a year to employers who recruit from amongst the ranks of the very long-term unemployed – while employers who hire the very long-term jobless do not incur NICs for such recruits until they have been employed for a year.

The impact of such recent reforms is as yet difficult to assess but what is clear is that they are very much the order of the day in policy circles. The degree of broad convergence between the Government and the opposition political parties on measures to improve work incentives is perhaps best demonstrated by frequent accusations that one party or another has 'stolen' another party's ideas. Politicians of all persuasions talk of the need to offer jobless people on benefit a 'hand-up, rather than a hand-out'. What divides the politicians is mainly differences in approach to reliance on means-tested in-work benefits.

While there is general support for some use of in-work benefit, two major concerns are often expressed. A fundamental problem arises because means-tested benefits of this kind give rise to the so-called 'poverty trap' i.e. recipients find that they are little better off if they try to raise their earnings because of the withdrawal of all or part of the benefit. Indeed, if one adds in the effect of tax rises as earnings rise, it is possible for some people on benefits to experience effective marginal 'tax' rates (EMTRs) in excess of 80 per cent (Duncan and Giles, 1996; OECD (1996a) provides examples of still higher EMTRs in excess of 90 per cent).

Another potential problem is that any such mechanism for supplementing pay will tend to reinforce downward pressure on wage levels at the lower end of the earnings scale. On the face of things this effect of in-work benefits should be of little concern, since the purpose of such benefits is, after all, to price low-productivity workers into jobs by enabling the labour market to clear at a higher level of employment. Some economists, however, are uneasy about having large numbers of people in work but part-dependent on state hand-outs (for example, Britton, 1996), while others fear that in non-competitive segments of the labour market in-work benefits act as a subsidy to inefficient exploitative employers at the taxpayer's expense. Those who take the latter view often favour setting a wage floor, such as a national minimum wage. The fear of course is that a minimum wage would itself destroy jobs for the very kinds of people who are most prone to unemployment, although an increasing amount of evidence suggests that such fears are groundless so long as a NMW is not introduced at too high a level (Philpott, 1996).

Another option – which could be introduced with or without a minimum wage – would be to switch the emphasis of wage supplements away from in-work benefits paid to workers and toward greater use of subsidies (or tax rebates) paid to employers. This would encourage hiring, without reducing pay rates. Both this option and a national minimum wage have been advocated by the 'new' Labour Party in the mid-1990s as part of a 'welfare to work' strategy designed amongst other things to effectively abolish long-term unemployment amongst 18–24-year-olds (Labour Party, 1996a, 1996b).

The assumption underlying Labour Party policy – which also includes a range of compulsory training and jobs programmes – is that job subsidies and employment schemes are self-financing in the medium term once savings in benefit payments and tax revenue 'flowbacks' from lower unemployment accrue (any short-run net cost, the Labour Party says, would be financed out of revenues raised by a 'windfall tax' on the profits of the privatised utilities). The Labour Party expects its programmes would become self-financing within the lifetime of a Parliament.

The validity of this assumption cannot be fully assessed in the abstract. However, critics of such an approach often point to the fact that employment programmes suffer from the well-known problem of deadweight (which means that the state supports jobs that would have been created anyway) as well as giving rise to job substitution and displacement effects. Taking such problems into account it is quite possible for the cost per additional job supported by the state to exceed any savings in benefit and tax flowbacks, resulting in a net cost to the Exchequer, although this remains a matter of some controversy amongst economists. If employment programmes *do* have a net cost they will have to be financed by cuts in other forms of public spending or by higher taxation or borrowing. This will have implications for jobs elsewhere in the economy and possibly also longer-run consequences for the overall performance of the economy.

FLEXIBILITY AND SKILLS

Ultimately the best way to deal with the problem of unskilled unemployment and remove the benefit trap is to ensure that workers have better skills, become more productive and thus command higher wages at work. As well as reducing structural unemployment such an approach would serve to enhance the overall competitiveness of the British economy. Britain's relative productivity performance has admittedly improved in the 1980s. But to the extent that public policy contributed to this, the main factor was probably reform of industrial relations, allied to efforts to enhance competition in product markets, rather than measures designed to create a much better educated and trained workforce.

The extent and precise nature of Britain's 'skills gap' with its competitors has been made somewhat clearer by the results of an official 'Skills Audit' which were published alongside the third *Competitiveness* White Paper in 1996 (Department for Education and Employment and Cabinet Office, 1996). The Skills Audit involved a comparison of skills attainment data in the United Kingdom and five other countries – the US, Germany, France, Singapore – plus interviews with a sample of multinational companies to ascertain their views on the supply of skills in these countries and Japan. As always with such exercises, comparison is made difficult by data problems. But the Skills Audit nonetheless underlines the long-standing strengths and weaknesses of skills provision in Britain. Britain performs relatively well in terms of providing higher (i.e. graduate-level) skills and – with the exception of Germany, which is streets ahead of everyone – holds its own against other countries when it comes to intermediate skills. But along with the US – the other Anglo-Saxon economy covered by the Audit – Britain was found to lag woefully behind in terms of providing such very low-level basic skills as literacy and numeracy.

Individuals lacking these skills are precisely those most at risk from structural unemployment. The problems they face often surface on government training programmes for the long-term jobless which, although ostensibly designed to provide work-related qualifications, often amount to little more than remedial basic education courses. Although the effectiveness of these programmes may have been increased somewhat by the activities of the private-sector-led Training and Enterprise Councils (TECs) – established in

1990 – still fewer than half of all participants gain a qualification (House of Commons, 1996). It is possible that reforms to basic education – stemming from amongst other things the introduction of the National Curriculum in the 1980s – will serve to improve prospects for the least skilled and subsequently make them easier to train. But even in the mid-1990s the jury is still out on the effectiveness of the education policy pursued by successive Conservative Governments.

On the positive side of the skills equation one can of course point to increased staying-on rates in further and higher education – as referred to earlier – as a sign that the overall supply of labour is gradually shifting in the right direction. Moreover it is true, as Government ministers highlighted in the mid-1990s, that the majority of jobs being created in Britain are in occupations offering above-average earnings. According to Waldegrave (*op. cit.*) one-fifth of jobs created in the two years to autumn 1995 were in professional occupations with gross hourly earnings 1.7 times the average for all employees, while a quarter were created in the managerial and administrative occupations on average paying 1.5 times the all-employees average.

To use the fashionable jargon, more skilled 'good' jobs – i.e. in managerial, professional or technical occupations – are being created than relatively unskilled low-grade 'McJobs' (hamburger flipping and the like). Ministerial rhetoric on this issue has with some justification been aimed at those commentators who criticise the deregulated UK labour market – and that of the US which has seen a similar bias toward good job creation in the 1980s and 1990s – on the assumption that it creates mostly low-wage jobs. But one should not necessarily see this as a vindication of the British version of Anglo-Saxon economics.

The tendency for highly developed market economies to create relatively more good jobs is part of a long-run trend and is precisely what one should expect to see in a world where, as already mentioned, the balance of demand is shifting away from unskilled labour. The true criticism of Anglo-Saxon economics, British-style, is not that it generates too many poor jobs but, on the contrary, that it fails both to generate enough such jobs for the least skilled and to provide such workers with the abilities required to gain access to better jobs. This is not to say that flexible labour market policies are irrelevant to the process of structural change in the demand for skills. For example, some amount of relative wage flexibility should be encouraged in order that the labour market can better signal the return to investment in skills. But flexible labour markets are unlikely to offer a sufficient response to the problem of unskilled unemployment in the absence of interventionist measures that can overcome the deep-rooted market and institutional failures that bedevil labour and training markets.

Discussion of the well-known externalities that are in theory the source of training market failure has tended to dominate the approach of economists to this issue. Some, however, have questioned this approach in the British context and focused instead on the lack of managerial capacity and/or the unwillingness of companies to use skills as the underlying source of Britain's skills problem. Keep and Mayhew (1995), for example, argue that too many British companies remain wedded to low-quality products requiring low skills because high-quality product strategies require substantial investment and radical changes in corporate organisation.

Unfortunately, this conclusion leaves policy-makers with a problem. It is far from easy in a free market economy to persuade companies to behave differently. Exhortation through the TECs may persuade more employers to become 'Investors in People' or to participate in similar initiatives – but many employers still present a deaf ear. Keep and Mayhew believe that more should be done in the first instance to encourage companies to think strategically – if they do this they are more likely to operate in ways designed to make use of skills. Whether this is a job for TECs, however, is a moot point.

Moreover, in similar vein, it might be argued that policy emphasis on external forms of labour market flexibility runs counter to the efforts of TECs and others to change business culture. It is often pointed out that one way of making companies think strategically about investment in people is to encourage long-term relationships between employers and workers. This, of course, is the antithesis of a 'hire and fire' business culture, having more in common with the so-called 'long-termist' or 'stakeholder' versions of capitalism said to operate in Japan and the Rhineland countries of continental Europe.

The underlying problem being described here of course is the short-termism that is often said to bedevil much of British industry, with the quest for quick profits and dividends taking precedence over long-term planning and investment (Hutton, 1995). If public policy and institutional reform could play a role in changing Britain's business culture so as to boost investment generally, the pay-off could in principle be substantial, in terms not just of higher skills but also of less structural unemployment. It can be argued that sustained investment of the kind that Anglo-Saxon economics has failed to deliver in the 1990s would, over time, raise productivity, boost growth and employment and increase living standards (although the links between investment and structural unemployment are a matter of dispute, an issue discussed by Rowthorn, 1995).

Fashionable talk of stakeholder capitalism by commentators on the political centre and left in Britain is derided by proponents of Anglo-Saxon economics who attribute the economic and employment problems experienced in many continental European economies in the 1990s to over-regulation and institutional rigidities. Yet the case against 'Europe' that one confronts in the popular parlance of Britain's political right is more often than not based upon a caricature of the so-called continental 'European model'. In reality, the European Union does not offer a homogeneous model. While it is likely that some EU states – for example France, Spain and

Italy – suffer under the weight of inappropriate labour market regulation, the stakeholder (or social market) states, notably Germany, have for most of the past twenty years performed better in terms of unemployment and adapting to change than the Anglo-Saxon economies (Goodhart, 1994).

For example, standardised unemployment rates as published by the OECD show that pre-unification West Germany until very recently out-performed both Britain and the US (the OECD figures refer to the former West Germany prior to 1992; see Table 14.9). Indeed even by 1995 the unemployment rate in post-unification Germany was still lower than that in the United Kingdom. Since then German unemployment has continued to rise to a rate – at the time of writing – of just over 9 per cent. But it is unlikely that this is the result of labour market rigidities; the main factor has been the decision of German policy-makers to follow the strict anti-inflation policy that accompanied unification with the economic stringency necessary to keep Germany on track to meet the Maastrict criteria for EMU.

Perhaps significantly, the Netherlands, the other key example of the Rhenish stakeholder model, has throughout the 1990s maintained a relatively healthy unemployment performance – certainly by UK standards – despite being directly affected by the macroeconomic traumas being suffered by its German neighbour. This suggests that the stakeholder model at least has the potential to hold its own against Anglo-Saxon economics, although the sharp rise in Swedish unemployment in the 1990s indicates ongoing strains in the once highly successful Nordic or Scandinavian model, which was the beacon for European social democrats in the 1970s and 1980s.

To the Anglo-Saxon economist, of course, the Rhenish stakeholder economies appear riddled with regulations and institutional rigidities which – because of his or her ideological preference for unfettered markets – must by definition reduce economic welfare, regardless of any evidence to the contrary. What the Anglo-Saxon economist cannot appreciate is the power of

Table 14.9 Standardised unemployment rates in major OECD countries

	1974 %	1983 %	1990 %	1991 %	1992 %	1995 %
United States	5.5	9.5	5.6	6.8	7.5	5.5
Japan	1.4	2.6	2.1	2.1	2.2	3.1
Germany	1.6	7.7	4.8	4.2	4.6	8.2
France	2.8	8.3	8.9	9.4	10.3	11.6
Italy	5.3	8.8	10.3	9.9	10.5	12.2
UK	2.9	12.4	6.9	8.8	10.1	8.7
Spain	2.6	17.0	15.9	16.0	18.1	22.7
Netherlands	2.7	12.0	7.5	7.0	5.6	6.5
Sweden	2.0	3.9	1.8	3.3	5.8	9.2

Source: OECD *Employment Outlook* (1996).

what are sometimes referred to as 'flexible rigidities', i.e. the ability of rules and regulations to compensate for market or other potential institutional failures and thereby enhance what we earlier described as internal flexibility. Marsden (1996), for example, points out that measures such as formal consultation procedures of the kind common in Germany facilitate what he calls 'co-operative exchange' between workers and employers and thus make labour markets more flexible and adaptable than is the case in the low-trust, insecure environment typical of the Anglo-Saxon economies.

One might conclude from this that statutory imposition of consultation procedures on large companies – such as proposed under the Social Chapter of the Maastricht Treaty, but opposed by the Conservative Government and many employers in the United Kingdom in the 1990s – should be seen as a development to be embraced. This remains a moot point, not least because it may be more appropriate to encourage or provide incentives for the establishment of stakeholder relations, as opposed to resorting to legislation. Nonetheless, it seems reasonable to draw the somewhat broader conclusion that the stakeholder model has the potential to challenge Anglo-Saxon economics. What is less clear is whether stakeholder capitalism offers a workable alternative model of economic and social development that could be easily translated into British form. At the time of writing, in the mid-1990s, the exponents of 'stakeholding' are not only fighting a battle of ideas with ideological opponents in Britain but also struggling to convey to potential sympathisers what the 'stakeholder economy' would entail in terms of specific public policy reforms (see Parkinson, 1996).

CONCLUSION

Britain's labour market is very different from that inherited by Mrs Thatcher's first administration in 1979. Developments in employment, unemployment and wage behaviour in recent years suggest that the policy changes wrought since that time have created a somewhat more flexible labour market, particularly if one means by this the greater ability of employers to hire and fire and greater relative wage flexibility. The jury is still out on the more fundamental issue of whether the structural (i.e. sustainable) rate of unemployment has fallen in Britain, although the virtual absence of pay pressure during the course of the 1990s' recovery offers cause for cautious optimism that the structural rate might now be as low as 6–7 per cent.

One should not forget, however, that a 6–7 per cent unemployment rate is still well above the 2–3 per cent that a generation ago was considered the norm for full employment. This, rather than the mass unemployment of the 1980s, is the true benchmark against which to judge the success of Anglo-Saxon economics and the performance of Britain's labour market. Moreover, in contrast to the era of full employment, the long-term unemployed now comprise a far higher proportion of total unemployment, while many able-bodied people – predominantly men with few skills or redundant skills – now eke out a meagre existence outside the labour market.

Whatever the merits of Anglo-Saxon economics, it seems unable to deal with this substantial hard core of people who, although structurally jobless, are not necessarily unemployable and could in principle be contributing to output and the well-being of society. Assuming that there are no major shocks to the economy in the next few years, and thus that unemployment is eventually able to fall to its current long-run sustainable rate, the question of how to deal with this continuing structural problem should be central in the minds of whoever is responsible for Britain's employment, training and welfare policies in the late 1990s and beyond.

NOTES

1　'Anglo-Saxon economics and the labour market', Speech by the Chief Secretary to the Treasury, Rt Hon. William Waldegrave, MP, to the American Chambers of Commerce, 11 June 1996.

2　Indeed, such has been the degree of deregulation that even the Employment Department was abolished in 1995, leaving Britain in an almost unique position amongst the developed economies in not having an all-embracing Ministry of Labour.

3　See HM government's third White Paper on Competitiveness (1996).

4　For details on the changing role of trade unions, see House of Commons (1995).

5　The LFS counts the number of *people* in employment, whereas the employee count contained within the WIE refers to *jobs*, so the two measures do not correspond directly (for example, a person with two jobs but working for different employers will appear once in the LFS but both his or her jobs should show up in the WIE). Moreover, the two surveys refer to rather different time periods throughout the year (the LFS is based upon seasons of the year, the WIE upon strict calendar quarters). The Office for National Statistics has investigated the discrepancy between the two data sets. Prior to the investigation it was thought that, aside from technical measurement differences, part of the discrepancy might be explained by the fact that the LFS is more closely attuned to the economic cycle. The WIE, for example, might be affected by delays in new companies registering for PAYE in the early stages of economic recovery. The LFS will immediately pick up people newly employed by these companies but the WIE will record the jobs they are performing only after a time. Similarly, the WIE may fail to pick up temporary or casual workers whom employers do not (or do not immediately) record as employees. However, an initial investigation failed to identify clear reasons for the discrepancy and further work is ongoing. See Perry (1996).

6　In 1994 the Law Lords ruled that the failure of the United Kingdom to grant part-time workers the same statutory rights as full-timers broke European equal opportunities legislation, given that the vast majority of part-timers are women. From spring 1995 employees working less that sixteen hours a week who have completed two years' service with the same employer have the same employment rights as employees working more than sixteen hours.

7　For a discussion of the concept of core or equilibrium unemployment and approaches to estimation, see OECD (1994); Layard, Nickell and Jackman (1991); Coulton and Cromb (1994). Note that the concept of core unemployment is not without its critics. See, for example, Ormerod (1994) and Solow (1995). There have also been recent developments in the theory of core unemployment which extend a role to factors other than those operating from within the labour market; see Phelps (1995).

8 'Strategic Reward Practice – Pay at the Crossroads'. Speech by Mr Adair Turner, Director-General of the Confederation of British Industry, to the IPD Compensation Conference, 25 January, 1996.

9 For a discussion of the 'speed limits' issue, see OECD (1994).

10 See George (1995).

REFERENCES

Beatson, M. (1995) *Labour Market Flexibility*, Employment Department Research Paper No.48; April.

Blanchflower, D.G. and Freeman, R.B. (1994) 'Did the Thatcher reforms change British labour market performance?', in R. Barrel (ed.) *The UK Labour Market: Comparative Aspects and Institutional Developments*, Cambridge: Cambridge University Press, pp. 51–92.

Britton, A. (1996) 'Full employment in a market economy', in J. Philpott (ed.) *Working Towards Full Employment*, London: Routledge, forthcoming.

Coulton, B. and Cromb, R. (1994) *The UK NAIRU*, Government Economic Service Working Paper No.124 (Treasury Working Paper No. 66).

Duncan, A. and Giles, C. (1996) 'Labour supply incentives and recent Family Credit reforms', *Economic Journal*, vol. 106, no. 434, pp. 142–155.

Department for Education and Employment and Cabinet Office (1996) *The Skills Audit: A report from an interdepartmental group*, June.

Freeman, R.B. (1995) 'The limits of wage flexibility to curing unemployment', *Oxford Review of Economic Policy*, vol. 11, no. 1, pp. 63–72.

George, E. (1995) 'Macroeconomic management and structural unemployment', *Bank of England Quarterly Bulletin*, vol. 35, no. 1, pp. 157–79.

Goodhart, D. (1994) *The Reshaping of the German Social Market*, London: Institute for Public Policy Research.

Gregg, P. and Wadsworth, J. (1996a) 'The importance of making work pay', Employment Policy Institute *Economic Report*, vol. 10, February.

—— (1996b) 'The polarisation of jobs', Employment Policy Institute *Employment Audit*, Issue 1, Summer.

Hutton, W. (1995) *The State We're In*, London: Jonathan Cape.

HM Government (1996) *Competitiveness: Creating the enterprise centre of Europe* (Cm 3300), London: HMSO.

House of Commons Select Committee on Employment (1995) *The Future of Trade Unions*, London: HMSO.

—— (1996) *The Work of TECs*, London: HMSO.

Keep, E. and Mayhew, K. (1995) 'UK training policy – assumptions and reality', in A. Booth and D. Snower (eds) *The Skills Gap and Economic Activity*, Cambridge: Cambridge University Press, pp. 180–205.

Labour Party (1996a) *Getting Welfare to Work*, June.

—— (1996b) *New Deal for a Lost Generation*, June.

Layard, P.R.G. Nickell, S.J. and Jackman, R. (1991) *Unemployment*, Oxford: Oxford University Press.

—— (1996) *Combating Unemployment: Is Flexibility Enough?* Paper for the OECD Conference on 'Interactions between Structural Reform, Macroeconomic Policies and Economic Performance', Paris 18-19 January 1996.

McLaughlin, E. (1992) 'Towards active labour market policies', in E. McLaughlin (ed.)

Understanding Unemployment, London: Routledge, pp. 1–21.

—— (1994) *Flexibility in Work and Benefits*, London: Institute for Public Policy Research.

Marsden, D. (1996) 'Regulation vs deregulation: which way for Europe's labour markets', in J. Philpott (ed.) *Working Towards Full Employment*, London: Routledge.

Minford, A.P.L. (1996) 'Is full employment attainable?', in 'Choices and Trade-Offs', Employment Policy Institute *Economic Report*, vol. 10, no. 7, May.

Minford, A.P.L. and Riley, J. (1994) 'The UK labour market: Micro rigidities and macro obstructions', in R. Barrel (ed.) *The UK Labour Market: Comparative aspects and institutional developments*, Cambridge: Cambridge University Press, pp. 258–72.

Morgan, J. (1996) 'What do comparisons of the last two economic recoveries tell us about the UK labour market?', *NIESR Review*, May, pp. 80–93.

Organisation For Economic Co-operation and Development (1994) *OECD Jobs Study: Facts, analysis, strategies* and *Evidence and Explanations*, Paris: OECD.

—— (1996a) OECD Economic Survey, *United Kingdom*, Paris: OECD.

—— (1996b) *Employment Outlook*, Paris: OECD.

Ormerod, P. (1994) *The Death of Economics*, London: Faber & Faber.

Parkinson, J. (1996) 'The stakeholder business', Employment Policy Institute *Economic Report*, vol. 10, no. 2, February.

Perry, K. (1996) 'Measuring employment: Comparison of official sources', *Labour Market Trends*, vol. 104, no. 1, January.

Philpott, J. (1996) *A National Minimum Wage: Economic effects and practical consideration*, London: Institute for Personnel and Development.

Phelps, E. (1995) *Structural Slumps: The modern equilibrium theory of unemployment, interest and assets*, Cambridge, Mass.: Harvard University Press.

Robinson, P. (1994) *The British Labour Market in Historical Perspective: Changes in the structure of employment and unemployment*, Centre for Economic Performance Working Paper no. 587.

—— (1996a) *Is There a Pay Problem?*, paper presented to a conference on 'Full Employment Without Inflation', Robinson College, Cambridge, May.

—— (1996b) *Study on the Labour Market in the United Kingdom*, Centre for Economic Performance, London School of Economics, June.

Joseph Rowntree Foundation (1995) *Inquiry into Income and Wealth*, vols 1 and 2, York: JRF.

Rowthorn, R. (1995) 'Capital formation and unemployment', *Oxford Review of Economic Policy*, vol. 11, no. 1, pp. 26–39.

Solow, R. (1995) 'Equilibrium theory goes askew', the *Guardian*, 27 February.

TUC (1996) *Social Costs and their Effect on Employment*, submission to the House of Commons Education and Employment Committee, Trades Union Congress.

15

VOCATIONAL EDUCATION AND TRAINING AND ECONOMIC PERFORMANCE

Ewart Keep and Ken Mayhew

This chapter examines the link between vocational education and training and Britain's economic performance, and seeks to evaluate the effectiveness of policy responses to Britain's perceived failings in this area. It will argue that the main thrust of current policy, which is to concentrate on reform of the institutional mechanisms through which VET is supplied, ignores fundamental underlying weaknesses in the demand for skills within the British economy and is therefore doomed to produce, at best, limited results.

INTRODUCTION: A NEW MODEL OF COMPETITIVE ADVANTAGE

Britain has experienced intermittent periods of worry about weaknesses in the education and training of its workforce, and their harmful effects upon economic competitiveness, since the later half of the nineteenth century. The latest wave of interest in this issue has extended unbroken since about the mid-1970s. Its start was marked by the publication of the various 'black papers' on education, and Prime Minister Jim Callaghan's 'Great Debate' speech in 1976. In this latest phase, long-standing concerns about insufficient training and skill formation have been amplified by a number of factors, including increasing international competition, and also by a number of comparative studies (Prais, 1990) which have shown British training practices and their effect upon productivity in an unfavourable light.

In the last decade there has emerged a clear consensus among policy-makers, embracing not only the major political parties but also the CBI, the TUC, the National Commission on Education (NCE), and the Commission on Social Justice (CSJ), which has centred around the type of theories about sustainable competitive advantage advanced by Reich (1983). These suggest that the rules of international competition have undergone a paradigm shift, and that skills now form the sole long-term source of competitive advantage. Thus Thurow (1994, p. 52) argues:

Show me a skilled individual, a skilled company, or a skilled country and I will show you an individual, a company or a country that has a chance to be successful. Show me an unskilled individual, company or country and I will show you a failure in the 21st century.

In the economy ahead, there is only one source of sustainable competitive advantage – skills. Everything else is available to everyone on a more or less equal access basis.

An illustration of the impact of these theories upon official policy is provided by the three recent White Papers on competitiveness (Department of Trade and Industry, 1994, 1995, 1996), which have all devoted considerable attention to the issues of VET, skill formation and the need to achieve what the CBI has dubbed 'a skills revolution'. The Department for Education and Employment (1996a, p. 4) has concluded that, 'international competition demands that our workforce is highly motivated, well educated, well trained and adaptable'.

THE POLICY RESPONSE

In terms of a resulting institutional change within the British VET system, a detailed picture of the institutional changes was provided in our contribution to the first edition of *Britain's Economic Performance*, and it is not our intention to repeat this here. Instead, we outline the main principles that have underlain the reforms, offer an overview of their effectiveness, and seek to identify whether, taken individually or as a whole, these changes have materially improved Britain's weak performance in the field of VET. Anyone wanting a more detailed institutional map and description should consult our earlier work (Keep and Mayhew, 1994).

Education

In 1980 Britain had an educational system which was generally regarded as providing an excellent academic education for an intellectual elite. For this relatively small group it was world class. However, it served those of average and below average ability less well. It was believed that, in comparison with other countries, too few people stayed on in full-time education beyond compulsory school leaving age (sixteen), whilst too many who left had inadequate standards of literacy and numeracy. A relatively small proportion of the age cohort went into higher education. Meanwhile the particular needs of the less able were poorly met in terms of subject mix and of teaching method and delivery. These failings, in conjunction with an inadequately trained workforce, meant that comparatively few of our post-16-year-olds were receiving adequate or appropriate education or training. This deficiency was particularly apparent in intermediate skills and competencies.

Policy response was hampered by the institutional oddity that different ministries were responsible for different elements of the system. The Department for Education looked after full-time educational matters, whilst the Department for Employment looked after work-based training. Not only did this lead to inconsistencies and lack of coordination, at times there was direct and purposeful competition for resources between the two departments. It has yet to be seen whether the merger of the two departments in 1995 will lead to significant improvements in this regard.

In the 1976 Education Act the Labour Government had introduced the policy of enforcing comprehensive secondary education. This involved abandoning the streaming of pupils at the age of eleven into either grammar schools (for those who passed the eleven-plus exam) or secondary moderns (for those who did not). Though an element of selection remained in some local education authority areas, comprehensive, mixed-ability schools came to dominate state secondary education. An important motivation for this change was the belief that such schools would provide a more effective education for the non-elite which was vital not just on distributional grounds but also to improve the skills base of our workforce. The Conservatives, when in opposition, had argued against the introduction of a comprehensive system and, when they came into power, they repealed the 1976 Act; but they did not attempt to dismantle the new edifice, rather chipping away at the edges. Thus they encouraged some element of selection by ability and more ability streaming within comprehensive schools. They also introduced an extensive assisted places scheme to enable the children of parents with modest means to enter the private secondary sector. This was symptomatic of increased emphasis on enhanced parental choice.

In ways other than comprehensivisation the 1970s Labour Government had started to show signs of a desire to transform the education system. Perhaps the watershed was Prime Minister Callaghan's speech mentioned above, when he decried the failure of our schools to deliver sufficient quality of teaching for the average pupil and also their broader failure to prepare people adequately for the world of work. The broad suggestion was that these deficiencies would not be solved simply by the introduction of comprehensivisation. This latter theme of the need to reorientate towards the vocational was to become a much more persistent one during the 1980s.

Initially, however, the post-1979 Conservative Government was relatively slow to turn its attention to education. Most of its early policies were motivated dominantly by restricted budgets. Real reform started to come only with the 1986 Education Act and with subsequent legislation. It then came very fast.

Many of these reforms were concerned with the governance of the education sector and were dictated by a belief that competition and the introduction of quasi-markets would deliver significantly better value for each

369

pound of Government money spent than the administered civil service type set-up these quasi-markets replaced. Important as these changes are, the details are not of direct relevance for the themes of this chapter and therefore we do not discuss them extensively. However, the faith exhibited in the introduction of markets in order to solve the problems of the supply of skills, also evident in the sphere of training, is central to one of our dominant themes. Much more will be said later, but here it is worth lingering on one aspect. The problem with introducing markets is that in the process one also encounters market failure, specifically the lack of adequate consumer information and the power of monopolies. Many of this Government's innovations are in large part an attempt to deal with such market failures whilst at the same time trying to capture the efficiency gains accruing from greater competition. The need to provide better information for consumers underlies the various parents' charters and the array of league tables. The attempt to control monopoly elements explains the apparent paradox of a government simultaneously preaching the virtues of markets whilst introducing a draconian and far-reaching system of supervision, monitoring and control. The key question is whether any gains accruing from enhanced competition are outweighed by the extra regulatory costs. The jury is still out.

Of particular importance were changes to the curriculum and to the qualification structure. The National Curriculum for 5–16-year-olds, first unveiled by the 1988 Education Reform Act, was the object of considerable controversy and significant subsequent amendment. The basic objective was to enforce the notion that a minimum percentage of class time should be spent on specified subjects. There were a number of aims behind this, amongst which was the desire to define what subject mix constituted an appropriate education for any given age group and also a wish to stress subject mix as it related to the subsequent labour market needs of the pupils. At the same time, great stress was put upon 'economic and industrial awareness'. The practice of national testing at a variety of ages was introduced, primarily as a means of monitoring the performance of schools and providing information to parents. A more rigorous system of school inspections was presumably designed to plug the gap left by the operation of the market in uncovering the poorly performing schools.

The qualification system was also transformed. We entered the decade with O levels, taken after four or five years at secondary school, with CSEs for the less able or academically orientated. After two years in the sixth form, A levels in three or sometimes four subjects were taken. In 1989 the O level and CSE examining structure was amalgamated into a single qualification, the GCSE, partly with the motive of preventing O levels from serving the purpose of an exclusionary exam indicating whether or not pupils were fit to proceed into the sixth form or on to A levels (see Finegold et al., 1990). Also in 1989, a new exam was introduced. This was the Advanced Supplementary (AS) level. Its aim was to provide a wider set of studies than was possible under the A level system alone. For each individual subject the standard is meant to be the same as for A levels, but only half the content is included. At the same time GNVQs were being developed as part of the NVQ complex (see below). These are meant to provide a vocational route through school life, and Advanced GNVQs are supposed to have parity of esteem with A levels.

However, ministerial reactions to the early results of some of these new exams suggest an unresolved tension between those who genuinely want to see wider access to further education and those who still take an exclusionary view (see, for example, Richardson, 1993). There is a further tension concerning the market philosophy. Thus far we have described this philosophy as accepting a trade-off between the gains from competition and the costs of regulation. But some commentators, notably Chubb and Moe (1992) drawing on the US experience, go further and suggest that the mode of regulation gives the managers of schools insufficient room to operate a market effectively. This is true even of the minority of schools which are grant maintained, that is free of local authority control. In any event, Chubb and Moe continue, if scope for supply response is limited (as it is), then the market mechanism is muted – in other words, the good schools are able to expand only to a limited extent in order to meet increased demand.

The late 1980s also saw major changes in the world of post-school education. These were driven by exactly the same philosophy as that which drove school reform. The so-called binary divide between universities and polytechnics was abolished . All universities – the old and the new – were put under a single funding body, the Higher Education Funding Council. Local authorities lost control of further education and sixth form colleges – instead they received funding from the Further Education Funding Council. In a variety of ways the theme of increased competition for funding and for students was dominant. The methods by which the Government attempted to achieve this were various and often highly experimental, but the thrust was consistent. As with school reform the aim was to put as many people through the system as possible. The great question here was could the lower end of the cohort achieve so much extra benefit as to offset any possible loss to the higher end of the ability spectrum.

In the case of schools the gains from comprehensivisation have been limited. Comparative studies show that Britain still lags its major competitors in mathematical ability for the lower reaches. At the very bottom end problems of literacy and numeracy remain considerable. Many more people are obtaining qualifications after five years at school, but it is far from clear how much real improvement of basic educational standards this implies. Meanwhile the gold standard of A Levels is being devalued in the eyes of many commentators. There is great controversy about whether or not there has been grade inflation, but what is certain is that the knowledge content of A levels has been reduced. It is less certain whether this has been accompanied

371

by slower cognitive development. Thus it is far from obvious what the mushrooming of qualifications represents in terms of improvements in the skills base of the country. By the same token, more and more people are obtaining degrees, but again the precise skills and capabilities gains derived from this are dubious. Problems have been exacerbated by the fact that the expansion has been accompanied by restricted government funding. For schools this has meant that the outcome of comprehensivisation has been prejudiced by, for example, the frequent lack of financial resource necessary to cater appropriately for the different needs of pupils of different abilities. At universities it has meant that the quality of the educational process and therefore of the end product must be open to doubt. The funding problem has been made worse by the fact that valuable resources have been spent on the regulation of the new quasi-markets at the expense of core educational activities.

Perhaps the main preliminary conclusion that can be drawn relates to the United Kingdom's major relative deficiency – that is in intermediate skills and capabilities. It is unclear that reforms of our full-time education system thus far have successfully addressed it. Furthermore it may be that some elements of expansion (notably in higher education) may turn out to have been wasteful given the structure of jobs presently on offer.

Training

During the 1980s, the British training system underwent a period of rapid and profound change. The sectorally based system of statutory training boards, which had existed since 1964, was abolished. It was replaced by two new sets of bodies. The first of these were the voluntary sectoral organisations – the Industrial Training Organisations (ITOs). These sectoral arrangements were subsequently overlain by a new set of local, employer-led Training and Enterprise Councils (TECs), and in Scotland, Local Enterprise Companies (LECs). A further key element in the new system was the introduction in 1986 of a revolutionary structure of competence based National Vocational Qualifications (NVQs), overseen by a National Council for Vocational Qualifications (NCVQ). In addition, a variety of often short-lived government-funded training initiatives and schemes – mainly aimed at the young entrants to the labour market and at long-term adult unemployed – were tried out. Of these, by far the most important was the Youth Training Scheme (YTS), more latterly titled Youth Training (YT).

In terms of design principles, the new structures were expected to provide local delivery of training to nationally agreed standards. In the view of the Government and bodies such as the CBI, the underlying rationale for the move to an employer-led, voluntary system was that it produced a training market in which individuals and employers are free to determine levels and types of skill investment and acquisition.

In contrast to education, the pace of institutional reform in training has slackened quite considerably in the last three or four years. The main recent development has been the merger of the Employment Department and the Department for Education to form the Department for Education and Employment (DfEE). The architects of the new training system appear to believe that, with this last change, a state of maturity has been achieved, and that further major institutional restructuring is unnecessary (although more minor changes remain a constant feature of the scene). This belief notwithstanding, it has become increasingly apparent, both to outside commentators and to those within the system itself, that there are serious problems with both the design of major elements within this new system and with the quality of some of the 'outcomes' that it is producing. In the space available, we cannot hope to cover every aspect of this institutional landscape, but the section below highlights some of the most important issues.

National Vocational Qualifications

Introduced in 1986, NVQs were intended to act as the 'superglue' that holds the new, devolved voluntary training system together, so that its training output is delivered to nationally recognised and agreed standards. NVQs are also expected to play a key role in providing a set of measurable performance indicators for progress of the VET system towards the National Targets (for details of which, see below). A DfEE review of the operation of the NCVQ concluded that 'the functions delivered by the NCVQ remained key to securing the Government's general and vocational education and training strategy' (1996b, p. 1). Given this pivotal role, problems with NVQs have considerable significance for the operation of the new VET system.

Unfortunately, NVQs have faced sustained and widespread criticism from both academics and educationalists, and also from many employers (CBI, 1994a). Adverse comment from academics has centred upon the inability of NVQs to provide a satisfactory level of underpinning theory and knowledge, and weaknesses in workplace assessment systems (Prais, 1991; Smithers, 1993); while employers have pointed to poor design, bureaucracy, and an overly-technical approach to assessment (Beaumont, 1996; Pickard, 1996). Underlying these criticisms has been the slow and very limited take-up of NVQs. Despite the fact that government and TEC-funded training programmes must aim for NVQs, latest figures suggest that just 7 per cent of employers are using NVQs (Spilsbury, Moralee and Evans, 1995), and there are indications that their take-up has plateaued.

Moreover, it was intended by government that the NVQ framework would subsume existing vocational qualifications and simplify the complex range of awards on offer (MSC/DES, 1986). This goal has not been realised. In the year 1994/5, 613,000 non-NVQ vocational qualifications were awarded, as against 281,838 NVQs in 1995 (DfEE, 1996c), and an official review of the work of the NCVQ concluded that 'success has eluded NCVQ with regard to establishing a national framework for all (or even the majority) of vocational awards' (DfEE, 1996d, pp. 14–15).

These problems and failings, taken together, have meant that NVQs have not yet fulfilled the pivotal role within the VET system that was expected of them. Unless the take-up of NVQs increases significantly in the next few years, this failure will continue.

Youth Training

One of the most important and far-reaching of the failures that has dogged the new voluntary training system has been its inability to develop and sustain a coherent, high-quality vocational training scheme for young entrants to the labour market. Despite having been in existence since 1983, Youth Training (originally known as the Youth Training Scheme – YTS) has failed to deliver a comprehensive programme for both young workers and the young unemployed. The Dearing Report (1996) on 16–19 education underlined the depth of this problem. A fifth of all 17-year-olds are in neither education nor training; one in eight of 18–20 year-olds are not in education, work or training (Nash, 1996); and only 40 per cent of the 280,000 youngsters on government-sponsored training programmes achieve any qualifications – often an NVQ level 1 (Times Educational Supplement, 1 March 1996). The completion rate for YT is 46 per cent, meaning that the majority of trainees never finish their agreed course of training (Dearing, 1996). In the context of the new training market, YT has a poor reputation among many of its customers – young people – who often see it as offering low-paid, exploitative work and poor-quality training (Wilkinson, 1995).

The Dearing Report proposed that, given the failure of YT to perform to an adequate standard, it be replaced by a new system of National Traineeships. These should be offered at a number of levels, lead to vocational qualifications, offer clear routes into Modern Apprenticeships (for details of which, see below), and cover broader as well as narrowly job-specific skills. The Government has agreed in principle to these recommendations.

The prospect for a successful transition from YT to National Traineeships is open to serious doubt. Previous attempts to provide an effective, high-quality work-based vocational training route have foundered upon the generally limited demand for more highly qualified young workers from employers. As Professor Alan Smithers has noted, it is unclear why, if employers have refused to offer adequate support to YTS and YT, they should be any more forthcoming towards National Traineeships (Pyke, 1996).

Modern Apprenticeships

In 1993, the increasingly apparent failure of YT to offer a high-quality vocational training route for young people, coupled with the continuing sharp decline in the number of apprenticeship training places being offered by British employers (down from 149,000 in 1980 to just 53,000 in 1990 on figures provided by employers to the Employment Department), forced the Government to introduce the Modern Apprenticeship scheme. These are training schemes for young workers that aim to provide job-related training to NVQ level 3, as well as covering broader, transferable core skills, such as communication, numeracy, and information technology. Modern Apprenticeships have been set up in industries and sectors where traditional apprenticeships have a long tradition, such as shipbuilding, as well as areas where such traditions are absent, such as childcare. Government financial support for the scheme covers only part of the costs, with employers expected to provide significant support.

Early indications are that, though well received by those employers who are participating, the scheme is not without its problems. Take-up of Modern Apprenticeships has been well below target, with just 23,500 on the scheme in February 1996 , as opposed to a hoped-for 60,000 by September 1996 (*The Observer*, 16 June 1996), and the quality of training on offer in some of the early modern apprenticeship pilots was low (*Times Educational Supplement*, 15 March 1996). It is also apparent that at least in the early days of the scheme, some TECs, anxious to meet their targets for Modern Apprenticeship places, have been more concerned with volume than quality, and have given scant heed to the needs of their local labour markets, or the competitive impact of the skills being created. In some cases this has meant a heavy concentration of apprenticeships being created in areas such as hairdressing, retailing and child care. Overall, in February 1996, 7.1 per cent of all Modern Apprenticeships were in hairdressing (*The Observer*, 16 June 1996). If these trends continue the impact of the scheme in helping make good Britain's oft-reported comparative deficit in craft and technician skills in manufacturing may be limited.

National Targets

The recently revised NTs for education and training, which have been established by the National Advisory Council for Education and Training Targets (NACETT) and endorsed by the Government in the 1995 White Paper on competitiveness, represent a minimum standard which it is believed the British workforce must achieve if the nation's international competitiveness is to be maintained. The National Targets also set the overall strategic performance indicators for the British VET system.

Unfortunately, there are already strong indications that many of the new, revised targets will not be achieved. NACETT noted in its 1995 progress report, that, unless there was a marked change of attitude and approach on the part of some employers, the lifetime learning targets would not be met (NACETT, 1995), a problem underlined by DfEE data (Employee Development Bulletin, January 1996, p. 3). A leaked draft of the Government's consultation paper on lifelong learning admitted that 'the scale of current lifetime learning remains well below the level required' (Ward, 1995)

There are also problems with the new Foundation Learning targets. Work undertaken for the Learning for the Future project suggests that there is little chance of hitting the first Foundation target of getting 60 per cent of young people to A level or its equivalent by the year 2000 (Richardson *et al.*, 1995), indeed there is doubt as to whether 50 per cent can be achieved by that date (Nash and Nicolls, 1995). Furthermore, research for the TEC National Council confirmed that, because of the number of 18–20-year-olds failing to find work, or enter education or training (about 230,000 in 1995, and set to rise to 280,000 by the year 2000), the Foundation targets were at risk (McGavin, 1996).

We will have to wait until 2000 to be certain of the effects of these trends, but of the three original Lifetime Learning targets originally set by the CBI in 1991, to be achieved by 1996 (CBI, 1991), none was met. Instead of all employees taking part in training and development activities, perhaps a third of adult workers are excluded from any training by their employer (Gallie and White, 1993; DfEE, 1996c, p. 71); rather than half of the employed workforce aiming for qualifications or units within the NVQ framework, no more than about 9 per cent of the workforce was doing so in 1995 (Spilsbury, Moralee and Evans, 1995); and instead of half of all large and medium-sized employers having achieved the Investors in People (IIP) standard, only 6 per cent of the relevant employers had achieved this by mid-1995 (NACETT, 1995). The scale of the mismatch between aspiration and reality underscores the depth and scope of the problem. The original targets were not simply missed, they were missed by miles.

Training system's general performance

These specific difficulties aside, how has the new training system performed? Chapter 11 details the overall levels of training currently taking place. In general terms, the data available support the conclusion that the overall volume (as measured in the proportion of employees receiving job-related training) has increased since the mid-1980s, with a particularly sharp increase in the late 1980s (DfEE, 1995, p. 72). In 1984, just over 8 per cent of the workforce reported being trained in the four weeks prior to the LFS interview. In spring 1994 (the last date for which we have figures comparable with earlier data), the proportion had risen to 13.1 per cent.

Large numbers of adult workers are however being left out. As mentioned above, Gallie and White's survey found about a third of adult employees were receiving no training, and recent Labour Force Survey figures appear to confirm this picture (DfEE, 1995), with 47 per cent of all employees who had received no training in the 13 weeks preceding the survey claiming that they had never been offered training by their current employer. The DfEE noted that 'this group represents one in three (34 per cent) of all employees' (*ibid.*, p. 71). Moreover, Machin and Wilkinson (1996) found that whereas half of all employees with degrees reported receiving training in the preceding year, just one-sixth of employees with no qualifications received any training. In general terms, training opportunities tend to be heavily skewed towards the best-paid and the best-qualified. Those lower in the organisational pecking order often receive little if any training, older workers tend to be neglected, and there are indications that the problems are worst for 'flexible', non-core workers, especially those in semi-skilled jobs (DfEE, 1995; CBI, 1994b; White, 1996).

Moreover, there remain questions about the quality of much of the training being provided. Data on training quality are limited, but what is available suggests significant weaknesses. One indicator is training course duration, which tells us something about the level of skills being imparted. Labour Force Survey data from spring 1994 indicated that 43 per cent of training courses lasted less than one week (Employment Department, 1994, p. 80), and 1993 LFS data showed that a quarter of training courses lasted a day or less (*Employee Development Bulletin*, November 1993). Moreover, only about 40 per cent of employer provided training is aimed at external qualifications, and where courses are aimed at qualifications these tend to be at the lower end of the spectrum – 79 per cent of all NVQs awarded in 1995 were at levels 1 and 2, and of non-NVQ vocational awards about 70 per cent were at the equivalent of NVQ levels 1 and 2 (DfEE, 1996c). As Felstead and Green remark, 'only a small proportion of those employees in training are working towards qualifications that would seem to equip them for the sorts of high/skill technology frontier jobs upon which it is regularly said that future prosperity depend' (Felstead and Green, 1996, p. 279).

Finally, changes that are currently taking place in companies' training systems raise doubts about the degree to which employers will deliver adequate levels of training in transferable or general skills, or meet the qualification levels specified by the NETTs. As Ashton, Storey and Felstead (forthcoming) demonstrate, some firms are removing specialist training departments and devolving responsibility to line managers. They are placing a much greater emphasis upon on-the-job training and are moving to a just-in-time, just-enough (as one of the big four retail banks puts it) approach to training spending and delivery. These developments are taking place against the backdrop of models of human resource management (HRM) that treat the company as an island and which have very little place for externally awarded, 'portable' national qualifications, which suggests at least in part the reason why the take-up of NVQs has proved so disappointing.

These difficulties, combined with the apparent impending failure to meet the baseline levels of training specified in the NETTs, suggest that, while there has been improvement, it has been too patchy, and far too slow. If the Reichian model of internal competitiveness is correct, significant parts of the British economy are likely to be in trouble in meeting overseas competition.

Inconsistencies and tensions within the new VET system

Besides the apparent inability of the new system to deliver the results which were originally promised, the system is also riddled with features that appear to contradict the basic ideology and design principles outlined above. For example, if the CBI believes in a training market (and it was the CBI that originally coined the phrase), why then does it also believe that the NETTs are necessary? For proponents of a free market solution to training problems, a genuine training market would be one where individuals and employers, acting in accordance with their own self-determined best interests, would decide the levels and types of training undertaken. Whatever level of activity took place as a result of those decisions would be the optimal level. The work of NACETT represents an attempt to second guess the market, and to impose what might appear to be centrally planned production targets. Hence the existence of NACETT and the National Targets suggests either confusion, or an implicit recognition by the CBI and others of the inherent dangers of market failure in the current system, with the decisions of individual employees and firms producing results that are economically rational when viewed from the perspective of those making the decisions, but which taken in total produce levels of training that are suboptimal from the point of view of society and the British economy as a whole.

Moreover, in a genuine training market, employers and individuals should be free to use any type of vocational qualification, and this choice should be made without the introduction of distortions in the competition between the various qualification providers. As noted above, the Government has instead chosen to introduce substantial distortions in competition, by effectively offering a heavy subsidy to NVQs. Those on government-sponsored training schemes (such as YT and Training for Work) must be aiming for NVQs, and, until very recently, only courses leading to NVQs have qualified for tax relief for the individual paying for such courses.

A more fundamental contradiction is the fact that many employers have criticised the architecture and operation of aspects of a system which, ostensibly, they have designed and are now responsible for running. A clear example here would be employer complaints about NVQs (Beaumont, 1995; CBI, 1994b). At an even more basic level, we are faced with the paradox of what is ostensibly an employer-led training system in which many employers have never heard of some of its major institutional components. Thus, for example, the *Skill Needs in Britain* survey (Spilsbury, 1996) suggests that slightly more than a third of employers were unaware of the Investors in People initiative, 63 per cent were not acquainted with Youth Credits, and, most worryingly of all, 73 per cent were unaware of the National Targets. If more than two-thirds of all employers do not know that the Targets exist, it is unlikely that they are gearing their training efforts to meet them.

Besides casting further serious doubt on the likelihood that the National Targets will be achieved, this situation also raises questions about what we mean by an employer-led training system. The employers who sit on NACETT (and its Scottish sister organisation, SCACETT) can hardly be said to be representative of the majority of British employers, if only because they actually know what the Targets are. More generally, there is a clear danger that the largely self-selected groups of individual managers who sit on bodies such as the TECs, LECs, NACETT, and the CBI's various education and training committees and sub-committees, hold views about training that do not accurately reflect those of the majority of employers.

In summary, even if one accepts the argument that improvements in the supply of skills can bring about a transformatory 'skills revolution' in Britain, the at best partial success of many of the main institutional reforms, coupled with a number of deep-seated inconsistencies in the design and operation of the new employer-led training market, suggest that many difficulties remain to be overcome. While there have been improvements in the levels of training activity, a skills revolution has not only not yet been achieved, but is by no means assured as a realistic goal in the future.

THE UNDERLYING PROBLEM

We would argue that underlying these institutional failings is a much deeper problem which centres on the level of demand for skill within the British economy. We have argued elsewhere (Keep and Mayhew, 1995, 1996) that policy-makers may be mistaken in concluding that a policy thrust aimed almost exclusively at the supply side, and therefore at changes to the institutional mechanisms of skill formation and delivery, will of itself prove to be sufficient to crack a problem that has confronted Britain for well over a hundred years. There is a considerable body of evidence that weakness in the underlying demand for skills and qualifications has been a long-standing phenomenon within our economy (Glynn and Gospel, 1993), and that this problem persists (Keep and Mayhew, 1995, 1996).

The reasons why demand for skill is currently limited within the UK economy are various, complex, and, we would argue, often closely inter-related. Taken in total, they may represent a form of systems failure, of a type which represents a major challenge to policy-makers (see Hutton, 1995, for details of the argument that there is a general systems failure in British political and economic life). In the space available we can only seek to highlight some of the most important facets of this problem. For a more detailed exposition of the difficulties relating to education and training, see Keep and Mayhew, 1995, 1996)

Market failure

Current training policies are aimed at creating a 'training market'. As with any market, there is a danger of market failure. In the case of training, the problems of the poaching of skilled labour and the inability of the firm to be certain of securing an adequate return on any investment in enhancing their employees' human capital, means that companies may decide upon levels of training that make sense for them as individual companies, but which in aggregate, produce a suboptimal level of activity when viewed from the perspective of society as whole (for a fuller exposition, see Stevens, 1996; Greenhalgh and Mavrotas, 1996). These problems are liable to be more acute in Britain than some other European countries because there is no legal compulsion on employers to train, and also because Britain has a relatively high level of job mobility compared to other EC and OECD countries (Van Ours, 1990).

As has been suggested above, a recognition of the danger of market failure is implicit in the adoption of the National Targets, and has been explicitly acknowledged by the CBI in relation to the training of non-core or 'flexible' workers (CBI, 1994b, p. 33). Greehalgh and Mavrotas (1996, p. 141) indicate that the problem is particularly acute for younger, more qualified workers in the private sector, and suggest that 'further attention must be given to resolving under-investment in training arising from high turnover in the British labour market'.

Structure of domestic demand

In the last twenty years the British economy has seen increasing levels of inequality and a dramatic rise in the numbers of those living in relative poverty (Goodman and Webb, 1994). Overall, a fifth of the EU's poor reside in the United Kingdom (Commission for Social Justice, 1993, p. 22) and one in four of the British population now live in households with less than half the average disposable income (Joseph Rowntree Foundation, 1996).

This has implications for the demand for skills within the economy. A large group of people living on limited means implies that within the domestic UK market there will be a significant demand for goods and services sold on the basis of price rather than quality, with knock-on effects on the demand for skills from those companies seeking to cater to this market segment. Kempson's (1996) study of research on the lives of those on low incomes confirms the importance of price as the dominant criterion for purchasing decisions among this group, and their general exclusion from the 'consumer society'. It is perhaps no coincidence that the director-general of the CBI – a body publicly committed to the concept of a high-skills economy – has suggested that increases in real incomes are needed in Britain. 'In the long term', the CBI believes, 'business cannot flourish without the broad mass of people enjoying the benefits of economic success at the same time' (Turner, 1996) – a view endorsed by the OECD in its most recent *Employment Outlook* (OECD, 1996).

The changing structure of the labour market

The changing structure of the British labour market also raises doubts about the viability of the Reichian model of competition based on enhanced workforce skills, and upon the relevance of current VET policies. Britain now possesses (jointly with America) the most deregulated labour market in the developed world (OECD, 1994), and government policies have sought to foster this development as part of a strategy of creating the United Kingdom as an 'enterprise economy', which in part competes on the basis of low labour costs. This policy and the changes it has helped encourage in the labour market, coupled with shifts in the pattern of employment growth, may make it harder for Britain to become a high-skill, high-wage economy.

Government commentaries have tended to place a gloss on occupational trends that stresses the growth of professional, managerial and technical occupations, taking this as an indication of a rising demand for higher-level skills within the economy (Employment Department, 1994). The DfEE's latest volume of *Labour Market and Skill Trends* advances the view that 'for many years the occupational mix of employment in the UK has been moving towards higher level occupations and away from manual, particularly lower skilled manual jobs' (DfEE, 1995, p. 41).

Unfortunately, this tells us only part of the story. While both unskilled and skilled manual employment in manufacturing has been in sharp decline since the early 1980s, and managerial and professional work for the more highly qualified has been growing, there has been a less well heralded parallel growth in relatively lowly skilled (though in official definitional terms, non-manual) employment in the services sector. Thus, the latest Institute of Employment Research (IER) projections of occupational growth to the year 2001 indicate that, along with increases in managerial work (set to rise 15 per cent between 1994 and 2001), professional occupations (up 18 per cent), and associate professional and technical (up 14 per cent), employment in personal and protective services is likely to increase by 24 per cent. This group grew by over a third between 1981 and 1994, and the rises in the near future will be steeper still (*ibid*, pp. 41–2). The other growing sector will be sales and service occupations. The IER expect that growth in sales, and in personal and protective services will be concentrated in 'less-skilled and frequently part-time posts' (*Employment Development Bulletin*, november 1995, p. 15). What the projections suggest therefore, is not a general rise in demand for higher-level skills across the whole economy, but a continuing polarisation of employment opportunities, with more highly skilled managerial and professional jobs, a continuing decline in skilled manual occupations in manufacturing (such as craft and technician posts), and further significant increases in relatively poorly paid employment in the service sector's equivalent of unskilled and semi-skilled manual work.

The picture in terms of sectoral growth within the economy is perhaps even less reassuring. Between 1996 and 2001 the fastest-growing sectors of employment will be distribution, hotels and catering, which will generate the biggest job gains in absolute terms (642,000). By 1994, with 5.4 million workers, this sector already accounted for nearly 22 per cent of UK employment (81). The record of the hotels and catering industry, in terms of its personnel policies, provision of training and use of skills, is not impressive, even by UK standards (Price, 1994; Lucas, 1996).

Moreover, recent years have witnessed other structural shifts in employment that are liable to undermine attempts to improve training provision and enhance skill supply. For example, between 1981 and 1994 increases in part-time employment accounted for about 1.5 million new jobs, while the number of full-time employees fell by 1.9 million over the same period, resulting in an increase in part-timers' share of total employment from 21 to 28 per cent. Part-time work is projected to rise by a further 1.3 million (22 per cent) between 1994 and 2001, while full-time work falls by another 0.2 million, so that part-timers will make up 32.4 per cent of the workforce at the start of the next millennium (DfEE, 1995, pp. 11–19). Self-employment will increase by 13 per cent over the same period, accounting for almost 14 per cent of all employment by 2001 (*ibid.*, p. 17). Finally, the CBI reports (1994b) that the use of temporary workers may have risen rapidly since 1993, and could account for 7 per cent of total employment. Hence, in overall terms, if the projections for the increases in part-time work and self-employment prove correct, and if the number of temporary workers stays static, then by the year 2001, official projections suggest that about 40 per cent of the workforce will either be part-timers, self-employed, or temps.

Unfortunately, the evidence available indicates that self-employment, employment in small firms, and part-time and temporary working are all strongly associated with lower than average levels of training activity (Employment Department, 1994; CBI, 1994b; DfEE, 1995), and the Employment Department admitted in 1993 that the growth of employment within these areas could have serious negative consequences for both training activity and demand for skills (Employment Department, 1993). Dex and McCulloch (1995, p. 137), in their comprehensive overview of flexible employment in Britain, concluded that, because of the impact of a deregulated labour market and the increasing use of flexible employment practices,

'Britain is sliding into being a low wage, low skill, economy in which the quality of jobs is declining'.

Learning pays?

Pay differentials have risen in Britain in the last ten to fifteen years, this being accounted for largely in terms of the increased earnings of those with degree-level qualifications, and the decline (as a percentage of the median earnings of all males) experienced by those with no qualifications, or with CSEs below grade 1 and its equivalent (DfEE/Cabinet Office, 1996, pp. 20–1). Nevertheless, a straightforward assumption that learning pays is not as easy to substantiate as is sometimes suggested. As the DfEE (1995) recently admitted, a factor influencing individual's willingness to train 'is uncertainty about what benefits they personally would gain from training . . . individuals may be doubtful whether employers will recognise the value of their training (In contrast they can be quite certain of most of the costs they will incur.)'.

Such doubts may be well-founded, as the role of formal skills and quali-fications in recruitment and selection, both for initial entry to employment, and for promotion, are often limited (Collinson, 1988). For example, a report by the organisation Industry in Education (which is sponsored by a number of large firms) suggests that employers are increasingly using informal chan-nels to recruit 16–18-year-olds and that many employers appear to 'discount qualifications in favour of candidates' personal qualities' (Industry in Educa-tion, 1996). The report goes on to criticise young people for an over-reliance on qualifications as a means of securing employment. In today's labour market, at best, qualifications may be a necessary rather than sufficient precondition for employment.

THE LINK BETWEEN SKILLS AND ECONOMIC SUCCESS

Finally, the relationship between training, skills, qualifications, and economic success is far less simple and direct than many commentators and policy-makers choose to assume. At the level of nation state there seems to be a link between fast economic growth, high productivity, and high levels of educa-tion and training (more so education than training) within the general popu-lation. The 'tiger' economies of South East Asia are frequently cited as examples of countries whose rapid growth can, in part, be attributed to significant investment in education and training. The NIESR studies have demonstrated a positive relationship between levels of skill and qualification in the workforce, and higher productivity and enhanced quality of goods and services (Prais, 1990). However, a clear link between training and profit-ability, or training and earnings per share, or training and dividend pay-outs – all measures of crucial importance to investors and managers – is difficult, if not impossible, to prove (for further discussion of this problem, see Lee, 1996). The DfEE and the Cabinet Office, in the *Skills Audit* which they undertook as part of the preparations for the third White Paper on competitiveness, admit that 'while there is much research into UK management, none has established to what extent good training contributes to good management, and good management to company performance' (DfEE/Cabinet Office, 1996, p. 43).

The problem with linking training to economic success suggests that a single model of competitive advantage based solely on skill, as advanced by Reich and Thurow, may not accord with present-day reality in Britain. In fact, companies are faced with a choice of product market strategy and with a variety of means of securing competitive advantage in the short, medium and long term. Some of these can be pursued in parallel with attempts to upgrade skills, but others are more or less incompatible with a high-skill, high-wage, high-value-added approach.

A number of these alternatives are outlined below. They are presented in two groups, the first of which comprises a number of individual strategies that companies can pursue, and the second of which covers a set of mutually reinforcing sources of competitive advantage which can serve as an alternative to a high-skill, high-spec strategy.

Seek protected markets

The first alternative, though one available to only a relatively limited number of firms, is to operate, as far as possible, within protected markets. In the United Kingdom, defence procurement provides opportunities for high-tech manufacturers to operate in markets where the strategic nature of the defence systems they are supplying to the British government effectively preclude exposure to overseas competition. The contest between two of Britain's leading high-tech manufacturers – GEC and British Aerospace – to takeover the VSEL shipbuilding concern illustrates this tendency. The market to supply the Royal Navy with nuclear-powered submarines may be limited, indeed in the long term dwindling, but it has the advantage of being one in which overseas shipyards are effectively debarred from competing. Outside of defence, the growth of international competition has meant that, in the manufacturing sector, other such opportunities are now rare. However, in the service sector there still remain substantial areas of activity, such as garages, retail banking, and personal and protective services (for example, security guards and private nursing and retirement homes), where international competition is limited.

Growth through acquisition

As recent economic history shows, another route to apparent competitive advantage is the use of take-overs as a means of easing competitive pressures and as a source of rapid growth. The economy has witnessed a number of major merger waves in recent times, and, despite the poor evidence for the success of mergers as a means of improving company performance (Dickerson, Gibson and Tsakalotos, 1995), this competitive strategy continues to receive enthusiastic endorsement from British companies and financial institutions. In 1995, UK acquisitions totalled 1,500 with a combined value of £66 billion (10 per cent of the value of London Stock Exchange) (Springett, 1995). Proportionately, merger activity in the United Kingdom runs at far higher levels than in most other countries, being well ahead of even the United States (Richards, 1996). Banks, building societies, electricity and water companies, pharmaceuticals, hotels, and the media have all been sectors where mergers and acquisitions activity has been particularly high.

It can be argued (Hutton, 1995) that by concentrating on mergers, rather than upon organic growth, British business has tended to under-invest in the conditions that might support higher levels of organic growth, such as a highly skilled workforce, or more up-to-date plant and machinery. It is certainly noticeable that, by contrast with the vast sums being expended on the market in corporate control, manufacturing investment in plant remains extremely sluggish.

Outward investment

A complementary strategy, and one that has become of increasing importance for many large firms, has been to shift investment and capacity overseas. As we have pointed out elsewhere (Keep and Mayhew, 1996) more and more big 'British' firms are, in fact, becoming multinational corporations, the majority of whose workforces are employed outside the United Kingdom. This is happening for a variety of reasons, for example, to get closer to the customer and the fastest-growing markets. During the 1980s as a whole, for every pound of inward investment attracted into Britain, British companies exported two pounds of capital abroad. In 1995, the ratio of capital export to imports was three to one (Halsall, 1995).

These changes are having a profound effect upon skilled manufacturing employment in Britain, as well as upon skill supply mechanisms, such as the modern apprenticeships, which tend to rely upon large companies to provide a disproportionate amount of the total skills training undertaken. As British operations become increasingly marginal to the well-being of the group as a whole, this expectation may become less and less realistic. Big British-headquartered multinational manufacturers may be competing successfully in world markets, with highly skilled workforces, but, in many cases, more and more of these workforces are employed and trained overseas.

Monopoly power and industrial concentration

Another avenue is the pursuit of monopoly power and of high levels of industrial concentration as a protection against the rigours of competition. Many of the privatised utilities are in the happy position of facing little real competition in the market-place. Their major strategic consideration is to contain and reduce costs in order to continue to make profits under their regulatory regimes, and thereby to maintain dividend records that allow them to fend off hostile takeover bids. Where competition has loomed, the response has not been to invest in people and thereby improve the quality of product or service, but instead to look to further cost reductions, and to mergers leading to vertical integration and tied customers, as the preferred strategy. Elsewhere, there is evidence that some of the large retail chains are willing to pursue predatory pricing policies as a means of wiping out competition from smaller, independent retailers (a point discussed at greater length below).

The new Fordism, cost-cutting and business process re-engineering

This brings us to a set of related strategies, which can of course be combined with some of those outlined above, that centres upon standardisation and rationalisation of product lines, often allied with utilising economies of scale, in order to drive down costs. Fordism and mass production may be unfashionable in manufacturing, but many of the large service-sector firms, in areas such as retail, banking and insurance, are delivering relatively narrow ranges of highly standardised goods and services, and are using the economy of scale advantages that accrue from this to compete on the basis of cost, and to drive out smaller competitors. Changes in the high streets of most towns in the United Kingdom are testimony, at least in part, to the efficacy of such a strategy.

Putting pressure on suppliers can be another element in this approach. In some cases, supplier chain pressure is concerned with upgrading quality, and in these cases the skills and training of suppliers' workforces may be directly targeted for improvement by the retailer. In other cases, particularly in food retailing, the purchasing power of the giant supermarket chains appears to be being used largely to squeeze the margins of food manufacturing companies.

An over-arching consideration within this type of strategy is often a desire to build competitive advantage on the basis of low costs, and to compete in the market-place on the basis of price advantage. Where considerations of price rather than product specification or product quality have primacy in determining competitive strategy, skill requirements will normally be lower than would be the case if delivery of a high-spec good or service was seen as the key to business success. Competition on the basis of cost also often brings in its wake a range of cost-cutting measures, such as de-layering, subcontracting, and the casualisation of the workforce. It is worth noting that in America, from whence the fashion for strategies based upon these types of corporate 'downsizing' and 'business process re-engineering' sprang, there is an increasingly strong perception that they have often failed to improve long-term corporate performance (Bridges, 1996; Sherman, 1995; Mumford and Hendricks, 1996).

In Britain, such measures certainly have very direct effects upon the style of personnel management techniques that are deployed, not least in terms of creating a large, peripheral workforce towards whom the employer feels minimal commitment and in whose training they are generally unwilling to invest (CBI, 1994b). Insofar as companies are choosing pathways to success other than one based on using the skills and knowledge of the workforce to upgrade product quality and product spec, their demand for skills and qualifications is liable to be limited, as is their need to practice any developmental form of human resource management (HRM).

The evidence suggests that, whereas many firms have taken up the rhetoric of HRM, or implemented in a very piecemeal fashion isolated elements of the HRM model, the full-blown adoption of 'soft', developmental HRM remains relatively rare (Sisson, 1994; Millward, 1994; Ezzamel, Lilley and Wilmott, 1996). In terms of judging the underlying priorities afforded to different competitive strategies by British firms, this suggests that, whatever the rhetoric, in reality most managements are either unwilling or unable to put in place the types of people management systems that would support a strategy of competitive advantage built around an employment relationship that stressed high levels of trust, commitment and skills. Indeed, an approach based around Taylorism, the threat of increased job insecurity, and a 'hard' variant of HRM that stresses control rather than real commitment, appears to hold the deep-seated appeal of familiarity to many in senior British management. The adoption of this approach to 'sweating' the human assets, may also, in part, stem from the fact that it is seen as producing results within a short timescale.

Nowhere is evidence of this strategy, and of the ingrained reluctance to believe in the competitive benefits of commitment, trust, and of helping people to develop and deploy their skills to best effect, rather than simply forcing them to work harder, more apparent than in the field of managerial employment. Recently, attention has been focused on the increased threat (whether real or imagined) of job insecurity, and the growth of long working hours, particularly among managers.

On working hours, a survey found that British men work longer than any of their European counterparts (Austin Knight, 1995), and pressure to put in excessive hours being greatest upon male senior managers, just under half of whom were found to be working 50 hours or more a week. The survey also revealed that many employees felt under pressure to work longer hours or face the risk of being singled out for redundancy. As one senior manager recently admitted, 'what we actually practice is Taylorism, chaining people to their desks and just turning the wick up under them to get more out of them' (Guest and Mackenzie Davey, 1996, p. 23). Ironically, even while implementing policies and practices that implicitly support this culture, companies admitted that longer working hours reduced performance and lowered morale (Austin Knight, 1995).

'Turning up the wick' under managerial employees has in some cases been achieved through decreasing levels of job security for managers, and a unilateral renegotiation of the 'psychological contract' of employment by the employer. These changes, brought about by de-layering, downsizing, and, in some cases by a simple desire to manage through fear, have seen companies holding the threat of redundancy over many of their employees. Research by Hallier and Lyon (1996) in the engineering sector underlines the negative impact that this threat can have upon managerial attitudes and commitment. They suggest (p. 39) that:

> The traditional psychological contract is not only under threat directly from employer action, but also indirectly from managerial reactions to the 'new order' being created in many firms. If the experiences of these managers mirror those of others in the UK, there may be considerable long-term damage being wrought on employers' most valuable asset – managerial commitment . . . the proliferation of more cautious managers may mean an even greater gulf opening up between HRM rhetoric and current organisational realities.

These findings are replicated by the work of Kessler and Undy (1996), and Hirsch and Jackson (1996).

Growing concern about personnel management practices in British firms has led the Institute of Personnel and Development (IPD) to call for a major inquiry into the state of employment relations in the United Kingdom (IPD, 1996). The IPD's director-general commented: 'too many employers have failed to recognise that a cowed, compliant workforce will not deliver competitive success . . . if managers want people who will stick their necks out rather than keep their heads down, they will have to rebuild the trust that has been lost' (*IRS Employment Trends*, August 1996, p. 4).

COMPETITIVE STRATEGIES AND SKILLS – AN OVERVIEW

Unfortunately, it is extremely difficult to obtain a precise and up-to-date picture of what proportion of employers are following the different approaches to competitive advantage outlined above. Besides the volatility of many companies' strategies, a major problem is that the vast majority of firms have adopted the rhetoric of human resource management (HRM), and total quality management (TQM), and its near universal usage serves to obscure the diverse range of practices and policies that is in reality being pursued. Indeed, as Gerald Ratner discovered, honesty about your firm's product market strategy may prove very expensive. Thus, with the exception of the discount retail chains, few firms in the service sector will admit in public that their competitive advantage stems primarily from economies of scale, a highly standardised range of products, and the use of relatively low-cost, casualised labour; rather than from the supply of high-quality goods and services, and the provision of excellent customer care.

These problems notwithstanding, looking across the British economy it is apparent that some companies are attempting to follow the type of trajectory advocated by the Reichian model, particularly in those sectors of manufacturing and services most exposed to international competition. There is evidence, however, as suggested above, from the poor take-up of sophisticated models of HRM, that the number of firms seeking to maximise skills and commitment may be relatively limited.

Some companies appear to be attempting a mixed model, with limited efforts at upskilling parts of their workforce as one element within competitive strategies that also place a heavy stress on cost-cutting, increasing casualisation (and sometimes de-skilling) of parts of the workforce, and organisational restructuring aimed at achieving significant economy of scale advantages. UK retail banking, with its moves to casualise some areas of staffing, and the 'factoryisation' of areas of work into large, mass production units (such as customer enquiry and customer care telephone services), while introducing advanced IT systems, would appear to be an example of this approach.

Other employers give every indication that they are heading in the opposite direction to the Reichian model. Their competitive strategy is based on price rather than quality or high product spec, and on standardisation and economy of scale advantages rather than the supply of higher value-added goods and services. Any substantial enhancement of general workforce skills plays a minimal role in such a model. In the service sector, the discount food retailer chains would be good examples of this trend. In manufacturing, a significant proportion of the clothing industry appears to remain locked into this style of operation (Lloyd and Rawlinson, 1992; Harijan, 1991). As has been suggested above, there are reasons embedded within the structure of domestic income distribution and demand that dictate that, at least within those organisations that cater primarily for the domestic market, the adoption of a cost-based product market strategy will make sense for at least a proportion of organisations operating in this market.

Overall, the prognosis is not particularly encouraging. The present major thrust of current personnel policies in many large British employers is to reduce headcounts and to cut labour costs by whatever means are necessary. Far from treating employees as a potential source of competitive advantage, they are seen as a source of costs that must be minimised. Moreover, there are indications that at least some parts of the economy are locked into a 'low skills equilibrium' (Finegold and Sosfice, 1988), where cost-based, low-spec competitive strategies limit the demand for additional skills (Prais, 1990; Temple, 1994; Oulton, 1993; Doyle, Saunders and Wong, 1992; Prais and Jarvis, 1996). As Buxton, Mayers and Murfin noted in the first edition of this volume (1994, p. 147), in relative terms Britain has been shifting towards 'a less skilled, less technically intensive product mix'.

The long-term success of the cost-driven focus being adopted by many firms is open to question. The alternatives to a high-skills, high-spec, high-wage strategy, for some companies at least, may prove to be culs-de-sac, rather than avenues to sustainable competitive advantage. Unfortunately, there is a danger that the use of business strategies that centre around cost reduction and growth through acquisition, may leave firms so anorexic, and so stuck in a routine of rounds of cost-cutting, that they lack the strategic vision, managerial capacity, up-to-date plant and equipment, and skills base that would enable them to have the option of moving in any other direction. Even if firms decide that a different competitive strategy is required for their long-term survival, they may find themselves lacking the wherewithal to render such a change feasible (Doyle, Saunders and Wong, 1992).

A final problem is that in thinking about the influence of competitive strategy upon skill levels and training, there is a tendency to focus on the effects within the single company whose policies are being examined. In fact, particularly in the case of large companies, the impact may be much wider. Supplier chain pressure is one example of this, but there are others. For instance, as mentioned above, the growth of large retail chains and the associated development of out-of-town retail centres has revolutionised the face of the British high street. Many small, specialist retailers have been squeezed out of business. The net effect of this process upon the overall level of demand for skills in the economy may have been negative.

For example, many traditional hardware shops, staffed by assistants who could advise customers about the use of tools and materials, have been replaced by DIY chains that are often little more than warehouses staffed by personnel whose expertise is limited to shelf-stacking and bar-code scanning. Another instance, would be baking. At present, a number of the large supermarket chains are alleged to be selling bread at cost price or less in an attempt to wipe out competition from both the large-scale plant bakeries and also smaller, independent craft bakers (Blythman, 1996; *The British Baker*, 9 February 1996, pp. 4–5; 23 February 1996, p. 11; 1 March 1996, p. 9). Moreover, the 'fresh' bread sold by the supermarkets is increasingly being mass-produced as pre-formed loaves at a central factory and then simply re-heated at the supermarket 'bakery' (*The Bakers Review*, February 1996, p. 10; Blythman, 1995), a move with obvious implications for the long-term skill requirements of bakery staff in supermarkets. Thus, even where the big retailer has itself a generally good record on the training and upskilling of its own workforce, it is by no means clear that the overall impact of its outlets upon the local economies and their resultant skill requirements, will, in aggregate, be positive. The big retailers may, through competitive strategies based on predatory pricing, be wiping out skilled employment elsewhere in the retail sector, in this case in small craft bakeries where production staff are normally required to possess the skills to undertake the production of bread from raw ingredients to finished product.

FINAL THOUGHTS

It will be apparent that the types of issue outlined above reflect trends and preferences that are deeply embedded in the fabric of British economic life and reflect the structural imprint of, among other factors, national history, the course of economic development, corporate culture, and perhaps also the evolution of the Anglo-Saxon model of corporate finance. These traits are not easy to reconfigure, and the type of policy focus that has stressed voluntarism, and an employer-led, market-based approach appears one that holds out limited prospects for rapid and fundamental change. In particular, the stress on reforming the institutional mechanisms of skill supply, while doing little to try to change the underlying structural circumstances that affect levels of demand for skills, appears unlikely to produce either the level or speed of results desired by policy-makers. Thus, it is hard to see how or why, of themselves, TECs, NVQs, or the National Targets, can make any rapid or significant impact upon changing the British economy's structural characteristics in ways that would seriously enhance the perceived role for training and skills within corporate competitive strategies.

At present there appears to be limited interest on the part of policy-makers at any point on the mainstream political spectrum in confronting many of the fundamental problems which the later part of this chapter has raised. There is hence a danger that policy-making will remain, for the fore-seeable future, stuck in the tramlines of supply-side initiatives aimed at boosting the numbers of those being trained and perhaps also aimed at improving, at the margins, the quality of some of the training on offer. Whether these policies take the form of current initiatives, or of individual learning accounts and a learning bank, they will, we would argue, tend to produce suboptimal results unless and until they are coupled with wider measures that seek to link improvements in the supply and delivery of VET with major efforts to stimulate employers' demand for skills and to improve the utilisation of skills within the workplace.

As a study undertaken in Leeds, Sheffield and Wakefield reported, in the face of a rising supply of better educated and trained labour, employers were reacting by recruiting the available qualified people without regard to the actual needs of the job. The study concluded that 'having qualified people at work is one thing, using them to generate a competitive advantage – as envisaged by the National Targets – is quite another' (Rajan and Jasper, 1995). The great danger of current policies is that we will end up with a more highly qualified workforce, many of whom will occupy low-paid, insecure, dead-end jobs, producing low-cost, low-spec goods and services, with no discernible improvement in competitive performance resulting.

REFERENCES

Ashton, D., Storey, D. and Felstead, D. (forthcoming) 'Towards the learning organisation? Current trends in training practice in the UK', *Human Resource Management Journal.*

Austin Knight (1995) *The Family Friendly Workplace*, London: Austin Knight.

Beaumont, G. (1996) *Beaumont Report on the Most Used National Vocational Qualifications and Scottish Vocational Qualifications (NVQs/SVQs)*, London: DfEE.

Blythman, J. (1996) 'A slice of life', *The Guardian Weekend*, 1 July, pp. 36–7.

Bridges, W. (1996) 'A requiem for loyalty', *Human Resources*, January/February, p. 15.

Buxton, T., Mayers, D. and Murfin, A. (1994) 'Research and development and trading performance', in T. Buxton, P. Chapman and P. Temple (eds) *Britain's Economic Performance*, London: Routledge, pp. 144–59.

Chubb, J. and Moe, T. (1992) 'How to get the best from Britain's schools', *The Sunday Times Magazine*, 9 February, pp. 18–36.

Collinson, D. (1988) *Barriers to Fair Selection: A multi-sector study of recruitment practices*, London: HMSO.

Commission for Social Justice (1993) *The Justice Gap*, London: Institute of Public Policy Research.

Confederation of British Industry, (CBI)(1991) *World Class Targets: A joint initiative to achieve Britain's skills revolution*, London: CBI.

—— (1994b) *Flexible Labour Markets – Who Pays for Training?*, London: CBI.

Confederation of British Industry (1994a) *Quality Assured – the CBI Review of NVQs and SVQs*, London: CBI.

Dearing, R. (1996) *Review of Vocational Qualifications for 16–19 year olds*, York: Schools Curriculum and Assessment Authority.

Department for Education and Employment (DfEE)(1995) *Labour Market and Skill Trends, 1996/97*, Sheffield: DfEE.

Department for Education and Employment/Cabinet Office (1996) 'The Skills Audit – a report from an interdepartmental group', *Competitiveness Occasional Paper*, London: DfEE/Cabinet Office, pp. 20–1.

Department for Education and Employment, (1996a) *Maximising Potential New Options for Learning After 16*, Sheffield: DfEE.

—— (1996b)'NCVQ 1996 quinquennial review – executive summary', London: DfEE (mimeo).

—— (1996c) 'Awards of vocational qualifications 1991/92 to 1994/95', *DfEE Statistics Bulletin*, No. 4/96, May.

—— (1996d) 'NCVQ 1995–1996 Quinquennial Review – Stage Two Report', London: DfEE (mimeo).

Department of Trade and Industry (1994) *Competitiveness – Helping Business to Win*, Cm 2563, London: HMSO.

—— (1995) *Competitiveness – Forging Ahead*, Cm 2867, London: HMSO.

—— (1996) *Competitiveness – Creating the Enterprise Centre of Europe*, Cm 3300, London: HMSO.

Dex, S. and McCulloch, A. (1995) 'Flexible employment in Britain: a statistical analysis', *Research Discussion Series*, No. 15, Manchester: Equal Opportunities Commission.

Dickerson, A. P., Gibson, H. D. and Tsakalotos, E. (1995) 'The impact of acquisitions on company performance: evidence from a large panel of UK firms', *Studies in Economics*, no. 95/11, Canterbury: University of Kent, Department of Economics.

Doyle, P., Saunders, J. and Wong, V. (1992) 'Competition in global markets – a case study of American and Japanese competition in the British market', *Journal of International Business Studies*, vol. 23, no. 3, pp. 419–42.

Employment Department, (1993) *Labour Market and Skill Trends 1994/95*, Sheffield: ED.

Employment Department (1994) *Labour Market and Skill Trends 1995/96*, Sheffield: ED.

Ezzamel, M., Lilley, S. and Wilmott, H. (1996) 'The view from the top: senior executives' perceptions of changing management practices in UK companies', *British Journal of Management*, vol. 7, issue 2, pp. 155–68.

Felstead, A. and Green, F. (1996) 'Training implications of regulation compliance and business cycles', in A. Booth and D. J. Snower (eds), *Acquiring Skills*, Cambridge: Cambridge University Press, pp. 255–83.

Finegold, D. *et al.*, (1990) *A British Baccalaureat: Ending the division between education and training*, London: Institute of Public Policy Research.

Finegold, D. and Soskice, D. (1988) 'The failure of training in Britain: Analysis and prescription', *Oxford Review of Economic Policy*, vol. 4, no. 3, pp. 21–53.

Gallie, D. and White, M. (1993) *Employee Commitment and the Skills Revolution*, London: Policy Studies Institute.

Glynn, S. and Gospel, H. (1993) 'Britain's low skill equilibrium: a problem of demand?', *Industrial Relations Journal*, vol. 24, no. 2, pp. 112–25.

Goodman, A. and Webb, S. (1994) *For Richer, For Poorer: The Changing Distribution of Income in the United Kingdom, 1961–91*, London: Institute of Fiscal Studies.

Greenhalgh, C. and Mavrotas, G. (1996) 'Job training, new technology and labour turnover', *British Journal of Industrial Relations*, vol. 34, no. 1, pp. 131–50.

Guest. D. and Mackenzie Davey, K. (1996) 'Don't write off the traditional career', *People Management*, February, pp. 22–5.

Hallier, J. and Lyon, P. (1996) 'Managing to look after number one', *People Management*, 2 May, pp. 38–9.

Halsall, M. (1995) 'The foreign fields of England', *The Guardian*, 30 December.

Harijan, L. (1991) 'New technology, management strategies and shop floor workers', unpublished PhD thesis, University of Leicester.

Hirsch, W. and Jackson, C. (1996) *Strategies for Career Development*, Brighton: Institute of Employment Studies.

Hutton, W. (1995) *The State We're In*, London: Routledge.

Industry in Education, (1996) *Towards Employability*, London: IiE.

Institute of Personnel and Development (1996) 'IPD statement on employment relations', London: IPD.

Joseph Rowntree Foundation (1996) 'Life on a low income', *Findings – Social Policy Research* no. 97, York: JRF, June.

Keep, E. and Mayhew, K. (1994) 'The changing structure of training provision', in T. Buxton, P. Chapman and P. Temple (eds) *Britain's Economic Performance*, London: Routledge, pp. 308–41.

—— (1995) 'Training policy for competitiveness', in H. Metcalf (ed.), *Future Skill Demand and Supply*, London: Policy Studies Institute, pp. 110–45.

—— (1993) 'Evaluating assumptions that underlie training policy', in A. Booth and

D. J. Snower (eds), *Acquiring Skills*, Cambridge: Cambridge University Press, pp. 305–34.

Kempson, E. (1996) *Life on a Low Income*, York: Joseph Rowntree Foundation.

Kesler, I. and Undy, R. (1996) 'The new employment relationship: examining the psychological contract', *Issues in People Management*, no. 12, London: IPD.

Lee, R. (1996) 'What makes training pay?', *Issues in People Management*, No. 11, London: Institute of Personnel and Development.

Lloyd, C. and Rawlinson, M. (1992) 'New technology and human resource management', in P. Blyton and P. Turbull (eds) *Reassessing Human Resource Management*, London: Sage, pp. 185–99.

Lucas, R. (1996) 'Industrial relations in hotels and catering, neglect and paradox', *British Journal of Industrial Relations*, vol. 34, no. 2, pp. 267–86.

McGavin, H. (1996) 'Jobless teenagers face a grim future', *Times Educational Supplement*, 8 March.

Machin, S. and Wilkinson, D. (1996) *Employee Training: Unequal Access and Economic Performance*, London: Institute of Public Policy Research.

Manpower Services Commission/Department for Education and Science (1986) *Working Together – Education and Training*, London: HMSO.

Millward, N. (1994) *The New Industrial Relations*, London: Policy Studies Institute.

Mumford, E. and Hendricks, R. (1996) 'Business Process Re-engineering RIP', *People Management*, 2 May, pp. 22–9.

Nash, I. (1996) 'Youth exodus costs £350 million', *Times Educational Supplement*, 1 March.

Nash, I. and Nicolls, A. 'Britain wide of the mark', *Times Educational Supplement*, 1 December.

National Advisory Committee for the Education and Training Targets (NACETT)(1995), *Report on Progress Towards the National Targets*, London: NACETT.

Organisation for Economic Cooperation and Development (1995) *Employment Outlook 1994*, Paris: OECD.

—— (1996) *Employment Outlook 1996*, Paris: OECD.

Oulton, N. (1993) 'Workforce skills and export competitiveness: An Anglo-German comparison', *National Institute of Economic and Social Research Discussion Paper* No. 47, London: National Institute of Economic and Social Research.

Pickard, J. (1996) 'Barriers ahead to a single currency', *People Management*, 21 March, pp. 22–7.

Prais, S. J. (1990) *Productivity, Education and Training*, London: National Institute of Economic and Social Research.

Prais, S.J. (ed.) (1990) *Productivity, Education and Training*, London: National Institute of Economic and Social Research.

Prais, S. J. (1991) 'Vocational qualifications in Britain and Europe', *National Institute Economic Review*, May.

Prais, S. J. and Jarvis, V. (1996) *The Quality of Manufactured Products in Britain and Germany*, London: National Institute of Economic and Social Research.

Price, L. (1994) 'Poor personnel practice in the hotel and catering industry; does it matter?', *Human Resource Management Journal*, vol. 4, no. 4, pp. 44–62.

Pyke, N. (1996) 'Lack of skills locks youth into low wages', *Times Educational Supplement*, 8 March.

Rajan, A. and Jaspers, A. (1995) *Achieving the National Targets: Obstacles and solutions*, Tunbridge Wells: CREATE.

Reich, R. (1983) *The Next American Frontier*, Middlesex: Penguin.

Richards, H. (1996) 'Takeovers are bad for health', *Times Higher*, 12 April.

Richardson, W. (1993) 'The 16–19 education and training debate', in W. Richardson *et al.* (eds), *The Reform of Post-16 Education and Training in England and Wales*, London: Longman, pp. 1–37.

Richardson, W., Spours, K., Woolhouse, J. and Young, M. (1995) Learning for the Future – Initial Report, London: Institute of Education/Centre for Education and Industry.

Sherman, S (1995) 'Stretch goals: the dark side of asking for miracles', *Fortune*, 13 November.

Sisson, K. (1994) 'Personnel management: paradigms, practice and prsopects', in K. Sisson (ed.), *Personnel Management*, second edn, Oxford: Blackwell, pp. 1–50.

Smithers, A. (1993) *All Our Futures: Britain's education revolution*, Manchester; Manchester University, Centre for Education and Employment Research.

Spilsbury, M. (1996) *Skill Needs in Britain 1995*, High Wycombe: Public Attitude Surveys Ltd.

Spilsbury, M., Moralee, J. and Evans, C. (1995) *Employers Use of the NVQ System*, Sussex: Institute of Employment Studies.

Springett, P. (1995) 'Bid kids set for a long party', *The Guardian*, 30 December.

Stevens, M. (1996) 'Transferable training and poaching externalities', in A. Booth and D. J. Snower (eds) *Acquiring Skills*, Cambridge: Cambridge University Press, pp. 19–37.

Temple, P. (1994) 'Evaluation of UK trading performance', in T. Buxton, P. Chapman and P. Temple (eds) *Britain's Economic Performance*, London: Routledge, pp. 76–97.

Thurow, L. (1994) 'New game, new rules, new strategies', *RSA Journal*, vol. CXLII, no. 5454, November, pp. 50–6.

Turner, A. (1996) 'Link pay to performance and we'll stay on track', *People Management*, 8 February, p. 21.

van Ours, J. C. (1990) 'An international comparative study of job mobility', *Labour*, vol. 4, no. 3, pp. 33–55.

Ward, L. (1995) 'Failure to lure students', *Times Educational Supplement*, 1 December.

White, M. (1996) 'Flexible response', *People Management*, 21 March.

Wilkinson, C. (1995) *The Drop Out Society – Young People on the Margin*, Leicester: Youth Work Press.

Part V

EUROPEAN INTEGRATION

16

OVERVIEW: THE EUROPEAN UNION

The impact of membership on the UK economy and UK economic policy

Valerio Lintner

INTRODUCTION

It is clear that participation in the process of European integration has had a fundamental influence on economic affairs and on economic policy in the United Kingdom since the country joined the then European Economic Community (EEC) in 1973.[1] One way or another, it seems inevitable that this influence will persist and may indeed intensify. Any understanding of Britain's economic performance, its policy stances and options, and its future economic prospects consequently necessitates some detailed consideration of the nature and implications of the process of European integration under the aegis of the EU, and of Britain's position *vis-à-vis* this process. Such an analysis is the principal aim of this chapter.

Membership of the EU involves acceptance of the *acquis communautaire*, i.e. the entire range of legislation and regulations which are contained in the Treaty of Rome and which the Union has developed since then.[2] It therefore has far-reaching consequences, not all of which are economic. It is indeed important to emphasise from the outset that a real understanding of the issues that the EU throws up involves political and social, as well as economic perspectives. Reality is interdisciplinary, and nowhere more so than in this field, although the emphasis here will naturally be on the economic aspects of membership. From an economic point of view the main consequences of membership can conveniently be divided into four categories:

1 the impact of the EU customs union on trade policy;
2 the impact on the mobility of the factors of production (the common market aspect of the EU);
3 the implications of participation in the Union's common policies; and
4 the consequences of the process of monetary integration and in particular the recent moves towards European Monetary Union (EMU).

These will be discussed in turn. We will consider the impact of each on the UK economy and on UK economic policy-making, with an emphasis on the central issue of monetary integration.

An important theme which runs through any study of the effects of the EU on UK policy-making is the impact of membership on the United Kingdom's national economic sovereignty, or its ability to determine and achieve its own first preferences in economic policy, in isolation of events and policies elsewhere. Indeed, in recent times it is this that has implicitly or explicitly dominated the economic and political debate on the United Kingdom's relationship with 'Europe'. Naturally, a feature of economic and political integration is that it implies joint determination, or at least close cooperation, in the formulation and implementation of policy in agreed areas. It is therefore axiomatic that it will result in some reduction in sovereignty at the local level among those who choose to participate: shared decision-making implies that any single participant cannot always do whatever it considers most appropriate to its individual needs. The important issue, it is argued here, concerns the extent of any such losses – whether UK membership of the EU results in the surrender of real sovereignty in important areas of economic policy, or whether it may in fact enhance such sovereignty by a process of pooling.

As essential background to the discussion that follows, it is useful to establish clearly some of the main features which seem to characterise the process of integration in Europe. First of all it is a process that seems to develop cyclically. Since 1957, one can broadly identify phases of rapid forward momentum, followed by periods of stagnation or even reversal. These cycles seem to be related to an extent to the economic cycle. Thus the period from the mid-1960s until the early 1980s were a period when little of real significance happened in the EC. Yet the mid and late 1980s were a period of hectic development, centred around the implementation of the '1992' programme to complete the internal market and by the Maastricht Treaty and its timetable for EMU. The early 1990s saw a period of slow-down, with the Maastricht process called into question by the deflationary nature of the convergence criteria during a recession, by German unification, by the power of capital markets and by uncertainty surrounding the democratic control of the institutions that are contemplated.

Secondly, the process of integration is essentially cumulative in nature, since each development provides the rationale for further ones. Thus the completion of the internal market gave more weight to the arguments in favour of monetary union. At this point it is also important to note that there is a strong link between developments in economic integration and those in the political integration sphere. Monetary union in particular is difficult to envisage without some development of integration in the political field.

Thirdly, the process of economic integration is in some senses a circular one. Integration is to an extent a reaction to the growing openness and interdependence of the European economies, but at the same by freeing markets it in itself reinforces the processes that are making the European economies interdependent.

Finally, it should also be noted that the institutional structure of the EU is such that nation states have retained and continue to retain most of the power. The real decision-making power has always lain with the Councils of Ministers,[3] which are inter–governmental bodies rather than supranational ones. Of the supranational bodies in the EC, the Commission has played a significant role in proposing and policing legislation, but it is the 'civil service' of the Community and as such it cannot take decisions. The European Parliament is not a legislative body,[4] despite its name, and the European Court of Justice interprets and enforces EC law (which, however, supersedes national law). Individual countries can still exercise a veto over fundamental developments, although decisions are being increasingly taken by (qualified) majorities, and much of the debate in the latter 1990s is centring around the extent to which the power of veto should be curtailed. The institutional balance of power is important not only in order to understand how the EU works, but also as an indicator of the progress of the integration project towards a supranational dimension.

It is of course well known that the United Kingdom's relationship with the whole integration project has been a distinctly difficult one, with the country coming to be regarded in recent years as an uncooperative and unenthusiastic participant. Broadly, the United Kingdom's relationship with the EC/EU can be divided into a number of different phases.

At first there was a period of what one might term disdain, in which Britain refused to participate in the foundation of the EEC, and in fact attempted to scupper the project by creating an alternative in the form of EFTA. This was followed by a period of rebuttal, in which the British application for membership was famously vetoed by DeGaulle. When the United Kingdom did eventually join, it was arguably too late, since the 'rules of the game' had been created without British participation and thus without specific regard to British interests. Membership has been characterised by lukewarm enthusiasm, the tone being set by the referendum on whether membership should continue at all. There followed a period of relative enthusiasm under the Heath government (perhaps facilitated by the fact that nothing much was actually happening in the EEC at this time), to be replaced in the 1980s by a phase of distinct hostility under Margaret Thatcher, typified by her refusal to join the ERM and by the interminable budget squabbles of the early 1980s. Nevertheless this period throws up a fascinating paradox, since it was Mrs Thatcher who was the prime instigator of the 1992 programme which then provided the impetus for the EMU.[5] She clearly did not realise the chain of events that completing the internal market would precipitate: perhaps a case of the economic liberal triumphing over the political Atlanticist anti-European. There followed a period of relative rapprochement during the latter part of Thatcher's time as PM and the early part of

401

the Major administration. The United Kingdom joined the ERM and then ratified Maastricht, even if opt-outs were negotiated on the EMU clauses and the social chapter. Most recently we have seen the emergence of so-called 'Euroscepticism', the difficulties within the Conservative Party and the advocacy of a further referendum by the likes of Sir James Goldsmith.

An interesting point here has been the position of the two major political parties. Labour was initially hostile, since the EEC was seen as a 'rich man's club' acting as an impediment to the implementation of socialist policies in the United Kingdom. After the 1983 general election defeat, however, the position of the Party shifted rapidly towards support for the integration project, on the realisation that many aspects of social and economic policy would in future need to be conducted in some way at the supranational level.[6] As far as one can tell, Labour Party economic policies are now inexorably rooted within an EU context. If the Labour Party, or at least its leadership, has shifted the length of the spectrum towards a pro-European stance, then it has been passed along the way by a Conservative Party travelling rapidly in the opposite direction. The pro-Europe party of Edward Heath has changed into the divided and 'Eurosceptic' one we have today.

THE CUSTOMS UNION AND TRADE POLICY

We move now to specific policy areas. The EU's customs union essentially involves three obligations on the part of its members:

1 the removal of all tariffs on imports from partner countries – a measure long since implemented by members;
2 the removal of non-tariff barriers (NTBs), or at least some of them, on intra-union imports. This has, to an extent, been achieved as a result of the '1992' programme; and finally
3 the adoption of a common policy towards trade with the rest of the world. This involves implementing the EU's Common External Policy (or Variable Levy in the case of agricultural products), but it also implies adopting a common stance in international negotiations such as the last Uruguay round of the GATT.

The rationale for this is analysed within the branch of economics known as customs union theory. In essence this shows that, under the usual restrictive assumptions, a customs union can improve welfare. The tariff changes that result alter relative prices in such a way as to promote changes in the inter-national and inter-regional structure of production and a more rational allocation of resources. Customs unions will have a broadly welfare-enhancing 'trade creation' effect, to the extent that they result in the displacement of higher cost and less efficiently produced domestic products by relatively more efficient and cheaper imports from partner countries. They will also have welfare-reducing 'trade diversion'[7] effects, in that cheap and efficiently produced imports from third countries will be displaced by inherently more expensive products from inside the customs union. The hope is that trade creation will exceed trade diversion and thus render the customs union on balance welfare-enhancing. The empirical evidence that exists in this area in fact suggests that the EEC customs union was on balance trade-creating and resulted in GNP gains of around 1 per cent.[8] It is important, however, to note that customs unions are inherently discriminatory devices, which from a theoretical point of view are strictly second-best *vis-à-vis* non-discriminatory free trade.[9]

In addition to these 'static' effects, customs unions are also assumed to have 'dynamic' effects: more scope for economies of scale, improved terms of trade, improved 'X-efficiency', increased growth. Studies tend to suggest that the first two of these are significant within the EC, and are indeed probably more important than the static effects.[10]

It should be noted, however, that the traditional theory of customs union provides a somewhat imperfect analysis. It has yet to take full account of recent developments in international trade theory. It also tends to ignore the issue of how welfare gains are distributed between member states, as well as the distribution of changes in the international location of production that result. Trade creation can hardly be considered as welfare enhancing to a worker who loses his or her job with no alternative employment available in expanding sectors. Furthermore, traditional customs union theory sheds little light on alternative reasons why customs unions might be formed. Harry Johnson (1965) and Cooper and Massell (1965), showed that, as usual under certain assumptions, a customs union might reduce the cost of and allow an increase in the extent of industrial protection, suggesting a possible protectionist motive for their formation.

The implications of all this for UK economic policy are clear. Ostensibly, control is lost over tariffs and NTBs as an instrument of economic policy. These can no longer be employed as a means of altering intra-union trade flows, and their use to control imports from the rest of the world is subject to the limitations imposed by collective decision-making. However, one must remember that these tools of intervention have become increasingly redundant in the modern world. Tariffs were undoubtedly widely used in Europe and elsewhere during the early part of the century, when protectionism became part and parcel of the spiral of decline into nationalism that resulted in the Second World War. However, since the late 1940s tariffs on trade between developed countries have been greatly reduced by the various rounds of the GATT as well as by the emergence of regional trade groupings and bilateral arrangements between countries. To this extent the lessons of the 1930s have been heeded. In any case one could argue that the increased concentration of production in the hands of multinational enterprises (MNEs) has further reduced the importance of tariffs, since direct investment has emerged as an alternative to trade.

Even in the past there were of course severe limits to the effectiveness of tariffs, given the welfare costs which had to be borne by domestic consumers and the probability of retaliation. Nevertheless, as recently as 1983 one finds the British Labour Party advocating an 'Alternative Economic Strategy' which relied heavily on protectionism as a means of facilitating the development of infant industries and promoting industrial regeneration. The message on tariffs has clearly taken a long time to sink in.

The demise of explicit tariffs in the post-war world led many EC countries to revert increasingly to NTBs as a means of protection. NTBs can take various forms: from the obvious quotas to the (slightly) less evident Voluntary Export Restraint Agreements (VERs, which are in reality anything but voluntary), state subsidies, discriminatory public procurement practices and indirect taxation regimes, restrictive frontier practices, obstructive health and safety and other standards, and so on.[11] In general NTBs represent a more serious impediment to trade than is the case with tariffs, since many of them prevent trade directly rather than through the price mechanism.

The EC's ubiquitous '1992' programme has made it increasingly difficult for these methods to be used as a means of economic policy. Some remain, but many have disappeared, thus in one more way apparently reducing the ability of individual states to control their own economies. For the United Kingdom, the loss of sovereignty argument carries more weight for NTBs than it does in the case of tariffs. For example, the new EU rules on competitive tendering for public contracts have in many cases severely restricted the ability of local authorities to use their expenditures to promote economic development and local multiplier effects by awarding contracts to suppliers in their own localities. In addition, restrictions on the use of indirect taxes such as excise duties increasingly constitute a significant loss of control over fiscal matters.

An important point here is that it is difficult in practice to differentiate between measures that are explicitly designed to restrict trade and those that represent a bona fide expression of a country or region's legitimate right to determine its own priorities in areas such as social policy. For example, how does one regard the imposition of VAT on fuel, or on books and newspapers? How does one classify regional policy, which may have laudable social and economic intentions but which also results in 'unfair' trade by reducing the costs of some producers? Thus the elimination of NTBs may have the additional side effect of reducing sovereignty in areas that are not purely economic.

It is also important to note that any losses of the sort outlined above are likely to be mitigated by the advantages the United Kingdom has probably enjoyed as a member of a powerful trading bloc, exerting increased influence in agreements such as the GATT and benefiting from more favourable terms of trade and some of the other effects outlined above, including the welfare gains, as well as distributional losses, discussed above.

The effects of membership on UK trade and production are predictably hard to estimate, since it is difficult to isolate the EC effect from other influences, such as long-term trends of falling competitiveness and inappropriate economic policies, on the UK position. Nevertheless, the best estimates tend to suggest that membership of the Community reduced UK output of manufactures and significantly worsened the trade balance in this area. Alan Winters, for example, suggests that the loss of output that resulted from accession was at least £3 billion (1.5 per cent of GNP), but that these losses might well have been outweighed by gains in welfare enjoyed by UK consumers as a result of cheaper imports from EC partners.[12] In general, it is probably fair to say that the net loss for UK manufacturing from the process of trade creation has been particularly great in areas such as consumer durables, while the United Kingdom as a whole has probably suffered from the effects of trade diversion in areas such as agriculture.

What is absolutely clear is that the EU has now become the United Kingdom's most important trading partner. The growing importance of intra–EU trade to the United Kingdom and its imbalanced trading position is shown in Table 16.1.

This should be seen in the context of the very considerable increases that took place in world trade during this period. It is interesting to note that

Table 16.1 Share of intra-trade in total trade: imports and exports by member state

	1980		1985		1990		1992	
	Imports	*Exports*	*Imports*	*Exports*	*Imports*	*Exports*	*Imports*	*Exports*
Original six member states								
BL	61.6	73.2	68.6	70.2	70.7	75.1	71.2	74.8
F	52.0	55.4	59.4	53.7	64.9	62.7	65.7	63.1
D	49.4	51.1	53.1	49.7	54.3	54.3	54.7	54.1
I	46.2	51.6	47.1	48.2	57.4	58.2	58.8	57.7
NL	54.7	73.5	55.8	74.7	59.9	76.5	58.8	75.4
First enlargement								
DK	50.3	51.6	50.7	44.8	53.8	52.1	55.4	54.5
IRL	75.3	76.0	71.7	68.9	70.8	74.8	71.9	74.2
UK	40.9	45.0	47.3	48.8	51.0	52.6	50.7	55.5
Second and third enlargements								
GR	40.9	48.2	48.1	54.2	64.1	64.0	62.8	64.2
P	45.3	58.6	45.9	62.5	69.1	73.5	73.6	74.8
E	31.3	52.2	37.9	53.3	59.1	65.0	60.3	66.3
EUR 12	49.2	55.7	53.4	54.9	58.8	61.0	59.3	61.3

Source: European Economy.

much of the increase in intra-trade (an estimated 71 per cent between 1959 and 1967) took the form of increased inter-industry trade, suggesting a strong trade creation effect within the EEC customs union.

THE FREE MOVEMENT OF LABOUR AND CAPITAL

The EU common market establishes the famous four freedoms within the Union: freedom of movement for goods, services, people and money, thereby creating a so-called 'level playing field' in these areas. Thus membership of the EU common market also involves accepting the free movement of the factors of production, labour and capital, within the Union. It also involves adopting a common stance on factor flows with the rest of the world.

It is important in this context to consider briefly the impact of these commitments. There is a certain amount of theoretical controversy among economists as to the impact of unhindered factor mobility. From a neoclassical perspective, free movement within an area should increase economic welfare by facilitating a more efficient allocation of resources. This is the basic rationale that neoclassical economic theory provides for a common market. It should also promote the equalisation of factor earnings between participating countries and regions, and thus promote economic convergence within the common market.

However, freedom of movement can be regarded, from another perspective, as resulting in the exacerbation of national and regional differences in real income and welfare, with more prosperous areas benefiting at the expense of less well-off countries and regions. This critique of the neoclassical approach is largely an offshoot of the work of Gunnar Myrdal. Myrdral held that the free movement of capital results in 'polarisation effects' through a process of 'cumulative causation'. Broadly, the inflow of capital into areas where its marginal productivity is greatest sets in motion a dynamic process that further increases productivity in these areas and reinforces their attractiveness to the owners of capital. Host areas therefore become more prosperous, attracting more and more capital from the source areas, which gradually become relatively less developed. The free movement of labour may lead to similar effects, since it may drain human capital from the source areas. There may be some flow of capital from the prosperous economic centre to the less well-off periphery as a result of factors such as low labour costs, congestion etc., but these 'spillover' effects are unlikely to be sufficient to compensate for the polarisation effects referred to above.

It is very difficult to test these hypotheses empirically, although it is arguable that the United Kingdom[13] has suffered from a polarisation effect, partly as a result of EC membership. To the extent that polarisation effects do exist they provide a strong case for an active and well-resourced regional policy within a common market, as well as a salutary warning to some of the less prosperous states currently seeking accession to the EU.

The impact on economic sovereignty of the unhindered mobility of capital is considerable. In the case of portfolio investments, it can effectively subvert national economic policy, as was made abundantly clear at the time of the United Kingdom's ignominious exit from the ERM in 1992. Then, the power of foreign exchange markets forced the abandonment of a policy which, let us not forget, at the time enjoyed almost total support across the political and economic spectrum. The role of speculation in this process is often highlighted, but it should be noted that other forms of market adjustment can have similar effects. It is a sobering fact, for example, that the investments of the UK financial services industry alone are roughly equivalent to 100 per cent of the United Kingdom's GDP, and that a mere 5 per cent shift of these holdings out of sterling would effectively neutralise the whole of the United Kingdom's foreign exchange reserves – the front-line means of intervention to support the currency. Even in the absence of speculation, prudent portfolio adjustment alone can thus affect the Government's ability to control the economy and pursue its economic objectives.

Direct investment can also have potentially serious longer-term effects on sovereignty: for example, if multinational enterprises dislike a tax regime, controls over borrowing, or labour market regulation, they can subvert these by locating elsewhere.

In the context of the United Kingdom's position, the pertinent questions concern the extent to which European integration has contributed to the mobility of capital (and thus contributed to the erosion of sovereignty in this area), and whether integration can enhance control over the forces of capital (and thus enhance sovereignty by pooling).

In practice, capital is highly mobile within the EU, but this is probably due mainly to factors which are out of the Union's direct control: the well-known developments that have led to the increased 'globalisation' of world capital markets, for example the 'communications revolution', world-wide deregulation of capital markets, increases in the supply in internationally mobile capital.[14] It is also, however, partly due to the actions of the EU itself, an example being the abolition of exchange controls as part of the '1992' programme. Britain had removed exchange controls as early as 1979, for reasons which had nothing to do with the EC.

Thus the view taken here is that although increased capital mobility has had important effects on the UK economy and on UK policy-making, the 'EU effect' in this area has been marginal. The mobility of capital has increased dramatically as a result of forces outside the EU's direct control. However, it must surely be the case that a united front on the part of fifteen or more of the richest countries in the world offers the potential of enhancing control over capital markets and even MNEs. Unless, that is, it induces MNEs to locate outside Europe and thus accelerates the loss of comparative advantage (to the NICs) in key areas of production which has so conditioned the strategic position of the European economy in recent years.

The evidence on intra-European capital movements is sparse, but it seems clear that changes in capital flows have not been as great as changes in trade flows (Mayes, 1994), and foreign direct investment has been low in relation to investment outside of the EU. For example, between 1975 and 1983, 83 per cent of the outward FDI of the EC 12 went outside the Community, most of it to the USA. Table 16.2 shows how UK FDI has increasingly been directed towards the EU. Figure 16.1 in turn shows how portfolio investment between the main EC countries increased during the 1980s.

Another dimension of the capital mobility debate concerns the impact of the common market on investment from outside. It is argued that the EC/EU attracts inward FDI as a result of fear of such events as the '1992' programme, and in order to circumvent trade barriers and to ensure the strategic placement needed to service such an important market. There has been in fact a large increase in inward FDI since the 1980s. The USA has been the main source of FDI, around 45 per cent of its entire FDI stock being in Europe by the 1980s (Dunning, 1989), but there has been an extra-ordinary acceleration of Japanese investment since the early 1980s. Since the late 1980s Japan has been the largest foreign investor in Germany, and the third largest in the United Kingdom (after the USA and Germany). The United Kingdom's ability to attract Japanese and other FDI has been of course much trumpeted by the British government as a sign of the success of its deregulation policies. What evidence exists does point to the United Kingdom having fared relatively well here. Dunning (1989) shows that between 1972 and 1985, investment by US companies in the United Kingdom increased marginally more rapidly than in the rest of the EC, increasing

Table 16.2 Foreign direct investment of the UK ($ billion)

	Inward		Outward	
	EEC	*% of total*	*EEC*	*% of total*
1962	133.7	9.4	272.9	8.0
1965	178.4	8.9	392.2	9.3
1968	278.2	10.2	628.9	11.3
1971	472.9	12.4	985.2	14.8
1974	1107.9	16.9	2282.0	21.9
1978	2034.7	18.3	4570.2	23.9
1981*	6502.0	22.6	8254.8	18.8
1984	1143.0	29.7	1594.9	21.1

Note: *From 1981 includes oil, insurance and banking.
Source: C.A. Schenk, 'Foreign Trade and Payments in Western Europe', in Schultz (1996).

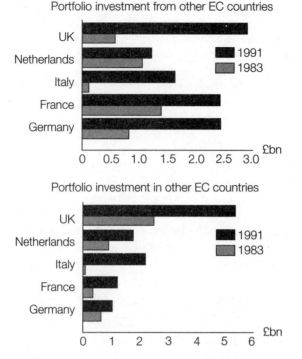

Portfolio investment from other EC countries

Portfolio investment in other EC countries

Figure 16.1 Intra-EC portfolio investment in selected European countries
Source: European Economy.
Note: data are based on non-harmonised national data.

the UK share of the EC capital stake of US companies from 36.7 per cent
to 40.7 per cent. However, by 1991 the United Kingdom's share of the
total stock of US direct investment in the EC had fallen to 36.2 per cent,
while the percentage in Germany, the Netherlands and France had risen
to 17.5, 13.1 and 10.9 respectively (Mayes, 1994). By 1987, the stock of
Japanese manufacturing FDI in the United Kingdom amounted to $488m
out of an EC total of $2,357m. The next most favoured location was Spain
($461m), followed by France ($310m) and West Germany ($277m). If we
consider Japanese non-manufacturing FDI, the United Kingdom's position
was even more striking, with a stock in 1987 of $3,586m out of an EC total
of $10,375 (West German stock was $1,025m – O'Cleireacain, 1989). Subsequently, Japanese investment flows into the United Kingdom accelerated
rapidly (to $6,855m in 1990 from $2,531m in 1987), but not as rapidly as in
France (from $330m in 1987 to $1,257 in 1990) and in Germany (from
$409m to $1,242m). In 1991, Japanese FDI fell dramatically in the United
Kingdom (to $3,690m) and in France (to $817m) but held up in Germany
and the southern EU states.

Labour mobility in the EU remains restricted, for time-honoured reasons which have been exacerbated by a lack of employment opportunities in the contemporary European economy. The actions that the Union has taken to promote the free movement of labour have been either symbolic in their importance (for example, the new burgundy European passport and the attempts to minimise frontier controls), or largely aimed at limited strata of society (for example, the ERASMUS programme and mutual acceptance of qualifications, which affect the academic community and professional people). Arguably, the most energetic efforts of European countries in this field have been directed at excluding people from outside; hence the Schenegen Treaty and the activities of the Trevi group.

The impact of the free movement of labour on the UK economy is thus probably negligible, and in the long run may be confined to an exodus of human capital or 'brain drain' from low-earnings areas to high-earnings areas. The main sovereignty losses here are the symbolic ones which arise from the removal of frontiers, as well as some loss of control over immigration policy.

THE COMMON POLICIES OF THE EU

The most important of the EU's common policies is undoubtedly the Common Agricultural Policy (CAP), currently accounting for approximately 60 per cent of the EU budget and affecting the price and supply of the most basic of commodities. The CAP essentially consists of a mechanism for subsidising agriculture through the price process. The EU Council of farming ministers sets minimum prices for most agricultural products. These are usually above world market prices, so they are kept up to the desired level by a tariff[15] which is fine-tuned on a daily basis to allow just enough imports into the EU. Prices are often set with little regard for what people actually want to buy, and so frequently they have been set above the internal equilibrium between supply and demand. The result has been not only expensive food, but also surpluses, which have been mopped up by the EU's 'intervention buying'. These surpluses have been stored, generating the infamous 'butter mountains' and 'wine lakes' which have scarred the public image of the EC and EU in the 1980s. Alternatively they have been 'dumped' (exported at below cost price) on world markets, to the detriment of food producers elsewhere. The CAP, it should furthermore be noted, has redistributed resources between states and individuals in member countries in a generally regressive fashion. It has also arguably contributed to the continent's ecological degradation by promoting the indiscriminate use of chemical additives, since the subsidy system rewards quantity of production rather than the quality of what is produced.

The CAP has resulted in some benefits to European societies: Europe is now a substantial net exporter of food where once it was a net importer;

food is plentiful, if you can afford it; agricultural incomes have been increased, however inefficiently and inequitably this may have been done; there have been vast improvements in agricultural technologies and in agricultural productivity, albeit at the cost of the environmental damage and the threat to the purity of what we eat, discussed above. Nevertheless, the consumer has had to pay heavily, twice over, for the policy, mainly through high food prices, but also via the EU budget, 60–70 per cent of which has typically been swallowed up by the CAP. There have been attempts to modify the excesses of the policy: in 1989 in the wake of the budget reforms that doubled the size of the structural funds following the establishment of the '1992' programme, and through the McSharry Plan and the Uruguay GATT round. In general one can say that reform from inside the Community has proved to be difficult, and real change has been precipitated by external forces such as pressure from the USA and others in the GATT negotiations.

Over the last few years prices have fallen, surpluses have been reduced, and the budgetary cost of the CAP has been moderated to an extent. The fundamental problem lies, however, in the very nature of the policy, which is based on millions of consumers paying heavily to protect the interests of a minority of large farmers. Such regulation has been distinctly unavailable to other industries such as steel and coal-mining, which have had to live (and die) in the free market. Nevertheless, there is a shortage of alternatives available. The obvious other approach to agricultural protection is through some system of direct cash transfers on the model of the former UK 'deficiency payments' system, which would probably be politically unacceptable because of its tax implications and because of the transfer of direct spending power to the EU that it would involve.[16]

Participation in the CAP thus constrains control over food policy. It has also had a significant impact on the UK economy, First of all it has consistently resulted in food prices (often considerably) higher than world market levels, with the welfare losses and regressive effects on the personal distribution of income that this entails. Higher prices resulted initially from abandoning the 'deficiency payments' system discussed above, as well as the highly favourable arrangements that existed with food suppliers from the Commonwealth. In fact food prices in the United Kingdom increased by something like 300 per cent in the decade between 1971 and 1981, partly no doubt reflecting increased world food prices during this period, while the Labour Party (1989) estimated that in the late 1980s every family was paying £13.50 each week to finance the CAP. The indirect impact of the CAP on employment has also been considerable. The best estimates suggest a job loss of around 860,000 in the largest four EC countries, with the United Kingdom and Germany suffering most severely, as the result of a loss of potential gross output of between 1.1 per cent and 2.5 per cent (and between 4.4 per cent and 6.2 per cent of exports in manufacturing industries) in these countries (Demekas *et al.*, 1988).

411

In addition, the CAP has precipitated the so-called 'British problem' with the EC/EU budget: a large proportion (typically 60–70 per cent) of the budget has been spent on the CAP; the United Kingdom has a relatively small (but generally very efficient) agricultural sector which employs approximately 2.5 per cent of the population, and therefore receives a disproportionately small share of transfers from the EU budget (Ardy, 1988). The result is the United Kingdom's position as a net contributor to the EU budget, when its relatively low GNP[17] would suggest that it should in fact be a net recipient. The net budgetary contributions of course precipitated the much publicised haggling over UK rebates that took place during the early Thatcher administrations.

The CAP is of course not the only common policy to be pursued at EU level. Other major policies are operated at EU level through the 'structural funds': the European Regional Development Fund (ERDF), which is the main instrument of the EU's regional policy, and the European Social Fund (ESF), the principal means of implementing the Union's social policy.[18] In addition, important aspects of European industrial and competition policy, fiscal policy, transport policy, environmental policy and fisheries policy are now conducted at EU level, while the common regulatory frameworks established in the 1992 programme and elsewhere affect a wide range of aspects of economic and political life, from employment contracts to the cleanliness of beaches, from local economic development to government subsidies to industry.

The importance of the other common policies is severely constrained by their limited claim on the EU budget, which is in any case modest in size at around 1.2 per cent of EU GDP. In general the United Kingdom has benefited more than proportionately from non-CAP EU expenditure, partly to mitigate the country's net contributions to the budget. The transfers involved in these policies are not of great macroeconomic impact, but they do have important effects in specific sectors. However, the real impact of these policies often lies in the legislation which accompanies them, and which nation states are obliged to adopt. Many EU common policies (the regional policy, fiscal harmonisation, the competition policy etc.) are designed to facilitate the working of, or mitigate the adjustment costs that result from, the internal market. Most also have the effect of promoting the economic cooperation and convergence necessary for integration at the macroeconomic level. The structure of the EU budget, how the money is spent and how it is financed, is shown in Tables 16.3 and 16.4.

Space constraints preclude a detailed examination of the impact of the various EU common policies, although these undoubtedly play a major and increasing role in developments in their respective fields. However, a significant example in the context of this book is technology policy. Here the Treaty of Rome provides limited powers for the Commission to act as a promoter of technological development.[19] Nevertheless, the fostering of European technology has been an important concern. Up to the 1970s, the emphasis was on encouraging large-scale projects in high-tech industries as a means of confronting US innovation. Since then the Community's policy has been based on promoting cooperation in high technology. In the late 1970s the Industry Commissioner Davignon facilitated ventures involving joint basic research, which precipitated the ESPRIT programme for R&D in information technology. This involved firms of various sizes and academic institutions across Europe. It was followed by similar ventures, funded by the Framework Programme research budget, in other high technology sectors. The Single European Act incorporated research as a central Community concern into the Treaty, thus ensuring some degree of continuity in its funding.

Technology policy may be predominantly a question of entirely desirable cooperation, but as discussed above, EU common policies may severely constrain the ability of countries and regions to pursue independent economic policies in certain areas, such as local economic development, taxation, social and environmental affairs. They may thus constrain sovereignty in areas where national and regional authorities could claim to have the greatest scope for independent action. One could argue, however, that this process is not always negative in its results. In the case of the United Kingdom, acceptance of EU standards in areas such as environmental affairs and employment rights has involved levelling up in recent years, although the British government would of course emphasise what it regards as the negative indirect effects of these regulations on the functioning of the market system. Hence the opt-out from the Maastricht Social provisions.

MONETARY INTEGRATION

This is probably the central issue of the day as far as Europe is concerned, and accordingly requires careful analysis. After the failed attempt at EMU in the 1970s and the successes of the EMS in the 1980s (see below), monetary union remained a remote prospect until the mid-to late 1980s. That it has moved to the top of the agenda, with the Delors Report eventually precipitating the timetables and conditions for full monetary union in the Maastricht Treaty, is testament to the rapid advance in the integration process in the few years up to late 1992. Whether this momentum can be maintained into the near future is a moot point. One perspective (outlined above) is that the process of integration tends to move in cycles, and that we are now involved in a plateau or downswing phase. It may logically be expected that monetary union, at least of the sort envisaged in the Maastricht Treaty, may accordingly have to be changed and/or postponed for a while. Nevertheless, an impressive political momentum has been maintained despite the difficulties, and this may just result in some sort of EMU within something like the Maastricht timetable.

One should note from the outset that monetary union is merely the limiting case in an overall process of monetary integration in which the United

Table 16.3 Budgetary expenditure of the European Communities (ECU m.[a])

| | ECSC operational budget | European Development Fund | Euratom[b] | EC general budget | | | | | | | Total |
				EAGGF[c]	Social Fund	Regional Fund	Industry, energy, research	Administration[d]	Other	Total EC	
1958	21.7	—	7.9	—	—	—	—	8.6	0.0	8.6	35.5
1959	30.7	51.2	39.1	—	—	—	—	20.3	4.9	25.2	146.2
1960	23.5	63.2	20.0	—	—	—	—	23.4	4.9	28.3	135.0
1961	26.5	172.0	72.5	—	8.6	—	—	27.9	2.9	39.4	305.0
1962	13.6	162.3	88.6	—	11.3	—	—	34.2	46.8	92.3	356.8
1963	21.9	55.5	106.4	—	4.6	—	—	37.2	42.3	84.1	267.9
1964	18.7	35.0	124.4	—	7.2	—	—	43.0	42.9	93.1	271.1
1965	37.3	248.8	120.0	102.7	42.9	—	—	48.1	7.4	201.1	607.2
1966	28.1	157.8	129.2	310.3	26.2	—	—	55.4	10.4	402.3	717.3
1967	10.4	105.8	158.5	562.0	35.6	—	—	60.4	17.1	675.1	949.8
1968	21.2	121.0	73.4	2,250.4	43.0	—	—	91.8	23.5	2,408.7	2,624.2
1969	40.7	104.8	59.2	3,818.0	50.5	—	—	105.6	77.1	4,051.2	4,255.9
1970	56.2	10.5	63.4	5,228.3	64.0	—	—	114.7	41.4	5,448.4	5,578.5
1971	37.4	236.1	—	1,883.6	56.5	—	65.0	132.1	152.2	2,289.3	2,562.8
1972	43.7	212.7	—	2,477.6	97.5	—	75.1	177.2	247.1	3,074.5	3,330.9
1973	86.9	210.0	—	3,768.8	269.2	—	69.1	239.4	294.4	4,641.0	4,937.9
1974	92.0	157.0	—	3,651.3	292.1	—	82.8	336.7	675.2	5,038.2	5,287.2
1975	127.4	71.0	—	4,586.6	360.2	150.0	99.0	375.0	642.8	6,213.6	6,412.0
1976	94.0	320.0	—	6,033.3	176.7	300.0	113.3	419.7	909.5	7,952.6	8,366.6
1977	93.0	244.7	—	6,463.5	325.2	372.5	163.3	497.0	883.4	8,704.9	9,042.6
1978	159.1	394.5	—	9,602.2	284.8	254.9	227.2	676.7	1,302.4	12,348.3	12,901.8
1979	173.9	480.0	—	10,735.5	595.7	671.5	288.0	863.9	1,447.9	14,602.5	15,256.4
1980	175.7	508.5	—	11,596.1	502.0	751.8	212.8	938.8	2,056.1	16,057.5[e]	16,741.7
1981	261.0	658.0	—	11,446.0	547.0	2,264.0	217.6	1,035.4	3,024.6	18,546.0[f]	19,465.0
1982	243.0	750.0	—	12,792.0	910.0	2,766.0[g]	346.0	1,103.4	3,509.7	21,427.0[h]	22,420.0

Year										
1983	300.0	752.0	—	16,331.3	801.0	2,265.5	1,216.2	1,161.6	2,989.9	24,765.5[i]	25,817.5
1984	408.0	703.0	—	18,985.8	1,116.4	1,283.3	1,346.4	1,236.6	2,150.8	26,119.3[j]	27,230.3
1985	453.0	698.0	—	20,546.4	1,413.0	1,624.3	706.9	1,332.6	2,599.8	28,223.0[k]	29,374.0
1986	439.0	846.7	—	23,067.7	2,533.0	2,373.0	760.1	1,603.2	4,526.2	34,863.2	36,148.9
1987	399.0	837.9	—	23,939.4	2,542.2	2,562.3	964.8	1,740.0	3,720.5	35,469.2	36,706.4
1988	567.0	1,196.3	—	27,531.9	2,298.8	3,092.8	1,203.7	1,947.0	6,186.8	42,261.0	44,024.3
1989	404.0	1,297.0	—	25,868.8	2,676.1	3,920.0	1,353.0	2,063.0	9,978.9[l]	45,859.8	47,560.8
1990	488.0	1,256.5	—	27,233.8	3,212.0	4,554.1	1,738.7	2,298.1	7,567.9	46,604.6[m]	48,349.1
1991	495.0	1,191.0	—	33,443.2	3,869.6	5,179.9	1,918.8	2,519.2	9,655.6	56,586.0[m]	58,272.0
1992	535.3	1,910.0	—	38,461.6	4,817.2	7,578.7	2,423.7	2,927.4	6,619.0	62,827.6[m]	65,272.9
1993	551.8	1,750.0	—	38,824.0	5,536.0	8,358.0	2,892.6	3,400.9	6,511.1	65,522.6[n]	67,824.4
1994	393.0	1,960.0	—	40,750.8	5,939.9	7,941.9	3,194.3	3,617.6	8,569.0	70,013.5[o]	72,366.5

Source; Eurostat.

Notes:

[a] UA until 1977, EUA/ECU from 1972 onwards.

[b] Incorporated in the EC budget from 1971.

[c] This column includes, for the years to 1970, substantial amounts carried forward to following years.

[d] Commission, Council, Parliament, Court of Justice and Court of Auditors.

[e] Including surplus of ECU 82.4 m. carried forward in 1981.

[f] Including ECU 1,173 m. carried forward to 1982.

[g] Including ECU 1,819 m. UK special measures.

[h] Including ECU 2,211 m. carried forward to 1983.

[i] Including ECU 1,707 m. carried forward to 1984.

[j] There was a small deficit in 1984 in respect of the EC budget due largely to late payment of advances by some member states.

[k] There was a cash deficit in 1985 of ECU 25 m. due to late payment of advances by some member states.

[l] Including a surplus of ECU 5,080 m. carried forward to 1990.

[m] 1990–92; Court of Auditors' report.

[n] General budget of the Community for 1993.

[o] General budget of the European Union for 1994. The figures for Social and Regional Funds do not include Community initiatives as these have not yet been decided.

Table 16.4 Budgetary receipts of the European Communities (ECU m.[a])

| | | | | | EC budget | | | | | |
| | | | | | | Own resources | | | | |
Year	ECSC levies and other	European Development Fund contributions	Euratom contributions (research only)	Miscellaneous and contributions under special keys	Miscellaneous	Agricultural levies	Import duties	GNP contributions or VAT[b,c]	Total EC	Total
1958	44.0	116.0	7.9	0.02	—	—	—	5.9	5.9	173.8
1959	49.6	116.0	39.1	0.1	—	—	—	25.1	25.2	229.9
1960	53.3	116.0	20.0	0.2	—	—	—	28.1	28.3	217.6
1961	53.1	116.0	72.5	2.8	—	—	—	31.2	34.0	275.6
1962	45.3	116.0	88.6	2.1	—	—	—	90.2	92.3	342.2
1963	47.1	—	106.4	6.7	—	—	—	77.4	84.1	237.5
1964	61.3	—	124.4	2.9	—	—	—	90.1	93.1	278.7
1965	66.1	—	98.8	3.5	—	—	—	197.6	201.1	366.0
1966	71.2	—	116.5	3.9	—	—	—	398.3	402.2	590.0
1967	40.3	40.0	158.5	4.2	—	—	—	670.9	675.1	913.9
1968	85.4	90.0	82.0	—	—	—	—	—	2,408.6	2,666.0
1969	106.8	110.0	62.7	78.6	—	—	—	3,972.6	4,051.2	4,330.7
1970	100.0	130.0	67.7	121.1	—	—	—	5,327.3	5,448.4	5,746.1
1971	57.9	170.0	—	—	69.5	713.8	582.2	923.8	2,289.3	2,517.2
1972	61.1	170.0	—	—	80.9	799.6	957.4	1,236.6	3,074.5	3,305.6
1973	120.3	150.0	—	—	511.0	478.0	1,564.7	2,087.3	4,641.0	4,911.3
1974	124.6	150.0	—	—	65.3	323.6	2,684.4	1,964.8	5,038.2	5,312.8
1975	189.5	220.1	—	—	320.5	590.0	3,151.0	2,152.0	6,213.6	6,623.1
1976	129.6	311.0	—	—	282.8	1,163.7	4,064.6	2,482.1	7,993.1[d]	8,433.7
1977	123.0	410.0	—	—	504.7	1,778.5	3,927.2	2,494.5	8,704.9	9,237.9
1978	164.9	147.5	—	—	344.4	2,283.3	4,390.9	5,329.7	12,348.2	12,660.6
1979	168.4	480.0	—	—	230.3	2,143.4	5,189.1	7,039.8	14,602.5	15,251.0

1980	226.2	555.0	—	1,055.9 [e]	2,002.3	5,905.8	7,093.5	16,057.5 [f]	16,838.7
1981	264.0	658.0	—	1,219.0	1,747.0	6,392.0	9,188.0	18,546.0 [g]	19,468.0
1982	243.0	750.0	—	187.0	2,228.0	6,815.0	12,197.0	21,427.0	22,420.0
1983	300.0	700.0	—	1,565.0	2,295.0	6,988.7	13,916.8	24,765.5 [h]	25,765.5
1984	408.0	703.0	—	1,060.7 [i]	2,436.3	7,960.8	14,594.6	26,052.4 [j]	27,163.4
1985	453.0	698.0	—	2,491.0 [k]	2,179.0	8,310.0	15,218.0	28,198.0	29,349.0
1986	439.0	846.7	—	396.5	2,287.0	8,172.9	22,810.8	33,667.2	34,952.9
1987	399.3	837.9	—	74.8	3,097.9	8,936.5	23,674.1	35,783.3	37,020.5
1988	567.0	1,196.3	—	1,377.0	2,606.0	9,310.0	28,968.0	42,261.0	44,024.3
1989	404.0	1,297.0	—	4,018.4	2,397.9	10,312.9	29,170.6	45,899.8	47,600.8
1990	488.0	1,256.3	—	5,191.5	1,875.7	10,285.1	29,252.4	46,604.7 [l]	49,349.1
1991	495.0	1,191.0	—	3,749.2	2,486.8	11,476.0	38,874.5	56,586.5 [l]	58,272.5
1992	535.3	1,910.0	—	385.9	2,328.6	11,599.9	48,513.2	62,827.6 [l]	65,272.9
1993	551.8	1,750.0	—	457.7	2,239.3	13,118.6	49,707.0	65,522.6 [m]	67,824.4
1994	393.0	1,960.0	—	516.1	2,038.9	12,619.3	54,839.2	70,013.5 [n]	72,366.5

Source: Eurostat.

Notes: From 1988 onwards agricultural levies, sugar levies and customs duties are met of 10% collection costs previously included as an expenditure item.

[a] UA until 1977, EUA/ECU from 1978 onwards.

[b] GNP until 1978, VAT from 1979 until 1987; GNP from 1988 onwards.

[c] This column includes for the years to 1970 surplus reserves from previous years carried forward to following years.

[d] As a result of the calculations to establish the relative shares of the member states in the 1976 budget, an excess of revenue over expenditure occurred amounting to 40.5 m. UA. This was carried forward to 1977

[e] Including surplus brought forward from 1979 and balance of 1979 VAT and financial contributions.

[f] Including surplus of ECU 82.4 m. carried forward to 1981.

[g] Including surplus of ECU 661 m.

[h] Including surplus of ECU 307 m.

[i] Including ECU 593 m. of repayable advances by member states.

[j] See note j to Table 16.3.

[k] Including non-repayable advances by member states of 1981, ECU 6 m.

[l] 1990–92; Court of Auditors' Report.

[m] General budget of the Community for 1993.

[n] General budget of the European Union for 1994.

Kingdom has been participating, with varying levels of enthusiasm, for a couple of decades. A complete monetary union is popularly conceived as consisting of a situation in which countries agree to dispense with their own national currencies and replace them with a single common currency. However, from one perspective it could be argued that a European single currency is not strictly an essential prerequisite for a monetary union, which would *de facto* exist in the presence of irrevocably fixed exchange rates between the European countries and full convertibility of national currencies, within a completed European common market.

A single currency would, however, certainly constitute a desirable or even crucial addition to the above. It would be an important symbol of the monetary union (creating a 'European monetary identity'), it would save on the transaction costs of changing currencies, and it would make the common market and other joint policies work better by increasing the transparency of prices. Most crucially, the single currency might safeguard the long-term integrity of the European monetary union. While different currencies exist, there will always be a doubt about the truly irrevocable nature of fixed exchange rates, given the political temptation to engineer a 'quick fix' for the economy via a devaluation.

The essential feature of monetary union in the EU is that it requires substantial macroeconomic (and to an extent microeconomic) convergence in order to be implemented without prohibitive economic (and political) costs, especially for the weaker economies that choose to participate.

A full monetary union would necessitate a common policy towards other currencies outside the union, requiring agreement on whether to fix or float the joint currency, as well as a pooling of reserves (or at least a commitment to make reserves available to partners), and a common policy towards exchange controls. Most significantly, monetary union requires a considerable degree of convergence in rates of inflation. In the absence of this, relatively high inflation countries experience losses in competitiveness and thus in relative levels of economic activity. Since there are no exchange rates, devaluation cannot compensate for differential rates of inflation. The alternative to devaluation is to make the 'burden of adjustment' fall on more painful areas such as the level of employment, investment, real incomes and growth.

On the face of it, all this would seem to involve the surrender of substantial economic sovereignty, for economic convergence of this kind clearly requires a substantial degree of cooperation and joint policy-making at the supranational level. First of all, countries lose control over important objectives of economic policy. There is a body of economic theory, pioneered by Fleming and Corden, which examines the welfare costs involved here in terms of countries having to accept second-best preferences in any Phillips trade-off between inflation and unemployment.[20] For example, a country involved in a monetary union cannot pursue a policy designed to reduce unemployment when its partners are involved in pursuing policies designed primarily to reduce the level of inflation. If the country wants to pursue its preferred policy stance it must first of all win the political battle over the objectives of economic policy. The distribution of these losses will be determined by the nature of joint decision making in the union. If the process is 'democratic', or based on some concept of averaging of preferences, then the costs will be more or less equally shared. If there is a 'leadership' outcome, then the leader (Germany, in the case of the EU) suffers none of the losses, which are then borne exclusively by other participants.

Countries furthermore lose individual control over the tools of policy. Policy has to be implemented in close cooperation with other countries, or, more probably, jointly implemented by supranational bodies such as the European Monetary Institute (EMI), the European System of Central Banks (ESCB) or the European Central Bank (ECB). Such authorities will need to implement a common monetary policy for the EU, with central determination of variables such as (assuming this were possible) the money supply and the rate of interest. There is clearly a good deal of scope here for sovereignty costs to be incurred. It may be, for example, that a macroeconomic stance that is appropriate for the union as a whole is not at all appropriate for individual regions. Or, as we have arguably seen in the wake of German unification, that the most powerful country in the union imposes a policy stance that is appropriate to its own needs but not to those of the union as a whole.

The prevailing wisdom among the economics profession is that inflation is predominantly a monetary phenomenon and is thus best controlled by monetary policy. Hence the emphasis in the Maastricht Treaty (see below) on developing a common monetary policy in the EU. To the extent that other factors also impinge on the rate of inflation, it may be necessary jointly to determine other policies as well, for example in the fiscal, microeconomic and structural areas. Additionally it should be noted that the current emphasis on inflation as the main item on the convergence agenda represents a particular ideological stance. In future it may be necessary and desirable to extend the convergence criteria to include more real variables such as perhaps the rate of unemployment, the rate of growth, indicators of regional disparity and personal income distribution and poverty. Another unresolved issue concerns the political accountability of economic policy. In the Maastricht scenario, the ECB would be an independent central bank, based on the Bundesbank model and with price stability as its prime institutional objective. There is a democratic deficit to the extent that at present there is no way to control or alter its activities through the political process. To begin to tackle this will require significant institutional reform within the EU.

The real question here, and the issue at the very centre of the monetary union debate, concerns the extent to which these apparent losses of national economic sovereignty are in fact real. Does real national economic sovereignty exist in today's world, or, to take an extreme stance, is it a total illusion fostered for ideological purposes? Put another way, to what extent could individual European nation states hope to exercise their own individual macroeconomic policies outside the EU? The specific answer to this will depend on a number of factors.[21] Nevertheless, one can make general observations in this context. Recent history is not too encouraging for what one may call the 'isolationist' stance. The experiences of the last Labour Government in the United Kingdom and of the Mitterrand administration in France from 1981–83[22] suggest that 'alternative' policies that go against the grain may be precluded by interdependence. At the same time the futile attempts by the UK Government to control the money supply in the mid-1980s and the recent ERM crisis provide examples which would suggest that there are limits to the power of 'mainstream' governments to exercise control over their own economies in an interdependent and deregulated world with large amounts of internationally mobile capital. The view taken here is that, in important aspects of macroeconomic policy at least, real national sovereignty is in practice somewhat limited. The alternative approach is that nations retain considerable freedom to diverge from what everybody else is doing. Proponents of this point to the UK devaluation and its consequent early emergence from recession. Whether this recovery is a real one and whether it can be sustained remains to be seen. Only time will tell who is right and who is wrong, and presumably even then history will be interpreted in different ways.

It is clearly premature to postulate that we have reached an historical phase in which the medium-sized European nation state has become obsolescent as a sovereign economic entity, but few would question that there are limits to its powers. If only large states can influence their own economic destinies, then this is surely a powerful case for monetary and other forms of European integration. In such a scenario integration does not imply loss of sovereignty, but rather enhancement of real sovereignty by a process of pooling.

To these potential sovereignty losses for the United Kingdom can be added the possibility of further losses of a distributional nature that may result from EMU, since there are grounds for believing that monetary union might disproportionately benefit the stronger participants at the expense of weaker areas.

While there may be losses, participation in an EMU would also offer some other important advantages to the United Kingdom. Apart from those mentioned above, one of the possible benefits of a monetary union lies in the fact that it allows countries to adopt what accountants refer to as 'best practice', i.e. the policy stances of the most successful. This might well be regarded as a distinctly attractive policy anchor in the United Kingdom as well as many other parts of Europe. At the same time there is a high probability that the UK financial sector[23] would benefit from participation.

However, in the end, the participating countries must believe that the benefits of a monetary union outweigh its costs – otherwise the union would presumably not take place.

WERNER TO MAASTRICHT: MONETARY INTEGRATION IN PRACTICE

Moving from the abstract and theoretical to a more immediate level, the current proposals for EMU are contained in the Maastricht Treaty of 1993, which has since been ratified by referenda and parliamentary votes in EU countries, often after a somewhat tortuous process. In this section we will examine the Maastricht Treaty and its antecedents.

The EU's progress towards monetary integration can be divided conveniently into three phases. Historically, monetary integration was not covered by the Treaty of Rome and was thus never an explicit objective of the EC. The issue first appeared on the European agenda at the Hague summit in 1969, partly as a strategy aimed at restoring stability after the political events of May 1968. The debate at the time centred on the extent to which Europe was in fact an 'optimum currency area',[24] and on the best strategy for constructing a monetary union. On the latter issue, there were two points of view, which came to be referred to as the 'economist' approach and the 'monetarist' position (nothing to do with Milton Friedman). The former, mainly supported by the Dutch and the Germans through the Schiller Plan, favoured a gradualist approach to EMU, involving the promotion of harmonisation and convergence in order to prepare the ground for the single currency. The latter, canvassed by the Commission, France and Belgium through the Barre Plan, supported a 'shock theory' approach, involving the introduction of fixed exchange rates as a *fait accompli*, leaving countries to adjust to these *ex post facto*.

The outcome was predictably a compromise between the two, in the shape of the Werner Plan of 1970, most of which was adopted by the Council of Ministers in March 1971 and which the came into effect in March 1972. This provided for some efforts to harmonise economic policies, but also created the 'snake in the tunnel' system of fixed exchange rates. The 'snake' consisted of fixing the exchange rates between the ten participants (the original six plus Britain, Denmark and Ireland, who were in the process of joining the then EEC) within bands of ±2.25 per cent. The 'tunnel' involved fixing the parity of the snake currencies against the dollar and other world currencies within the 4.5 per cent bands established in the Smithsonian Agreements of December 1971. The overall objective was a 'monetary union by 1980'. The observant reader will conclude therefore that the plan failed, collapsing in the wake of the disarray which followed the oil crisis. When the chips were down, European nation states were fundamentally unwilling to subordinate their own interests to those of European integration. Thus sterling floated away in June 1972, Italy left in February 1973, France in January 1974 and again in March 1976, and EMU faded away.

After the Werner Plan, the impetus towards monetary integration was revived in 1977 by Roy Jenkins, and the EMS was set up at the Bremen and Copenhagen Councils of 1978, coming into existence in March 1979. The EMS basically consisted of two features: the European Currency Unit (ECU), which was the European 'currency in waiting' and the fulcrum of the ERM. It is based on a weighted basket of all the currencies involved. Secondly, the Exchange Rate Mechanism (ERM), which attempts to fix the exchange rates between the participating countries and between these currencies and the ECU originally within a band of ±2.25 per cent and ±6 per cent for weaker currencies such as the lira and sterling. The bands following the sterling crisis of 1992 became ±15 per cent, putting into question whether the ERM had survived at all. There is thus a 'snake', but this time no 'tunnel', since the European currencies involved can float *vis-à-vis* the dollar, the yen and other world currencies. The mechanism for maintaining exchange rates within the system consisted of agreements for supportive central bank intervention in foreign exchange markets, a (limited) reserve pooling obligation, and a (largely unused) divergence indicator. This was backed up by some measures to promote policy convergence and by a limited redistributive mechanism.

There was considerable scepticism about the EMS at the time of its launch, and it encountered early instabilities. But to many people's surprise it weathered the storm in the early 1980s and proved to be a considerable success. It in fact promoted exchange stability in Western Europe, since there were only eleven realignments (twelve if one includes the exit of sterling and the lira in late 1992) altogether, and none at all between January 1987 and the exit of sterling. Currencies outside the ERM experienced considerably greater instability. The EMS also probably contributed to lower and increasingly convergent rates of inflation in Europe, although it must be said that price stability was also facilitated by the neoliberal consensus on economic policy in this period. Finally, it managed to establish an increasing role for the ECU as a private sector currency in the course of the 1980s.

However, the EMS was weakened by the United Kingdom's refusal to join the ERM (although sterling was always part of the ECU basket) until 'the time was right' in October 1990,[25] and arguably by excessive reliance on German leadership. Nevertheless, it paved the way for what was to follow, for the very success of the EMS provided the stimulus in the late 1980s for a debate on the way forward for the system. The Commission's response was to set up the Delors Committee which produced what is usually referred to as the Delors Report in April 1989, calling for a full monetary union to be set up in three stages. This spawned two InterGovernmental Conferences (IGCs, one of which was on the subject of political union, which had not originally been on the agenda) then the Maastricht Treaty, which has now been ratified in EU member states. This is the third and current phase of the monetary integration process.

It is important to note that the Maastricht Treaty deals with more than just monetary union, for it constitutes a wide-ranging reform of the Community and a significant step forward for European integration on a number of fronts. Its principal feature is the Treaty on European Union, but there are also seventeen assorted protocols (additional agreements not signed by all members) as well as thirty-three Declarations (guidelines on the interpretation and implementation of the Treaty, which however are not legally binding).[26]

The Treaty of European Union amends the Treaty of Rome and it consists of five aspects.

1 The European Union, based primarily on the EC and its institutions, but also on a common intergovernmental foreign and security policy, a common home affairs and justice policy (conducted on an intergovernmental basis), and a number of common policies in areas such as education, training, youth, public health, the labour market, industrial policy, communications, research and development, regional policy, environmental policy and development policy.
2 Subsidiarity,[27] which was introduced into the Treaty largely to allay the fears in certain quarters that too much power might be transferred to the EU level. Paradoxically, it might also pave the way for regionalism and the marginalisation of the nation state in the (very) long run.
3 A Committee of the Regions, with solely advisory powers.[28]
4 EMU, as we shall discuss below.
5 European Citizenship, which is considered in many quarters to be a somewhat controversial concept, but the proposals include giving European citizens the right to stand for election and vote in local and European elections in all EU states, to be represented by the consuls of all EU states, and to complain to the European Ombudsman about deficiencies in EU institutions.[29]

All this is to be supplemented by some limited institutional reform granting a little more power to the European Parliament, some provisions for tackling fraud and ensuring financial rectitude (the Court of Auditors becomes a full EC institution), and an enhancement in the powers of the European Court of Justice to improve the implementation of EU legislation. Finally there is the Social Chapter, a separate protocol outlining basic employment rights, to which the United Kingdom has not adhered. The United Kingdom and Denmark also have the right to 'opt out' of the provisions for EMU.

The specific proposals and timetable for EMU are shown below. The first of the three stages is undertaken under existing Community powers, while the final two stages require an amendment to the Treaty of Rome.

1 Stage one consists of the completion of the single market, increased coordination and cooperation in economic and monetary fields, strengthening the EMS, an extended role for the ECU and an enhanced role for

the Committee of Governors of EU members' central banks. This stage began in July 1990 and should have been completed by January 1993. It was in fact thrown into disarray by the currency crisis of late 1992.

2 Stage two essentially involves the groundwork for the single currency: all members are to be included in the narrow band of the ERM, the European Monetary Institute (EMI) is to be set up to promote the coordination necessary for EMU. This stage began in January 1994, but the turmoil in the ERM has meant that it is far from complete.

3 Stage three is then complete monetary union, with the introduction of the Euro as the single currency for Europe. A specific agenda has been prepared for this, with deadlines and convergence criteria that are to be met. The timetable is as follows:

- by December 1996, if the EC Council of Finance Ministers decide by a qualified majority that a 'critical mass' of seven states (six, if the United Kingdom opts out) have met the convergence criteria, then a date is to be set for introducing the ECU in relevant states. Failing that,
- by December 1997, the start of an automatic process leading to complete monetary union among a minimum of five states by January 1999. Additionally,
- 1998 is to see the start of the creation of the European central bank (ECB), which takes over from the EMI, and is seen as the independent issuer of currency, and of the European System of Central banks (ESCB), the independent conductor of monetary policy and foreign exchange operations. If these institutions are not yet in place, then national central banks are to become independent at this time. The numbers involved are necessarily modified in the light of the 1995 EFTA enlargement.

The Maastricht convergence criteria are as follows:

1 states must have a maximum budget deficit of 3 per cent of GDP per annum;
2 countries must have a maximum total public sector debt of 60 per cent of GDP;
3 there are to be no realignments within the ERM;
4 countries are to have a rate of inflation a maximum of 1.5 per cent above the average rate in the three lowest inflation EU countries in the year before the decision (1996 or 1998). This qualification rate (4.7 per cent when the Treaty was signed) must be judged as 'sustainable';
5 long-term (government bond) interest rates should be a maximum of 2 per cent above the average of those in the three lowest rate countries.

Table 16.5 shows the situation regarding these convergence criteria in 1993, just after the Treaty was signed, as well as giving some indication of the prospects of countries meeting them by 1999.

Table 16.5 Current position on, and prospects for, the Maastricht convergence criteria

Member state	Inflation in 1993 %	Pass test by 1999?	Public deficit 1993 % of GDP	Pass test by 1999?	Long term interest rate 1993 %	Pass test by 1999?	Public debt 1993 % of GDP	Pass test by 1999?	Feasible to join EMU by 1999?
Belgium	2.8	✓	7.4	≈	7.3	✓	138	⊙	✓
Denmark	1.4	✓	4.4	✓	8.9	✓	79	✓	✓
Germany	4.3	✓	4.2	✓	6.3	✓	50	✓	✓
Greece	13.7	⊙	15.5	⊙	23.9	⊙	114	⊙	⊙
Spain	4.7	≈	7.2	≈	10.2	≈	56	✓	≈
France	2.3	✓	5.9	✓	6.8	✓	45	✓	✓
Ireland	2.3	✓	3.0	✓	7.7	✓	93	✓	✓
Italy	4.4	≈	10.0	⊙	11.3	⊙	116	⊙	⊙
Luxembourg	3.6	✓	2.5	✓	6.9	✓	10	✓	✓
Netherlands	2.1	✓	4.0	✓	6.7	✓	83	✓	✓
Portugal	6.7	⊙	8.9	⊙	12.4	⊙	70	✓	✓
UK	3.4	≈	7.6	✓	7.9	✓	53	✓	≈
EU average	3.8		6.4		8.1		66		
Target	<1.5% above 3 best		3.0%		<2% above 3 best		60%		
Austria	3.7	✓	2.9	✓	6.6	✓	57	✓	✓
Finland	2.2	≈	9.1	⊙	10.0	≈	60	✓	≈
Norway	2.3	✓	3.2	✓	6.9	✓	47	✓	✓
Sweden	4.5	≈	14.7	≈	8.8	✓	67	≈	≈

✓ Should achieve the criterion relatively easily.
≈ Will have difficulties meeting the criterion and may not manage to do so.
⊙ Unlikely to meet the criterion.
Source: European Parliament (1994).

Table 16.6 European Union: key economic projections

	GDP growth* 1996	GDP growth* 1997	Fiscal deficit** 1996	Fiscal deficit** 1997
Belgium	1.1	2.3	−1.2	−3.7
Denmark	1.3	2.7	−0.9	−0.6
Germany	0.5	1.8	−3.9	−2.9
Greece	2.0	2.5	−8.1	−6.9
Spain	2.0	2.9	−4.8	−3.7
France	1.0	2.1	−4.2	−3.0
Ireland	5.6	4.9	−2.0	1.6
Iceland	1.8	2.7	−8.3	−5.2
Luxembourg	2.6	3.0	−0.7	0.3
Netherlands	1.8	2.5	−3.5	−2.9
Austria	0.7	1.1	−4.6	−3.1
Portugal	2.3	2.8	−4.4	−3.7
Finland	3.0	3.6	−3.3	−1.6
Sweden	1.2	2.0	−5.2	−3.1
UK	2.4	3.0	−4.4	−3.7
EU	1.5	2.4	−4.4	−3.4

Source: European Commission.
Notes: *GDP annual growth (%).
 **Fiscal deficit as % of GDP.

Since then we have seen governments throughout Europe desperately tailoring their economic policies and stances to meet the criteria, often with severe deflationary consequences and in face of severe political opposition. The latest Commission forecasts (May 1996) suggest that Britain, Belgium, Spain, Italy, Austria and Portugal are all likely to fail to meet the budget deficit criterion (a maximum of 3 per cent of GDP to enter EMU in 1999) in 1997. Negotiation and political wheeling and dealing on the final conditions of entry are thus likely to be the order of the day in the run up to 1999. Table 16.6 shows the Commission forecasts in mid-1996.

CONCLUSION

The immediate future of the European integration project is closely tied up with EMU, and the future of EMU is uncertain. There are many difficulties, a point emphasised by factors such as British reluctance, the difficulties in ratifying Maastricht, the difficulties Germany has experienced over unification, the costs involved for some of the outlying states in meeting the convergence criteria in a recession, and the disarray within the ERM that turbulent foreign exchange markets have precipitated.[30] However, a rump of the most economically advanced countries in the EU (Germany, France, Austria, Belgium, Luxembourg, the Netherlands, and perhaps Sweden and

Table 16.7 Introduction of a single currency/sequence of events

Phase A Launch of EMU	Phase B Start of EMU	Phase C Single currency fully introduced
Start of the phase	*Start of the phase*	*Start of the phase*
• List of participating member states • Date of start of EMU announced (or confirmed) • Deadline for the final changeover to the single currency • Setting up of the ESCB and the ECB • Start of production of notes and coins	• Fixing of conversion rates • ECU becomes a currency in its own right • Monetary and exchange-rate policy in ECU • Inter bank, monetary, capital, and exchange markets in ECU • New government debt issued in ECU • Corresponding wholesale payment systems in ECU	• ECU notes and coins introduced • Banks have completed the changeover (retail business payment systems) • Notes and coins denominated in national currency are withdrawn • Public and private operators complete the changeover • Only the ECU is used
Throughout the phase	*Throughout the phase*	
Stepping-up of preparations and implementation of measures that will, if possible, have been adopted beforehand • Legal framework • National steering structure • Banking and financial community changeover plan	• Banks and financial institutions continue the changeover institutions continue the chageover • Public and private operators other than banks proceed with the changeover circumstances permitting	
1 year maximum	3 years maximum	Several weeks

Source: EC Commission (1995).

even the United Kingdom) seem to be both ready and willing to proceed within something like the conditions and timetable set out in the Maastricht Treaty. The EU institutions, meanwhile, continue with their planning, the current plans being illustrated in Table 16.7.

Discussions are currently taking place within an IGC on the future of Maastricht and EMU. Various outcomes are possible, including a two-speed or even a 'variable geometry'[31] Europe. The view taken here is that it is by no means certain[32] that EMU will take place as envisaged in the Maastricht Treaty, but that the political momentum towards it on mainland Europe is such that some kind of EMU might well happen by the millenium. In any case, in the medium term monetary union is likely, given the forces that are driving it and the political will which still exists to achieve it. Whether the

United Kingdom participates will be determined by a variety of factors, principally the nature of UK governance when the time arrives. Whatever decision is taken is likely to be an historic turning point for the United Kingdom.

NOTES

1 The original Community of six countries (West Germany, France, Italy, Belgium, the Netherlands and Luxembourg) had existed from March 1957, when the Treaty of Rome was signed. In 1973 the United Kingdom, Ireland and Denmark became members to complete the first enlargement of the EC. The second phase of enlargements, usually referred to as the Southern enlargement, involved the absorbtion of Greece (in 1981) and the Iberian states of Spain and Portugal in 1986. The Community of twelve that was thus created was unchanged for nearly a decade until the former EFTA states of Austria, Sweden and Finland joined the EU in 1995. Post-Maastricht we thus have a European Union of fifteen states, and the possibility of a number of others joining in the foreseeable future.

2 Notably as a result of the EC's '1992' programme to complete the internal market, and of the 1993 Maastricht Treaty (see below).

3 Among which Councils of Heads of State, or Summits, are the most important. It is these that are responsible for strategic decisions.

4 Despite the existence of some cooperation and co-decision procedures.

5 There is a view that Mrs Thatcher's obstructiveness actually facilitated further progress, since it served to unite the other leaders involved against her.

6 Cynics might claim that this also had something to do with the supposition that any development that Margaret Thatcher disliked so much must have some good in it.

7 The terms 'trade creation' and 'trade diversion' were first devised by Jacob Viner in the 1950s. Customs union theory was then developed by a number of eminent international economists such as Bhagwati and Lipsey. For a full discussion, see a number of books on the economics of European integration, including Lintner and Mazey (1991).

8 For a good survey of empirical studies of the effects of the EC customs union, see Robson (1987).

9 In fact the original EEC customs union infringed the 'most-favoured-nation' principle of the GATT, which then had to be suitably amended.

10 See Petith (1977) and Cecchini (1988).

11 See Lintner and Mazey (1991).

12 These 'impact costs' were to an extent foreseen, but were expected to be outweighed by longer-term 'dynamic' gains. For example, it may well be that membership has helped the United Kingdom to attract a greater amount of foreign direct investment from the USA, Japan and elsewhere. The overall impact of accession is impossible to quantify, and is in any case largely immaterial, given that, despite the political lurch towards 'Euroscepticism', there seems now no realistic prospect of the United Kingdom withdrawing from the EU.

13 As well as other countries such as Greece.

14 See, for example, Edye and Lintner (1996).

15 The variable levy.

16 For a fuller consideration of the impact of the CAP, see Lintner and Mazey (1991).

17 United Kingdom per capita GDP expressed in ECU was 89.2 per cent of the EU

average in 1994, and it has been below the EU average every year since 1969, except for the period 1981–5.

18 There is also a structural element to the CAP. This is, however, insignificant in relation to the price support aspect of agricultural policy.

19 EURATOM, despite its endemic problems, was much more strongly directed at promoting European development in its technological sphere..

20 Whatever form this trade-off takes, and indeed whether it exists at all – the expectations-augmented approach would imply that common rates of inflation can be achieved without serious long-term employment effects.

21 See Lintner, in Brouwer *et al.* (1994).

22 Mitterrand was elected with a mandate to pursue a French version of the 'altern-ative economic strategy', based on Keynesian reflation and increased state inter-vention in industry. This happened at a time when Thatcher, Reagan and others were busy experimenting with monetarism. Thus France expanded demand when its trading partners were contracting theirs, and the result was a balance of pay-ments crisis and a policy U-turn towards the ERM and the 'franc fort' stance which eventually laid the base for economic success in the late 1980s.

23 And other sectors, to judge by the position adopted by the CBI.

24 An area in which it is possible and beneficial to have fixed exchange rates, see Mundell (1961).

25 Arguably the worst time imaginable, in the context of German unification and the coming recession.

26 For an excellent interpretation of the Maastricht Treaty, see Church and Phinnemore (1994).

27 The principle by which policy in the EU should be pursued at the lowest effective level of government.

28 See Brouwer, Lintner and Newman (1994).

29 Non-EU citizens who are legally resident in the EU also have this right.

30 At the time of writing the ERM technically continues to exist without sterling and the lira, and with fluctuation bands of ±15 per cent.

31 Countries being left to an extent free to opt in or out of various EU developments.

32 Or even necessarily desirable, given that (a) the convergence criteria are rigid and ideologically biased to the exclusion of real criteria such as unemployment and regional disparities; (b) the issue of the democratic accountability of EU institu-tions such as the ECB remains unresolved; and (c) there is a largely insufficient redistribution mechanism within the EU.

REFERENCES AND FURTHER READING

Ardy, B. (1988) 'The national incidence of the European Community Budget', *Journal of Common Market Studies*, vol. XXVI, pp. 401–30.

Brouwer, F., Lintner, V. and Newman, M (eds) (1994) *Economic Policy-making and the EU*, London: Federal Trust.

Cecchini, P. (1988) *1992: The Benefits of a Single Market*, Report of the Cost of Non-Europe Steering Committee, Aldershot: Wildwood House.

Church, C. H. and Phinnemore, D. (1994) *European Union and European Community*, Hemel Hempstead: Harvester Wheatsheaf.

Coates, K. and Barrett Brown, M. (eds) (1993) *A European Recovery Programme*, Nottingham: Spokesman.

Cooper, R. C. and Massell, B. F. (1965) 'A New Look at Customs Union Theory', *Economic Journal* vol. 75, December.

Corden, W. M. (1971) *Monetary Integration*, Princeton Essays in International Finance, no. 73.

Demekas, D. G., Bartholdy, K., Gupta, S., Lipschitz, L., and Mayer, T. (1988) 'The effects of the common agricultural policy of the European Community: A survey of the literature', *Journal of Common Market Studies*, vol. XXVII, pp. 61–78.

Dunning, J. (1989) 'European integration and transatlantic foreign direct investment: The record assessed', paper presented at the *Fulbright International Colloqium, "1992: Europe and America"*, Reading, December.

Edye, D. and Lintner, V. (1996) *Contemporary Europe*, Hemel Hempstead: Prentice-Hall.

European Commission (1995) *One Currency for Europe*, Green Paper on the Practical Arrangements for the Introduction of the Single Currency, Brussels.

European Parliament (1994) *The Social Consequences of Economic and Monetary Union*, Working Paper, Social Affairs Series, Luxembourg.

Fleming, M. (1971) 'On exchange rate unification', *Economic Journal*, vol. 81.

Holland, S. (1983) *Out of Crisis*, Nottingham: Spokesman.

—— (1993) *The European Imperative*, Nottingham: Spokesman.

Johnson, H. (1965) 'An economic theory of protectionism, tariff bargaining and the formation of customs unions', *Journal of Political Economy*, vol. 73, pp. 256–83.

Labour Party (1981) 'Withdrawal from the EEC', Research Papers, *Labour Party Research Department*, September.

—— (1989) 'Meeting the Challenge in Europe', *Labour Party Manifesto*.

Lintner, V. and Mazey, S. (1991) *The European Community: Economic and political aspects*, Maidenhead: McGraw-Hill.

McGowan, F. (1994) 'EC Industrial Policy', in A. M. El-Agraa, *The Economics of the European Community*, 4th edn, Hemel Hempstead: Harvester Wheatsheaf.

Mayes, D. (1994) 'Factor mobility' in A. M. El-Agraa, (ed.) *The Economics of the European Community*, 4th ed, Hemel Hempstead: Harvester Wheatshef.

Mundell, R. A. (1961) 'A Theory of Optimum Currency Areas', *American Economic Review*, vol. 51, pp. 657–65.

Myrdal, G. (1957) *Economic Theory and Underdeveloped Regions*, London: Duckworth.

Oates, W. (1972) *Fiscal Federalism*, London: Harcourt, Brace, Jovanovitch.

O'Cleireacain, S. (1989)'EC Policies towards Japanese trade and Investment: Implications for US–EC relations', paper presented at the *Fulbright International Colloqium, "1992: Europe and America"*, Reading, December.

Petith, H. (1977) 'European integration and the terms of trade', *Economic Journal*, vol. 87, June, pp. 262–72.

Robson, P. (1987) *The Economics of International Integration*, 3rd edn, London: Allen & Unwin.

Schultz, M. (1996) *Western Europe since 1945: Economic and social change*, Harlow: Longman.

Sharp, M. L. and Pavitt, K. (1993) 'Technology policy in the 1990s: Old trends and new realities', *Journal of Common Market Studies*, vol. 31, no. 2.

Winters, L. A. (1987) 'Britain in Europe: A survey of quantitative trade studies', *Journal of Common Market Studies*, vol. XXV, no. 4, pp. 315–35.

17

COST COMPETITIVENESS, THE ERM AND UK ECONOMIC POLICY[1]

Tony Buxton and Valerio Lintner

INTRODUCTION

In joining the Exchange Rate Mechanism (ERM) of the European Monetary System (EMS) in 1990, as well as any benefits to its trade performance, the United Kingdom hoped to secure a stable base for low inflation and sustainable economic growth. Joining would provide an 'anchor' which would reinforce anti-inflationary policy, accepting the disciplines that membership involves and removing the temptation to manipulate the economy for political ends which arguably had generated the 'stop-go' of the post-war period. It was therefore a highly laudable scheme for John Major to promote as the centre-piece of his economic policy and had the support of all the major UK political actors, of the Bank of England,[2] as well as the practical support, if necessary, of the other central banks in the EU. An anchor it turned out not to be. On 16 September 1992, the United Kingdom left the ERM after a period of intense pressure on sterling and considerable political remonstrations.

In the days leading up to that incident, the then UK Chancellor, Norman Lamont, described devaluation as 'fool's gold'. That and similar statements were of course necessary as evidence of the Government's determination not to resort to leaving the ERM to relieve pressure on the pound, and therefore hopefully to stave off slippage of the anchor. Once the pound was free to float, its value fell. By 18 September its rate had fallen by 5 per cent from its ERM 'floor' of DM 2.78. On the same day Mr Lamont was reported to have said 'we have not resorted to devaluation, the pound is now currently floating and we will have to see what level it finds'.[3] On the same day, the same source also reported the not entirely unrelated 'Britain's jobless total rises to five-year high'. Following 1992, the pound further drifted down relative to the DM, amounting to a total devaluation/float of about 20 per cent against the DM until 1996 when it recovered.

It is now commonly held that, along with many other policy 'tricks and levers', devaluation does not 'work' in stimulating the economy; that any short-term benefits to exporters are eventually eroded by the inflationary effects of higher import prices, and furthermore that such manoeuvres reduce the authorities' credibility.[4] Devaluation may 'work' in reducing real incomes to levels commensurate with external balance, however. Devaluation beginning in 1981 amounted to more than 30 per cent over the 1980s. Whether it 'workd' is an interesting question. It was accompanied by a 30 per cent rise in the real output of manufacturing industry and a 65 per cent rise in the volume of that sector's exports, up to the cyclical peak in 1990.2. The next logical question is therefore: will the devaluation since September 1992 'work' in the longer term?[5] The Government's view is that the apparently strong, inflation-free recovery in the economy since then is due to the broad thrust of its policies and not to the devaluation of the pound and has had support in high places.[6] So does the United Kingdom still need an external anchor in the form of the ERM, or is it now big enough to stand on its own two feet?[7] Can things be different now, or will the economy again suffer the agonies of an apparent boom which turns to slump and puts another notch on the inflationary/unsustainable growth scenario?[8] If this is to happen then it essentially means that, should real incomes need to be reduced, consistent with internal and/or external balance, the authorities will have the political will to carry it out without resorting to devaluation. Or, on the other hand, the authorities can be trusted not to attempt a 'competitive devaluation' for short-term political advantage. If it is the case that rejoining would not involve looking to the ERM for an anchor because the authorities can now be trusted and/or because they know that the City cannot be fooled into thinking that the ERM can provide one, then the debate concerning re-entry could involve the possible trade benefits and the sovereignty and policy restrictions which membership entails, presuming that the common currency is just around the corner.[9]

The events around September 1992 brought considerable political repercussions in their wake. It was a deeply significant phase of contemporary British economic history, putting into focus a number of key issues relating to the conduct of UK economic policy. This chapter asks whether, given the economic incidents of the medium to long term that preceded this, the departure from the ERM was inevitable – was this anchor[10] a pipedream? It goes on from there to consider whether the possible internal anchor is strong enough to ensure stability in the ERM in the future, and the role that involvement in the process of monetary integration in the EU may play in the conduct of UK economic policy in the medium and longer term – whether this or any other anchor is feasible. Arguably an answer to this question is vital to the debate about the long-term future of the pound. It does this by particular reference to the productivity performance of the United Kingdom relative to its major competitors.

BACKGROUND TO UK ENTRY TO THE ERM

It is important in answering these questions to examine some aspects of the United Kingdom's involvement in the process of monetary integration and in particular the ERM. The United Kingdom has always been a member of the EMS from its inception in 1979. Sterling has always formed part of the ECU weighted basket; the United Kingdom has deposited the required 20 per cent of its foreign exchange reserves with the European Monetary Cooperation Fund in exchange for ECU; and the country has participated in developments designed to strengthen the system, for example the Basle/Nyborg agreement of September 1987.

However, the British government consistently refused explicitly to join the ERM during the 1980s. At first a variety of arguments were used against joining, mainly to do with the particular structural characteristics of the UK economy: sterling's anomalous position as an international currency and as a 'petro-currency'; the characteristics of the local labour market; the United Kingdom's position as a high-inflation country relative to the other major actors in the system; even the nature of the UK housing market.[11] All this would, in the minds of the authorities, render the impact costs of membership of a fixed exchange rate system too onerous in terms of unemployment and the reduction in the level of economic activity, notwithstanding any long-run benefits from an effective anchor.

Arguably, however, the underlying reason for the British government's reticence was political: a reluctance on the part of factions within the Conservative Party to contemplate the required surrender of national economic (and thus political) sovereignty in monetary and other areas of policy.[12] Thus membership was felt to be incompatible with the Medium Term Financial Strategy, and would open the way for further monetary integration requiring 'political union, a United States of Europe, which is not on the agenda'.[13] This view is in line with the generally suspicious attitude which the British Government has adopted on matters European, and would seem to be borne out by subsequent events, such as the Maastricht 'opt-out', as well as the very recent ructions caused by the 'Eurosceptics' in the Conservative Party,[14] not to mention Sir James Goldsmith's Referendum Party.

When the impetus towards deeper European integration intensified during the mid/late 1980s,[15] and the prospect of the ERM developing into a European Monetary Union became a distinct possibility, the British Government's position changed from one of rejection to one of prevarication: we would join 'when the time is right'. At this time, some of the potential benefits of participating in the European monetary integration project were being strongly canvassed. French economic prospects had been transformed by membership after the failures of the first Mitterrand government of 1981–3 and here was a real chance to break the post-war UK cycle of wage increases exceeding productivity growth leading to higher inflation, loss of competitiveness and devaluation. If this involved accepting welfare losses of the Fleming-Corden type,[16] then it might be a price worth paying. In any case, real UK sovereignty over economic policy was increasingly regarded as a questionable concept in an interdependent world characterised by open economies, multinational production, high capital mobility and deregulated capital and foreign exchange markets.[17] As a result, a policy of 'shadowing the D-Mark' was adopted by Nigel Lawson, with the exchange rate as the major policy target following the 'official' abandonment of monetarism in 1986,[18] with a view to proving that the United Kingdom could keep up with the DM and that ERM entry was feasible.

Tracking the DM outside the EMS is a completely different matter to when on the inside, however. 'Credibility' when outside is important, but is everything on the inside. Gaining credibility takes time, however, and in the event, when the United Kingdom did join in October 1990, it could hardly have chosen a worse time. This was the month of German unification, which was to lead to German policy stances that would exacerbate the coming recession[19] and effectively scupper attempts by European governments to meet the Maastricht convergence criteria and perhaps even destroy the ERM itself. The UK economy had peaked in the second quarter of 1990 and was going into decline. In addition, sterling entered the ERM at a rate (Dm 2.85) that was arguably far too high, even allowing for the wider fluctuation bands that were to be allowed to the United Kingdom. The immediate costs of ERM membership were thus substantially greater than they otherwise might have been and, as we shall argue, made short-run credibility very difficult and rendered permanence within the EMS highly problematic.

THE SIGNIFICANCE OF PRODUCTIVITY IMPROVEMENTS

It is in this context that this chapter examines productivity and cost competitiveness in the United Kingdom. Productivity growth is a key element in economic development. In the short run the ability of the economy to satisfy the demands upon it depends upon the productivity of its resources. When this is inadequate, the resultant excess demand tends to generate balance of payments or inflation problems that have been so prevalent in destabilising much of the United Kingdom's economic evolution. In the medium term, the path of productivity can strongly influence international competitiveness. This in turn can raise output and improve living standards in the long run.

In the United Kingdom much attention has been focused on the extent to which productivity improved in the 1980s as a result of the new regime with its emphases on 'supply-side' policies rather than the 'demand-side' ones that had dominated the post-war period. The issue was regarded as particularly important because the growth of productivity seemed in the mid- to late

1970s to have fallen to a dangerously low level and also because of the link between productivity and competitiveness in international markets, where the United Kingdom's share of world manufactured exports continued to fall and the balance of trade of manufactures followed a similar downward trend until, in 1983 for the first time, it went into deficit. Whether there had been a sustainable change in productivity became a key economic issue. The word 'miracle' was often used to describe the claimed turnaround that took place in the 1980s and was professed to have arisen out of the new economic policies.[20]

Both labour and capital are important in maintaining or improving competitiveness, but only labour is considered here. This is not because capital is unimportant for productivity improvement. The ultimate resource though is people, and the extent to which they can fashion improvement determines long-run growth so that in the end labour productivity is paramount. The paper also looks only at manufacturing industry. This is not because the rest of the economy is unimportant, but manufacturing is often seen as the driving force for exports and therefore the balance of payments, an area where strong performance is vital and has been found somewhat wanting in the United Kingdom over the years.[21]

A high proportion of UK output is sold directly or indirectly in competitive international markets. Maintaining and improving 'competitiveness' is therefore vital to overall economic success.[22] While price is of central importance, competition in quality, in design and process, in selling, and in matching design to markets are also crucial. Strong impressionistic evidence suggests that UK non-price competitiveness and product quality, delivery date, design, reliability and after-sales service improved over the decade of the 1980s,[23] and may well have contributed significantly to improving competitiveness in the short run and, if maintained, in the longer term as well. But non-price factors are hard to quantify, and good statistical indicators are generally not available[24] so that only price factors are considered here.

The early 1990s' UK recession and subsequent recovery has to some extent put into abeyance a verdict on whether the new policy regime has established a sustainable new order. Nevertheless the aim of this chapter is to investigate whether there is evidence of a break with the past; namely a fundamental sustainable improvement in productivity and cost competitiveness by providing a straightforward collection of evidence making comparisons of aspects of UK manufacturing productivity and linking it to international competitiveness. Given its economic history, this is vital if readmission to the ERM is viable at some future date. The evaluation forgoes parametric statistical analysis and tests. While not denying them their place, a more intuitive approach is taken here to be put beside other evidence.

THE UK EXPERIENCE

The debate about the United Kingdom's relative improvement received much analytical attention and revolved around the basic question – was it sustainable or not? The issue was whether the UK economic policy changes of the 1980s[25] had a fundamental effect or whether it was just another cyclical recovery. On the positive side the potential for catch-up on the other countries was thought significant. But other countries have not been standing still. They too had to respond to the increased harshness of international competition as impediments to free trade were lowered and removed and the world economy became more competitive. The process of 'catching-up', however, may be easier than setting the pace, so that the UK economic policy changes in the 1980s may have had a stronger effect than elsewhere. The 'supply-side revolution' which most countries strove to achieve may have been more beneficial to the UK economy because reform was much more radical. The freeing-up of markets and the return of the 'right to manage',[26] the 'enterprise culture'[27] and the 'fear factor'[28] in the United Kingdom may have made firms more responsive and competitive in world markets. Furthermore the severity of the slump at the turn of the decade was greater in the United Kingdom than in most other countries.

Additionally, the UK recovery was longer and stronger than in previous cycles so that confidence to invest in advanced technology may have been greater and this might have been self-generating. The 1980s also saw an acceleration in the use of stock control systems such as 'just-in-time' and 'right-first-time,' and of team-working and similar methods. The effects of these can be dramatic, and may not only raise the level of productivity but also increase its growth rate by imposing flexibility so that firms can respond quicker to changing demand patterns. A related factor is the redesign of products to eliminate some operations and components, a route adopted by the Japanese which the United Kingdom has been following.

The combination of a deep recession between 1979 and 1981, supply-side measures designed to complement a stable macroeconomic stance, and a relatively long recovery may therefore have created the conditions for a sustainable improvement in manufacturing productivity growth. On the negative side, however, the length and strength of the recovery might have simply reflected the depth of the 1979–81 slump, which was undoubtedly severe and which saw the end of many companies. This may have boosted productivity simply by the 'batting average' effect, where low productivity companies were put out of business. Furthermore those that went to the wall may have been potentially the most dynamic, but in investing in the longer term had stretched themselves too far when the recession deepened and lengthened.[29] The effect on unemployment was prolonged, so that 'precariousness'[30] may have reduced 'flexibility' and labour increasingly failed to reallocate quickly and efficiently.[31] Furthermore in the latter part of the 1980s the economy was run at a very rapid rate so that output growth was very fast and productivity may have benefited simply in a 'Verdoorn' manner not dissimilar to the past.[32]

So whether or not the improvement in productivity growth in the 1980s over the later 1970s is sustainable is hard to say. The extent to which the 1980s differed from earlier periods is obviously basic to the debate. Figure 17.1 gives productivity growth in UK manufacturing industry over eight cycles up to 1990. While the UK economy as a whole experienced relatively steady growth after the 1979–81 recession – a single cycle spanning eleven years – as far as manufacturing was concerned, the 1980s must be split into two.[33]

In both 1980s' cycles, productivity grew rapidly but the rate was faster in the later period, partly of course because the early 1980s included a very big recession. Productivity growth in the 1980s was not the fastest in the post-war period, however – the most rapid was in the late 1960s – but the progression in the 1980s over the 1970s is again clear. Only a comparison with an 'ideal' or what was potentially achievable can tell if this was above expectations, or whether it reversed a potential further decline, and this is not possible. On the surface, though, the long period of rapid productivity growth does suggest an improvement.

Whether the strong performance of the 1980s is sustainable remains to be seen. Analysis of cycles in terms of the output and employment changes that

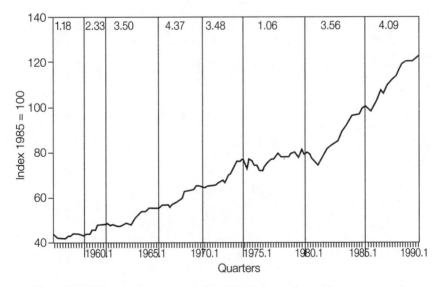

Figure 17.1 UK manufacturing productivity: index and growth rate over cycles
Source: CSO.

437

accompanied those in productivity can help in the clarification of the process of productivity growth.[34] This suggests that until the mid-1960s, productivity and output increased at fairly equal rates so that employment remained relatively stable. After this a different order began to emerge: output grew less than productivity, and employment fell away until midway through each cycle – the so-called 'shake-out' of labour – but then recovered to some extent. This divergence between the paths of output and productivity became more marked cycle by cycle, and culminated in the period between 1979.2 and 1985.2 when employment fell monotonically and faster than ever before – the massive 'shake-out' of employment in the early 1980s which amounted to a quarter of the employed labour force in manufacturing.

An obvious explanation for this was that employers were able to reduce overmanning and trade-union restrictive practices – the *raison d'être* of the labour market reforms which had been carried out as part of supply-side policy. Was this a once-and-for-all improvement, where productivity rose as monopoly power in the labour market was lessened by trade union reform, or did the change generate a fresh start, enabling the continuous accomplishment of new technology and efficient work practices which accelerated the underlying growth path – was it short run or longer term? The experience of the 1980s suggests that in the second 1980s' cycle the earlier growth pattern seen until the mid-1960s was to some extent restored – productivity and output grew at similar rates and employment actually rose slightly after its trough in 1987.1.

Which of these patterns is more desirable and more likely to be sustainable – productivity from a shake-out where employment falls, or from more rapid output increase where employment is maintained or increased? The answer is obvious and is supported by the experience of Japanese manufacturing. Improvements in productivity over cycles which is dominated by shake-outs and relatively poor output growth cannot be the way forward if manufacturing is not to go into terminal decline. The striking question is whether developments in the late 1980s portend a return to the opposite, or even an improvement? It is relatively early days since the peak in 1990.2, but events since then suggest that the recovery in manufacturing is more like the mid-1970s to mid-1980s than the late 1980s, as shown in Figure 17.2.

The graph shows output falling by nearly 4 per cent. After 1990.2, productivity fell for two quarters but then picked up and grew by nearly 13 per cent to the second quarter of 1992 with employment falling rapidly *ipso facto* – the 'shake-out' source of productivity improvement seems to have come round again. To the extent that output is the superior basis, the portents for the future of UK manufacturing productivity are not good.

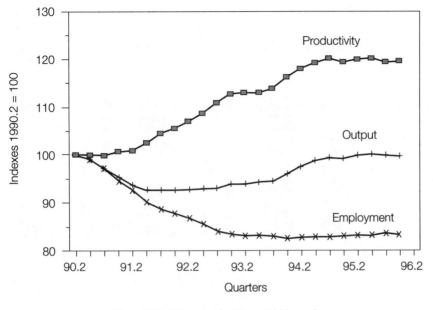

Figure 17.2 UK manufacturing: 1990s cycle
Source: CSO.

PRODUCTIVITY ACROSS COUNTRIES

International differences are at the heart of many comparisons in the literature but present difficulties. Countries are generally at different stages in their
economic development. Since the United Kingdom was the first country to
industrialise then arguably it is the furthest down the road and industrial
comparisons with others are inappropriate. And while it is manufacturing
which is under investigation here, the other parts of the economy are linked.
This does not rule out such comparisons of course.

Figure 17.3 begins the story by displaying the extent to which the United
Kingdom was still behind the other G6 economies in 1990, the year in which
the United Kingdom joined the ERM. It shows the *level* of productivity,
rather than its rate of increase, in manufacturing industry measured in terms
of purchasing power parity (PPP) exchange rates.[35]

The US had the highest level of labour productivity, despite the strong
dynamic performances of some other countries. *Per contra*, Japan had a lower
level than the others except the United Kingdom. The United Kingdom was
behind the rest by a significant amount. On the negative side, immediate
evidence of a 'miracle' is not forthcoming, but for this an analysis over time
is required. The corollary of this of course is that the United Kingdom is a
relatively low-wage economy,[36] and therefore a low-cost one, but this may
not be a desirable state to be in except perhaps in the very short run, despite

439

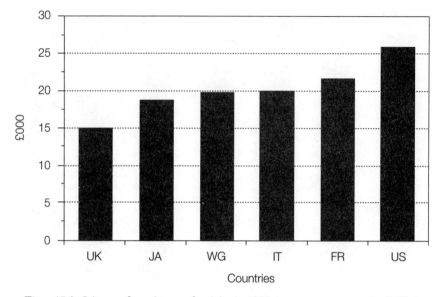

Figure 17.3 G6 manufacturing productivity in 1990 (output per person in £PPPs)
Source: OECD.

the claim of the recent DTI White Paper claiming the United Kingdom to be the 'Enterprise Centre of Europe'.[37] This is explored more fully in the conclusions.

Meanwhile, Figure 17.4 looks at the dynamic evidence by showing changes over the longer term. While evidence is hard to come by, the faster growth of GDP in competitor countries than in the United Kingdom in the 1950s and 1960s was arguably founded on rapid productivity growth in manufacturing. To some extent this was inevitable, given differences in the stages of economic development. By the 1970s, though, the playing field was probably level in this respect and relative improvement was on merit. When making comparisons over time it is important to make them between cyclically comparable dates, and the usual way is peak to peak. Economic coordination between nations in the world means that cycles of economic activity tend to be similarly timed, and this was certainly the case in 1973 following the first oil shock. There are often cyclical differences across nations though, both in timing and amplitude, and this means that taking the cycles which each country individually experiences is one approach to making comparisons. The United Kingdom's recent peaks in GDP were 1974.2, 1979.2 and 1990.2, so that Figure 17.4 shows growth of labour productivity in the G6 economies using this criterion, making comparisons over the United Kingdom's last two GDP cycles.[38]

The United Kingdom was significantly behind the other countries in

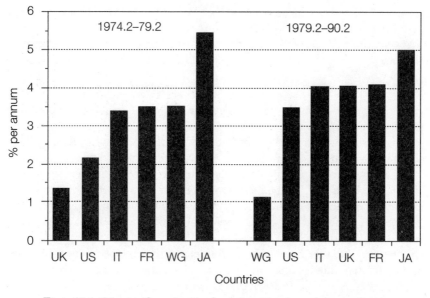

Figure 17.4 G6 manufacturing productivity: annual average growth rate
Source: OECD.

the later 1970s. This was then reversed so that over the 1979–90 economic cycle the United Kingdom was about equal to France and Italy. This is a significant move up the growth-rate league table. If the new position were to be maintained, then some progress up the levels would inevitably follow.

PRODUCTIVITY AND COST COMPETITIVENESS

The portents for productivity are therefore mixed, with strong evidence for a relative improvement internationally, but less from the start of the 1990s cycle. But what does that matter for international competitiveness? Since productivity in manufacturing grew at least as fast in the United Kingdom in the 1980s as in most other countries, how responsive has 'competitiveness' been to the improvement over the 1970s?

Productivity is clearly an important aspect of international competitiveness. While all costs are important for exporters, labour is often regarded as the key element in pricing, so that if wages are low in relation to output, competitiveness is higher. The typical line of thought is that if productivity in the United Kingdom grows less quickly than in competitor countries, to maintain competitiveness for any given exchange rate, relative wages must do the same. The standard method of analysis is therefore to compare unit labour costs – the cost of labour required in relation to the output it produces. This can be measured by comparing average wage costs with the

441

amount of output produced per person.[39] When contrasting across countries the measure is put in relative terms where the United Kingdom is compared to a weighted average of competitor countries[40] and in terms of a common currency giving 'relative unit labour costs' $(RULC)$.[41] The whole formula is:

$$RULC = (RWCPP/RLP) * EER$$

where $RWCPP$ = relative wage costs per person, RLP = relative labour productivity, EER = effective exchange rate.

How can $RULC$ be used to show the value of productivity? Relative unit labour costs and its three elements – wage costs, productivity and the exchange rate can be distinguished separately to help to identify the source of changes. Figure 17.5 begins by comparing the course of wages and productivity in relation to those of competitors in the build-up to ERM entry.

Progress on the relative productivity front comes across clearly in the rising trend of RLP and this is partly because of the relatively large weight given to the US and West Germany whose productivity experiences were somewhat inferior to the United Kingdom's. However, relative wage growth was also on a rising trend in the 1980s and a faster one at that – the traditional UK malaise of paying ourselves more than we deserve seems from this not to have been eliminated, but significantly reduced.[42]

In Figure 17.6 the two other components of the story are graphed – $RULC$ and EER. Clearly, a devaluation can, holding wages and productivity constant, improve unit labour costs relative to competitor countries while a revaluation can do the opposite. Wages and productivity are obviously not

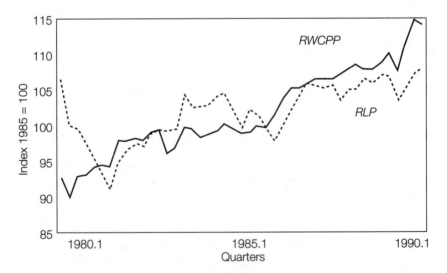

Figure 17.5 Relative wages and productivity, 1979.2–1990.2
Source: CSO, IMF.

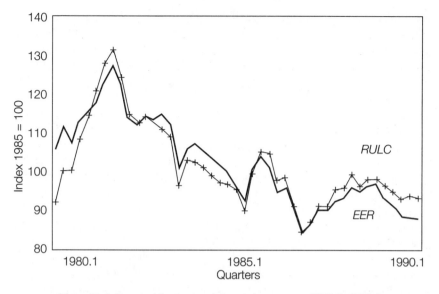

Figure 17.6 Competitiveness and the exchange rate, 1979.2–1990.2
Source: CSO, IMF.

held constant in this scenario and any causation is not straightforward, as discussed later. Notwithstanding, the course of the two is very similar suggesting at least a close short-term association by whatever line of causation.

What comes across very clearly in this analysis is that the exchange rate follows *RULC* much more closely than relative wages and productivity. Causation is obviously not directly from the exchange rate to relative unit labour costs. Rather more likely is that relative wage increases, when too excessive to keep unit labour costs in the United Kingdom below those of competitors, needs to be compensated for by either a relative wage change, a productivity increase, or a movement of the exchange rate. Relative wage changes and productivity seem to play a small part in this in the short run, compared with the exchange rate. In the longer term the difference between these two plays the major part but the *EER* compensates in the short term.

This is an extreme scenario, in which manufacturing and the exchange rate are the jointly determined variables. The opposite extreme is where the exchange rate is exogenous, determined by events outside manufacturing, and the experience of oil production is one possible cause. Under this, *RULC* follows the *EER* and to the extent that productivity changes differ from competitors, wages take up the slack. This might explain why, despite the big fall in the *EER* and the rise in relative labour productivity, UK wage growth remained at a steady rate after the 1979–81 recession.

The true explanation is somewhere between these two. But whichever, it is still the case that manufacturing industry in the United Kingdom benefited in

443

the 1980s from a big equivalent fall in costs from the *EER* decline. In the ERM, should the United Kingdom rejoin, this is not impossible but less likely, on anything other than a short-term basis. If we continue to pay ourselves more than we collectively earn in terms of productivity in the future, then for the same wage/productivity pattern, *RULC* will rise and competitiveness will suffer.

What, then, can we conclude about relative productivity and cost competitiveness from the above? The 'supply-side' policies of the 1980s were designed to reverse the relative decline of the UK economy. This was thought to be especially relevant in the manufacturing sector, where labour relations were considered particularly poor yet its importance was thought to be especially weighty because of the potential tradability of its produce. The performance of UK manufacturing in terms of productivity growth did indeed turn round when compared with the 1970s, and in the later 1980s the pattern of productivity, output and employment seemed to have returned to the arguably superior one of the 1950s and 1960s, when output grew strongly along with productivity, and employment was stationary or even increased, as in the successful Japanese model. In this sense, notwithstanding the earlier comments on timing, ERM entry was right in 1990, with productivity making an historically very strong contribution to competitiveness.

The fact that membership could not be sustained despite this is one pointer to any future rejoining of the ERM, or for that matter, any other anchor for the economy. Another pointer is that the pattern of the new cycle since 1990 suggests that the United Kingdom appears to have reverted to labour shedding as a foundation for productivity improvements discussed earlier. But equally important is the course of *RULC* since leaving the ERM. *RULC* values in the cycle beginning in 1990.2 are shown in Figure 17.7.[43]

The sharp fall in the last quarter of 1992 reflects the devaluation on leaving the ERM. Following that, however, *RULC* in the United Kingdom has been rising and, given the relative stability of the *EER* since then, this has been because relative wages have exceeded productivity. Unless this is reversed, or there is a devaluation, relative export prices will be put under pressure and balance of payments problems will follow – the same old story. In the event, the pound has been revalued in 1996 and 1997 which will make matters worse for *RULC*.

The evidence of a fundamental change in the 1990s therefore is, like the 1980s, not strong. The scope for a successful re-entry to the ERM is consequently weak. On the one hand, productivity improvement has been on the back of labour-shedding rather than output growth, a process which must get increasingly harder. And on the other hand the productivity gains which have been made have been more than taken up by wage increases compared with those of competitors. This has meant that the United Kingdom's *RULC* has risen which in turn, without some sort of compensation – either spontaneous or in the form of policy change – will inevitably lead to

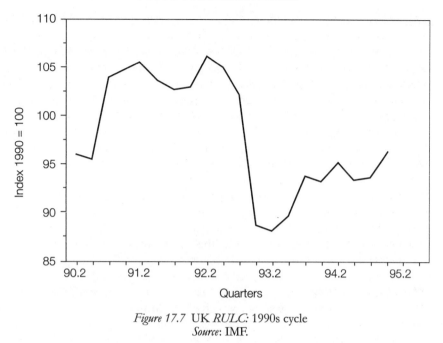

Figure 17.7 UK *RULC*: 1990s cycle
Source: IMF.

pressure on the exchange rate. The United Kingdom therefore shows no evidence of providing its own anchor to remain competitive. The markets, on past performance, arguably would not believe that the ERM could provide one. So the case for re-entry under current policies seems somewhat shaky.

FUTURE POLICY DIRECTIONS

What, then, are the policy options facing the United Kingdom? Productivity improvement in relation to wage increases *vis-à-vis* the United Kingdom's competitors is vital in the context of finding an anchor in membership of the ERM, and even more so if the United Kingdom contemplates participation in a monetary union in the longer term – arguably an even stronger anchor. But will this be the framework in which UK economic policy will be conducted in the medium to long term? To what extent will progress towards monetary union in the EU continue, and to what extent will the United Kingdom be a participant in such developments? It is likely that the process of monetary integration in Europe will continue and that there will eventually be a European monetary union of one form or other, though when this will be is difficult to say. There does seem to be a strong political head of steam building up in continental Europe for some sort of EMU by the millenium.

However, it is worth noting the view that the process of integration moves

445

in cycles and that Europe is currently entering a plateau, or even a downswing phase. Moreover the Maastricht model of EMU has a number of flaws.[44] All of which would imply that EMU of the sort envisaged in the Maastricht Treaty may have to be postponed. Be that as it may, we would argue that the objective pressures on the United Kingdom to be involved in such developments when they do occur are likely to be irresistible. The imperatives which the United Kingdom will face are likely to be at least twofold.

First, there is the need to change some of the basic parameters referred to above that have so conditioned the United Kingdom's post-war development – 'short-termism', price-wage spirals, stop-go political and economic cycles, the predominance of finance capital over manufacturing, and the like – in order to create the conditions under which a fundamental and sustainable improvement in productivity and cost competitiveness can take place.[45] The evidence presented here suggests that, despite the rhetoric, no such permanent change has occurred during the last decade, nor is it ever likely to in a situation in which devaluation is available to provide a 'quick fix'. Or, looked at the other way, as discussed earlier – as Norman Lamont found out in the autumn of 1992 – defending the currency of an economy in which the underlying conditions are weak as perceived by an unrestrained City, is not easy. External discipline over an extended period of time may be the only real hope of a solution.

Secondly there is likely to be a continuing loss of 'real national economic sovereignty', the ability of the British government in an interdependent and deregulated world to pursue its first choices in economic policy in isolation from events elsewhere. The precise nature and extent of such sovereignty losses is open to debate,[46] but it is clear that they are considerable for a country such as the United Kingdom. In the late twentieth century there are clear limits to the power of medium-sized nation states to behave as sovereign economic entities. What is more, this trend is likely to intensify, for example as new technology leads to the 'delocalisation' or reduction in the size of the non-traded goods sector.[47] In this scenario there is little choice: control over economies can only be maintained, if at all, by the joint determination and implementation of economic policies. Sovereignty is not lost in such a situation, but it may be enhanced by pooling.

Fundamental to this argument is an analysis of why the United Kingdom was forced out of the ERM. The evidence presented here suggests that the United Kingdom's productivity performance in relation to wage growth, though improving, was out of line with that of other members in the build-up to, and eventual entry to the ERM, and that therefore exit from the system was in some senses inevitable. But then the period of membership had hardly been sufficient to begin to achieve credibility. Of greater fundamental importance may have been the timing of entry, the rate at which the United Kingdom entered, and the highly restrictive and deflationary nature of the Maastricht convergence criteria. One could also point to inherent weaknesses in the ERM itself, which may have been too restrictive in a situation of insufficient economic convergence amongst its members, and which may have suffered from inadequate resources to maintain parities in the face of the scepticism of the markets.[48]

If the above scenario is true, then the evidence presented in this paper throws up some real problems for the United Kingdom, for it seems that there is a worrying propensity to achieve productivity gains by shedding labour, but that even these are eroded by wage growth. The United Kingdom has clearly not found a long-term solution to this, especially if we are to create what Galbraith refers to as 'the good society', which 'does not allow some of its people to feel useless, superfluous and deprived'.[49] The OECD *Employment Outlook* (1993) shows that nearly half of the EU's jobless have been unemployed for over a year. The social effects of this are exacerbated by what are arguably some inappropriate labour market policies. The United Kingdom, more enthusiastically than other EU governments, has followed the US model of promoting deregulated and flexible labour markets and downward wage flexibility in order to encourage the creation of low-wage/low-skill jobs. Hence the concern about 'social dumping' and the refusal to accept the very modest proposal contained in the 'social charter' and the 'social chapter' of Maastricht, which for the United Kingdom would involve some levelling up of basic social protection in the labour market. The United Kingdom's current policy places the burden of adjustment on the economically most vulnerable, and is in many ways akin to a new form of 'beggar thy neighbour' protectionism.[50] And, from the evidence presented, it does not work. In addition, such a policy carries with it the risks of locking the United Kingdom into a permanent low-wage trap, and of creating a low-wage, low-skill underclass where the necessary productivity increase will not come because the stimulus is not there – employers can lower unit labour costs by reducing wages and employees will not strive for anything other than the basic minimum to stay in the job.[51] It seems inconceivable that the United Kingdom can compete with the newly industrialised countries on the basis of wage costs. A change of tack is clearly required.

CONCLUSIONS

This paper has argued that, despite the UK economy performing relatively well in the late 1980s, the underlying tensions created by insufficient productivity growth in relation to wages meant the inevitable departure from the ERM, sooner rather than later. The markets believed essentially that the anchor which the United Kingdom strived for would slip because the 'paying-ourselves-too-much' syndrome had not been broken and that something had to give. The potential longer-term benefits from membership were, as a result, not realised. Evidence on the situation since departure from the ERM suggests that it has still not been broken and that rejoining would create similar tensions and possibly the same result. The supply-side policies – essentially to reduce workers' rights and their participation in the productive process – which were designed to raise productivity but also reduce the extent to which any gains are eroded away in wage increases, have therefore failed. The alternative is that the interests of the United Kingdom's population would best be served by a marked shift in the emphasis of economic policy towards the more 'social market' approach to be found in other EU countries.[52] Arguably, it is inevitable and desirable that in the medium term some of this be conducted at the EU level.[53]

This would of course require a radical shift in UK policy orientations, as well as an objective evaluation of the United Kingdom's real position in the world in the late twentieth century. Nevertheless, it is our view that such a change of philosophy is essential to improve long-run prospects. Without this, the UK economy will continue to drift without the anchor which membership of the EMS could provide and the real income benefits which it could yield.

NOTES

1 A version of this paper was delivered at the XLVIth Conference of the Applied Econometrics Association at Stuttgart in March 1995. The authors are grateful to Ciaran Driver for helpful comments.
2 The Governor (1991).
3 *Financial Times*, 18 September 1992.
4 Although views may be changing, as in Dornbusch (1996).
5 The authorities are curiously reticent on this matter, claiming that the sustained economic recovery since then is due to its other economic policies.
6 The IMF (in 1996).
7 In the sense discussed above.
8 Even if this is the case, of course, there may be other strong reasons for wishing to rejoin.
9 With the possibility of a single currency, the debate about ERM membership of course turns into a debate about UK participation in EMU, as discussed in Chapter 16.
10 Remembering that the monetarist one had come and gone. The money supply anchor eventually slipped through a combination of loss of credibility – targets consistently missed – plus the world stock market crash (which may not be unconnected) and the subsequent apparent need to avoid the likely loss of world liquidity which had happened after the 1929 crash, plus fiscal expansion on the back of so-called 'incentive' tax reductions.
11 Timothy Congdon's assertion that the high degree of home ownership and mortgage indebtedness which results from the United Kingdom's 'property owning democracy' makes the elasticity of demand for money with respect to the rate of interest in the United Kingdom greater than that in other EU countries, with obvious implication for the joint conduct of monetary policy.
12 For a full discussion of the relationship between European integration and national economic sovereignty, see Lintner (1994).
13 Nigel Lawson, 17 April 1989.
14 Who, it will be recalled, John Major suspended from the party, and who effectively

precipitated the crisis which led him to stand for re-election as party leader (and thus effectively as Prime Minister).

15 Ironically, this development was at least in part the result of policies that the British government had itself championed: the highly successful '1992' programme, and the deregulation of capital and foreign exchange markets, for instance.

16 Fleming (1971) and Corden (1972).

17 Lintner (1994), Strange (1994), and, for slightly different views, Harris (1994) and Newman(1994).

18 Nigel Lawson in his Mansion House Speech in September 1986.

19 Pugh (1993).

20 'There can be no doubt that the transformation of Britain's economic perform- ance during the eighties, a transformation acknowledged throughout the world, is above all due to the supply side reforms we have introduced to allow markets of all kinds to work better.' Chancellor Nigel Lawson, Institute of Economic Affairs special lecture, 21 July 1988.

21 Coutts and Godley (1992), Thirlwall (1992) and Thirlwall and Gibson (1992) are contributions which discuss the issues.

22 Stressed in the recent *Competitiveness* White Paper (HMSO, 1995).

23 Buxton (1994) and NEDC (1989), for instance.

24 See Buxton (1994), i.e. Chapters 5 and 6.

25 The main policies are outlined in HMT (1989) and Dicks (1991).

26 Jackman *et al.* (1990).

27 Hughes (1992).

28 Metcalfe (1989).

29 Oulton (1987).

30 The extent of security of employment.

31 OECD (1986) and (1991).

32 NEDC (1988). Other contributors to the debate include Bosworth (1989), Feinstein and Mathews (1990), Glyn (1992), Kay and Haskell (1990), Muellbauer (1986), Muellbauer and Murphy (1989) and Spencer (1987).

33 Using the Wharton School criterion where a peak is defined by a two quarter or more fall in output. Manufacturing output in fact did not exceed its 1985.2 level until a year later.

34 Buxton (1996).

35 PPPs for individual sectors are unavailable, so that the GDP rates are used instead. The resultant errors are unknown, but obviously depend on the relative sizes of the manufacturing sectors across countries and their representativeness.

36 Buxton (1994).

37 HMSO (1996).

38 Notwithstanding the break in the mid-1980s in UK manufacturing discussed earlier.

39 Hughes (1992) and Muellbauer (1986).

40 The weights used are exports.

41 NEDC (1987).

42 NEDC (1987) where *RLP* is shown to be declining slowly but *RWCPP* increasing rapidly in the 1970s.

43 There has been a delay in the publication by the IMF of the data used to compile the series, so that the graph is not as up-to-date as would be desirable.

44 See Chapter 16.

45 For further discussion of these issues, see Hutton (1995).

46 See Lintner (1994).

47 See Soete (1994).

48 Although one should note that in any event this would be extremely difficult. For

example, the investments of the United Kingdom financial services industry alone amount to something like 100 per cent of GDP, and a precautionary 5 per cent shift of assets out of sterling on their part would be sufficient to neutralise the whole of the United Kingdom's foreign exchange reserves.

49 In a recent lecture to the Cardiff Law School.
50 See Soete (1994).
51 While they look for another.
52 Hutton (1995).
53 Which policies should be conducted at the various levels of government – regional, national and supranational – is a matter for research and political debate. In general we favour the true subsidiarity principle of conducting policy at the most local level compatible with efficiency.

REFERENCES

Bosworth, D. L. (1989) 'The British productivity miracle', Institute of Employment Research, University of Warwick, mimeo.

Brouwer, F., Lintner, V. and Newman, M. (1994) *Economic Policy-making and the European Union*, London: Federal Trust.

Buxton, T. 'The competitiveness of UK manufactured exports', in T. Buxton, *et al.*, (eds) *Britain's Economic Performance*, London; Routledge.

—— (1996) 'Maintaining international competitiveness: Is the UK reverting to labour shedding and is it working?', *The Business Economist*, vol. 27, no. 1, pp. 38–49.

Corden, W. M. (1972) 'Monetary Integration', *Princeton Essays in International Finance*, no. 73, Princeton, N.J.

Coutts, K. and Godley, W. (1992) 'Does Britain's balance of payments matter any more?', in J. Michie (ed.) *The Economic Legacy 1979–92*, London: Academic Press, pp. 60–7.

Dicks, G. (1991) 'What remains of Thatcherism?', *Economic Outlook*, vol. 15, no. 5, pp. 11–19.

Dornbusch, R. (1996) 'The effectiveness of exchange-rate changes', *Oxford Review of Economic Policy, International Competitiveness*, vol. 12, no. 3, pp. 26–38.

Feinstein, C. and Mathews, R. (1990) 'The growth of output and productivity in the UK', *National Institute Economic Review*, vol. 133, pp. 78–90.

Fleming, M. (1971) 'On exchange rate unification', *Economic Journal*, vol. 81, pp. 467–88.

Glyn, A. (1992) 'The "productivity miracle", profits and investment', in J. Michie (ed.) *The Economic Legacy 1979–92*, London: Academic Press, pp. 77–88.

Harris, L. (1984) 'Financial integration and economic sovereignty in Europe', in Brouwer *et al.*, pp. 61–70.

HMSO (1995) *Competitiveness: Forging Ahead*, Cm 2867, London.

—— *Competitiveness: Creating the Enterprise Centre of Europe*, Cm 3300, London.

HMT (1989) 'Helping markets work better', *Economic Progress Report*, no. 203, August, London: HMSO, pp. 4–8.

Hughes, A. (1992) 'Big business, small business and the "enterprise culture"', in J. Michie (ed.) *The Economic Legacy 1979–92*, London: Academic Press, pp. 296–311.

Hughes, K. (1993) 'Introduction: UK competitiveness and industrial policy', in K. Hughes (ed.) *The Future of UK Competitiveness and the Role of Industrial Policy*, London: PSI, pp. 1–6.

Hutton, W. (1995) *The State We're In*, London; Jonathan Cape.

Jackman, R., Layard, R. and Nickell, S. (1990) *Unemployment*, Oxford; Oxford University Press.

Kay, J. A. and Haskell, J. E. 'Industrial performance under Mrs Thatcher', in T. Congdon *et al.*, *The State of the Economy*, London: IEA, pp. 20–8.

Lintner, V. (1994) 'National economic sovereignty and European integration', in Brouwer *et al.*, pp. 9–18.

Metcalfe, D. (1989) 'Water Notes Dry Up', *British Journal of Industrial Relations*, vol. 27, pp. 1–31.

Muellbauer, J. (1989) 'Productivity and competitiveness in British manufacturing', *Oxford Review of Economic Policy*, vol. 2, pp. i–xxv.

Muellbauer, J. and Murphy, A. (1989) 'How fundamental are the UK's balance of payments problems?', mimeo, Nuffield College, Oxford.

NEDC (1987) *British Industrial Performance*, London: NEDO.

—— (1988) 'Pay and productivity', memorandum by the Director General, London: NEDC(87)8.

—— (1989) 'Trade performance', memorandum by the Director General, London: NEDC(89)9.

Newman, M. (1994) 'Sovereignty, public power and the economy', in Brouwer *et al.*, pp. 1–8.

OECD (1987) *Flexibility in the Labour Market*, Paris.

—— (1991) *Employment Outlook*, July, Paris.

—— (1994) *Employment Outlook*, no. 94, December, Paris.

Oulton, N. (1987) 'Plant closures and the productivity "Miracle"', *National Institute Economic Review*, no. 132, August, pp.71–91.

Pugh, G. (1993) 'The economics of German unification', *Greenwich Papers*, no. 1, Summer.

Soete, L. (1994) 'European Integration and Strategies for Employment', in Brouwer *et al.*, pp. 27–42.

Spencer, P. (1987) *Britain's Productivity Renaissance*, Credit Suisse, First Boston.

Strange, S. 'The power gap: Member states and the world economy', in Brouwer *et al.*, pp. 19–26.

The Governor (1991) 'The economy and ERM membership', *Bank of England Quarterly Bulletin*, February, pp. 53–5.

Thirlwall, A. (1992) 'The balance of payments and economic performance', *National Westminster Bank Quarterly Review*, May, pp. 2–11.

Thirlwall, A. and Gibson, H. D. (1992) *Balance of Payments Theory and the United Kingdom Experience* (4th edn), London: Macmillan.

Part VI

STRUCTURAL CHANGE, INDUSTRIAL POLICY AND ECONOMIC PERFORMANCE

18

OVERVIEW: ECONOMIC POLICY AND THE CHANGING INTERNATIONAL DIVISION OF LABOUR[1]

Mohammad Haq and Paul Temple

Full employment . . . is an adventure which must be undertaken if free society is to survive. It is an adventure which can be undertaken with confidence of ultimate success. Success, however, will not come by following any rigid formula but by adapting action to circumstances which may change continually.

(W. Beveridge, *Full Employment in a Free Society*, p. 192)

INTRODUCTION

The longer-term development of capitalist economies is based upon an evolving division of labour. The role of economic policy in that process has always been a contentious issue. This overview explores some of the features explaining the changing relationship between policy and performance, especially in the field of microeconomic policy aimed at stimulating industrial competitiveness – a branch of policy that has come to embrace not just industry policy but also science and technology policy (as discussed further by Margaret Sharp in Chapter 19) and, increasingly, regional policy.

Attempts to summarise secular change have not generally found prevailing economic orthodoxy to be a helpful guide to the processes involved or the implications for society. Instead, a plethora of ways of describing longer term structural change has developed: 'economic maturity', 'deindustrialisation', 'globalisation', 'sclerosis', 'technological regimes' are just a few examples of the concepts that have been used to describe deeper-seated economic development.

This overview cannot hope to survey them all. Instead, two significant processes are reviewed which would, by common consent, be regarded as vital for the understanding of the advanced capitalist economies. The first is the growth of the service sector; this is examined in the next section. The second is the rapid increase in international (or cross-border) investment, which appears capable of effecting the most far-reaching changes in the world in which we live. This chapter then examines the role that micro-economic policy has played, and perhaps could play, in shaping this changing economic environment.

ECONOMIC MATURITY AND THE GROWTH OF SERVICES

Economic maturity

The rise of the service sector in the more industrially developed economies has provoked considerable debate as to its economic significance. In this section we comment upon three aspects of this new division of labour with important ramifications for policy debate: differential productivity growth rates between goods and services and its relationship to the fiscal problem, potential market failures in service provision, and the international tradability of services.

Structural change is most often described and assessed in terms of shifts in the division of labour in an economy. In fact, economic development has certain features which all economies appear to have shared in the transition from an agrarian base to an industrial one.

Initially the agrarian sector provides the major share of employment. Industrialisation begins when a sustained process of economic growth establishes itself; this involves, *inter alia*, a rapid shift in the share of employment away from the land toward the so-called 'secondary' sector – manufacturing, construction, and energy. The service sector provides an important accompaniment to this process – especially in transport and distribution activities, which permit markets to expand, although other service activities, associated with domestic service, urban development, and trade, are also important.

As Rowthorn and Wells (1987) show, this pattern of development is not sustainable. Widening employment opportunities eventually tend to reverse the process of increasing domestic service, and the shrinking employment share on the land means that agriculture can no longer act as a huge labour reserve for the expansion of industry. On the other hand, immigration can in certain circumstances prolong the period where the supply of labour to industry is highly elastic, and this was of course very relevant to the pro-longed post-war boom both in Europe and in the US. When employment shares in domestic service and agriculture cease to be significant in terms of those of the secondary and tertiary sector, then expansion of the share of the service sector necessitates declines in the share of industry. This provides one possible definition of economic maturity. In the United Kingdom at least, this stage was decisively reached by the 1960s when the share of manufacturing employment peaked and the rapid expansion in the employment share in health and education – activities primarily associated with the emerging welfare state – could no longer be accommodated from sources in agriculture, domestic services, and the post-war run-down in the armed forces.

In other advanced economies, and with the exception of the US, the stage of maturity was reached rather later than in the United Kingdom. In the 1960s, this produced a lively debate as to whether the United Kingdom had reached a point of 'premature maturity', and whether there was disguised unemployment in the service sector as in agriculture. By the 1970s the debate concerned the apparent relationship between the growth of public (and non-marketed) services and the decline of manufacturing. Aspects of the reasons for, and the implications of the shift from manufacturing to services are explored by Hadjimatheou and Sarantis, in Chapter 20.

None of this answers the question of why the share of the labour force engaged in service sector activities should rise so rapidly once a certain stage of economic maturity is reached, nor why it might be important to distinguish services from manufacturing or other industrial activities. Reasons for both phenomena are now considered further.

Productivity, prices, and the fiscal problem

It is of course important to understand why the employment share of services tends to rise through time. A number of powerful, but sometimes contradictory, forces are at work which combine to determine the size of the sector. The first of these is how the demand for goods, *vis-à-vis* services, responds to the demands of an increasingly wealthy society. It is sometimes suggested that the demand for services is particularly 'income elastic'. However, empirical studies have not actually confirmed that the demand for marketed services in general is any more responsive to growing income than that for manufactured products. Other considerations suggest that productivity and prices have as big, if not a bigger, role to play. Moreover technological change has set up fundamental possibilities for the substitution of goods for services which are well documented: television for the services of live entertainers; the automobile for public transport; the washing machine for the laundry, and so on. All these cases are well documented.[2] The element on which we focus here is that key parts of the service sector are inherently less 'progressive' than other economic activities, limiting possibilities for technical and productivity advance.

In a seminal paper on 'unbalanced growth', written over twenty years ago, William Baumol drew attention to some of the simple, but quite startling, implications for economies characterised by a dichotomy between 'progressive' activities and those which, by their very nature, were not susceptible to the beneficial effects of advances in technology and labour productivity (Baumol, 1967). In these activities, it is the labour itself which is essential to consumption – a theatre production or waiter service in a restaurant would be suitable examples. In such cases the quality of the labour performed is, to a large extent, the quality of the output itself. Many, but by no means all such occupations are to be found in the service sector – manufacturing, for example, makes use of designers, marketers, many of whom may well fall under the heading depicted by Baumol. Moreover, a large number of these kinds of service fall within the public sector – the most important of which can be found in education and health care. In any of these cases, opportunities for productivity growth, if not entirely absent, are at least severely circumscribed. As Baumol himself remarks, we tend to judge the quality of education in terms of labour input – declining average class sizes being frequently used as an indicator of 'progress'.[3]

Given some simplifying assumptions, the most important of which is that wages in the long run will tend to equality in both the progressive and the non-progressive sector, then there will be a persistent tendency for prices in the non-progressive sector to rise in terms of those in the rest of the economy, so that what is happening to relative output cannot be inferred from either expenditure data measured at current prices, or from employment data. What happens to demand will depend upon both price and income elasticities; many services will simply disappear (except perhaps in luxury niches) either because prices become prohibitive, or else because wages for those services fall behind those obtainable elsewhere – the 'shoe-shine' and domestic servants are examples. Under certain circumstances, such activities may return. Indeed there is plenty of evidence that some such phenomenon is occurring in the United Kingdom today – a reflection in part of growing inequality in incomes and wealth.

In other sectors the existence of 'family workers' or the labour of illegal immigrants may prevent wages from growing as fast as in the progressive sector. However, some services are clearly relatively income elastic and here price and income effects may tend to cancel out.

For this reason it is equally interesting to consider what would happen if, either through market or non-market forces, the relative output of the two sectors were to be maintained. In this case, the unprogressive sector will (over time) absorb an ever-increasing fraction of the nation's workforce. Moreover, the overall rate of growth in the economy will tend (asymptotically) toward that recorded in the unprogressive sector.

It is an empirical question as to how far productivity growth in services as a whole actually falls short (if at all) of that in manufacturing, although one not easily resolved, not least because of the difficulties we have mentioned of measuring 'quality' in services.

It is important to realise that it is often in the public sector where activities most closely resemble those classified by Baumol as unprogressive. Official output statistics are more or less useless in this regard since, in the United Kingdom, the Office for National Statistics actually measures the output of many public sector activities by means of employment, so nothing can be said about productivity growth without circular reasoning. Nevertheless we may be able to infer something about productivity movements on the basis of changes in relative prices. The issues raised by Baumol are particularly relevant when the output is publicly provided, since there is no direct counterpart to rising prices from the consumer's point of view. What people do experience is the ongoing debate about the level of funding of the educational and health services. The often-expressed disagreement about whether there have, or have not been, 'real cuts' in education or health services (or for that matter, police, fire, street-cleaning, etc.) often boils down to a question of the standard of measurement. Figure 18.1 shows some relevant deflators estimated from the National Income *Blue Book* for three major components of government spending: health, education and the

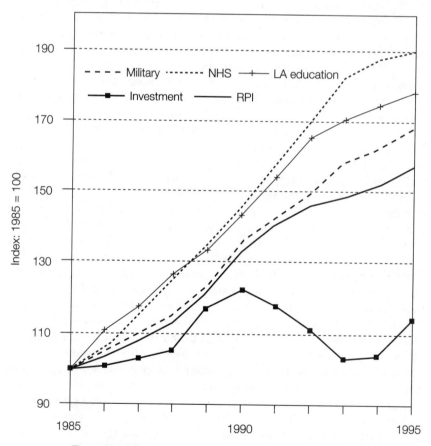

Figure 18.1 The prices of public services (implicit deflators)
Source: UK National Accounts, 1996.

military. On this evidence, the prices of defence, health and education all rose relative to the headline retail price index. When measured in 'own prices', it turns out for example that the volume of government spending rose between 1985 and 1995 by 2.1 per cent per annum for the National Health Service, against 2.2 per cent in the whole economy. The comparable figures for defence provision and local authority expenditure on education both actually fell – by 2.9 per cent and 0.8 per cent per annum respectively.

Of course, measuring spending in terms of an overall standard – the retail prices index or the GDP deflator – does have meaning as an indicator of the 'opportunity cost' of utilising resources in that particular way – what must be forgone in terms of other goods and services not produced. In practice this is what most commentators tend to do, but this can be severely misleading if the point of contention is the *volume* of the service being delivered.

The fact that all these areas are largely financed by general taxation of course adds a certain spice to the fiscal problems of government. The French have a saying: 'avoir le coeur a gauche et le porte-feuille a droite',[4] which may go some way to explaining how people's expressed desire for a better health service is not necessarily matched by any corresponding vote at the polls. As far as current debate in the United Kingdom is concerned, it needs to be stressed that the relative cost of education and health provision will tend to rise through time quite irrespective of whether provision is in the public sector, the private sector, or a 'pseudo' market. This is not to deny that 'efficiency' cannot be improved in these areas by more effectively marshalling resources, but this is going to be a short-run, *level* of productivity effect and does not affect the argument based on trends. Nor is it to deny that technological change is important and may become increasingly so in these areas, but that this seems unlikely to raise crude measures of productivity (pupils per teacher, patients per nurse) by very much. It follows that if these activities are to be funded through general taxation, a rising burden of taxation as a percentage of GDP seems the inevitable price that must be paid if standards are to be maintained in the longer term.

Although areas of low productivity growth do tend to cluster within the service sector, it must not be supposed that this is an essential characteristic of all services. In some, productivity growth can be quite rapid and it is clear, for example, that technological change in the ability of machines to process many thousands of relatively homogeneous transactions may have profound effects in some areas of finance and insurance. Moreover, in these areas management strategies are actually designed to make such things as loan advances much more homogeneous in nature – changes only made possible with the development of huge data bases describing personal credit ratings. In transport and communication there is also considerable scope for productivity advance and in these industries recorded growth over the 1980s was very similar to that recorded for manufacturing. Distribution also has shown gains, comparable to those seen in the economy as a whole. In hotels and catering by contrast, productivity growth has apparently been negligible (Smith, 1989; NEDO, 1992).

Market failure and the tradability of services in international markets

In addition to secular trends in productivity performance, two other aspects may be important in assessing the significance of the service sector: potential market failures in service provision, and the issue of international tradability.

Services can be distinguished from goods on a number of counts, including their tangibility, their stockability, and the frequent need for close interaction between buyer and seller or between producer and user. Intangibility, for example, leads to a classification which includes distribution and transport, financial, business, and professional services, health care, education and other personal services, public administration, etc. But the economic significance of these possible distinctions is somewhat elusive and it is generally more satisfactory to speak of tendencies which typify services as a whole, rather than every individual service. As we have seen, a tendency for lower long-term productivity growth is one example with clear implications for the structure of economies in the course of development, but not one which can be applied to all services. Other tendencies include one toward market failure and hence for provision to occur within the public sector, or for regulation within the private sector; also of vital importance is a tendency toward lower tradability in international markets.

The market failure literature recognises the public good argument for government provision – provision by private firms is problematic; because of the free-rider problem, firms are unable to appropriate the returns. The classic example is the service provided by the armed forces. However, there are many examples of rather more imperfect public goods, in which a case can be made for public provision. Research and development activity is an especially important example where private returns may fall short of the underlying social benefits. In areas such as this, the involvement of the public sector varies enormously across countries. In Japan, for example, state involvement is much lower in R&D than is the case in the United Kingdom. This might reflect missed opportunities for increasing welfare in Japan but it may also (and more likely) reflect the relative ability of firms in the United Kingdom and Japan to exploit innovation successfully.

A rather different strand to the market failure argument is based on the quality of provision. Informational asymmetries may create a strong case for regulation of service-sector activities. Although Akerlof (1970) originally applied the idea to the market for second-hand cars, his strictures may be even more generally applicable to the supply of services, not least because 'irreversibility' is an essential aspect of many services (e.g. once your hair has been cut or a court case lost, there is no return to the *status quo ante*). If customers have difficulty in either observing the characteristics of the

461

supplier or the diligence with which the duties are undertaken, then better-quality practitioners may have difficulty extracting premia for quality: a form of Gresham's Law applies in which the 'bad will drive out the good'. The market itself has devices for improving information flows which include guarantees, reputation effects, consumer and producer organisations, and so on. Sometimes contracts can be drawn up which are contingent upon certain outcomes (e.g. the 'no win no fee' contract is common in US legal practice) but the sharing of risk in these situations is not necessarily optimal.

Systems of intervention (such as licensing) aimed at reducing these informational sources of market failure are generally more common in the service sector (and especially in professional services) and they can create potent barriers to entry, especially across national boundaries and these of course have been important in the EU's attempt to create a unified market. The principle behind the European Single Market has been one of 'mutual recognition' rather than 'harmonisation' of bodies and standards, which is generally seen as a second-best strategy in which a downward spiral of standards is seen as a possibility.[5]

Interventions in markets based on the need for ensuring quality in provision may for such reasons reduce the international tradability of services, but there are of course many other reasons for lower tradability, largely stemming from two factors: first that many services exist which are dependent upon the close proximity of the customer (a haircut, or a visit to the cinema) and secondly because many services depend upon special national circumstances (e.g. a tax consultant). However, as Kierkowski (1987) points out, services can be traded through other means, e.g. by:

1 moving the customer to the location of the supplier (international tourism is the most important example of this, but education and health may be increasingly relevant);
2 moving the supplier to the location of the customer (e.g. civil engineering consultancy);
3 relocating services overseas through foreign direct investment.

It is clear that the generally lower tradability of services is not immutable but is highly contingent. Innovation in the field of information technology may be having the effect of making services rather more tradable, while economic integration can be expected to increase the contestability of markets. Both the Single European Market and the Uruguay Round are clearly important in this respect. Nevertheless, estimates of world trade in services indicate that it is only a fraction of trade in goods. According to the data presented in Hoeckman (1993), world merchandise exports totalled $3,500 billion in 1990, against $820 billion for service exports. Low tradability in services has meant that foreign investment in service activities has been a key feature in the globalisation of the world economy, as we see below.

The UK Experience

As we have seen, a shift of labour into the service sector can be regarded as quite normal for mature economies. To what extent is the United Kingdom atypical in this regard, and to what extent has the growth of the service sector been, in any important way, 'unbalanced', as suggested by some commentators (e.g. Wells, 1989)? The answer depends upon a more precise picture of the nature and causes of service sector growth in the United Kingdom. More especially, to what extent is it a reflection of a comparative advantage in services which is now getting greater opportunity to assert itself as markets become more open and services become more internationally tradable?

As we have seen, the share of total employment in services rises with economic development. In the United Kingdom this share has reached a comparatively high level – the third highest in the OECD area in 1993, behind the US and Canada. When viewed over time, it can be seen from Figure 18.2 that the United Kingdom already had a relatively high level of employment in services in 1960. But it can be seen that this was also true for manufacturing, where in 1960 the United Kingdom had the highest share of employment, not just in terms of the six economies displayed in Figure 18.3, but also in the entire OECD area. This was possible because the share of employment in agriculture had already dwindled far below that of anywhere else. By way of illustration, the share of civilian employment in agriculture in the United Kingdom in 1960 was 4.7 per cent, compared to 14 per cent in

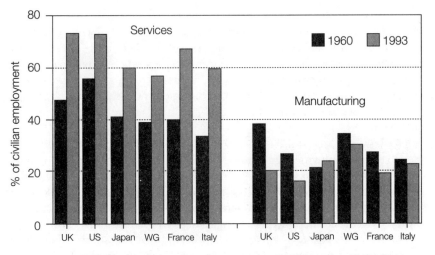

Figure 18.2 Changes in employment structure: G6 economies, 1960–93
Source: OECD Historical Statistics, 1960–93.
Note: data for West Germany are for 1990.

463

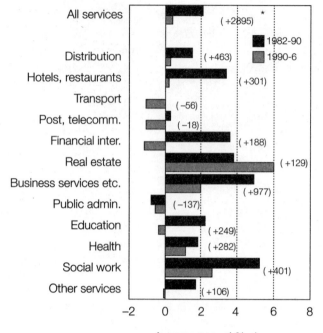

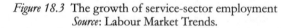

Average annual % change

Figure 18.3 The growth of service-sector employment
Source: Labour Market Trends.
Note: * absolute change in employment in thousands for sector over 1982–96 are in
parentheses. Employees only.

Germany, 22.5 per cent in France and 32.6 per cent in Italy. Even in the US, it
was higher, at 8.5 per cent. Because this reservoir of labour in agriculture was
so much smaller in the United Kingdom than elsewhere, the rapidly rising
share of services in employment has mainly come from a declining share of
manufacturing employment. Other economies, notably Japan, Italy, and
Germany, have seen more modest changes in the share of employment in
manufacturing.

The United Kingdom has therefore seen a particularly rapid increase in
the share of employment in services, with the most rapid changes coming
only after the oil shocks of the 1970s and especially during the 1980s. Within
the service sector, however, it is important to realise that employment
growth has been far from even across the different industries. Figure 18.3
shows that in all there were 2.9 million additional employees in service
industries in 1996 as against 1982. Business and financial services have been
the biggest contributors to new jobs. Growth in jobs in distribution have also
been important, as well as in hotels and catering. Health, education, social
work have also grown steadily, while over the whole period only post,

telecommunications, and public administration have shed jobs. The major change in comparing the most recent period, 1990–6, with the period 1982–1990, has been the loss of jobs in financial intermediation.

One interesting aspect of the pattern of growth in the 1980s and 1990s compared with the growth of service sector employment earlier in the post-war period has been the increasing relative importance of 'marketed' services (which are essentially produced for a profit) against 'non-marketed' services in public administration, health, and education, which had dominated growth in the period 1945–73 (Temple, 1994).

To what extent does the rapid growth of service sector employment, and of financial and business services especially, reflect domestic factors or a shifting pattern of specialisation in international trade? One way of assessing the role of trade is to examine the components of the balance of payments. Figure 18.4(a) illustrates the major components of the current balance of payments expressed as proportion of GDP for the fifty years since the end of the Second World War. It can be seen that swings in the current balance have, in the main, been determined by movements in the balance of visible trade (excluding oil) which is predominantly composed of manufactured goods. The balance on (non-factor) services has generally been in surplus throughout the post-war period, peaking as a proportion of GDP in the 1970s. The decade of the most rapid increase in the employment share of services – the 1980s – in fact coincides with a slow *deterioration* in the contribution of services to the current balance.

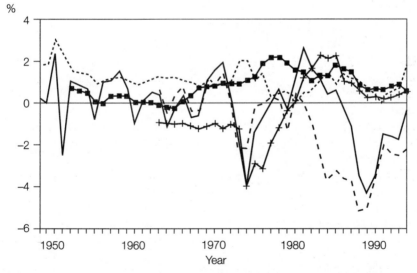

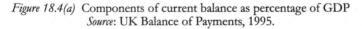

Figure 18.4(a) Components of current balance as percentage of GDP
Source: UK Balance of Payments, 1995.

A more detailed picture of the contribution of services is presented in Figure 18.4(b), which indicates the important role of the financial services sector. The surplus generated by the balance on financial and business services has shown no tendency to rise as a proportion of GDP in the course of the 1980s. However, some of the activities of the City appear not in the service export figures but under the guise of investment income (interest, profit, and dividends). Here, as Figure 18.4(a) shows, while there is a surplus, it has shown no secular tendency to increase in relation to GDP. The other sector worth noting is travel and tourism, where a growing deficit has emerged over the course of the 1980s and 1990s. The general lack of dynamism in service sector exports is exemplified in *Blue Book* estimates of volume growth – which despite the difficulties in choice of deflator, are surely indicative; these show that the growth in the volume of service exports managed only 1.6 per cent over the period 1979–95, against 3.2 per cent for imports of services (Office for National Statistics, 1996). The corresponding figures for goods were both 4.2 per cent. In value terms the share of manufactured exports in total credits from trade actually rose considerably – from 56 per cent to 64 per cent between 1979 and 1994 – while the share of service exports fell from 26 per cent to 23 per cent (CSO, 1995).

The direct contribution to trade of the service sector therefore displays

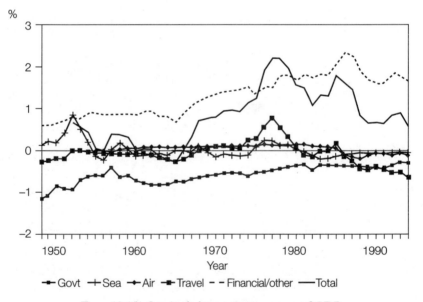

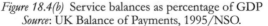

Figure 18.4(b) Service balances as percentage of GDP
Source: UK Balance of Payments, 1995/NSO.

little of the dynamic character of the growth in service employment, suggesting that domestic factors have played the lead role. However we may be ignoring an indirect contribution, with services acting as an input in the manufacturing or other tradable sectors. A variant on this possibility is a 'pseudo' deindustrialisation story in which much of the growth in services is attributable to increased purchases of services by other sectors, which may be due to technical changes and the growing sophistication of production (which requires greater use of professional services in design, R&D, legal expertise, marketing and so on). Alternatively, some of the growth of services may simply be the result of the contracting out of services which were formerly carried out 'in-house'. This latter trend is consistent with more recent managerial moves toward greater concentration on so-called 'core' business activities and toward the leasing or renting of capital equipment. To consider more generally the respective roles that intermediate and final demand have played, recourse is needed to important (but rather unfashionable) input–output methods. A recent study along these lines by Gregory and Greenhalgh (1996), showed that a large part of the rising demand for financial services over the period 1979–90 emanated from rising inputs of financial services into the production process of other sectors. The change directly attributable to the growth of domestic final demand for financial services was, however, very important in generating the boom in financial services of the period 1985–90. This domestically oriented boom probably delayed the impact of new technology and restructuring until the 1990s.

Offering something by way of conclusion on the developing role of services in the UK economy is not easy. Of course the service industries are not anything like a homogeneous whole and they vary enormously in terms of the sophistication of the technology employed and the wages they offer. Certainly some of the growth witnessed in the boom years of the late 1980s was highly unbalanced, and this is being corrected in the 1990s in areas such as banking. Indeed some service sectors such as banking, transport, and telecommunications are going through the same kind of structural transformation that manufacturing went through in the 1980s. One point stands out, however, and that is that the service sector as a whole is not currently providing a dynamic element to the nation's trading performance. The once fashionable idea that the United Kingdom possesses a considerable comparative advantage is not really sustainable. Nor has the impact of the Single Market really had much obvious impact thus far. Nevertheless, services will be crucial if full employment is to be established. In many services, such as catering and the leisure industries and personal services, technology is sufficiently flexible for them to be relatively free of the capital constrained prospects for employment in manufacturing or other parts of the service sector (see above, Chapter 13). Beyond that, the provision of services as inputs into other sectors is a vital ingredient of national competitiveness.

This may be particularly true in the United Kingdom where reliance on the external market may be stronger than elsewhere. If this is the case, then ways of addressing issues of market failure will be paramount.

INTERNATIONAL INVESTMENT AND TECHNOLOGICAL CHANGE

Phases of development

A changing international division of labour has been an essential accompaniment of industrialisation from its beginnings in the eighteenth century, while capturing the benefits of technological change provides the fundamental motive driving the accumulation activities through which change occurs in the structure of production.

Increasingly, this process is being articulated through truly international firms, able to organise the functional activities of production, marketing, finance and R&D on a world scale. The 'globalisation' of the world economy through international firms in this sense is the term frequently used to describe this latest phase in the developing international division of labour. The integration of world capital markets is an essential adjunct to the whole process. For Britain, economic integration within the European Union provides a further and significant dimension to the changing place of Britain in the international division of labour. By and large, policy changes world-wide have reinforced the underlying forces at work, with by far the greater proportion of newly enacted legislation in the direction of liberalisation of existing controls on international direct investment (UN, 1995).

The economic theory which helps to explain foreign direct investment (FDI) stresses the importance of market imperfection and how efficiency gains can be made by internalising transactions within the firm. Early examples of multinational enterprise before the Second World War were mainly based on simple exercises in vertical integration, especially where this involved access to natural resources. The big international oil companies were of course exemplary in this regard. However, the first phase of development after the war, up to the 1970s, primarily involved a one-way flow of investment from the US to Europe, Japan, and the developing world. Underpinning this relationship was a combination of the big technological lead then enjoyed by US firms at this time, combined with their sheer size. The problem for these large US corporations was not only how best to utilise their technological advantage (e.g. Hymer, 1979) but also the accumulation of other intangible assets such as brand names and corporate images (in short, highly mobile proprietary assets) in a world where national markets were still highly fragmented and trade barriers for competitive products remained high. The important point of course is that these owner-specific assets can be input jointly across plants, wherever located, and can therefore act as a source of competitive advantage. The other prong to this was the line of reasoning suggested by the concept of the product cycle where competitive advantage could be gained for firms by locating the standardised production of mature goods in developing economies where labour costs were lower.

This phase of development persisted only as long as US technological leadership could be maintained. In national markets outside the US, local firms often held competitive advantages *vis-à-vis* the US firms, which meant that domestic production was not often entirely displaced and that the form of competition remained relatively benign. However, the situation did begin to change in the 1970s. US technological supremacy was effectively squeezed from two sources. The first involved the ability of the US economy to produce technological change on a broad front. According to Mowery and Rosenberg (1989), the effects of the heavy concentration of the US R&D efforts in defence and space activities – a build-up heavily contingent upon the Cold War – may have changed considerably between the 1960s and the present. Such changes mainly concerned the extent of 'spillover' between military and space technologies on the one hand, and civilian technologies on the other. For example, although the development of the jet engine had tremendous possibilities for civilian aircraft, military developments became less and less appropriate as military performance requirements increasingly became dominated by the demands of supersonic travel. Other examples, from microelectronics and communication satellites, also point to an increasing divergence in performance demands. Moreover, the whole direction of spillover seems to have shifted in a number of key technologies. Most of these problems operate (on a much smaller scale) in the United Kingdom, where differences in organisational culture (even within firms) are also seen as significant barriers to effective interaction between military and civilian research (Smith and Smith, 1992). Slowly, then, the appropriateness of US technological capability for commercial exploitation began to change.

The second squeeze on the technological domination of the US came from the simple fact of technological transfer. Largely based on so-called 'Fordist' techniques of mass production in manufacturing, American production technology was not especially difficult to assimilate in economies with very similar levels of educational attainment. Moreover, the 'Fordist' model of competitiveness, based on dedicated and inflexible capital equipment, and the heavy use of unskilled labour, was increasingly being challenged, especially in areas such as the motor car, where problems posed by successive oil shocks had left their mark.

Although in 1980 the US continued to dominate flows of foreign investment, the following decade clearly marked a change in both the direction and nature of investment flow. Notwithstanding the continuing importance of flows based on gaining access to markets to exploit some proprietorial advantage, the new phase of accelerating foreign investment was increasingly based on the need to access resources, especially those associated with the generation of new technology and innovation. Much evidence has been accumulated showing that the processes involved in innovative activity are highly complex and geographically rather immobile in nature. In knowledge-based activities, much knowledge transfer is 'tacit' in nature and geographically sticky. Below, Martha Prevezer (Chapter 21) discusses the role that localised industrial clusters play in the high technology industries of biotechnology and computing, discussing the implications for policy. More generally, access to resources has become a much more important reason not only for international investment but also for the spectacular growth in a variety of forms of industrial extra-market linkage – joint ventures, cooperative research agreements, cross-licensing and so forth. These alliances are seen to be especially important in developing generic technologies such as information technology and biotechnology. Many alliances can be thought of as extending the technological reach of transnational firms (Hagedoorn and Schakenrad, 1993).

Central to the latest phase of development in the integration of the global economy has therefore been the drive for the extraction of rents from technical change and innovation – necessitating competitive strategies increasingly common to Japanese and European corporations as well as those based in the US. In the later 1980s and especially after 1985, the growth of FDI was remarkable, with the total flow generated by the OECD economies growing by over 31 per cent per annum between 1983 and 1989. The early 1990s did, however, see an FDI recession (indicating that it is a cyclical phenomenon) but nevertheless, FDI had recovered substantially by the middle of the decade, especially outflows from the US, where domestic recovery began earlier. Japanese FDI remained depressed by the level of 1990. As a result of the substantial growth of international investment over more than a decade, it is estimated that global sales of foreign affiliates exceeded world-wide exports of goods and non-factor services (UN, 1995).

Currently, international investment is highly concentrated within the developed economies of the US, Japan, and Europe. By 1993, 75 per cent of the FDI inward stock was in the developed economies. However, the share of the developed economies in the flow of FDI in that year was only 62 per cent, indicating that the share of the stock in the developing economies may be starting to change. FDI by European firms in the 1990s has emphasised locational advantage which follows from the creation of the Single Market. Moreover, despite the attention that has been focused on Japanese FDI, the outward Japanese stock in the EU and the US ($25 billion and $96 billion dollars, respectively), has been dwarfed by the EU-owned stock in the US – $249 billion in 1993 – and the reverse stock of $232 billion (all data UN 1995). The EU-owned stock in the US may be compared with the EU-owned cross-border stock within the EU itself which stands in excess of $339 billion.[6] By these standards The EU-owned stock of investment in Japan is very modest at $10 billion.

Inward and outward UK foreign direct investment

The United Kingdom has played a major part in the story of FDI, not least because government policy has so actively favoured both inward and outward investment. This is not perhaps so surprising as Britain has always played a key part in the internationalisation of production. For inward investors, the well-developed market for corporate control is obviously a significant factor, as is the positive attitude of the British government to many of the issues raised, the United Kingdom's low labour costs, and the English language. However, the share of the FDI inflows in the EU has been much smaller in the 1990s than it was in the period 1983–90, when the UK share was around one-third, and by far the highest of any country. Over the period 1991–4 the share has been 18 per cent (UN, 1995).

On the other side of the coin, the sheer magnitude of UK investment overseas raises important questions about the commitment of British management to the United Kingdom (see, for example, Keep and Mayhew, 1993 and above, Chapter 15). During the 1980s, the numbers of acquisitions of US businesses comfortably outstripped those made by Canadian, German, or Japanese firms (OECD, 1992). Evidence presented by Williams *et al.* (1990) suggested that no more than 40 per cent of the turnover of the top twenty UK-owned engineering companies is now generated within the United Kingdom. Outward FDI from the United Kingdom went into sharp recession in 1990, but recovered during 1993 and 1994, representing about 12 per cent of the total of the five major home economies for FDI (which is rather lower than the share of the 1980s).

It is clear from the evidence discussed that, despite the prominence given to it, Japanese inward investment in the US or EU is small compared to EU–US flows, and it is largely in areas outside manufacturing in distribution and finance – distribution activities, for example, have always bulked large in Japanese strategy for market penetration (Williamson, 1990). Prevailing impressions to the contrary may have something to do with the feverish pitch of Japanese FDI in 1988 and 1989, as well as the impact of Japanese production methods on indigenous economies, not to mention just a hint of xenophobia in the literature. The timing of the surge in Japanese investment into the EU makes it clear that there was a perceived need to be in position prior to the creation of the Single Market, although investment in Europe was a logical next step following the build-up of considerable local supply capacity in the US.

As far as Japanese manufacturing investment in the EU is concerned, the UK share seems to have been the largest (Yamawaki, 1993). However, the sectoral composition of this investment varied across countries, with the United Kingdom being a favoured location for electronic and electrical equipment and (along with Spain) for transportation equipment. The debate on the nature of this Japanese inward investment on the UK economy and its longer-term implications for performance is far from complete, and still further from being conclusive.

Implications for national competitiveness

Clearly FDI is undertaken by firms for reasons of their own competitiveness and profitability. Most international investment in the developed economies takes the form of acquisition of other firms rather than new 'greenfield' investment, in contrast to the situation in developing countries (UN, 1995). Acquisition frequently involves access to resources, especially technology, which raises difficulties because the system of corporate governance in different countries may make the acquisition of technology by this means easier in one direction compared to another. It is frequently contended, for example, that access to Japanese technology is difficult not only because a much higher proportion of R&D is conducted in private firms in Japan than say in the US, where the proportion of publicly funded research in universities is greater, but also because corporate governance mechanisms in Japan make takeover a rare event. In conditions of full employment, of course, even greenfield FDI may not generate additional physical investment, as domestic investment is crowded out. In these circumstances, gains from national competitiveness are dependent upon a beneficial ownership effect and the possibility of favourable spillovers or externalities – whether in terms of organisation, the training of personnel, or through some other means.

Encouraging inward investment has been a central plank of government policy and been stressed in all of the recent *Competitiveness* White Papers (HMSO, 1994, 1995, 1996), with some additional discussion of the reasoning in Eltis and Higham (1995). The latter correctly point out the importance of foreign-owned companies in UK manufacturing and the fact that they generate higher levels of labour productivity and higher investment per worker. They also place much emphasis on various 'spillover' effects, arguing that such things as 'management style' and quality control have 'spread very widely' to UK-owned companies. Since technology transfer is generally agreed to be easier and less costly within firms and within national borders, they also appear to argue that the greater internationalisation of UK physical assets may be a substitute for the fact that the proportion of GDP spent on R&D is lower in the United Kingdom than in the US or Japan. Although they point to the gap in R&D spending being of the order of 0.5 to 1 per cent of GDP, it is of course much larger in the case of manufacturing GDP (see above, Chapter 4). However, this argument is little more than unadorned assertion, and the essential point is that policy needs to have technology transfer as a specific objective of policy (see Temple, 1995, and below).

A very liberal policy toward inward investment in the advanced economies usually has a corollary in terms of greater outward investment and the

United Kingdom is no exception: taking the period since 1979 as a whole, outward investment has been considerably greater than inward investment. The beneficial impact of outward investment is critically dependent upon the existence of full employment. A choice between foreign and domestic investment can be assumed to be taken on the basis of potential profit income (the private rate of return). If for financial or other reasons, foreign investment comes at the expense of domestic investment, then in conditions of unemployment the social rate of return on domestic investment (which should include both profit and at least a portion of employment income) may comfortably exceed the private rate. Whether domestic and foreign investments do in fact act as substitutes has been examined in a number of empirical studies. In Sweden where, as in the United Kingdom, outward FDI has been a very important aspect of corporate strategy, empirical research has shown that foreign investment did have a negative impact on domestic investment (Svensson, 1993). Evidence for the US tends to show by contrast that foreign and domestic innovation may be complementary (Stevens and Lipsey, 1992).

The impact of foreign on domestic investment is not of course the only effect that needs to be considered. Recent research in the United Kingdom has looked at the impact on exports. Blake and Pain (1994) found a negative long-run relationship between outward FDI and manufacturing exports for the United Kingdom between 1972 and 1992, while also finding a positive relationship between inward FDI and exports. On the other side, the most recent White Paper (HMSO, 1996) refers to a KMPG survey which asked respondents about the impact of their last investment. A clear majority thought that the impact on exports and domestic employment was positive or neutral. For the more specific case of firms in the food and drink industry, Balasubramanyam (1993) finds a positive relationship between exports and sales by foreign affiliates, although it is statistically insignificant.

Although it has formed a vital component of economic policy, a very liberal regime toward FDI has never been subject to systematic scrutiny. Given the importance of the subject, empirical evidence remains rather thin, and while there are clearly benefits from these substantial inflows of FDI, the overall effect when outflows are taken into account remains far from clear. The question of spillovers from the inward investor to the domestic economy is a particular area where much harder evidence is required.

MICROECONOMIC POLICY AS AN AGENT OF CHANGE

General considerations

Economic policy represents the final agent of change to be discussed, one just as hotly disputed as deindustrialisation and international economic integration. It is not the intention here to discuss the whole range of economic policy but to concentrate upon the role of a subset of policies specifically aimed at stimulating technical change, innovation, and more generally the competitiveness of industry. The first part outlines some general considerations about the role of the state in improving economic performance before the next part analyses industrial and other microeconomic policy in more detail. One aspect of policy of great importance in Britain – privatisation – is then considered in detail. The final section offers some concluding remarks.

This narrowing of focus for the present discussion is not perhaps as restrictive as it seems, since in the United Kingdom, as elsewhere among the advanced economies, the scope for independent economic policy in various areas (such as macroeconomic policy) has clearly diminished. Even within microeconomic policy the rules governing membership of the EU have placed constraints on what might be done under the rubric of industry policy. The EU is determined, for example, to curb the use of direct cash aids to industry, applying Articles 92 and 93. More general European disillusion with subsidies has been reported (Lehner and Meiklejohn, 1991), and this may help the Commission in its objectives. At the present time the United Kingdom has a relatively low level of state aid for manufacturing (comparable as a proportion of manufacturing GDP with Germany and significantly less than France or Italy; Commission of the European Communities, 1991). The increasing importance of European competition policy will also tend to curb some 'restructuring' policies aimed at declining industries and ailing firms. A process of substitution can of course be expected as new policy instruments are designed and evaluated, and it can be anticipated that technology-cum-innovation policy will loom increasingly large.

In evaluating the role of the state in economic change, the contribution of neoclassical orthodoxy has never been of great assistance. One reason for this is that major structural change in capitalist economies frequently involves significant revaluations of existing assets which governments, but not apparently economists, must take into account. Physical capital, workforce skills, firm-specific competencies, and whole technologies, are subject to the process of 'creative destruction' originally described by Schumpeter. The consequential redistributions of rents that structural change entails may affect not just individuals in the form of redundancy, or firms in the form of bankruptcy, but the prosperity of whole regions or economies. In short, sidestepping questions regarding the impact of such powerful forces as technological change, or freer trade and capital flows, on the distribution of income is inappropriate from any kind of political perspective. At the very least, the liberal market-based solution to the problems created by changes in asset valuations, i.e. allowing changes to go uncompensated, requires a 'strong' state, able to prevent countervailing political processes – a paradox pointed out by Gamble (1987) and more recently by Chang and Rowthorn (1995).

A second important reason why orthodox economics is found wanting in discussing the role of the state lies in its insistent opposition between 'markets' on the one hand, and 'intervention', on the other. In advanced capitalist economies, however, the state is and will remain a major player on its own account. Despite the declared objective of right-wing politicians and economists to roll back the frontiers of the state, this has simply not happened on anything like the scale envisaged. Government actions in the fields of taxation, military defence, education, science and technology, health, and the welfare state, have considerable implications for the competitiveness of indigenous firms, and it is quite misleading to conceive of government as in principle some kind of neutral entity doing little more than helping to set the 'macro-climate' in which business operates.

Despite these reservations about traditional economics and the liberal doctrines associated with it, they have jointly helped to create an important transformation over the last twenty years in the relationship between state, society and economy. Nowhere is this more so than in the United Kingdom. The basis of economic policy for the first thirty years after 1945 has been broken. This involved not just the attack on the Keynesian principles deployed in the macroeconomy but also on the principles of welfare economics – which asserted that market failures at the micro level were important but in many instances could be corrected or ameliorated by government action. The countervailing idea of 'government failure' was central to the rise of 'public choice' theory and the 'new political economy'. The former emphasises that the state can effectively be controlled by self-seeking individuals or groups who can, and do, use their power to pursue interests different from those of society. Austrian forms of political economy by contrast point to the inadequacy of a notion of market failure because of its dependence on the idea of a market in a state of competitive equilibrium, which is held to be an inappropriate basis for policy in a dynamic and complex world.

Both these strands of modern thought are undoubtedly correct to point to the simplistic character of received welfare economics, but they tend to obscure the essential point, noted above, that the state is a vital player in any modern economy and must be involved in creating the myriad of institutions through which market processes work. A way of thinking about this which is relatively conventional but does not depend upon the crude vision of the state as 'intervening' in a set of preordained market processes is to think of the state in relation to public good provision. It needs to be remembered that public goods are outputs which for well-known reasons are under-provided (rather than not provided) by the private market. They might therefore be regarded as a potentially fruitful arena for partnership between the public and private sectors. Arguably, the strength of public good provision is at the very heart of the idea of national competitiveness.

An excellent example of public good provision has been provided by

Chang and Rowthorn (1995), who emphasise the role of the state in providing 'visions' of the future around which the coordination of investment can occur – a process they describe as being 'entrepreneurial' in character since in addition to the vision itself there is also the ability of governments to marshall resources around that vision. Examples cited include not only the familiar case of Japan in the 1970s when that economy managed a radical shift of resources toward knowledge-intensive sectors of production (on this see Freeman, 1987), but also the example of a Bismarckian Germany in the nineteenth century, where government provided a focal point for the development of German heavy and chemical industries. In fact, the point about the coordinating role of the state in providing visions of the future has not been lost in the United Kingdom, as the recent Technology Foresight exercise, a deliberate attempt to create a domestic version of Japanese forward visions, makes clear (for further discussion, see Sharp below, Chapter 19; Stout, 1995). While it may be too early to judge the outcome of Foresight, the failure of government to make substantial financial commitments to the process may have damaged its credibility (see Temple, 1997).

The role and evolution of competitiveness policy

The growing attention being devoted to economic policy at the microeconomic level has at least two sources. The first is a reflection of the growing dissatisfaction with the outcomes from macroeconomic policy increasingly constrained by international economic integration and especially within the EU by the Maastricht convergence process. Macro policy today clearly targets inflation above everything else, and despite the achievement of low inflation rates throughout the advanced economies, the promised benefits, notably in terms of lower unemployment, have simply not materialised. The second emanates from the changing microeconomic climate itself. It has been argued more or less throughout this book that competitive success for firms will depend increasingly upon the ability to make both physical and intangible investments which make better use of the competitive advantages of their economies – i.e. that these investments should make increasing use of knowledge-based resources. This point needs development in more detail.

The translation of the competitive potential of the advanced economies – their knowledge base – into actual performance, is dependent upon a number of conceptually distinct and highly complex processes discussed more fully in Temple (1997). They are:

- the generation of new knowledge;
- the translation of new knowledge into innovative products and processes;
- the diffusion of innovations;
- the exchange of knowledge intensive goods and services;

- the absorption of knowledge and learning and its coordination within the technological infrastructure.

All of these processes are widely acknowledged to be subject to considerable market failure and are highly dependent upon public good provision for their effectiveness. For these reasons they all could be – and to a varying extent have been – regarded as potentially fruitful areas for government policy. The first process is generally seen as the preserve of science policy, while the second and third are generally regarded as the concern of technology policy. Taken together with the more neglected fourth and fifth processes they could be regarded as constituting the domain for a competitiveness policy.

Increasingly, the microeconomic policies of the OECD have been directed toward diffusion processes and away from generation of new knowledge (e.g. Limpens *et al.*, 1992). Reasons for the increased emphasis on diffusion processes include the recognition of the vastly greater importance which attaches to diffusion (as compared with innovation) in the generation of economic wealth, a greater awareness of costs of technology transfer, and the potential for market failure where network externalities are present (as is the case in many communications and information-processing technologies). There are various implications of this change of emphasis, including meeting the problems of smaller firms for whom the informational problem may be particularly acute.

Some years ago Henry Ergas showed how technology policies in a number of countries, notably Germany and Sweden, which emphasised diffusion as an objective through attention to the provision of public goods, outperformed policies which were 'mission-oriented' and which focused on new knowledge generation and radical innovation as aims of national importance. The public goods in question include aspects of the education and training system, cooperative R&D, and industrial standardisation. By contrast, the technology policy of the United Kingdom was taken as a prime example of the mission-oriented approach and came in for especially sharp criticism. Projects such as Concorde and the AGR reactor are usually summed up as hugely expensive failures (e.g. Henderson, 1977) and they almost certainly crowded out other innovatory paths. Despite impressions to the contrary, these kinds of project are not yet dead, even in the non-defence private sector: BT, for example, continued to rely on its System X at the instigation of OFTEL, and the nuclear industry is still heavily subsidised (Ergas, 1993). These missions are all heavily centralised in terms of decision-making and tend to involve only a few key players. France has also pursued a mission-oriented technology policy, but with apparently a greater degree of success, based on superior administrative capacity and concentration on far less radical innovation – a good example being the high speed train (TGV) which was essentially based on 'stretching' rather than supplanting existing

477

technologies. But failures also are apparent in areas such as VCRs and computing. Nowadays, as we shall see, the technology policies of both France and the United Kingdom display much more attention to diffusion, even if the legacies of a different approach remain.

Beyond the consideration of diffusion, competitiveness policy needs also to address issues posed by the fourth and fifth processes listed above. The exchange of knowledge intensive goods and services poses particular problems in situations of information asymmetry. Trust may be an important ingredient if firms are to undertake investments subject to opportunistic behaviour. Quality assurance (such as the ISO 9000 series of standards) and other mechanisms which help to reduce the problem of informational asymmetry, may be important, especially if, for cultural or other reasons, trust is difficult to establish. The ways in which trust can become a source of competitive advantage has been stressed in the sociological literature surrounding the concept of the geographically localised industrial cluster (e.g. Sabel, 1989).

It is also important for policy to be alive to the fact that private rates of discount for knowledge may differ systematically from social rates. The ability of a firm to generate rents from knowledge may disappear long before the usefulness of a piece of knowledge is lost to society. Ways of absorbing knowledge into the technology infrastructure (e.g. into educational and training syllabuses or industrial standards) need to be designed and implemented and form a vital component of competitiveness policy.

Finally, it is worth remarking that the key processes of technological change are interdependent. For example, strengthening the patent system may (through higher prices) retard the diffusion of an innovation. Competitiveness policy therefore has to be formulated in ways which enable public good provision to be flexible and systemic in character.

In the United Kingdom, as elsewhere, various strands of microeconomic policy have tended to converge on the objective of enhancing national competitiveness. We shall briefly discuss here industry, science and technology, and regional policy. In these areas, and in clear distinction to policies focused on labour market reform, although change has been implemented in line with a *laissez-faire* programme, it has been pursued in less dogmatic fashion. The exception to this has been privatisation policy which, outside the labour market, is the one area where political, theoretical and ideological considerations have proved important.

Until the end of the 1970s industry policy in the United Kingdom mainly took the form of support for fixed investment, often to aid restructuring in declining industries such as shipbuilding. In the early 1980s this was partially replaced by policies aimed at support for technology and R&D (see, for example, Shepherd, 1987); notable initiatives included the creation of a new ministerial post and the Alvey programme aimed at stimulating linkages between industry and the universities (e.g. Quintas and Guy, 1995). However, a major review of the support for technology removed much aid to near market development work where the Government was not convinced that there was a strong market failure case. There was a new emphasis at the time on collaborative R&D and a subordination of domestic R&D programmes to those initiated in the EU. However, a different set of emphases embraced aid for small firms, and which broadly assisted diffusion processes, e.g. subsidies to design and other advisory services which recently have been brought under the umbrella of the Business Link programme (the so-called 'one stop shop'). Although the mission of Business Link encourages the establishment of horizontal and vertical collaborative networks between firms, the programme has been criticised for its emphasis on bilateral linkages between the agency and the firm.

Whatever the rationale for the current emphasis of industry policy, it needs to be remembered that this should be seen against a backdrop of very substantial reductions in government support for industry. To understand the reasons why, even in areas such as R&D provision, which is very much against the international trend, it is important to understand the very general disillusion with industry policy and the widespread perception that it has failed in the past to achieve any significant objectives. The redirection of industry policy since the 1970s owes much to this sense of failure, not just within the field of high technology, but also with the exercises in industrial 'restructuring'. In many of these exercises, the idea of static economies of scale have in the past featured strongly. This owes much to the widely held view throughout Europe in the 1960s that national fragmentation of markets in Europe meant that the size of indigenous firms was inadequate for competition with the US giants. This resulted in considerable laxity in the United Kingdom and elsewhere with regard to merger policy and a legacy for Europe of 'national champions', each close to the ear of government and partly protected through domestic policies. Assessing the desirability of this should be about assessing the trade-off between economies of scale on the one hand and weakened competition on the other. In the event, the latter has been allowed to occur but the reduction in costs due to economies of scale has been more questionable. A number of studies have indicated that across most industries the minimum efficient scale of production falls far short of even national markets in the EU (see for example Geroski and Jacquemin, 1985; Adams and Brock, 1988; Geroski, 1989). According to some, the result has been a key ingredient in the phenomenon of so-called 'Euro-sclerosis' in which European firms have failed to adapt and respond to the challenges posed by a variety of shocks, including technological change and freer international trade.

Static economies of scale are generally much less important from the point of view of innovation than dynamic economies, i.e. cumulative processes of learning by doing, learning by using, etc. The significance of dynamic increasing returns stems from the advantages of an early start or at

479

least that of a rapid response. Outcomes are 'path dependent' and there is (for example) no reason for superior technologies to prevail (e.g. Arthur, 1989). Here the importance of size is also debatable. Although there is a Schumpeterian idea that large size and market power are essential for innovativeness,[7] the role of small and medium-sized firms in innovation is increasingly being stressed. Pavitt *et al.* (1987) have, by studying several thousand innovations in the United Kingdom between 1945 and 1983, suggested that smaller firms do play a leading role in innovation which is consistently underestimated because they lack the formal R&D projects and departments of the bigger organisations. However, there are reasons for supposing that smaller firms have particular difficulties exploiting innovation and this is connected with a lack of assets needed to complement the purely technical aspects of innovation – in finance, marketing, design and so on. Improving their access to these assets would certainly be a justifiable aim for an industrial policy and would clearly assist in enhancing competition for larger firms.

In UK science policy, the role of government has never seriously been questioned, and recent government pronouncements, and in particular the important 1993 White Paper *Realising Our Potential*, which established Technology Foresight, clung to the belief that Britain has a very strong science and engineering base which only needs to be tapped to gain competitive advantage. This particular view, although widespread, has not gone unchallenged. A study by Martin *et al.* (1990) showed that, in a comparison with four Europen countries, UK spending per head of population by government was higher than the average in only mathematics, computing and environmental sciences. However, outputs from the science base are also important and here the picture does appear to be better, although it may be weakening (Martin, 1992). In common with other countries, it is now explicitly argued that science is about creating strategic opportunity and that research programmes need to be designed with an assessment of the 'match between potential research outputs and the likelihood that they can be appropriated by firms and organisations' (HMSO, 1993).

Regional policy has also seen significant changes and, like industry policy, these have involved considerable reductions in the resources devoted to it. The old emphasis involved the redistribution of resources to reduce inequalities, with an attempt being made to divert investment into the problem regions, including a deliberate policy which skewed infrastructure investment (e.g. Britain's motorway system) to the assisted areas. By the 1980s the recession and the growing urban problem put paid to the more purely redistributive policies (for a discussion, see Gudgin, 1995). What assistance remains is targeted at fewer areas, and is channelled through independent organisations such as the Training and Enterprise Councils, and in Scotland by the Local Enterprise Councils. Many diverse local efforts have, however, been substituting for the old national regional policy and have the stimulation of the competitiveness of their indigenous firms as an objective. We may include here the development of such entities as science parks and business parks, where cheaper technology transfer was seen as at least an important secondary objective.

Industry, science and regional policy have therefore, and for possibly different reasons, tended to converge into a set of policies which emphasise the development of technological capability and competitiveness. The question is, however, whether the different strands of policy, conveniently brought together in the *Competitiveness* White Papers (HMSO, 1994, 1995, 1996) really add up to a coherent strategy, and whether the financial resources that are necessary are really being committed. In this, Technology Foresight provides an excellent example, for it can be reasonably argued that it is more a vehicle for administering cutbacks in provision for scientific research than it is one for generating commercial value and additionality from increased resources. The difference is important and perhaps sets out the previous government's position more clearly than pronouncements about the determinants of competitiveness.

In general, however, the elements of a competitiveness policy discussed above take a back seat in comparison with the attention devoted to privatisation policy as a source of national competitive advantage. To this we now turn.

Privatisation policy

In its broadest interpretation privatisation uses ownership change to reduce the role and influence of the state in providing goods and services to individuals, and has been an integral part of the economic policies pursued by the nations of Western and Eastern Europe during the 1980s and the 1990s. It marked a reversal of the nationalisation programmes which had been set up in many advanced economies, especially after 1945 and for a variety of reasons such as the need to improve industrial relations and efficiency. Outside the restructuring and reform of the labour market, privatisation has been centre stage of the British government's microeconomic policy, dwarfing other areas such as competition policy. Indeed, it can be seen from the ensuing discussion that ownership change has been implicitly placed above the need to introduce competition in the policies pursued.

The public corporations were a particularly suitable target for the public choice theorists. Managers' utility was held to depend partly upon the size of the operation, suggesting that the corporations might be overstaffed, while the monitoring of management was held to be especially ineffective. Since taxpayers are a diffuse body, there is little incentive to undertake much monitoring activity. Moreover the relationship between the taxpayer and the agent was highly mediated; the direct monitoring was the responsibility of government ministers, who in their turn were responsible to parliament. In these circumstances the ballot box was regarded as a rather feeble alternative to the rights of shareholders.

It is important to distinguish here between privatisation *per se*, which involves a change of ownership, and the raft of other measures which may precede or accompany it, and which may be termed restructuring. An important aim of restructuring was, in some instances, to increase competition, it being recognised that while a so-called 'natural monopoly' (e.g. a network such as the national grid, a railway line, etc.) may form the core of the industry, many activities of the former corporations were not natural monopolies at all (e.g. in power generation, retail activities, etc.). Changes in performance consequent upon privatisation may therefore be the result of many simultaneous changes, not all of which will be due to the change in ownership. Empirical evidence regarding the impact of privatisation is further complicated by the fact that the nationalised industries usually had a public interest obligation (involving, for example, the use of more expensive domestically produced coal in electricity generation). This affects the relevant counterfactual case when considering what might have happened to performance under public ownership, had restructuring taken place anyway.

The Government motives behind the privatisation process were not of course simply economic, they were also clearly political. In addition to the efficiency gains predicted by the public choice theorists, the substantial proceeds from privatisation would impact on the public sector's borrowing requirement and allow a faster tax-cutting strategy, especially important when it was realised that curbing public expenditure was no simple thing at a time of rising unemployment. Moreover, it was hoped that extending share ownership might have similar repercussions on attitudes to the council house sale programme (one of the earliest acts of the incoming Conservative government in 1979). The ownership change itself has taken different forms – from stock exchange flotation, to outright sale to a private sector company, or management buy-out. The British government also adopted the policy of contracting out to the private sector activities being carried out within the public sector.

A major objective of privatisation policy throughout Western Europe was to shift the balance of power from the public to the private sector. In the United Kingdom the programme began earlier and today remains more extensive than in other EU economies. Figure 18.5 shows the impact of the privatisation on the proportion of the net capital stock of the British economy from 1979 to 1994, i.e. prior to rail privatisation. In 1979, around 18 per cent of the stock was in the control of the managers of public corporations; by 1994 this had fallen to just 5 per cent. The proportion in the hands of industrial, commercial, and financial companies (which excludes those in the personal sector) rose from 30 per cent to around 40 per cent. The impact of the biggest sell-offs can clearly be discerned: British Telecommunications in 1984; British Gas in 1986; the water companies in 1989, and electricity generation and distribution in 1990. At the time of writing British Rail is in

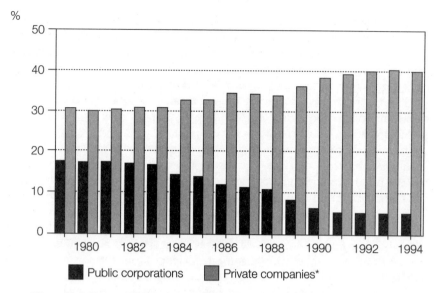

%

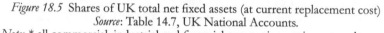

Figure 18.5 Shares of UK total net fixed assets (at current replacement cost)
Source: Table 14.7, UK National Accounts.
Note: * all commercial, industrial and financial companies not in personal sector.

the process of being privatised, while the privatisation of the Post Office remains on the agenda.

The economic and political unacceptability of allowing natural monopolies complete freedom in the market-place after privatisation meant that privatisation policy in practice has been tempered by some degree of regulation in order to safeguard the consumer and promote competition. The regulatory regime that has evolved over the past fifteen years in the United Kingdom is based on the principle of price capping (PC), rather than controlling the required rate of return on investment (ROR). The price-capping formula that is applied to the telecommunications, gas, electricity and water industries is some variant of RPI − X, where RPI represents the rate of growth in the retail price index and X is some number which represents efficiency savings the benefit of which is to be passed on to consumers. The formula was first put in place when British Telecom was privatised in December 1984. At that time it was thought that competition would spontaneously emerge within a very short period and that regulation therefore would be a temporary requirement. Littlechild (1985) was of the view that 'competition is by far the most effective means of protection against monopoly. Vigilance against anti-competitive practices is also important. Profit regulation is merely a "stop-gap" until sufficient competition develops'. In reality, however, the history of privatisation policy in the United Kingdom over the past fifteen years is one of a systematic increase in regulation. It is generally believed that the price-capping approach to regulation is superior to that of ROR, frequently adopted in the US, because there may be incentives for the regulated monopolist to hit the target rate of return by raising capital inputs above that indicated by the cost-minimising output mix – so called 'gold plating' (Averch and Johnson, 1962; Doyle, 1993).

So what has been the impact of this massive programme on economic performance, in areas vital for the supply side – in energy, water, and communications?

The focus of the economic performance debate in the area of privatisation has been whether change in ownership from the public sector to the private sector would produce efficiency gains, and would therefore be desirable from the point of view of improving overall economic performance. The concept of efficiency that is generally brought under scrutiny in this debate is that of 'productive' efficiency, which concerns the production of a given output at minimum cost. This implies that a firm is not only producing on the technological frontier ('technical efficiency') but is also using the most efficient combination of inputs, given input prices ('price efficiency'). While the public choice theory relates perhaps particularly to technical efficiency, public interest obligations also constrained the way in which nationalised industries were forced to operate (e.g. a requirement to buy output from domestic producers, or to pay a price above that ruling in the world market). Parker (1995) points out that these efficiency concepts are all essentially static and make no allowance for dynamic efficiency gains, i.e. the generation of benefits through technological change in processes and products. This aspect of economic efficiency, which has been crucial in the performance debate in other areas, has not however been much considered in that concerning ownership.

The broad consensus seems to be that in the cases where the costs of market failure arising from monopoly power are insignificant, transfer of ownership to the private sector will produce technical efficiency gains by providing the incentives to minimise costs. Examples of such cases are public enterprises operating in markets where there already exists some degree of competition (e.g. BA, Jaguar, British Aerospace and so on).

The argument in favour of privatisation becomes less clear if the degree of market failure is substantial as is the case when monopoly power is significant. For instance, the privatisation of a monopolistic utility may create opportunities of internal cost savings, but its profit-seeking behaviour may lead to the abuse of monopoly power in terms of higher prices to consumers and a lower level of overall output, and hence may generate considerable allocative inefficiencies. Whether there is a net gain or a net loss from privatisation in such cases depends upon the relative magnitudes of the two effects and may go in either direction. In competitive markets the issue of allocative efficiency becomes insignificant and the technical efficiency gains from change of ownership provide the rationale for privatisation.

Proponents of privatisation argue that technical efficiency gains from privatising state-owned monopolies can still be achieved, if the transfer of ownership to the private sector is supported by a regulatory framework, designed to curb monopolistic behaviour and promote competition. This has been the underlying rationale in the evolving approach towards privatisation adopted in the United Kingdom. However, when the possibility of imperfections in the regulatory system and the costs of regulation are taken on board then the link between privatisation policy involving state-owned monopolies and economic performance becomes somewhat unclear. Indeed the opponents of the sale of public property argue that technical efficiency gains can be reaped by restructuring public enterprises by changing their legal form, introducing competent management and opening the market to entry. Public sector enterprise reforms in West Germany have been developed along these lines over the past fifteen years. The theoretical debate thus seems to come to rest in a choice between efficiently operating state-owned monopolies in the public sector as a result of restructuring, versus privatisation and efficient independent regulation in the market-place. Perhaps what matters in the end is hard evidence on what privatisation policy has achieved.

There is no unique measure of technical efficiency. Moreover, since accounting records do not usually contain sufficient information about costs, empirical analysis has to use other indicators such as productivity measures to draw inferences about changes in efficiency. Even then it is difficult to isolate changes in efficiency from business cycle effects. It is not therefore surprising that the evidence that is available on efficiency gains following the change in ownership is not clear-cut in all cases, with the results often being sensitive to the efficiency measure used.

Parker (1995) examines the issue of change in ownership and the impact on performance using measures of both labour and total factor productivity. Privatised companies included in this study, which while under public ownership could be regarded as being part of a market where they faced some competition, are British Airways, British Airports Authority, Britoil, British Aerospace, Jaguar, Rolls-Royce, and National Freight. Taking the period just prior to privatisation together with the post-privatisation period, the study shows that with the exception of Jaguar, Rolls-Royce and British Airports Authority, there were gains in labour productivity as compared to the nationalisation period. Using total factor productivity, however, i.e. after allowing for a change in capital input, the picture changes as only British Airways emerges with gains as compared to the nationalisation period. The study also shows that the most significant gains in productivity were made in the period just prior to the privatisation and hence begs the question as to whether change in ownership was really essential, or whether improved monitoring, which almost certainly occurs as an industry becomes the centre of attention prior to privatisation, was the cause. Indeed, a sociological 'Hawthorn effect' cannot be ruled out in these circumstances. Parker's work also covers two of the state-owned monopolies which were privatised, namely British Gas and British Telecom. In both cases labour productivity gains are reported in the period just before privatisation and post-privatisation, as compared to the nationalisation period. This picture, however, is completely reversed when total factor productivity is considered. Earlier empirical work on productivity by Yarrow (1986 and 1989) and Bishop and Kay (1988), also indicates mixed results with regard to improvements in efficiency. In an earlier study Foreman-Peck and Manning (1988) compared the performance of British Telecom with some of its state-owned counterparts in Europe and could not conclude that it performed better. Hunt and Lynk (1995) provide evidence that the abandonment of the Integrated River Basin Management system after privatisation has denied the water industry significant efficiency-enhancing effects through lost economies of scope.

In an important recent study, Newbery and Pollitt (1996) examine the social costs and benefits emanating from the restructuring and privatisation of the Central Electricity Generating Board in England and Wales. They show that efficiency gains have been reaped in electricity generation resulting from the privatised generating companies being able to move away from nuclear fuels and expensive British coal to cheaper imported coal and gas. Furthermore this also provided the incentive to British Coal to lower its costs of production, as well as reducing the nuclear power programme. However, this raises the question whether these efficiency gains could have been achieved under public ownership had the Central Electricity Generating Board been relieved of its obligation to buy British coal, and which could then also presumably engage in its own 'dash for gas'. It should also be taken into account that these gains need to be balanced against the losses suffered by having to import electricity from France. Newbery and Pollitt also consider the vital question of the distribution of the benefits from improvements in technical efficiency – is it the consumers or the shareholder? They show what happens to real final prices to consumers (which of course includes the unknown impact of the privatisation of distribution). Domestic prices (with the introduction of VAT at 8 per cent in 1994) are back where they were at the time of privatisation, a similar situation to larger industrial customers; however, lighter industrial consumers are being charged rather less. More generally, Stern (1994) has shown that consumers of energy in Britain have not benefited from fuel price falls to the same extent as in other European economies, or that, outside telecommunications, utility consumers have fared better in general than in comparator countries (Helm, 1994).

Cost savings have been demonstrated in contracting out services to the private sector in the National Health Service and local authorities (Ascher, 1987; Domberger et al., 1987). Once again, the question has not been addressed as to whether these savings could have been realised through internal restructuring.

Consider the question of privatisation and the emergence of subsequent competition in the utility sector. For the successful promotion of competition the privatisation programme should have contained provisions for restructuring the utilities so that their monopoly power, emanating from their vertically integrated structures, could not be retained after privatisation. However, evidence suggests that the manner in which privatisation was carried out created firms with significantly dominant positions in their markets, and hence benefits from competition could not be fully reaped. British Telecom was privatised with its vertically integrated structure intact, as its management was strongly opposed to a break-up. Mercury, a subsidiary of the recently privatised Cable and Wireless, was granted the licence to operate a nationwide fixed-link telecommunications network and hence was to be British Telecom's first potential competitor. However Mercury's share of the telecommunications market was insignificant as compared to British Telecom. While the passage of time has seen the growth of vigorous competition in the areas of network operation and apparatus supply, in the primary business of fixed-link telephony British Telecom's domination remains and hence the industry continues to require extensive regulation. The electricity industry was vertically separated at the time of privatisation, but given that nuclear power was not taken up in privatisation a duopoly was created in generation in the form of National Power and PowerGen. Robinson (1992) is quite clear that the Government did not restructure the electricity industry properly so as to promote competition. The creation of a duopoly in generation provided the scope for collusion and abuse of monopoly power by National Power and PowerGen. In February 1994, the Director General of Electricity Supply decided not to refer these companies to the Monopolies and Mergers Commission after they gave undertakings that they would divest themselves of some generation capacity and would bid for the next two years into the pool such that the average pool price does not exceed a cap. Privatisation does not appear therefore to have produced sufficient competition in electricity generation. Mechanisms for the promotion of competition, and hence the necessity of further restructuring, have also been part of the post-privatisation debate in the gas industry.

Imperfections in the regulatory framework can also create distortions in the market. Regulators require a substantial amount of information on operating costs and capital expenditure from the regulatee who can be selective in the provision of this information, and hence can influence in its favour the price cap set by the regulator. As each of the privatised utilities has its own independent regulatory body, Helm (1994) argues that this provides scope for regulatory arbitrage, an important aspect of which is that regulators acting independently of each other may set the price caps in such a manner which encourages substitution between utilities and generates under- or over-investment, with detrimental consequences for economic performance.

In short, the fact that the regulatory regime in Britain was set up in ways that were deliberately intended to be innovative (e.g. the price cap formula) has meant that there has been a rather steep learning curve for the regulators. Initially this created high rates of return for shareholders, partly perhaps because of the laxness of the regulatory regime. This has led to demands for tougher regimes and/or new utility taxes and a consequential increase in investor uncertainty. Evidently, much remains to be done and learnt if the regulatory regime is to develop effectively. The idea that competition would develop more or less spontaneously, rather than by design, has proved far too simplistic.

SOME CONCLUSIONS

Change is endemic in capitalist economies. Trying to summarise its nature through concepts such as deindustrialisation and globalisation can present only partial, distorting, and ultimately ephemeral characterisations. Nevertheless they are useful aids precisely because the emphasis is on *processes* of change, and therefore can be used to counter more orthodox 'equilibrium' approaches to economic thought. By illustrating a few of these ways of characterising economic change, it is hoped that some idea has been gleaned of how Britain fits into the evolving international political economy.

The concept of deindustrialisation has been around for at least two decades and has proved useful in establishing a common trend across the more advanced economies. Today all the advanced economies have seen the share of employment in manufacturing decline over the period since 1960. In the United Kingdom this has been particularly rapid but this appears to be due to a number of factors. Importantly, however, it does not appear to suggest that the basis of the UK pattern of specialisation in international trade has shifted to any significant degree out of manufacturing and into services. Services do form an important part of UK exports but the data indicate that the United Kingdom is just as dependent upon its manufacturing sector today as it was twenty years ago. More significant than the changing pattern of international specialisation have been differences in productivity growth. This may have particular implications for the fiscal problems of the advanced economies, especially in attempts to deliver ever-higher volumes of public sector services – in education and health especially. Also important in the case of the United Kingdom has been the increasing use of producer services in other parts of the economy. Comparatively little is known about this trend, but it may partly be a symptom of increasing knowledge specialisation in production activities, and the increased demand for professional services in areas such as finance and design. The use of the market for these sophisticated services is a crucial area for national competitiveness and one where market failure may be particularly important. The provision of public goods in the form of standards, and industrially relevant qualifications, as well as a far-sighted and flexible education system are vital in making the use of the market (as opposed, for example, to 'in-house' training) effective.

Foreign investment, especially that driven by the process of European integration, has been an extremely powerful source of structural change in the British economy, and one moreover which has been actively encouraged by government. Much of the inward investment into the United Kingdom has involved a change of ownership and is not of the 'greenfield' kind. In theory these ownership changes should be beneficial to profits, but this is not of course the same thing as the welfare of the local inhabitants. There is of course a potential for fruitful spillover to local firms, but this needs to be addressed specifically in the formation of policy. Another major plank of the Government's industry policy – privatisation – has also hinged critically upon ownership change. The increase in competition which has resulted has not, perhaps, been as great as anticipated, with far more weight thrown onto a regulatory regime than expected. In this department much still needs to be learnt.

Together with action in the labour market, privatisation and encouraging international investment have been key components of the previous Government's micro-economic policy. Whatever one's views on the impact of these policies, the future direction of policy, if it is to be based upon the constructive enhancement of national competitiveness, will need to consider more directly the challenges faced by the tradable sector of the economy and manufacturing in particular. As the Government recognises, at least in one of its hats (e.g. the *Competitiveness* White Papers), this will require a general shift of resources into earlier stages of the product cycle – innovation and diffusion. But as Margaret Sharp points out in Chapter 19 below, this cannot be achieved by mere exhortation, but will require a coordinated industry policy aimed at building up technological capacity, not just in a few sectors but across the range of industries – new and traditional alike (see above, Chapter 4).

Ways must be found to develop investment strategies which expand both technological capabilities and, given the constraints on new job creation (see Chapter 13), physical capacity. As Ciaran Driver shows in Chapter 9, this will require greater risk-taking. In addition it will require an industrial strategy, for many of the problems have a structural dimension, especially in terms of corporate governance and capital market issues, and the need to bolster the competitive process by encouraging the smaller firms to challenge the giants. These things can only be achieved by enhanced public good provision to stimulate innovation and market entry.

Using an industrial policy approach to achieve macro objectives sounds attractive, but the difficulties are enormous. The arguments against any such strategy are powerful and well organised. In theoretical terms, the vision of the economy that has guided the development of policy in Britain has been that of the universal efficacy of the market. The credibility of this position has been stiffened by the widespread belief, whether misguided or not, that industrial policy has in the past failed in Britain, and that 'intervention' is often worse in its effects than the market failure that it is intended to ameliorate. In Britain especially, more positive ways of conceiving of government action need to be developed. It has been argued above that public good provision is one of way of thinking which really involves 'partnership' between the private sector and government if provision is to be effective. At the heart of a competitiveness policy are measures which provide the coordination of investment and trust, and which would induce, as a result, greater entrepreneurial risk-taking. To assist in this, what is required first and foremost is a frank audit of the institutional framework that underpins Britain's industrial and technological structure and hence the indigenous competitiveness of firms. It would embrace areas such as corporate governance and the takeover mechanisms, the institutions involved in the generation and transfer and diffusion of technology, and the provision of finance for business, especially in the small-firm sector. Despite three White Papers devoted to the competitiveness issue, such an institutional audit has not been carried out. Temple (1997) has argued that it would reveal two key weaknesses – in regard to institutions promoting technology transfer and diffusion, and in the field of finance, especially in relation to smaller-scale entrepreneurial start-ups. Much current policy recognises the problem in these areas, but not perhaps their scale. Other weaknesses also exist – especially in relation to corporate governance mechanisms – but they may prove rather more intractable, at least in the shorter term. However, institutional innovation in these areas may require a much more fundamental rethink of the way in which government is organised. Most important, effective public good provision may require considerable devolution of government power if the potential for technological communities (firms and research centres) are to reap the benefits of economies of agglomeration which are discussed more fully by Martha Prevezer in Chapter 21 below. It should never be forgotten that in Britain, the deep scepticism surrounding government, and national government in particular, poses a formidable obstacle to imaginative industry policy. Temple (1997) argues that an extension of local democracy by the creation of strategic capacity at a regional level may be one way out of this dilemma.

NOTES

1 Funding from Gatsby Foundation gratefully acknowledged.
2 See for example Gershuny and Miles (1983).
3 In fact, attempts have been made in the United Kingdom to assess 'outputs' in terms of success rates in nationally comparable exams. In principle these could be used to generate productivity measures. Critics have suggested that the nature of the input (the student's level of attainment at entry) should be taken into account, so that it is 'value added' that is being assessed.
4 'To have one's heart on the left and one's wallet on the right.'

5 See, for example, Gatsios and Seabright (1989). Under these second-best conditions, although no institutions can be prevented from trading, products can, which may still constitute a formidable barrier to entry.

6 This figure is for the outward FDI stock of Austria, Finland, France, Germany, Italy, Netherlands, Sweden, and the United Kingdom only.

7 Because, it is contended, only firms with market power can generate the rents from innovation to make it worthwhile. Very competitive industries may be unable to generate the necessary rents if innovations can be quickly copied.

REFERENCES

Adams, W. and Brock, J. (1988) 'The bigness mystique and the merger policy debate: An international perspective', *Northwestern Journal of International Law and Business*, vol. 9, pp. 1–48.

Akerlof, G. (1970) 'The market for "Lemons": Quality uncertainty and the market mechanism', *Quarterly Journal of Economics*, vol. 84, pp. 488–500.

Arthur, W. B. (1989) 'Competing technologies, increasing returns, and lock in by historical events', *Economic Journal*, vol. 99, pp. 116–31.

Ascher, K. (1987) *The Politics of Privatisation: Contracting out public services*, Basingstoke: Macmillan.

Averch, H. and Johnson, L. (1962) 'Behaviour of the firm under regulatory constraint', *American Economic Review*, vol. 52, pp. 1052–69.

Balasubramanyam, V.N. (1993) 'Entrepreneurship and the growth of the firm: The case of the British food and drink industries in the 1980s', in J. Brown and M. B. Rose (eds) *Entrepreneurship, Networks, and Modern Business*, Manchester: Manchester University Press.

Baumol, W. (1967), 'The macroeconomics of unbalanced growth: The anatomy of urban crisis', *American Economic Review*, vol. LVII, pp. 415–26.

Bishop, M. and Kay, J. (1988) *Does Privatisation Work? Lessons from the UK*, London: London Business School.

Blake, A. P. and Pain, N. (1994) 'Investigating structural change in UK export performance: The role of innovation and direct investment', NIESR Discussion Paper no. 71.

Central Statistics Office (1995) *The UK Balance of Payments: The pink book*, London: HMSO.

Chang, H.-J, and Rowthorn, R. (1995) 'Entrepreneurship and conflict management', in H.-J. Chang, and R. Rowthorn (eds) *The Role of the State in Economic Change*, Oxford: Oxford University Press.

Commission of the European Communities (1991) *Fourth Periodic Report on the Social and Economic Situation and Development of the Regions*, Luxembourg: Office of Official Publications of the European Community.

Davis, E. and Smales, C. (1989) *1992: Myths and realities*, London: Centre for Business Strategy, London Business School.

Domberger, S., Meadowcroft, S. and Thompson, D. (1987) 'The impact of competitive tendering on the costs of hospital domestic services', *Fiscal Studies*, vol. 8, no. 4, pp. 39–54.

Doyle, C. (1993) 'Regulating firms with monopoly power', in R. Sugden (ed.) *Industrial Economic Regulation*, London: Routledge.

Dunning, J. (1993) *The Globalization of Business*, London: Routledge

Eltis, W. E. and Higham, D. (1995) 'Closing the competitiveness gap', *National Institute Economic and Social Review*, November.

Ergas, H. (1987) 'Does technology policy matter?', in B. R. Guile and H. Brooks (eds) *Technology and Global Industry*, Washington, D.C.: National Academy Press, pp. 191–245.

—— (1993) *Europe's Policy for High Technology: Has anything been learnt?*, Paris: OECD.

Foreman-Peck, J. and Manning, D. (1988) 'How well is BT performing? An international comparison of telecommunications total factor productivity', *Fiscal Studies*, vol. 9, pp. 54–67.

Freeman, C. (1987), *Technology Policy and Economic Performance*, London: Pinter.

Gamble, A. (1987) *The Free Market and the Strong State*, Basingstoke: Macmillan.

Gatsios, K. and Seabright, P. (1989) 'Regulation in the European Community', *Oxford Review of Economic Policy*, vol. 5, no. 2, summer, pp. 37–60.

Geroski, P. (1989) 'European industrial policy and industrial policy in Europe', *Oxford Review of Economic Policy*, vol. 5, no. 2, summer, pp. 20–36.

Geroski, P. and Jacquemin, A. (1985) 'Industrial change, barriers to mobility, and European industrial policy', *Economic Policy*, no. 1, November.

Gershuny, J. and Miles, I. (1983) *The New Service Economy: The transformation of employment in industrial societies*, London: Francis Pinter.

Gregory, M. and Greenhalgh, C. (1996) 'The labour market consequences of technical and structural change', *Centre for Economic Performance*, DP 1, Institute of Economics and Statistics, University of Oxford.

Gudgin, G. (1995) 'Regional problems and policy in the UK' *Oxford Review of Economic Policy*, vol. 11 no. 2, pp. 18–63.

Hagedoorn, J. and Schakenrad, J. (1993) 'Strategic technology partnering and international corporate strategies', in K. Hughes, (ed.) *European Competitiveness*, Cambridge: Cambridge University Press, pp. 60–87.

Helm, D. (1994) 'British utility regulation: Theory, practice, and reform', *Oxford Review of Economic Policy*, vol. 10, no. 3.

Henderson, P. D. (1977) 'Two British Errors: Their probable size and some possible lessons', *Oxford Economic Papers*, vol. 29, no. 2, pp. 159–205.

HMSO (1993), *Realising Our Potential*, Cm 2250, London: HMSO.

—— (1994), *Helping Business to Win*, Cm 2563, London: HMSO.

—— (1995), *Forging Ahead*, Cm 2867, London: HMSO.

—— (1996), *Creating the Enterprise Centre of Europe*, Cm 3300, London: HMSO.

Hoeckman, B. M. (1993), 'New Issues in the Uruguay round and beyond: An assessment', *Economic Journal*, vol. 103, no. 421, pp. 1528–39.

Hunt, L. C. and Lynk, L. (1995) 'Privatisation and efficiency in the UK water industry: an empirical analysis', *Oxford Bulletin of Economics and Statistics*, vol. 57, no. 3, pp. 371–388.

Hymer, S. (1979) *The Multinational Corporation: A radical approach*, Cambridge: Cambridge University Press.

Keep, E. and Mayhew, K. (1993) 'UK training policy – assumption and reality', paper presented to the CEPR conference *Training and the Skills Gap*, Birkbeck College, April.

Kierkowski, H. (1987) 'Recent advances in international trade theory: A selective survey', *Oxford Review of Economic Policy*, vol. 3, no. 1, pp. 1–20.

Lehner, S. and Meiklejohn, R. (1991) 'Fair competition in the internal market: Community state aids policy', *European Economy*, vol. 48, pp. 7–114.

Limpens. I, Verspagen, B. and Belan, E. (1992) *Technology Policy in Eight European Countries*, Maastricht: MERIT.

Littlechild, S. C. (1985) *Regulation of BT's Profitability*, London: HMSO.

March, D. (1991) 'Privatisation under Mrs Thatcher', *Public Administration*, vol. 69, winter, pp. 459–80.

Martin, B. (1992) 'Struggling to keep up appearances', *New Scientist*, vol. 136, November, no. 7, pp. 23–5.

Martin, B. *et al.* (1990) 'UK government spending on academic research', *Science and Public Policy*, vol. 17, no. 2, pp. 1–13.

Mayes, D., Hager, W., Knight, A. and Streeck, W. (1993) *Public Interest and Market Pressures: Problems Posed By Europe 1992*, Basingstoke: Macmillan.

Mowery, D. C. and Rosenberg, N. (1989) *Technology and the Pursuit of Economic Growth*, Cambridge: Cambridge University Press.

NEDO (1990) *Memorandum by Director General: The challenge of ERM entry*, London: NEDO.

—— (1992) *UK Tourism: Competing for growth*, Report of the Working Party on Competitiveness in Tourism and Leisure, London: NEDO.

Newbery, D. M. and Pollitt, M. G. (1996) 'The restructuring and privatisation of the CEGB: Was it worth it?', *Department of Applied Economics*, Working Paper No. 9607, University of Cambridge.

Odagiri, H. (1992) *Growth Through Competition, Competition Through Growth*, Oxford: Oxford University Press.

OECD (1992) *Technology and the Economy: The key relationships*, Paris: OECD.

Office for National Statistics (1996) *United Kingdom National Accounts: The blue book*, London: HMSO.

Parker, D. (1995) 'Measuring efficiency gains from privatisation', *Occasional Papers in Industrial Strategy*, no. 36, University of Birmingham.

Pavitt, K. and Patel, P. (1990) 'Large firms in the production of the world's technology: An important case of non-globalisation', *Journal of International Business Studies*, vol. I, pp. 1–21.

Pavitt, K., Robson, M. and Townsend, J. (1987) 'The size distribution of innovating firms in the UK: 1945–83', *The Journal of Industrial Economics*, vol. 35, no. 3, pp. 297–316.

Piore, M. and Sabel, C. (1984) *The Second Industrial Divide*, New York: Basic Books.

Quintas, P. and Guy, K. (1995) 'Collaborative pre-competitive R&D and the firm', *Research Policy* vol. 24, pp. 325–48.

Robinson, C. (1992) 'Memorandum to the House of Commons', Energy Committee: Special Report, vol. 1, London: HMSO, p. 48.

Rowthorn, R. E. and Wells, J. (1987), *Deindustrialization and Foreign Trade*, Cambridge: Cambridge University Press

Sabel, C. (1989) 'Flexible specialisation and the re-emergence of regional economies', in P. Hirst and J. Zeitlin (eds) *Reversing Industrial Decline?*, Oxford: Berg.

Shepherd, J. (1987) 'Industrial support policies', *National Institute Economic and Social Review*, vol. 122, pp. 59–71.

Smith, A. D. (1989) 'New measures of service sector outputs', *National Institute Economic and Social Review*, vol. 128, May, pp. 75–88.

Smith, R. P. and Smith, D. (1992) 'Corporate strategy, corporate culture and conversion: Adjustment in the defence industry', *Business Strategy Review*, vol. 3, no. 2 Summer.

Stern, J. P. (1994) 'The Government's public policy towards gas', in D. R. Helm (ed.) *British Energy Policy in the 1990s: The transition to the competitive market*, Oxford: The OXERA Press.

Stevens, G. V. G. and Lipsey, R. (1992) 'Interactions between domestic and foreign investment', *Journal of International Money and Finance*, vol. 11, pp. 40–62.

Stout, D. K. (1995) 'The foresight process', *Science, Technology, and Innovation, Science Policy*, vol. 8, no. 2, pp. 22–5.

Summers, R. (1985), 'Services in the international economy', in R. P. Inman (ed.) *Managing the Service Economy: Prospects and problems*, Cambridge: Cambridge University Press, pp. 27–48.

Svensson, R. (1993) 'Domestic and foreign investment by Swedish multinationals', The Industrial Institute for Economic and Social Research, working paper no. 391, Stockholm.

Temple, P. (1994) 'Notes on the changing international division of labour', in T. Buxton, P. Chapman and P. Temple (eds) *Britain's Economic Performance* (first edn), London: Routledge.

—— (1995) 'The competitiveness white papers. What lessons for industrial policy?', *Centre for Industrial Policy and Performance Bulletin*, no. 8, summer.

—— (1997) 'Clusters and competitiveness: A policy perspective', in G. M. P. Swann, M. Prevezer and D. K. Stout *The Dynamics of Industrial Clustering: International comparisons in computing and biotechnology*, Oxford: Oxford University Press.

United Nations (1995) *World Investment Report 1995*, New York: United Nations.

Wells, J. (1989) 'Uneven development and deindustrialisation in the UK since 1979', in F. Green (ed.), *The Restructuring of the UK Economy*, Hemel Hempstead: Harvester Wheatsheaf, pp. 25–57.

Williams, K., Williams, J., and Haslam, C. (1990) 'The hollowing out of British manufacturing and its implications for policy', *Economy and Society*, vol. 19, no. 4, November, pp. 456–90.

Williams, K. *et al.* (1992) 'Against lean production', *Economy and Society*, vol. 21, no. 3, August, pp. 321–54.

Williamson, P. J. (1990) 'Winning the export war: British, Japanese, and West German exporters' Strategy Compared', *British Journal of Management*, vol. I, pp. 215–30.

Yamawaki, H. (1993) 'Location decisions of Japanese multinationals', in K. Hughes (ed.) *European Competitiveness*, Cambridge: Cambridge University Press, pp. 11–28.

Yarrow, G. (1986) 'Privatisation in theory and practice', *Economic Policy*, vol. 2, pp. 323–78.

—— (1989) 'Privatisation and economic performance in Britain', *Carnegie-Rochester Conference Series on Public Policy*, vol. 31, pp. 303–44.

19

TECHNOLOGY POLICY

The last two decades

Margaret Sharp

INTRODUCTION

Technology policy is about promoting technological innovation. Mowery (1992) defines it as 'policies that are intended to influence the decisions of firms (and public agencies and enterprises) to develop, commercialise and adopt new technologies'. It has come into prominence in the last two decades for a number of reasons.

First, developments in new technologies have themselves been in the news – computers, mobile phones, the internet, are all examples of new technologies which are now having an effect on our everyday lives; biotechnology is transforming the process of drug discovery in pharmaceuticals and is about to have a profound effect upon agriculture and food production.

It can be argued that it was ever so – at any point in time, new products and processes are making their impact. There is, however, some evidence to show that the process is not as continuous as may appear. Many years ago the Russian statistician Kondratieff noted long, fifty-year cycles in global economic development, and economists such as Mensch (1975) and Freeman (1984) have suggested that these might be associated with the introduction of radical new technologies such as steam power (in the first industrial revolution) and electricity (at the turn of the twentieth century).

Freeman, in particular, has suggested that such radical developments have been associated with a clustering of associated innovations (e.g. electricity brought the electric light, electric motors and a range of equipment in the home and workplace which has since transformed life-styles) which in turn have knock-on effects on the overall economic performance of the economy (Freeman, 1984; Perez and Freeman, 1988). The upswing of the long cycle has in the past been marked by a prolonged investment boom as industry and consumers invest in the range of new products and processes thrown up by the new technologies. Such long booms have been preceded by periods of turbulence as the new technologies jostle for position beside the old, gradually establishing dominance and, in so doing, making obsolete the equipment and skills associated with the old technologies. Viewed in such a way,

495

the developments in microelectronics and the associated information and communication technologies of the last two decades can in retrospect be seen as a period of changeover and turbulence bringing radical and pervasive change in its wake.

Secondly, even though many economists remain sceptical about long wave theories, the demise during the same period (1975–95) of faith in Keynesian (and for that matter monetary) demand management techniques has led to a new emphasis on 'supply-side' policies which includes, besides emphasis on 'flexible' labour and capital markets, consideration of the importance of 'intangible' capital in terms of both education and training and research and development. In particular, the 'new growth theory' has identified a number of potential 'engines for growth' in total factor productivity, including externalities in investment in physical capital (Romer, 1986), externalities from investment in human capital (Lucas, 1988), and investment by firms in R&D and new product development (Aghiou and Howitt, 1990; Grossman and Helpman, 1990; Romer, 1986, 1990).

Such wider investments are sometimes dubbed 'investment in broad capital' and the models are referred to as 'endogenous growth' models because the externalities help to make the process self-generating. Investment in physical capital, for example, because it tends to be in the latest 'vintage' of machine, etc., is seen to embody a considerable element of R&D/ innovation. Romer's so-called 'expansion in varieties' model (1986) picks up the Schumpeterian discussion of the role of monopoly in innovation. It suggests that purposeful investment in R&D (in order to introduce new products and differentiate them from competitors) needs to see reward in a period of monopoly profits, monopoly in this instance being secured through patent rights on innovation.

The new growth models have for the first time moved away from the neoclassical view of technology as an exogenous variable, explained as a 'residual factor' in growth,[1] and begun to recognise the feedbacks within the system. Even so, there remains among economists a tendency to rely too much on the distinction between invention and innovation, and to see the process of innovation as a linear one which starts with scientific research and ends with the successful introduction of a new product. Such a view is implicit, for example, in the frequently heard statement that Britain is 'good at invention but poor in innovation'.

In reality, life is much more complex than this linear model would imply and the innovation process characterised by continuous interaction and feedback (Kline and Rosenberg, 1986). These models emphasise the linkages between upstream and downstream phases of R&D and the extensive feedback between the scientific, technological and process phases of development. Far from being able to apply new scientific ideas costlessly and effortlessly (as implied by neoclassical economic theory), innovating firms have to meet the costs of developing and maintaining up-to-date R&D

facilities, and employ scientists and engineers who understand state-of-the-art developments elsewhere. In developing new products and processes, firms will therefore use much knowledge that is not in the public domain but is embedded in the firm itself – and its employees – knowledge of how to get the best out of particular types of equipment; how to approach specific problems. Such knowledge has been acquired over many years of experience, experiment and innovation. It is *tacit* knowledge and comes from *within* the firm and its organisation, built up cumulatively over the years. In normal circumstances it gives existing firms and organisations inherent advantage over newcomers trying to break into the industry.

The importance of these changed perceptions should not be under-estimated. The neoclassical model, with its exogenous role for science and technology, is predicated upon the assumptions of science as codified information, costlessly and effortlessly transferred as needed – a sort of well-spring of knowledge which can be tapped when necessary. In its place now is a model in which much science and technology are developing endo-genously; where much knowledge is tacit, passed on by word of mouth and learning by doing, and by institutionalised routines within the organisation; and where knowledge and information are therefore acquired cumulatively over time, giving advantage to existing players over new entrants. In essence, it is no longer a world in which firms are the passive recipients of knowledge, but one where firms are active participants in learning and creating new knowledge.

As the OECD's Sundqvist Report summed it up: 'Society is shaped by technical change, and technical change is shaped by society. Technical innovation – sometimes impelled by scientific discovery, at other times by demand – stems from within the economic and social system and is not merely an adjustment to transformations brought about by causes outside that system' (OECD, 1988, p. 117). In other words, the whole process of innovation should really be seen as a system in which both the generation of new products and processes and their diffusion and application become an integral part of the economic and social environment.

This systemic view of technology means that technology policy casts its net far wider than just measures to promote new technologies. It means we are interested in the broad range of issues that affect Britain's system of innovation – on the one hand, investment performance, both in new plant and equipment and in R&D and education and skills training for the work-force; on the other, the institutional framework within which the system works, including such issues as the ease (or otherwise) of obtaining loans for new ventures or the mechanisms for technology transfer from academic to industrial environments. Much of this is covered in other chapters of this book, and this chapter seeks in particular to review developments in the institutional framework, although inevitably it casts its net wider than what might narrowly be regarded as technology policy.

The aim in this chapter is to set developments within this broader context. It is arranged as follows. The next section considers the historical legacy which helped shape Britain's system of innovation. More recent developments in the 1980s and 1990s are then examined, followed by policy developments of the recent past. The final section assesses what, if anything, has been achieved, and attempts to draw some conclusions.

THE STATE AND TECHNICAL ADVANCE, PRE-1979

The historical legacy

By and large, the state in Britain has not acted as a catalyst to industrial and technological development. Between the mid-eighteenth and last quarter of the nineteenth centuries, its economic role was largely confined to regulatory functions and to the advancement and military protection of foreign trade. The next hundred years brought a rising tide of state intervention but it was often hesitant, usually resisted, and seldom as determined and forthright as in other countries. It tended to be reactive, not proactive. Contrast this with France, where the state has generally seen itself as a creator of new modes of production and as an entrepreneur in its own right.

There are, however, a number of characteristics which were formed in Britain's early years of industrialisation and which, having survived the upheavals and policy changes of the last century, have become deeply embedded in the British culture. As such, they help to explain current developments. As the systems of innovation literature stresses – history matters.

First, it is worth recalling that the first industrial revolution is often associated with names – Tull and the seed drill; Hargreaves and the Spinning Jenny; Watt and the steam engine; Brunel and railways and steamships. In the early part of the nineteenth century it was possible for the individual entrepreneur to command the range of practical and theoretical knowledge required to develop the most sophisticated innovations of the day. Technology in general preceded science – theories came later to explain the empirical phenomena. It was predominantly, as Landes has described it 'tinkering technology' and as he and other historians have argued, the tradition which it encouraged was ill-adapted to the more institutionalised, systematic and science-based technological systems which underpinned the second industrial revolution (Landes, 1969; Hobsbawm, 1968).

A second theme of British economic history is that the industrial innovators of the eighteenth and nineteenth centuries were outsiders to the social elite, and very often religious dissenters or non-conformists. With the occasional exception of financiers, very few came from the established middle classes. A phenomenon much remarked upon by social historians is the speed with which entrepreneurs and their offspring were 'captured' by the aristocracy, with its anti-industrial values, while continuing to enjoy the rent from accumulated commercial assets (Jessop, 1989). This goes a long way to explain the long cultural ascendancy in British society of the City over industry, of finance over commerce, and of pure over applied research (Weiner, 1981).[2]

Thirdly, education is not a new issue in British performance. Early industrialisation ignored education and until the late nineteenth century (perhaps even later), there was no proper education 'system' in Britain. In contrast, in Germany, Japan and even the United States, organised education was the prelude and springboard for industrial advance. Economic historians are now agreed that this failure to establish an adequate education system was an important cause of Britain's difficulty in adjusting to late nineteenth- and twentieth-century industrial requirements.

Fourthly, it is important to remember that British economic expansion in the nineteenth century was an international phenomenon. The imperial trading system hinged on the export of finance, technology and manufactured goods, and the import of raw materials and food – what has been referred to as a 'vertical' division of labour (Sharp and Shepherd, 1987). While Britain's geopolitical ascendancy depended ultimately on technological and military (especially naval) superiority, it was also characterised by:

1 its extra-European nature – Britain's trading strength lay in the markets opened up in North America, Australasia and Africa, not in Europe;
2 the City as a source of capital – London provided much of the investment capital for the infrastructure necessary to open up these markets, reinforcing the City's ascendancy over industry;
3 the importance of multinational traders – Britain became the hub of an elaborate raw material, food and energy trading system. The firms that developed around it were as much traders as manufacturers, and even today resource trading remains one of Britain's strongest specialisations, with firms such as BP and Shell (oil/gas), Unilever (food and oils), and RTZ (minerals) amongst the largest of their kind in the world.

One of the results of these developments was a divergence between manufacturing and those sections of the economy dealing with financial and material flows (which should now be extended to include retailing). While the former has declined, the latter has flourished; and while the former has remained occupationally unpopular among the educated elite, the latter has provided its principal source of new employment and income, including unearned income.

Finally, the sheer brutality of British industrialisation needs emphasising. The enclosures which drove people off the land, the terrible health and safety conditions in factories, mines and cities, the effects of pollution, the lack of any economic safety net – all were in their way traumatic and engendered a deep ambivalence in the population about the benefits of industrialisation. This led to the growth of a particularly adversarial form of trade unionism, and a distrust of industry and capital amongst both working and middle classes (Thompson, 1968). Over time, it also led to a duality of policy: efforts to arrest Britain's (relative) economic decline from 1900 onwards were accompanied by equal and even more persistent efforts to develop more humane forms of economic organisation. This duality of policy was evident well into the post-1945 period, but was decisively over-turned in the 1980s. By meddling, the state had, it was argued, both stifled the economy and prevented the poor from bettering themselves.

Post-war optimism

The two world wars and the Cold War were especially important in changing attitudes towards technology. They gave legitimacy to state sponsorship of technological and industrial development and they brought the first direct funding of R&D, the establishment of government R&D laboratories, the use of procurement as an instrument for creating new production capabil-ities, and the use of industrial planning in areas such as energy. In general, the success of the new products, such as radar, emerging from wartime activity, gave credence to the notion that the state could usefully play a part in accelerating the development and diffusion of new technologies.

Continuing military demands on industry had the added effect of creating industrial sectors that were predominantly under the wing of the state. Brit-ain's leading role in the defence of north-west Europe and its adherence to nuclear weapons meant that substantial state resources were committed to the nuclear, aerospace, shipbuilding and electronics industries. Britain was second only to the United States in its per capita commitment to defence R&D, and since military technologies (or quasi-military technologies, like nuclear energy) were assumed to represent the leading edge of technology, the state took upon itself the role of prime mover.

The 1960s, and particularly the period 1964–9, when the Labour Party was in power, was a period of considerable optimism about technology and what state intervention might achieve (Sharp and Shepherd, 1987, chapter 6; Mottershead, 1978). The following features of policy in this period are worth noting.

Keynesian rationalism The Keynesian macroeconomic management practised at this time, the adoption of indicative planning, and the use of various interventionist measures to restructure industry and induce technical advance can all be seen as part of the same rationalist approach. The future was considered sufficiently predictable, and the industrial system sufficiently malleable, to allow the state to play a central role in control.

Partnership Industrial progress was seen as best achieved through part-nership between government, the trade unions and industrial management, as manifested in the National Economic Development Council (NEDC). Consensus between these parties would, it was hoped, bring greater control over incomes, agreement on industrial strategy and an end to the traditionally adversarial style between management and trade unions.

Expansion of education Education was seen as holding the key to equality of opportunity, as well as being necessary to support economic and technical advance. The reform of primary and secondary education to encourage more open, child-centred learning, was accompanied by a major expansion of higher education in the universities and polytechnics. This was to be the age of opportunity for all.

Emphasis on manufacturing The increasingly grave balance of payments problems gave manufacturing, and especially the engineering industries, pride of place in economic policy-making. Efforts were made to bolster capabilities through import substitution and export promotion, and to stem the drift of employment from manufacturing to other sectors via a selective employment tax which hit the service industries.

The role of technology Industrial decline was attributed particularly to the failure to develop and apply new technology. Britain's good record in scientific discovery and invention was not translated into innovation, nor were new products or new manufacturing processes rapidly taken up by industry. Efforts were made to hasten the application of new process technologies, such as numerically controlled machine tools, via investment grants, demonstration projects and a host of other measures.

Scale economies Enlarging enterprises to give them greater opportunities for reaping economies of scale was regarded as a key to higher productive efficiency. Fragmentation was viewed as a source of weakness. Thus the Government, through the Industrial Reorganisation Corporation, supported the wave of mergers which created 'national champions' such as GEC in electrical and electronic engineering, British Leyland in motor vehicles, ICL in computers and Alfred Herbert in machine tools.

The 1970s

The retreat from this post-war optimism began in the 1970s. The oil crises and stagflation of that period brought disillusionment with Keynesian policies of macroeconomic management, and greatly eroded belief in the Government's powers of omniscience. In spite of perceptions to the contrary, the industrial strategy of the 1970s, with its panoply of sector working parties and tripartitism, was predicated on an economic philosophy which suggested that there were, for Britain, no winners, but a huge backlog of missed opportunities across the industrial board. The basic problem was diagnosed as being that Britain was producing products that were frequently ten years out of date, on machines that were twenty years out of date (Stout, 1978). The solution required a wholesale upgrading of quality, attention to detail and the pursuit of high value-added opportunities. Selective grants were available to encourage re-equipment on a sector-by-sector basis, big was no longer necessarily beautiful and, increasingly, international competitiveness became the key success indicator.

Old habits, however, died hard. When Rolls-Royce, and subsequently British Leyland, ran into difficulties, they were bailed out by the state, which subsequently became the largest shareholder. The National Enterprise Board (NEB), set up in 1975 to catalyse new technologies, was rapidly turned instead into a rest home for 'lame ducks'. Meanwhile, major decisions of the 1960s – particularly Concorde and the programme to build a succession of nuclear power stations based on the advanced gas-cooled reactor (AGR) – continued to drain scarce technological resources to 'big projects' rather than dispersing them more generally across industries (Henderson, 1977). Despite all the efforts to revive economic fortunes, the domestic economy did not prosper, international trade shares continued their decline, and many interventionist policies came to be regarded as failures.

More than anything else, the discontinuities brought about by the oil crises shook industrial confidence. Manufacturing investment slumped, unemployment rose, but so too did inflation. Struggling to control inflation, governments gradually allowed the maintenance of full employment to slip from the top of the politico-economic agenda. Henceforth, pride of place was given to the reduction of inflation and public borrowing. The former was achieved mainly through the administration of a tough incomes policy run in conjunction with the trade unions – the so-called Social Charter. The *quid pro quo* was a succession of labour laws which considerably strengthened the role of the trade union movement – indeed, one cabinet minister subsequently described the Social Charter as a matter of 'all take and no give'.[3] When successive rounds of the incomes policy hit increasing opposition from rank-and-file members, the spirit of cooperation rapidly caved in, culminating, in the autumn of 1978, in a succession of inflationary wage claims and a wave of public sector strikes which were dubbed the 'winter of discontent'. For many this was the last straw in a decade of vacillation during which the power of the trade unions had grown to excess and that of managers was too severely curtailed.

THE CONSERVATIVE RECORD – 1979–95

The election of the Thatcher-led Conservative government in 1979 was in many respects a response to the perceived failure of earlier years. This goes some way towards explaining the three main prongs of economic policy in the 1980s: the retreat from industrial intervention and the return to a *laissez-faire* approach to industrial issues; the use of monetary instruments as the foundation of a macroeconomic policy whose main task was to control inflation; the reining-in of trade union power and the end to any attempt at tripartite consensus.

Thatcherism also marked the end of the post-war consensus of successive British governments that it was their responsibility to help strengthen technological capabilities. The Thatcher government of the 1980s largely disavowed this responsibility, partly out of the belief that industry should look after its own affairs, and partly because it had little understanding of the importance of technological capabilities to performance. As we shall see, although there have been changes during the 1990s, many of the attitudes engendered in the 1980s have survived to influence policy.

Three recurring themes – the free market, enterprise and value for money

Until the 1980s, the starting point for British (and other) governments in formulating industrial policy has been to begin with a set of observations about industry's international performance and then to develop a series of analyses identifying areas of strength and weakness at both national and international level. These analyses formed the basis of policy formulation – the state acted like a doctor, making diagnoses and specifying regimens and medicaments. And, like any good doctor, it did not follow the Darwinian principle of the survival of the fittest, but preferred to see the sick returned to health alongside the fit.

It was this concept of the pragmatic 'doctor state' which was so thoroughly rejected by Thatcherism. In its place was substituted a far more doctrinaire approach built deductively upon three concepts at the centre of their own philosophy – the free market, enterprise and value for money.

The free market was seen as the natural, most efficient, stable yet dynamic regulator of the economy. As good Hayekians, the Thatcherites considered that previous governments, both Labour and Conservative, had committed a number of cardinal sins. They had wrongly assumed that their knowledge and judgement, *qua* governments, were superior to those of firms in the market-place; their interventions had disturbed market mechanisms and diminished perceptions of risk (by providing a safety net for erring companies); and they had encouraged too cosy and corporatist a relationship to develop between industry and state.

The Thatcher concept of enterprise was more idiosyncratic. To start with, it denoted a broad cultural movement. In the words of the DTI's 1988 White Paper, 'the key to continued economic success lies in the further encouragement of the enterprise of our people' (UK Government, 1988). Behind it lay some romantic vision of the natural state which should be enjoyed by 'our people'. At the same time, it was a highly individualistic concept. The principal actors were individuals and individual firms – notably small firms – whose essential qualification was that they operated a new or expanding business. The entrepreneur did not have to be a creative force, generating and exploiting new scientific and technical knowledge. The enterprise might just as well be a sweatshop, a software house or a property company.

Value for money, for its part, provided the central key for action in areas where the state has been unable to shift the locus of activity into the private sector. It served the twin objectives of improving public sector performance and reducing public expenditure. The implicit, and on many occasions explicit, assumption was that the public sector was by definition parasitic and wasteful of resources while the private sector was efficient, productive and virtuous. Wherever possible, therefore, public sector services were to be subcontracted out to private sector concerns and decisions devolved to firm level. Ironically, where this proved impossible and government retained responsibility for allocation decisions – in areas such as basic research and education – its search for value for money led instead to increasing centralisation and *dirigisme*.

... and three phases of policy

Taking the period 1979–96 as a whole, there have been three distinct phases of policy. Up to 1984, and roughly coinciding with the first Thatcher administration, policies in support of innovation showed surprisingly little change from those of previous administrations. Sir Keith Joseph, Secretary of State for Industry from 1979 to 1981, who was a strict non-interventionist with an avowed intention to abolish his own department, in fact found himself in the thick of recession and forced to hand out unprecedented subsidies to the then state-owned steel, shipbuilding and car industries. His successor, Patrick Jenkin, determined to give priority to supporting new, sunrise firms rather than the old, sunset industries and resurrected many of the 1975–9 schemes for promoting and supporting new technologies. In general support was provided by technology rather than industry (e.g. there were schemes for supporting biotechnology, robotics, computer-aided design, etc.) and emphasis was put on raising knowledge and awareness, especially amongst small firms. He appointed, for the first time, a Minister for Information Technology and, via its incumbent, launched the Alvey Programme, modelled on the Japanese fifth generation computer scheme, and one of the most ambitious initiatives for promoting high technology ever seen in Britain. Aimed at supporting pre-competitive R&D in electronics, the programme was highly successful in promoting collaborative R&D between industry and higher education, but found the next stage of developing the interface with corporate R&D more testing (Guy *et al.*, 1991).

A distinct change of course came in the mid-1980s and reflected two developments. One was the insistent pressure from the Treasury to limit public expenditures. The other was the growing strength of the non-interventionist, deregulatory wing of the Conservative Party, which had received a boost from the unexpected popularity of the privatisation of British Telecom. From 1984 onwards, efforts were made to bring innovation policy, and for that matter industrial policy more generally, into line with neoliberal orthodoxy. This led to a gradual withdrawal from innovation support schemes, including the Alvey Programme, and culminated in the 1988 Enterprise Initiative when it was announced that, with the exception of the European Eureka Initiative, the Government would support no 'near-market' R&D.[4]

The advent of the Major administration in late 1990 brought yet another change of course, especially after the 1992 general election when Michael Heseltine became Secretary of State for Industry and President of the Board of Trade. Technology and competitiveness leapt to the top of the agenda. An Innovation Unit was established within the DTI; league tables, benchmarking, best practice seminars were introduced. Yet by this time, neoliberal orthodoxy had taken hold. While the DTI adopted a more proactive stance, its budget was cut dramatically (which meant it had no resources with which to back up initiatives) and the privatisation of the R&D infrastructure continued apace. Indeed, ironically, what has become known as Thatcherism emerged in its starkest and most uncompromising guise under the Major administration.

Levels of R&D expenditure and patenting

By international standards, British expenditure on R&D as a proportion of GDP was relatively high in the early 1980s but by the 1990s had fallen below

Table 19.1 R&D expenditures as a proportion of GDP, 1981–94

	1981–5			1990–4		
	*Total**	*Govt*	*Industry*	*Total**	*Govt*	*Industry*
UK	2.30	1.10	1.00	2.19	0.71	1.11
Germany†	2.54	0.99	1.52	2.54	0.92	1.56
France	2.12	1.14	0.88	2.42	1.13	1.08
Italy	0.97	0.49	0.45	1.29	0.61	0.63
USA	2.70	1.30	1.34	2.73	1.10	1.57
Japan	2.34	0.52**	1.66	2.82	0.49**	2.15

Source: UK Government (1992) *Annual Review of Government Funded R&D*, Table 2.6.7; *1996 Forward Look: Science Engineering and Technology Statistics*, Table 7.4.
Notes:
* There are small amounts of funding from other sources, e.g. charities, which means that the total is more than straight aggregation of government and industry expenditures.
† Germany 1981–5 is West Germany; 1990–4 Germany as a whole. The two series are not therefore comparable.
** Japanese figures for government spending relate only to expenditures on national science and engineering and are OECD estimates.

the levels of the leading industrial nations (Table 19.1). In the earlier period, government expenditure on R&D as a proportion of GDP was less than in the USA but similar to that of France, and considerably higher than in Germany, Italy or Japan, reflecting the relatively high spending on defence R&D (Table 19.2). By the early 1990s, the British government contribution had fallen well below French and German levels, reflecting, in part, the falling levels of defence R&D spending. But as Tables 19.2 and 19.3 show, in fact, the relative fall in civilian R&D was more severe than the fall in defence R&D, and by 1994 the British government's support for civilian R&D was lower than in any other major industrial economy. The fall in the DTI's R&D budget has been particularly severe. As Table 19.3 shows, in 1986–7 the

Table 19.2 Government funding of R&D – civilian and defence as a percentage of GDP, 1986 and 1994

	1986			1994		
	Total	*Civilian*	*Defence*	*Total*	*Civilian*	*Defence*
UK	1.11	0.61	0.50	0.78	0.43	0.35
Germany*	1.11	0.98	0.13	0.96	0.86	0.08
France	1.42	0.94	0.48	1.27†	0.84†	0.43†
Italy	0.72	0.66	0.06	0.63	0.57	0.06
USA	1.26	0.39	0.87	1.03	0.46	0.57
Japan**	0.48	0.46	0.02	0.50	0.47	0.03

Source: OECD (1996) *Main Science and Technology Indicators.*
Notes:
* 1986 refers to West Germany only. Figures therefore not strictly comparable between two years.
† 1993
** OECD estimates. Civilian figures reflect only expenditures supporting natural sciences and engineering.

Table 19.3 UK government expenditure on science and technology, 1986–7 to 1994–5 in real terms (1995 prices, £m)

	1986–7	*1994–5*	*% change*
Total science vote	1,980.9	2,240.0	+13
R&D in science base	1,936.5	2,137.0*	+10
Civil departments	1,792.5	1,116.5	−38
of which DTI	⎰ 695.7	345.1	−65
D Energy	⎱ 297.3		
Defence	2,898.1	2,031.5	−30

Source: UK Government *1996 Forward Look: SET Statistics*, Table 2.2.
Note: * Excludes cost of OST administration and pensions.

Table 19.4 Shares of West European patenting in the US, 1975–94

	1975–80	1981–5	1986–90	1991–4
Germany*	38.60	41.56	41.35	40.40
France	14.46	14.70	15.20	16.59
United Kingdom	17.93	15.66	14.94	13.76
Switzerland	9.00	8.05	7.08	6.81
Italy	4.98	5.50	6.36	7.03
Netherlands	4.45	4.68	4.88	4.94
Sweden	5.70	5.03	4.61	3.79
Belgium	1.78	1.62	1.65	1.90
Finland	0.72	1.04	1.37	1.83
Denmark	1.04	0.99	1.00	1.14
Spain	0.57	0.42	0.65	0.83
Norway	0.64	0.56	0.63	0.65
Ireland	0.11	0.16	0.25	0.30
Portugal	0.02	0.03	0.03	0.02
Total	100.00	100.00	100.00	100.00

Source: Data supplied to SPRU by the US Patent and Trademark Office.
Note: * Includes the former East Germany in 1991–4. Before that date West Germany only.

combined R&D budgets of the DTI and the Department of Energy were £993m. (in £1995 terms) while the R&D budget of the merged departments in 1994–5 was £345m. – a fall of over 65 per cent during the nine-year period. Of this £345m. only £195m. was devoted to innovation and technology support, with £95m. going to aerospace and £54m. to energy R&D.

The United Kingdom's record in R&D is mirrored by its record in patenting. As Table 19.4 shows, while France, Germany and Italy have all held or improved their positions over the course of the last two decades, the UK position has steadily declined.

Industrial R&D

Table 19.1 also illustrates the disappointing performance of industrial R&D. In the early 1980s British industry performed better than their French and Italian counterparts, although even then well below the performance level of German, US or Japanese industry. By the 1990s, in spite of a somewhat improved performance, the French had all but caught up and only Italian industry was clearly doing less well. In particular, the differential between US and Japanese industrial performance had widened. (The German figures between the two periods are not really comparable because of the assimilation of the former East Germany into Germany in 1990–1.)

Table 19.5 presents the sector breakdown of industrial R&D expenditures for 1987 and 1994 respectively. The figures are converted to 1994 prices to enable comparison to be made in real terms. The outcome shows clearly that

Table 19.5 Sectoral breakdown of UK R&D expenditures (in real terms)
1987–94

	£m. (1994)		% growth 1987–94
	1987	*1994*	
Chemicals	909	828	−9
Pharmaceuticals	953	1,825	+91
Mech. Eng.	417	589	+41
Elec. mach.	1,917	1,542	−20
Transport	690	685	−1
Aerospace	1,245	7,059	−15
Other manuf.	833	927	+11
Total manuf.	6,965	7,454	+7
Total manuf. *without* pharm	6,011	5,630	−7
Services	2,090	2,075	−1

Source: 1996 Forward Look: Science, Technology and Engineering Statistics, Table 4.4.

during this period only two sectors, pharmaceuticals and mechanical engineering, have shown significant growth, with the former registering an overall growth of 91 per cent for the eight-year period. Indeed, without the pharmaceutical sector, far from registering a 7 per cent *increase* in overall R&D, the manufacturing sector would register a 7 per cent *decrease*. Nor has the service sector increased to take up the slack. As Table 19.5 shows, for the period 1987–94 the service sector actually showed a slight fall in R&D expenditures. Figures 19.1(a), (b) and (c) taken from the 1996 *R&D Scoreboard* (DTI, 1996) bring home the exceptional nature of the pharmaceutical industry. It is the only industry in Britain where the R&D/sales ratio (usually referred to as R&D intensity) has exceeded the world average. In other industries, even the chemical industry, which is usually regarded as a strong R&D performer, UK industry remains persistently below its international competitors.

Inward investment and foreign R&D in Britain

With the exception of the pharmaceutical/chemicals sector, British manufacturing has also come increasingly to depend on the activities of foreign multinational companies. As Chapter 8 shows, during the 1980s direct foreign investment into the United Kingdom grew substantially, with Britain retaining its status as the favourite location of US, and now Japanese, investment in the European Community. In a number of vital sectors foreign firms now predominate: Ford, GM, Peugeot and now Nissan, Toyota and BMW in car manufacturing; IBM, DEC and Fujitsu (ICL) in computers; Matsushita, Sony and Hitachi in consumer electronics; Intel, Texas Instruments and NEC in semi-conductors. Indeed, the encouragement of import substitution via foreign investment has arguably become the central

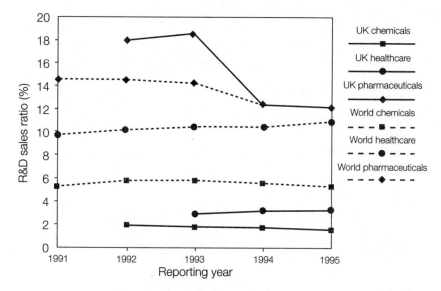

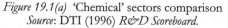

Figure 19.1(a) 'Chemical' sectors comparison
Source: DTI (1996) *R&D Scoreboard.*

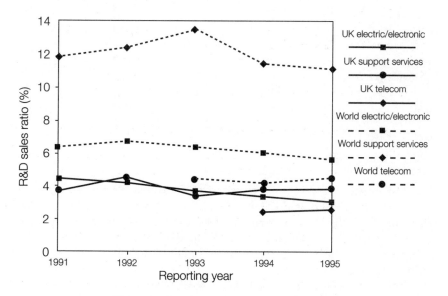

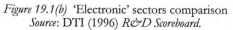

Figure 19.1(b) 'Electronic' sectors comparison
Source: DTI (1996) *R&D Scoreboard.*

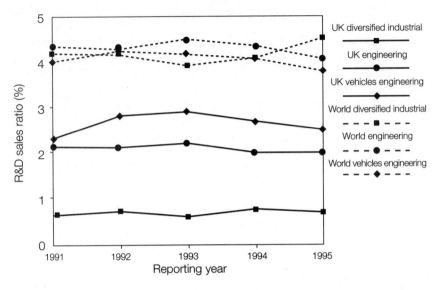

Figure 19.1(c) 'Engineering' sectors comparison
Source: DTI (1996) *R&D Scoreboard.*

Table 19.6 Sources of funding for UK R&D in real terms, 1985–94 (£m)

	1985	%	1994	%
Government	5,369	43.0	4,718	32.0
HE	76	<0.5	110	0.5
Business	5,849	47.0	7,407	51.0
Private non-profit	264	2.0	521	3.5
Abroad	993	8.0	1,857	13.0
Total	12,551	100	14,613	100

Source: 1996 Forward Look: Science, Engineering and Technology Statistics, Table 6.3.

industrial policy response to the trade deficit. But it also means that in important sectors there is no major British-owned company still operating. For example, with the exception of defence electronics, there is now no major British-owned company operating in the electronics sector. These foreign-owned companies are also increasingly important contributors to R&D, as Table 19.6 shows.

By 1994 foreign sources (mostly UK-based subsidiaries of foreign multi-nationals) were contributing as much as 13 per cent of total R&D funding in the United Kingdom.

Profitability and R&D

Why should there be such disappointing levels of industrial R&D and above all such low growth outside the pharmaceutical sector? In the early 1980s, the Conservatives' answer was that profits had been squeezed too tightly by wage inflation under Labour. Once levels of profitability were restored, they claimed, investment in R&D would pick up, alongside investment expenditure as a whole.

Table 19.7 casts doubt on this suggestion. It shows that while manufacturing income as a whole rose between 1979 and 1989 by only 4.3 per cent, profits rose ten times faster, by 44 per cent. However, the proportion of those profits reinvested in productive capacity was relatively small – over the whole period manufacturing investment (including leased assets) rose by 12.8 per cent, whereas dividend distributions increased by 73.2 per cent.

The recently published 1996 *R&D Scoreboard* shows that UK companies in the year 1994–5 devoted 1.7 per cent of sales revenue to R&D and 17.1 per cent of profits, whereas the average for the world's top 300 companies was 4.4 per cent of sales revenue devoted to R&D and 62.1 per cent of profits (DTI, 1996).

Ingham, writing about the development of modern capitalism, noted the difference between the Anglo-Saxon equity-based financing and bank-financed industrial sectors:

> One paradoxical . . . feature of the contrast between stock market and bank finance economies is that the former have lower levels of overall capital investment, generate less external finance and exhibit lower growth rates, but also declare company profits which are significantly higher than those in the latter.

> (Ingham, 1984, p. 72)

This was well demonstrated in the 1988–9 joint GEC-Siemens takeover of Plessey. International comparison showed GEC and Plessey to have been consistently more profitable than their competitors, but to have equally consistently slipped down the international league table of electronics companies measured by size and market share.[5] A further twist is added by the ease of corporate takeover in Britain (as in the United States). High profits and dividends have been sought in order to maintain stock ratings but the relatively open market in corporate assets has encouraged British firms to give growth by acquisition a higher priority than organic growth. As a result the 1980s saw the triumph in Britain of management by financial criteria. It was the age of the financial conglomerate (Hanson Trust, BAT, even GEC) managing disparate assets as distinct profit centres. While encouraging cost-cutting and thus productivity growth, such firms seldom showed concern for the longer-term processes of technological accumulation and organic (i.e. internally generated) output growth. It is notable that many have been leaders in the de-merger movement of the 1990s.

511

Table 19.7 Distribution of UK manufacturing productivity growth,
1979–89

	1989 *(relative to 1979 = 100)*
Manufacturing sector output	
Output	112.2
Employment	74.0
Productivity[a]	151.6
Manufacturing compared to all business	
Manufacturing/business prices[b]	95.0
Business/manufacturing productivity[c]	84.1
Manufacturing income	
Real income[d]	104.3
Real profits[e]	143.9
Real wage income[f]	94.5
Real wages per head[g]	127.8
Real profits per unit of capital[h]	127.7
Use of manufacturing profits	
Investment[i]	112.8
Real dividends[j]	173.2
Real share prices[k]	224.8

Sources: Table 4.2 from J. Michie (ed.) *The Economic Legacy 1979–92*, London: Academic Press. Sources cited are as follows: CSO, *UK National Accounts 1991*, Tables 1.7, 2.1, 2.4, 13.7, 17.1, plus 1979 data from CSO *OECD Labour Force Statistics*, UK Tables III, IV; *IMF Financial Statistics*; CSO *Business Monitor P5*, No. 21, Table 2 and No. 14.

Notes:
[a] Manufacturing real value-added per person employed.
[b] Manufacturing value-added deflator divided by business sector (GDP less dwellings, public administration, health and education) deflator.
[c] Business-sector total factor productivity divided by manufacturing total factor productivity (with labour and capital stock inputs weighted by 1979 income shares).
[d] Manufacturing output divided by ratio of consumer prices to manufacturing prices, i.e. purchasing power (in terms of consumer goods) of manufacturing incomes.
[e] Manufacturing gross profits (including excess of self-employment incomes over average wage) deflated by consumer prices.
[f] Manufacturing income from employment, adjusted for self-employment, deflated by consumer prices
[g] Real-wage income divided by manufacturing employment.
[h] Real profits divided by manufacturing (gross) capital stock.
[i] Gross fixed capital formation including assets leased by manufacturers.
[j] Estimated from dividends on accounts of manufacturing companies operating mainly in the UK, deflated by consumer prices.
[k] Industrial share prices deflated by consumer prices.

Conclusions on the record 1979–95

Looking back over the sixteen years 1979–95, it seems fair to conclude that technical progress in Britain related more to the use of new technology than to its development. Productivity has improved, but process change has taken precedence over product innovation. The priority given to cost reduction and higher profits led firms to shed labour, adopt modern working practices, and to seek growth by trading in assets (mergers and takeovers) rather than by creating new technological capabilities. Moreover, the growing share of services, particularly financial services, enhanced the economic power and influence of the City. The incentive structure this created, with its emphasis on realising short-term gains, has had a pervasive influence over risk-taking and vitiated against investments with long-term and uncertain pay-offs, precisely those involving the use and exploitation of new technologies.

THE POLICY RESPONSE

How far has policy sought to address these issues? As noted earlier, under the Thatcher government, there was a surprising lack of interest in science or technology and the three principles – the free market, enterprise and value for money – dominated policy developments. These three principles have been applied rigorously to the support of both basic and applied research.

Basic research

As far as basic research was concerned, the Thatcher regime from the start regarded the academic world as a prime example of the parasitic tendencies of the public sector. Budgets were tightly controlled, barely rising to meet inflation, let alone to recompense for the increasingly capital-intensive nature of all fields of academic research;[6] emphasis was put on 'relevance', with industrialists being imported onto research councils and university courts to advise on industrial needs, while the search for 'value for money' led to increasingly complex exercises in accountability in an area where, by its nature, much of the pay-off is long-term, uncertain and non-quantifiable.

This whole approach culminated in the 1993 White Paper on Science and Technology introduced by John Major's new Cabinet-level Minister for Science (an innovation introduced after the 1992 general election), William Waldegrave (UK Government, 1993). Under its auspices, the research councils, long the bastion of basic research, were re-organised, provided with mission statements which made explicit the subservience of science to industrial competitiveness, and given new boards of management with a strong industrial orientation.

The key innovation introduced in the White Paper was the Foresight Exercise. Derived from the Japanese practice of developing every five years a forward 'vision' of the major threats and opportunities likely to confront the economy within the next twenty years or so, it involved extensive discussions and consultations – consensus building – across a wide variety of industrial sectors, bringing together experts from industry, academia and government. The objectives were not only to provide a framework for government to focus on the future, but, perhaps more importantly, to use the process to encourage British industry to focus on longer-term horizons (Martin, 1993). This has proved more difficult than envisaged. Those involved in the Foresight discussions tended to be research and technical personnel from industry who needed little conversion; getting the message across to their bosses is the tricky part of the exercise and, to date, as the latest R&D Scoreboard figures illustrate, shows little sign of success (DTI, 1996).

The exercise, however, can be been seen as an attack on basic science. Even before the Foresight exercise there had been a growing proportion of research council money devoted to 'directed' rather than blue sky research. Such programmes at their best identify growing areas of research and, by ear-marking resources, flag them as areas of interest and develop academic capabilities ahead of demand. For the purists amongst academics, curiosity-led research is, by definition, the best, ultimately yielding the greatest benefits to society. They argue that in a world where, as with basic research, outcomes are unknown, no one can best-guess which outcomes will prove the most effective: it is better, therefore, to leave the scientists to judge each other through peer review, rather than to impose some outside criterion. The emergence of 'directed programmes' of research in the 1980s was bitterly attacked for diverting resources away from what was regarded as higher-quality research (Balmer and Sharp, 1993).

By the 1990s the battle was lost. The post-White Paper reorganisation of the research councils under a single Director General in the Office of Science and Technology (OST), whose first appointee, Sir John Cadogan, was formerly R&D director for British Petroleum, brought the requirement that all research proposals state the contribution the research will make to the United Kingdom's competitiveness. The increasing prevalence of directed programmes, deliberately focused on areas highlighted by the Foresight exercise, sealed the fate of 'responsive mode' grants (i.e. where research funding responded to proposals coming from academics). At the same time the reorganisation of the university sector, with increasing pressures for quality assessment both in the research and teaching areas and the doubling of student numbers, left many academics with teaching loads and paperwork spiralling out of control. The days of the 'trust relationship' were over.[7] Academic research is now well and truly accountable: value for money and enterprise rule the day. Symbolically, in 1995 OST was absorbed into the DTI. The days when science had an independent voice in the Cabinet were short-lived.

The promotion of innovation

Government support for applied R&D has never recovered from the 1988 Enterprise Initiative which axed support for near-market R&D. In the mid-1980s, as noted earlier, the Alvey Programme, combined with other special initiatives and the Support for Innovation (SFI) Scheme meant that, in spite of themselves, the British government were spending £300m. a year on innovation technology support, the equivalent of £450m. in 1995 terms (UK Government, 1986). Table 19.8 details the equivalent expenditures for 1994–5.

Leaving aside the standards/regulatory support item, the main thrust of DTI spending is on technology transfer and technology development. The latter includes some £45m. accounted for by the UK contribution towards the European EUREKA and Framework programmes, £15m. towards the LINK university/industry collaborative programme and £30m. for initiatives supporting R&D in small and medium-sized firms (SMEs).

The small business sector has been a major area of focus in recent years, partly because it has been growing very fast as large companies have slimmed down, 'delayered' and shifted to outsourcing their requirements. Indeed, whereas in the 1970s only 17–18 per cent of the population were employed in establishments of less than 100 people, by 1989 this had risen to 25 per cent (Hughes, 1992) and by 1994 to 30 per cent . Nevertheless, in spite of its fast growth, Conservative policies towards small business have carried more rhetoric than reality. Table 19.9 below compares UK and West German aid to SMEs in 1988/9. What is notable is, first, that, in spite of the stated target of restricting help to SMEs in the 1988 White Paper (UK Government, 1988), UK support for the sector as a percentage of GDP was less than half that of West Germany. Secondly, that whereas 20 per cent of the German

Table 19.8 DTI expenditure on innovation and technology support, 1994–5

	£m.
Innovation climate	3.0
Management best practice	13.8
Technology transfer and access	27.5
Technology development	90.8
of which	
EUREKA & EU programmes	45.00
SMEs	30.80
LINK	15.00
Standards/regulatory support	63.1
Total	198.2

Source: UK Government, *1996 Forward Look*, section 12.

Table 19.9 Support for small and medium-sized enterprises in the UK and West Germany, 1988–9

	UK		West Germany	
Type of support	*£m.*	*per cent*	*£m.*	*per cent*
Special regional assistance	108.5	21.2	167.1	9.1
R&D, technology	10.0	2.0	375.2	20.3
Loans, grants and guarantees	3.8	0.7	1,093.4	59.3
Start-up assistance	199.0	39.0	61.7	3.3
Training	110.0	21.5	81.5	4.4
Information and consultancy	77.9	15.3	64.7	3.5
Other	1.6	0.3	0.3	—
Total support	510.8	100.0	1,843.9	100.0
Total support as percentage of GDP	—	0.10	—	0.25
SME activity as percentage of GDP	—	32.2	—	46.0

Source: Bannock, G. and Albach, H. (eds) (1991) *Small Business in Europe: Britain, Germany and the European Commission*, London: Anglo-German Foundation.

expenditures went to R&D support, only 2 per cent of UK expenditures did so. Although this has increased (Table 19.8 records £30m. now devoted to SME R&D), £30m. is paltry compared to German levels of support. Yet, as is now widely recognised, the small firm sector is critical to future developments. Dynamic high-technology small firms are part of the modern success story around the world – from Italy to California and from Taiwan to Baden-Wurttemberg. Clusters of small firms, often working in vertical supply chains with other small and large firms – sometimes referred to as the Fifth Generation Innovation Process[8] – are increasingly seen as the way forward for industry. While sectors such as biotechnology have a good record in Britain, the general picture is depressing. For example, a study of the employment of scientists and engineers in British manufacturing industry found that from a sample of 700 firms in all size ranges, only 50 per cent undertook any R&D, and 50 per cent of these did not employ a graduate scientist on R&D work. Confronted by recession and aggressive competition from, amongst others, foreign firms, too many British companies cut out R&D altogether and resorted to the low-price, low-cost, low-productivity route to competitiveness, even though there was clear evidence that those that chose the alternative high-productivity (and high R&D) route outperformed their competitors over the longer run (Bosworth and Wilson, 1993).

It would be unfair to the development of policy during the 1990s to suggest that these problems – the low capability of British industry to use and develop modern production methods – were not recognised. The previous section highlighted the continuing poor R&D record of British industry (with the major exception of pharmaceuticals and chemicals). As the

Bosworth and Wilson study shows so clearly, spending on R&D is not only about developing new products, but about being able to use and understand new production methodologies.

This message is well understood by government. The latest statement on R&D policy – the *1996 Forward Look on Government Funded Science, Engineering and Technology* – states quite explicitly:

> Innovation – the successful exploitation of new ideas – is essential for sustained competitiveness and wealth creation. Innovation is not just about science, engineering and technology, but reflects an essential process of continuous improvement in all spheres of business. Successful innovation requires the provision and co-ordination of many interdependent factors, particularly important being the availability of skilled manpower, long term finance and high quality management.
>
> (UK Government, 1996a, section 12)

This message has been developed and spelt out in three successive papers on competitiveness issued by the DTI and forming part of their innovation initiative (UK Government, 1994, 1995, 1996b). Together with the Waldegrave White Paper on the science base and the Foresight Initiative which has emerged from this, there has developed a consistent attempt to raise the profile of innovation and, in particular, to raise industry's awareness of its own failings and of the need to improve performance.

The thrust of policy is, however, still largely exhortation. As the *Forward Look* makes plain:

> Industry has the prime responsibility for funding its own R&D and the DTI aims to focus its resources on those areas where it can add greatest value. To do this, the Department's innovation support concentrates on five broad areas: fostering a favourable climate for innovation; promoting best practice techniques; assisting technology transfer and access; supporting technology development in appropriate cases; and fulfilling statutory and regulatory requirements.
>
> (UK Government, 1996a, section 12)

These sentiments are fine – but, as the earlier comparison with German support expenditures made clear, what is actually being done is paltry. Whereas Germany has a thick web of well-established support mechanisms for small firms, developed very much at the local level, Britain is now trying to develop similar mechanisms, on the cheap, imposed top-down from the centre. The Government is establishing a series of regional 'prefectures' in the regions and linking these to the DTI's Business Link offices, aimed at providing advice at a local level to business and staffed by their Technology and Design Counsellors. Other initiatives include the *R&D Scoreboard*, league tables of how companies perform in R&D terms; the annual innovation lecture; publicity given to Britain's best firms aimed at promoting best practice; promotion of Teaching Companies, a scheme which links universities with R&D departments – all highly worthy schemes aimed at changing attitudes and practice with the minimum commitment of funds. What is absent is any attempt to encourage local or regional governments to play a part in fostering enterprise – a coalition that has proved powerful in other countries. Treasury control of local expenditures excludes this.[9] Only in Scotland and Wales, where regional development agencies have had some autonomy, is there evidence of the same, bottom-up, dynamism as is happening in other countries.

Privatisation

Since the privatisation of British Telecom in 1984, all of Britain's major public utilities, with the exception of the Post Office, have been sold off to the private sector. Privatisation has often been accompanied by deregulation, and the explicit injunction to the utilities to seek the lowest-cost source of supply, whether it be British or foreign, has already had a major impact in the transport, telecommunication and energy sectors. This is aptly illustrated by the situation in the coal industry where a knock-on effect of the privatisation of electricity has been to destroy the market for British-mined coal (in favour of, on the one hand, gas and, on the other, cheaper imported coal). The privatisation of what is left of that industry has led to the almost total demise of deep-mined coal extraction in favour of open-cast developments. This in turn has largely destroyed the British mining equipment industry which had benefited over the years from a close and mutually beneficial 'maker–user' relationship with the nationalised coal industry and which had helped to contribute to its impressive productivity record (Surrey, 1996).

While many of the nationalised industries may have overspent on R&D, privatisation has led to substantial falls in expenditures, with the emphasis shifting from longer-term research towards shorter-term development. Figures of the trend in R&D in the energy sector give some indication of the impact privatisation has had, with expenditures in real terms falling by approximately 50 per cent (see Table 19.10).

Privatisation has extended to the Government's own research laboratories (Public Sector Research Establishments – PSRE), the aim being as far as possible to create an 'open market' for government funded research. An 'efficiency scrutiny' published in July 1994 (UK Government, 1994) made recommendations for wholesale privatisation but was widely criticised for failing to understand the functions of these laboratories (as key advisory units for the Government). The House of Commons Select Committee on Science and Technology commented: 'We fear that the remit and conduct of the scrutiny were such that it has, at best, diverted much time and energy from the PSRE's main functions and may have been profoundly and

Table 19.10 R&D in the privatised fuel sector in the UK in real terms,
1986/7–1994/5 (1994 £m.)

	1986–7	1988–9	1994–5
Electricity*	280	306	113
Nuclear Fuels/Nirex	111	119	66
Coal	57	38	11
Gas	111	107	75†
Total	559	570	265

Sources: Annual reports of relevant utilities, pre- and post-privatisation. SPRU
Energy Progamme.
Notes:
* A substantial proportion (approximately 75 per cent) of R&D pre-privatisation
went on nuclear energy and much of the fall in expenditures in this sector is
accounted for by the very substantial reductions under this head.
† 1994.

unnecessarily damaging to their morale' (House of Commons, 1994). The
Government have nevertheless pressed ahead with privatisation. In some
cases, as with the National Physical Laboratory and the Royal Observatories,
the Government retain ownership but operating contracts are being put out
to competitive tender. In most cases, however, the aim is full privatisation.
For example, the National Engineering Laboratory and the Laboratory of
the Government Chemist were privatised in November 1995 and March
1996 respectively (UK Government, 1996a, p22). The aim, as stated
explicitly in the *1996 Forward Look*, is to develop competition 'wherever
possible'. This means that services, such as weights and measures, which over
the years have become internalised within the Government machine, have
now been externalised and are required, like so much else, to justify their
existence in terms of value for money.

European programmes

The period since 1984 has also seen the emergence of a strong programme
of technology policies from the European Union. Science and technology
played no part in the Treaty of Rome, partly because in 1957 the dominant
new technology was nuclear power and this was dealt with by the separate
Euratom Treaty. Although there was talk in the late 1960s of creating a
European Technological Community, nothing in fact emerged until the early
1980s when the double threat of Japanese and American multinationals
challenging Europe's somewhat sclerotic national champions led Davignon,
then Commissioner for Industry and Research, Technology and Development, to introduce the ESPRIT (European Strategic Programme for
Research in Information Technology) programme, in 1983. The latter was

aimed primarily at electronics and, like the Alvey programme in the United Kingdom, looked to collaborative R&D between corporate and academic players as a means both to mobilise resources and to alerting the sleeping giants of the corporate world to the realities of global competition (Guzzetti, 1995). European programmes looked to shared cost funding (50 per cent industry; 50 per cent Commission), required collaboration across country boundaries, dealt only with pre-competitive R&D, and awarded grants on the basis of peer-reviewed excellence. ESPRIT marked the beginning of a whole series of further programmes which in 1986 were grouped into a four year Framework Programme (FP). The first FP ran (retrospectively) from 1983–86; FP2 ran from 1987–90; FP3 from 1990–4; and FP4 runs from 1994–8 (Sharp, 1993).

FP4 expenditures were budgeted at ECU 12.7 bn (£9 bn) for the four year 1994–8 programme, or approximately £2.25 bn per annum across the fifteen countries of the European Union. Even at this level of expenditure, it amounted to less than 5 per cent of the amount all fifteen countries were spending on R&D. In other words, in most countries, what national and regional governments are doing to promote R&D and innovation is much more important than EU expenditures. Nevertheless, the European programmes have become highly influential. In a country such as France, for example, evaluation has revealed that 'nearly all heavy R&D spenders in industry, most French high-tech SMEs and most large public laboratories' are involved in one programme or another (Laredo, 1995). In Britain, while there is active company involvement, the main gainers are universities and research institutes (Georghiou et al., 1994) Most universities participate actively in Framework Programme initiatives, seeing them not only as a valuable supplement to the increasingly scarce research council funds, but also as opening doors to networking with other European institutions.

Britain's Conservative governments have, from the start, been innately suspicious of these European programmes. In 1985 the government backed the alternative, nationally (as distinct from community) based collaborative programme EUREKA in the hope that this would kill the nascent Framework Programme. In the event, both have flourished, EUREKA emerging as the 'nearer market' complement to the FP's commitment to backing pre-competitive R&D (and also the home of Europe's 'grands projets' in areas such as high-definition TV and semiconductors). Far from killing off the Community initiative, as Mrs Thatcher had hoped, it has added to the panoply of pan-European policies which now dominate the innovation agenda.

The overall result is that, in the field of civilian technology, Britain is now very much the follower rather than the leader in Europe, partly through its attachment to *laissez-faire* policies, partly through industrial weakness, and partly through the Conservatives' instinctive distrust of things European. For British high-technology firms, as for many others, Europe provides the only means of achieving the requisite scale of innovative activity. Thus

ESPRIT, RACE and EUREKA in electronics, and Airbus and the European Space Agency in aerospace, are the primary contexts within which British firms, and especially large firms, pursue their technological objectives. The British government has played a minimal – and at times obstructionist – role in these developments. The lead has come instead from industries and governments in France, Germany, Italy and (in electronics) the Netherlands, as well as from the European Commission itself. Britain has ceded its leadership in civil aerospace to France (although Rolls-Royce remains the pre-eminent aero-engine manufacturer); is a belated participant in the European space programme; and is not involved in the large semiconductor programmes (JESSI, etc.). In electronics generally no British firms have joined with Siemens, Thomson, Philips or Olivetti in trying to mobilise resources to respond to the technological challenge coming from the US and East Asia. Instead, many British firms have been prey to takeover – or, strictly speaking, acquisition – by foreign competitors, leaving very few British-owned companies operating in front-line technological activities in electronics. Only in pharmaceuticals and defence has Britain taken the lead in the emerging integrated European market.

CONCLUSIONS – *PLUS ÇA CHANGE*

This chapter began by focusing on the systemic nature of the innovation process and of the importance, within that process, of both people (and the skills and knowledge that they embody) and also the infrastructure of institutions that supports them. It suggested that Britain's rapid industrialisation in the early part of the nineteenth century shaped a system of innovation that was to prove inadequate and out of date by the end of that same century. As knowledge-based production systems grew in importance the British system was exposed for giving too little attention to education, training and skills (or for that matter to treating people as people) and too much on the trading of assets (including monetary assets) rather than the trading of goods.

Cushioned by the emergence of protectionism, colonial markets and pervasive restrictive practices during the inter-war years, it was not until this imperial system unravelled itself in the late 1960s that the seriousness of the British failings were exposed. Even so, the cures prescribed too frequently attacked symptom, not cause. Inflation, chronic imbalances of payments, rising levels of unemployment – all symptoms of the underlying poor productivity performance – were subjected to sweeping macroeconomic prescriptions which did nothing to improve performance, let alone to address the underlying systemic nature of failure.

Meanwhile, technology came to be viewed as a sort of *deus ex machina* – a potential saviour of the system. But there was no understanding of mechanisms. The implicitly linear view of the system assumed that money spent on science would inevitably create 'good things' in terms of technology, while faith in economies of scale created national champions to exploit them. Failure on both fronts led to widespread disillusion and a general view that interventionism does not work.

In this respect Thatcherism was no different. The evil, in 1979, was inflation: the cure was to embrace a new formulation of the old deflationary policies of the gold standard, known as monetarism. And as with earlier sweeping macroeconomic remedies, it failed to change the system, although, as noted, so deep was the purge on this occasion that productivity *did* improve, but mainly because the very inefficient tail of the distribution was lopped off, thus shifting average performance significantly upwards. Fundamentally, as far as technology is concerned, little else has changed: Britain still lags in terms of R&D performance, investment in new plant and equipment and above all in terms of investment in human capital.

Ironically, the failures of monetarism have helped promote a more realistic diagnosis. With both Keynesian demand management and monetarism discarded, the focus of policy has switched to the 'supply side'. For Thatcher, the answer was simple – non-intervention. The market, the entrepreneur and value for money were the prescription and it was applied relatively ruthlessly, dominating 'the Enterprise Initiative' at the end of the 1980s.

The Major government of the 1990s was more pragmatic. The wide-ranging Waldegrave consultation exercise and the detailed analyses undertaken by the DTI's Innovation Unit, followed up by the Science Policy White Paper *Realising Our Potential* and Heseltine's three *Competitiveness* White Papers have, at last, pointed in the right direction, identifying cause not symptom and putting innovation, and the innovation system, at centre stage. Above all, they have recognised the systemic nature of the innovation process and the need, not just to pull one or two levers, but to improve the system as a whole.

Sadly, while the diagnosis may now be correct, the policy prescription is still dominated by the three Thatcherite principles of the free market, enterprise and value for money. As a result there is emerging a giant mismatch between policy and prognosis.

Take the two issues highlighted at the beginning – skills and infrastructure. Chapter 15 has examined the record on education and training. This chapter has sought to analyse policy on the development of infrastructures. Both areas have seen major, and in the case of education and training, more or less continuous, change. But in both cases the changes risk becoming self-destructive. Where there should have been support for system development, the constant search for 'value for money' is squeezing public expenditures, demanding non-existent efficiency gains and seeking to substitute private money for what has traditionally been provided by the state. In the pursuit of market principles, targets, league tables and opt-outs are encouraging individualised competition at a time when discussion should focus on team-building and collaboration. Year-by-year public expenditure changes for all public sector institutions make short-termism endemic and strategic planning impossible. Constant assessment, retargeting and review are destabilising these institutions at a time when they need support. Stress and low morale have led to a haemorrhage of the older and more experienced staff. In other words, far from developing and realigning institutions to meet new priorities, policy has in fact led to a serious disintegration of traditional support mechanisms.

Looking beyond the public sector to the private, while the importance of R&D, small firms and technology transfer are now understood, the sums being put behind initiatives aimed at 'oiling the wheels of change' have been derisory. Likewise, at a time when decentralisation, both in spatial and organisational terms, has been seen to promote vitality and creativity, the Treasury-imposed controls prevent the decentralised, local initiatives which can be tailored to the needs of the firm and region as happens in Emilia Romagna and Baden-Wurttemberg. The demands of accountability leave no room for the old pluralism of the system. Business Links, TECs and LECs are all central government creations imposed on the regions, run by central government officials and accountable to central government appointed business leaders. At the same time, central government has been weak in relation to control of the business sector itself. Privatisation has recreated substantial private sector monopolies, but weak regulatory and competition policies mean that record profit levels have resulted in a dividend bonanza to private shareholders, rather than an upturn in investment or spending on R&D. Again, as Chapter 10 has described, no serious attempt has been made to tackle the endemic short-termism of the financial sector.

Once again, it would appear, the opportunity has been missed. The last twenty years have seen a revolution in our understanding of the role and importance of technology within society. Policy, unfortunately, still has to catch up with understanding.

NOTES

1   The term 'residual factor' was coined by Abramovitz (1956) in the first growth accounting exercise. For an overview of the extensive discussions of the issue since then see Mairesse and Sassenou (1989).
2   Because, as Weiner (*op. cit.*) explains, the mark of the aristocracy was to send their sons away to public school and Oxbridge to study the classics, this being seen as the best training in logic. By the end of the nineteenth century, mathematics was seen as an acceptable substitute, and the 'pure sciences' were the next best thing to mathematics. Engineering and the applied sciences came considerably lower in the social pecking order.
3   The phrase was used by Joel Barnett, who had been Chief Secretary to the Treasury during the period of the Social Contract, in the television series 'The writing on the wall', produced by Channel 4 in the early 1980s.
4   The terms 'pre-competitive' and 'near market' define R&D that, on the one hand, is generic across a range of possible uses/products, and, on the other, is aimed specifically at helping launch a particular product. The Conservatives maintained that the latter was the responsibility of the firm and, if a product was viable,

should pose no finance problem. In fact with new products and processes there is often what is known as the 'pre-production development gap' – small and medium-sized firms in particular find it difficult to raise finance for an untried product. Its existence had led, in 1978, to the introduction of a scheme called the Pre-Production Development Scheme (PPDS), with grants available to cover up to 30 per cent of the launch costs of innovative new products and processes. This was extended in 1981 and converted into the Support for Innovation (SFI) scheme with the rate of subsidy reduced to 25 per cent, but it still proved to be one of the more popular schemes. The 1988 White Paper axed it completely. In its place was put the LINK schemes, which offered up to 50 per cent grants for collaborative R&D schemes involving several firms and an academic partner. By definition, when several firms club together, the R&D supported must be of a general nature (i.e. pre-competitive) and useful to any one of them.

5   The takeover battle was explored in detail in 'The GEC-Siemens bid for Plessey: the wider European issues', by Kevin Morgan, Bernard Harbor, Mike Hobday, Nick von Tunzelmann and William Walker. PICT Working Paper No. 2, SPRU, University of Sussex.

6   Table 19.4 shows the money devoted to R&D in the universities and research councils increasing between 1986/7 and 1994/5 by 10 per cent in real terms. From 1993/4 the statistics include imputed VAT payments whereas the 1986/7 figures do not. Allowing for this, the real increase over these years is in fact only 8 per cent. In addition, the deflator used is the GDP deflator which takes account of general price rises rather than those associated with specific areas. The problem for the universities is that in order to remain in the forefront of research, equipment needs frequent renewal and updating, which is expensive. OECD figures show Britain now bottom of the league in terms of funds devoted to academic research per capita of the workforce – measured in terms of 1994 values, the funds devoted in the United Kingdom amounted to £57 pa, compared with £95 in France, £100 in Germany £115 in Holland and £110 in the USA, and £70 pa for Italy. OECD (1995) Science and Technology Indicators.

7   The 'trust relationship' refers to a situation when, by virtue of their record, professional qualifications, etc. those who are employed are 'trusted' to perform well. For many years public sector professions in the United Kingdom, whether in teaching, universities, the health services, etc. were in this position. The introduction of performance indicators, league tables, etc. has signalled the end of this era: professionals, like the rest of the world, are accountable and must show that they are performing as expected. For the basic scientist, whose experimental work may result in a dead-end, it poses some problems, especially if they are young and unknown (success indicators for academics being based on publications and citations).

8   The term Fifth Generation Innovation Process was coined by Roy Rothwell (Rothwell, 1994) to describe a process dominated by systems integration and networking in which external linkages with suppliers and customers form an integral part of the development process. See Rothwell (1994).

9   The UK Treasury's control of public expenditure extends to local authority spending which, like government departments, is effectively cash limited. Local authorities are set spending targets, on which central government grants (75 per cent of expenditures) are based. Spending over target gets no grant – effectively adding a gearing factor of four in relation to local tax levels for any over target spending – and if local authorities raise taxes above levels the Government judges prudent, they are capped. This leaves little, if any discretion on expenditures for local decision.

REFERENCES

Abramovitz, M. (1956) 'Resource and output trends in the United States since 1870', *American Economic Review*, vol. 46, pp. 5–23.

Aghiou, P. and Howitt, P. (1990) 'A model of growth through creative destruction', NBER Working Paper pp. 3223.

Balmer, B. and Sharp, M. (1993) 'The battle for biotechnology', *Research Policy*, 22, 1993, pp. 463–78.

Blackaby, F. (ed.) (1978) *British Economic Policy 1960–74*, Cambridge: Cambridge University Press.

Bosworth, D. and Wilson, R. (1993) *The Role of Scientists and Engineers in Technology Change*, ESRC Innovation Update Series.

Department of Trade and Industry (DTI) (1996) *The UK R&D Scoreboard 1996*, Edinburgh: Company Reporting Ltd.

Freeman, C. (1984) *Long waves in the World Economy*, London: Pinter.

Georghiou, L. *et al.* (1994) *The Impact of European Community Policies for RTD upon Science and Technology Committees in the UK*, DG XII, Commission of Europe.

Grossman, G. and Helpman, E. (1990) 'Trade, innovation and growth', *American Economic Review*, Papers and Proceedings, May.

Guy, K., Georghiou, L., Quintas, P. *et al.* (1991) *Evaluation of the Alvey Programme for Advanced Information Technology*, London; HMSO.

Guzzetti, L. (1995) *A Brief History of European Union Research Policy*, Brussels: European Commission.

Henderson, P. D. (1977) 'Two British errors: Their probable size and some possible lessons', *Oxford Economic Papers*, July, pp. 159–205.

Hobsbawm, E. J. (1968) *Industry and Empire: an Economic History of Britain since 1750*, London: Weidenfeld & Nicolson.

House of Commons, Science and Technology Select Committee (1994–5) 'Efficiency unit scrutiny of PSRE', First Report, vol. 1, Report and Minutes of Proceedings.

Hughes, A. (1992) 'Big business, small business and the enterprise culture', Chapter 13 in J. Michie (ed.) *The Economic Legacy 1979–1992*, London: Academic Press.

Ingham, G. (1984) *Capitalism Divided? The City and Industry in British Social Development*, London: Macmillan.

Jessop. B. (1989) *Thatcherism: The British Road to Post-Fordism?* Paper in Politics and Government, University of Essex.

Kline, S. J. and Rosenberg, N. 'An overview of innovation', in R. Landau and N. Rosenberg (eds) *The Positive Sum Game: Harnessing technology for economic growth*, Washington, D.C.: The National Academy Press.

Landes, D. (1969) *The Unbound Prometheus*, Cambridge, Cambridge University Press.

Laredo, P. (1996) '*The Effects of EU Research Programmes: Towards a reappraisal of the formulation and implementation of EU Research Policy*', paper presented to Triple Helix Conference, Amsterdam, mimeo.

Ledoux, M.-J. *et al.* (1993) 'Economic evaluation of the effects of the BRITE-EURAM programmes on the European Industry', final report for DG XII-4 Evaluation Unit, January.

Lucas, R. (1988) 'On the mechanics of economic development', *Journal of Monetary Economics*, vol. 22, pp. 3–42.

Mairesse, J. and Sassenou, M. (1989) 'R&D and productivity growth: An overview of the literature', paper prepared for OECD Conference on the Contribution of Science and Technology to Economic Growth, OECD, June.

Mench, G. (1975) *Stalemate in Technology: Innovations overcome the depression*, New York: Ballinger.

Mottershead, P. (1978) 'Industrial policy', in F. Blackaby (ed.) *British Economic Policy 1960–74*, Cambridge: Cambridge University Press.

Mowery, D. (1992) 'Finance and corporate evolution in five industrial economies', *Industrial and Corporate Change*, vol. 1, pp. 1–36.

OECD (1988) *New Technologies in the 1990s: A socio-economic strategy* (The Sundquist Report), Paris.

Perez, C. and Freeman, C. (1988) 'Structural crises of adjustment, business cycles and investment behaviour', in Dosi *et al.* (eds) *Technical Change and Economy Theory*, London: Pinter Publishers.

Romer, P. (1986) 'Increasing returns and long run growth', *Journal of Political Economy*, vol. 94, October, pp. 1002–37.

—— (1990) 'Endogenous technological change', *Journal of Political Economy*, vol. 98, pp. S72–S102.

Rothwell, R. (1994) 'Industrial innovation – success, strategy, trends', chapter 4 in M. Dodgson and R. Rothwell (eds) *The Handbook of Industrial Innovation*, Basingstoke: Edward Elgar.

Sharp, M. (1993) 'The Community and new technologies', chapter 11 in Juliet Lodge (ed.) *The European Community and the Challenge of the Future*, London: Pinter Publishers, pp. 200–23.

Sharp, M. and Sheperd, G. (1987) 'Managing Change in British Industry', vol. 5 of *Studies in Employment Adjustment and Industrialisation*, Geneva, ILO.

Stout, D. (1978) 'Deindustrialisation and industrial policy', in F. Blackaby, *op. cit.*

Surrey, J. (ed.) (1996) *The British Electricity Experiment. Privatization: the record, the issues, the lessons*, London: Earthscan Publications Ltd.

Thompson, E. P. (1968) *The making of the British working class*, Hammondsworth: Penguin.

UK Government (1986) *The Government's Expenditure plans: 1986–7 to 1988–9*, Pts 3 and 4, vol. II, Cmnd 9702. London: HMSO.

—— (1988)*DTI – The Department for Enterprise*, Cmnd 278, London: HMSO.

—— (1993)*Realising Our Potential: A strategy for science, engineering and technology*, Cmnd 2250, London: HMSO.

—— (1994)*Competitiveness: Helping business to win*, Cmnd 2563, London: HMSO.

—— (1995)*Competitiveness: Forging ahead*, Cmnd 2867, London: HMSO.

—— (1996a)*1996 Forward Look: Annual review of government funded R&D* (vol. I): *Science, engineering and technology statistics* (Vol. II), London: HMSO.

—— (1996b) *Competitiveness: Creating the enterprise centre of Europe*, Cmnd 3300, London: HMSO.

Wiener, M. J. (1981) *English culture and the decline of the industrial spirit, 1850–1980*, Cambridge: Cambridge University Press.

20

IS UK DEINDUSTRIALISATION INEVITABLE?

George Hadjimatheou and Nicholas Sarantis

INTRODUCTION

Since about 1960 the share of manufacturing employment in total employment in the United Kingdom has been declining. In the 1960s the decline was very gentle. It accelerated sharply in the 1970s and since then has continued at a steady and significant pace. The decline in the manufacturing employment rate, although more pronounced than in many other countries, is not confined to the United Kingdom. Other industrially advanced countries exhibit a similar trend.[1] The observed pattern raises a number of questions: Why is it happening? What determines its pace in general and its different manifestation in various countries in particular? Is it a phenomenon of major concern that governments should address by pursuing policies to arrest its continuation?

It is not surprising that studies of these related issues have failed to produce any form of consensus. Brown and Julius (1993), for example, draw a historical analogy with an earlier downward trend in the share of agricultural employment and suggest that:

1 Manufacturing employment may continue to fall across OECD countries, reaching levels of 10 per cent or less within the next thirty years. For them there is little doubt that the trend will continue.
2 Employment in manufacturing should be expected to fall faster in those countries where manufacturing employment is currently highest.
3 It would be a critical mistake for policy-makers to try to arrest the decline by pursuing traditional industrial policies that involve direct support to industry. In other words, the trend should not be resisted.
4 The proposition that manufacturing has special growth-inducing characteristics not to be found in services is, for a number of reasons, no longer true as manufacturing loses its past pre-eminence as the fountain of all foreign exchange and as the major source of critical breakthroughs in productivity and wealth creation.

A somewhat similar view is expressed by Crafts (1993, 1996) who does not

527

consider deindustrialisation as an unmitigated disaster for future growth prospects. He suggests that in the hands of populist politicians it could be allowed to become a dangerous obsession and a potential distraction from addressing directly specific issues of the human capital formation and technological capabilities of British industry. In his 1996 contribution he concludes a review of theoretical issues and empirical evidence as follows:

> Deindustrialisation of the labour force was an inherent part of a process of raising the growth rate by improving the appropriability of returns to innovation and liberalising the economy. Better design of macroeconomic and labour market policies could and should have made this process less painful. Regarding the reversal of deindustrialisation as *per se* good for growth and long-term economic welfare and setting policy accordingly would be a serious error.

(p. 181)

At the other end of the spectrum, Bazen and Thirlwall (1989), reflecting the views of a significant number of economists in the United Kingdom, suggest that:

1 The deindustrialisation experienced by the United Kingdom has been predominantly of the negative kind, where the fall in manufacturing employment is associated in a causal way with stagnation and unemployment.
2 The performance of the manufacturing sector is of vital importance for economic growth.[2] There is a real danger that contraction of the manufacturing industry may lead to stagnation of the whole economy through a lack of technological dynamism and severe balance of payments constraints on growth.[3]
3 A coherent strategy of export-led growth should be developed. The industrial strategy, based on tax incentives, investment grants and subsidies, should aim to induce an allocation of resources in favour of technologically progressive industries.

Kitson and Michie (1996) echo these views and suggest that the poor industrial performance of the United Kingdom can be attributed to under-investment, harmful macroeconomic and industrial policies, an unduly competitive and destructive *laissez-faire* Anglo-Saxon productive system, and a financial system that does not address the interests and needs of industrial capital. They believe that a strong manufacturing sector is a necessary condition for a flourishing United Kingdom and that governments have an important and active role to play in the recovery of manufacturing employment and production.

This chapter does not pursue the debate on the effects of deindustrialisation on the economy. It rather concentrates on providing a formal and empirical account of the main arguments for the phenomenon of deindustrialisation. This is done by using annual observations for the period 1921–93 to examine the determinants of the manufacturing employment rate in the United Kingdom. There is then a brief description of the timepaths of the major variables used in the formal analysis, followed by a review of the main theoretical arguments for deindustrialisation, and specification of the employment equation. The econometric estimates are then reported and discussed, followed by some simulation results for manufacturing employment over the next fifteen years. The final section draws up the main conclusions of the study.

STYLISED FACTS

The measurement of the variables, over the period 1921–93, used in the empirical work reported in the following section, is explained in the data appendix to this chapter. The construction of long-term time series covering the Second World War period is always vulnerable to criticism about the reliability of data. We feel, however, that the adjustment of pre-war data to make them consistent with those for the post-war period reported in the latest publications, which are more reliable, combined with the use of five overlap years for computing the adjustment factors, makes the time series fairly consistent and reliable over the long sample period. One area where we are less happy concerns manufacturing output for the war years 1939–1945. The lack of data for that period has forced us to interpolate the observations on the basis of proxies. Therefore the data for manufacturing output for the war years should be treated with caution.

The behaviour of individual variables is displayed in Figures 20.1–20.5. The manufacturing employment rate, *RME*, the proxy for deindustrialisation in this study, shows a decline in the 1930s, a period coinciding with the great depression, followed by an unusually strong expansion in the period approaching and during the Second World War. After the war there was a downwards adjustment, though it remained fairly stable up to the late 1960s. Since then, however, there has been a dramatic and accelerating fall in the manufacturing employment rate, most notably during the 1980s and early 1990s when the average rate stood at 23.5 per cent, compared with 36.5 per cent in the 1950s and 34 per cent in the 1920s. The average rate for the post-war period was 31.6 per cent, compared with 33.5 per cent during the pre-war period, reflecting the eventual and persistent decline in the share of manufacturing employment in the last thirty-five or so years.

Considering output, with the exception of the war years and the immediate post-war period adjustment, the share of manufacturing output in total output, *RMO*, exhibited a steady upward trend from the 1920s up to 1970. Since the early 1970s there has been a dramatic reversal of this trend, with the manufacturing output rate falling to an average of 23.8 per cent during the 1981–93 period, compared with a peak of 31.2 per cent during the 1960s.

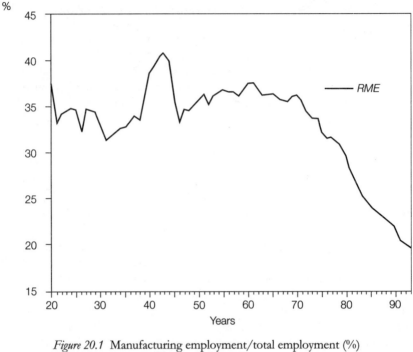

Figure 20.1 Manufacturing employment/total employment (%)
Source: see Appendix.

This was equivalent to its level in the 1920s, when the average rate stood at 23.5 per cent. The dramatic fall of the 1970s coincides with the collapse of employment in manufacturing.

Unlike employment and output, net manufacturing exports as a proportion of nominal GDP, *RMX*, declined steadily throughout the 1920s and 1930s, turning into negative figures during the war years. There was a considerable expansion from the end of the Second World War up to the middle of the 1950s. Afterwards, however, net manufacturing exports took a big dive, declining at an accelerating rate and turning into a deficit from 1983 onwards. The average rate stood at −2.1 per cent in the 1980s and early 1990s, compared with 8.7 per cent during the 1950s. Looking at the post-war period, the average rate was 3.3 per cent, compared with 5.5 per cent during the pre-war period. The overall picture indicates a long-term deterioration in the trade balance of manufactures. The decline in the trade balance in manufacturing comes much earlier than the decline in manufacturing shares in output and employment.

Manufacturing is a sector expected to exhibit substantial productivity gains over time. Relative manufacturing productivity, *RMQ*, has been rising steadily throughout the sample period, except for the Second World War years and the

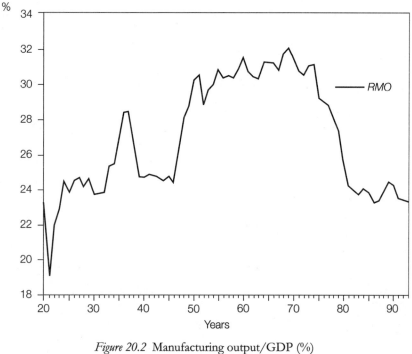

Figure 20.2 Manufacturing output/GDP (%)
Source: see Appendix.

1977–81 period. The average ratio, i.e. manufacturing productivity as a percentage of productivity in the whole economy, stood at 105 per cent during the 1981–93 period, compared with 82.8 per cent in the 1950s and 69.7 per cent during the pre-war period. This evidence indicates a widening gap between productivity in manufacturing and that in the rest of the economy.

The graph for unemployment in the whole economy shows a familiar picture: very high unemployment rates during the 1920s and 1930s, followed by low and stable rates during the 1950s and 1960s. Unemployment started rising again very sharply after the 1973–4 oil-price shock, and most noticeably, during the 1980s when the average rate stood at 9.2 per cent compared with 1.8 per cent during the 1951–70 period.

THEORETICAL CONSIDERATIONS

The literature on the subject suggests a number of major explanations for the observed decline in the share of manufacturing employment.

Maturity thesis   After a certain stage of economic development there is a continuous shift of demand away from industrial products towards services.

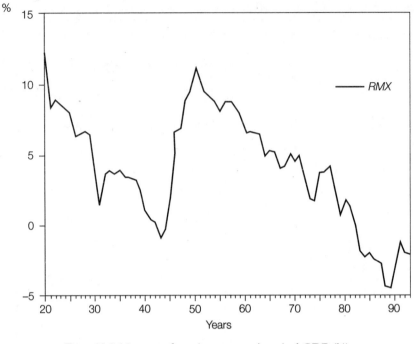

Figure 20.3 Net manufacturing exports/nominal GDP (%)
Source: see Appendix.

Assuming that productivity in the service sector is not higher than productivity in manufacturing, the change in demand patterns would be manifested in a shift of employment away from manufacturing towards the production of services. The obvious test of the validity of this hypothesis is whether, when observed at constant prices, expenditure on manufacturing output declines relative to spending on services. Evidence would tend to suggest that the decline in the share of manufacturing employment is not matched by a shift of demand in favour of services. This is especially the view put forward by Baumol *et al.* (1989) who suggest that the ratio of service output to GDP, when measured at constant prices, exhibits no upward trend. But Rowthorn (1992) observes that even after allowing for the problems of measuring the volume of service output, there is now increasing evidence of a shift in demand towards services. This is certainly the case in the United Kingdom, where the growth of service output during the 1970s and 1980s was significantly greater than the growth of manufacturing output.[4] What seems to be true is that the shift in employment in favour of the service sector cannot be fully explained in terms of a shift in demand toward services (Kitson and Michie, 1996).

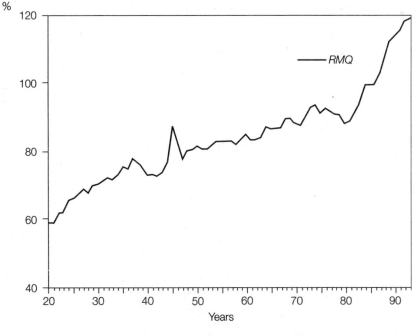

Figure 20.4 Manufacturing productivity/total productivity (%)
Source: see Appendix.

International competitiveness Under conditions of free trade the decline in the share of manufacturing employment in a particular country can be explained in terms of movements in productivity performance across countries. A continuous erosion of a productivity advantage could result in deindustrialisation in favour of competitor countries.[5] Given, however, that most industrially developed countries seem to be afflicted by deindustrialisation, this line of argument would suggest that the competitiveness of their manufacturing is losing ground *vis-à-vis* the developing world which is taking advantage of increasing possibilities, mainly through technology transfer, to catch up. The implications of this hypothesis would be manifested in the form of a shift of manufacturing production away from industrially advanced countries towards an increasingly strengthened developing world.[6] The increasing ability of the developing world to enter manufacturing production in a more extensive and at the same time a more competitive way is largely assisted by the greater ease of transfer of modern technology (see Brown and Julius, 1993). Differences in the rate of deindustrialisation associated with different countries could be accounted for by changes in the relative productivity and competitiveness across countries over time. In the case of the United Kingdom the higher degree of deindustrialisation has been

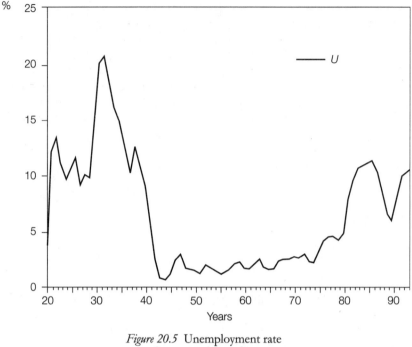

Figure 20.5 Unemployment rate
Source: see Appendix.

attributed to a number of factors: the low profitability of the British manufacturing sector associated with a fragmented structure of industrial relations, poor and/or inappropriate educational, training and management
skills, high tax rates, and an unstable macroeconomy (see Eltis, 1996); a
balance of payments constraint that results in relatively low rates of growth
of the economy and especially of the manufacturing sector, which in turn
depresses the potential for productivity growth – an argument associated
with the view that manufacturing production generates positive externalities
that spill over to the rest of the economy (see Kaldor, 1966, and Thirlwall,
1979); and a financial system that tends to serve the interests of the financial
sector at the expense of those of the industrial sector (Hutton, 1996).

The cost disease hypothesis   Probably the most influential hypothesis is
Baumol's (1967) cost disease model according to which technologically stag-
nant services tend to rise in price at a faster rate than industrial goods
produced in technologically progressive sectors. In other words, because of a
higher growth of productivity in the manufacturing sector the cost of production in manufacturing falls relative to the cost of production in the
service sector. The hypothesis implies that even if demand is such that the

ratio of manufacturing real output to real output in the service sector remains fairly constant, the share of employment in the service sector would tend to increase. Also, when measured at current prices the ratio of service output to manufacturing output would tend to increase. This relative price effect has also been used to explain the long-run rise in the ratio of public expenditure to total final expenditure in many industrially developed countries. A major issue with this hypothesis is that the measurement of productivity in the service sector is a very difficult task, especially in view of the fact that a great deal of output in the service sector is not marketed (e.g. see Smith, 1989). The same approach to the problem in question would suggest a rather gradual, persistent and uniform shift over time of employment towards the service sector. Since the data do not conform to this pattern, this line of argument is unlikely to provide a full explanation of deindustrialisation.

In considering the tendency of the share of manufacturing employment in the United Kingdom to fall, it is possible that all three factors mentioned above were at work in tandem. In addition to long-term trends, addressed by the approaches outlined above, the share of manufacturing employment is subject to cyclical influences (Rowthorn and Wells, 1987). Stylised facts suggest that the manufacturing employment share exhibits a pro-cyclical pattern.

Rowthorn and Wells (1987) use data from twelve industrially advanced countries over the period 1953–78 to estimate the following simple relationship:

$$M_t = a + b\ln Y_t + c(\ln Y)^2_t + dU_t + eB_t + u_t \tag{20.1}$$

where M = manufacturing employment as a percentage of total civilian employment in the economy, Y = GDP per capita at constant prices, U = percentage unemployment, B = net manufactured exports as a percentage of GDP.

The two income terms are supposed to capture the overall effect of 'fundamental forces, in the realm of demand and productivity, which cause the share of industry in total employment to rise during the early stages of economic development and then to fall later on, once the stage of economic maturity has been reached' (*ibid.*, p. 30). This explanation of the decline in industrial employment is called the 'maturity' thesis. The unemployment variable is used as a proxy for the stage of the business cycle, whilst B allows for the proposition that the higher the volume of net manufactured exports as a percentage of GDP the more likely it is that the country will be more industrialised and will employ more of its workforce in the manufacturing sector. This is fully discussed by Rowthorn and Wells in the section on the 'specialisation thesis' (*ibid.*, pp. 218–20). Rowthorn and Wells obtained OLS estimates using both cross-section data and pooled data for all countries over the 1953–78 period. They found that all three regressors are significant in explaining the observed variation in M, with Y and U being predominant in accounting for intertemporal variations in M, and B accounting for much of the international variation in M.

Baumol's (1967) cost disease model implies that the higher the gap between productivity levels in the manufacturing and service sector the higher will be the shift in employment from manufacturing to services.[7] To allow for this, the list of explanatory variables in our empirical work is extended to include the influence of relative manufacturing productivity, RMQ (i.e. the ratio of manufacturing productivity to productivity for the whole economy).

The major theoretical implication of the analysis in this section is that in the long-run a downward trend of the share of manufacturing employment will be largely dictated by an upward trend in real per capita incomes. The time path would exhibit pro-cyclical fluctuations and the pace of the decline would be influenced by the competitiveness of British industry and aggregate unemployment. Consequently, the model used for estimation takes the form[8]

$$(RME)_t = e[Y_t, (Y)^2_t, U_t, (RMX)_t, (RMQ)_t]$$ (20.2)
$$+ \quad - \quad - \quad + \quad -$$

where RME is the share of manufacturing employment in total employment, Y is real income per capita, U is the unemployment rate, RMX is the ratio of trade balance in manufactures to nominal gross domestic product, and RMQ is relative manufacturing productivity. The signs below the variables indicate the anticipated effect.

The first two terms in equation (20.2) represent the maturity thesis, with the manufacturing employment rate first rising as economic development improves and, beyond a certain point of economic maturity, starts falling. Unemployment is used to capture the influence of cyclical factors. The trade variable (RMX) indicates the structure and specialisation of the country's foreign trade, while the productivity variable (RMQ) indicates the extent of efficiency in the manufacturing industry relative to the rest of the economy.

EMPIRICAL RESULTS

The employment equation (20.2) is basically an equilibrium relationship. But in the short run the manufacturing employment rate is likely to deviate from its long-run equilibrium level due to the presence of adjustment costs. Consequently, the empirical implementation of the model consists of two stages. In stage one, we examine whether there is a long-run equilibrium relationship consistent with the theoretical model (20.2). In the second stage we investigate the short-run dynamic behaviour of the manufacturing employment rate. Our tests produced the following estimates for the long-run manufacturing employment rate.[9]

$$\ln(RME) = -4.415 + 3.431\ln Y - 0.188(\ln Y)^2 - 0.029\ln U +$$
$$0.021RMX - 1.713\ln(RMQ) \quad (20.3)$$

We notice that the signs of all parameters correspond to those anticipated for the employment model (20.2). Deletion tests confirmed the significant effect of all factors on the long-run manufacturing employment rate, with per capita income and relative productivity exerting the strongest influence.

To investigate the short-run dynamic behaviour of the manufacturing employment rate, we have used an error correction formulation which utilises the long-run parameter estimates. The usual practice by economists is to set up an error correction model where the residuals from the long-run equilibrium equation (20.3), say Z, enter in a linear form Z_{t-1}. The coefficient on Z_{t-1} measures the speed of adjustment towards equilibrium. Given the long historical period covered by our sample and the nature of the topic, our *a priori* belief is that there may well be non-linearities in the adjustment of the manufacturing employment rate towards its equilibrium. To investigate this possibility we followed Escribano (1987) in replacing Z_{t-1} in the error correction model by a quadratic function $f(Z_{t-1})$. The estimates of the short-run equation are reported in Table 20.1.

The explanatory performance of the regression is quite good. What is particularly remarkable is the ability of the model to capture almost all turning points (see Figure 20.6), despite the fact that the sample period was

Table 20.1 Estimates of the short-run employment model

$$\Delta\ln(RME)_t = -0.005 + 7.146\Delta\ln Y_t - 0.431\Delta(\ln Y)^2_t - 0.052\Delta\ln U_t$$
$$ (1.8) \quad (6.3) \qquad (5.9) \qquad\qquad (6.9)$$

$$+ 0.027\Delta\ln U_{t-1} + 0.004\Delta(RMX)_{t-3} - 0.384\Delta\ln(RMQ)_t + 0.208\Delta\ln(RMQ)_{t-2}$$
$$ (4.0) \qquad\quad (2.3) \qquad\qquad (5.4) \qquad\qquad (2.7)$$

$$-0.850Z^2_{t-1}$$
$$(2.9)$$

$\overline{R}^2 = 0.784$, SER $= 0.015$, DW $= 1.766$, LM(1) $= 0.810$, RESET(1) $= 0.235$, BJ(2) $= 0.397$, HET(1) $= 0.004$, ARCH(1) $= 0.216$, STAB(9, 51) $= 1.470$.

Note: Estimation period 1925–93; $\overline{R}^2$ is the coefficient of determination adjusted for degrees of freedom; SER is the standard error of the regression; DW is the Durbin–Watson statistic; LM(1) is the Lagrange Multiplier test for first order serial correlation [$\chi^2(1)$]; RESET is Ramsey's reset test for functional form [$\chi^2(1)$]; BJ is the Bera–Jargue test for normality [$\chi^2(2)$]; HET is the Lagrange Multiplier test for heteroscedasticity [$\chi^2(1)$]; ARCH is the autoregressive conditional heteroscedasticity test [$\chi^2(1)$]; STAB is the CHOW structural stability test [$F(v_1, v_2)$], sample split 1958; numbers within parentheses below regression coefficients are t-values.

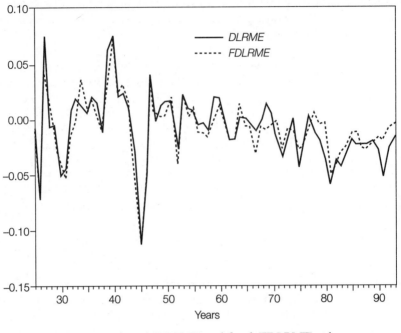

Figure 20.6 Actual (DLRME) and fitted (FDLRME) values
Source: Table 20.1

characterised by some important events. The regression passes very comfortably a wide range of diagnostic statistics even at the 1 per cent significance level. The residuals are normally distributed, serially independent and homoscedastic. The quadratic error correction term is correctly signed and highly significant (even at 1 per cent significance level), which provides strong support for the nonlinear specification of the adjustment mechanism.

All variables exert a strong influence on the manufacturing employment rate and have the *a priori* expected signs. Acceleration in the growth of per capita income or an increase in unemployment and manufacturing productivity cause a decline in manufacturing employment, whereas an increase in real income per capita or expansion in net manufacturing exports brings about an improvement in the manufacturing employment rate. These empirical findings suggest that all competing hypotheses discussed above play a role in the deindustrialisation of the UK economy, with the maturity thesis and cyclical factors exerting the strongest influence, followed by the relative productivity thesis and the structure of foreign trade. Our results for the maturity thesis and unemployment confirm those obtained by Rowthorn and Wells (*op. cit.*) for the post-war period. The importance of cyclical factors supports Kitson and Michie (*op. cit.*) who attribute part of Britain's poor industrial perform-

538

ance (since 1960) to inadequate macroeconomic and industrial measures. Our evidence for the importance of net manufacturing exports, on the other hand, contrasts with the insignificant effect reported by Rowthorn and Wells from their time series study.

Given the long period covered by our study and the occurrence of many important episodes during that time, stability in the estimated equation could be of vital importance. We investigate this problem by using both the Chow structural stability test and the Recursive Least Squares method. The Chow stability statistics are considerably smaller than their critical values. Figures 20.7–20.8 show the CUSUM of recursive residuals and the estimated values of the regression coefficients throughout the recursive period, together with plus/minus twice their estimated standard errors. The CUSUM statistic remains within its 5 per cent significance bounds and fluctuates around the zero line. As the sample period becomes longer and information accumulates over time, all coefficient estimates based on recursive OLS quickly converge and remain remarkably stable throughout the sample period. These findings, combined with the values of the Chow tests, provide firm evidence of parameter stability.

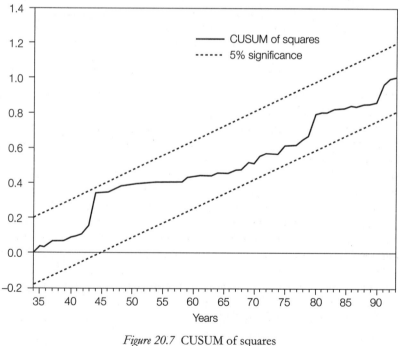

Figure 20.7 CUSUM of squares
Source: Table 20.1.

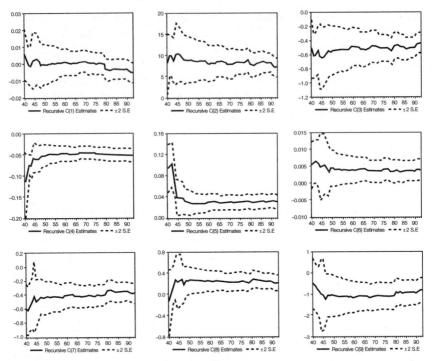

Coefficients: c(1) = constant; c(2) = DLYH; c(3) = DLYHS; c(4) = DLU; c(5) = DLU(–1); c(6) = DRMX(–3); c(7) = DLRMQ; c(8) = DLRMQ(–2); c(9) = Z^2(–1)

Figure 20.8 Recursive coefficients

THE OUTLOOK FOR THE MANUFACTURING EMPLOYMENT RATE

Brown and Julius (1993) argue that the share of manufacturing employment to total employment will continue falling throughout the industrial world. To get some idea of the future time path for the United Kingdom manufacturing rate, we have carried out a number of simulations using the long-run and short-run estimates of the employment model. The simulations are based on the following assumptions.

Scenario 1 All exogenous variables grow at their average growth rates over the last decade, 1984–93. i.e. $\Delta \ln Y = 0.01704$, $\Delta \ln(RMQ) = 0.02281$, $\Delta(RMX) = -0.01928$, $\Delta \ln U = -0.00192$.

Scenario 2 All exogenous variables grow at their average growth rates over the last five years, 1989–93. i.e. $\Delta \ln Y = -0.00057$, $\Delta \ln(RMQ) = 0.02021$, $\Delta(RMX) = 0.45189$, $\Delta \ln U = 0.04560$.

540

Scenario 3 The deficit in manufacturing exports is steadily falling so net manufacturing exports revert to a balance by 2005. The unemployment rate is continuously declining and converges to 5 per cent (roughly the NAIRU rate) by the year 2005. Per capita income and relative manufacturing productivity are growing at the steady rates of 1.7 per cent and 20 per cent respectively, which are approximately equal to their average growth rates during the last fifteen years.

Scenario 4 Assumptions as in scenario 3, except that there is no growth in per capita income, which was the experience over the 1989–93 period.

Scenario 5 Assumptions as in scenario 4, except that the deficit on manufacturing exports is falling faster and converts to a substantial surplus (similar to the average level of the 1960s and 1970s) by the year 2005.

The simulation results up to the year 2010 are shown in Table 20.2. The striking finding is that the share of manufacturing employment to total employment is sharply declining in all simulations. In the most pessimistic case (scenario 1), the manufacturing employment rate falls to 11.5 per cent in 2010, down from 20 per cent in 1993, a decrease of almost 50 per cent. Even in the more optimistic case (scenario 5), it declines to 14.5 per cent by the year 2010. These results support the pessimistic view expressed by Brown and Julius (1993). Indeed their prediction of a 10 per cent manufacturing

Table 20.2 Simulation values for the manufacturing employment rate

Year	Scenario 1	Scenario 2	Scenario 3	Scenario 4	Scenario 5
1994	19.592	19.691	19.683	19.812	19.683
1995	19.067	19.303	19.225	19.460	19.239
1996	18.636	19.008	18.869	19.187	18.908
1997	18.174	18.725	18.519	18.896	18.615
1998	17.681	18.410	18.153	18.563	18.315
1999	17.163	18.069	17.773	18.812	18.007
2000	16.629	17.707	17.384	17.805	17.695
2001	16.086	17.329	16.987	17.395	17.378
2002	15.541	16.940	16.587	16.974	17.059
2003	14.999	16.546	16.185	16.548	16.738
2004	14.465	16.149	15.783	16.121	16.417
2005	13.940	15.753	15.384	15.697	16.096
2006	13.428	15.359	14.988	15.278	15.776
2007	12.930	14.971	14.597	14.866	15.457
2008	12.445	14.589	14.212	14.462	15.141
2009	11.976	14.214	13.833	14.066	14.828
2010	11.521	13.847	13.461	13.680	14.518

employment rate in thirty years seems to be an under-estimate. Ironically, this decline (both in the short and long term) is fundamentally due to the strong negative influence of accelerating growth in per capita income (the maturity hypothesis) and in relative manufacturing productivity (the cost disease hypothesis), both of which represent major economic objectives.[10] The positive influence of lower unemployment and larger net manufacturing exports can slow down the speed of the decline in the manufacturing employment rate, as shown by simulations 3, 4, and 5, but these are not sufficient to reverse the trend.

CONCLUSIONS

The evidence reported in this chapter provides no comfort to those concerned about the declining share of manufacturing employment in total employment. The estimated model seems to provide a reasonable account of both the trend and short term fluctuations in the UK manufacturing employment rate over the period 1921–93. It suggests that the sharp downward trend in the manufacturing employment rate during the post-war period was the result of a concerted and sustained impact from a number of ongoing processes: increasing per capita incomes in a mature industrially developed economy where changing demand patterns favour the service sector; an economy in which the growth of productivity in the manufacturing sector increasingly outstrips productivity gains in the rest of the economy; an open economy that experiences a substantial decline in the volume and relative importance of its net manufacturing exports; high overall unemployment rates which exert stronger influence on the manufacturing sector relative to the rest of the economy.

Assuming a growing economy, further technologically driven gains in productivity with a disproportionate depressing effect on the demand for labour in manufacturing, and sustained competition from overseas economies, our projections appear to suggest that the share of manufacturing employment in total employment is set to continue its downward trend. Reasonable projections of the determining factors would seem to indicate that a ten per cent employment share for manufacturing within the next twenty years is not at all an unlikely scenario. These results imply that the Government may only be able to slowdown the speed of the decline, but not to reverse the trend, through appropriate macroeconomic and industrial measures aimed at improving manufacturing exports and reducing aggregate unemployment. As discussed in the introductory section of this chapter and in Chapter 18, there is considerable disagreement as to whether the overall impact of government intervention through macroeconomic and industrial policies will be beneficial to the economy.

NOTES

1 See the evidence in Kitson and Michie (1996).
2 This is also stressed in a House of Lords Select Committee Report: 'Manufacturing industry is vital to the prospects of the United Kingdom. . . .Our manufacturing base is dangerously small; to achieve adequate growth from such a small base will be difficult' (House of Lords, 1991, pp. 3, 43).
3 This point is also made by Kitson and Michie, *op. cit*. These authors add two further arguments: first, deindustrialisation can create a depressing environment for training, thus seriously obstructing the successful shift of labour into other sectors. Second, much of the service sector itself depends crucially on the size and growth of the manufacturing industry.
4 See Graham *et al.* (1989), Eltis (1996), Kitson and Michie (*op. cit.*).
5 Empirical evidence (see Crafts, 1996) indicates that productivity in UK manufacturing has lagged behind the other industrialised countries, though the gap has been narrowed during the 1980s.
6 Unfortunately there are no historical (and reliable) data on productivity in the developing world for testing this hypothesis.
7 A similar outcome can result from what Eltis calls 'defensive investment', which has led British industrial companies 'to cut costs and therefore employment to produce a product range which changed relatively little' (Eltis, 1996, p. 184). Kitson and Michie also argue that 'in the 1980s the benefits of this productivity growth went overwhelmingly into cutting employment and increasing dividends rather than developing new products and expanding output' (Kitson and Michie, 1986, p. 199).
8 Notice that in the estimation of the model all variables are measured in natural logarithms, except *RMX* which has negative numbers.
9 These estimates were obtained by applying the Johansen cointegration tests. For a good introduction to these tests and the error correction model used for investigating the short-run behaviour of manufacturing employment, see Holden and Thompson (1992).
10 This evidence on the negative influence of productivity on the share of manufacturing employment seems to substantiate the claims of some economists (e.g. Kitson and Michie, *op. cit.*) and political commentators that the major productivity gains in UK manufacturing during the 1980s were largely due to job cuts rather than increased output (see also Figure 20.2).

REFERENCES

Baumol, W. J. (1967) 'Macroeconomics of unbalanced growth: The anatomy of the urban crisis', *American Economic Review*, June, pp. 415–26.

Baumol, W. J., Blackman, S. A. B. and Wolff, E. N. (1989) *Productivity and American Leadership: The Long View*, Cambridge, Mass.: MIT Press.

Bazen, S. and Thirlwall, T. (1989) *Deindustrialisation*, London: Heinemann.

Brown, R. and Julius, D. (1993) 'Is manufacturing still special in the new world order?', in R. O'Brien, (ed.) *Finance and the International Economy*, Oxford: Oxford University Press.

Crafts, N. (1993) *Can Deindustrialisation Seriously Damage your Wealth?*, London: Institute of Economic Affairs.

—— (1996) 'Deindustrialisation and economic growth', *Economic Journal*, vol. 106, pp. 172–83.

Eltis, W. (1996) 'How low profitability and weak innovation undermines UK industrial growth', *Economic Journal*, vol. 106, pp. 184–95.

Escribano, A. (1987) 'Cointegration, time co-trends and error-correction systems: An alternative approach', CORE Discussion Paper no. 8715.

Feinstein, C. H. (1972) *Statistical Tables of National Income, Expenditure and Output of the U.K. 1855–1965,* Cambridge: Cambridge University Press.

Graham, N., Beatson, M. and Wells, W. (1989) '1977 to 1987: A decade of service', *Employment Gazette*, January, pp. 45–54.

Holden, K. and Thompson, J. (1992) 'Co-Integration: An introductory survey', *British Review of Economic Issues*, vol. 14, pp. 1–55.

House of Lords, (1991) *Report from the Select Committee on Science and Technology*, London: HMSO.

Hutton, W. (1996) *The State We're In,* London: Vintage.

Kaldor, N. (1996) *Causes of the Slow Rate of Growth of the United Kingdom,* Cambridge: Cambridge University Press.

Kitson, M. and Michie, J. (1996) 'Britain's industrial performance since 1960: Under-investment and relative decline', *Economic Journal*, vol. 106, pp. 196–212.

Rowthorn, R. (1992) 'Productivity and American leadership', a Review of Baumol *et al.* (1989) *Productivity and the American Leadership: The long view, Review of Income and Wealth*, December, pp. 475–96.

Rowthorn, R. and Wells, J. R. (1987) *Deindustrialisation and Foreign Trade,* Cambridge: Cambridge University Press.

Smith, A. D. (1989) 'New measures of British service outputs', *National Institute Economic Review*, no. 128, May, pp. 75–87.

The British Economy Key Statistics 1900–1970, published for the London & Cambridge Economic Service by Times Newspapers Ltd.

Thirlwall, A. P. (1979) 'The balance of payments constraint as an explanation of international growth differences', *Banca del Lavoro Quarterly Review*, vol. 128, pp. 44–53.

DATA APPENDIX

Data for the pre-war period and, in many instances, up to the 1950s, are taken from *The British Economy Key Statistics 1900–1970* (thereafter referred to as *BEKS*). Whenever data for the war years are missing, these were taken from Feinstein (1972). Data for the post-war period were taken mainly from *Economic Trends Annual Supplement* 1993 and 1994 (thereafter referred to as *ETAS*). In constructing consistent time series, our policy has been to adjust earlier data to the latest series available, since we regard the latter as more reliable. Therefore, all variables at constant prices are based on 1985 prices. The individual variables are measured as follows:

ME: Manufacturing employment (employees in manufacturing industry)

A. 1920–58: *BEKS.*

B. 1959–70: *Department of Employment Gazette*, March 1975.

C. 1971–93: *ETAS* 1993, 1994, *ET* September 1994.

Series B was adjusted to make it consistent with series C by using the three common data points 1971–3. Subsequently series A was spliced so as to make it consistent with the latter series using an adjustment factor based on the overlapping years 1959–63.

TE: Total employment (employees in employment)

A. 1920–49: *BEKS.*
B. 1950–93: *ETAS* 1993, 1994, *ET* September 1994.
Series A was adjusted to make it consistent with series B by applying an adjustment factor based on the five overlapping years 1950–54.

RME: Ratio of manufacturing employment (ME) to total employment (TE), in percentages

GDP: Gross domestic product at factor cost (average estimate), 1985 prices

A. 1920–38, 1946–47: *BEKS.*
B. 1939–45: Feinstein (1976).
C. 1948–93: *ETAS* 1993,1994, *ET* September 1994.
Series B (after being rebased from 1938 prices to 1963 prices) was used to fill in the missing observations for the series A. The latter was then made consistent with series C by applying an adjustment factor based on the overlapping years 1948–52.

Y: Income per capita at 1985 prices (gross domestic product at factor cost per capita)

Data for 1948–93 were obtained from *ETAS* 1993, 1994 and *ET* September 1994. Data for 1920–47 were constructed by dividing GDP at 1985 prices by total population (*PO*) and then adjusting the computed data to the 1948–93 series, using a splicing factor based on the common years 1948–52.

NGDP: Gross domestic product at current prices (average estimate at factor cost)

A. 1920–47: Feinstein (1976).
B. 1948–93: *ETAS* 1993, 1994, *ET* September 1994.
Series A was made consistent with series B by applying an adjustment factor based on the common data points 1948–52.

U: Unemployment rate (in percentages)

A. 1920–64: *BEKS.*
B. 1965–93: *ETAS* 1993, 1994, *ET* September 1994.
Series A was made consistent with series B by applying a splicing factor based on the overlapping years 1965–69.

NMX: Net exports in manufactures at current prices

This variable is calculated as the difference between the values of manufacturing exports (f.o.b.) and manufacturing imports (c.i.f.) of both finished
and unfinished goods. Data for the period 1964–93 were obtained from
Monthly Digest of Statistics (various issues), and were adjusted wherever necessary to make them consistent with those reported in the issue of April 1993.
Data for 1920–70 are available in *BEKS*. The observations for 1920–63 were
adjusted to the 1964–92 series by using an adjustment factor for a five-year
overlap (1964–8).

RMX: Ratio of net manufacturing exports (NMX) to nominal gross domestic product (NGDP), in percentages

MO: Manufacturing output at 1985 prices

This variable was constructed as follows: First we constructed a consistent
index (1985 = 100) of output for total manufacturing industry. Data for
1950–93 were obtained from *ETAS* 1993, 1994, *ET* September 1994. Those
for 1920–49 (excluding 1939–45) were taken from *BEKS*. This series is based
on 1963 = 100 and was rebased to 1985 = 100 by using an adjustment factor
for a five-year overlap (1950–4). Given the value of real GDP in 1985
(£307,901 million at factor cost) and a weight of manufacturing output to
GDP in that year of 238/1000, we transformed the index of manufacturing
output into values at 1985 prices. Since we were unable to find any data on
manufacturing output for the war years 1939–45, the values for these years
were interpolated by employing the implied GDP growth rates to proxy the
growth path of manufacturing output.

RMO: Ratio of manufacturing output (MO) to GDP in percentages

MQ: Manufacturing productivity (output per person employed in manufacturing industry), 1985 = 100

A. 1920–59: *BEKS*.
B. 1960–93: *ETAS* 1993, 1994, *ET* September 1994.
Series A was made consistent with series B by applying a splicing factor
based on the common data points 1960–4. Series A does not include observations for the war years 1939–45. Data for these years were constructed by
applying the implied growth pattern of the ratio of manufacturing output
(*MO*) to manufacturing employment (*ME*), converted to an index based on
1985 = 100.

TQ: Total productivity (output per person employed in the whole economy), 1985 = 100

A. 1920–59: *BEKS.*

B. 1960–93: *ETAS* 1993, 1994, *ET* September 1994.

Series A was adjusted to series B by applying a splicing factor based on the overlapping years 1960–64. Series A misses observations for the war years 1939–45. These were constructed by the same method as for *MQ*, but using the implied growth pattern of the (*GDP/TE*) ratio.

RMQ: Relative manufacturing productivity; ratio of manufacturing productivity (MQ) to total productivity (TQ), in percentages

PO: Population

A. 1920–59: *BEKS.*

B. 1961–93: *IMF International Financial Statistics* (various issues).

No adjustment is required for these series since the common data points are the same.

21

INDUSTRIAL CLUSTERS IN HIGH TECHNOLOGY INDUSTRIES

Differences between the US and UK

Martha Prevezer

INTRODUCTION

There has been considerable recent interest in the geography of innovation – why in innovative high-technology industries, in particular the computing and biotechnology industries, companies have tended to locate close to each other. For example, the transformation of Silicon Valley from an agricultural district in the 1950s to the world's centre for the growth of the dynamic computing industry has been the subject of considerable interest (see, for instance, Larsen and Rogers, 1984, or Saxenian, 1994). There are various theories of why clustering occurs, with emphasis on both supply and demand sides of the market. Work at the Centre for Business Strategy at London Business School looks at the genesis of regional industrial clusters in computing and biotechnology and distinguishes between the benefits and attractions of a cluster to new entrants on the one hand and incumbent firms already located in a cluster on the other. Firms cluster at particular locations to take advantage of various sorts of spillovers: these may be due to agglomerations of specialised labour, specialised inputs or knowledge spillovers (Krugman, 1991). Commercial opportunities are particularly associated with knowledge spillovers in high technology sectors. In US computing and biotechnology, for instance, firms have clustered at particular locations due to synergies between firms from different sectors, and between the science base and the creation of new innovative firms. These synergies are a product of spillovers from research in the science base that create opportunities for new firms to commercialise that research, or of spillovers between firms that occur when firms are located close to each other, with communication and knowledge transfer between the people in those firms. The potential to absorb these spillovers has created the momentum for growth of industrial clusters in particular states, via the entry of new firms and through enhancing the growth of incumbent firms in particular sectors (Swann, 1993; Prevezer, 1996; Swann and Prevezer, 1996)

Individual countries in Europe appear to lack such a forceful dynamic to cluster in these industries. The United Kingdom, which is in the forefront of Europe in the commercialisation of biotechnology, having the greatest number of small biotechnology companies and centres of scientific excellence that compete with other European countries, has not experienced an equivalent process to that which has occurred in the San Francisco Bay area, with the creation there of several hundred small biotechnology companies of different types. The issue is not one of absolute geographical size. The markets for the products of biotechnology are global. The marketing and distribution is achieved through collaboration with world-wide multinationals. Such alliances are themselves not constrained by geography. The constraints appear to lie on the supply side of the creation of spillovers in a particular locality of a sufficient magnitude to set in motion the dynamic whereby new companies are attracted to that location. The spillovers are partly due to economies of scale. There are scale economies in both infrastructure and in supplies of specialised skills in the variety of disciplines needed and in auxiliary industrial activities, such as specialised equipment manufacture, access to which is essential if firms are to keep at the forefront of technological activity. It is also a question of whether there are opportunities for new entrants to absorb the spillovers, or whether the sector is dominated by incumbents which are adept in absorbing spillovers locally within their sector, leaving fewer opportunities for new firms to be created. In addition the structure of clusters has been important, with certain sectors of industry generating a more innovative dynamic to growth than other sectors. There are differences in the composition and innovativeness of clusters between the US and the United Kingdom.

This paper examines these issues and theories and describes how clusters have formed in the US in computing and biotechnology. It compares this with the formation of clusters in those industries in the United Kingdom. It then goes on to examine the mixture of spontaneous creation of clusters alongside policy inducements to exploit the local resource base and to encourage interactions between firms. These have been particularly prominent in biotechnology. These policies in various US states, centred in particular around the US Regional Biotechnology Centres and other high technology initiatives, have been a mixture of those providing infrastructural public goods, and those that have been designed to bring together specialist scientific research of interest to a particular sector with firms that might be interested in developing that research. We look at the range of these policies and what they are designed to do, with the United Kingdom in mind, to see whether similar regionally based initiatives might produce a clustering momentum. We go on to look at the spectrum of science and technology policy, regional policy and industrial policy in the United Kingdom and at how these might be reoriented and coordinated in order to create some of the critical features to the growth of industrial clusters in the United Kingdom.

THEORIES OF CLUSTERING

This section draws from a survey of the literature on industrial clusters and innovative performance (Baptista, 1995). Recent interest has stemmed largely from the high technology industries, in particular those clustered in Silicon Valley and Route 128, looking at what stimulated these clusters, with emphasis on the science base and on start-ups coming out of existing companies; the high quality of human capital in the regions, the support of venture capital and technological infrastructure also played important roles in establishing these clusters (Dorfman, 1983; Saxenian, 1985). Saxenian (1994) emphasises the role of informal networks of communication between commercial and professional people in Silicon Valley which have been more fluid, adaptable and innovative than the more hierarchical, insular firms that have dominated Route 128. She has attributed the continued innovativeness of Silicon Valley to this difference in industrial and commercial organisation.

Porter (1990) uses a diamond to describe the four facets that create competitive advantage: factor conditions; firm strategy, structure and rivalry; demand conditions; and relations with related and supporting industries. He emphasises domestic rivalry and geographical concentration as driving competitive advantage, with rivalry promoting competition and investment, and concentration increasing the intensity of interactions within a region. He also points to the roles of specialised factors such as skilled labour, knowledge of the market and specialised infrastructure, with geographical concentration and rivalry promoting higher-quality factors and attracting new sources of supply, and creating more sophisticated customers and hence superior demand conditions. In the high technology industries, the role of information is important, with universities and research centres creating local advantage as such information is hard to spread great distances.

Krugman (1991) stresses that industrial concentration is not a new phenomenon, and characterises very traditional non-technological industries as well as more recent high-technology industries. He restates Marshall's (1920) three main sources of such localization, which are supply-side externalities. These stem from labour market pooling, with advantages through a concentration of a large number of skilled labour with similar skills; this benefits both workers and firms and helps them to cope with the uncertainty of business cycles and unemployment. It creates increasing returns through specialization and possible scale economies. The second source of concentration of firms is concentration of intermediate inputs, with a greater number of specialised suppliers of inputs and services lowering costs and creating economies of scale and scope. Thirdly there are technological externalities or spillovers, particularly important in knowledge intensive industries. Recent interest has focused on these, and we return to explanations based on this theme below.

Arthur (1989) concentrates on the role of positive feedback and the lock-in or path dependence that follows from sometimes accidental historical events in establishing both technological or product standards and by analogy geographical regions of strength in a particular industry. This focus is therefore on the process by which agglomeration externalities lead to geographical concentration. The presence of increasing returns or network externalities can lead to one product or technology dominating (David, 1985; Arthur, 1989). Many products, such as computer hardware and software, require compatibility with each other, and once market share is gained in one brand, that becomes an industry standard (Swann, 1992). This also happens with locations, if the net benefits from locating in a region increase with the number of firms in that region. If such agglomeration economies are strong, firms will tend to cluster. The origins of the process may be historically accidental, and not determined by any intrinsic economic advantage of the area. The process will not normally continue indefinitely, but will cease when congestion sets in and diminishing returns predominate. Industries might therefore demonstrate concentration in one region or be spread over a few regions.

Demand sources of concentration and clustering that have also been highlighted (Swann, 1993) include local demand effects especially if there are strong input–output effects from related industries. Hotelling (1929) argued that firms might gain market share if they moved closer to each other. Other demand advantages include reducing consumer search costs, and increasing information about the strength of market demand through observing clusters of firms trading at one location.

Costs of clustering (Swann, 1993) include congestion effects, when competition in input and output markets creates scarcities and increasing costs. This congestion can create an upper bound to the increasing returns stressed above. The decline in clusters usually comes about abruptly and suddenly, when industrial development shifts to new centres. This can be brought about by the emergence of radical new ideas which makes old information obsolete (Brezis and Krugman, 1993), and makes the costs of clustering outweigh the benefits of agglomeration. Swann (1994) analysed the performance of a cluster in terms of the diversity of sectors or technologies and their convergence; if there is no convergence between technologies, there will be no benefit from proximity and single technology or single sector clusters will dominate. If technologies converge, multi-sectoral or multi-technology clusters will benefit from inter-sectoral benefits and will outperform single sector clusters.

What makes technological progress special is partly the fact that it is non-rival – it cannot be used up and can be replicated more easily than created – and that it is only partially excludable, as it is not easy to gain complete appropriability over it. These two conditions create the possibilities for spillovers to exist, whereby firms share knowledge with each other without paying for it in a market transaction. To balance this somewhat, Cohen and Levinthal (1989) have established that firms need competences in R&D in order to be able to exploit new knowledge: that it is not costlessly and easily transferable between institutions or firms without their having prior capabilities in similar fields with which to absorb that knowledge. There have been several empirical studies of spillovers, which have established evidence for substantial spillovers between firms and between industries leading to gains in productivity, to changes in the structure of production and to innovative activity (Griliches, 1991; Terleckyj, 1980; Scherer, 1982, 1984; Jaffe, 1986; Bernstein, 1989; and Bernstein and Nadiri, 1989, 1991).

There have also been studies identifying the sources and recipients of spillovers. Jaffe (1989) and Acs et al. (1992) have shown that spillovers can arise from university-based research leading to innovative activity in firms. The geographical localisation of such knowledge spillovers has been established by Jaffe (1989), Jaffe et al. (1993) and by Acs et al. (1992), showing that spillovers from university research are stronger within the same state as the origin of the research. Government expenditure creating knowledge spillovers has also been looked at by Nadiri and Manuneas (1991, 1994) establishing that government-financed R&D and public infrastructure have lowered costs and raised productivity in particular industries. Grupp (1994) has identified spillovers arising from public R&D infrastructure. There are also studies looking at which types of firms profit from such spillovers. The bulk of corporate R&D expenditure is known to be located within the largest firms (Scherer and Ross, 1990; Pavitt, 1987). But Acs and Audretsch (1987) have found that in some markets, small firms are more innovative. Acs et al. (1994) argue that there are differences between large and small firms in their capacity to absorb spillovers, with large firms benefiting from private corporate R&D and small firms benefiting more from spillovers from university research.

A differerence that we will pick up below was found between the pattern of industrial R&D in the United Kingdom with the dominance of the great corporate centre (Howells, 1984; Thwaites, 1982) and the pattern of spatial concentration of R&D in the US, where the corporate centre is not so predominant. Malecki (1980) found much industrial innovative activity in the US to be located at federal-supported centres in the 'Sunbelt region', close to universities and major research laboratories, partly reflecting the different scale of the US economy and the importance of regional policy (Baptista, 1995).

Another distinction made in the literature is between the different sources of innovation. It is now recognised that innovation can stem from various stages in the production process: from basic research, from product and process development and from nearer-market commercialisation and feedback from customers and users. Each stage can receive inputs from external sources and is capable of absorbing spillovers from the outside environment. Nelson (1993) argues that academic and basic research is more important for technological progress in the early stages of development of an industry and diminishes as the industry matures. The benefits of geographical closeness to the science base and research institutes or to related industries will be particularly strong when the knowledge is tacit and uncodified, requiring shared knowledge bases and shared language and considerable communication in order to understand and transmit the knowledge. The tacitness of knowledge will also be a function of the stage of development of a technology or industry, with less knowledge being codified and transmittable in the early stages of development of a technology or industry. Debresson and Amesse (1991) have argued that networks of localised innovators are more durable than formal alliances, illustrating the importance of informal communication over more formal channels through which information may be transferred. Von Hippel (1988), Feldman (1994), Dorfman (1983) and Saxenian (1994) all stress the importance of suppliers and users as a source of outside knowledge and ideas, providing another explanation for geographical concentration. Feldman (1994) tests specifically for the importance of specialised business services, and the presence of related industries as well as the presence of centres of private and academic research in establishing regional networks of firms in highly innovative industries, and finds them to be significant in influencing location decisions.

There is considerable overlapping and consensus between many of these explanations of geographical concentration or clustering, with some emphasising demand conditions and many more recently focusing on supply externalities and in particular the presence of various sorts of supply spillovers, especially in knowledge-intensive industries. In the work reported below, which focuses on the computing and biotechnology industries, many facets of these theories are relevant and we pick up various threads in explaining patterns of clustering in these two industries in the US and the United Kingdom.

CLUSTERING IN COMPUTING AND BIOTECHNOLOGY IN THE US

Figure 21.1 (page 560) shows how concentrated the US computing industry was in 1988 and the biotechnology industry in 1991. Three US states accounted for more than half of the computer companies in 1988 (California, Massachusetts and New York); in biotechnology the leading three states accounted for just under 40 per cent of biotechnology companies in 1991 (California, Massachusetts and New Jersey). More striking, perhaps, is the overwhelming concentration of both computing and biotechnology in California, with over 35 per cent of computer companies and 23 per cent of biotechnology companies located there. In biotechnology the distribution of companies between states is more even than in computing, with a larger number of states attracting a sizeable proportion of companies. The predominance of California and Massachusetts in a variety of sectors which are most developed in both industries suggests that clusters have been created in states with a mix of type of company and not through specialisation by each state in one sector.

Models of entry and growth: the main results

In order to analyse the main forces of attraction into a cluster and the benefits to firms' growth of being located in a cluster, Swann (1993), Prevezer (1996) and Swann and Prevezer (1996) developed a series of models to look at entry into clusters and at what forces were beneficial for growth of incumbent companies within a cluster. For details of the data and construction of these models of entry and growth, see the work cited above. Here we summarise the main findings.

The strongest effect on entry of new firms in computing were cross-sectoral attractors, with 'hard' sectors – components, hardware and systems – attracting 'soft' sectors – software and peripherals. In other words, strength of employment in hardware, components and systems at a cluster encouraged entry by software and peripherals firms. Own-sector strength of employment, however, discouraged entry – i.e. strength of employment in software discouraged further entry into the software sector, etc. In biotechnology, the science base exerted a strong pull to the entry of new companies at a cluster. Entrants were as attracted by proximity to centres of research as by proximity to other companies. The cross-sectoral attraction between sectors was restricted to a group of sectors, with employment in therapeutics at a cluster attracting equipment, agriculture and diagnostic companies and vice versa. However there was much less entry into the other four sectors: chemicals, food, waste and energy. This suggests that the positive feedback, prompting clusters to grow once entry of new companies is underway, was limited to one block of industrial sectors in biotechnology and was weaker in biotechnology than in computing.

The growth models were company-level models and examined how growth of employment in each company depended on the age of the company, exposure to own sector employment at that cluster and exposure to employment at a cluster in other sectors than the sector to which the company belonged, and also in the biotechnology case to employment in the science base at that cluster. In both industries it was employment within the company's own sector and cluster which promoted growth of the company, whereas strength of employment in other sectors at that cluster in general detracted from company growth. However, growth rates were almost twice as high in computing as in biotechnology overall. In computing the effect of own-sector strength at a cluster was particularly pronounced for the 'hard' sectors – components, hardware and systems, and was less strong for the 'soft' sectors of software, peripherals and services. In biotechnology, the strength of the science base at a cluster did not assist company growth: more often, coefficients were negative, suggesting that it discouraged company growth.

This implies that incumbent firms were effective at absorbing spillovers within their own sector. In the entry models, own sector employment discouraged entry of new firms into that sector, suggesting that, in absorbing spillovers in their own sectors locally, incumbents were competitively preventing any opportunities becoming available for new entrants. Incumbents did not, however, benefit from strength in a cluster in other sectors of the industry, nor from strength in their local science base in biotechnology. By contrast, entrants were attracted by strength in employment in other sectors and by strength of the local science base. Incumbents therefore were not effective in absorbing local spillovers in other sectors or in the local science base, and that left open greater opportunities for new entrants at that location, which were effective at absorbing spillovers created by the science base and by the presence of certain key sectors.

These results are largely supported by the findings of others especially the encouragement to clustering through entry of new firms into the biotechnology industry by the presence of a strong science base. In a study of the birth of US biotechnology enterprises, Zucker, Darby and Brewer (1994) determined that it was the presence of key 'star' scientists that influenced the timing and creation of new biotechnology firms. Audretsch and Stephan (1995) identified the role of scientists as founders of new firms as being particularly important in making firms locate near the science base.

There are differences in the structures of the two industries which affect the interdependencies between their different parts. In computing, sectors of the industry divide most naturally into the different technologies within the industry: components, hardware, software, peripherals, systems, etc. These are broad distinctions which encompass many differences within the sectors, but by and large each sector describes a particular set of technologies and companies specialise within a sector. These technologies are interdependent in the creation of the end-product: the computer and its services to an end-user. This in turn creates positive feedback between sectors, whereby change in one sector has a knock-on effect on other sectors. End markets for computing are not confined to one sector of industry but are spread across the industrial, financial and domestic structures.

The biotechnology industry is structured differently, with considerable similarity especially in the early days of the industry, between the different technologies used across sectors. Companies have tended instead to

555

specialise according to applications to a particular industry: therapeutics and diagnostics firms are broadly within the pharmaceutical industry; agricultural and chemical firms see their technologies applying to the agro-chemical market. This division into existing sectors of industry is not completely clear-cut: some new diagnostic firms address not just health care but water and food testing also; research tools and equipment companies supply both industry and research establishments; and environmental applications create a largely new sector. Nevertheless this structure broadly applies, with bio-technology start-ups dependent to a substantial extent on existing companies in their own sector for their market and for help in jointly developing tech-nologies. Many links are therefore vertically forward to particular user indus-tries for each sector, rather than between sectors where there is relatively little technological interdependence. Feedback between the sectors is there-fore more limited than in the case of the computing industry.

Finally in this section we would like to stress that a key characteristic of clusters in biotechnology in particular has been the role of collaboration of various sorts, which has required proximity in order to work. Collaboration has been within the science base, in the origins of the industry, in the bring-ing together and working together of different scientists based locally within the different disciplines that were harnessed to create the new technologies. This is documented in various histories of the origins of the industry (Hall, 1987; McKelvey, 1994), and its implications for clustering are looked at in more detail in Swann, Prevezer and Stout (forthcoming). Local collaboration was also important between different types of skills: scientists, entre-preneurs, and venture capitalists. Sometimes these skills were combined with-in particular people, with several important scientist-entrepreneurs who were both prominent in their scientific/academic environments and keen to commercialise their knowledge through founding new companies. More often, and especially once the industry had been established in a recognisable shape, venture-capitalists who were heavily involved in the process brought together entrepreneurs with managerial experience, often gained within incumbent companies, with scientists keen to exploit the commercial potential of their new technologies. This binding of people happened more frequently and more easily within growing clusters of firms, where communciation was more intense and connections were made more fluidly and readily, than outside such clusters. This is described more fully in Swann, Prevezer and Stout (forthcoming). This is a similar process to the networks of firms and social connections in the computing industry, stressed by Saxenian (1994) as being critical in maintaining innovation in that industry in Silicon Valley.

We return to some of these themes later when we discuss whether these ingredients of clusters are present in the United Kingdom, and what can be done to stimulate the types of interaction that appear to be necessary to generate the clustering momentum. Before that we compare clustering in the computing and biotechnology industries in the US with those in the United Kingdom. We then review the role of policy inducements in contributing to the diffusion of clusters in the US, in order to understand what types of lesson and policy might be useful in the UK context.

CLUSTERING IN THE US AND UK COMPARED

We have available a detailed comparison between clustering in the US and UK computing industries (Baptista and Swann 1996) and of clustering in US and UK biotechnology (Prevezer and Shohet, in Swann, Prevezer and Stout, forthcoming) which highlight some of the main structural differences between the industries in the two countries.

The UK computing industry is even more concentrated than the US industry. The three main states in the US accounted for 50 per cent of firms in 1988, whereas, in the United Kingdom, Greater London and the South East accounted for 62 per cent of firms. In terms of employment, concentration was even more marked in the United Kingdom, with Greater London accounting for 35 per cent of firms but 70 per cent of employment. Another difference between the US and UK computing industries is in the size of firms in highly concentrated regions: in the United Kingdom, the proportions of firms and employment (apart from in Greater London) are roughly equivalent. In the US the two top states – California and Massachusetts – in terms of numbers of firms have below-average numbers of employees per firm. New York, on the other hand, accounts for 22 per cent of total employment, having over ten times the number of employees per firm as in California.

There are key structural differences between the US and UK computing industries which go a long way towards explaining the difference in their success stories, despite the presence of clusters or the concentration of firms in both countries. The UK industry is concentrated around the services and distribution sectors, which accounted for 60 per cent of firms and 50 per cent of employment in 1990. The US industry, on the other hand, has been concentrated in peripherals and software, with 55 per cent of firms in those sectors (although only 16 per cent of employment in those sectors). The United Kingdom by contrast had only 15 per cent of firms (and employment) in peripherals and software.

In the core manufacturing sectors of components and hardware, both the US and United Kingdom have 15 per cent of firms in those sectors, but the US has 35.5 per cent of its employees in core manufacturing whereas the United Kingdom has only 10.5 per cent of employment. Perhaps equally important, the role of these core manufacturing sectors operates differently between the two countries. In the US these are leading firms with headquarters and decision-making about strategy and innovation taking place in the US; in the United Kingdom these firms are mainly foreign-owned with key operations and strategy formation occurring elsewhere, mostly in the US. These divergences in terms of development and sectoral specialisation are in part due to the different life-cycles and histories of the industry in the two countries, with the industry's origins firmly based in the US and key developments in the industry's technologies and structure occurring there. If one includes the development of the software and peripherals sectors as being equally 'core' to the industry as hardware and components, the US predominance in these sectors is even more marked. The UK structure has largely formed through being a provider of services and distribution outlet for the core of the industry located elsewhere.

Using a slightly altered version of the full model referred to above and reported in Swann and Prevezer (1996), Baptista and Swann (1996) found similarities in the entry effects between the two countries. In the United Kingdom, as for the US, strong entry effects came from strength at a cluster in components and hardware which encouraged entry into several sectors. Significant positive effects in the United Kingdom also came from the presence of the peripherals and services sectors on entry into the services, software and systems sectors which were not particularly attracted by strength at a cluster in hardware and components. It is not clear whether the magnitude of the effects is larger for one country or the other: components and peripherals may be more important in promoting entry in the United Kingdom, whist hardware exerts a stronger pull in the US.

The results of the growth models, with broadly similar models constructed in Baptista and Swann (1996) as in Swann and Prevezer (1996), also show broad similarities in the form of growth promoters but with marked differences in magnitude. In both countries own-sector employment at a cluster was the main promoter of growth, whereas employment in other sectors of the industry discouraged growth of firms at that location. The average rate of growth for US firms was, however, about twice that for UK firms. In addition, variables were added that tested for the effect of localised competition (through the presence of larger numbers of smaller firms than average in a region, based on Glaeser et al., 1992 and Feldman and Audretsch, 1995) and this effect was found to be significant in the US but not in the United Kingdom. The main contrast between entry attractors and growth promoters is consistent for both the US and United Kingdom. Entry is attracted by strength at a cluster in other sectors, i.e. cross-sectoral effects predominate. Growth in both countries, on the other hand, is promoted by strength at a location of employment in the firm's own sector.

So what is the difference between the two countries in their clustering processes in computing? One striking result is that the tendency for clustering or concentration regionally appears to be just as strong in the United Kingdom as in the US. The dynamics of the processes of entry attraction and promotion of growth of firms at particular locations also appear to be quite similar, with entry of new firms being attracted by the presence of other sectors and growth being promoted by strength at a cluster in the firm's own sector. However the success stories of the industries in the two countries appear to be quite different. In terms of growth rates of firms in the industry, US computing firms have displayed much stronger growth than UK firms. This may reflect the structure of the concentration of firms, with US firms being clustered around hardware and components manufacturing firms, in clusters of software and peripherals firms. UK entry, on the other hand, has been spurred partially by the presence of hardware and components firms into communications and distribution but also by the presence of peripherals firms into the peripherals, services, software and systems sectors. This may in part reflect the different stages of the lifecycles of the two industries, with the UK industry developing later and in response to developments in the US. The UK industry has been far more heavily based on the services and distribution sectors than on either the components and hardware sectors or the software and peripherals sectors. This feature too may have affected growth rates in the two countries, with greater synergies between software and hardware sectors in the US, leading to more innovative activity in the creation of new products, than between sectors in the United Kingdom with the services and distribution sectors not typically being the most innovative sectors in the computing industry in terms of the creation of new products and technologies. The greater significance of localised competition in the US on the growth rates of firms, with more smaller firms within a region creating more competitive conditions within that region, may also have played a role. This links us back to the descriptions of Saxenian (1994), who characterises success in the computing industry in Silicon Valley as due to the vibrancy and mobility of localised networks of information and people with fluid 'flat' informal structures of firms, in contrast to the larger, more insular and rigidly organised firms on the east coast. These features of networks do not appear to characterise the concentrations of computing firms that we see in the United Kingdom. Perhaps we should reserve the word 'clusters' to those regions exhibiting some of these less tangible qualities of high communication and innovativeness, and speak only of concentrations of firms in regions where these qualities are absent. There appears at any rate to be a qualitative difference between the type of cluster that one finds in computing in the US and that in the United Kingdom.

The Shohet study of the UK biotechnology industry brings out some of the key differences in clustering between the US and United Kingdom in that industry. There are differences in sectoral composition between the UK and US biotechnology industries, as there are between their computing industries. UK biotechnology is less concentrated in the therapeutics sector than is the US industry, and more dominated by reagents and supply firms, equipment and instrumentation firms and diagnostics firms. The reagent, supply and equipment sectors may be thought to be less innovative sectors and more auxiliary to the core of the industry than are the research-based

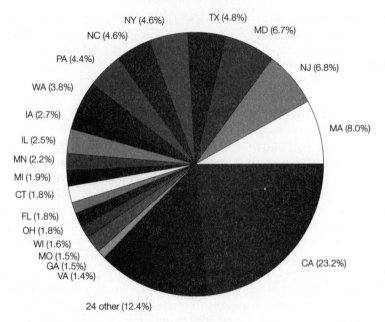

Figure 21.1(a) Distribution of biotechnology companies by US state (1991)

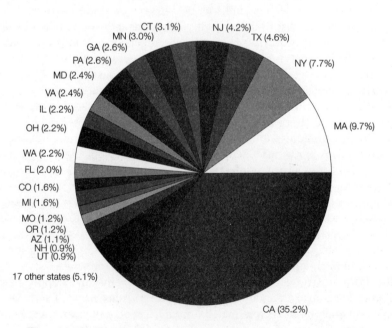

Figure 21.1(b) Distribution of computer companies by US state (1988)

therapeutics, diagnostics and agricultural sectors. As with UK computing, this difference in structural composition may reflect the different lifecycles of the US and UK industries, the UK industry being much younger and smaller, developing later than the US industry and being focused therefore more on the second stage of development of the industry and linked to key developments occurring within the US industry.

There is a regional specialisation between sectors of the industry in the United Kingdom with agricultural companies concentrated in East Anglia, pharmaceuticals in London and the South East, supply companies in the South East and chemicals in the North West. This differs from the situation in the US, where there appears to be a greater mix of sectors within the strong clusters. One might argue that this leads to ideas and technologies flowing more readily between sectors in the US, and that perhaps this inter-sectoral diffusion of technologies and information is less readily accomplished in the United Kingdom on account of regional specialisation and insulation between sectors.

A simple average entry model, (see Swann and Prevezer, 1996) was constructed for the UK biotechnology industry. The results for the UK biotechnology industry are somewhat different from those for the US. UK dedicated biotechnology firms do not appear to be attracted by the presence of the local bioscience base in the same way as are US companies. UK companies have tended to locate near universities generally, but not close to centres of particular bioscientific expertise relating to biotechnology. Such attraction to universities may in fact be related to the desire to be near generally highly qualified labour, rather than close to particular scientific skills. However, we have noticed for the US that close collaboration between the science base and companies requires proximity between them; and this lack of proximity in the United Kingdom may go hand-in-hand with a lack of collaboration between the UK science base and local industry. We return to this below. UK biotechnology companies in certain sectors are, however, attracted by clusters of employment in the bioscience industry. In the US, new biotechnology firms were only attracted by industry employment in certain sectors, whereas other sectors were less affected by the strength of employment in industry.

There is another general difference between the US and UK biotechnology industries that is likely to have affected clustering patterns, and that is the role of large incumbent companies in the industry, and in particular their relationship with the new dedicated biotechnology firms. First, as noted above, their large corporate R&D departments in the United Kingdom have been located near corporate headquarters, in contrast to the US where corporate R&D has often been located near universities. This links to the greater insularity of the UK companies than large US companies and has been reflected in their reluctance in the early 1980s to form alliances and become involved with the earliest UK biotechnology firms. This fits in with reports

561

from the relatively few key small companies in the early 1980s in the United Kingdom, that they found it easier to collaborate with and received more attention from large US and Japanese companies than they did from their home-based companies. This may have been related to the perception of the large UK companies that they had sufficient in-house research resources and an adequate background in biological research to keep abreast of developments in biotechnology without needing to foster an indigenous industry of small companies with links to the science base. So whereas alliances between small UK companies and large companies existed, they were mainly with non-UK companies in the 1980s and did not have a clustering element to them – they were formed across large distances. What has been entirely missing in the United Kingdom has been the local networks of alliances between small biotechnology firms, which have been central to clusters in California and Massachusetts.

This brings us onto the final but very crucial difference between the US and the United Kingdom in their clustering dynamics: the nature of collaboration and networks in the two countries. From interview work conducted in the United Kingdom (Prevezer and Shohet 1996), it appears that it is harder in the United Kingdom to cross the science community/industrial community divide than in the US. This has a variety of reasons: the absence of intermediaries such as the type of venture-capitalists found in the US, much less job mobility and less fluidity between the scientific and industrial environments. So whereas scientific networks exist in the United Kingdom, as do industrial networks, these networks are national and not regional and they tend not to cross the institutional barriers between the science and industrial communities. And the intense local collaborative links that have been important in making clusters grow, which are collaborations between different types of skill and specialisation, appear to be missing in the United Kingdom.

We return to these themes below, where we consider the policy implications of these differences in the United Kingdom, what types of policy help to create clusters and how the existing structure of UK policy has been inimical to correcting some of these institutional or structural failures. First, however, we turn to the role that regional policies in the US have played in assisting cluster formation, in biotechnology in particular.

THE ROLE OF POLICY IN THE FORMATION AND MIGRATION OF HIGH TECHNOLOGY CLUSTERS: REGIONAL POLICIES IN THE US

The role of policy in stimulating clusters to develop in US states other than those in which they took root when the industry came into being is an intriguing one. It is interesting for the lessons that may be learned more generally about the conditions which are necessary for regional policy to be effective in encouraging entry of new firms, and for established companies to come to that region and engage with the local communities of researchers and manufacturers and enable a new industrial network to emerge. In this section we look at the policy initiatives tried by particular states in the US to encourage biotechnology clusters and in some cases high-technology activity more generally to migrate and develop. We analyse these policies in terms of their specialisation in particular biotechnology niches and whether local conditions are propitious for that sort of concentration of activity. We compare the degree of policy momentum in biotechnology with the greater extent to which the evolution of the computing industry has been market-driven, once the initial dynamic was underway. We relate this difference back to the structure of the two industries.

As described above, the biotechnology industry, in its constituent sectors, is linked more critically to its user industrial sectors where the technologies are applied than to other sectors within the biotechnology industry. It is also argued (see Swann, Prevezer and Stout, forthcoming) that the impetus for innovation lies in different parts of the production process in different industrial sectors. Thus research is particularly central to innovation in therapeutics and diagnostics, production processes and manufacturing in chemicals and food, and the role of users in instrumentation and diagnostics. The success of policy initiatives hinges on focusing on initial conditions needed to foster particular sectors and the skills and resources that are appropriate to those sectors. Research conditions – its quality and concentration, conditions for transferability into the industrial sector, the availability of skilled research labour, the complementarity of research interests between the science base and pharmaceutical companies – are critical to encouraging clusters in therapeutics to develop. The strength and accessibility of the user community in the form of users of new instruments, medical technology or new diagnostic kits would be critical for the development of firms specialising in those sectors. For companies specialising in research, they have to be prepared to pay higher research labour costs at locations near leading research centres. For example Boston, San Francisco and San Diego have the highest research labour costs in the USA; but if specialisation is further downstream, then there are advantages in locating further away from these centres, as a different type of labour skill is required (see Prevezer, in Swann, Prevezer and Stout, forthcoming). Policies therefore need to be tailored to particular local strengths, and geared to encouraging those parts of an industry to which the location is most suited.

A variety of initiatives have been put in place across the USA in biotechnology, mainly through the Biotechnology Centres located in particular states as part of local government policy. These Centres vary enormously in their aims and focuses, but they have a number of common types of policy. Features of these policies are: encouraging the particular specialisms of that area, and enhancing and making use of local expertise, such as strength in

563

particular disciplines or industrial sectors, in research at Research Triangle Park, or in health regulation in the area near the National Institutes of Health; tax breaks or other fiscal inducements to entry of new companies and the setting up of subsidiaries of established companies; the creation of infrastructure that can be shared between small companies that would otherwise not have access to such facilities. Examples of these are research parks, incubator buildings, pilot plant facilities or DNA libraries and gene banks.

In biotechnology there have been what might be called successive generations of clusters within the industry, and these clusters have their own distinct characteristics and policies associated with them. The first generation of clusters is based in California and Massachusetts; the second generation is of two types: newer industrial clusters in Maryland and North Carolina, and clusters generated within older industrial districts in New Jersey, New York and Illinois, for instance. There are differences in policy between these two types, the first building on new skills and strengths of that area, the second aiming to regenerate former industrial strength on the basis of the stock of existing skills and strengths of established companies in those areas. The third generation of more recent clusters are based in states that have not previously been considered as core to the industry such as Washington, Idaho, Tennessee towards the west coast or Texas, Michigan and Delaware further east. These clusters have a different focus from the older clusters, aiming to specialise in different sectors and building on strengths resident in their particular regions (see Prevezer, in Swann, Prevezer and Stout, forthcoming).

The involvement of the spectrum of companies and research institutes, as well as the creation of linkage and transfer institutions have been critical in helping these distinct clusters to grow. There has been an awareness of the structure of industry in that particular region and where the innovative potential has lain. In terms of lessons that can be learned for UK policy-makers, focusing on local conditions and particular strengths in each region is key; also an understanding is needed of which sectors or parts of the industry it is appropriate to try to stimulate in each particular region. The importance of policies and agents which are capable of bringing together the appropriate range of skills and resources should also not be underestimated.

CONCLUSIONS: THE UK POLICY ENVIRONMENT AND ITS RELATION TO THE DYNAMICS OF CLUSTERING

This section acts by way of a conclusion and poses a number of questions that need to be answered in the context of the United Kingdom which might generate the type of clustering dynamic that has been seen in these high-technology industries in the US.

Temple (in Swann, Prevezer and Stout, forthcoming) argues that although the United Kingdom has industrial concentration or 'agglomerations', it lacks true 'clusters'. He identifies three main characteristics of clusters, on which policy attention should be focused. These are: the life-cycle of a cluster and its critical mass; the creation of innovative entrepreneurship and specialist services to assist the innovative entrepreneur; and the governance of clusters in the creation of shared visions regarding technological expectations, trust and coordination which are required to harness expectations towards clear objectives.

From the empirical studies reported above, it is clear that agglomerations below a certain size in terms of firms and employment would fail to display the feedback mechanisms that characterise the take-off of cluster growth. The precise size of critical mass would vary between industries and between sectors of those industries. It was also established that such feedback depended on the composition of the cluster: if there was convergence between different technologies, then clusters composed of those various technologies would outperform clusters specialising in single technologies. If on the other hand there was no convergence, then specialist clusters would do better (Swann, in Swann, Prevezer and Stout, forthcoming).

Assisting the creation of critical mass and take-off of a cluster requires a detailed knowledge of where UK strengths lie which are relevant to particular high-technology industries. The importance of shared public goods, especially to SMEs and start-ups, is very clear from the experience in the US. This raises further questions about the nature and scale of the infrastructural resources that are available in the United Kingdom. From the description of policies that abound in biotechnology throughout the US (see Prevezer, in Swann, Prevezer and Stout, forthcoming) it is clear that the scale of resources going into this industry dwarfs efforts in the United Kingdom that are being made to create the equivalent type of infrastructure. If such is the case, then greater efforts must be made to have access to resources at the European level, which in aggregate can compensate for the small scale of resources within the United Kingdom. Such networking with European institutions and companies, however, would have to be made on an informed and specialised basis, targeting strengths in particular research niches to complementary interests and resources elsewhere in Europe. These links will not be forthcoming without substantially greater awareness and information about what resources and strengths exist, and through the creation of new European-wide networks that ease access to, for example, the European Molecular Biology Laboratory or other leading facilities.

The creation of innovative entrepreneurship is also critical in the establishment of clusters, and this may be thought of in terms not so much of individuals but of collaboration and coordination between the capacities of different people or services (Temple, *op. cit.*) The role of venture capitalists in the US in forming linkages between scientists and industrialists, in finding appropriate management for nascent and growing companies, as well as in providing finance, has been essential in encouraging the entry of new firms, on which high-technology clusters in particular have been based.

In the United Kingdom there are obstacles to the creation and growth of small companies, which are already recognised in some quarters and which are being redressed. Considerable attention has been given to financing difficulties of high-technology start-ups in the United Kingdom and of SMEs generally. High-technology start-ups have had to work harder to raise funds via venture capital in the absence of a public stock market providing an exit route for private financiers. The burden of providing commercial justification and finding appropriate management has fallen more heavily on the shoulders of the small business in the United Kingdom than in the US, where the venture capitalists themselves have been more heavily involved and have taken on some of these functions (Prevezer, 1991). Small companies in the United Kingdom have had to rely more heavily on less flexible bank-based finance with a relatively small proportion of venture-capital financing going into high-technology businesses. The problems of finance for smaller businesses in the United Kingdom, along with the constraints that they face in introducing new technology, are dealt with more fully in Hughes (1994). In general, however, the range of supporting services and people have not been available to a similar degree in the United Kingdom, in the way that they appear to function in encouraging clustering in the US.

The importance of collaborative intensity was stressed as having been a key constituent in the establishment and growth of clusters. What Temple calls the governance of a cluster describes the creation of relationships of trust and partnership within communities that share the same vision. He argues that the Government's role in this may be through the promotion of cooperative precompetitive R&D, which has been a highly successful policy in Japan, for example, in encouraging technological information flows and technology transfer.

Such collaboration and fluidity between different types of institution – academic and industrial, different industrial sectors, financing and industrial – are weaknesses in much of the UK commercial structure. Easing collaboration between different types of skills, and combining such skills within particular people or within one institution, will need to be fostered specifically against the background of traditions of acute specialisation and insularity within particular disciplines. Such collaboration will need to be pump-primed by changes in constitutions and attitudes within institutions, encouraging and rewarding collaboration with industry by research institutes, or movement between different industrial or financing environments for example. Such changes in policy and attitudes accompanying them are already being seen in the United Kingdom, but there is a long way to go.

Temple argues that the formation of clusters in the United Kingdom requires the bringing together of three types of economic policy: industrial policy, regional policy, and science and technology policy which have operated in the United Kingdom hitherto in an uncoordinated manner. Also UK policies have tended to focus more on redistributive issues, on reducing the impact of declining industries, than on assisting the competitive market process. This requires more emphasis on competitive tendering, to a wider range of contenders for government contracts, and a willingness to open up inherently secretive government administrative procedures to greater outside scrutiny. This would encourage, in turn, the greater dissemination of knowledge from government projects and increase the potential spillovers from such projects into the rest of industry (Ergas, 1987).

The United Kingdom cannot run counter to the international trend and devote fewer resources to the knowledge base (Temple, in Swann, Prevezer and Stout, forthcoming). The creation of public goods and infrastructure as part of all three types of economic policy are vital. The creation of highly visible magnets for industrial location have been more effective in the US in the clustering process than more direct influence over the location of industry, again working with market processes rather than counteracting them. Such magnets should be linked to local industrial strength, in determining which bids for resources are successful. To create local technological communities, he suggests that some form of Faraday Centre (CEST, 1992) on a localised basis might be recreated, which would assist the movement of people between the science base and industry, would help with the tracking of R&D to complement firm-specific R&D, and provide a focus for collaborative R&D within industry.

In relation to the United Kingdom's science and technology policy, a stark contrast appears between the very local or regional policies that are promoted at the state level in the US and the much more centralized formation of policy in the United Kingdom. Also the states in the US have not been afraid of targeting resources into particular key technologies that are predicted to be important for industrial strength in the future. UK technology policy has tended until recently to be more arm's length and less directed to specific technologies. To some degree this is changing, with the advent of the United Kingdom's Technology Foresight Initiative. We await to see how far this will be taken and how it will be used (Stout, 1995). Science and technology policy could be harnessed to regional policy through regional technology centres, along the lines of the German regional economic councils, which in order to act as magnets would require greater regional autonomy and strategic capacity at the regional level. This too would run counter to the very powerful centralised direction of policy that has characterised much of UK economic policy and has been inimical to the growth of diverse yet highly specific and localised industrial clusters.

REFERENCES

Acs, Z. and Audretsch, D. (1987) 'Innovation, market structure and firm size', *Review of Economics and Statistics*, vol. 69, pp. 567–75.

Acs, Z., Audretsch, D. and Feldman, M. (1992) 'Real effects of academic research: Comment', *American Economic Review*, vol. 82, pp. 363–7.

Acs, Z., Audretsch, D. and Feldman, M. (1994) 'R&D spillovers and recipient firm size', *Review of Economics and Statistics*, vol. 76, pp. 336–40.

Arthur, W. (1989) 'Competing technologies, increasing returns and lock-in by historical events', *Economic Journal*, vol. 99, pp. 116–31.

Audretsch, D. and Stephan, P. (1995) 'How localized are networks in biotechnology', paper presented to the IFS Conference on R&D, Innovation and Productivity, London.

Baptista, R. (1995) 'Industrial clusters and innovative performance: A survey of the literature', Centre for Business Strategy Working Paper no. 156, London Business School.

Baptista, R. and Swann, P. (1996) 'The dynamics of firm growth and entry in industrial clusters: A comparison of the US and UK computer industries', presented to the International Schumpeter Society Conference, Stockholm.

Bernstein, J. I. (1989) 'The structure of Canadian inter-industry R&D spillovers and the rates of return to R&D', *Journal of Industrial Economics*, vol. 37, pp. 315–28.

Bernstein, J. I. and Nadiri, M. I. (1989) 'Research and development and intra-industry spillovers: An empirical application of dynamic duality', *Review of Economic Studies*, vol. 56, pp. 249–69.

—— (1991) 'Product demand, cost of production, spillover and the social rate of return to R&D', NBER working paper no. 3625.

Brezis, E. S. and Krugman, P. (1993) 'Technology and the life-cycle of cities', NBER Working Paper no. 4561.

Centre for Exploitation of Science and Technology (CEST) (1992) *Attitudes to Innovation in Germany and Britain: A comparison*, London.

Cohen, W. M. and Levinthal, D. A. (1989) 'Innovation and learning: The two faces of R&D', *Economic Journal*, vol. 99, pp. 569–96.

David, P. (1995) 'Clio and the economics of QWERTY', *American Economic Review Papers and Proceedings*, vol. 75, pp. 332–6.

Debresson, C. and Amesse, F. (1991) 'Networks of innovators: A review and an introduction to the issue', *Research Policy*, vol. 20, pp. 363–80.

Dodgson, M. (1991) 'Strategic alignment and organizational options in biotechnology firms', *Technology Analysis and Strategic Management*, vol. 3, no. 2., pp. 115–25.

Dorfman, N. (1985) 'Route 128: The development of a regional high technology economy', in Lampe, D. (ed.) *The Massachusetts Miracle: High technology and economic revitalisation*, Cambridge, Mass.: MIT Press.

Ergas, H. (1987) 'Does technology policy matter?', in B.R. Guile and H. Brookes (eds) *Technology and Global Industry*, Washington, D.C.: National Academy Press.

Feldman, M. P. (1994) *The Geography of Innovation*, Kluwer Academic Publishers.

Feldmen, M. P. and Audretsch, D. B. (1995) 'Science-based diversity, specialisation, localised competition and innovation', 22nd EARIE Conference, Sophia Antipolis, September.

Glaeser, E. L., Kallel, H. D., Scheinkmen, J. and Shleifer, A. (1992) 'Growth in cities', *Journal of Political Economy*, vol. 100, pp. 1126–52.

Grupp, H. (1994) 'Spillover effects and the science base of innovations reconsidered: An empirical macroeconomic approach', paper presented at the Munster conference of the International Joseph A. Schumpeter Society.

Hall, S. (1987) *Invisible Frontiers: The race to synthesize a human gene*, London: Sidgwick & Jackson, 1987.

Hotelling, H. (1929) 'Stability in competition', *Economic Journal*, vol. 39, pp. 41–57.

Howells, J. (1984) 'The location and organisation of research and development: Some observations and evidence from Britain', *Regional Studies*, vol. 18, pp. 13–29.

Hughes, A. (1994) 'The "problems" of finance for smaller businesses', in Dimsdale and Prevezer (eds) *Capital Markets and Corporate Governance*, Oxford: Oxford University Press.

Jaffe, A. (1986) 'Technological spillovers from R&D: Evidence from firms' patents, profits and market value', *American Economic Review*, vol. 76, pp. 984–1001.

—— (1989) 'Real effects of academic research', *American Economic Review*, vol. 79, pp. 957–70.

Jaffe, A., Trajtenberg, M. and Henderson, R. (1993) 'Geographic localization of knowledge spillovers as evidenced by patent citations', *Quarterly Journal of Economics*, vol. 63, no. 3, pp. 577–98.

Krugman, P. (1991) *The Geography of Trade*, Cambridge, Mass.: MIT Press.

Larsen, J. and Rogers, E. (1984) *Silicon valley fever: Growth of high technology culture*, London: Allen & Unwin.

McKelvey, M. (1994) *Evolutionary Innovation: Early industrial uses of genetic engineering*, Linkoping: Department of Technology and Social Change.

Malecki, E. J. (1980) 'Dimensions of R&D location in the United States', *Research Policy*, vol. 9, pp. 2–22.

Nadiri, M. I. and Mamuneas, T. P. (1991) 'The effects of public infrastructure and R&D capital on the cost structure and performance of US manufacturing industries', NBER Working Paper no. 3887.

—— (1994) 'Infrastructure and public R&D investments and the growth of factor productivity in US manufacturing industries', NBER Working Paper no. 4845.

Nelson, R. (1993) *National Systems of Innovation*, Oxford: Oxford University Press.

Pavitt, K. (1987) *On the Nature of Technology*, Brighton: University of Sussex, Science Policy Research Unit.

Porter, M. (1990) *The Competitive Advantage of Nations*, London: Macmillan.

Prevezer, M. (1991) *Financing biotechnology in the UK*, London: National Economic Development Office.

—— (1996) 'The dynamics of industrial clustering in biotechnology', *Small Business Economics*, vol. 8, pp. 1–17.

Prevezer, M. and Lomi, A. (1995) 'Networks for innovation in biotechnology', Centre for Business Strategy Working Paper no. 159, London Business School; forthcoming in *Knowledge, Technology and Innovation* (eds J. Butler and A. Piccaluga), Guerini e Associati.

Prevezer, M. and Shohet, S. (1996) 'New Knowledge: Production v diffusion; the case of UK biotechnology', Centre for Business Strategy Working Paper no. 162, London Business School, forthcoming in *International Journal of Technology Management*.

Saxenian, A. (1985) 'Silicon Valley and Route 128: Regional prototypes or historical exceptions?', in M. Castells (ed.) *High Technology, Space and Society*, Beverley Hills, Calif.: Sage.

—— (1994) *Regional Advantage: Culture and competition in Silicon Valley and Route 128*, Cambridge, Mass.: Harvard University Press.

Scherer, F. M. (1982) 'Inter-industry technology flows and productivity growth', *Review of Economics and Statistics*, vol. 64, pp. 627–34.

—— (1984) 'Using linked patent and R&D data to measure inter-industry technology flows', in Griliches, Z. (ed.) *R&D, Patents and Productivity*, Chicago: Univeristy of Chicago Press.

Stout, D. K. (1995) 'Technology foresight – a view from the front', *Business Strategy Review*, vol. 6, Issue 4.

Swann, P. (1993) 'Can high technology services prosper if high technology manufacturing doesn't?', *Centre for Business Strategy Working Paper no. 143*, London Business School.

—— (1994) 'Product evolution and the rise and fall of industrial clusters', paper presented at the EUNETIC Conference: Evolutionary Economics of Technological Change, European Parliament, Strasbourg.

Swann, P. and Prevezer, M. (1996) 'A comparison of industrial clustering in computing and biotechnology', *Research Policy*, 25, 1139–57.

Swann, P., Prevezer, M. and Stout, D. K. (forthcoming) *The Dynamics of Industrial Clustering: A comparison of computing and biotechnology*, Oxford: Oxford University Press.

Terleckyj, N. (1980) 'Direct and indirect effects of industrial Research and Development on the productivity growth of industries', in J. N. Kendrick and B. N. Vaccara (eds) *New Developments in Productivity Measurement and Analysis*, Chicago, Ill.: University of Chicago Press.

Thwaites, A. T. (1982) 'Some evidence of regional variations in the introduction and diffusion of industrial process within British manufacturing industry', *Regional Studies*, vol. 16 pp. 371–81.

von Hippel, E. (1988) *The Sources of Innovation*, Cambridge: Cambridge University Press.

Zucker, L., Darby, M. and Brewer, M. (1994) 'Intellectual capital and the birth of US biotechnology enterprises', NBER Working Paper no. 4653.

INDEX